A HISTORY OF THE DORA CAMP

A HISTORY
of the
DORA CAMP

André Sellier

TRANSLATED FROM THE FRENCH BY
STEPHEN WRIGHT AND SUSAN TAPONIER

WITH A FOREWORD BY MICHAEL J. NEUFELD
AND AN AFTERWORD BY JENS-CHRISTIAN WAGNER

Ivan R. Dee
CHICAGO 2003

PUBLISHED IN ASSOCIATION WITH THE UNITED STATES HOLOCAUST MEMORIAL MUSEUM

First published in France in 1998 by Editions La Découverte as *Histoire du camp de Dora*. Published in Germany in 2000 by zu Klampen Verlag as *Zwangsarbeit im Raketentunnel*. First American edition published 2003 by Ivan R. Dee in association with the United States Holocaust Memorial Museum. The assertions, arguments, and conclusions contained herein are those of the author or other contributors. They do not necessarily reflect the opinions of the United States Holocaust Memorial Council or of the United States Holocaust Memorial Museum.

The author and the publishers are grateful for the support of l'Amicale des déportés de Dora-Ellrich, Harzungen et Kommandos annexes; the French Ministry of Foreign Affairs and the Cultural Service of the French Embassy in the United States (as part of the program of aid for publication); the French Ministry of Culture; L'Union des Blessés de la Face et de la Tête (Les Gueules Cassées); and The European Community.

Sellier, André.
   [Histoire du Camp de Dora. English]
  A history of Dora Camp / translated from the French by Stephen Wright and
  Susan Taponier ; with a foreword by Michael J. Neufeld and an afterword by Jeus-Christian Wagner.
    p. cm.
   "Published in association with the United States Holocaust Museum."
   Includes bibliographical references and index.
   ISBN 1-56663-511-X (alk. paper)
    1. Dora (Concentration camp)—History. I. Title.

D805.5.D6 S4513 2003
940.53'1853224—dc21

2002035164

In memory of my father, who reached the front at Les Éparges in April 1915, the day he turned twenty, and who left the camp at Buchenwald in April 1945, the day he turned fifty; and in memory of all our comrades from that scarred generation.

Contents

Foreword ix

Introduction 3

PART ONE: BEFORE DORA

1   The State of Germany in August 1943   11
2   The Rocket Program Prior to Dora   19
3   Buchenwald and the Concentration Camp System in 1943   35

PART TWO: THE HELL OF DORA

4   The New Organization of Autumn 1943   49
5   Nine Months of Ordeal   58
6   Death in Dora   72

PART THREE: A TRUE CAMP, A TRUE FACTORY

7   Speer, Kammler, Dornberger, and von Braun in 1944 Germany   95
8   The Peoples of Dora   107
9   The Tunnel Factory and Its Workers   122
10   The Camp at Dora in 1944   149

PART FOUR: RENEWED HELL

11   Kammler's New Work Sites   179
12   Harzungen, Ellrich, and Woffleben   191
13   Rottleberode, Blankenburg, Langenstein, and Other Nearby Camps   222

PART FIVE: THE FINAL MONTHS

14   The End of Auschwitz and Peenemünde   235

Illustrations   243

15   The Final Months at Dora and the Boelcke Kaserne in Nordhausen   265
16   A Chronicle of the Last Days   288

PART SIX: EVACUATION, LIBERATION, RETURN

17 The Great Dispersion of April 1945 and the "Liberation" of Dora   307
18 From Dora, Ellrich, and Harzungen to Bergen-Belsen   319
19 The Five Convoys in Altmark, and the Gardelegen Tragedy   336
20 Death Marches Toward the East, and the Odyssey of the Blankenburg
    Kommando   352
21 From Sachsenhausen and Ravensbrück to the Schwerin Region   373
22 The Dora-Mittelbau Toll   395

EPILOGUE: FIFTY YEARS AFTER DORA

23 After the War: Between Missiles and Trials   407
24 Solidarity and Memory   434
25 Dora Today   446

AFTERWORD: MITTELBAU-DORA IN THE SYSTEM OF NAZI CONCENTRATION CAMPS   455

Biographical Glossary   469
Notes   473
Sources   498
Bibliography   501
Maps   505
Index of Prisoners   526
Index of Persons Other Than Prisoners   532
Subject Index   535

Foreword

A quarter of a century ago, concentration camp Dora—also known as Mittelbau or Mittelbau-Dora—was virtually unknown in the English-speaking world. Its brief twenty-month existence at the end of World War II had been covered up or ignored by the U.S. government and the Western media because of its inconvenient connection to an American hero: the rocket engineer Wernher von Braun (1912–1977), who had helped put the first U.S. satellite in orbit and the first Americans on the moon. It took the 1979 publication of *Dora,* the translated memoir of a French Resistance leader and camp survivor, Jean Michel, to begin to establish this camp in the public mind. Michel's book was influential in launching an investigation of the group of former German rocket engineers by the new Nazi-hunting unit of the U.S. Justice Department, which in turn led to the return to Germany in 1984 of one of von Braun's chief deputies, Arthur Rudolph. Rudolph, who had served as project manager of the Apollo Saturn V moon rocket for NASA, had been production manager of the underground Mittelwerk plant that produced V2 ballistic missiles using concentration camp labor from Dora, leading to thousands of deaths. The Rudolph case spawned muckraking books and television programs by journalists in the late 1980s and early 1990s, as well as scholarly research on the rocket program and the Mittelbau-Dora camp in German, French, and English. In 1997 a second important French survivor memoir, Yves Béon's *Planet Dora,* appeared in translation in this country.

In spite of all this activity, no full-length history of the Mittelbau-Dora camp system has ever been published in the English language—until now. This fact alone would make the book you hold in your hand an event. But what makes it particularly unique is that it is the product of a Dora survivor and former slave laborer on the V2 production line who also has historical training. In the foreword to the German translation of this book, Eberhard Jäckel, the eminent historian, has compared André Sellier to Eugen Kogon. A former Buchenwald prisoner, Kogon launched the study of the Nazi concentration camps in 1946 with his book *Der SS Staat,* which appeared in English as *Theory and Practice of Hell.* Like Kogon, Sellier examines the history of his camp with engagement but also with scholarly detachment, skillfully analyzing all the sources available to him. *A History of the Dora Camp* is not a memoir, yet Sellier is able to use his memories and those of his fellow survivors to supplement the somewhat meager written record. The extensive use of the memoir files of the Dora-Ellrich and Buchenwald-Dora survivor associations in France, supplemented by interviews and correspondence with French, Belgian, Czech, and Slovenian prisoners, gives the present book a powerful, personal dimension which does not undermine its restrained tone.

It is, to be sure, a French view of what happened in Dora and its subcamps, like the two memoirs that have preceded it in English. The voices of the Russian, Ukrainian, and Polish prisoners who formed over half the population of these camps have scarcely been heard, even in the new, excellent scholarly literature in German, because of the lingering effects of the division of Europe and the lack of expertise in Slavic languages in the West. (Jewish prisoners, mostly from Hungary, were only a small minority in the Mittelbau-Dora camps until the evacuation of Auschwitz and Gross Rosen in late January 1945.) We can only hope that this deficit, which is common to all works on the topic, will soon be remedied by new scholarly research. But even when it is, there is no doubt that André Sellier's *History of the Dora Camp* will continue to be revered as a standard work on the topic. I highly recommend it to all readers.

MICHAEL J. NEUFELD

Washington, D.C.
October 2002

A HISTORY OF THE DORA CAMP

INTRODUCTION

Since the end of the Hitlerian Reich, along with the concentration camps that were one of its essential characteristics, literature on the subject has never ceased to grow within Germany itself and in the other countries concerned, in Europe as well as in the United States and Israel. Thus on the fiftieth anniversary of the end of the war and the "liberation of the camps," a number of excellent commemorative works were published, most often in the form of anthologies. This particular study of the Dora camp, however, is of a quite different sort. It is a historical study, written by a historian, who also happens to have been a *Häftling*, a "prisoner," in the camp, where his identity was reduced to the number 39570. In undertaking to write this book, I was seeking to meet the expectations of my fellow prisoners, who wanted it to be done by a professional historian.

For a variety of reasons the concentration camp world was not, for many years, systematically studied from a truly historical perspective. In 1945 we were confronted with a previously unknown type of institution—unknown, at any rate, in terms of the extent of its criminal perfection. Its analysis was not made any easier by the mediocrity of information provided by those in charge of the camps themselves—that is, the SS. From 1933 to 1945, everything that had anything to do with the camps was secret, and many of the relevant documents were destroyed during the war's final weeks.

An essential explanatory role was played, in the first years after the war, by a handful of German and Austrian prisoners who had found themselves assigned to positions in the camps that had enabled them to gain an understanding of the workings of the system and to appreciate the behavior of all those involved, from the wardens to the various categories of prisoners. The writings of Eugen Kogon, Hermann Langbein, and Walter Bartel, in particular, made it possible to interpret both the contents of the remaining documents and the evidence given by the SS in the trials following the war.

The consequence of this absolutely unavoidable procedure was to give a somewhat stereotyped picture of the concentration camp universe—a picture stemming from the experience of the German political prisoners who had spent many long years imprisoned in one of the "big" camps. It was in this way that the specificity of the Shoah came to be inadequately emphasized—although this did not prevent the three above-named authors from proving themselves effective adversaries of attempts at revisionism. In the same way, too little weight was put on the shift in scale that took place in the last two years of the camps' history, between 1943 and 1945, because of the increase in the number of exterior Kommandos and the considerable growth in the number of prisoners.

Given that the Dora camp itself, including its annexes, was no doubt the most perfected expression of this transformation, it struck me as necessary, having read the testimonies of my fellow French, Belgian, Dutch, Czech, and Slovenian prisoners, to point out clearly the particular characteristics of this period as well as the complexity of what had been observed. My ambition was to replace the somewhat static picture of the concentration camp phenomenon with a narrative that both takes account of the chronology and integrates it into the history of the final period of the Nazi regime, that of its decline and collapse.

As I will explain further along, I have based my work on a large and somewhat eclectic collection of testimonies assembled by the Former Dora Prisoners' Association. Although it came as no surprise, I was struck by the extreme variety of individual "paths." While small groups, such as the one to which I belonged, whose stories were more or less the same, did come together, many of the stories are marked by individual incidents. Above all, we all lived in ignorance of what was happening to most of the others. My friends and I scarcely had any idea about what was going on outside of our underground factory. Conversely, many of our fellow prisoners never set foot in the factory.

I was therefore confronted with a collection of texts, all of which referred to a greater or lesser number of incidents that had occurred at given times and places. In isolating the episodes of each of these testimonies, I found myself with dozens of pieces of an enormous puzzle; it was putting them together that enabled me to reconstitute the history of the whole in a coherent way. I was thereby able to do extensive—and generally satisfying—cross-checking between the testimony of witnesses independent of one another. This procedure was only possible through the identification of some five hundred prisoners, witnesses, and witnesses' partners who were quoted on one or more occasions in clearly determined circumstances.

I now know, with assurance and precision, the sequence of events in the underground factory at Dora and in the neighboring camp, in the annex camps such as Ellrich and Harzungen, in the underground work sites in the Zorge valley, and on the railway work sites in the Helme valley. I know when the most dramatic as well as the calmest periods were, and where they took place. But this history makes sense only when illuminated by the development of the military and political situation in Germany at the time.

Recent historical studies make it possible to identify the series of decisions that determined our fate. The first was to make systematic use of the concentration camp labor force in the arms industry. The second, in application of the first, was to make use of prisoners in the factory at Peenemünde (on the Baltic) in the construction of V2s. The third, following the bombing of Peenemünde, was to transfer V2 production to an underground site in Thuringia, using prisoners alone alongside German civilians. The fourth was to situate German aeronautic production as a whole underground, having prisoners do the necessary digging and construction work.

Thus in late August 1943 the Dora camp was set up in Thuringia at the same time that the Dora "Tunnel" was re-built for the construction of V2s. Large underground or railway work sites were opened in the spring of 1944 in the surrounding area at the same time as the annex camps. Both in the case of the secret weapons—the V2 as well as the V1—and in the case of the aeronautics industry, we were caught up in a power struggle between the SS and the civil and military technocrats: in other words, between Arms Minister Albert Speer and his engineers, Wehrmacht artillery specialists, and the team of rocket specialists behind Wernher von Braun. In making use of the concentration camp labor force, the SS sought—and to some extent managed—to take control of the Reich's war industry.

The consequences of this escalation were dramatic for prisoners throughout Germany, but it was the factory in the Dora Tunnel—the sole production site of the V2s, and subsequently of the V1s—that was constantly at the heart of this strife, which was more or less clearly arbitrated by Hitler himself.

In the hierarchy of concentration camps and Kommandos (work details), the Dora camp was the last to be classed as an "autonomous" camp, a "main" camp. Far more recent than the other camps in this category, such as Dachau, Sachsenhausen, and Buchenwald, its importance stems from its association with secret weapons production. Ironically, though, this very association has proved detrimental to its notoriety.

All the other large camps bore unequivocal place names, such as Auschwitz. The Dora camp was situated in a secret region designated by a variety of code names, relatively disconcerting for the uninitiated historian but which wouldn't have raised many problems for Allied intelligence. Dora was one of these code names—as was Mittelbau, which in the final months designated all of Dora and the adjoining camps. There were thus two names for a single reality, to which circumstances conspired to add a third. When American troops reached the area in April 1945, the vast majority of the prisoners were no longer there, the SS having "evacuated" them in often murderous fashion. What they discovered was a combination of cadavers and near-dead survivors in a Nordhausen barracks. This discovery was to leave an impression, and the subsequent trial of the Dora war criminals came to be referred to as the "Nordhausen Trial."

These difficulties of terminology could have been overcome were it not for the fact that the very existence of the Dora Tunnel was concealed, as much by the Americans as by the Soviets, who, in their duel for the missile technology, each inherited members of the Peenemünde research team. It was not a problem to acknowledge the role of von Braun and his team; but it was unseemly to re-call the Dora Tunnel and its prisoners. And it was largely in reaction against this tendency to consign Dora to oblivion that the camp's former deportees wanted this book to be written.

In France after the war, associations were created made up of former deportees who had been in the same camps or same Kommandos. With regard to Dora, one association includes former prisoners from Dora, Ellrich, and Harzungen as well as the Kommandos attached to them in the framework of Mittelbau.[1] An-other association, that of Buchenwald-Dora,[2] is made up of former prisoners of Buchenwald and of the Kommandos that depended on Buchenwald—which was the case with Dora in its early days. Certain fellow prisoners are members of both associations, which, as far as the writing of this book was concerned, were never in competition with one another.

The initiative came from Dora-Ellrich, which in the late 1980s set up a his-torical commission. Its objective was to assemble the greatest number of testi-monies, whether in published form, simply put together by their respective authors for distribution among friends and family members, or even just left in manuscript form. A pamphlet brought out in 1989 made it possible to establish an initial schema, which I made use of when I embarked on a study of the his-tory of Dora, following historical research of another nature. From that point on, the various contacts I established with a variety of former prisoners from Dora-Ellrich, Buchenwald-Dora, and the corresponding Belgian association com-pleted my information and enabled me to understand what had taken place in those places I had not experienced personally.

Like so many others in the camps, I had been an ordinary prisoner. As op-posed to my father—with whom I was arrested and who was imprisoned at Buchenwald—I had not been a French *Résistance* leader. I held no position in the camp's functioning. I had the good fortune to be appointed as an "electri-cian" in a quality control Kommando in the tunnel factory, along with others as ill qualified for the job as myself, given that I had been a history teacher in the Cambrai high school. I could just as easily have had another fate, and not have lived. Given that I had the capability to write this book, I felt that it was my responsibility to do so, quite simply, in memory of those who did not return. Perhaps the fact of "having been there" enabled me to see it through.

In writing this book, I thought of the readers of today; of my children, and above all of my grandchildren. I wanted to make this period of history, which remains disconcerting for Europeans, intelligible to them. As a historian, I do not personally believe in the lessons of history. But I think that making an effort at lucid analysis of the events of the past is always an excellent exercise—especially when these events happen to have been dramatic, which is the case with Dora. The witnesses I quote have in no way exaggerated. That has alleviated any need for commentary on my part as well as any conclusion. Each reader remains free to draw his or her own.

In the course of the several years it took to prepare and write this book, I very deeply felt the confidence and friendship of my friends from Dora, which was a very great help to me. I am referring to Louis Garnier, to Jean Mialet, and to Jacques Brun, and to the members of the board and historical commission of the Amicale Dora-Ellrich, Yves Béon, André Cardon, Max Dutillieux, Étienne Eckert, Lucien Fayman, Jean Gineston, Étienne Lafond, André Rogerie, Pierre Rozan, Georges Soubirous. I am also referring to the president of the Buchenwald-Dora Association, Guy Ducoloné, and to its general secretary, Jean Cormont, who was himself one of our friends from Dora. I received the same cooperation from the Belgian association,[3] from Ernest Abel, Leopold Claessens, Xavier Delogne, Albert Van Hoey, Raymond Wautrecht, and the general secretary, Marie-Claire du Bois de Vroylande, daughter of a prisoner who died at Ellrich.

I must pay very particular homage to the two men, successively in charge of the historical commission, Lucien Fayman and Georges Soubirous. It was they who collected and sorted through the first large collection of testimonies, without which this book could not have been written. And they never ceased to help me thereafter.

I must also pay particular tribute to my Slovenian friend, Milan Filipcic. We are virtually the same age, with only a few days' difference. We were both young teachers when we met in Ko[mmando] Scherer. He already spoke French. I never got beyond the mere basics of Slovenian. I was thus unable to read the book he published on Dora with the help of his friends. But he kept abreast of my book as I was writing it, and I am happy he was satisfied with it.

I am greatly indebted to Étienne Eckert. Not only did he show me that I had mastered German words—which is now true to some extent—but he never ceased to share with me the discoveries he made in his reading, which were always in keeping with my own curiosities.

Various friends have shown close interest in my work on particular points: André Lobstein with regard to the *Revier,* Maxime Cottet about Harzungen,

Raymond Wautrecht about Harzungen and Oranienburg, Clément-Robert Nicola about Harzungen and the Boelcke Kaserne, Jean-Pierre Couture about Ellrich and the Boelcke Kaserne, Bernard d'Astorg about Bergen-Belsen.

I also took advantage of the friendly assistance of three specialists, Paul Le Goupil, Yves Le Maner, and Joachim Neander. Paul Le Goupil, former prisoner from Buchenwald's "tattooed convoy" and from the Langenstein Kommando, is remarkably skilled in using archives and always ready to provide assistance. Yves Le Maner, highly qualified teacher at the Saint-Omer high school, is the man behind getting the Wizernes site better known, and is well informed about the history of the V2s and the importance of the Dora Tunnel. In 1997, Joachim Neander defended his doctoral thesis on Mittelbau, and in particular on the April 1945 evacuations.

I was above all concerned not to betray the memory that my closest friends and fellow prisoners had retained of our common experience. Francis Finelli, Pierre Gáti, and Joseph Béninger died before the book was completed. André Fortané, René Bordet, and René Souquet are in agreement with regard to the content, and, perhaps most important, with the tone adopted.

I noticed recently that academics far younger than myself acknowledge the precious help provided by their children in overcoming computer problems. I could not have done this book without a computer, and it was my daughter Caroline who tutored me firmly and patiently.

My friend Anne Le Fur once again helped my son Jean produce original cartographic illustrations, which were truly adapted to the subject.

In the end, we all have to thank my wife for two important reasons. First, for several years running she accepted that the rooms of our house would be overrun, far more than usual, with dossiers and books. Then she was an attentive and demanding reader, tirelessly following all the phases of the work.

PART ONE

Before Dora

THE STATE OF GERMANY
IN AUGUST 1943

The Military Situation

The history of the Dora concentration camp begins on August 28, 1943, with the arrival of the first convoy of prisoners from the Buchenwald camp. Over the course of the previous year the military situation in Germany had considerably worsened, and Dora's beginnings were in many respects conditioned by this new situation.

On August 23, 1942, German troops had reached the Volga at Stalingrad, and the Swastika-emblazoned flag had been hoisted on Elbrus, the highest peak in the Caucasus. By November 1942 the Germans had even reached the territory of the autonomous Checheno-Ingush Republic. In Africa, Rommel, who had been made field marshal, had reached El Alamein, at the gates of Alexandria, in July. In the West, a Canadian raid had foundered at Dieppe on August 19, 1942. The Todt Organization was pursuing the building of the Atlantic Wall. The success of U-boat and Luftwaffe attacks on Allied convoys in the North Atlantic had led to the suspension of convoys to Murmansk. The cooperation of the Vichy authorities had enabled the Vél d'Hiv roundup on July 16, 1942.

By August 1943, however, the picture was entirely different—and above all on the Eastern Front. Encircled at Stalingrad since November 22, 1942, the German Sixth Army utterly capitulated on February 2, 1943. The retreat of German troops who had adventured into the Caucasus came to a close when the Soviets took back Rostov on February 14. The front line subsequently stabilized between Moscow and the Sea of Azov, leaving a large Russian salient around Kursk, reconquered on February 8, 1943.

Anxious to regain the initiative, Hitler set about to reduce this heavily fortified salient. Operation Citadel, put off on several occasions, was launched on July 5, 1943.[1] As the military historian Philippe Masson, among others, has put it, "At dawn on 5 July, began one of the most grandiose battles of all time." Both sides, convinced of the importance of what was at stake, pitted a large portion of their tanks, artillery, and airpower against one another. The fighting was bitter and the losses considerable. On July 12, aware of his failure, Hitler halted the offensive, but the battle spread northward and southward. The Soviets took back Orel on August 5 and Kharkov (definitively) on August 22. The reconquest of the Ukraine had begun, and the Germans were pulling back toward the Dnieper.

On the Mediterranean side, developments had been no more satisfying from a German perspective. Rommel, beaten at El Alamein on November 4, 1942, had quickly retreated toward the west, and the British rolled into Tripoli on January 23, 1943. Meanwhile, an Anglo-American landing had taken place in Morocco and Algeria on November 8, 1942, and a new front had been opened in Tunisia. The fighting in North Africa came to an end on May 13, 1943, with the capitulation of the last of the German and Italian troops in Tunisia.

The next phase came with the landing in Sicily[2] on July 10, 1943, the conquest of the island winding up on August 18. Meanwhile, on July 25 in Rome, Mussolini was overthrown and interned, and the king of Italy designated Field Marshal Badoglio to replace him. The month of August passed with uncertainty, but Hitler, who had no confidence whatsoever in King Victor Emmanuel and Badoglio, prepared for the occupation of Italy. It was only in September, however, that events grew precipitous. On the 8th the Italian government announced that it had concluded an armistice with the Allies and left Rome for Brindisi. On the 9th the Americans landed at Salerno and the British at Taranto. On the 10th the Germans occupied Rome and on the 12th freed Mussolini. Italian troops were taken prisoner by the Germans, both in Italy itself and in the Balkans.

In mid-1943 the Germans were faced with yet another crisis, due to the Luftwaffe's increasing inferiority compared to British, American, and Soviet airpower. In particular, German territory was more and more often the target of Allied bombing raids.[3] On three occasions, on July 24, 27, and 29, the RAF launched massive attacks on Hamburg, inflicting enormous damage. During the night of August 17–18, the rocket-testing center in Peenemünde was bombed. Simultaneously the Americans hit large factories in Regensburg and Schweinfurt. On August 18 the Luftwaffe's chief of staff, General Jeschonneck, committed suicide. Meanwhile, the most recent successes of the German submarines dated back to March, and by mid-1943 the Kriegsmarine was also in crisis.

Following the Anglo-American landing in North Africa, German troops had occupied all of France, entering the *zone libre* on November 11, 1942. On February 16, 1943, the STO (Service du travail obligatoire, or Compulsory Work Service) in Germany was established. There were a large number of *réfractaires*—people who refused this compulsory service—and a segment of French youth went underground, using fake identity papers. Some joined the Resistance movement—the maquis—while others sought to reach North Africa via Spain. Arrests of Resistance fighters increased.

This panorama of events makes it easier to understand what took place in Dora as of August 1943. The setbacks of classical weaponry, particularly at

Kursk, made new arms all the more appealing. Air raids on German factories provided impetus for the development of underground facilities. Events in the Ukraine, Italy, and France enabled immediate expansion of the concentration camp workforce.

The Armaments Ministry and Albert Speer

In August 1943, responsibility for setting up a new factory for the construction of V2s was above all in the hands of Albert Speer and his Armaments Ministry, whose title was still Reichsministerium für Bewaffnung und Munition. The ministry had been established on March 17, 1940, and put in the hands of Dr. Fritz Todt, born in 1891 and a member of the Nazi Party since 1922. In 1933, Todt had created the Todt Organization, a paramilitary group in charge of carrying out large works and fortification projects in Germany. It had first of all built the autobahn network, followed by the fortifications of the Westwall facing the Maginot Line.

The Armaments Ministry was created in 1940 to resolve problems in the manufacture of ammunition, but Todt had not been given responsibility for naval or aircraft construction and was not supposed to interfere with Hermann Göring's prerogatives in the execution of the Four-Year Plan. Todt remained, moreover, at the head of the Todt Organization, which was in charge of building the Atlantic Wall. This sort of bastardized system was characteristic of how the Nazi administration operated. From late 1941 on, Todt's essential preoccupation was to reestablish communications routes, especially railways, in that part of the Soviet Union occupied by the Germans, where they had been methodically destroyed. The principal difficulties were encountered in the Ukraine, where Todt was assisted by the architect Speer, who was also a member of the government.

While on a mission in Dnepropetrovsk in early February 1942, Speer, unable to take the train because of heavy snow, returned by plane on the 7th to Hitler's headquarters in Rastenburg in East Prussia.[4] Todt, who happened to be there, died on February 8 at eight o'clock in the morning in an airplane crash following takeoff, the circumstances of which were never elucidated. Five hours later, Hitler entrusted Speer with all the functions previously exercised by Todt. Speer returned to Berlin by train on February 9. He was thirty-seven years old.

Speer's career had already been exceptional. Born in 1905 in Mannheim, he was the son of a very wealthy architect. He too studied architecture in Munich and subsequently in Berlin, joining the Nazi Party in March 1931. He opened his own office and worked in the building where the *Gauleiter* of Berlin, Joseph Goebbels, had his headquarters. When Hitler came to power in January 1933, he directed various projects for Goebbels, who had become propaganda minister. It was at this time, in the fall of 1933, that Speer was noticed by Hitler, who had a passion for architecture, and became a part of his close circle. He did the lighting design (the "cathedral of light") for the Nazi Party congress in Nuremberg in 1934. In 1935 he was put in charge of studying the vast new complex planned for Nuremberg, the first stone of which was laid in 1937, which was to be completed by 1945. In 1937 he designed the German pavilion at the Paris Exhibition.

Hitler envisaged gigantic projects for the transformation of Berlin. It was in this perspective that, in January 1937, Speer was named Generalbauinspektor, giving him the rank of secretary of state. He was thirty-two years old. In 1939, while continuing to work on the Nuremberg and Berlin projects, he began studying airports, shipyards, factories, and air-raid shelters. In the summer of 1941 his organization became the "Baustab Speer." Hitler asked him to give thought to the future German settlements in the Ukraine, but he went there above all in order to get the railways and heavy facilities operational once again. Following in Todt's footsteps was a very heavy responsibility, but he had the requisite experience.

Speer kept Todt's principal collaborators in place. Xaver Dorsch stayed at the head of the Todt Organization, with substantial autonomy. Karl Otto Saur, head of the Technisches Amt, was his main deputy minister. In the course of a meeting on February 13, 1942, Hitler laid out the extent of Speer's responsibilities. He was given more leeway, for instance, with regard to Göring than Todt had been given.[5] With Hitler's support, Speer tended to rely on company technicians—whom he very frequently visited—rather than on bureaucrats or leaders of large industries. Some of these same technicians would later be involved at Dora.

One problem he faced was the distribution of raw materials and construction-related materials. The other problem had to do with the workforce, which was insufficient. Todt, like Speer after him, was unable to impose his point of view as to the need for total mobilization—of women in particular—as was by then the case in Great Britain.[6] Fritz Sauckel, *Gauleiter* of Thuringia and one of Hitler's old companions, did his best to overcome these difficulties by recruiting workers—both men and women—in the Ukraine and other occupied territories of the Soviet Union. Aside from these *Ostarbeiter*, other more or less forced workers were brought from Italy, France, Belgium, and the Netherlands. In France, the government itself established the STO in February 1943. But thought was also given to making use of the concentration camp labor force. What went on in Peenemünde in 1943 is entirely significant for the combining of these two sources of labor.

The Development of the SS Empire

Some people have argued that by mid-1943 in National Socialist Germany there existed an "SS empire" constituting a state within the state. The expression used is of little importance, inasmuch as there was nothing genuinely institutional about it; rather, it was a progressively established de facto situation, open to further development.

The SS itself, the Schutzstaffel (protection squad), was the name that, in 1925, was given to the small personal guard that had been created in 1923 for the protection of Hitler, head of the Nazi Party. In 1929 this SS was put under the command of Heinrich Himmler, designated Reichsführer-SS. Born in 1900, Himmler was a long-standing Nazi, having taken part in the attempted putsch in Munich in November 1923. Under Himmler the SS became a troop with a limited number—but a highly disciplined and fanatical corps—of members; a "black order" whose slogan "Your honor is your fidelity" referred to unconditional fidelity to the führer.

The SS was thus very different from Ernst Röhm's SA, the Sturmabteilung or assault section, a mass movement that engaged in street-level opposition to communist organizations. In the autumn of 1932 the SA counted some 700,000 men, as opposed to 50,000 in the SS. Nevertheless, right from the early years of the Nazi regime in 1933–34, the SS won out definitively over the SA and indeed played a decisive role in doing away with Röhm and his circle during the "Night of the Long Knives" on June 30, 1934. At the end of this period, Himmler was master of the concentration camps and the police. A veritable concentration camp system was set up in Dachau by Theodor Eicke, who, in July 1934, became Inspektor der Konzentrationslager. Other camps were later set up along the lines of this early model, including Sachsenhausen in 1936, Buchenwald in 1937, Mauthausen in 1938, and Ravensbrück in 1939. These camps were devised to intern and progressively eliminate opponents of the Nazi regime.

The takeover of the police was a long and complex operation. In 1931, Himmler had already created, within the Nazi Party itself, the SD, or Sicherheitsdienst (security service), in the hands of Reinhard Heydrich. With Hitler's coming to power in 1933, the political police depended on various states—Prussia, Bavaria, Saxony, and so on. Göring set up a Gestapo, or Geheime Staatspolizei (secret police) in Prussia, where he was minister-president.[7] Himmler established an equivalent force in most of the other states, then also successfully gained control of the Prussian Gestapo in April 1934. On June 17, 1936, these different police groups were brought together and Himmler became *chef der deutschen Polizei* while conserving his role as Reichsführer-SS.[8] Finally, on September 27, 1939, the Gestapo and the SD were also grouped together in the RSHA, Reichssicherheitshauptamt, or Central Security Office of the Reich.[9] In the meantime, the Kripo, or criminal police, and the Gestapo had formed the SIPO, or security police. Very often, members of the SS took charge of various branches of the RSHA, which ensured overall cohesion. Following Heydrich's death (he was killed in Prague in 1942), Ernst Kaltenbrunner replaced him at the head of this organization.

The SS managed to impose itself on German society. A number of its officers came from the aristocracy or intellectual circles. Executive members who continued to work in their field were members of the Allgemeine-SS, the general SS. Himmler even created the title of "honorary leader," which was awarded to upper civil servants, scholars, and diplomats without their actually having to carry out any real duty.[10]

Some SS members were quartered in barracks and comprised the Waffen-SS, the armed SS. It consisted of 7,000 men in 1935 and some 23,000 in 1939. In 1940, four SS divisions, including three motorized divisions, were deployed in Holland and then in France. One of them was Eicke's Totenkopf (Death's Head) Division, made up of camp guards. From 80,000 men in 1940, the Waffen-SS swelled to 140,000 men in 1942 and to 300,000 by the end of 1943.

The political and military power thus acquired, however, failed to satisfy the SS and Himmler. It had to be supplemented by economic power. In 1940 the WVHA, Wirtschaft- und Verwaltungshauptamt, or Central Office for the Economy and Administration, was set up under the command of Oswald Pohl, who was in charge of carrying out this project. According to a 1942 organization chart,[11] it had five departments, the first two of which, A (budget) and B (supplies and clothing), were purely technical. Department C (construction) was run by Hans Kammler, who was in charge, most notably, of building the gas chambers in Auschwitz. Department D corresponded to what had been Eicke's concentration camp inspection unit, following his transfer into the Waffen-SS and subsequent death on the Eastern Front in 1943. The switchover came into effect in April 1942 and Richard Glücks, who replaced Eicke, became head of Department D. Department W, dealing with the economy *(Wirtschaft)* in general, was put under Pohl's direct authority. A large part of the WVHA bureaucracy had already been in place since 1938 in buildings in Oranienburg—part of a vast complex, also comprising the Sachsenhausen camp, the SS barracks, and various workshops and factories.

The Economic Ambitions of the SS

For a long period the direct involvement of the SS in the economy was limited, and was exercised through the intermediary of the company Deutsche Erd- und Steinwerke, or German Earth and Stone Works, created on April 29, 1938.[12] The sadly famous Mauthausen quarry and Klinker Brickworks in Oranienburg served both repression and industrial activity. Elsewhere, in many camps, including Buchenwald as well as Dora, for example, the Quarry *(Steinbruch)* Kommando continued to have a disciplinary function.

On January 26, 1942, Himmler, writing to Glücks[13] with regard to the deportation of German Jews, added: "Large economic tasks are to be transferred to the camps in the coming weeks. Pohl will fill you in on the details." On March 16, on Himmler's instructions, Pohl went to Speer's office (minister only as of February 8) to determine the number of prisoners apt for work to be made available to the war industry.[14] It would appear that he offered 25,000 men—6,000 from Sachsenhausen and 5,000 from Buchenwald.

Several options for associating a factory with a camp were thus possible. The simplest, which seems to have been adopted in late 1942 for the prisoners of Sachsenhausen, was to establish a camp in the compound of an existing factory: the Heinkel Kommando was thus set up in a building of the Heinkel aircraft factory in Germendorf, near Oranienburg. It was a very large Kommando, in 1944 comprising as many as 7,000 or 8,000 prisoners, 1,000 of whom were French. Another option was to set up a camp next to a factory, as was the case with the large Falkensee camp set up in 1943 to the west of Berlin, next to the DEMAG factory, for building railway material and Tiger tanks. There too, prisoners from Sachsenhausen were used. The fact that this camp was close to the WVHA no doubt fostered these early arrangements in liaison with Speer's Armaments Ministry. There was even a "Speer" Kommando near the camp, devoted to the recuperation of nonferrous metals from old electric cables.

On the basis of muddled passages in Speer's last book,[15] it would seem that establishing a factory at Buchenwald next to a large existing camp (rather than putting a Kommando next to an existing factory) raised serious problems. The plan was to create a Gustloff factory for the manufacture of rifles, although the Gustloff Werke established in Weimar already employed prisoners from a Buchenwald Kommando. The factory was finally set up. As will be shown, Dora's beginnings were of an entirely different nature: right from the beginning the point was to set up a factory and a camp simultaneously, which would together form a whole.

Making camp prisoners available for industry, and especially for the arms industry, didn't entail any change of status for them. An extract from Pohl's instructions, dated April 21, 1942,[16] sheds light on this point: "The camp commander alone is responsible for the employment of the work potential. This employment has to be taken in the true and full sense of the word, in order to maximize the rate of yield. Work time is linked to no time schedule."

Judging by the memo that Glücks sent to SS camp doctors on December 26, 1942, it does not appear that the camp commanders were able successfully to adapt themselves to carrying out these instructions.[17] In it he states: "Attached for your information is a table of current arrivals and exits in all the concentration camps. It would so appear that of some 136,000 in-coming prisoners, 70,000 have died. With a mortality rate of this kind, the number of prisoners will never reach the level the Reichsführer-SS has ordered. [. . .] Camp doctors are to pay closer attention than previously to the prisoners' food. [. . .]

"Furthermore, doctors are to show concern for the work conditions on the different work sites in order to improve them as may be possible." The memo's conclusion is unequivocal: "The Reichsführer-SS has ordered an appreciable decrease in mortality." No heed whatsoever, of course, was paid to this memo, as can be noted, a year later, in Dora.

[[2]]

THE ROCKET PROGRAM
PRIOR TO DORA

The history of Dora, the tunnel factory, and the camp is part of the history of rocket development—part of the German period of that history at any rate. Literature on the subject is both abundant and uneven. The best and most recent overall work is Canadian historian Michael J. Neufeld's book, *The Rocket and the Reich,* published in 1995. It is a complete and well-balanced account of all the technical and political aspects of this adventure right from the 1920s until the capitulation in 1945. The following presentation of the events prior to the creation of Dora, particularly those in Peenemünde, owes a great deal to Neufeld's account and analysis.

Rockets Before the War

THE ERA OF THE AMATEURS. Space flight had been the object of major theoretical work in Russia (Konstantin Tsiolkovsky beginning in 1903), in France (Robert Esnault-Pelterie), and in the United States (Robert Goddard), but it was only in Germany and Russia that attempts were made to put theory into practice. Interest in rockets, in Germany, began in the 1920s, in the Weimar Republic, and was immediately associated with the futuristic aspect characteristic of the era. What took place at that time is well known, because the protagonists, concerned with securing financing for their experiments, did a considerable amount of self-promotion. A certain number of facts need to be pointed out.

First, the important role played by Hermann Oberth. Born in 1894, Oberth was a German professor of mathematics in Transylvania, and thus at the time a Romanian citizen. In 1923 he published in Germany *Die Rakete zu den Planetenräumen (Rockets to Outer Space)*, which, though it enthused only a limited number of readers, brought a new theme to the fore. In 1929, Fritz Lang brought out his film *Frau im Mond (Woman on the Moon)* with Oberth's scientific support.

Rocket enthusiasts set up a sort of club and, in September 1930, rented an abandoned military site, in Reinickendorf, north of Berlin, which they referred to as the Raketenflugplatz, for their activities. Their performances were varied. They were generally young, like Oberth himself. Youngest among them was Wernher von Braun, born in 1912 to an aristocratic, wealthy, and conservative family. In spite of their undeniable know-how and enthusiasm, these amateurs were not able to get very far in terms of conquering space. They lacked the money, organization, and simultaneous mastery of numerous technologies. Outside of Germany, this enthusiasm for rockets was found only—and to a lesser extent—in the Soviet Union. The key person there was Serge Korolev, born in 1907, who was to crop up once again after 1945.

THE ERA OF THE ARTILLERYMEN. The experiments of the amateurs on the Raketenflugplatz were followed with interest by professionals. Artillery officers made up Section 1 of the test division of the Heereswaffenamt—which Neufeld translates into English as "Army Ordnance Office."[1] In 1932 this section (Prüfwesen, Abteilung 1) was headed by Col. Karl Emil Becker. In 1938, Becker, promoted to general, became director of the office itself. The tests took place on the military training ground at Kummersdorf, south of Berlin near Zossen. In light of the clauses of the Treaty of Versailles, work in the field of heavy artillery was not allowed, but nothing forbade taking an interest in rockets.

Following a demonstration in June 1932 at Kummersdorf by a group of enthusiasts, Becker offered to assist them in the pursuit of their activities, but demanded absolute secrecy. The student von Braun was the only one to accept.[2] The divulging of the results attained by the others was forbidden in April 1934, once Hitler had come to power.[3] In December 1932, having obtained a research contract, von Braun began working at Kummersdorf while at the same time working on his doctorate at the University of Berlin under Dr. Erich Schumann, who was also an adviser to the Ordnance Office.[4] He defended his thesis "with distinction." The title and contents were not made public.[5]

Two important remarks have to be made here, following Neufeld. The first has to do with the considerable influence of the artillerymen within the German army. All the high-ranking officers were from the artillery: this was true during the Weimar Republic and remained the case after 1933. When the War Ministry, controlled by Werner von Blomberg, an artilleryman, was eliminated by Hitler in February 1938, it was Walther von Brauchitsch, another artilleryman, who became commander in chief of the army and who promoted Becker. This makes it easier to understand the continuity of support and credit accorded to rocket research between 1932 and 1940.[6] The other remark concerns the links between the army and the universities. Becker and his collaborators did specialized university studies in their capacity as officers. Many of those in charge at Peenemünde came from the university.

At Kummersdorf, von Braun worked in a wide variety of fields: metallurgy, rocket shape, ignition problems, guidance systems, and so on. He was joined by two former amateurs who were to play key roles at Peenemünde: Walter Riedel in January 1934 and Arthur Rudolph in August of that same year. When the first A1 rocket did not work, von Braun designed an A2 rocket, two prototypes of which were launched successfully in December 1934 on the island of Borkum. But the A2's dimensions remained limited.[7]

The initial A was taken from the word *Aggregat,* meaning aggregate or assemblage, and was deliberately meaningless. At Kummersdorf and later at Peenemünde a whole series of rockets bore this name, some actually built while others remained on the drawing board. Neufeld provides the characteristics of the whole series, from A1 to A12. The A4 was the only one to have been built in a series and to have been operational. When it was launched in September 1944, Goebbels nicknamed it the V2, the V coming from *Vergeltungswaffe* (retaliation weapon). In order not to confuse his readers, however, Neufeld speaks only of the A4, as did the German technicians at the time. Yet inasmuch as the general public has only ever heard of the V2, it seems impossible to avoid the term. For reasons of pure convention, in the first part of the present book, up until the bombing of Peenemünde, reference will be to the A4; beginning with its assembly in the Dora Tunnel, reference will be to the V2.

In March 1935, Germany denounced the restrictive military clauses of the Treaty of Versailles and revealed a rearmament program. Particular attention was given to aviation. In charge of developing Luftwaffe weapons was Wolfram von Richthofen (cousin of the famous Richthofen of World War I), who maintained excellent relations with Becker's team. Joint projects were envisaged.[8]

THE EARLY YEARS AT PEENEMÜNDE. In June 1935, the Kummersdorf facilities having become inadequate, von Braun suggested the creation of a special rocket base. An agreement in principle was arrived at for a base that was to be shared by the Armaments Office and the Luftwaffe. In late 1935, von Braun discovered an appropriate site on the north part of the island of Usedom, in the Baltic. The Ordnance Office and the Luftwaffe came to an agreement on financing, and the Peenemünde land was purchased on April 1, 1936. Work on setting up the site began in August.[9]

On the north of the island, "Peenemünde-West" was reserved for the Luftwaffe, and "Peenemünde-East" for the Ordnance Office's rockets. There were possibilities for extension toward the south in order to house the personnel working at the base, and a little railway to ensure links. In spite of good relations on the local level, cooperation with the Luftwaffe did not materialize. Richthofen was replaced in early 1937 by Ernst Udet. In April 1938 the formal separation of the two bases was decided.[10]

Two individuals took control of Peenemünde: Walter Dornberger and von Braun. Longtime collaborator of Becker's (and von Brauchitsch's protégé),

Walter Dornberger, born in 1895, was put at the head of the Office's new "rocket section" in the summer of 1936. Another artilleryman, Leo Zanssen, was to command the Peenemünde base as of the summer of 1938. Wernher von Braun, at twenty-five, was designated technical director in May 1937. Dornberger and von Braun got along well together. Beginning in 1938, Dornberger's Berlin-based section came to be known by the abbreviation Wa Prüf 11 (Heereswaffen-amt Prüfwesen 11). The base was to be designated HVP (Heeresversuchstelle Peenemünde). The A3 rocket, a larger version of the A2, was finished at Kum-mersdorf and testing took place in December 1937 off the coast of Peenemünde, on the little island of Greifswalder Oie. Three failures were registered, full of lessons to be learned, as von Braun would later claim.[11] A certain number of A5s—a rocket derived from the A3—were subsequently built and tested on a number of occasions. But effort henceforth focused on the A4 rocket—the one that was to be built at Dora and would become known in 1944 as the V2. Six years would be required, from 1938 until 1944, for this rocket to become opera-tional. It was in 1938–39 that, at Dornberger's instigation, considerable means were put into the project. He obtained from Becker the financing and personnel he asked for. Neufeld clearly shows the importance of the technological chal-lenges to be overcome in three essential areas. The first was that of the engine, of which chemist Walter Thiel was in charge. The second was that of aerody-namics, put in the hands of Rudolf Hermann, a junior physicist. The third was that of guidance systems, entrusted to a third academic, Ernst Steinhoff.[12]

Because of the new nature of these fields of research, which all had to be co-ordinated, Dornberger focused all available means on the Peenemünde site. Thiel, who had stayed at Kummersdorf, joined the others in 1940. A highly modern wind tunnel was built, along with a guidance-systems laboratory, launching pads, and an electric power station. A small urban center with a vari-ety of housing and sports facilities was set up, and a new electric line was also put in. This required the overcoming of major difficulties, in that the terrain was not propitious and access to the island was inconvenient.[13] As of September 1939, three thousand people worked at Peenemünde. Many would remain nos-talgic for these early years.

What is remarkable is that this exceptionally consequential program escaped political interference until 1940. Hitler's regime had been in power since 1933. A certain number of the technicians were notorious Nazi Party members—this was the case with Rudolph, Hermann, and Steinhoff but not Walter Riedel, Thiel, or military men Dornberger and Zanssen. Von Braun, when asked to do so, agreed to join the SS on Dornberger's recommendation; his membership took effect on May 1, 1940, and von Braun was registered as an *Untersturm-führer,* or second lieutenant.[14]

The project remained the affair of the artillerymen, and Neufeld emphasizes that they had a purely tactical conception of the rockets, which they saw as supercannons. Their objective was to exceed by far and away the performance of the Long Max (that Neufeld refers to as the "Paris Gun"),[15] which in 1918 had been used to shell Paris from a distance of seventy-five miles.

Wartime Work on the Rockets, 1940–43

UNCERTAINTIES IN THE FIRST YEARS OF THE WAR. Contrary to what one might suppose, German arms policy in the first years of the war was characterized by great confusion. Work on the rockets was scarcely affected by this, but Dornberger was constantly obliged to remain on guard. An initial scarcity of munitions was already being felt in November 1939, and the Ordnance Office was held responsible. To solve the problem, Hitler named Todt armaments minister on March 17, 1940. Becker, besieged by private problems, committed suicide on April 8.[16] He was replaced by Gen. Emil Leeb, another artilleryman, who held the position right up to 1945. Leeb continued Becker's policies but lacked his experience and influence. Dornberger benefited, however, from the support of von Brauchitsch, who remained commander in chief of the army until December 1941.

The fundamental problem was that of the respective priorities to be assigned to planes for the Luftwaffe, submarines, and rockets. This battle of priorities, described by Neufeld, was translated by a year and a half of confusion, with Hitler making no real choice. On August 20, 1941, Hitler received Dornberger, von Braun, and Steinhoff along with Fromm and Keitel in East Prussia. The offensive in the east was moving ahead favorably, and Hitler, envisaging a swift victory, planned to then turn on England, using rockets to do so. He wanted to have a large number on hand as quickly as possible. This priority was confirmed by the OKW (Oberkommando der Wehrmacht) the following month.[17]

All the research and development work to get the A4 operational was able to proceed normally, but there continued to be difficulties for the production factory, which, when the time came, would have to deliver the quantities of rockets Hitler demanded. Dornberger, like many officers of his generation, did not wish to entrust this production to private industry. And he wanted, moreover, production to be located at Peenemünde in order to maintain close links between development and production engineers. But inasmuch as the A4 rocket had still not achieved a perfectly successful launch, he had a hard time convincing his interlocutors of the importance of his immediate needs in terms of steel and labor.

SPEER'S SUPERVISION AND HIMMLER'S INTRIGUES. On February 8, 1942, replacing Todt, who had just been killed in an airplane crash, Albert Speer became armaments minister. His authority rapidly asserted itself, thanks to Hitler's support. He was favorable to developing the rockets, and he was familiar with

Peenemünde where he controlled a construction office. He had actually worked there himself as an architect and had met von Braun and the other young project leaders, with whom he had many affinities both culturally and socially.

As minister he did not have authority over aeronautical construction but got along well with Field Marshal Erhard Milch, the man in charge of it. The people in Peenemünde-East and Peenemünde-West were in constant contact, despite their administrative separation. The people in the eastern unit used the western unit's airport, and in turn, the western unit was housed by the eastern unit. Cooperation was established for the use of gyroscopes or antiaircraft missile projects. However, in early 1942, the Luftwaffe ventured alone into the conception of a flying bomb. The code name of the operation was *Kirschkern* (Cherry Pit). The device, designed by Argus Motorenwerke and the Fieseler company, was baptized "Fi 103."[18] It was to be known in 1944 as the VI and was ultimately manufactured underground at Dora.

Dornberger and von Braun's greatest problem, in the course of the year 1942, was to succeed finally in launching an A4. The first two launches, on June 13 and then on August 16, yielded only mediocre results. Dornberger could not keep from expressing his disenchantment.[19] It was only on October 3 that the launch was totally successful: the rocket climbed 50 miles into the air and fell to the ground 120 miles from the launching point after five minutes of flight.[20] The following launch, on October 21, was only a partial success. By contrast, the first launch of the Fi 103 at Peenemünde-West, on December 24, was a total failure.

Speer, who had until then kept his distance, decided to directly exercise his authority. In December 1942 he ordered the creation of a Sonderausschuss A4 (A4 Special Committee), putting responsibility for it in the hands of Gerhard Degenkolb, from the DEMAG company, who had successfully directed German locomotive production.[21] The headquarters was in Berlin, at the so-called Lokomotivhaus. A Nazi and an authoritarian, Degenkolb quickly ran into conflict with Dornberger.

Assembly-line production of a rocket—only one of which had ever functioned properly—is different than producing locomotives, whose technology has been well known for a long time. One of the points of contention had to do with the launch method to be used—against England obviously. Dornberger was in favor of a mobile launching device. In December 1942, Hitler declared himself favorable to the construction of a bunker in the north of France, in the Éperlecques Forest north of Saint-Omer; the Todt Organization was put in charge of building a seventy-one-foot-high concrete facility. English-language documents refer to it as the Watten Bunker, from the name of a small town slightly to the east, with a "mountain" serving as a reference point for aviators. In July 1943, Hitler ordered the building of another bunker in the Cotentin, in Sottevast, from which the southwest of England could be reached.[22]

Assembly of the A4s was scheduled to take place at Peenemünde, but also, as of late 1941, in Friedrichshafen, at the Zeppelin factories there. In March 1943 the Rax Werke factory in Wiener Neustadt, south of Vienna, was added to the list. A fourth site envisaged at Falkensee at the DEMAG, to the west of Berlin, was ultimately ruled out. Degenkolb set an objective of three hundred rockets per month at each site, to be reached by December 1943.[23]

At Peenemünde, an administrative distinction was established between development and production. There was, on the one hand, the development unit (*Entwicklungswerk* or EW), which pursued development of the rocket. On the other hand, the testing factory for the manufacture in series (*Versuchsserienwerk* or VW—that is, "test series works") had a hard time getting under way.[24] A heavy burden of responsibility weighed on Rudolph's shoulders as chief engineer. The collection of the plans and the list of the parts furnished by Walter Riedel's office were constantly incomplete as those in charge of development incessantly introduced new modifications—a fact that led to serious tensions.

There was, moreover, a constant dearth of labor, and the use of foreign workers raised security problems. For pure road and construction work, Italian and Polish laborers had often been used. But now, the nonqualified positions in the factory had to be filled by Polish workers and Soviet prisoners of war. This fell under the responsibility of Jäger, who was at the head of the Sonderausschuss A4 labor subcommittee (*Arbeitseinsatz*). In April 1943 there were more than three thousand foreign workers on the entire Peenemünde complex.[25]

In May 1943, to make things official, Speer set up a Commission for Long-Distance Bombings, presided over by Waldemar Petersen, director of the AEG. On May 26 at Peenemünde, Speer brought together his assistant Saur and Degenkolb, General Fromm, Field Marshal Milch, Adm. Karl Dönitz, and many other notables. Two A4 rockets were launched. The first was perfectly successful, the second was a partial failure. The two attempts of the Fi 103 were a total failure. Nevertheless, the commission recommended the construction of both devices, considered to be complementary. This decision had manifestly been made beforehand by Speer and Milch.[26]

Afterward, on July 7, Dornberger, von Braun, and Steinhoff were received by Hitler in Rastenburg in the presence of Speer and Keitel. Von Braun provided commentary on the film of the successful launch and Dornberger gave a lecture. Hitler was particularly impressed by von Braun, who was given the title of professor.[27] The enthusiasm spread to all those present, and to Saur in particular, who had hitherto been reticent.

Degenkolb brought in consultants, in particular Albin Sawatzki, who had brilliantly directed the construction of Tiger tanks at Henschel in Kassel. He was designated on August 4 to plan the production of the A4s, which had to begin by the end of the month.[28] As will be seen further on, the bombing of Peenemünde during the night of August 17–18 would quickly overthrow all these plans.

The meetings regarding the rockets did not include the SS and its chief, Himmler, who nevertheless showed his interest in various ways. On December 11, 1942, he came to Peenemünde and watched a failed launch (after the successful launch of October 3). In 1943, when the Stettin Gestapo carried out a number of arrests, Colonel Zanssen, who commanded the Peenemünde base, was accused. The affair, which reached very high levels in Berlin, quickly came to nothing and Zanssen, vigorously supported by Dornberger, was cleared.[29]

Himmler's second visit took place on June 28, 1943. For the occasion, von Braun apparently wore his SS uniform—one of the few times he is known to have done so. He was then promoted to *Sturmbannführer*—that is, major.[30] But this was not how the SS managed to get itself involved, in mid-1943, in rocket production. It was by providing a concentration camp workforce.

FIRST RECOURSES TO CONCENTRATION CAMP LABOR. The prisoners from the Buchenwald camp who arrived at Dora on August 28, 1943, were not the first to be used for rocket manufacturing. Others had already been put to work at Peenemünde, in Wiener Neustadt, and in Friedrichshafen. It all began with an initiative of Jäger's: following a discussion at Peenemünde, where Rudolph mentioned to him his concerns about a labor shortage, Jäger organized a visit for him to the Heinkel factories in Oranienburg, where a large Kommando of prisoners from the Sachsenhausen camp was employed and housed.[31] The visit, which took place on April 12, 1943, was the object of a detailed and highly favorable report by Rudolph, with instructions as to how to proceed in order to have the prisoners sent.[32] With Dornberger's approbation, a meeting took place on June 2 at Heinz Kunze's office—Degenkolb's assistant—and it was decided to request fourteen hundred prisoners through Jäger from Obersturmführer Maurer, of the SS's WVHA.[33]

Rudolph's report and the minutes of the meeting at Kunze's marked the beginning of a process that would lead to the deaths of thousands of prisoners in Dora. Some fifty years later, what is all the more striking is the utter banality of the documents. Rudolph appears concerned exclusively with solving his labor problems, both qualitatively and quantitatively, in whatever way necessary. He would have preferred more German specialists at his disposal, but several hundred were all he managed to obtain, by means of a complicated administrative procedure (point 3 of the minutes). Beyond that, he was advised to solicit the help of a development unit for the production factory, even though the rocket was far from being ready.

As for foreign workers, for security reasons, the French and all those who had the right to leave were to be excluded; *Ostarbeiter* and Russian prisoners of war would have to suffice. In any case, the latter were already locked up in the shacks of the Trassenheide camp. Thus prisoners remained the only option; it was to be hoped that they had the requisite professional skills. In any case, with regard to prisoners, there was no need to worry about housing, food, pay, etc. So much the less to worry about. The minutes of the meeting show that Jäger's indications were adopted without discussion, and the meeting then moved on to the next point.

The dominant impression is that of supreme indifference with regard to the lot of the prisoners. And this is the impression that Neufeld emphasizes on several occasions. Rudolph was well aware of the Heinkel Kommando prisoners' working and living conditions. He had made a special trip to Oranienburg to gather information. He himself, as already mentioned, was a Nazi of very long standing. But the others taking part in the meeting were also necessarily aware of what was going on. Kunze and Jäger were Speer's men, and the two officers in attendance were representing Dornberger.

At Peenemünde, the first 200 prisoners to arrive from Buchenwald, on June 20, were Germans and Russians. On July 11 the next convoy of 400 was made up essentially of French prisoners, bearing identity numbers in the "14,000" series (see chapter 4), who had arrived at Buchenwald in June.[34] In Wiener Neustadt, 500 prisoners arrived on June 20 from the Mauthausen camp. They arrived on June 22 at the Zeppelin factories in Friedrichshafen from Dachau. On August 14, another Kommando from Dachau was established in Saulgau, in the Upper Swabia, to manufacture for Zeppelin demifuselages for the V2s, intended to be put together at Peenemünde, and then at Dora.[35]

As for prisoners' conditions at Peenemünde, Neufeld found only one witness, a German nonpolitical prisoner, Willy Steimel, whom he did not consider entirely reliable.[36] But there are also the written testimonies of French political prisoners, Roger Berthereau,[37] André Cassier,[38] Eugène Laurent,[39] and above all Michel Fliecx, who devotes fourteen pages of his resistance and deportation memoirs to a sustained account of his time at Peenemünde, from July 11 to October 11, 1943.[40]

His narrative comprises three successive episodes: the month preceding the bombing, the bombing itself, and the aftermath of the bombing up until the return to Buchenwald. Fliecx, who suffered a great deal afterward at Dora and Bergen-Belsen, as will be clear in examining other excerpts from his memoirs, has rather good memories of his first month at Peenemünde. The prisoners were housed on the ground floor of the factory in specially reserved and carefully enclosed quarters that were clean and had new bunks and earthenware washbasins. Food was more or less adequate.[41]

The prisoners were guarded by the SS, with a camp commander who was "fairly above board with us, except when he was drunk," in which case he was liable to be dangerous. Among the wardens was a "Romanian" nicknamed "Mustache"—a *Volksdeutsch*, a Romanian German—who would lash out wildly.[42] On the prisoners' side, the camp senior was a Red, a respected German politician. The other Germans were Greens—that is, criminals of all kinds.[43]

French prisoners who had professional qualifications were employed normally. Others, like the student Fliecx, more or less easily found themselves small jobs. One Peenemünde director complained that he did not find as many qualified workers among the French as he had been promised.[44] Relations with the German civilians appear to have been acceptable. Fliecx confirms that the mortality rate was low. Steimel mentions, among others, four deaths due to the consumption of methanol. Fliecx confirms this, adding that the four were German criminals.[45] It was a classic—and awful—story that comes up again and again. At Peenemünde it was necessary to mix ethanol with methanol in order to reduce the impact on the potato harvest. This more or less bearable situation came to an end with the bombing. The factory was hit, and the prisoners' quarters destroyed. The camp senior was killed, and the Greens took power. The final weeks of the Peenemünde camp and the transfer of the prisoners to Dora will be dealt with in chapter 4.

Several members of the Kommando from Wiener Neustadt were French, and had remained at Mauthausen since their arrival from Compiègne in April 1943. An enclosed complex was reserved at once for the new factory and the camp, with solid buildings. This complex was close to the Rax Werke, a railway construction factory specializing in tenders, whose very name was unknown to the prisoners. The conditions of existence were at first acceptable, before the arrival of further Polish and Russian prisoners, also from Mauthausen, accompanied by a control team, the most frightening member of which was the *Kapo* Georg Finkenzeller, known as "Big George," a former member of the French Foreign Legion who would turn up once again in Dora in 1944. With respect to the SS, the prisoners recall two *Rapportführer*, known as the "black panther" and the "blond panther," mentioned by Louis Crotet,[46] Pierre Lucas,[47] and Paul Bochet.[48] With them was Jean Maupoint, a cabaret artist in Clermont-Ferrand, then in the camp of Compiègne, as well as Arsène Doumeau.

THE BOMBING OF PEENEMÜNDE. The activity on the north of the island of Usedom, which had been going on since late 1936, could not go unnoticed by the British indefinitely. First of all, in November 1939, the British naval attaché in Oslo had been tipped off by an unknown informer, no doubt German, as to rocket testing taking place on a remote Baltic island, in all likelihood Greifswalder Oie. Subsequent rumors had come from Scandinavian countries about rockets being spotted by fishermen off Bornholm. Then more precise information was passed along by the Polish resistance movement, originating from workers employed at Peenemünde. And finally, on May 15, 1942, following a photographic reconnaissance mission of destroyers moored at Swinemünde, a reconnaissance pilot had taken several pictures of Peenemünde on his way back, revealing surprising details. All the evidence seemed to converge.

In April 1943, Duncan Sandys, a young (thirty-four-year-old) member of Parliament and Churchill's son-in-law, was put in charge of looking into the matter. He had himself been an artilleryman before suffering foot injuries and had some notion about rockets. He had a systematic aerial investigation carried out, which revealed the presence at Peenemünde of two long objects in the form of torpedoes (on June 22) and the existence of various buildings that had recently been put up in the north of France. The key person in carrying out this research was Dr. R. V. Jones, scientific adviser with the intelligence services of the Air Ministry.[49]

On June 29, Churchill, following the recommendations of the Defense Committee, decided to launch a massive nighttime air raid—code-named Hydra—on Peenemünde.[50] As it happened, the bombing raid caught those in charge completely off guard, although security measures had been increased. The problems linked with using foreign workers have already been mentioned above. Attempts were made to eliminate the very name Peenemünde from new documents. As of June 1, 1943, the base ceased to be called Heeresanstalt Peenemünde and became Heimat-Artillerie Park 11, with the same abbreviation of HAP. It was located at Karlshagen, a village further to the south on the island of Usedom.[51] Karlshagen was also the name of the prisoners' Kommando. It is quite unlikely that these subterfuges caused much bother to British intelligence services, but they did hinder the work of historians.

The attack took place during the night of August 17–18, 1943, taking advantage of the full moon. The British, by means of a diversionary tactic, managed to draw German fighter planes all the way to Berlin. More than six hundred aircraft took part in the bombing, which lasted almost an hour. In the end, forty bombers were shot down by antiaircraft units or fighter planes that subsequently arrived on the scene.[52] The damage was not as great as was believed in London. The test stands, wind tunnel, and measurement room were not hit. Von Braun was able to save the plans and archives from the fire. But human losses were high because the bombs hit first and foremost the living quarters to the south. There were 735 casualties, above all among the Russian prisoners and Polish workers housed in the Trassenheide camp barracks. Also, 178 German technicians were killed, including Dr. Walter Thiel along with his family.[53]

But the most important consequence was that the Germans knew henceforth that the Peenemünde base was not secure enough for building rockets, and that a factory had to be put up elsewhere, as sheltered as possible from air raids. The large complex set up by Dornberger had to be largely dispersed. Coincidentally, on the 13th of that same month of August 1943 the Rax Werke factories in Wiener Neustadt were bombed and on the 27th it was the Éperlecques blockhouse, which was, this time deliberately, rendered unusable.

FROM PEENEMÜNDE TO DORA. It took the German leaders only some ten days to draw their conclusions about the bombing of Peenemünde. On August 18, Speer traveled by plane successively to Peenemünde, Schweinfurt, and Ratisbonne to get an idea of the extent of the destruction caused by the British and American bombing raids. During this time, Himmler left his headquarters in

Hochwald in East Prussia to meet with Hitler in Rastenburg and urged him to take three steps: move A4 production facilities from Peenemünde to an indeterminate underground site; move the test base to an SS training camp in Blizna, Poland; and use only concentration camp labor in the factory, alongside the German personnel.

On August 20, at Hitler's request, Speer and Saur came to Hochwald to discuss the implementation of these decisions with Himmler. Brigadeführer Dr. Hans Kammler was put in charge of the SS's side of the operation. On August 25, Dornberger, brought up to date in Berlin, entrusted von Braun by telephone with organizing a meeting of those in charge of Peenemünde in order to plan the transfer of production. There seems to have been some discussion of an installation in the Saar area. Sawatzki and Rudolph were put in charge of the operation.

On August 26, in the course of a meeting in Speer's office between Dornberger, Kammler, Saur, and Degenkolb, the Kohnstein site was decided upon. The site had been located in mid-July (that is, before the bombing) by one of Degenkolb's collaborators, who had been looking for a suitable underground setup. The site had been dug out by the WIFO company for its own purposes, as will be seen shortly. The company endeavored to hold on to the site but was soon obliged to relinquish it, in spite of Göring's intervention.[54] On August 28, Kammler had the first prisoners sent from Buchenwald to commence work on the site.

WIFO and Kohnstein, South of the Harz Mountains

The underground complex where it was decided, on August 26, 1943, to transfer the Peenemünde production factory had been dug in the Kohnstein hill, to the south of the Harz Mountains. The successive waves of prisoners from Buchenwald that were sent there knew nothing about this underground facility, which they discovered with alarm; they did not even know the name of the hill itself, about which they would remain ignorant. The geographical landmarks—Thuringia, the Harz Mountains, Nordhausen—would all come later, and in generally imprecise fashion. Thus care must be taken not to rely excessively on notations of this kind to be found in the memoirs.

Interesting indications with regard to the surroundings of Dora are to be found in the writings of the German historian Manfred Bornemann, who comes from the region and is very familiar with its past and geography. A new and expanded edition of his book, *Geheimprojekt Mittelbau,* was published in 1994.

THE HARZ MOUNTAINS AND SURROUNDING AREA. The whole region is dominated by the wooded massif of the Harz Mountains, which stand out clearly on any map of Germany—even a simple road map. It is the most northerly part of the chain of hills, valleys, and mountains that comprise the Harz range and that make up most of the relief of what is now central Germany. The summit, the

Brocken, reaches 3,712 feet, but the plateau is between 1,600 and 1,900 feet high.[55] There has always been a great deal of human activity in the Harz Mountains because of the metal mines, but no normal-gauge railway crosses the massif, which has to be circumnavigated to the east or west. This topography was decisive for the way in which evacuations took place in April 1945.

Because of its proximity to such large urban centers as Berlin, Hamburg, and Leipzig, the Harz Mountains were, before 1939, a resort area, and the presence of numerous hotels and villas facilitated setting up offices and housing for the management transferred from Peenemünde in 1943. The Harz climate is harsh, but the towns and villages of the southern part are relatively protected; the winds were less severe at Dora than at Buchenwald, which was built on the Ettersberg heights, facing north.

The Thuringian basin—a fairly complex sedimentary basin with a variety of rock from the Mesozoic era—spans from the south of the Harz Mountains all the way to the Thüringerwald. At the edge of the Harz Mountains, at the level of Dora, is a thick layer of anhydrite, which makes up the Kohnstein (culminating at 1,079 feet) as well as the neighboring rises, dominating Dora to the north. To the south of the site of the camp, on the other hand, the horizon opens onto a virtually flat subsidence plain, the Goldene Aue. It was in that direction that fragments of civilized life could be perceived.

ANHYDRITE AND ITS USE. It was thus in a layer of anhydrite that the underground galleries of the Kohnstein had been dug. But one wonders whether, at the time, the prisoners were ever able to identify this rock: some spoke of white quartzite, others simply of crystalline rock. Anhydrite is an anhydrous calcium sulfate, and gypsum is the corresponding hydrated form; on the surface, due to rainfall, the anhydrite may turn into gypsum. Anhydrite and gypsum are both used in making plaster. The German word *Gips*, in everyday usage, refers at once to anhydrite, gypsum, and plaster. Anhydrite is also a raw material of the chemical industry.

In the Zorge valley, at the foot of the Harz Mountains, the exploitation of anhydrite in quarries is a dominant feature of the landscape—similar to the exploitation of gypsum in Cormeilles, in the Paris area. But the extraction sometimes takes place in galleries in the interior of the hills—as was the case for gypsum for many years in Montmartre. This extraction is facilitated by the relatively horizontal character of the layers of anhydrite and the homogeneity of the rock, which generally requires no special props. The Kohnstein to the south of the Zorge, and to the north, the Himmelberg and the Mühlberg, are all part of one geological formation. At the level of the Zorge, several rifts can be detected, and digging the tunnels was a somewhat more difficult undertaking, as will be seen shortly.

Bornemann's very-well-documented study shows the importance of the plaster industry in the region, particularly at Ellrich, before the First World War. In the 1920s, anhydrite, extracted in Niedersachswerfen, was above all used by the Leuna synthetic fertilizer manufacturer, near Merseburg. Then came the crisis that affected all the activities right across the board.[56] It was in 1935 that the involvement of the WIFO factory was to change the conditions of exploitation.

WIFO AND THE DIGGING OF THE KOHNSTEIN. The WIFO company was founded in 1934 by the Reich Ministry of Economics. Its full name was Wirtschaftliche Forschungsgesellschaft—that is, economic research society—which made a wide variety of activities possible. Foremost among them was to stockpile reserves of hydrocarbon in various sites throughout Germany. It was also involved in the exploitation of tanker trains and pipelines (in Romania).[57]

It was in order to set up a depot in Niedersachswerfen that, in 1935, the WIFO struck an original bargain with the IG Farben company, linked to the joint digging of an underground complex under the Kohnstein. The anhydrite extracted in the operation was to be used by IG Farben (principally) for the Leuna factory, and the WIFO was to be able to take advantage of an underground depot without having to worry about getting rid of the rubble. The operation was profitable for both parties.[58]

The project, which would be completed in 1944 under different conditions, consisted of digging two parallel tunnels from north to south, then linking them together as the digging advanced with regularly spaced, perpendicular galleries. Tunnel A to the east can be distinguished from tunnel B to the west. The perpendicular galleries were numbered, in Arabic numerals, from north to south. The length of each tunnel was approximately 5,850 feet (a little over a mile), and each gallery was 490 feet long. There was also an emergency gallery *(Notstollen)* that started from tunnel A and ended up on the eastern flank of the Kohnstein.

The digging began in June 1936 and took place in three successive phases. The first, rapid phase ended in May 1937 with gallery 18. In the second phase, from June 1937 to August 1940, after a shift in direction toward the east, gallery 30 was reached in tunnel A and gallery 32 in tunnel B. It was then that a median gallery was undertaken, halfway between tunnels A and B, extending from gallery 20 to gallery 45. The third phase, with a smaller work crew, began in July 1941 and was interrupted in August 1943 by the change in plans regarding how the complex was to be utilized. By then, tunnel B was finished, but not tunnel A, which had no southern exit. A new gallery *(Grenzstollen)* went from tunnel A to the eastern flank of the Kohnstein.[59]

From one phase to the next, the tunnels' cut was modified, though the overall dimensions remained more or less the same: thirty feet wide and twenty-three feet high. Overall, according to Bornemann, more than 35 million cubic feet of anhydrite were extracted—in other words, some 3 million tons. None of the prisoners knew how the tunnels and galleries had been dug out. Various rumors spread. Sadron simply wrote: "I was told that the digging of the tunnels had begun toward the end of World War I." Others added that it had been done by Russian prisoners. The idea that it may have been the outcome of a common-place mining activity, of the kind that had been ongoing in the Harz region for centuries, sprang to no one's mind.

At the end of the 1930s, the WIFO had transformed the halls into a hydrocar-bon depot, with gasoline reservoirs and tanks. When the war started, its activity increased, and a wide variety of goods came to be stockpiled in the underground halls. The labor force required for this stockpiling activity was initially German. In 1943 it comprised a certain number of foreign workers, in particular Czechs and French from the STO.

THE WIFO'S OTHER ACTIVITIES. In 1940, the WIFO was put in charge of the material recovery of war booty and requisitioned raw materials. Branch opera-tions were set up, in particular in Paris and Brussels. Their activity was looked into, after the war, by the French Service for Financial Investigations in Ger-many. The French historian Jacques Delarue devoted the first part of his book *Trafics et Crimes sous l'Occupation (Trafficking and Crime During the Occupa-tion)* to the "underside of the black market" and the role played in this domain by various German organizations, paying particular attention to the Rohstoff-handelsgesellschaft or Raw Materials Trading Company, known as the ROGES, a filial of the WIFO, created in 1940.[60]

Delarue describes its functioning as follows: "The role of the ROGES com-pany, though purely administrative, and consequently unspectacular, was never-theless of capital importance. It was this company that centralized, first of all through book-keeping, as well as materially, all goods sent to Germany. Every forty-eight hours, the purchasing organizations would announce the delivery of goods by category. The ROGES supervised the accuracy of the deliveries, which it had shipped duty free, as the property of the Wehrmacht, taking full responsi-bility for the duration of the whole shipping operation, which was carried out by an accredited transport company.

"It was also the ROGES which received the funds attributed by the delegate of the Four-Year Plan, and which advanced the necessary currencies to the pur-chasing offices for buying goods on the black market. And, lastly, it was the ROGES that resold these same goods, in Germany, to the firms designated by the distribution service, at prices fixed by the national economic offices. The re-sale prices being lower than the purchase prices, a compensation fund at the Fi-nance Ministry covered the difference as well as the ROGES' operating expenses. But all of this was, of course, nothing but a book-keeping game and a means of control, the 'purchases' in France being covered by the occupation ex-penses, which meant that the goods cost nothing whatsoever."

It is clear that the WIFO, either directly or through its filial the ROGES, played a leading role in Germany's war economy. And it is clear that it had the ability to take on and carry out an undertaking as large as the digging out of the

Kohnstein underground passages. It is also clear that, set up by the Ministry of the Economy and linked to the Four-Year Plan administration, it depended on Göring,[61] for whom, moreover, it facilitated the "acquisition" of artworks. It is not surprising that Göring, in vain as it turned out, intervened to avoid the WIFO's eviction from the Kohnstein in late August 1943. Nor is it surprising that it was necessary to move the metals and various goods out of the Kohnstein halls, as will be seen further along.

[[3]]

BUCHENWALD AND
THE CONCENTRATION CAMP
SYSTEM IN 1943

Buchenwald, a Large Camp, Typical of the Concentration Camp System

BUCHENWALD, DORA'S ANTECHAMBER. In mid-1943 the Buchenwald concentration camp sent a large Kommando to a fairly distant site to build the V2s at Peenemünde/Karlshagen. It is not surprising that from the end of August its role was to supply a workforce to Dora, the future camp to be built at the foot of the Kohnstein in Thuringia. Moreover, one of the ongoing functions of Buchenwald for over a year was to receive convoys of prisoners from outside Germany or from other camps within Germany, only to send them on—by thousands and tens of thousands—mostly to external Kommandos, and in particular toward Dora.

From the outset, however, Dora was a very particular Kommando—as will be shown in chapter 4—since the prospective camp was to be closely linked to a factory within a company, the commander of the camp being one of the directors. Dora then became, in the autumn of 1944, an autonomous camp—the last of the main camps created in Nazi Germany. For a year the link between Buchenwald and Dora continued, and the prisoners in Dora who went through Buchenwald—the vast majority, that is—kept their number from Buchenwald right to the end. Thus the recollections of Dora veterans generally begin with a chapter on Buchenwald.

It would be difficult, however, to discuss Buchenwald in a coherent manner on the basis of survivor testimonies alone, for two reasons. First of all, the experience of the majority of these witnesses was limited in time. And the camp at Buchenwald itself greatly evolved between mid-1943 and the liberation in 1945, quite often resulting in various misunderstandings. Therefore it is essential to take a closer look at Buchenwald before turning to a detailed discussion of Dora.

IMAGES OF BUCHENWALD. The images of Buchenwald are varied and in large part contradictory, above all on account of the conditions in which the liberation of the camp came about in 1945. There is no question here of going back into the—altogether passionate—1976 controversy concerning the chronology of events of that afternoon of April 11, 1945. Amouroux—among others—dealt with the subject in 1993.[1] What is important to bear in mind is that when the American troops from Patton's army arrived at Buchenwald they found a camp intact, being administered by the prisoners—a small number of whom had recently armed themselves—with an international organization that had taken things into hand. These exceptional circumstances allowed for the best resolution—given the conditions of the period—of the problem posed by the existence of some twenty-one thousand men to be fed, treated, and then repatriated. There was no disorder, no epidemics, and the repatriation of the French could actually be described as "efficient."[2]

Unfortunately, this concerned only half of what the camp population had been on April 6: the SS had meanwhile managed to haul twenty-three thousand prisoners into the evacuation convoys. The often tragic situation of the Kommandos outside of Buchenwald will be dealt with in part 6. Thus, it was not in fact a single camp that was liberated but rather two side-by-side camps. The normal camp was the "large camp," in which the prisoners were generally able-bodied. But there was also a "small camp" for the ailing that had a very high mortality rate, into which the others were normally not permitted. The image the Americans made public, after their discovery of Ohrdruf on April 5, followed by Eisenhower, Patton, and Bradley's visit to Ohrdruf on April 12, was one of beds in a small camp with its emaciated sick, one of whom was Elie Wiesel. This, along with the crematorium, was what was shown to journalists and delegations coming from the United States—particularly the congressional delegation that arrived at Buchenwald on April 24.[3]

There are no complementary photographs of able-bodied men, in particular those who had taken up arms. This has resulted in a blurry image that has since been quite troubling to readers—as shown by a page in the weekly, *Candide,* in 1965, where Joseph Kessel published a review of *L'Arbre de Goethe (Goethe's Tree)* by Pierre Julitte. Beneath Kessel's signature is a picture of a bed in the small camp followed by the surprising caption: "Thus lived those who undertook one of the most remarkable acts of resistance of the last war."

There is no confusion, however, in the minds of Buchenwald survivors speaking out today. The young Charles Lavallard, having laid down his weapon, thus became a nurse in the former *Revier* of the SS, to help save the sick, often moribund, whom the stretcher-bearers, particularly the American soldiers, were evacuating from the small camp.[4] Jorge Semprun, who stated that "to live in the small camp, during the last winter of the war, was a nightmare; and to survive it was a miracle,"[5] does not know if a French doctor—a prisoner—actually managed to save the Jewish man from Budapest, whom he and his friend Albert had heard singing the Kaddish—the prayer of the dead—in a block of the small camp, lying among the corpses.[6]

It should not be assumed, however, that the Americans were interested only in the corpses and the moribund. Already on April 16, 1945, as Eugen Kogon recounts, "an Intelligence Team from the Psychological Warfare Division arrived in the camp at Buchenwald."[7] "Its mission was to study the living conditions and to show, in a comprehensive report addressed to the SHAEF (Supreme Headquarters of the Allied Expeditionary Forces), how a German concentration camp was set up, what role it played in the national-socialist state, and what the fate of those placed by the Gestapo in these SS-guarded camps had been. Buchenwald was the first large concentration camp to fall intact into the hands of the Western Allied Forces. It was to serve as an example for studying the system prior to this institution."

Kogon notes that this team, under the direction of Lt. Albert G. Rosenberg, was made up of Max M. Kimenthal, Richard Akselrad, Alfred H. Sampson, and Ernest S. Biberfeld. Slightly more is known about Lieutenant Rosenberg, thanks to Semprun's recollections in *L'Écriture ou la vie*.[8] Semprun was one of his sources in the camp—naturally in German. It was Rosenberg who brought those who lived in Weimar to visit Buchenwald. It was he who, on Saint George's Day, brought Semprun to see Goethe's summerhouse on the banks of the Ilm, in the vicinity of Weimar. Rosenberg was a twenty-six-year-old Jewish Berliner who had emigrated to the United States in 1933 with his family. Though he had become an American, he remained very immersed in German culture. One can assume, going by their names, that the other members of his group were also Jews of similar origin.

Whatever the case may be, the members of this team played a key role in gaining understanding of the German concentration camp system, by getting Eugen Kogon to write *L'État SS*. In the introduction to the book, Kogon tells how, in response to their questioning, he ended up writing a report as early as May 1945, in Buchenwald itself, which he had confirmed by fifteen camp leaders, both communist and noncommunist. The interest of this report—passed along by Rosenberg—led British and American leaders to push Kogon to write a book for the general public, extending the subject from the camp at Buchenwald to all the camps. Kogon, housed along with his family in the Frankfurt area, finished the book in November 1945.[9] *Der SS Staat* was published in Germany in 1946 and translated into French in 1947 under the title *L'Enfer organisé (Organized Hell)*. It has remained the basic reference on the camps and was reprinted in France under its real title, *L'État SS*, in 1970 and later in 1993. As for the *Buchenwald Report* itself, it got lost in the archives before being later published in the United States, in 1995, from a copy kept by Rosenberg—who himself went on to become a professor at the University of Texas at El Paso. He will be mentioned again in the epilogue.

It was in this way that the camp at Buchenwald was to become something of a model camp, civilized by the victory of the Reds over the Greens; of the political prisoners, and above all communists over common-law criminals. It is worth pointing out that Kogon, of Austrian origin, was in no way a communist himself and later went back to a university career in West Germany.

The book's success was important for another reason: having been written by a German, it revealed the length of the purely German period of the camps, prior to the mass arrivals of the "deportees," French or otherwise. In this sense it is an excellent starting point from which to assess the camp realities in the summer of 1943—at the very outset of Dora. These realities were very different from those prevailing a year later, particularly with regard to the French.

THE EICKE-STYLE CAMP. In terms of its aims and operation, the camp at Buchenwald in mid-1943 was still very close to the concentration camp model worked out to the last detail by Theodor Eicke, first commander of Dachau, then general-inspector of the camps until 1939. At the head of each camp was a *Kommandant* (along with his *Kommandantur*), who was both the head of an SS garrison, of the *Totenkopf* unit, and of the prisoners' camp, the *Konzentrationslager*. This camp fell under the authority of one of the *Kommandant*'s assistants, the *Lagerführer,* or camp leader. SS members fell into one of two categories: the first was made up of those who were involved, in one way or another, in the camp or at the work sites; the second was comprised of *Posten*, guards posted in the watchtowers or patrolling with dogs around the camp perimeters.

Camp administration was looked after by the prisoners, with those principally in charge being chosen by the commandant. The main person was the *Lagerältester* (LÄ), or camp elder. In the major camps there were sometimes several *Lagerführer* and *Lagerältester* (LÄ1, LÄ2) who would take shifts. The prisoners were normally divided, for housing purposes, into blocks, which were either permanent structures or wooden sheds. Constant surveillance of the prisoners was carried on within the blocks. A prisoner, the *Blockältester* or block elder, assisted by several *Stubendienst,* was in charge of each block under the authority of an SS member, the *Blockführer,* or block leader. The latter could, at any moment, come and inspect the block; he came at any rate at least once a day, to initial the registers kept by the *Schreiber*, or block secretary. The information in these registers had to tally with the figures established by the *Schreibstube*, or central camp office. At the same time, the prisoners were subjected to head counts, or "roll calls," that took place on the parade ground in the middle of the camp. The roll calls could be very drawn out if the various figures put together by the *Rapportführer*—the SS member in charge of the operation—did not match up. Sometimes the roll calls were also prolonged as a form of collective punishment.

Other organizations kept files on the prisoners. One of them, outside the camp, was the Politische Abteilung, or political section, a creation of the Gestapo and the Kripo. It held the prisoners' political or criminal files, and these files followed them from camp to camp. Moreover, they could be opened at any time by whatever level of the police administration had compiled them. This represented a significant bureaucracy, in which the employed prisoners were the mere secretaries.

The other organization was the Arbeitsstatistik, based within the camp, and was, at Buchenwald at any rate, truly managed by the prisoners. Its role was the allotment of work to everyone. Some were assigned a quiet administrative role. Other Kommandos, like those working in the quarries, were especially hard. Skilled laborers who found work in factories dependent on the camp were better off than those who did heavy manual tasks. Thus the Arbeitsstatistik had significant power; it became significant when it was time to draw up the "transport" lists for the outside Kommandos. This was the case, for example, when it was necessary to supply the SS with the five hundred prisoners they demanded one particular day for Dora, Langenstein, or Ohrdruf. This especially delicate subject will be dealt with later.

The functioning of a camp required the existence of a variety of general services. The fate of the majority of prisoners depended, to a large extent, on how these services were managed. Most important among them was the *Revier*—a common term referring to a hospital—which could as easily be the SS *Revier* as the camp *Revier.* There was also the kitchen, clothing store, showers and disinfection area, laundry, and so on. Finally, there was a sort of internal camp police, whose members were called the *Lagerschutz.* At the head of all this one finds the *Kapos,* who were prisoners, each one being under the control of an SS member.

There was another category of *Kapos:* those who directed the Kommandos, the work teams in the camp or those working in companies. These Kommandos were of various sizes and also more or less stable. The *Kapos* were assisted by a highly variable number of *Vorarbeiter,* who could loosely be described as foremen. Certain Kommandos had a *Schreiber.* In concentration camp jargon, the term Kommando had a very wide range of meanings. It could refer to a small group of prisoners in charge of some temporary duty in a camp, or all the prisoners of Ohrdruf, considered as a Kommando dependent on Buchenwald, in turn broken down into Kommandos of various sizes. The context alone makes it possible to know.

All those in charge who had been chosen among the prisoners wore armbands and enjoyed a variety of privileges—more or less, depending on their importance—in terms of dress, hair length, etc. These were the *Prominente.* These positions were the object of bitter competition between clans, especially between political prisoners and common criminals—and possibly between prisoners of different nationalities.

IDENTITY NUMBERS AND TRIANGLES. Up to now, "prisoner" has referred to all those interned in a concentration camp, and this will continue to be the case.

It is the translation of the German word *Häftling*, normally used in this sense. The word "deportee" is suitable only for those who had been transferred from their country to Germany—such as the French or the Belgians. It cannot be applied to citizens of the Reich. But the word "deportee" will be used with regard to convoys leaving from Compiègne, for example.

One characteristic common to all the prisoners, whatever their function may have been, was no longer to be referred to by name but rather by an identity number. Everyone had to be able to state his number in German and above all to recognize it when it was called out. The number was assigned upon arrival in a large camp, a main camp often referred to as the *Stammlager*. Someone leaving a large camp for a Kommando that depended on it did not change his identity number. Thus prisoners from Dora continued to wear the number they had been assigned upon their arrival at Buchenwald, just as the prisoners from Wiener Neustadt continued to wear their number from Mauthausen. But the moment they were transferred—as will be seen later—from Wiener Neustadt to Dora via Buchenwald, they were given numbers from Buchenwald. Michel Fliecx and André Rogerie's changes in identity numbers will be pointed out further on. The recollection of their identity number or numbers is not only a sort of proof of deportation for former prisoners—as it has been alleged—but also a way of situating them amid successive convoys. Reference will frequently be made, with regard to Dora, to the "14,000s," the "20,000s," and the "21,000s" or, later on, of the "77,000s." This way of speaking is convenient for those concerned, as for the author who is himself a "39,000."

The identity number was not the only element of identification used in the camps. There was also the color of the triangle sewn onto the jacket, at least as far as the Germans were concerned, which of course also included Austrians, Sudetens, and so on. Green triangles designated criminals, some of them serving sentences, others considered to be so many professional delinquents (along the lines of those shipped off to prison colonies in former times). Black triangles designated asocial types—a vague category. On the eve of the 1936 Olympic Games in Berlin, in order to clean up the city, there was a roundup of beggars, bums, pimps, and so on, who were then interned in Sachsenhausen and made to wear a black triangle; most of them died shortly thereafter.[10] Repeated absenteeism from work was all that was required to fall into this category. Red triangles were for political prisoners, a portion of whom were well-identified activists: communists, social democrats, Austrian monarchists, etc. Many others were there for having at some time or other expressed opinions hostile to the regime. At Dora, former soldiers from the French Foreign Legion could also be found.

There were other colors of triangles as well. Pink triangles designated homosexuals, condemned for offense to the German race. For this reason, only Germans—or those considered to be German—were concerned. During the war an

Alsatian from Mulhouse was lumped into this category. Purple triangles were reserved for *Bibelforscher*—that is, "fundamentalists" or Jehovah's Witnesses. Also in the camps were those who had been condemned by military tribunals: French SS members were thus interned in Dachau and Stutthof.

Except for the Germans, as well as the Jews and Gypsies, all the prisoners wore red triangles. Overall they really were political prisoners in the broad sense of the term (including hostages), but the Germans also deported individuals with whom they had various problems in conjunction with the black market, procuring, brawling, and so on. This was true for the French, the Belgians, and the Dutch, among others. But criminals in the occupied countries were judged by the courts in their countries and were not deported to Germany. Because Poles and Czechs, however, were at the time citizens of the Reich, it seems that their criminals were interned in the camps in the same way as German Greens.

An initial on the triangle indicated nationality: F for the French, B for the Belgians, P for the Poles, and so on. In certain cases, determining nationality raised problems, which will be examined in chapter 8. Jews and Gypsies who were interned as such had yellow or brown triangles. Their history at Dora was, generally speaking, distinct from that of the other prisoners.

QUARANTINE. Some of the Dora prisoners, as will be seen, spent various lengths of time at Buchenwald before being registered on a "transport" list for Dora. They thus experienced Dora at different times. But for most of the others, their only experience of Buchenwald was the "quarantine"—and it should be pointed out what this entailed. Originally it consisted of the period during which the newcomers were isolated in order to avoid the possible spread of epidemics. Typhus above all was feared in the camps; indeed, it killed many people at the time of the liberation in 1945 at Bergen-Belsen and Dachau. This preoccupation was very real at Buchenwald, where a quarantine was prolonged in March 1944 following the outbreak of a contagious illness.

But quarantine took on another dimension in 1943–44, once there was a sustained demand for putting together convoys of prisoners for external Kommandos—and especially for Dora. The time of the quarantine was thus put to use for choosing between those who were to be admitted into the Buchenwald camp and those who were to be put "in transport." Immediately after the end of the quarantine period, the latter were sent on their way to their destination.

The quarantine took place in a complex of quarantine blocks, which made up the little camp separate from the large camp. When quarantine came to an end, as a sanitary measure, with the end of the convoys of foreign prisoners, the small camp was transformed into an enclosure filled with the sick and the moribund mentioned above. Dora survivors would, upon their return, see photographs in which they recognized their quarantine pallet beds but not their occupants.

With regard to the French, it seems that quarantine conditions changed greatly between the summer of 1943 and the beginning of 1944. In a recent article,[11] Daniel Chlique, the author's brother-in-law, provided the lyrics (and music) of the "Chant des déportés" ("Prisoners' Song"), which he composed in quarantine in Block 47. He adds: "The song was sung, at the request of a Block leader—a German political prisoner—by a chorus of three hundred French prisoners, designated for the convoy of 25 February heading for Mauthausen." Various testimonies of singing and popular-song sessions that took place during this period, in quarantine, have been provided by Tauzin,[12] Rassinier,[13] and Brother Birin.[14] Even today they give rise to great surprise among those from the earlier convoys.

The 1943 Transformation

THE STATE OF THE BUCHENWALD CAMP IN THE SUMMER OF 1943. The Buchenwald camp was set up in 1937 with the arrival of a first group of Greens on July 19. On August 6 there were 1,400 prisoners on the site—at once Reds, Greens, and Purples. Kogon's account of the camp's beginnings is accurate.[15] On this well-known subject, Rassinier put together a totally mythical text to illustrate his theories about the camps.[16] The first years were very hard for the Germans and Austrians who, at the time, made up the mass of the prisoners. The "fundamentalists" and the Jews particularly suffered. The observation that, in 1944, the camp had become a "sanitarium" was widespread among survivors at that time, and although surprising for those who had only recently arrived, was no doubt sincere.

In early 1943 work within the concentration camp complex itself still exceeded industrial activities. The most striking example is the construction of the eight-mile-long railway line linking Weimar to Buchenwald, decided on in March 1943. On June 21, the appointed date, after working day and night at a maniacal pace, the line was inaugurated by the SS elite, led by Kammler. The very next day, work had to start up again on a six-month project.[17] The prisoners coming from Compiègne on September 18, 1943, arrived at the Weimar station and were subsequently transported to Buchenwald by truck.[18] The January 1944 railway convoys, however, went right to Buchenwald. The transport list of arrivals at Buchenwald, which was not available until after March 1943, indicates that prisoners came from Wewelsburg in April. They carried out work in one of the SS's major centers, south of Paderborn.

Nevertheless, in Buchenwald itself, arms-industry-related factories were set up. That of the DAW—Deutsche Ausrüstungswerke—belonged to the SS and was located inside the barbed-wire fences. Himmler finally obtained Speer's authorization to construct the Gustloff's thirteen halls outside the camp; a large Kommando, however, was already set up in the Gustloff factories in Weimar. There was also the Mibau Werke factory, where gyroscopes were built.[19] A more distant Kommando was set up in the Junkers factories in Schönebeck, near Magdeburg.

All these factories required personnel, which the managers imagined they could find among the prisoners who were arriving—the French for instance. It was thus recommended that those arriving present themselves as *Facharbeiter,*[20] that is, as qualified workers, or at least as *Handwerker,* manual laborers. The others, intellectuals or farmers, could be used for outside Kommandos, for the terrace.[21]

In actual fact they were far more likely to be registered on transport lists heading for Dora or Laura—another Buchenwald Kommando that will be mentioned further on. Guy Raoul-Duval, before arriving at Dora in January 1944, remained in Buchenwald, assigned to an outside Kommando in October 1943. According to his recollection, this experience was not too bad.[22] In the concentration camp universe, where nothing was ever really sure, many prisoners had a succession of contrasting experiences. This was the case for the Czech prisoners Benès[23] and Litomisky,[24] who passed through Buchenwald in the autumn of 1943 on their way from Auschwitz to Dora. They felt that they had landed on another planet.

They were struck above all by two things: on the one hand, the limited nature of the brutalities inflicted by the prisoners wearing armbands and the SS, not overly present in the camp; and on the other hand, the regularity with which rations were handed out and packages distributed. The definitive takeover of the camp administration by the Reds—communists as it happened—was decisive in this regard. It came about in June 1943.

Hermann Langbein, an Austrian who spent a long time in Dachau, then in Auschwitz, is—along with Kogon—the best analyst of the Nazi concentration camp system. In two chapters of his work, *La Résistance dans les camps de concentration nationaux-socialistes,* he successively examined "The prisoners' autonomous administration" and "The struggle between the Reds and the Greens."[25] He insists on the need to avoid an excessively black-and-white view of events in seeing Evil on the side of the Greens and Good on the side of the Reds. He nonetheless concludes that, overall, the Reds were by far and away preferable to the Greens, both in the case of communist control as at Buchenwald or Sachsenhausen, or social democratic and Catholic control as in Dachau. The omnipresence of Greens at Dora, in the difficult periods, on the other hand, had tragic consequences.

THE TRANSFORMATION OF THE CONCENTRATION CAMP SYSTEM THROUGH STATISTICS. The supply by the SS of an ever larger concentration camp labor force to arms manufacturers and several other factories, starting in 1943, had major consequences on the structure and operation of the camps, which underwent a veritable transformation. The incomplete and inconsistent character of the available documents makes it impossible to carry out a complete statistical study on this subject, but the information that has been gathered is no less significant.

One important indication concerns the number of camps and Kommandos based in them. Wolfgang Sofsky provides some numbers, taken from G. Schwarz.[26] "In December 1942, there were only 82 external work Kommandos (*Außenkommandos*), 29 of these were in Dachau alone. A year later, the total had climbed to 196. Most of the satellite camps were not set up until 1944; in June of that year, there were 341, and by January 1945, there were 13 main camps with a total of 662 *Außenkommandos*." The (benign) terminological confusion is of little consequence. What matters is the exceptional progression of the totals. To fill all the camps and Kommandos, an increasing number of prisoners was required. On the basis of three documents stemming from the SS, Sofsky points out the following progression of the total:[27] 115,000 in August 1942, more than 200,000 in May 1943, 525,000 in August 1944, and 714,000 in January 1945.

With regard simply to "entries" in the Buchenwald camp alone, Kogon drew up a table[28] on the basis of the following figures: 14,111 in 1942, 42,177 in 1943, 97,866 in 1944, and 43,823 in the first quarter of 1945. These figures, which correspond to identity numbers, comprise both newcomers into the concentration camp system and prisoners coming from other camps (organized transfers or evacuations). For Buchenwald, the progression appears with the series of identity numbers having to do with the arrivals of French prisoners. In June 1943 the numbers were into the "14,000s," the "small numbers" having been reused, occasionally several times over, following deaths since the beginning of the camp. The arrival of the "20,000s" and "21,000s" took place in September 1943, the "39,000s" to "44,000s" in January 1944, and the "77,000s" in August 1944. These and other convoys will be studied in greater detail later.

However one looks at these figures, established according to a variety of criteria, what stands out is that the situation in late 1944, before the evacuation of the camps in the east, was incommensurable with that in early 1943, both in terms of the number of prisoners and their geographical distribution.

The observed rise in the number of prisoners results from the conjunction of various factors that Sofsky,[29] among others, has enumerated. There was first of all, in late 1942, the transfer into the camps of inmates from prisons in the Reich—those serving sentences of more than eight years in the case of Germans and Czechs, and more than three years for Poles, as it was specified. There was also, progressively, the transfer of more or less free workers into the camps on the basis of a wide variety of accusations, the most often targeted being the Polish and the *Ostarbeiter,* Ukrainians, or others; the same lot was reserved for many Soviet prisoners of war. It was then decided to use a Jewish or Gypsy labor force outside of the Auschwitz complex. Rather curiously, in his assessments, Sofsky seems to overlook the "deportees" from the occupied countries in the west and south of Europe.

One of the very important consequences of this overall growth in the number of prisoners in the camps was that it made the Germans very much a minority. Langbein provides several examples of this.[30] "In Buchenwald, they made up twelve percent after the liberation, almost a third of whom were Austrian; in Mauthausen, in March 1945, the proportion was approximately nine percent, and eight percent in Dora, including all the sub-camps, on 1 April 1945. Twelve prisoners from Sachsenhausen, who were still there immediately after the Liberation, wrote up a report according to which there was, after 1942, no more than a minority of eight to ten percent Germans, very few of whom were political. Dachau, on Liberation day, had no more than three percent Germans and 0.8% Austrians." Langbein followed up with percentages for Gross Rosen (2 percent), Flossenbürg (5.5 percent), and for Auschwitz (1.9 percent).

This development was to the Greens' benefit in that they had an easier time finding jobs as *Kapos,* in particular in exterior Kommandos rather than in the large camps. The de facto complicity between them and the SS was reinforced in these Kommandos, as was the case at Ellrich. In the large camps, on the other hand, though not without some difficulty, a link was established between German and Austrian Reds and foreign politicians, in Buchenwald and Dachau for example, as will be shown.

CONVOYS FROM BUCHENWALD AND DORA. Examining the convoys that came to Buchenwald, most of them heading for Dora, between June 1943 and January 1944, makes it possible to appreciate the mechanisms of the transformation in the life of the camps.

What is first of all noticeable is the volume of convoys coming from the Ukraine. The origin was initially Dnepropetrovsk, on July 26, August 26, August 29, and September 19, 1943, then Kirovograd on October 11 and November 17, 1943, and Nikolaiev on October 6, November 27 and 30, 1943, and then March 23, 1944. These convoys correspond to the progressive evacuation of the camps in the Ukraine, accompanying the German retreat after the defeat at Kursk in early July. This amounted to 4,140 deportees from Dnepropetrovsk, 847 from Kirovograd, 1,569 from Nikolaiev, and 233 from Kiev, for a total of 6,789. A very significant portion of these "Ukrainians," virtually all of whom were young, were transferred to Dora after the quarantine. Thus they showed up again in the tunnel, where they did not go unnoticed. The other group of convoys came from Compiègne: 962 on June 27, 900 on September 4, 989 on September 18, 911 on October 30, 921 on December 16, 1943, 1,939 on January 19, 1,990 on January 24, and 1,580 on January 29. The total of 10,192 deportees is considerable; they were mainly French, with a few foreigners from France; the convoy of January 19 included a group of Spanish Republicans.

From January to May 1943 there had been three large convoys from Compiègne to Sachsenhausen (3,650 deportees at the outset) and two others to Mauthausen (2,000 deportees). Subsequently, right up until March 1944, all the convoys were sent to Buchenwald. The first convoys were made up largely of young people, who, not wanting to do their STO, had gone underground or had attempted to cross the Pyrenees to get to North Africa through Spain.

Subsequently, the proportion of more elderly French Resistance fighters seems to have been greater, the Germans having notably decided to deport those men whom they had long since arrested and had been holding in Fresnes, Romainville, or Compiègne. Three examples can be mentioned: Marcel Baillon, arrested on August 26, 1942, Father Jean-Paul Renard, on November 11, 1942, and Jean-Henry Tauzin, on November 26, 1941.

This series of convoys in the direction of Buchenwald, followed by still others in May and August, accounts for the large proportion of French who were in the camp at the time of the Liberation. But, above all, it accounts for the fact that Dora has occasionally been called the "French cemetery," the deportees from various convoys very often having been sent to Dora, and then Ellrich and Harzungen. It was pointed out above, in chapter 1, that the Italian government of Badoglio had concluded an armistice with the Allies on September 8, 1943, and that the German troops had occupied Rome on the 12th. The SS then took control of the camps where Yugoslavian partisans were interned: given the zones annexed or occupied by Italy, these were Slovenians, Croatians from Dalmatia, and Montenegrins. Many of them arrived in Dora several weeks later, via Dachau and Buchenwald. With them came Italian soldiers, who had been disarmed and taken prisoner by the Germans in the Balkans or in Italy itself. They had, as will be seen, a special status without really being privileged.

The ethnic makeup of Dora's original population, to a large extent due to the political circumstances of the moment, is out of keeping with the usual makeup of large German camps. Germans from Buchenwald, a large majority of whom were Greens, were sent to supervise this rarely German-speaking population. The Reds, having control of the Arbeitsstatistik, thus had the chance to get rid of a certain number of them—and not necessarily the most friendly ones. To fill out the numbers, prisoners were brought in from other camps, particularly from Auschwitz. In the first weeks there were several convoys of Poles from Buchenwald to Dora. Czechs also arrived, who, according to available testimony, seem to have already passed through Auschwitz. It was in this way that, in a few months, a diverse population of prisoners came together, the majority of them novices in the universe of the concentration camps, and no doubt for this reason all the more liable to suffer from the conditions that were to be imposed on them.

PART TWO

The Hell of Dora

[[4]]

THE NEW ORGANIZATION OF AUTUMN 1943

The decisions made in August 1943 after the bombing of Peenemünde had two important consequences. The first was to break up the geographical and administrative unity of the V2 design and production apparatus, until then held together only through Dornberger's obstinacy. The second was to establish an organic, indissoluble link between the German rocket venture and the Nazi concentration camp system—under the worst conditions for the prisoners concerned. The new organization will be described in this chapter. The following chapters deal with "the Hell of Dora" between September 1943 and May 1944.

Setting Up Mittelwerk

The most important organization-related decision was the immediate transfer of the V2 production factory from the Peenemünde base to the underground complex at Kohnstein—that is, the Dora Tunnel. This represented the transfer of materiel, German staff, and the prisoners already sent from Buchenwald to Peenemünde/Karlshagen. The two men in charge of the operation were Sawatzki, given the task of planning the entire operation, and Rudolph, who was to set up the factory and get it running. Rudolph was one of the senior rocket specialists, while Sawatzki had recently arrived from another industrial sector. Both were Nazis.

At the same time, V2 production, having escaped the control of the Ordnance Office, was entrusted to a new limited liability company called Mittelwerk GmbH, set up in Berlin on September 21, 1943, in the course of a meeting presided over by Speer (assisted by Degenkolb and Kunze), in which Professor Hettlage took part, representing the Amt für Wirtschaft und Finanzen, which was looking after the financing. Also attending were Kammler, representing the SS, and Franz Wehling, manager of the WIFO, owner of the Dora Tunnel.[1] The capital was held by the Rüstungskontor GmbH, or Armament Fund Ltd., set up on May 4, 1942, and given charge of various tasks including the distribution of steel and nonferrous metals. This organization also had offices in the occupied countries and particularly in France.

Kurt Kettler, director of the Borsig locomotive factory in Hennigsdorf, near Berlin, was also present at the meeting and was appointed manager. The Mittelwerk offices were, in principle, to be set up in Berlin-Charlottenburg, but in actual fact were in the premises (a former convent, secularized in the sixteenth century) occupied by the Napola at Ilfeld.[2] A certain number of directors were subsequently appointed—including Sawatzki and SS-Sturmbannführer Otto Förschner, the Dora camp commander, who was put in charge of security.

Replacing a hydrocarbon and raw materials depot with a mechanical-engineering factory in the tunnels required heavy work and much manual labor. Moreover, the tunnels themselves were unfinished. As the WIFO already had staff and material on location, either directly or through subcontractors, contracts were concluded with it for renting premises and managing the conversion work. Mittelwerk's partner was the WIFO's Ni Agency (derived from Niedersachswerfen), directed by Karl Wilhelm Neu since 1936.[3]

Beginning on October 1, 1943, Sawatzki established plans for the new underground factory.[4] With an overall surface area in the order of 1.04 million square feet, the factory was meant to employ in the long run some 18,000 people, including 2,000 German civilians and 16,000 prisoners of all nationalities. Before the Peenemünde bombing, it should not be forgotten that three sites were chosen for assembling the V2s: Peenemünde, Friedrichshafen, and Wiener Neustadt. In November 1943, following the bombings, Wiener Neustadt was dropped from the list: the equipment and some of the personnel (Germans and prisoners) were transferred to Dora. In Friedrichshafen, that portion of production intended for V2s was limited to the fuel tanks and center section. The assembly of the V2s was concentrated in the Dora Tunnel.

Dispersion of the Sites

The transfer of the production factory was not the only repercussion felt in Peenemünde after the August 18 bombing. The whole base was split up into various units for which new locations had to be found. The damage had been extensive in the inhabited zones—hardest hit—but the factories and annexed installations could have continued to function following more or less extensive repairs. That, at any rate, was what Dornberger hoped.

There exists a late (1989) testimony by a French prisoner, Roger Berthereau, who was part of a group of electricians, that has to do with the damage suffered by one of the electrical power stations. With several friends, whose names he provides, he managed to discreetly but effectively worsen the damage. He provides the first precise indications of successful sabotage on the basis of favorable circumstances, by a small group that was at once competent and able to keep a secret.[5]

There was one transfer from Peenemünde that in the end did not come about until evacuation in February 1945: that of the development unit, whose technical director was Wernher von Braun. In October 1943, however, it had been decided to install the unit in the early months of 1944 at Ebensee (in Upper Austria, on the south shore of Lake Traunsee) in an underground complex still to be dug. Prisoners from Mauthausen arrived on location on November 18, 1943, to begin the digging, which was to continue right up until April 1945, with other uses in mind. Von Braun took advantage of the various technical difficulties that cropped up in order to stay on at Peenemünde, in what remained an army base.[6]

Peenemünde ceased, however, to depend on Dornberger, whom General Fromm—commander of the army of the interior—appointed *Beauftragter zur besonderen Verwendung Heer,* or "army commissioner for special tasks," on September 4. The objective, in fact, was to create and train units in charge of launching the rockets. Dornberger set up his headquarters in Schwedt, on the Oder, upstream from Stettin, and thus not far from Peenemünde. Collaboration between him and von Braun was able to continue easily. It was Zanssen, initially, who replaced him at the head of the "Wa Prüf 11."[7]

The most important transfer, aside from that of the production factory, was that of much of the rocket testing. Instead of firing V2s from Peenemünde out over the Baltic toward the east, it was decided to fire them northward from Blizna—a former firing range of the Polish artillery taken over by the SS and which was situated within the General Government of Poland, ninety miles northeast of Krakow near the confluence of the Vistula and the San. The SS gave it the name of Heidelager.[8]

The schema decided on was as follows. The rocket would be designed in the development unit, which remained at Peenemünde, until its planned transfer to Ebensee. It would be assembled by Mittelwerk in the Dora Tunnel and sent from there to Blizna for a test flight—no small journey. When the conclusions to be drawn from the launch at Blizna implied modifications to the rocket, they would be brought back to Peenemünde where they would be studied, in order to introduce them into the assembly by Mittelwerk, before another rocket would be sent to Blizna for another trial. Things had really been far simpler when everything took place at Peenemünde. The British pilots no doubt overestimated the destruction they had wreaked on Peenemünde; they nevertheless did succeed in disorganizing the German system.

But at the end of 1943 this schema existed in theory alone. Indeed, no rocket was produced between August 1943 and January 1944, and only the eight built at Peenemünde in early August still remained.[9] It took more than four months—four terrible months for the prisoners—to get the V2 production factory up and running in its new underground site. Other transfers were decided in late 1943, such as that of Rudolf Hermann's wind tunnel to Kochel, on the edge of the Alps, south of Munich. A company bearing a code name was set up for this purpose.[10] The new wind tunnel would operate only until October 1944.[11]

The setting up of test centers for the V2 engines in two locations—Lehesten and Redl-Zipf—was much quicker. At Lehesten, a large slate quarry situated on the border of Thuringia and Bavaria south of Saalfeld was converted for these purposes.[12] At Redl-Zipf, in Upper Austria northeast of Salzburg, a hill behind a brewery had to be dug into.[13] In both cases the labor force came from concentration camps. The Redl-Zipf work site was opened on October 4, 1943, by prisoners from Mauthausen. It was a Kommando from Buchenwald that, at the same time, opened the work site at Lehesten. Thus the new phase of V2 development was in all cases associated with the concentration camp system: in Dora and Lehesten as well as at Ebensee and in Redl-Zipf.

The Wizernes Bunker

In his new functions, on October 4, Dornberger visited Hitler, who, ignoring his advice, decided on the construction of a new bunker at Wizernes,[14] south of the northern French city of Saint-Omer, to replace that of Éperlecques, once again bombed on September 7. The new site was some twelve miles from the previous one, next to the Saint-Omer/Boulogne railway line. It was an enormous chalkworks, whose base could be dug out in order to safely store, within its four and a half miles of tunnels, a large number of V2s prior to their launch.

The central part had to be transformed to ready it for firing rockets in a vertical position. And, in order for the entire complex to be sheltered from bombings, an impressive-sized dome of concrete was poured over the central section: 16 feet thick and 234 feet in diameter, it had an overall mass of fifty thousand tons. The Todt Organization contracted the work out to a large Rhineland company, Philipp Holzmann. The labor force was made up of German workers, including Westphalian miners, and forced laborers, in particular Russian and Polish prisoners of war. Three teams worked around the clock.

The Éperlecques site was not totally abandoned, however. The bunker was re-built there, where a liquid oxygen factory was to be set up.

The Rocket in the Power Struggle

In order to appreciate the responsibilities of the various parties in subsequent events, it is worthwhile pointing out the relative positions, in the autumn of 1943, of the army, the Armaments Ministry, and the SS. The dominant authority was the minister Albert Speer, who enjoyed the führer's full confidence. In September 1943 his ministry changed names. Since Todt had created it in 1940, it had been the Reichsministerium für Bewaffnung und Munition, giving it authority for arms and munitions production. Its new title, Reichsministerium für Rüstung und Kriegsproduktion, broadened its domain of competence to all armament and war production. This had already been the de facto situation, but it was significant that it be thus made official.

Regarding rocket production, there were three hierarchical levels. At the head of it was Speer, and his assistant Saur, head of the Technisches Amt. Beneath him was the Sonderausschuss A4, with Degenkolb and his assistant Kunze. At the base was the Mittelwerk company, directed by Kettler along with Sawatzki. The SS provided the concentration camp labor force, based on Kammler's instructions, who had received full powers from Himmler in this regard. The fact that Förschner was one of the directors of Mittelwerk was symbolic, given his lack of competence.

Von Braun appeared isolated in Peenemünde, but with his team of specialists he alone was in a position to push the project forward, with the help of the artillerymen Dornberger and Zanssen. Indeed, the V2 was still not operational, and would only become so in September 1944, in the wake of further tests carried out by Dornberger and von Braun.

While waiting for the Mittelwerk factory to provide the V2s for these tests, von Braun kept the Peenemünde installations operational away from the ruins, which were left deliberately "intact" to mislead aerial observations. He traveled a great deal in the final months of 1943 to sort out the technical problems raised by the installations in the Dora Tunnel, in Lehesten, and in Redl-Zipf. That time frame coincided with the most painful period for the prisoners at all three sites.

Systematic Secrecy

As already seen in chapter 2, a preoccupation with secrecy had ultimately led to name changes—Karlshagen replacing Peenemünde, for instance. Beginning in August 1943 the practice of coding became systematic, and it is necessary to take a closer look at this issue in order to avoid confusions and recognize the synonyms. "Dora" designated the Kommando that was sent to the Mittelwerk factory at Kohnstein and later to the corresponding camp. Though its usage became generalized, the name was not official at first. "Laura" referred to the Kommando working in Lehesten. Dora and Laura depended on Buchenwald.

The work sites opened in Upper Austria by the prisoners from Mauthausen were assigned names of minerals. Ebensee was given the name *Zement* (cement). Redl-Zipf became *Schlier,* a rock typical of the region. This type of coding was later applied to the work sites near Dora. There was also a coding system based on animal names. As of September 1943 the Peenemünde unit was called *Kitz,* the kid.[15]

The first plan laid out by Sawatzki on October 1, 1943, was allegedly written in Hammersfeld—a place that does not exist. This name was soon dropped. The WIFO report of December 31, which will be referred to further on, was dated "OU," which corresponds to *Ort ungenannt,* or "unnamed place," the height of camouflage.[16] The postal address of the Dora camp was first Block 17 of the Buchenwald camp, and then Sangerhausen, a city some thirty miles to the east of Nordhausen, whose name, on the other hand, never appears.

The whole region around Dora—that is, the region of Nordhausen and the neighboring zones of the Harz Mountains—constituted a whole secret network. It was the *Mittelraum,* where the Mittelbau complex was to be found, including the Mittelwerk company.[17] One can merely guess that it had to do with central, or "middle," Germany.

The First Nine Months at Dora

From September 1943 until March 1944, "transports" of prisoners to Dora from the Buchenwald camp—chosen for the most part from within the quarantine blocks—never ceased. In general they concerned a round figure: 250 prisoners in the case of the February 11, 1944, transport, of which the author was part, including a very large majority of French prisoners who had arrived from Compiègne with the first major convoy in January.

Eventually the goal was to attain the requisite number of workers to satisfy the Mittelwerk company's manpower needs and ensure the functioning of the neighboring camp. But first, it was above all necessary to have an indefinite mass of prisoners to carry out the task of transforming the factory and the camp. Because this transformation work led to numerous victims, whose corpses were transported to Buchenwald to be incinerated, they had to be replaced, and it was this kind of occurrence that gave Dora its justifiably detestable reputation. Further on, an attempt will be made, on the basis of available information, to draw up a statistical table of this period. But its essential features must first of all be described.

Until February 1944 inclusively, newcomers to Dora, with the exception of several rare *Prominente,* were immediately sent into the tunnel, where they were housed, as Sawatzki had intended right from his initial plan. On the outside, the SS barracks, indispensable collective buildings such as the kitchen, and the few prisoners' barracks that will be discussed later (*Revier, Schonung,* Italian POW block) were built. Absolute priority was given to getting the factory ready, and the construction of an external camp was deliberately postponed. It was only in January 1944 that the prisoners of the Kommandos working on the outside began to be housed outside the tunnel. The others remained there until

April–May. The last to come out, in May (May 29, as Henry Bousson points out), were the electricians of the Kommando AEG. Among them was Léon Bronchart and his young friend Georges Argoux, who arrived there in September 1943. Their underground stay lasted nine months.[18]

The ordeals common to all that resulted from overcrowding in the "dormitories," which took the place of blocks, as well as the total absence of hygiene, will be dealt with later. But it must be added that these dormitories were not situated amid an operating factory but at the very heart of an unimaginable work site, full of noise and dust. In the tunnels and galleries at Kohnstein, the WIFO's underground stockpile had to be evacuated, the boring of tunnel A completed, and various redigging, filling-in, and concrete-laying jobs carried out. Electrical and other networks had to be set up, with all machines, workshops, and offices installed. With everything being done in improvisation and precipitation, the disorder was as apparent as it was real. Those in charge were increasingly overwhelmed the lower one went in the hierarchy, and the blows just rained down on basic prisoners. It is an open question as to whether the outside Kommandos doing the "earthwork" for road and railway building in the mud and cold were better or worse off than those in the tunnel. In any case, for months on end the prisoners concerned returned to sleep in the tunnel.

Only at the very beginning of 1944 was the tunnel factory in a position to deliver its first V2 for trials at Blizna. And only in March–April was the factory itself more or less completed. It was then and only then, when construction of the camp was finished, that the last Kommandos were able to leave the tunnel dormitories for real blocks outside. The transports from Buchenwald to Dora in March provided the requisite workforce that did not sleep in the tunnel.

The Succession of "Transports" from Buchenwald to Dora

The "transports" from Buchenwald to Dora having been set up essentially for those prisoners in quarantine, their order corresponded with the convoys that arrived in Buchenwald. The progression can be tracked with regard to both French prisoners and prisoners of other nationalities arrested in France. The same could be done for the Ukrainians, for instance, but the information is not easily available. The first convoy arriving in Buchenwald from Compiègne on June 27, 1943, was comprised of 1,000 deportees, who were numbered in the "14,000" series (beginning at around "13,800"). A group of them left for Peenemünde/Karlshagen, where they arrived on July 11. The others remained in Buchenwald. Certain among them would later be part of the first transports to Dora, at the very beginning of September.

A second convoy of 900 arrived in Buchenwald on September 4. This group was numbered in the "20,000" series. A large number of them got to Dora on September 28 and 29. The convoy of a thousand who arrived on September 18 made up the "21,000" series. Beginning on October 13, many of them arrived in Dora.

A transport of sixty-one prisoners was registered on September 20 in Buchenwald, coming from Sachsenhausen. They were immediately sent to Dora. The group was made up of sixty miners from the Pas-de-Calais and from Huy in Belgium, and of Léon Bronchart, who had the number 21983. The numbers of the others went beyond "22,000." The return of prisoners sent to Karlshagen was registered in Buchenwald on October 14. They were renumbered, some toward the end of the "22,000" series, some at the beginning of the "28,000" series. Both groups were immediately sent to Dora.

Some French deportees were numbered in the lower "30,000"s, such as Louis Girard, Marcel Baillon, and Georges Virondeau. They did not come from Compiègne but had passed through a variety of prisons in both France and Germany. The convoy of October 30 coming from Compiègne was initially made up of a thousand deportees. There were 911 when they arrived (the number of deportees who died in the course of the "journey" varies from one convoy to another). Their numbers fell between the "30,000"s and "31,000"s. They arrived at Dora on November 20. On that same day a convoy arrived in Buchenwald from Mauthausen made up in fact of a number of the prisoners from the Wiener Neustadt Kommando. They were numbered above "31,500" and transferred to Dora as of November 23. The convoy of one thousand deportees who arrived from Compiègne on December 16 fell into the "38,000" series. But the last of the "38,000"s were from Alsace-Lorraine, coming from Natzweiler (that is, Struthof). They were transferred to Dora in December, followed by the others in January 1944.

In January 1944, in the framework of Operation Meerschaum (sea foam), fifty-six hundred French (or foreigners arrested in France) were deported in three convoys that arrived in Buchenwald on January 19, 24, and 29. The numbers subsequently go from 39400 to the upper "44,000"s. Overall, the prisoners of the two first convoys sent to Dora arrived there in several transports in February and went into the tunnel. Those from the third convoy arrived in March and remained in the camp. Of course, these indications are schematic. Some French prisoners remained at Buchenwald for some time before being sent on to Dora. André Guichard (14890) arrived only in December 1943, and Guy Raoul-Duval (21693) in January 1944.

It can be seen that in the course of this period, French deportees continued to arrive in Dora. The resulting variety of the testimonies makes it possible to have as complete a knowledge as possible of events in these dramatic months. Less is known about the prisoners of other nationalities. It is known that at the end of October 1943, Yugoslavs bearing numbers in the "32,000" series arrived indirectly from Italy; and that in mid-November, many Poles with numbers in the

"33,000" and "34,000" series arrived. Italian prisoners of war were sent from various *Stalag* between October 14 and November 2.

The Transports from Peenemünde, Wiener Neustadt, and Sachsenhausen

Until the August 18, 1943, bombing, life for Buchenwald prisoners sent to Peenemünde had been tolerable, as mentioned earlier. The bombing brought on two major changes. The first was that the German Greens took power that was unleashed on the others: one of their number, known as Mischka, replaced the Red LÄ, who was killed. The second was the overcrowding in the shelters, the dormitories having been destroyed. Michel Fliecx devoted several pages of his memoirs to narrating the more or less useless recuperation activities in which he had to engage in the general disorder that followed the bombing: loosening and taking off bolts, scraping dirt off bricks, and so on.[19] Ultimately, all the prisoners were transferred to Buchenwald, then to the Dora Tunnel, where the material saved from the production factory had been shipped along with a number of the German civilians.

Because the Wiener Neustadt site was threatened by air raids (the most recent on November 2, 1943), it was decided to stop production there. The evacuation of the site took place on November 17. The material and some of the civilians and prisoners were transferred to the Dora Tunnel. It seems that the rest of the prisoners were then sent to the Redl-Zipf work site, which had just opened with prisoners from Mauthausen.

The miners who arrived from Sachsenhausen in a special transport were designated to finish digging tunnel A at Kohnstein. They very erroneously imagined that they were being sent to a coal mine in the Saar.[20] Léon Bronchart, who was with them, was an extraordinary individual, whose name will be mentioned later in connection with the AEG Kommando.

[[5]]

NINE MONTHS OF ORDEAL

Life in the Tunnel

ARRIVAL IN THE TUNNEL. To the north of the Kohnstein, in the Zorge valley, there was no room for any major new installations. To the south, on the other hand, it was possible to build a shunting yard with areas for stockpiling as well as an SS camp to the east and the concentration camp in the small valley.

In September 1943 an embryonic version of the camp was first set up near tunnel B's south exit; it was surrounded with barbed wire and had army tents for the SS and the *Prominente*. As tunnel A was not yet finished, there was no other access. But it meant entering the tunnel from the wrong side. The work undertaken by the WIFO had started in the north, where lighting and flat ground had existed for some time. In the south, on the other hand, work was still under way on a full-scale work site.

For many months the prisoners' first sight of the tunnel was an even greater shock than their arrival in Buchenwald had been several weeks earlier. The narratives frequently make reference to a descent into hell—and these are not literary reminiscences.

A few phrases taken from these narratives help reconstitute the scene. "The huge wooden door, which barred the entrance, creaked shut behind us. [. . .] We were suddenly engulfed in darkness. Now and again, however, an acetylene lamp threw its sooty glow on the very high walls. We climbed over piles of sand, catching our feet in cables, bumping into beams or railway ties which were scattered over the floor." "We went into the tunnel, walked for a long while, then on the right, we entered an excavation that had been dug out to establish a temporarily abandoned hall. The ground was rough, water seeped from the rocks, pools of water lay stagnant." "Water seeped from everywhere. The ground was sticky and slimy, causing our wooden soles to slip." "In the tunnels where we suddenly found ourselves, there were heaps of stones piled in stagnant water." These testimonies, given by Jiri Benès, Léon Bronchart, and Jean Mialet, date from September–October 1943.[1] Benès and Bronchart add, regarding conditions when they arrived in September: "There was a pile of half-stuffed straw mattresses. We all took one and tried to stretch out somewhere." "We spent the night amidst shouts and blows, lying in water, the points of the rocks bruising our bodies." That was Hall 39.

THE TUNNEL "DORMITORIES." In October 1943, Halls 43 to 46 were transformed into "dormitories;" Émile Nérot and Jean Rieg recall having taken part in cobbling pallet beds together and moving straw mattresses in.[2] This arrangement would last until May 1944, that is, for more than seven months. These four halls were on the right at the very end of tunnel A, the digging of which was just being completed. They were reserved for housing the prisoners, whereas the preceding halls made up the factory. After the dormitories were eliminated in the summer of 1944, V1 production—which had previously been carried out, above all, by the Volkswagen factory in Fallersleben—took their place. Contrary to the others, these halls did not lead to tunnel A; they were dead-ends, which did nothing to improve ventilation. Beyond the entrance to Hall 46 was the digging site. Digging went on twenty-four hours a day, in two twelve-hour shifts. That was also the rhythm of the factory, such that the dormitories were occupied almost permanently. The rear of the digging site, from where the earth was evacuated, was across from the dormitories. The digging site and the dormitories were thus closely associated, and the prisoners, once they left work, were unable to get away from the dust and noise of the drill-hammers, the explosions, and the movements of the stone-filled carts. When the dormitories were evacuated, digging was still unfinished.

During this period there was still no running water in the tunnel. There were of course pipes, but the water in them was not drinkable but rather intended for jobs like making concrete, and the prisoners had no access to the few taps there were. This meant that washing oneself was utterly impossible, which is a serious problem for people working in a mine in the dust or outside in the mud. It also meant that it was impossible to drink anything other than the soup broth. It was always possible to burst the pipes, but that was an act of sabotage and very dangerous. Moreover, consuming undrinkable water was a surefire way of contracting dysentery, the most feared disease at the time.

Nor, consequently, were there proper hygienic facilities. Because the prisoners were not outside, the solution of going into the bushes or using makeshift outhouses did not exist. They had recourse to half barrels with a plank on top, installed in tunnel A, in front of the dormitories. They were barrels that the WIFO had used for storing gasoline. Raymond Jacob notes: "I was affected into a Kommando where, using a hammer and a chisel, we were supposed to cut the barrels into two pieces to make latrine buckets."[3]

Benès was part of the latrine-bucket Kommando for a while. The half barrels had to be carried to the latrine holes outside, and the SS's toilets needed to be cleaned. "It was very unpleasant, but also very dangerous work because of the risks of typhus and dysentery."[4]

In the first quarter of 1944 the total number of prisoners in the Dora camp was somewhere between 11,500 and 12,000. At least 10,000 were still housed in the tunnel, which means there were permanently some 5,000 prisoners in the four dormitories. Other figures have spread, based on an incorrect reading of the WIFO report of December 31, 1943, according to which 5,500 were allegedly housed in the camp barracks. These numbers, put forth by Bornemann[5]—which Neufeld relied upon[6]—greatly surprised the survivors, and an inquiry carried out by the Dora-Ellrich association showed that these statistics were erroneous. The building of the camp began in earnest only in March.

The dormitories were some 400 feet long, 40 feet wide, and 30 feet high. They were comprised of rudimentary wooden partitions at each end, and a three- or four-story double partition in the middle. Movement was possible along the aisles on either side of the central partition. This resulted in a scarcely imaginable cramming together of filthy individuals, at times suffering from dysentery or coughing up their lungs in the dust caused by the blasting at the work site.

In this close and muggy atmosphere, lice ended up in the straw mattresses and then in the clothes. Each day each prisoner would try to kill his own lice without ever really managing to do so. As Paul Butet recalls: "At the beginning, I would only find a few in the folds of my shirt or the seams of my underwear. It was relatively easy to squash them between our thumb nails, but because of the conditions of hygiene, they multiplied so quickly that by the end of February there was nothing more to be done. I had been lucky enough to have a home-made wool sweater. I had to get rid of it in a corner of the tunnel: there were almost as many lice as there were stitches."[7]

THE GREAT DISINFECTING CAMPAIGN OF FEBRUARY 29, 1944. The lice began to spread from the prisoners to the SS and the German civilians. The authorities then feared—not without cause—a large typhus epidemic, and the decision was made to carry out a general disinfecting campaign. It began on February 29, 1944, and lasted several days and nights. The ten-thousand-odd prisoners in the tunnel were subjected to it one after the other. The operation has been related at length by Charles Sadron,[8] who at the time had only just recently arrived in Dora and, like everyone else, was already covered in vermin. He describes the disinfecting itself, after the long wait that preceded it.

"We were brought shivering into the compound of the sleeping camp, in front of the large shower building. A confused ruckus issued from its lit-up windows. Nearby, the large rolling steam-room periodically gave off a cloud of white steam, which vanished into the darkness. The air smelled of disinfectant. We had to wait in the snow for the group ahead of us to come out. The cold was very keen. We warmed one another up by rubbing our backs together. Fatigue gripped our temples in a merciless vise.

"Finally, it was our turn. There was a fight to get into the large room first, where the warmth penetrated us and livened us up. But we had no time to savor this well-being. We had to quickly undress. Shirts were to be thrown on the right-hand pile, underpants onto the left-hand pile, we hurriedly rolled them up into a ball, and, naked, lined up in front of the unlikely 'barbers,' who shaved us from head to foot. At times, a gust of freezing-cold air made us shiver. The odor of three hundred filthy bodies, covered with scabs and sores was nauseating.

"The shearing finished, we entered the shower room in single file, our shoes in hand. Immediately to the right of the entrance was a large cement bathtub, which we got into by climbing three steps. It was full of a solution which smelled strongly like disinfectant. The water may have been clear and hot at the beginning. But a thousand dirty men, with muddy feet had been through it before we arrived. And so it was into a cold and murky liquid that we had to plunge, one after the other, under the surveillance of a brute, who first tore off any bandages and made sure that, in keeping with the rules, we completely disappeared, including the head, into this slop. We emerged almost suffocating, our eyes burning, shivering, and crowded under the showerheads. When we were all there, the shower began. It was a wonderful moment. The very hot water brought on an unimaginable sense of well-being. We rubbed our skin—which was red with ulcers and vermin—with voluptuous frenzy. The men shouted with joy and sang. It was a deafening racket that only came to an end when the showers stopped.

"Then things got less amusing. We went into the room next door, holding our by-now soaking-wet shoes in our hands. It was here that we were to retrieve our disinfected clothing. The room, the same size as the shower room, opened onto the outside through five windows and a door, all of which were wide-open onto the night. A glacial wind blew onto our soaking-wet bodies: there was nothing to dry ourselves with, and we had to wait like that for many long minutes. We rubbed ourselves with our hands and smacked our skin violently and repeatedly, anxious to avoid the pneumonia—that is, the death—that threatened us.

"Finally, we were allowed to approach the table where the wash was piling up. Quick, quick, a shirt, some underpants, a sweater, pants and a jacket, and we had to move on a little further to put them on. An SS walked about, speeding up the operation. We had to move more and more quickly. With his cane, he lashed the bare backs of any laggards. It nonetheless took us a bit of time, because we had to wring out the clothes before putting them on, even though they had only been soaked and not washed. God only knows where the shirt I received came from: it was trimmed with wide embroideries. It was dotted with lice specks, and the breast was smudged with black spots. But that was of no consequence: it had been disinfected. I pulled it on quickly. It only went halfway down my stomach. Soaked like the rest, the boxer shorts had only half a right leg, and obviously neither buttons nor trim; but that could be fixed with some thread. As a matter of fact, I couldn't really complain: the guy next to me pulled on a pair of boxer shorts that must have belonged to someone with dysentery, because there was still a patch stuck to the bottom of them. I nearly threw up; but one day, I too was to be subjected to the same experience.

"The SS guard started getting angry. We quickly pulled on the remnants of sweaters, pants that were too short, vests with the buttons missing, and off we went! At the exit, we were thrown a grimy beret, also wet, and there we were, back outside. It was perhaps three o'clock in the morning. Standing in the snow, we fastened on as best we could the rags which were falling from our bodies. The Kapo called for us to group together. Our wet clothes gave off steam in the cold air. Once again we had to wait. My God, we thought, that pneumonia is sure to get us! After an hour, we were all there. We headed for the dormitory at full speed, where each of us huddled under his blanket, which was also wet." The author shall confine himself to the following remark: "That night, a few of us friends were there with Charles Sadron."

HUNGER, RATIONS, AND CARE PACKAGES. The prisoners in Dora suffered a great deal from hunger in the early months, but also, as will be seen, in the final months. Reactions varied, however, as in all the camps, from one individual to another. Marcel Pierrel states: "The most striking memory was the constant hunger that gnawed at us."[9] Others stress different aspects. In this respect, Max Dutillieux's remark sheds light on these differences in attitude: "Real hunger starts by just tickling the stomach, then twisting it for a few hours; then it doesn't hurt anymore at all, but it eats away at your reserves, wearing you down, consuming your muscles and ends up killing you."[10] In Dora, as in all the camps, some prisoners would imagine extraordinary menus "for the day when freedom had returned with abundance"; others never thought about it.

The daily ration consisted of a quart of rutabaga-based soup, a piece of bread, a pat of margarine, and one other element, which could be a sort of cottage cheese, a sort of jam, or a sort of sausage, in small quantities. Only the bread didn't have to be consumed immediately, which led Fliecx to explain the reasons for not keeping the bread for later:

"The first was that we were terribly hungry, which was only stimulated by the soup, far too inconsistent and inadequate; it is really very hard to have hunger in your stomach and bread in your pocket. There is no way to stop thinking about that confounded piece of bread; whereas, if you ate it, there was no more thinking about it. The torture wasn't worth it in my opinion. In my two years of experience, nibblers were a species that rarely lasted long. The other reason is that there was a good chance that when you woke up, delighted at the idea of sinking your teeth into some bread, your delight quickly turned into useless rage: no more bread! A dexterous thief had relieved you of it during the night."[11]

This was one of the serious problems of daily life in the first months of Dora: that of insecurity—and in this regard the contrast with Buchenwald is striking. There are any number of anecdotes regarding provisions. They have to do, in the first place, with the distribution of rations, initially carried out in the "blocks" represented by the tunnel dormitories. The Czech, Otakar Litomisky, became the *Schreiber* of one of them whose *Blockältester*, Kurt Kemeter, was a German Red who had fought in Spain. Litomisky relates with pride that the Czechs in his block built a wooden distribution counter with a window for handing out food while checking identity numbers. He adds that in the other blocks it was impossible to do so without the help of the SS.[12]

The bread still had actually to arrive in the blocks. Fliecx tells the following: "The bread was back-packed in from the outside in sacks, with twenty breads per sack. Thus there was a long column which moved in the tunnels, duly escorted by the Stubendienst, club in hand to ward off those who sought to get too close. If there was an electrical failure, which was not uncommon, you would hear yells, sounds of tearing fabric, and a stampede of feet [. . .]. When the light came back on, there was nothing but ripped-open bags whose content had sometimes completely disappeared."[13]

Prisoners who received care packages, distributed in the tunnel blocks, were immediately threatened and were smart to quickly consume the contents, sharing it with their fellow prisoners. In any case, Litomisky points out, "The packages' contents, even if they arrived in good condition, soon went bad because of the humidity in the Tunnel."[14] Thefts took place in the blocks while prisoners were sleeping: it was better to put bread rations, food from care packages, and shoes in good shape under one's head as a makeshift pillow. There was never any doubt as to the thieves' nationality. They were young Ukrainians, organized in gangs, and the stolen objects circulated quickly. Practically no one was ever caught in the act.

Attacks also took place in the camp as was observed by several French prisoners from the barracks of the *Revier*. Jacob and Fliecx[15] witnessed attacks on the rutabaga wagons before they got to the kitchens. The Greens in charge did not get involved when those carrying the soup drums being attacked were, for instance, Italian prisoners of war, who had their own block in the camp.

Soup drums brought near the camp entrance also had to be protected when the day-shift tunnel Kommandos were allowed out for approximately an hour to eat their soup, instead of having to eat it in the dormitories. Fliecx, from the *Schonung* (rest-period block for prisoners), contemplated the scene. "In groups of five, they were white as sheets for lack of air, light and food, unshaven, filthy, and dressed in blue and gray rags, which made them look even more pitiful."[16]

The mere conditions of internment of the Dora prisoners would have been enough to produce a high rate of mortality in the nine months of imprisonment in the tunnel. But they were accompanied by equally detestable working conditions.

From the WIFO Stockpile to the Mittelwerk Factory

In respect of the decisions made at the highest level, after August 18, 1943, the WIFO had to leave its underground installations at Kohnstein to allow the V2 production factory to be set up. The problem thus arose of who was to look after the dismantling and evacuation of the WIFO stockpile, followed by the work required to start up the factory. Following the bombing, the people in Peenemünde lacked the teams needed to deal with this task. Moreover, the Trassenheide camp, which housed the Russian and Polish workers in charge of carrying out work in the camp, had been particularly hard hit. There was, in any case, no further question of using anything but a concentration camp workforce in the tunnel, aside from German civilians.

The WIFO, on the contrary, had experienced German personnel and a certain amount of equipment on location, and was in contact with subcontractors whom they could rely on. Thus the WIFO was put in charge of converting Kohnstein on behalf of Mittelwerk, and under the authority of the Armaments Ministry.

THE WIFO'S ROLE. The contract concluded on September 5, 1943, put the WIFO's Ni Agency in charge of implementing, for Mittelwerk, a program designated as Bauabschnitt Erweiterung III, that is, it corresponded to the extension of phase three, then underway, of the digging of the Kohnstein tunnels.[17] In fact, the program went well beyond this subterranean work. Indeed, it not only included the full-scale conversion of the factory but also, outside, the construction of offices *(Bürounterkunft)* of the departments of Oberingenieur Sawatzki, the *Barackenlager* for the German civilians in Ilfeld and in Harzungen, a barracks for the SS (SS-*Unterkunft*) as well as a concentration camp, referred to as a *Häftlings-Erholungslager* (prisoners' rest camp).

There is a long list of a wide variety of categories in the assessment signed on December 31, 1943, by Neu, director of the WIFO.[18] His responsibility, at the implementation level, was thus total. It should be noted in passing that the assessment included, along with what was completed *(fertiggestellt)*, categories where work was still under way *("50% der Baracken aufgestellt")* or merely planned *(vorgesehen)*. It is not always perfectly clear.

What, at any rate, is highly revealing is that the concentration camp and the SS barracks formed a whole along with the factory and the Mittelwerk camp administration. Any subsequent attempt at dissociation was ruled out. In this complex there were German civilians (and several soldiers, as will be seen), the prisoners, and the SS, none of whom could be unaware of the others' presence.

THE FATE OF THE "WIFOS." In late August 1943, in Niedersachswerfen, a certain number of foreign workers with legal working papers were employed by the WIFO—Frenchmen from the STO and Czechs who had been recruited and given contracts from within the Protectorate as well as three Belgians. They were still working in the north part of the tunnel in October and lived freely outside after their work hours. They had only a very discreet relationship with the prisoners.

At the end of October, for reasons unknown—but doubtless for security-related motives—these foreign workers were all arrested and fitted out in striped prison uniforms with a white triangle bearing the initial W. Their hair wasn't cut and they initially formed a Kommando all on their own. Their families continued to receive a portion of their pay, but the workers were forbidden to indicate their change of status. Several prisoners—Dunouau, Nérot, Soubirous—refer in their memoirs to these arrests, which they witnessed.[19] Gradually the "Wifos" were mixed in with the other prisoners.

THE EVACUATION OF THE WIFO FUEL DEPOT. In order for the factory to be installed in the tunnels, the fuel depot that had been set up there first had to be removed. The underground passages, it must be remembered, had been dug and set up with this in mind. In particular, the shape of the halls was circular in order to house the enormous cylindrical tanks. The latter thus had to be emptied and taken apart, which was a long job, no doubt carried out essentially by the Wifos prior to their arrest. Sermot and Dunouau mention this dismantling work.[20] It seems that the fuel was transferred to Bohemia-Moravia.[21]

There were also stockpiles of gasoline tanks, and Mialet relates their being moved and loaded onto railway cars in insane conditions, under the supervision of a perfectly hysterical German civilian. It was barrels of this kind, cut in two, that served as latrines. Bornemann[22] and Neufeld[23] also refer to the existence of a stockpile of poison gas; but Neander, after further investigation, does not believe this to be the case.[24]

Benès, Demuyter, Dutillieux, and Martin refer to all manner of material and objects, in particular copper and chemical products.[25] The (Russian) prisoners who drank methyl alcohol died in awful conditions. But there were also cases of tinned goods and even bottles of port wine. Dutillieux notes: "I remember having seen several fellow prisoners, French and Russian, in an inebriated state after having discovered the cases of port!"[26] There was thus a full range of the WIFO's acquisitions, particularly from France, through the black market operations described above.

THE COMPLETION OF TUNNEL A. The task of boring tunnel A through to its southern end was, under the conditions in which it was carried out, one of the most murderous work sites of this whole period. The teams followed one upon the other in twelve-hour shifts, and the "miners" would then sleep, without washing, in the nearby dormitories, full of dust and noise. It was here that Bronchart's friends—who had come with him from Sachsenhausen—were transferred. At the time of the Liberation, in Bergen-Belsen, he met again with only one of them, a miner from Sallaumines, near Lens.[27]

Bronchart testifies to what he saw: "In spite of the risk involved given the chaos, I managed to visit my friends the miners on their work site. My intention was to get back in touch with them, given that for the time being I was alone, mostly to find out if their work was less inhuman. What I saw left me horrified! First off, as I approached the sector, I encountered a layer of dust, which had invaded the tunnel, a half-light due to a defective lighting system, made worse still by this dust; a dreadful din, the explosion of charges, the noisy crash of jackhammers, drills, the grinding of pails and spades; carriages rolling along makeshift, unpinned rails, and a twisted track that could, at any moment, cause a derailing, which gave the Kapos and the Vorarbeiter the pretext, as if they needed one, to hit the men who were exhausting themselves to 'get it back on track,' but who were doing so without any suitable means, because they were not given the opportunity."

He adds: "The carriages were unloaded down below the railway cars, which, in turn, were loaded. Whereas, turning the system the other way round, the carriages could have been unloaded straight into these cars, sparing the men unimaginable pain, as they worked right up against one another, hindering one another, fighting to dig and shovel on the rough ground, white as shrouds from the dust that entirely covered them, grunting from the effort, and the never-ending blows, the massacres."[28]

Paul Butet gives his own personal account in identical terms:[29] "I was assigned to a Kommando of miners. [...] I spent twelve hours a day in the 'stones,' as we said amongst ourselves. [...] The civilian Meister who directed the work had the holes packed with explosives; a blast of the horn was followed by the explosion, and then right away, in the dust and smoke, with the others, I had to pick up the stones, load them into a carriage on a 24-inch track, then push the carriage further along, where it was hooked onto a work-site locomotive.

"We had to lift enormous stones to load them, and there was no question of going about it two or three at a time. Push the carriages at a run, then run back for another load. If only these stupid carriages had been in good shape, but they were forever derailing, and even in a group it was no easy thing to get a loaded carriage back onto its track. [...] We managed however, with the help of the Kapo, who would reach out and smack all our taut backs, shouting himself hoarse about what bastards, saboteurs, or even 'Scheisse Stück' (pieces of shit) we were. [...] The dust from the rock, the smoke from the explosives all went into our lungs, of course, but also stuck to our skin. After two weeks, we had become gray, swarthy, the color of the rock."

The rubble was transported further along in the tunnel. After the large cylindrical reservoirs were dismantled, it was used to fill in the lower part of the circular-section halls: Halls 25–28, 30–32, 34–37, 39, and 42. Conversely, one hall had to be dug deeper still in order to put the rockets into a vertical position. The concrete-pouring Kommandos, such as the Sievers Kommando, were particularly feared.[30] They dealt with the concrete work on the ground but also on the arches at certain places in the southern part of the tunnel, in those places where the layer of anhydrite was cut with fissures that allowed water to leak in—the effects of which were felt by the first prisoners to arrive. At the level of Hall 42, a sinkhole (like those frequently found on karstic plateaus, because of the transformation of the anhydrite into gypsum that had been dissolved) was discovered. Special retaining work had to be carried out.[31]

"EARTHWORK" FOR THE OUTSIDE KOMMANDOS. For months, Kommandos left the tunnels every day for "earthwork" outside. The survivors have only a vague and indistinct memory of it. They did *Strassenbau,* road building, and laid ties and rails so that the factory could finally be connected to the outside world from the south and the first rockets be shipped to Blizna.

They all remember the cold and above all the mud, recalled by Benès: "In the soft and sticky earth in the temporary roll-call area, the autumn rains formed a pond between twelve and twenty inches deep. On the unfinished roads, it was worse still. When a truck passed by a column of prisoners, they were all sprayed from head to foot with a deluge of mud. Even good socks wouldn't have been enough, because the mud came in over the top. This was the state in which people returned to the Block [of the tunnel] to sleep for two or three hours. Most climbed onto their bunks still in their socks, without getting undressed or even taking their shoes off. The straw mattresses turned into mud pies."[32]

The worst Kommando appears to have been the "Kabelsir" Kommando, according to the testimony of Auchabie and Alabert, who describe it in few words: "The Kabelsir Kommando, working for the AEG firm, was put in charge of laying a large buried electrical cable to provide Dora with electricity from Nordhausen. It existed for a three-month period: roughly December 1943, January and February 1944, and consisted of digging the trench with spades, laying the cable and filling in the trench. [. . .] Made up of 100 *Stücke* (units) at the outset, reduced to less than twenty by late December, reinforced to 100 once again, only to be reduced to some fifteen by late January, and ten or so by late February, at the completion of the job. The prisoners having made it through were thus very rare, a mere handful, or even a fingerful."[33] *Kabelsir* is a gallicized version of *Kabelzieher,* "cable pullers." As these jobs were carried out far from the camp, there were attempts at escape, which were ferociously punished by the SS guards.

BUILDING THE BARRACKS. A concentration camp's history generally starts with the construction of the camp itself, preceded by that of the SS barracks. At Dora, given the absolute priority given to getting the tunnel factory up and running, it seems that the SS were left for some time in their tents alone and that their barracks were first set up by prisoners requisitioned to build the quarters after their work hours in the tunnel or in the earthworks. The SS ultimately obtained the use of special Kommandos, who also built the kitchen and various other camp buildings.

A special Kommando was also sent to build the camp intended for German civilians in Ilfeld. Exceptionally, tension does not appear to have been particularly high in this Kommando, referred to in the narratives of Albert Amate[34] and Jean Michel.[35]

SETTING UP THE FACTORY IN THE TUNNEL. Setting up the V2 production factory in the Dora Tunnel does not seem to have been an easy operation. According to Rudolph's late narrative, it was only on December 31, 1943, that symbolically the first four or five rockets, actually still imperfect, were loaded onto railway cars.[36] But Rudolph makes no reference to the difficulties encountered and the means used to overcome them. Based on the witnesses' identity numbers, it is known when they arrived. On the basis of their narratives, one can assume that dismantling the WIFO and the basic improvements of the tunnels and halls (concrete work, lighting, and so on) took longer than expected.

It is likely that merely deciding where to locate the various facilities was the object of multiple orders and counterorders, because all the competent people were still in Peenemünde. As soon as everything was under the same roof, as Dornberger wished, these kinds of problems were quickly resolved. There is, on this topic, a text by Jiri Beneš who, as a Czech, sought to demythologize the celebrated German organization in his memoirs.[37]

"In tunnel B, where the assembly cradles had to be moveable along the line, the prisoners put in rails. Under the supervision of five engineers, the rails were laid on a thick layer of reinforced concrete. Scarcely had the concrete really hardened in our sector of the tunnel than a sixth engineer arrived and ordered that the rails be taken up and moved two and a half feet to the left. This was very hard work because we had a lot of difficulty breaking a mile-and-a-half-long, six-inch-thick layer of reinforced concrete, with chisels and hammers. What, at the time, we found very funny was that while we in the south sector started to rip up the rails, still other prisoners, in the north sector, continued to methodically lay concrete, carrying their job through to the end.

"Finally, the rails were moved thirty inches to the left. Assembly cradles arrived from Wiener Neustadt, but they turned out to be heavy and impractical. So we waited for other assembly cradles from Swinemünde. These cars arrived, but they were for narrow-gauge track. We therefore set rails corresponding to the narrow gauge between the normal gauge rails. We laid them up as far as the switches, but at that point we didn't know what to do. So we wrote to engineer number 6. He arrived surrounded by his assistants, took all the measurements once again, then decided to eliminate one of the rails of the narrow gauge, which required re-pouring concrete where it had been.

"The two rails of the narrow gauge were finally torn up in the forward (south) section of tunnel B, where only the normal gauge track was left in place. New assembly cradles were ordered for this 400-yard-long segment of track. In the middle part, only one rail of the narrow-gauge track was used. In the rear (north) part, all the rails were finally torn up to facilitate the installation of the airplane-motor factory, separate from that of the V2s."

Benès deliberately pushed his narrative to the point of caricature, but this type of situation must have been frequent and provoked a good many delays and arguments. Which points to the issue of interpretation problems, raised by a well-known text of Speer's. In his office's "chronicle," one finds the following account: "On the morning of 10 December [1943], the minister traveled to the Harz Mountains to visit a new factory. Carrying out this monumental task had forced those in charge to go to the limit of their energy resources. Some were so exhausted that they had to be forced to take their vacation to rest their nervous systems."[38]

Many years later, in his book about the SS, Speer took up this passage once again to point out that the prisoners' conditions of existence had so shocked the minister's entourage that some had to be given leave.[39] This interpretation is not convincing at all. The chronicle's text is perfectly explicit—moreover, it is in no way surprising. It is likely that the rocket experts were subjected to a great deal of tension at the time, their reputations and careers being on the line. The consequences of the situation on the prisoners were necessarily dramatic, because the ongoing race against the clock implied an unbearable rhythm. Many testimonies detail the condition in which the machines and various parts of the framework were carried from the cars, unloaded outside the tunnel, to where they were to be installed in the factory. Dutillieux sums up how the machines were moved: "To manipulate them, our tools were planks, beams, jumpers, rolls of steel, ropes. [...] We pushed and pulled."[40] But those involved had neither the experience, nor the strength required. Rogerie,[41] Douay,[42] Benès[43] wore themselves out carrying girders. Like the mine, like the earthworks, setting up the factory equipment gave rise to a very large number of victims.

THE AEG KOMMANDO AND THE KOENIG KOMMANDO. It happened that certain tasks required real or more or less real specialists, who thereby escaped the hardest jobs. The electricians, inside the tunnel, were relatively privileged. Several excerpts from the testimonies of French prisoners show how they ended up being fairly numerous in the AEG Kommando. Bronchart tells how it got started:[44] "[The Dutch interpreter] asked me: 'Are you an electrician?' When I answered that I was, he said: 'I am signing you up as an electrician in the AEG Kommando, make sure you show up tomorrow at the Arbeitsdienst.' A group of six Frenchmen thus came together, including Bronchart, his friend Georges Argoux and Koehren, 'who spoke decent German and was, moreover, a genuine electrician.' " "The AEG was reinforced, and we recommended to all the newly arriving Frenchmen that they declare themselves to be electricians."

"Our first job in the AEG was to install lighting in the main hall. [...] We finished the lighting installations in the two lateral tunnels. In the constructed halls the lighting was then abundant and harsh. The ground was leveled. We began installing the machines on their cradles. We dug the trenches for the high-tension cables."

Méfret describes his experience: "Arriving in the Dora tunnel on 3 November 1943, I was immediately affected to the AEG service [...] with Marcel Berthet, who was a professional, and who taught at the watchmaking school in Besançon. [...] Our job was to fix the lines for the light as the boring of the tunnel moved forward. We worked on the main cables of the two tunnels to service the perpendicular halls."[45]

Jacob got himself into the group when coming out of the *Revier*: "I met someone I knew, a '20,000' like myself, who boasted up all the advantages of being an electrician in the AEG. Replying that I had a paper to return from whence I came, he offered to falsify it for the AEG, and introduced me to the Kapo who accepted me."[46] Vagnon also indicates: "I was affected to the Transportkolonne, and then to the AEG Kommando (which allowed me to survive)."[47] Bronchart's influence, even on the *Kapo,* was thus determinant.

There was also another Kommando of electricians, the Koenig Kommando, whose *Kapo* was initially a Frenchman, but he lacked authority. Very amateur electricians, such as Georges Soubirous[48] and Raymond de Miribel, who were poorly supervised, were unable to stay in the group and the *Kapo* was replaced. On the contrary, the *Vorarbeiter* Berthereau, who had come from Peenemünde with his friend Choquet, spent the winter of 1943–44 there, "in less horrible conditions than the others."[49]

LÉON BRONCHART. In September 1943, Bronchart was forty-seven years old. He was born in Bapaume, in the Somme region in the north of France. His father, of Belgian origin, was a stonecutter and trade unionist. He himself started working in a glassworks when he was eleven. In 1914 he signed up as a soldier in a mountain brigade and was quickly taken prisoner. He passed through different camps, including Ohrdruf,[50] attempting escape several times, unsuccessfully. In November 1917, released as a member of the medical corps, he returned to France through Switzerland. He joined up as a stretcher-bearer in the Foreign Legion and was awarded the Croix de Guerre and the Médaille Militaire. He joined the Orléans railway company in 1919, working first of all as a stoker, then as a locomotive engineer out of the Tours depot in 1931. He was active as a socialist and above all as a trade unionist, becoming general secretary of his network's section of engineers and stokers.

He took part in the war in 1940 as part of the railway corps and was then transferred to Brive. He joined the Resistance and was arrested, after being denounced in January 1943 with a variety of fellow Resistance fighters, including his eldest son. The group was transferred to Compiègne, then to Sachsenhausen. From there, with his son, he went into the Staaken Kommando that built the Falkensee camp, then on to Falkensee. On September 11, 1943, he was brought back to Oranienburg for interrogations, in the wake of further arrests in France. He made it out but was sent to Dora, via Buchenwald, with a group of miners, as mentioned above. He had several advantages. He had spent three years in prisoners' camps in Germany from 1914 to 1917. He spoke German. He was an experienced manual laborer in different fields. He was a seasoned activist. At Staaken and then at Falkensee he got on with his block leader, a German communist. In Dora he skillfully maneuvered the *Kapo* and the *Meister*. Very proud of his military past, he particularly supported the young, particularly those from the officers' school of Saint-Cyr.

After he retired in 1947, he remained active and in 1969 published his memoirs, with the appropriate title *Ouvrier et Soldat (Worker and Soldier)*.

GROWING NEEDS FOR LABOR. It seems that, as of December 1943, the engineers in charge of V2 production were concerned about training the team that would be needed to assemble the rockets under the orders of the *Meister*—ordinary German civilians—most of whom were from Peenemünde and supposed to be competent. It was then that, little by little, Kommandos of "specialists" came together; they would remain fairly stable, reinforcements notwithstanding, right up until the final weeks. We shall return to this organization in chapter 9. What must be emphasized is that the members of these Kommandos, generally advantaged in terms of work, were subjected to the common condition of being housed in the tunnel right up until May 1944. Charles Sadron's delousing narrative is that of one of these so-called specialists.

There were also specialists in outside activities, such as the painter Jacques Vern, who tells the following; "They asked for painters, I raised my hand and was taken. First, we did camouflage work on the stones which came out of the Tunnel, then camouflaged the Tunnel entrance, then the buildings intended for the prisoners."[51]

[[6]]

DEATH IN DORA

Death, Ever-Present

THE DORA *REVIER*. All the concentration camps had some sort of hospital, which was called the *Revier*. Certain camp maps indicated *Häftlingskrankenbau* or HKB, which was the same thing. There was a wide variety of *Revier*, depending on location and time period. The quality of a *Revier* was dependent on the personality of the SS doctor who supervised it, and that of the *Kapo* under whose command it fell; it also depended on the genuine medical competency of the "doctor" and nurse prisoners who worked there. In any case, means and particularly medicines were generally lacking.

The setting-up of a *Revier* at Dora was part of the makeshift conditions of the early months. Initially there was only a tent close to the tunnel entrance, followed by a sort of shanty *(Bude)* in the tunnel; and finally, one of the first blocks to be built in the camp—on the north side of the valley, no doubt Block 16—was turned into a *Revier* at an unspecified date.

Normally there was a sort of infirmary for external care *(Äussere Ambulanz)* that treated—with a limited number of ointments—wounds of all types. There was also the *Innere Ambulanz,* where a decision was made either for a patient's hospitalization, or a limited period of rest *(Schonung),* or simply a return trip right back to the Kommando. One way or another, only a fever of at least 39 degrees Celsius was considered as truly ill; for a long time an initial selection was made on this basis in a barracks at the very end of a hall in the tunnel—apparently Hall 36.

Information on Dora's *Revier* personnel is often uncertain, but this is not particular to Dora. The SS doctor, the *Lagerarzt,* was at first a certain Heinrich Plaza, described by Jean Michel as "a tall guy, with the mug of a brute"; he was dangerous when drunk and insulted the prisoners.[1] He came from Buchenwald where he was in charge of pathology and entirely incompetent. After Dora, he passed through Struthof before being appointed to Ohrdruf. He was replaced at the beginning of 1944 by Dr. Karl Kahr, who remained there until December and who will be mentioned in a later chapter.

It is difficult to know if the *Kapo*—in the initial months—was Ernst Schneider, a builder, or Karl Schweitzer, a stove fitter. They were both Reds and filled in as surgeons as the case required.[2] The arrival of Fritz Pröll in April 1944 brought with it major improvements. Little by little and in an erratic manner the prisoners became part of the *Revier* personnel. The main figure was a Dutch doctor, Dr. Groeneveld, who arrived in Dora with the first convoy of August 28, 1943, remaining there until the evacuation in April 1945 with the last convoy. The first French "doctor" (in fact a dental surgeon) seems to have been Dr. Jacques Desprez, who arrived in September with the other "20,000"s. He cropped up again in Harzungen. Then came Dr. Maurice Lemière, who maintained his duties up until April 1945. Among the dentists were René Laval, Georges Croizat (dental technician, who passed through Peenemünde), and Jean Michel—recruited thanks to Jacques Desprez—who looked after the files as he had no medical training.[3] It was during the first months of 1944 that the French team grew significantly, as will be seen, with the presence of Louis Girard, René Morel, and Marcel Petit among others. The Czechs, equally present, were principally represented by a dentist, Otto Cimek, and by a surgeon, Jan Cespiva.

GROENEVELD, THE DUTCH DOCTOR. Born in 1907, H. L. (known as Hessel) Groeneveld set up his medical practice in Nijmegen in 1935. He belonged to the Mennonite Church, an important church in the Netherlands, where it was created in the sixteenth century. Groeneveld joined the Resistance, was arrested, and escaped. He tried to reach the Pyrenees but was once again arrested during a roundup in the Paris *métro* in November 1942. Imprisoned for many months in Paris, he was then transferred to Compiègne in the spring of 1943 and deported in June to Buchenwald, where he was assigned the identity number 14340. Some Dutch friends managed to place him as a nurse in the *Revier.*

On August 28, 1943, he was in the first convoy of 107 prisoners sent from Buchenwald to Dora; in his memoirs, Groeneveld noted that only 7 of them were left in 1945. Initially he worked in the tunnel, then became a nurse again once the *Revier* was set up. He finally managed to have himself recognized as a doctor. After him, many prisoner-doctors arrived—French and Czech in particular. But Groeneveld's authority remained. Those attesting to his competence and kindness are numerous, French prisoners like Sadron foremost among them.

Chapter 19 will deal with the role he played in the evacuation and how he got back home.

GETTING INTO THE *REVIER,* AND GETTING OUT. Quite naturally, prisoners who fell ill sought medical help and thus turned to the *Revier.* But it was difficult to get into the *Revier,* as many prisoners have explained. For a number of weeks it was necessary to first go through the tunnel infirmary. The following accounts were made by Fliecx, followed by Butet.

"I went to the [tunnel] infirmary. It was a horrible barrack built at that time in the large gallery that led to the Blocks. [. . .] We waited outside. It wasn't very well lit and we were squeezed together in the shadows. Off and on, the door would open, throwing light upon the strange combination of the wounded, the sick, the dying and those who wangled their way in. On the other side of the barrack was the morgue, a pompous title for the canvas curtain that didn't even hide the lifeless, dirty bodies that piled up behind it. Sometimes men that still had some life left in them—but not enough life to bother with—were brought in there."[4]

"I was coughing constantly [. . .] I decided to go to the doctor's office by reporting sick. The infirmary, the Revier, had just been set up in a barrack in the camp. For those of us from the Tunnel, it was simply out of the question to go there alone. You first had to check in at the Tunnel infirmary, a small barrack set up at the far end of the gallery. Lording over the operation was a Russian prisoner, with several assistants. His only equipment was a medical thermometer and a few papers. We started lining up in front of the door; no doubt to set the mood, several dead bodies were piled up at the side.

"When it was my turn, he handed me the thermometer, without a word. I took my temperature under the arm—it was almost 39 degrees Celsius. He wrote my number down on a piece of paper, stamped it and motioned for me to wait outside. [. . .] We were thirty or so to leave the Tunnel under the supervision of a Kapo, feet treading through mud, the French prisoners rubbing one another's backs to get warm. The examination was quickly done by a prisoner doctor, he listened with his stethoscope, gave me two aspirin and the secretary wrote out four days of Schonung on my paper.

"I don't know if it was the aspirin or the prospect of not working for four days that gave me back some hope, but I returned to my Schlafstollen (dormitory) saying to myself that 'they' may get my fat, but surely not my skin and bones, and that I was going to fight 'to the death' to live."[5]

Fliecx managed sometime later, in the first weeks of 1944, to get himself hospitalized in a *Revier* that was transformed inside: "The Revier is a barrack at the top of the camp. You miserably flounder about in a horrible quagmire to get there. Once there, you wait in front of the door no matter what the weather, those with forty-degree fevers mixed in with the others. Obviously, it's always the strongest who push the others out of the way and slip in as soon as the door opens. The sick and disabled remain several hours shivering in the wind and snow. Some collapse, exhausted, to the ground. [. . .]

"Medical care? Oh excellent if you're fortunate enough during the visit to be sent to the Revier, all the prisoners' dream. It was my good fortune that the doctor—a German political prisoner—after giving a rough feel at the two pigeon eggs that were developing under my arm, sent me there. Before entering the room, there was a delightful moment: I was undressed and bathed in a real bathtub with hot water.

"In room eight, it was a French doctor who gave the orders; the nurse was Russian. Here in the Revier the change was one-hundred percent from the rest of the camp. Everything was clean, everyone had a wooden bed, a sheet, a pillow and a warm blanket. There were twenty of us. Lots of Italians. [. . .] We didn't know what to do with all the food there. [. . .] In the mornings, I woke up naturally for the first time in ages. Everything was calm. [. . .] There we were well taken care of, pampered even, and the next day you'd be thrown back, with the same indifference, into the hellish life of the KL. . . ."[6]

Dutillieux had the same type of experience: "During the days that followed [the disinfecting campaign of February 1944], I no longer itched from lice, but I started to cough. The fever had hit me. [. . .] Roland told me the trick: 'Just before roll call, smoke a cigarette dipped in machine oil. When the Kapo gets you to step out of the line up, you'll be at forty. When you get to the Revier and the nurse takes your temperature, you'll still be over thirty-eight.' [. . .] Everything went as planned. [. . .] After having me swallow an aspirin and gargle with permanganate, they led me to my bed. It was the top bunk of a bed with only two levels. [. . .] With sheets! [. . .] My closest neighbors were three feet away on each side, I was out in the middle! Compared to the Block, this Revier was very comfortable, sumptuous. [. . .] I spent eight days there, with absolutely nothing at all to do, a total rest. [. . .] I was unable to swallow anything other than milk, my mouth was so full of canker sores. [. . .] For eight days I spat blood. [. . .] My pneumonia cured up without any medication—except for the aspirin and the mouth wash the day I entered the Revier. [. . .]

"The remedy for bringing down a fever and curing pneumonia or pleurisy was simple: dip a blanket in a bucket of cold water, wring it out well, fold it into fours the way you would a sheet, and wrap it around the sick person's bare chest. [. . .] It was left there for about a quarter of an hour, the time it took the blanket to heat up a bit. After eight days of this treatment, the result was surefire: if the patient wasn't already dead, he could go into convalescence. In any case, the fever would have fallen."[7]

Rieg was saved by the same type of treatment: "From 7 February to 13 March, 1944: in the Revier with a bronchial pneumonia. It seems I moaned for eight days with a fever and nothing to eat. A Czech male nurse made me chipped-ice packs to put around the chest, the only remedy at his disposal."[8]

Minor surgical operations were also carried out, such as the one meant to rid Fliecx of his abscesses: "That morning, they operated on my abscesses. Laid out on the operating table, I watched the doctor preparing his scalpel. It was dull and it tore at me; I heard the flesh rip under the blade; on reflex I sat bolt upright. The male nurse laid me back down with a violent slap in the face. I sweat off my last fat molecules. Next, my arm was wrapped in paper bandages which were to remain on for approximately twenty-four hours. It didn't matter, I was very relieved. It was terrible how abscesses could wear you down."[9]

Quite obviously, the prisoner personnel of the *Revier*—with the support of the SS doctor—did what it could with the scant means at its disposal to help the small number of sick who were authorized to receive medical care for a limited time. There were those who succumbed, and who justified the opinion—common in the camp—that the *Revier* was the antechamber to the crematorium. However, there were those whose state of health apparently improved, and who were allowed a rest, in the *Schonung*.

THE *SCHONUNG*. The *Schonung* was initially a short rest period of a few days, access to which depended on obtaining a paper stamped by a doctor from the *Revier*. The recipient was authorized to return to his block and do nothing, as Butet did for four days in his sleeping quarters in the tunnel. Possibly the SS considered one day that all these prisoners lazing about seemed disorderly, and so it was decided to regroup them into a special block of the camp.

As André Rogerie has noted: "Monday came and this time Buchet went up to the Revier with me. It was his turn to be examined; we both had pneumonia. This time, we preciously guarded the note which I was so lacking and we spent the day in Schonung. But, at that point a change occurred: those in Schonung didn't go back to sleep in the Tunnel. They stayed where they were and went to roll call. Oh! These deadly evening roll calls, on your feet for hours, we standing in the snow and shaking with a severe fever. We no longer ate. We had to drink, drink. [. . .] During the day, we had to sit on stools without backrests. [. . .] In the evening, the stools were taken away and straw mattresses were laid on the floor. And, as if that weren't enough, I contracted dysentery.

"The 27 January, I received my first care package. [. . .] The sugar brought my appetite back and I ate everything that day. [. . .] The day after, I found a little box of pills in my pocket, [. . .] in fact it was for dysentery—Stovarsol—that had been given to me in Compiègne. [. . .] Because the Schonung was full, the doctor decided to send me back to work."[10]

Fliecx and Dutillieux went to the *Schonung* after going through the *Revier*.

"Done with the hospital! I was sent to the Schonung. It was no longer in small barracks, but now in a Block of the new camp. We slept on straw right on the floorboards. [. . .] We stayed sitting on stools all day long, so much so that our backsides hurt; but, all the same, we were happy not to be working. [. . .] The guard was a Czech, Victor, who yelled stupidly morning and night. [. . .] I stayed in the Schonung for a while. Then, I went back down into the Tunnel."[11]

"Leaving the Revier meant therefore either the crematorium or the Schonung, the rest or convalescence building. [. . .] To the left of the entrance was a large room without any furniture. Hundreds of 'convalescents' were packed in. At night, all the bodies laid out covered the entire floor. [. . .] In the morning, the corpses were taken out and thrown into a heap in front of the building, where a special Kommando, the Totenträger, came to pick them up. [. . .] As for the large room to the right of the entrance, I never went in. I only know that it is much worse than the room in which I find myself resting. It was reserved exclusively for those with diarrhea. [. . .]

"Several times a week, a camp doctor, a prisoner, came to the Schonung building and pointed out, after a quick examination, those who were well enough to return to work. I was lucky enough to be seen by a French doctor. [. . .] The doc asked me if I wanted an extra eight days in Schonung. [. . .] But, eight days in that hell was enough for me. [. . .] So, I went back to the Tunnel."[12]

Fliecx's last visit to the *Schonung* was to the dysenteric room: "I was transported on a stretcher from the Tunnel to the camp. [. . .] When I got up there, I was hoping they'd send me to the hospital. But no, they judged me still to be in too good shape; you had to be in the throes of death to get in now. I was again sent off to the Schonung, to the room reserved for those with dysentery. [. . .] They had me take my clothes off, and sent me into the 'Scheisserei' room. The first thing that hit me was a foul stench, then I moved a few steps forward. On all sides, lying on disgusting straw mattresses, were skeletons, their dirty gray skin hanging from them.

"The next day, I was really not well. [. . .] Then I too collapsed into the torpor that seemed to wipe out all the sick there. [. . .] How many days did I remain like that in the Schonung? I couldn't tell anymore—between three and eight days, I suppose. [. . .] I received another package. Maybe that was what saved me, because I was at the end of my tether. I managed to eat a pot of quince jam, one of honey, and drink a bottle of syrup."[13]

THE "TRANSPORTS." At the beginning of 1944 a significant number of prisoners—in the *Revier, Schonung,* tunnel, and in the camp—were unable to work. Many of the prisoners had already died; but others still, sometimes referred to as *Muselmänner*, were perhaps going to take awhile to die. Space was lacking, sleeping quarters in the tunnels were full, and the camp was still very rudimentary. And new prisoners were expected to arrive from Buchenwald at the moment when the factory in the tunnel would finally be able to produce the V2s. Those of no use in Dora had to be gotten rid of.

Therefore it was decided in January 1944 to organize a "transport" to the Maïdanek camp, close to Lublin, within the Polish General Government. The affair was planned with the greatest secrecy, and the destination remained unknown. Officially, it was to be to a rest camp. Later it was referred to, no doubt sarcastically, as a *Himmelkommando*, a heaven Kommando.

There were apparently no survivors from that transport, for which the date varies from one source to another, the most likely being January 6. According to Jean Michel, it was Dr. Jacques Desprez who knew of the destination.[14] Michel also quotes the account given by Pierre Rozan, who met a completely drunk SS man who had taken part in the transport. He complained of the work he was made to do: "I was disgusted: forced to do a job that made me sick to my stomach. Might as well have me work in the latrines, wallow in the shit. I had to deal with the sick who could no longer get out of the railway cars. They didn't want to stand up. I had to crush their larynxes by stomping on them with my boots to finish them off."[15]

It was necessary for this transport, as for so many others, to have everyone accounted for after a roll call in order to proclaim, "Die Rechnung stimmt!" The transport comprised one thousand sick men. Michel told how Raymond de Miribel avoided the departure in the nick of time by speaking in his approximate German to an SS officer, who he knew bore the same name.[16]

There is more known about the second transport, also made up of one thousand men, leaving Dora on February 6 and arriving in Maïdanek on February 9. André Rogerie provided a highly detailed account of the journey and period spent at the Maïdanek camp from February 9 to April 15. When he left the camp to go to Auschwitz, he observed: "Of the 250 Frenchmen who left Dora with me, there were only eight left and it wasn't over yet." According to his testimony, the Polish, in general, fared much better.[17]

The third transport left Dora on March 26 and arrived at Bergen-Belsen on March 27. Fliecx's is the most detailed account of the trip and the first weeks at Bergen-Belsen. Like a few other French, he remained on at Bergen-Belsen and survived. He ended up being the orderly of the *Lagerältester.* He relates: "In the office I consulted the camp registers. Often I took the first one, the transport from Dora. All you could see were gallows crosses in red pencil! Pages practically covered in them. On 27 March 1945, the anniversary of our arrival in Belsen, I counted the survivors: fifty-two out of a thousand! And of the 600 French, only seventeen remained. Three percent. The last handful, the toughest."[18]

To explain these deaths, over a year, it must of course be taken into account—but to what degree?—the circumstances particular to Bergen-Belsen. It must also be taken into account the (rare) cases of those who, considered cured, were sent back in August 1944 to Buchenwald and from there to Dora. This was the case of Didier Bourget and Roger Tricoire. It was also the case of the Slovenian Matija Zadravec. The first convoy took those involved by surprise. Afterward, some of the sick became suspicious. Rieg had only barely recovered than he got out of the *Revier.*[19] Dutillieux didn't linger in the Schonung. Others let themselves be dragged along through lassitude. As Rogerie has revealed: "I coughed off and on along with violent coughing fits. But, tonight there was some excitement in the Tunnel. A 'transport' was being prepared. Everyone unable to work had to leave the premises that night: the Revier, the Schonung, the sick, everyone had to take the train the very next day—Sunday—to an unknown destination—to a better camp, so it seemed. In fact, it was an extermination transport, but I wasn't aware of that yet and it was—my God—with great satisfaction that I saw my name noted down so I could also take part in this expedition."[20] Bronchart pointed out that he wasn't able to convince Étienne Bordeaux Montrieux not to go.[21]

Fliecx, like so many others, was in no position to react: "And then one day we were given striped outfits and we all left the Schonung. [. . .] We were around a thousand [in a barrack]. [. . .] Then, they led us out. In a blurry dream, I went down the camp pathway. What a strange marching parade we must have made! The camp head and the whole gang of Greens surrounding him hung to the sides: 'Nach Sanatorium!'. . . . they screamed as we passed by. [. . .] Below, on the tracks, the cars were open. I was heaved in. Instinctively, I dragged myself into a corner and waited, passively, for what would happen next."[22]

A strange thing happened to Simonin: "One night, I was taken out of the Block by a green Kapo (Kurt), then led to an administrative building where a Schreiber asked me if I had been sick. When I said I had not been, he opened a door to the outside for me and ordered me to quickly return to the Block. I later learned that it was in order to fill up a transport to Lublin."[23] Another victim would have to be found.

Another story is told by Joseph Jazbinsek, whose young brother François died in the second convoy to Maïdanek. Himself laid up sick in the *Revier,* he was forcibly marched to the tunnel by his *Kapo* Willy, who came to get him with two other prisoners. The next day Willy took him back to the *Revier,* which had meanwhile been largely emptied of its occupants, who had left in the transport for Bergen-Belsen. It was in this way that he survived.

THE TUNNEL'S VICTIMS. Not all the deaths in Dora occurred in the *Revier* or the *Schonung.* There were all those who, in the tunnel, died suddenly because they simply could not hold out any longer.

I shall quote just one example: "Among our fellow prisoners arrested the same time we were, was Marius Reimann, from Albert in the Somme, and his son Claude. Upon arrival in Buchenwald, Marius was given the number 39568, Claude number 39569, and myself number 39570. We arrived at Dora together on 11 February 1944. One morning, Claude found his father dead beside him. That day, Marius was one of the 'deaths in the Tunnel.' He appears on the list dated 28 February 1944." Rogerie quotes another: "Then Buchet got up a last time and all of a sudden collapsed to the ground. He was dead. His body was immediately thrown onto the heap of the day's dead. There were easily fifteen there, piled up any old way."[24]

Corpses were placed in heaps, particularly in front of each of the dormitories, as noted by Butet and Mialet.

"I was picked out by the Kapo of the Schlafstollen who hit me, but especially conscripted me to take out the night's dead. And indeed, when the 'reveille sounded,' ten to fifteen prisoners, or more, did not get up and remained huddled on their straw mattresses. They died in their sleep. [. . .] They had to be taken out and carried to the Tunnel entrance. [. . .] I didn't much appreciate this duty, and the next day I went back to loading rocks into the carriages."[25]

"Only seven corpses [at the door of the block], stiffs we called them. The bodies are bare-footed, with shaved heads. We see the enormous nails, the filthy toes, and the emaciated faces. All the dead looked alike in their ugliness and extreme thinness."[26]

These deaths posed an administrative problem, as pointed out both by the Czech Litomisky, at the block level in the tunnel, and the Dutchman Van Dijk, at the level of a large Kommando.

As Litomisky explains, "Every morning and every evening, the Block personnel brought the dead bodies to the entrance, where the Schreiber established a list of the dead prisoners' identity numbers and passed them along to the Arbeitsstatistik. The bodies were then put in a special enclosure in the Tunnel, where they were stored for several days. In the end, wagons were brought around to pick them up and take them out of the Tunnel. Meanwhile, it often happened that prisoners would get into the enclosure to exchange their clothes for whatever they found that was better on the dead bodies. But these clothes bore the identity numbers of the dead. After a while, the SS no longer knew who was dead and who was alive. They relied on the Arbeitsstatistik, whose information was also perfectly inaccurate. For this reason, it was one day decided that the identity number would be written on the foreheads of the cadavers with a special marker.

"One evening, an incredibly filthy and dusty Italian crept into the Block, looking for some food. After a while, the Block personnel noticed he had his matriculation number written on his forehead. He was one of the morning's 'dead.' We were all dumbfounded. The Italian, meanwhile, as filthy and dusty as ever, couldn't understand why we were all laughing so much at the very sight of him. He kept repeating, 'Pane, pane!' He was actually very fortunate to have landed in Block 4. Most of the Blockältester would have clubbed the poor Italian to death, in order to bring him into line with the registers."[27]

Van Dijk's recount is no less evocative of the problems confronted: "As [my Kommando's] messenger, one of the most disagreeable duties fell to me: I became an accountant of the dead. After the roll call, I went with Wladi and two on duty helpers—a Ukrainian by the name of Joseph and a Tartar with an unpronounceable name—to the Blocks in search of those who did not show up for the roll call. It wasn't difficult to find them. Most often, they were found dead or dying in the 'clutches' (the name given to the dormitories), or outside on the excrement-spattered ground. I would write down 'verstorben' behind the corresponding number on the list and I copied it onto the forehead or the chest of the dead man with the help of an aniline pencil which I wet with my saliva.

"It happened that we would arrive too late, and we'd find the dead, or even the dying, already unclothed. It was therefore impossible to identify the body. I had my own method: I just used one of the numbers remaining on my list and that we couldn't find. For the prisoner who, through exhaustion, was no longer able to get up, I wrote that number on his arm. That way he'd be identifiable once dead. I then wrote down the corresponding number under the list 'krank.' Most often, the sick man was already dead by the next roll call but he was still listed as part of the Kommando for his food ration. It happened that there remained still other missing numbers. So, we went in search of them in other Kommandos to complete my lists.

"While Wladi and I continued our search in the 'clutches,' the two helpers dealt with the dead that we had found. That is to say that they took off the still usable clothes, and sometimes extracted the crowns in gold or silver from the mouths of the corpses. After this preparation, they put a sliding knot round the two legs, or the neck, and dragged the corpse behind them all the way to the heap in the main tunnel."[28]

Bronchart, Fliecx, and Auchabie each in their own way recall the next step in the operation.

"From the Blocks [. . .] the dead were brought to hall 36, which we called the boulevard of the flat-out. So were the latrines. There, two Kommandos dealt with the evacuation. For the dead, it was two bodies to a wheelbarrow. By pulling them, dragging them by the feet, they were piled in a heap at the Tunnel exit. [. . .] The latrines were evacuated by hand. We didn't pass through this hall lightheartedly. Often we were forced to by the SS."[29]

"The dead were more and more numerous. Every morning they were piled up at the exit to the Blocks. From there, they were transported to hall 36, where the undertakers loaded them onto iron wheelbarrows, two by two, dragging their feet on the ground, their heads banging against each other on the wheel. The undertakers received quite a few perks, so they could allow themselves the sport of racing the wheelbarrows to see who would arrive first to the Tunnel door, with hearty laughs when the wheelbarrow bumped into something and tipped over. These macabre chariot races had long since ceased to upset anyone."[30]

"The dead from underground were transported to gallery 36, where a carriage transported them out of doors. In gallery 36, it was not unusual to see a prisoner, no doubt having fainted, make every last effort to get out from under the heap of corpses. It was said, on the other hand, that the Russians hid themselves there to avoid work. [. . .] To survive, underground, when a corpse was found, his identity number was unsewn, and then resewn on top of our own with a very thin electrical wire, which allowed us to get his soup and his ration of bread for as long as his corpse remained undiscovered."[31]

INCINERATION AT BUCHENWALD. There are few testimonies on the transport of the corpses to Buchenwald. It was Fliecx who described what happened: "From the window of the Schonung, the small carriages could be seen coming from down below, at the Tunnel exit, loaded with the dead. [. . .] Not far from us, the convoy stopped and the corpses were transported into a small shed close to the Revier. There they were kept up to three days until the truck came to take them to Buchenwald. There were about a hundred each time. . . ." (These were not only the dead from the tunnel, but those from the *Revier* and the *Schonung*.)[32]

He adds: "One time the driver of the truck had quite an experience. In a sharp curve in Nordhausen, one of the slatted sides broke off and all the bodies were thrown onto the road. Public commotion. Immediately a Kommando of prisoners was sent to fix up the incident."[33]

Until the end of March 1944 it was at the Buchenwald crematorium that the bodies regularly arriving from Dora were incinerated, which gave it its terrible reputation. As will be shown in chapter 10, a "countryside crematorium" was then set up in the camp. Dora's ultimate crematorium, which has been conserved, was much later.

THE DEATH TOLL. Survivor accounts, whether published or not, often include number estimates of losses suffered up to 1945, at least as regards the French. This is true of Bronchart's book.[34] Such information is generally not acceptable. It is based, for example, on the census of the French carried out at Bergen-Belsen in April 1945 before the repatriation, whereas the evacuations had in fact led many French off in other directions. Because of various circumstances, the author did not actually get back from Mecklenburg until the end of May, without any particular difficulty; he was therefore absent at Bergen-Belsen. Rigorous work—starting with the convoys from Compiègne—such as that carried out by Paul Le Goupil, will ultimately provide a clearer picture.

Concerning the first months of Dora there exists no uncertainty. The number of prisoners incinerated month by month at Buchenwald is known. A total of 2,882 dead can be broken down as follows:

1943	October	18
	November	172
	December	670
1944	January	719
	February	536
	March	767

A breakdown on the basis of nationality is also available:

Russian	839	or	29.1 percent
French	708		24.6
Polish	407		14.1
German	373		12.9
Italian	264		9.2
Yugoslav	91		3.2
Czech	41		1.4
Dutch	32		1.1
Belgian	15		.5

| Various | 5 | .2 |
| Undetermined | 107 | 3.7 |

This breakdown corresponds overall to arrivals in Dora. The "Russians" were above all Ukrainians, evacuated from camps in the Ukraine once the German troops had retreated in the second half of 1943. The convoys of French that left Compiègne in the second half of 1943 were directed toward Buchenwald. The Italian capitulation in September 1943 was followed by Italian soldiers being sent to Germany as prisoners of war after they stopped fighting on the German side; some of them were sent to Dora. The Yugoslavs who had been political prisoners in Italy were sent to German camps. The Poles and the Czechs came to Dora via other camps, especially Auschwitz it would seem. The high number of German deaths is surprising, as they essentially occupied the positions of *Kapo, Blockältester, Lagerschutz,* and so on.

It is known month by month the number of prisoners from Dora incinerated at Buchenwald. It is also known that one thousand prisoners were shipped off from Dora in transports for each of the months of January, February, and March 1944. On the other hand, the total figures are available of all those present in Dora at the beginning of each month from October 1943 to April 1944. It is possible to derive, from this information, the number of prisoners who arrived in Dora between the end of August 1943 and the beginning of April 1944.

There were some 17,535 prisoners. As the number of prisoners at the beginning of April was 11,653, the number of prisoners dead was 5,882: 2,882 incinerated and 3,000 taken away in transports. In total the number of dead represents a third of all those who arrived at the camp in a period of seven months. It is true that at the beginning of April there were still some survivors of the three transports to Maïdanek and to Bergen-Belsen. But the majority of them would more or less not have long to live.

The total number of prisoners at the beginning of each month grew as follows:

1 September 1943	380
1 October 1943	3,290
1 November 1943	6,276
1 December 1943	8,976
1 January 1944	9,923
1 February 1944	11,957
1 March 1944	11,521
1 April 1944	11,653

Arrivals, for each month, were as follows:

August	1943	380
September		2,910
October		3,004

November		2,872
December		1,617
January	1944	3,753
February		1,100
March		1,899

In spite of their large numbers, the prisoners who arrived during the first quarter merely allowed the level to remain at between 11,000 and 12,000 prisoners.

LESSONS TO BE DRAWN FROM THE "GREFFIER LIST." An attempt can be made to describe with greater precision what actually happened by using the data provided in a precious document with regard to the French alone, and which is known by the name of the "Greffier List," from the name of the man who brought it back to France in 1945.[35]

It is made up—in alphabetical order—of the names and surnames of the French prisoners who died at Dora, including identity numbers, dates of birth, and dates of death. This document, like all documents of this type, is not perfect because it contains numerous errors, particularly regarding names. But various cross-checking has shown that, essentially, it is a reliable source. For the period up to the end of March 1944, the number of identified dead was 685, corresponding roughly to the number of French indicated above in the breakdown by nationality, which was 708.

On the basis of the alphabetical Greffier List, it was possible to draw up two other lists, one with a classification of identity numbers and the other with a classification of time of death, providing information of particular interest.[36]

Starting from the chronological list of deaths, it is indeed possible to establish a ten-day chart that indicates the great number of deaths between the beginning of December 1943 and the end of March 1944. The highest number of deaths were initially registered in the last ten days of December and the first ten days of January, and then during the three ten-day periods of March, following the great disinfecting campaign. The death rate fell abruptly in April. It is difficult to draw a conclusion because of the three transports in January, February, and March: many of the sick evacuated in March, for example, would without a doubt have been dead by April had they remained in Dora. Whatever the case may be, the slaughter, with regard to Dora, then drew to a close. The fact that it then started up again, in Ellrich and the Boelcke Kaserne, is another aspect of a complex historical whole.

A STEEP DEATH RATE. Using the Greffier List, it is possible to plunge still further into what can be known about the first months of Dora by cross-referencing the information on the times of death with that of the dates of arrival inferred from the identity numbers. It can be assumed then that the prisoners who had similar identity numbers—the "21,000"s for example—all arrived at

Dora at the same time, that is, after being released from quarantine at Buchenwald. However, it is known that some of the French remained in Buchenwald for a more or less long while before being sent to Dora. But examination of the survivor list shows that the number of such cases was limited during the time frame under consideration.

Statistics have been established on the dates of death for the French who had identity numbers up to "32,000," in other words, those who arrived at Dora before the beginning of December 1943. It has been observed that 554 of them were dead before April 1, 1944, and 141 in the course of the entire time period that followed until the evacuation in April 1945. Only a few weeks were required each time after the arrival of a transport for massive numbers of deaths to be registered. Several accounts bear witness to this situation.

Mialet noted the first death among the French prisoners as André Commandeur (21684), on October 27, 1943, age nineteen. In fact, it was Maurice Cauchois (22815), on October 23, age thirty-eight. "It was the first death. We prayed for him. A Protestant minister who was part of the Kommando, led prayers for believers, and offered thoughts upon which to meditate for free-thinkers. Everyone discovered their true selves. The cropped heads bowed. The little French guy went up to paradise, escorted by the ardent pleas of these men who, all now, continued to waste away and of whom a good many, as Christmas approached would, like him, be dead.

"A little Russian guy watched the scene. At the end of the prolonged silence, he touched my arm and asked: 'Was ist das?' I explained as best I could. The little deportee had a smile of understanding and perhaps of pity; with his left hand, he made the sign of the cross. The deaths that followed Commandeur's were not favored with these pious words to accompany them. They were just too numerous."[37]

Bernard d'Astorg spoke of his father, Colonel d'Astorg, deported from Compiègne in one of the January convoys: "I was in the Tunnel with the AEG Kommando. At the end of March, I met a Frenchman whose name I've forgotten who informed me with urgency that my father was in the Revier, very sick. I was completely surprised and I somehow managed to get permission to go up immediately to the Revier. I remember that the sun was blazing and that crossing the roll call area to reach the Revier was for me a dream-like moment.

"When I arrived at the Revier, I was shown where to find my father. And indeed, there I found him lying on a straw mattress which he was sharing with another dying man. He was practically naked, had dysentery and pneumonia (or pleurisy), was very thin and already difficult to recognize. But, his morale was incredible. He told me how happy he was to see me in a somewhat healthy state, and told me to hold out because, he added, the landing wasn't far off, 'a few months.' The Stubendienst put an end after a few minutes to this reunion and I went back to the Tunnel.

"I started out once again a few days later on this expedition to the Revier. I learned that my father had left on a transport to a rest camp. I later learned it was on the 29 March transport to Bergen-Belsen. He died on 4 April 1944. The landing occurred two months and two days later."[38]

André Rogerie (31278) arrived at Dora on November 21, 1943, and gave the names of those closest to him: Paul Corbin de Mangou (31276) died on January 2, 1944, Marius Buchet (31283) died on January 25, Jean Bourgogne (31300) died on February 4. Rogerie himself left on February 5 with Maurice Estiot (31298) for Maïdanek, where Estiot in turn died. He remained the only one left from the initial group.[39]

Pierre Auchabie (30750) also arrived on November 21, 1943, at the same time as twenty-one other deportees from the Corrèze, Dordogne, and Haute-Vienne. He drew up a death toll: died on November 26, Henri Julien (30438); on December 11, André Lizeaux (30775); on December 12, André Eymard (31069); on December 15, Sylvain Combes (30471) and François Paucard (30690); on December 22, Émile Dupuy (30751); on January 18, Valentin Lemoine (30493); on February 4, Jean Blanchou (30665); on February 6, Pierre Maisonnial (30659); on February 22, Jean Lanemajou (30816); on March 8, Antoine Maisonnial (30603); and on March 26, Fernand Ratineaud (30704). Those leaving on a transport and not returning: Fernand Astor, Jean de La Guéronnière, Abel Lalba, Albert Lizeaux, Pierre Lizeaux, Antonin Mazeau, André Paucard, and Antoine Pouget, all from the "30,000"s. Alfred Maloubier (30673) died on February 6, 1945, at Ellrich.[40] Pierre Auchabie was the only one to make it home, via Ellrich and the Boelcke Kaserne!

Rogerie and Auchabie, like many others, fell upon bad Kommandos. This was not the case for everyone; if so the only survivors would have been saved by a miracle, as they were. To some extent this was what some people upon their return thought had happened. Rassinier wrote in 1948 still, regarding convoys "20,000" and "21,000," that only a dozen remained on June 1, 1944 out of the fifteen hundred who arrived in October.[41] Which was, very fortunately, highly exaggerated.

Where Lies the Blame?

It is altogether undeniable that in a few months tens of thousands of men, perhaps not deliberately but in any case knowingly, were killed at Dora. The impression is given that these deaths just simply didn't matter. It was the price to pay. It is, under these circumstances, at once necessary and difficult to determine where responsibilities lay.

INDIVIDUAL CRIMES OR COLLECTIVE RESPONSIBILITY? When one looks closely at what happened at Dora during the first few months, it is striking to note the low number of individual acts directly causing a man's death. There were certainly executions by hanging, but in small number, not more, so to speak, than in the everyday life of a normal concentration camp. Of the some seven hundred French dead, not one had been executed.

Some prisoners were savagely beaten after trying to escape from the outside work sites and died some days later. Such was the case of Paul Belin, who died on November 19, 1943,[42] and André Legrand, who died on December 29.[43] But if a trial for the murders of this period had taken place, it would have no doubt been very difficult to find and expose the guilty parties.

If so many prisoners died, it is due to a certain number of converging factors: the fact that they were forced to work beyond their limits; the fact that they were forced to live in inhumane conditions; the fact that they were not given medical attention. All of which has to do with collective responsibility. First it is necessary, for clarity's sake, to examine the information known about the various groups having participated in the surveillance of the average prisoner and about their behavior.

THE GERMAN CIVILIANS. The prisoners' work in the tunnel and on the outdoor work sites was supervised by German civilians, generally described as *Meister.* Relations with the engineers at this period were exceptional. Most of the people involved in setting the factory up were no doubt transferred from Peenemünde. The others for the most part came from the WIFO or subcontracted companies.

In the German organization of trades, the *Meister* ("master") was a tradesman with a recognized qualification and in a position to employ apprentices. In Dora the term was debased: it applied—for any task—to the civilian who gave orders to members of a Kommando, passed along by the *Kapos* and *Vorarbeiter.*

The names of the Kommandos most of the time were not very revealing. There was certainly no hesitation about the name of the AEG Kommando, whose activity was well defined. The name WIFO, curiously enough, does not come up often; there existed, however, a Kommando of masons, the WIFO Maurer, about which Jean Mialet has retained an atrocious memory.[44] The large Kommandos bore Sawatzki's name: there existed at least three, Sawatzki I, II, and III, which were involved in the development of the tunnel[45] without a noticeable direct link to the *Oberingenieur* concerned. It is possible that these designations were relevant only to the Arbeitsstatistik files.

The *Meister* left the disciplining to the *Kapos* and SS. They were moreover prohibited from personally punishing the prisoners. Some, like the characters involved in removing the gasoline tanks, were frankly hostile.[46] The majority were indifferent. Some were discreetly benevolent, and Max Dutillieux felt it important to give a moving homage to "his old Meister [who] took a real risk" for him.[47]

PRISONERS WEARING ARMBANDS. It would be interesting to know how Buchenwald's Arbeitsstatistik—under the control of the Reds—established the first lists of "transports" of German prisoners (Greens or Reds) to Dora. We are reduced to conjecture. Concerning the Greens, there is every reason to think that it was a very good occasion to get rid of both unsavory individuals and potential competitors for the good positions at Buchenwald. It was of course a very nasty trick to play on the French and Soviet deportees who had been sent to Dora to have them accompanied by German (or even Polish) criminals, who were destined to keep an eye on them as *Kapos* and *Vorarbeiter.*

A certain number of Greens, reduced to very subordinate positions at Buchenwald or even sent to the quarry, thus had the chance to vent their frustration—and did not deprive themselves. Their deep-seated xenophobia could then be played out on the Russians, the French, and the Italians without any holding back. Many of the Greens who wore armbands were somber brutes, shamelessly striking average prisoners in the Kommandos working on excavation, in the "stones," machine transport, or frame building. Through their physical abuse, but no doubt just as much from their demented overseeing of the work, they were responsible for working many prisoners to death.

Dutillieux mentioned the *Kapo* Rudi Schmidt, who "was a piece of garbage," and his acolyte, the *Vorarbeiter* nicknamed Jumbo. He clarified: "Seventeen Frenchmen were under the orders of Rudi at the end of October 1943. There were only three left alive by the end of winter."[48] Slightly later the situation altered: "Changing Kommandos, I changed Kapo; I left Rudi Schmidt for Willy Schmidt. I left a scum for a crook. Willy was bigger than Rudi, stronger, more intelligent and no doubt for that reason better considered by the organization."[49] It might have been that a certain selection was made in favor of certain Kommandos. Bronchart was able to have a cordial relationship with the *Kapo* of the AEG Kommando, who had been condemned only for counterfeiting.[50]

Concerning the Reds, it is immediately striking to note how few of them were sent to Dora. Quite plainly, the prisoner leaders at Buchenwald didn't wish to risk the lives of their comrades in this altogether uncertain venture. Doubtless the commander of Buchenwald must have insisted on the appointment of two of their own for the positions of *Lagerältester* I and II of Dora. It ended up being a Bavarian mechanic, Georg Thomas, and a miner from Upper Silesia, Ludwig Sczymczak, both German communists, who were chosen. They arrived, so it would appear, already on August 28, 1943, along with the *Kapo Lagerschutz* Otto Runke.

Based on information quoted by Bornemann, next came Karl Schweitzer as *Kapo* of the *Revier,* Albert Kuntz as *Lagertechniker* and August Kroneberg as *Kapo* of the *Zimmerei* (carpenters), then Ludwig Leineweber (in October) as *Kapo* of the Arbeitsstatistik.[51] A later chapter will focus on the role they would come to play.

Thomas and Sczymczak were, after the war, considered heroes for two reasons: they refused to serve as hangmen in February 1944, and they were killed in April 1945 with other communist leaders after weeks of imprisonment. Hermann Langbein noted that Thomas's and later Sczymczak's refusal had numerous witnesses. He added, without being more exact, that after a period in the bunker "they took up their camp functions again." They appeared, in any case, to have been replaced as LÄ by a Green.[52]

The two Czechs who provided testimonies, Litomisky[53] and Benès, were not in favor of Thomas, who apparently didn't like the Czechs, perhaps because he was Bavarian. It appears that he had something against the "Czech Legion."[54] This was no doubt an allusion to the Czech Legion, made up of prisoners of war—from the Austrian army—who had fought in 1918 against the Bolsheviks while retreating eastward through Siberia. Benés, who was mixed up at that time in various intrigues between *Kapos* and other *Prominente*, Greens or Reds, provides a confused account, which brings out the great mediocrity of all these people.[55] To want to pass onto some *Häftlingsführung* or other, as Rassinier did,[56] the fundamental responsibility for the tragedy of the first months at Dora is to forget rather hastily the role of the SS and especially of those in charge of the manufacturing operation of the V2s—to which the camp was intrinsically linked.

THE ROLE OF THE SS. In all the prisoners' accounts of the first months, the SS were in the background in the tunnel or with the outside Kommandos. In the tunnel they hunted down all those they considered layabouts from every nook— of which, at the time, there was no lack, in particular young Ukrainians. It was a reign of terror. The minimum punishment, for a long time codified in the regulations by Eicke, was "fünf und zwanzig," twenty-five whacks on the backside. Outside the tunnel, the SS and their dogs were responsible for preventing escapes. As has been shown, the crackdown on those attempts could go almost to the extent of murder.

The SS's direct responsibility was greater still, especially in the first weeks. First, they considered Dora to be a camp like the others, like all those they had seen up until then. It was thus out of the question to give up the outside roll call, even for those living completely inside the tunnel. As told by Bronchart:

"Every Sunday, for the Kommandos which were not at work, a roll call took place regardless of the weather. We exited the Tunnel and were made to stand to the left of the entrance, in the area where the sugar beet crops were. To get there in rows of five, we went arm in arm, so that the column wouldn't break up, because sometimes the sick could no longer keep up. Watched over by the SS, with their dogs which intervened every time too large a gap swelled between two rows, we climbed the hill to reach the gathering site, the mud as thick as ever, sticking to and leaking into our miserable canvas boots. This march was real agony, and entailed fights amongst the prisoners for positioning; so much the worse for those who found themselves at the edges where the beatings rained down. . . ."[57]

Nor is there any question of considering that the prisoners were not, first and foremost, at the service of the SS. Maronneau explained: "Half of the convoy was led toward the Tunnel and put to work straight away in a drilling gallery. After a short night, we were taken outside to transport various parts meant for the construction of the future SS camp barracks. This system lasted around three weeks. Following the visit of high-ranking Nazi officials, it was decided to make two teams, one working outside constructing the camp, the other continuing the drilling and setting up of the Tunnel."[58]

It seems, indeed, that the Buchenwald commander's visit of inspection was needed to get things adjusted. According to Kammler's instructions, absolute priority was given to the setting up of the tunnel factory and its access points.[59] Everything concerning the camp was deferred. The outdoor roll calls disappeared. Sunday became an ordinary day. A general roll call took place later, in February, in the snow.

THE FACTORY CAMP. From November 1943 on, and for a period of several months, only the factory mattered: it had to get finished and get going. The camp was only a vast formless annex of which the essential element was the kitchen. It supplied the soup that the inhabitants of the tunnel came to eat at the door before withdrawing to the sleeping quarters and the work halls, with their dirt and their lice. When lice were discovered, a disinfection block was added to the kitchen. Because all available space was required for the factory, there was no possibility of building a crematorium for the corpses the factory "produced" with efficiency greater than that with which it produced the V2s. The months from November to March were the deadliest in Dora's history.

All those in charge on the German side were involved in a frenetic race against time because they were all committed to Hitler and to supplying Germany with this famous rocket capable of changing the course of the war. Whether they really believed it or feigned—consciously or not—belief in it is of little consequence. The degree of collective illusion is surprising today, but that is a judgment after the fact. Many prisoners at that time were seriously worried when they discovered what they commonly referred to as the "torpedoes."

The Germans in charge were the artillerymen as well as all the scholars and engineers working with them, since 1932, to perfect this new weapon—to which they had already devoted so much effort and money—perhaps to the detriment of other research. It was also the Armaments Ministry technocrats, who had not flinched in their support for the project since 1942 but were worried about the delays that were accumulating. It was, of course, the SS that sought obstinately to take control of the operation.

When examining the structure of competencies at the end of 1943, Albert

Speer, then at the height of his influence, appears—as concerns the rockets—to have been in control of the situation. It was he who came to see the tunnel factory in December 1943 and who passed on to Kammler a message of satisfaction for the work accomplished. Perhaps this satisfaction was moreover excessive, because the reconversion of a fuel depot into a virtual aircraft-engineering factory was not such a feat in a country with Germany's industrial tradition. But this country no longer had, at the end of 1943, the purely German labor force and the material means necessary to carry out such an undertaking in a normal time frame.

In the spring of 1943, before even the bombing of Peenemünde, resorting to the concentration camp labor force appeared to be the only way to confront the difficulties that had arisen. From that moment on everyone was aware of what was at stake and necessarily in agreement: Dornberger, Rudolph and von Braun, Speer, Degenkolb and Sawatzki, and Kammler. In the end, Neu had no choice but to follow.

The hell of Dora was a result of this mixture of personalities, all perfectly indifferent to the fate of these subhumans who were the prisoners. The author has found no criteria for placing individual responsibility on one person or another, or exonerating one or the other. It was the entire operation, as it had been conceived, that was nothing if not criminal.

To go further in placing liability, it would be necessary to have all the messages, instructions, minutes of meetings, and reports exchanged in all directions between those concerned. It would be necessary to have the dossier on the high-tension underground line running from Nordhausen to Kohnstein, or on the placing of the rails in tunnel B. It would be necessary to follow the process that culminated in the organization of the first transport to Maïdanek or to the general disinfecting campaign. There is nothing of this kind. There are not even any bits and pieces of dossiers. And it is better thus, as it avoids uncertain conclusions.

There were simply on one side thousands of victims, and on the other a group of leaders. That group of leaders was accountable, collectively, for the thousands of victims.

PART THREE

A True Camp, a True Factory

[[7]]

SPEER, KAMMLER, DORNBERGER, AND VON BRAUN IN 1944 GERMANY

In the course of 1944, the fate of thousands of prisoners in the Dora camp and the tunnel factory as well as in the various camps and Kommandos that were being set up throughout the *Mittelraum* depended on initiatives and rivalries between teams in positions of power that were not always homogeneous, each of which had its own ties to the führer with his shifting priorities. The aim of this chapter is to attempt to introduce some order into a confusing story based in large part on the later memories of some of the protagonists, which have been used by other authors with varying degrees of goodwill or hostility. The most recent studies, which are more qualified, nevertheless give us a fairly good idea of what happened.

On the one hand, a Mittelwerk complex, including the tunnel factory and the Dora camp properly speaking, was still intact along with a few ancillary Kommandos. The chapters in part 3 of this book deal with this complex and its relationship to what was left of the Peenemünde base. On the other hand, the SS under the direction of Kammler undertook a major works project using a workforce made up of prisoners in various parts of the Reich, particularly the *Mittelraum.* Those work sites and the corresponding camps will be mentioned in part 4.

Some of the workforce was initially moved around between the Mittelwerk complex and the new work sites, under the authority of the Buchenwald command. In the autumn of 1944, however, the SS put up Dora as an autonomous camp, bringing most of the *Mittelraum* sites under its authority. This was the situation prevailing in particular in the first quarter of 1945, which will be described in part 5.

Whereas the notion of *Mittelraum,* encompassing the Harz region and northern Thuringia, is a convenient geographical expression, there was a well-defined Sperrgebiet Mittelbau under the direct authority of Kammler, within a radius of twenty and later thirty miles from Nordhausen.[1]

The Military Situation in 1944

Chapter 1 dealt with the military situation in Germany in mid-1943, when the story of Dora first began. From then on, the situation gradually grew worse on all fronts.

On the Eastern Front the retreat first became obvious in the Ukraine: the Soviets took back Kiev on November 6, 1943, Odessa on April 10, 1944, and Sebastopol on May 9. In the north the siege of Leningrad ended on January 27. In July 1944 the Soviets arrived first in Minsk, then in Vilnius, Lublin, Lvov, and Brest-Litovsk; they were at the gates of eastern Prussia and on the Vistula across from Warsaw. Blizna had to be evacuated. In August 1944, Romania switched camps, followed by Bulgaria in September, while Finland laid down its weapons. In October the British were in Athens. By the end of 1944 the Germans had abandoned Macedonia, Serbia, and Albania. On December 27, Hungary was invaded and Budapest was surrounded.

In Italy the Allies took Monte Cassino in May 1944, entered Rome in June, Florence in August, and Ravenna in December.

The Allies landed in Normandy on June 6 and in Provence on August 15. They reached Paris on August 25, Lyon on September 3, Antwerp on September 4, Luxembourg on September 10, and Strasbourg on November 23. By this time German territory was directly threatened: the Americans took Aachen on October 21 and Düren on December 12. Hitler decided on a counteroffensive in the Ardennes that began on December 16, but Bastogne was relieved on December 26.

By the end of 1944 in the East as well as the West, the conquest of Germany was drawing near.

Internal Rivalries Before the July 20 Assassination Attempt

The various teams or factions involved in German politics in 1944 paid close attention to Hitler's decisions, either in order to comply with them as best they could or to attempt to influence them in one direction or another. Various alliances developed or dissolved depending on the moment, but the power relationships were never perfectly clear. It took an event like the failed assassination attempt of July 20, aimed directly at the Führer, to generate clear-cut decision-making. It seems legitimate to divide the story of 1944 into two periods, before and after that date.

It is striking, as Speer reported, that the landing in Normandy did not disturb the routine of daily life in Berchtesgaden, where Hitler had been settled for several months.[2] The date of June 6 made no difference in this respect. Hitler's residence was called variously the Berghof, or Obersalzberg or Berchtesgaden. All three names are still used, according to each author's preference.

As mentioned earlier, at the end of 1943, Albert Speer's influence had reached its peak. He had all of German industrial production under his authority, since Walter Funk, minister of the economy, had handed over to him all prerogatives stemming from the Four-Year Plan in September. He was neither in charge of aircraft construction, which was under the authority of Marshal Erhard Milch, nor of shipbuilding, which came under the authority of Adm. Karl Dönitz, though he had no personal conflicts with either Funk or Milch or Dönitz.

In fact, if his memoirs are to be believed, it was with Hitler's "inner circle" that Speer was not on good terms; this included Martin Bormann, head of the Chancellery, his deputy Hans Lammers, and Marshal Wilhelm Keitel.[3] The old cronies from the early days of Nazism, who often became *Gauleiter,* such as Fritz Sauckel in Thuringia, also took a dim view of him. Each one tried to preserve his authority over his own territory against the initiatives of the minister of armaments. As for Göring and Goebbels, his relationship with them varied according to circumstances. On the whole he had solid support in the army, from Gen. Heinz Guderian, for example, but he ran up against the ambition of Himmler and the SS.

He relied on the technicians, civilians and military, who held him in esteem and sought his support. He was particularly involved with the specialists at Peenemünde and Mittelwerk, and therefore particularly anxious to see V2 testing resume rapidly, using rockets produced by the Mittelwerk factory, the factory of the Dora Tunnel. The first tests in Blizna came to nothing.

Speer's situation was seriously compromised when he fell ill in January 1944. He was suffering from an inflammation of his left knee and had to be hospitalized on January 18. He was treated by Dr. Gebhardt at the Hohenlychen Hospital, which was under the authority of the SS.[4] Hohenlychen is located north of Brandenburg, about seven and a half miles from Ravensbrück. (This same hospital will be mentioned once again in connection with events in April 1945.)

Speer was above all completely exhausted, and he had trouble running his ministry from his hospital bed. On February 10 he fell into a coma for three days with various complications: Friedrich Koch, sent by Hitler's physician, remained at his bedside. He recovered and was able to leave Hohenlychen on March 18 for a period of convalescence. He spent a few days in Klessheim, near Salzburg, where he received a number of visits, including one from Hitler, and then went on to Meran (Merano) in South Tyrol, which was attached de facto to the Reich since the Italian capitulation. There he was informed of the decisions taken in his absence.[5]

During the three-month period when Speer was removed from power, a number of events took place, including the arrest and later the release of von Braun. What is known about this subject comes from the testimony of von

Braun and Dornberger, which Neufeld has scrupulously analyzed.[6] The dates indicated here are only approximate, for want of conclusive documents.

It all began when von Braun (who was an SS officer, as has already been
noted) was called by Himmler to his Hochwald headquarters in eastern Prussia
sometime in February 1944. Himmler recommended that von Braun work more
closely with Kammler to solve the problems of the V2. Von Braun claims to
have replied that the problems were purely technical and that he was confident
Dornberger would help him. It appears that von Braun had been under surveillance since October by the SD, which was drawing up a report against him as
well as against Klaus Riedel and Helmut Gröttrup. They were said to have expressed regret at an engineer's home one evening that they were not working on
a spaceship, and that they had the feeling the war was not going well. Kohler,
who was eager to share anecdotes, noted that they were denounced by "a young,
very attractive woman dentist."[7]

Von Braun was arrested on the above-mentioned grounds, no doubt on February 22, and taken to Stettin. Riedel and Gröttrup were arrested the next day as
well as von Braun's younger brother, Magnus, a chemical engineer and pilot in
the Luftwaffe who had been assigned to Peenemünde on the Wasserfall project.
Von Braun remained imprisoned for two weeks without any idea of the charges
against him. Dornberger was called to Berchtesgaden (from Schwedt) to be informed of the arrests by Keitel, but he was not allowed to intervene on their behalf with Hitler. It was only through the Abwehr in Berlin that he was able to
obtain the conditional release of von Braun, who was never bothered again, nor
was his brother. It appears that Speer, too, despite his illness, intervened on their
behalf. Riedel and Gröttrup were also criticized for their political sympathies
prior to 1933, yet they, too, were released. Riedel died in an accident in August.
Gröttrup appears to have been under surveillance for a longer period. He was to
be found in Thuringia in 1945, and later on, in Russia.

At the time of the "duel for the conquest of space,"[8] all this history would be
used to enhance von Braun's image. At the time it was one more episode in the
rivalry between Speer and Himmler, who thus suffered a temporary setback.

On April 19, Speer sent a memorandum to Hitler from Meran in response to
the latter's decision to build six huge underground factories to protect the aviation industry from bombing and Dorsch's assurance that the project could be
completed in six months. Gitta Sereny recalls in detail[9] the events that followed
the receipt of Speer's memorandum: Hitler's hostile reaction, rumors of Speer's
resignation, a message of affection addressed by Hitler to Speer, and Speer's return to his position of authority, as Hitler could not do without him at the head of
industry. On May 8, 1944, Speer was back in his office in Berlin and started out
on a new round of inspection tours throughout Germany. Dorsch remained at the
head of the Todt Organization in the occupied countries. He was a personal
friend of Himmler and had taken part in the 1923 putsch in Munich.[10] Nevertheless, Speer retained his authority over building within the Reich.

The Kammler Sonderstab *Is Set Up*

During Speer's absence the SS was successful in one endeavor, however. Kammler was placed in charge of equipping the underground sites for the aviation industry using concentration camp workers. Hitler promised to provide him with contingents of Hungarian Jews for that purpose.[11] The project was independent of the one that he examined with Dorsch. In both cases they were at the time priorities for Hitler, who was very concerned about the intensity of the American bombing in late February.

At the beginning of the process, a *Jägerstab,* a headquarters for fighter plane production, was formed as a result of an agreement on March 1 between Speer and Milch to see to it that aircraft construction would not be penalized in relation to the weapons industry.[12] Sauer was appointed head of this headquarters, which included Kammler. It was on this basis that Göring gave orders to Kammler to put the aviation industry underground.

Kammler immediately set up a *Sonderstab,* a special headquarters bearing his name, which launched construction projects in various parts of the Reich, particularly in the *Mittelraum.*[13] The complex organization of the Kammler *Sonderstab* was further aggravated by the use of a rather unfamiliar coding system. This will be discussed later in chapter 11 in part 4, which deals mainly with projects B3, B11, B12, etc., and the corresponding camps such as Ellrich and Harzungen resulting from the Kammler *Sonderstab*'s activity.

While these projects were getting under way, transfers were soon being made to the existing underground sites, but they could offer only a very partial solution to the problem. From the Junkers-Betriebe company, production units from Magdeburg, Köthen, and Leipzig were taken to Nordwerk Niedersachswerfen, the name given as of April 1944 to the northern part of the Kohnstein Tunnel, which had been handed over to Hall 20 by Mittelwerk.[14] Other Junkers production units, from Schönebeck, made up the Thyrawerke Rottleberode. There the underground site was a natural gypsum grotto, known as the *Heimkehle,* the largest of its kind in Germany, located near Rottleberode.[15]

V2 *Tests and the May 6, 1944, Meeting*

The first V2 firing toward Paris, and then London, would not take place until September 8, 1944, more than a year after the bombing of Peenemünde and eight months after the first rockets were rolled out from the Mittelwerk factory. The Blizna testing center operated until June, but tests were being performed simultaneously on the island of Greifswalder Oie, near Peenemünde.[16]

Apparently the first rockets that were delivered in early 1944 had a number of defects, which were not surprising given the condition of the factory at the time. Leaks and poor soldering were noted, and the electrical system had to be systematically revised by DEMAG in Falkensee, which meant more time and therefore delayed the tests. Serious problems continued at the launches until the spring: rockets exploded or fell back, damaging the firing equipment. In the following months the rockets were observed to disintegrate several thousand feet above the target.

There was still considerable uncertainty about these technical problems when a major meeting was held on May 6, 1944, in the office of Georg Rickhey, the new head of Mittelwerk since April 13. He had been chosen by Speer and had a background in industry as manager of a Ruhr subsidiary of DEMAG and manager of the Technical House in Essen.[17] The participants at the meeting included, first, General Dornberger, General Rossmann, commanding officer of "Wa Prüf 10," and five officers from the army's Ordnance Office (artillerymen); second, four directors of Sonderausschuss A4, including Kunze and Storch (whose name will come up again soon); third, von Braun and Steinhoff; finally, nine representatives of Mittelwerk, including Rickhey, Kettler, Sawatzki, Rudolph, and Förschner, and a representative of Askania, a subcontracting company.

It was actually a summit meeting of all the parties concerned about the success of the rockets, which may have been an exception in terms of its size. One is struck, in passing, by the number of university degrees the participants held. Most of them appear to have had links with Speer in one way or another, and this rapport no doubt explains the "spirit of camaraderie" that characterized the discussion. It was announced that Speer was going back to work full-time, which was a cause for celebration.

The participants toured the factory on this occasion, naturally without going to visit the still occupied "dormitories," but they might have crossed paths with hundreds of despised prisoners in the factory, even in the mildest Kommandos. The SS was represented at the meeting only at the level of Förschner, who was the camp commander, and as such, one of the directors of Mittelwerk. The minutes of the meeting contain no mention of his taking part.

Indeed, many of the questions discussed were of an ordinary, technical nature and could well have been brought up in any large firm in peacetime, such as production delays due to modifications resulting from tests, the problem of not having an up-to-date list of spare parts, the need for double-checking, once at the subcontractors' and again upon receipt at the Mittelwerk factory, and so on.

As was customary in this type of meeting, the lack of manpower was used to explain some of the problems, and it was not surprising that Kammler was asked to provide eighteen hundred additional prisoners. The latter ignored the request in any event, as the prisoners sent from Buchenwald at the time went on to Ellrich, Harzungen, or Wieda.

In the minutes, which seem, by their sheer banality, to have been very faithfully recorded, one sentence stands out, attracting the reader's attention some fifty years on. The discussion concerned the disadvantages of having production of the *Rudermaschinen* (the servomotors for aerodynamic control of the rocket) too widely dispersed from a geographical standpoint. They were being manufactured in Mittelwerk, Saarbruck, Litzmannstadt (the new name of Lodz), and by two Parisian companies ("2 Pariser Firmen"). It appeared advisable to group all this special production together at Mittelwerk and transfer both the machines and the workforce.

At this point a remark was made (it happened to be made by Storch, but that is neither here nor there) without drawing any conclusion: "Einsatz französischer Arbeiter im MW nur Einkleidung möglich" [We cannot use French workers unless they are made to wear the uniform]—by which everyone understood he meant "striped prisoner's pajamas." For Storch it was a banal observation given the situation. The fact that it would mean arresting and deporting French civilians was not his concern, and there is nothing to indicate that he himself was in favor of this solution. On the other hand, if the Gestapo and the SS were to take care of supplying the manpower, they would know how to put it to use. In any event, it never occurred. Yet the degree to which the concentration camp system had become widespread, which leaps out of the page from this simple, isolated sentence, is no doubt significant.

Whatever may have been their manpower needs, there was no question at the time of relying on Hitler to give priority to manufacturing V2s. Indeed, the Luftwaffe's V1s were practically ready to be launched on London. The first firing in that direction took place on June 13, only one week after the landing in Normandy, when it was still possible to harbor some illusions. The device could be quickly mass-produced, which pleased Hitler.[18]

The fact that, for a number of weeks in mid-1944, Hitler showed less interest in V2s was an obstacle to giving it priority, but it allowed Dornberger and von Braun time to analyze the problems. In Blizna they went so far as to station themselves on the actual targets to see more clearly what was happening, and von Braun nearly got himself killed. The story of that adventure is one of the reasons behind the later "gesture" toward von Braun.[19]

It now appears after the fact that this period served above all to draw up an indispensable list of parts, taking into account the constant changes resulting from the tests, to be applied both at Peenemünde and Mittelwerk. It was said that by the end of the war some sixty-five thousand changes had been made, usually in details, which, from a technical standpoint, is not aberrant.[20] At the time, prisoners who found themselves working as "inspectors" or warehouse keepers had an impression of gentle chaos that hardly disturbed the *Meister.*

At Peenemünde, von Braun and the others were not restricted to developing V2s. They had other tasks, particularly designing an antiaircraft missile for the Wasserfall (waterfall) program initiated in 1942. In August 1944, one-fourth of the workforce at Peenemünde was assigned to the program.[21] The Luftwaffe was officially in charge, though in June 1944 aircraft production was transferred to the Armaments Ministry (and Milch resigned).[22]

Various tests failed until June 13, when a V2, equipped with Wasserfall missile guidance, was launched in Peenemünde. The rocket veered off course and burst in the air above the Swedish town of Kalmar, which would later make it possible for the Allies to collect a great amount of varied debris from the site.[23]

Allied Concerns and Operation Crossbow

The intense bombing of Peenemünde in August 1943 shows that the British took very seriously the risk of a German rocket attack on England, which would have been likely to cause massive destruction and compromise preparations for the landing in Western Europe. At the end of 1943, top-level meetings were held between the British and Americans.[24]

Their worries were compounded by the discovery that new installations, obviously intended for firing, were being built in the north of France. Corroborating information on the subject was provided by French Resistance fighters[25] and British agents in France. Aerial photographs revealed the existence of "ski sites" in particular, edifices resembling giant skis laid backwards, that had to be launching ramps facing London. There were also much larger concrete buildings.

These constructions were scattered between the Pas-de-Calais and Somme regions on the one hand and the Cotentin on the other, designed to send rockets to either London or ports in southern England. Within the scope of Operation Crossbow, launched in December 1943, an air offensive was launched on the installations and severely damaged them. The Germans then changed their technique, pretending all the while that they were maintaining their activity on the "ski sites." They built dozens of modified sites that were rudimentary and camouflaged, where the ramp would not be mounted until just a few days before the beginning of the offensive.[26]

It began on June 13, after the Normandy landing, and on June 15 244 V1s were launched within twenty-four hours. The two-thousandth firing took place on June 29. By early July the rate had reached 200 a day from Pas-de-Calais and the Somme. They caused considerable damage, especially in London, and a million Londoners abandoned the city for the provinces. Starting on June 17 the term V1 was used in the press by Propaganda Minister Goebbels to designate the Fi 103. V stood for *Vergeltungswaffen*—or retaliation weapons.

The V1s were not the Allies' sole preoccupation. The fact that Peenemünde was being little used for launchings intrigued the Allies until the Polish Resistance supplied information drawing attention to the Blizna site at the end of

December 1943. Photographs finally made it possible to identify a rocket on May 5, 1944.[27]

It was not until June, however, that more specific information was obtained from the debris that had fallen onto Kalmar, Sweden, from the rocket that went off its path and exploded there. After vigorously protesting, the Swedish refused to return the debris to the Germans but agreed to turn it over to the British. A cargo plane was discreetly sent over from England to pick it up. The reconstruction carried out in Farnborough in July was deceptive, for, as mentioned earlier, the guidance system belonged to a Wasserfall missile.[28] Yet the Allies did find out the weight of the nose cone, which had hitherto been overestimated, and the presence of serial numbers indicated that the offensive was drawing near.

McGovern tells the long story of the recovery of another V2 by the Polish Resistance and the transport of the main parts (with the real guidance system) by a Dakota which was sent to pick them up from the base in Brindisi.[29] It was ultimately brought to Great Britain after the Swedish V2.

The New Organization After July 20, 1944

The failed assassination attempt against Hitler on July 20, 1944, resulted in Himmler's being appointed head of the army inside Germany to replace Fromm. The conspirators were members of Fromm's staff, and he could not have been totally in the dark about their plans. He was quickly imprisoned and would be executed in March 1945.[30] Since September 1943, Himmler had been Reichsminister of the interior. Now he controlled the country from both a civilian and military standpoint. In actual fact, Fromm's real successor was SS-Obergruppenführer Hans Jüttner, who was head of the headquarters of the Waffen-SS.[31]

Fromm, to whom the artillerymen of Peenemünde reported, had long been one of Speer's allies against the SS. When he was arrested, Speer lost a key figure in his system. Dornberger, Zanssen, and Gen. Erich Schneider had been Becker's deputies in the Ordnance Office in the early thirties. Schneider, who had been head of the office since 1943, was arrested and then released through Speer's intervention and had the charges dismissed, but he did not resume his position.[32] Zanssen took up a command position on the Western Front.[33] Dornberger, whose loyalty was unquestionable, remained isolated.

On August 6, Himmler gave full authority to Kammler to speed up the use of V2s,[34] which had become the focus of German hopes as the V1s had merely spread panic in London. By this time the English were stopping them with barriers of antiaircraft guns and captive balloons, and fighter planes also shot them down. On July 31, the Americans finally broke through the lines at Avranches.

The Allies were advancing quickly by the end of August and the beginning of September: Paris was liberated on August 25, Amiens on August 31, Brussels on September 3, and Antwerp on September 4. As a result, any firing sites that had not been destroyed fell into their hands between the lower Seine and the lower course of the Meuse. That was exactly what happened to the Wizernes Bunker, intended for V2 launching, which was bombed and left uncompleted,[35] along with the liquid oxygen plant in Éperlecques.

The first V2s were fired on September 8. A rocket launched from the Ardennes towards Paris landed in Maisons-Alfort. Two rockets fell on London, in Chiswick and Epping. From now on the firings were carried out from mobile ramps, as Dornberger had advised from the beginning. They circulated in the wooded expanses of Haagsche Bosch, behind The Hague, in Holland, and in Western Germany. The targets were London and Antwerp as well as Liège.

Jüttner, eager to avoid being outflanked by Kammler on Reich territory, put Dornberger in charge of training battery personnel and delivering V2s to the borders of Germany.[36] This balance of responsibilities was to remain in place until the country was invaded. The Luftwaffe remained in charge of V1 firing, and manufacturing was then transferred to the Dora Tunnel as will be shown further on. The firings were aimed at Antwerp and Liège.

The Last Months of Peenemünde

After July 20 the final reorganization of Speer's production system took place, which no doubt had been in the works for some time. The main change concerned the Peenemünde base, which had remained a military establishment. As mentioned earlier, it had been the Heimat-Artillerie Park 11, or HAP, of Karlshagen since June 1, 1943.

As of August 1, 1944, a new company was set up under the name Elektromechanische Werke GmbH, Karlshagen, or EW, which took over the development unit's activity for the Armaments Ministry, just like Mittelwerk. The managing director was Paul Storch, a director of Sonderausschuss A4, who came from Siemens.[37] He had taken part in the May 6 meeting at Rickhey's office. Peenemünde continued to belong to the military, which rented it to EW. The Versuchsplatz Karlshagen, the operations base, remained under the command of General Rossmann, the head of Wa Prüf 10.[38]

At the same time Kunze was placed at the head of Sonderausschuss A4 and Degenkolb pushed aside. After making insulting remarks about various Nazi leaders, he was interned in a clinic from which he reappeared in April 1945 as a liaison agent between the ministry and Kammler.[39] Kunze, whose offices had been transferred to Thuringia in early 1944,[40] was thus coordinating three companies: Mittelwerk with Rickhey, EW with Storch, and a third company managing Rudolf Hermann's wind tunnel in Kochel. The companies that had been set up for the engine testing centers in Lehesten and Redl-Zipf[41] merged with Mittelwerk, which also took over the Ni Agency of WIFO on August 15.[42]

The new organization was less complicated and did not disturb Dornberger or von Braun or their deputies, whose expertise protected them completely from any interference. It was impossible to do without them, just as Hitler could not do without Speer at the head of industry. Kammler was powerful but he knew nothing about rockets, and they could not be abandoned.

From August 1944 to January 1945, work continued at Peenemünde despite a diminished workforce resulting from transfers to Mittelwerk as well as American bombing on July 18, August 2, and August 25, and frequent air raid warnings.[43] Von Braun saw to it that the employment of his staff was justified by various tasks.

A great deal of work was still required on the V2s and for Wasserfall.[44] The team took up earlier studies on a winged A9 rocket, renamed the A4b, and tests took place in December 1944 and January 1945, unsuccessfully, which was not a surprise to anyone.[45] At the request of the Luftwaffe they also worked on a small antiaircraft missile called the *Taifun* (typhoon).[46] They even went so far as to devote a considerable amount of time to imagining a sort of platform towed by a submarine from which V2s could be launched on New York. A production contract was concluded with the Vulkan shipbuilding company in Stettin.[47]

Von Braun remained in close contact with Mittelwerk and sometimes went into the tunnel factory. One occasion is recalled in a letter he sent on August 15, 1944, to "Dear Mr. Sawatzski," including, among other things, the following paragraphs: "During one of my latest visits to Mittelwerk, you spontaneously suggested that we take advantage of the good technical training of prisoners available to you and at Buchenwald to organize additional development work and construction in small units. On that occasion, you introduced me to a French physics professor and prisoner who has been working until now on checking mixing devices *(Mischgeräte)*, who would be particularly capable of running such a production unit. I immediately accepted your proposal. Together with Dr. Simon, I went to Buchenwald to see other able prisoners, and as you suggested, managed to have Standartenführer Pister transfer them to Mittelwerk."

This text is interesting for a number of reasons. It shows that von Braun was making frequent visits to Mittelwerk, that his visits gave him an opportunity to talk about various topics, including the prisoners, and that he was quite capable of conducting procedures within the concentration camp system, even with the camp commander at Buchenwald.

As it happens, the rest of the story of the French professor assigned to the *Mischgeräte* is known. His name is Charles Sadron, and he gave the firsthand account of the disinfecting process mentioned earlier. This is how he tells it:[48] "To be honest, however, I have to point out that I did meet one man who showed an almost generous attitude towards me. It was Professor von Braun, a member of the technical HQ, who developed the aerial torpedoes. Von Braun came to see me in the production unit.

"He was a young, very Germanic-looking man who spoke perfect French. He expressed his regret, in courteous, measured terms, at seeing a French professor in such a state of misery, and then he proposed that I come and work in his laboratory. Of course, it was out of the question that I accept his offer. I harshly refused. Von Braun excused himself and smiled as he left. Later on, I was to learn that, despite my refusal, he had nevertheless tried several times to improve my situation—in vain by the way." This text was published in 1947, before von Braun had become famous.

In chapter 6 the close relationship between the concentration camp system and the factories working on the V2s was mentioned. Two further components should be added.

The first was the existence of an underground factory in a closed down railway tunnel where special vehicles were equipped to transport V2s. Its code name was *Rebstock* (vine plant) because it was located in a winegrowing region near Dernau/Ahr in the Rhineland. The prisoners who worked there came from the Natzweiler-Struthof camp.[49]

The second was the existence of a new concentration camp at Peenemünde itself,[50] with prisoners taken mainly from Sachsenhausen. This camp will be discussed at the end of chapter 10.

[[8]]

THE PEOPLES OF DORA

In every Nazi concentration camp the population was deliberately mixed, with varying nationalities and reasons for internment. The point was to avoid any solidarity among prisoners in one way or another. Nevertheless, due to circumstances the mixture was never quite the same from one camp to another, and the relationships established among the different groups was peculiar to each camp. The following information concerns Dora and the annex camps and Kommandos, until the end of 1944—i.e., prior to the arrival of prisoners evacuated from Auschwitz and Gross Rosen.

In order to understand the position of each of the populations involved, we must refer to the structure of Europe at the end of 1943, which was dominated by Nazi Germany. It comprised three main groups: 1. The German Reich with its two dependent territories: the Bohemian-Moravian protectorate and the General Government of Poland. 2. The conquered territories of the Soviet Union that were administered by the Reich commissariats of Ostland and the Ukraine. 3. The occupied countries of Western Europe: France, Belgium, and the Netherlands, Denmark and Norway, and Italy.

We can leave aside the Allied countries or vassal states of Central Europe and the Balkans, which had few nationals at Dora, except for the Hungarian Jews who, in any case, formed a special community.

In this chapter we will discuss the Germans and those assimilated to Germans, the Czechs and the Poles; then Russians, Ukrainians, and other Soviet peoples; and finally the French, the Belgians and the Dutch, the Italians, and the Slovenians. The last paragraphs will be devoted to the Hungarian Jews and the German Gypsies.

Germans and the Assimilated

Hitler's Germany was called the Deutsches Reich, which, since 1871, had already been the name, first of the Hohenzollern Empire, and second, of the Weimar Republic.[1] Its citizens were therefore *Reichsdeutsche*—i.e., Germans of the Reich. This included Germans prior to 1938 as well as Austrians, Germans from Sudetenland, Memel, and Danzig, and all the German-speaking people of Bohemia-Moravia and the former Poland. In some camps, such as Dachau, one might encounter political prisoners—monarchists or social democrats—who called themselves Austrians. That was not the case at Dora.

The SS were *Reichsdeutsche* regardless of their origin. Among them were also *Volksdeutsche*, German nationals of foreign countries who could not be in the Wehrmacht and therefore joined the SS. They came from Slovakia, Hungary, Romania ("Saxons" from South Transylvania or "Swabs" from Banat). The "Romanian" SS who appear in the accounts were *Volksdeutsche* from Romania (Hermann Oberth, one of the rocket pioneers [see chapter 2], who spent several years at Peenemünde, was also one). The term was used at least for a while to refer to natives of Alsace-Lorraine, Luxembourg, and Belgians from Eupen and Malmédy, before they were drafted "in spite of ourselves" in the German army.

The Germans were the only prisoners whose status was differentiated by the color of their triangles. In Dora there were hardly any except Greens ("common-law" prisoners), who accounted for the great majority, and Reds, the political prisoners.

The Greens belonged to two categories, which are defined by Kogon.[2] "The Gestapo distinguished between the 'BV prisoners' who had already been punished for criminal acts, and the 'SV prisoners' who were still purging their punishment. The first were said to be 'held preventively for a temporary period' (Befristete Vorbeugungshäftlinge), from which was derived the general expression, using the same initials, of 'professional criminals' (Berufsverbrecher). The second were called Sicherungsverwarte or 'prisoners for security reasons.'" (Some people believed that SV meant *Schwerverbrecher* or "dangerous criminals.") The testimonies of other prisoners hardly make any distinction between these two categories, or with the rare "black triangles," who were usually pimps. The whole range of criminals could be found there, from bloodthirsty brutes to peaceful crooks.

The Reds were not only in the minority; as Langbein remarked, "At Dora there must have been barely 40 politically-aware Germans and hundreds of criminals." The fact that the political prisoners usually held important positions corresponded to a deliberate choice on the part of the camp commander, who was eager to keep peace in a camp linked to a secret weapons factory. As a result, in annex camps such as Ellrich, the least recommendable Greens held sway to the misfortune of the others.

Among the Reds, the French prisoners met a number of former members of the French Foreign Legion, who had been imprisoned for that reason. Their behavior toward the French was highly variable.

The Czechs

The Czechs became part of the Deutsches Reich when the Bohemian-Moravian protectorate was proclaimed on March 15, 1939. Hence the Czech prisoners wearing a red triangle with a T could belong to any category, including that of common-law prisoners. There were a number of these at Dora, but the vast majority of Czechs were former partisans. Despite the traditionally large size of their party, there were not many Czech communists at Dora; they stayed, well organized, at Buchenwald.

After the events of 1938–39, the Czechs were politically extremely hostile to the Germans, a fact that they later demonstrated by expelling the German-speaking population from the Czech Republic in 1945–46. Yet they were closely linked from a cultural standpoint, as Bohemia and Moravia had belonged for centuries to the Holy Roman Empire and then to the Austro-Hungarian Empire. Most Czechs at Dora spoke German and were well educated, which ensured them secretarial positions both in the camp and in the factory and a role at the *Revier.* It is hard to estimate the pace of their arrival at Buchenwald, and then at Dora, as none of the convoys—this is inside the Reich, remember—were readily identifiable. We know from the testimony of Benès[3] and Litomisky[4] cited previously that Czech prisoners arrived at Dora in the very first weeks, after a difficult stay at Auschwitz. Another large group was present when the camp was built. Some could also be found at Ellrich.

Although they were Slavs, the Czechs were not treated like the Poles and the Russians. There were no Czech prisoners of war, since there had been no war against them. The Czechs had been conscripted for compulsory labor and there were Czechs among the free workers who became the "Wifos" of the Dora Tunnel. In some ways their discipline and taste for organization were surprising in a concentration camp world, and they were rewarded for it by earning a certain amount of esteem. As we saw earlier, Litomisky explained with pride how he had overseen the distribution of food in a tunnel block, and Benès mocked so-called German organization in laying the tracks for tunnel B.

The Poles

After the Austrians in 1938 and the Czechs in March 1939, the Poles appeared in the camps at the end of 1939. Once Warsaw had capitulated on September 27, the German authorities were determined both to reduce the territory that would keep the name of Poland and to deprive the Polish people of their traditional elite. In any case the Soviet Union annexed the eastern part of the country, which was divided up between Ukraine and Belorussia, and transferred the Polish population of these territories to Siberia and Kazakhstan. The Russian massacre of Polish officers at Katyn took place in the spring of 1940.

The German portion of Poland was itself cut in half. One part was directly attached to the Deutsches Reich with a view to its Germanization. Once again Poznan became Posen, and it was there in the setting of the castle that Himmler made his great speeches. Oswiecim, in Upper Silesia, became Auschwitz, and a camp was set up there in May 1940, whose first occupants along with Germans were Poles. The other part formed the General Government of Poland, attached to the Reich and placed under its direct administration. The General Government had its headquarters in Krakow; Warsaw was in ruins. Polish prisoners of war were distributed throughout Germany, along with millions of Polish civilian workers, usually forced laborers. Above all, the nation's managers, functionaries, academics, and officers were sent to camps such as Sachsenhausen and Mauthausen.

In 1943–45 a number of Poles arrived at Dora. Quite often they were civilian workers who had been sanctioned under various pretexts. There was also a diverse group of delinquents, and the number of sentences requiring internment in a camp was lower for the Poles than for the Germans or the Czechs. Generally speaking, the Poles at Dora formed a proletariat deprived of practically any national political or cultural framework. A number of them spoke German, which earned them positions as *Kapos* and even as block leaders, especially if they were delinquents linked to their German counterparts. Others were *Vorarbeiter, Stubendienst,* or nurses. They did not have a good reputation; in fact, they were often detested by Western prisoners, particularly the French.

Two accounts seek to give a better image of the Poles at Dora, relying on limited, but real, examples. The first is from J. B. de Korwin-Krokowski[5] on the one hand, an officer who managed to leave Poland in 1939, fought in France in 1940, and was arrested as a Resistance fighter in December 1943. The second is from Tadek Patzer, arrested in Poland in 1941 and transferred from Auschwitz to Dora in 1943. Both of them, who were quite familiar with camp life, corresponded after the war with Langbein, who refers several times to their accounts.

The political vicissitudes of Poland, which was divided until 1918 among Germany, Austria, and Russia, were such that problems of nationality were sometimes difficult to sort out. Krokowski commented about a certain Janek, *Stubendienst* in Block 8, that he was "more Ukrainian than Polish." No doubt he had originated in Eastern Galicia, as we shall see later. He also mentioned the case of Hans Kaczmarek, who was a German political prisoner (communist) at Dora, and after the war was decorated with the highest Polish military distinction for his resistance action at Dora. In fact, the Polish partisans imprisoned at Dora claimed allegiance to the Polish government in London, and the communists were in the minority.

Russians, Ukrainians, and Other Soviets

A particularly large number of prisoners at Dora came from the Soviet Union. They arrived in two ways. The first were interned in Ukraine and deported to Buchenwald when Soviet troops began reconquering the territory, as we saw earlier. The others were already prisoners of war or civilian laborers in Germany and were transferred to the concentration camps with or without reason.

We know that the young Ukrainians, organized into groups of looters, were preying on others during the first few months at Dora, inside the tunnel as well as outside. Kogon evokes those that remained at Buchenwald as follows:[6] "Whereas the prisoners of war formed well-disciplined teams who were very skillful, as well as fair, in protecting their collective interests, the mass of Ukrainians made up a crew that is difficult to describe. In the beginning, they were so favored by their German comrades that it was almost impossible to make the slightest complaint against a 'Russian.' Soon, however, due to their insolence, laziness and the lack of camaraderie among many of them, the situation was rapidly reversed, and they could no longer hope to obtain important positions." Other authors show the perplexity of the German communists in the face of this unforeseen side of the new "homo sovieticus."

Until the spring of 1942 the Germans were hardly concerned about using the manpower constituted by Soviet prisoners of war, whom they massacred or left to die. Civilians in the occupied countries were at the time simply conscripted on the spot by military authorities. The attitude of the Germans changed in 1942 when they had to mobilize fresh troops to offset their losses on the Eastern Front and were starting to encounter a lack of manpower in Germany. Sauckel was in charge of recruiting laborers from the occupied countries, particularly in the East. Millions of *Ostarbeiter*, both men and women, were thus transferred to highly varied jobs. When the SS, under the impetus of authorities such as Kammler, needed to extend its hold over economic life, the Gestapo had only to arrest a suitable number of *Ostarbeiter* and dress them in prison stripes—an operation known as *Einkleidung*.

It was above all in 1944 that these new prisoners arrived at Dora; they were either former prisoners of war or *Ostarbeiter* and belonged to all the nationalities of the Soviet Union: Russians, Ukrainians, Belorussians, and others. Recently Joseph Béninger[7] and the author, in discussing their experiences of the Scherer Kommando, evoked the memory of one of their friends, a young Bachkir who had been a film projectionist and had read (in Russian translations, of course) the works of Balzac, Victor Hugo, Alexandre Dumas, and Jules Verne. Miller says the same thing in talking about his friend Vladimir at Ellrich: "Like all of his compatriots, he had read much of our literature, and never ceased expressing his admiration for Victor Hugo, Balzac and Alexandre

Dumas. There was not a village in the USSR where the young people were not familiar with the father of *The Three Musketeers* and admired him, he explained."[8]

There were some Estonians, Letts, and Lithuanians, but generally most residents of the Ostland were sent to the Stutthof camp near Danzig. The Soviet prisoners were primarily Russian and Ukrainian. The difference between them was clear-cut in the beginning but faded with time. In all probability the other prisoners had trouble distinguishing them. François Heumann,[9] who was more familiar than others with Slavic languages, notes that the much-discussed Ukrainians spoke Russian, whereas he had heard a group of *Ostarbeiter* speaking Ukrainian in Metz before his arrest. Indeed, the Ukrainians at Dora, who were deported from Dnepropetrovsk, east of Ukraine, came from a region in which Russian was commonly spoken—and still is today—whereas the *Ostarbeiter* who were transplanted to Metz no doubt came from the western part of Ukraine where only Ukrainian was—and is—used.

We should add that Eastern Galicia, which passed from Polish hands to those of the Soviet Union in 1939–41, had by this time been incorporated into the General Government of Poland and thus into the Reich, even though its population was mainly Ukrainian since the Poles had been transferred to the interior of the Soviet Union. In the face of such confusion, even Krokowski limits himself to describing Janek as Polish-Ukrainian. One final point that is not without interest: the SS recruited black-uniformed Ukrainian militiamen in this region, who became guards at concentration camps. On occasion guards and prisoners would exchange a few words in Ukrainian in the Kommandos outside.

A large number of these Russian-Ukrainians were restricted to excavation works and transport at Dora as well as at Ellrich, Harzungen, and Wieda. At Peenemünde and Wizernes the *Ostarbeiter* made up the basic workforce. Others at the camp were *Stubendienst* or *Kalfaktor* (orderlies) in the *Revier.* Still others, more rarely, had jobs as "specialists" in the tunnel, such as the young Bachkir.

The prisoners of other nationalities suspected the existence of an internal organization within this community, with leaders whose authority was recognized. The arrests and hangings during the final weeks were, as will be seen, a serious blow to the group. After the liberation of Bergen-Belsen, the two leaders who appeared as representatives of the Soviets were Lt. Col. Alexander Manko from Leningrad and Capt. Mikhail Piskunov of Minsk.

The French

Most of the deportations from France to Germany, aside from those of the Jews deported as such, originated at the camp of Compiègne. It was a complex of French military buildings that had been installed in Royallieu, south of the town. The buildings were used by the Germans starting in 1940, first as a prisoner-of-war camp (Frontstalag 122), and then as an internment camp, with one part of the buildings reserved for American nationals and the other for French (or foreigners in France) arrested by the German services.

The latter stayed at Compiègne camp for varying lengths of time, but it usually served only as a transit camp. The internees came from all the German prisons of France and were grouped together there while awaiting the next convoy leaving from the Compiègne train station for one of the large concentration camps in Germany. Jews were deported from another camp, located in Drancy, northeast of Paris. The prisoners were not all deported from Compiègne to the major camps. Some were sent to German prisons after passing through special camps such as Hinzert, near Trier, or Neuenbremme, south of Saarbrücken. This latter group of deportees generally belonged to the category "NN," i.e., they were the subject of a decree of December 7, 1941, concerning some of the Resistance fighters arrested in the occupied countries in the West. No one was to know what happened to them, and they were unable to write about their news. NN stood for *Nacht und Nebel* ("night and fog"). Contrary to what Alain Resnais's film suggests, this regime did not concern all camp prisoners.

The aforementioned organization underwent two changes in 1943–45. Some NN prisoners were transferred from prisons to camps, such as Neuengamme or Gross Rosen. In the later period Compiègne was no longer the sole departure point. Convoys were organized in August 1944 in various other train stations in France.

As we mentioned earlier in chapter 3, all the deportation convoys that left from Compiègne between June 1943 and January 1944 went to Buchenwald, and a large proportion of the French prisoners involved were transferred from there to Dora between September 1943 and March 1944. After that the distribution changed: convoys from France and "transport" from Buchenwald both had more varied destinations.

From April to August 1944, Buchenwald and Neuengamme received the greatest number of deportees, ahead of Mauthausen and Dachau. Of the five convoys that arrived at Buchenwald, two in particular were used to populate the camps of Ellrich, Harzungen, and Wieda; the deportees in the other convoys were in large part transferred to Flossenbürg or into one of the increasing number of Kommandos. In all, only a small percentage of newcomers were assigned definitively to Dora itself. The first of the convoys in question left Compiègne on May 12, 1944, and arrived in Buchenwald on May 14. The corresponding matriculation numbers ranged from "50,000" to "53,000." Among the deportees were victims of the roundup, particularly at Saint-Claude on April 9, Easter Sunday. The transfer to Wieda or Harzungen took place in early June. The other convoy is called the "77,000"s, as the matriculation numbers went from "76,000" to "78,000." This convoy left from the Pantin train station on August 15, 1944, with deportees taken, in particular, from Fresnes prison. It arrived in

Buchenwald on August 20, and the transport to Dora took place in late August or early September. Most of the prisoners involved were quickly transferred to Ellrich.

Aside from the transport corresponding to convoys from France, French prisoners with quite varied matriculation numbers were sent from Buchenwald to Dora in small groups, especially after the August 24, 1944, bombing that destroyed the Gustloff factory.

The French represented a large percentage of the population of Dora, Ellrich, Harzungen, and Wieda, but they did not form a homogeneous group. They came from every region and had been arrested under different circumstances and at different times.

In 1943, among the prisoners were numerous *frontaliers,* i.e., those who had tried to cross the Pyrenees to reach North Africa. These included students like Raoul-Duval, Dutillieux, and Soubirous, and military men like Demuyter. Dora also had many graduates of the officers' academy of Saint-Cyr, some *frontaliers* and others not. Bernard d'Astorg and Xavier Lamothe were among the "20,000"s, Louis Mével and Jean Mialet among the "21,000"s, André Rogerie among the "31,000"s, Luc Clairin and René Haentjens among the "38,000"s, Guy Tartinville among the "40,000"s, Michel Delaval and Louis Garnier among the "44,000"s, Roger Couëtdic and Jean de Sesmaisons among the "49,000"s, and Pierre Dejussieu among the "77,000"s.

Beginning in 1943 the number of Resistance fighters who were arrested increased, along with the number of roundups. Among those who arrived at Dora there was only a very small group of active communists while the others remained at Buchenwald when they were detected by the "Red" leaders in the camp who tried their best to spare them bad "transports." In general, noncommunist Resistance leaders in the three convoys of January 1944, whether members of Parliament or not, also remained at Buchenwald. It was not until September 1944, amid the disorder following the bombing, that such leaders belonging to the "77,000" convoy were sent on to Dora. Yet this did not suffice to give a real structure to the French group from a political standpoint.

Small, very lively units were formed, however, mainly out of the work Kommandos in the tunnel factory, when their composition remained unchanged. Some groups that were formed in Compiègne subsisted in spite of the difficulties. People from the same area such as those from Saint-Claude also maintained certain ties. That was the case of the three "Vendéens," Maurice de la Pintière, Xavier de Lisle, and Robert de Lépinay, who were arrested together while trying to get across the Pyrenees. Lépinay died in March 1944, before leaving for Bergen-Belsen.[10]

Indeed, the French were not all political prisoners, despite the red triangle with an "F" that they were all required to wear. Some of them, a very small number incidentally, had been arrested in France for common-law violations af-

fecting the German authorities: theft, swindling, etc. French criminals or delinquents who were judged by French courts, however, remained imprisoned in
France. Most of the time these prisoners behaved in the camp like the rest of
their fellow Frenchmen, and some were even exemplary.

Little mention is made of them in the accounts. The best accounts were
given by Max Dutillieux of three prisoners in the Rossla Kommando, whom we
will encounter in the next chapter. In the Dora Tunnel, Francis Finelli, a high-
ranking civil servant in the Interior Ministry, had the chance to chat in Corsican
in a neighboring hall with a certain Martin Colonna. While inspecting a prison
after the war, he found him again: he had "fallen again," according to his own
expression. Other French prisoners were interned in concentration camps for of-
fenses committed in Germany. It was mainly in Dachau that Edmond Michelet
ran into them when he arrived in the camp.

Alsace-Lorraine Natives and the Struthof Camp

At Buchenwald and Dora, a significant number of prisoners came from
Alsace-Lorraine. They ended up there in two ways: either they were professors
and students from the University of Strasbourg, which had retreated to Clermont-
Ferrand in 1939, or they were Alsatians or Mosellians who had been arrested at
home since Alsace and Lorraine had been annexed by Germany in 1940.

After occupying the "free zone," the German authorities were not pleased at
the prospect of having the University of Strasbourg continue in Clermont-
Ferrand. An initial roundup took place on June 25, 1943, another on November
25, 1943, and isolated arrests continued during the first few months of 1944.
Thus Jean-Pierre Ebel, Étienne Eckert, Robert Gandar, André Gérard, Eugène
Greff, Paul Hagenmuller, Jean Lassus, André Lobstein, and François Schwertz
arrived sooner or later at Dora. Charles Sadron, a native of the Berry region and
a professor at that university, was also arrested on November 25, 1943. They
were all deported as French prisoners after spending some time, like all the others, in Compiègne.

From the German point of view, the situation of the Alsatians and Mosellians
who were arrested at home was quite different. Though not *Reichsdeutsche,* they
were at least *Volksdeutsche.* In the camps, most of them ended up being recognized as French with an F on their triangle. Similarly, natives of Luxembourg
were often able to keep their identity. Natives of Lorraine, such as Joseph
Béninger, François Heumann and Albert Schmitt, went through the Struthof
camp before being given identity numbers at Buchenwald among the "38,000"s
and sent to Dora in late December 1943.

The Struthof camp was not, however, reserved for prisoners from Alsace-
Lorraine. It was not located in France, any more than Auschwitz was located in
Poland or Mauthausen in Austria. According to the delimitation of the period, all

these camps were in the Deutsches Reich. Struthof was set high up in the Vosges Mountains of Alsace. For the SS it was the Natzweiler camp, built by German and Polish prisoners in 1941. Kramer was commander of the camp for a long time, before going to Auschwitz and then Bergen-Belsen, where he was stationed in 1945 at the time of the evacuations. For a while Fritz Pröll was a nurse there before coming to Dora. Plaza was the camp's SS doctor between the beginnings of Dora and Ohrdruf. It was a very harsh camp. As at all the large camps there were outside Kommandos. Some were close by, like Sainte-Marie-des-Mines (then called Markirch). Others were more remote, like *Rebstock* in the Rhineland, which was working on the vehicles to transport V2s, or those in the Neckar valley where the Kammler *Sonderstab* had underground tunnels dug, as we shall see in chapter 11.

The prisoners that came through Struthof were of varied nationalities. This was the case of the Slovenians who were sent to Sainte-Marie-des-Mines in particular. There were numerous French prisoners, especially the NN, in the final weeks, when the massacres occurred. The camp, which was evacuated to Dachau in August–September 1944, was not liberated by the Americans until November 23.

The Belgians

There were few Belgians at Dora during the terrible early months. As we saw in chapter 6, there were 15 deaths among them compared to 708 among the French prisoners. No convoys from Belgium arrived before May 8, 1944. The first Belgians who arrived at Dora were already at Buchenwald or were in the convoys from France, or had gone through prisons in Germany.

Four convoys brought deportees from Belgium between May 8 and August 11, 1944.[11] Some remained at Buchenwald, at least for a while. The others, who were sent to *Mittelraum* camps,[12] were usually not used in the Dora Tunnel on assembling V2s or V1s. They quickly joined the new underground work sites under Kammler, which will be discussed in part 4. Many of them died. According to later studies, "The mortality rate was higher than average: taking into account those that perished during the evacuations or shortly after their liberation, there were about 1,400 deaths, which corresponded to nearly 55% of the Belgians at Dora-Mittelbau." The fact of remaining or not remaining at Buchenwald was therefore of great importance, and the conditions governing the choice are still being hotly debated fifty years later.[13]

The 967 deportees who arrived in Buchenwald on May 8 came from Breendonck, a camp set up in a fort west of Malines that was particularly harsh. They found living conditions at Buchenwald much more bearable than at Breendonck. They were assigned identity numbers in the "48,000" and "49,000" series. In May and June 1944, 502 of them were transferred to Dora, and most of them were quickly assigned to Ellrich. The Breendonck camp, which opened in September 1940, was run like all the other camps in Germany, with an SS commander, Sturmbannführer Philipp Schmitt, and guards who were members of the Flemish SS. The SS from the Walloon Legion of Léon Degrelle were not concerned by this camp. We will talk about the French SS of the Charlemagne Division in chapter 21.

Of the 891 deportees in the May 23 convoy that departed from Brussels, who were given identity numbers in the "54,000" series, 699 were transferred to Dora, and most of them landed in Harzungen on June 10. A third convoy arrived from Brussels on June 20 with 574 deportees (the "60,000"s), and by July, 391 of them were in the Dora complex. The last convoy arrived from Brussels on August 11. Of the 824 deportees, 369, classified among the "75,000"s and "76,000"s, were sent directly to the new Blankenburg camp.

Later, at the time of the evacuation of the eastern camps discussed in chapter 14, numerous Belgian prisoners arrived from Gross Rosen who were NN internees initially sent to the Gross Strehlitz prison in Upper Silesia.

In Belgium as in France, the convoys included some foreigners who had been living in the country. They concerned, moreover, Frenchmen from North Pas-de-Calais, the region then under the control of the *Militärbefehlshaber,* and the Gestapo in Brussels.

Joseph Woussen

Joseph Woussen,[14] born in 1893 and at the time a lieutenant colonel in the Belgian army, arrived at Dora in October 1943 with the number 30060. One of the leaders of the Secret Army, he was arrested in 1942 and spent time in a series of prisons before being sent to Buchenwald. He stayed in the tunnel until April 1944. While in the camp he tried to "visit his fellow Belgians to boost their morale as far as he was able." One of them added: "His personality, age and experience, perhaps, too, the fact that he was the highest-ranking Belgian officer in the camp, account for the influence he exerted over the other Belgians who saw him as a moral leader in whom they could confide." Since he could speak German he served as the "public scribe," writing postcards to the prisoners' families. He gathered and disseminated news on military events.

He ended up being assigned for many long months to peeling potatoes and was able to supply a few friends. Despite his age and the length of his deportation, he was one of the essential witnesses of the evacuation to Ravensbrück and Malchow.

When he returned to Belgium, General Woussen became president of the Belgian Association of Political Prisoners of Dora and Kommandos, until his death at age 102.

The Dutch

There were never more than a few Dutch prisoners at Dora. They arrived through various itineraries, as two examples illustrate. Doctor Groeneveld was arrested in Paris. Van Dijk, conscripted for compulsory labor, was arrested in Germany while trying to get back to the Netherlands. Thanks to their knowledge of German they often found quite acceptable positions in the factory or the camp. The solidarity in their group was very high.

Italian Prisoners of War

In September 1943, when the Badoglio government concluded an armistice with the Allies, the Germans disarmed the Italian troops in all of the territories they were able to control, both in Italy itself and in the Balkans. The soldiers were transferred to Germany, and a small proportion of them agreed to continue fighting. Although there was, generally speaking, no resistance, the others were considered as "prisoners of war" and interned in the *Stalag*.

Between October 14 and November 2, 1943, 748 prisoners were transferred from various *Stalag* to the Dora camp, where a barracks, Block 18, was reserved for them. They kept their uniforms. They were given their own series of identity numbers, beginning with 01.

Some of them refused to work on rocket production, which they considered contrary to the Geneva Convention of 1929 concerning the protection of prisoners of war. Six were shot to death in early December 1943 in the camp: Emmine Blanchet (0276), Giovanni Scola (0278), Ernesto Moz (0279), Elisio Flamatti (0456), Giuseppe Bacanelli (0457), and Carlo Massoni (0458).

The Italian prisoners of war were not in a privileged situation. They were harshly treated by the Greens and subjected to looting by the young Ukrainians, as noted in chapter 5. Like the Wifos, they gradually melted into the mass of prisoners and could be found at Dora, Ellrich, and Harzungen. In the end, 264 of the 728 prisoners did not make it home.

The Yugoslavians

When we speak of Yugoslavs in 1943–44, it is somewhat difficult to define them after the border upheavals in April 1941 and September 1943.

The Yugoslavia of 1919 was completely shattered by 1941. Parts of the territory went to neighboring countries: northern Slovenia to the German Reich, the Vojvodina to Hungary, Macedonia to Bulgaria, Kosovo to Albania under Italian domination, and southern Slovenia and Dalmatia to Italy. Three entities were created: Serbia under the control of the Germans, Montenegro under an Italian protectorate, and Croatia which also included Bosnia-Herzegovina. Germany dominated the interior part of former Yugoslavia and Italy the coastal area.

In 1943 the Germans replaced the Italians and directly administered southern Slovenia as well as Istria, Trieste, and Frioul within the scope of the Adriatisches Küstenland. The "Yugoslavs" at Dora were former Italian nationals: Slovenians, Croats from Istria and Dalmatia, and Montenegrins. They were differentiated from the Serbs and the Croats. In February 1945 there were thus thirty Serbs, five Croats, and forty-eight Yugoslavs.

The majority of the Yugoslavs were interned in Italy when the Germans occupied the country. They were in a camp in Renicci, near Perugia. On September 23, 1943, they were placed in a transport of 700 people that ended up, by mistake, at a prisoner-of-war camp in Nuremberg. From there they were transferred to the Flossenbürg concentration camp. Then, 506 of them were sent to Buchenwald and given identity numbers in the "32,000" series. Finally, 350 arrived at Dora on October 28.

Other Slovenians, arrested later on, were quarantined in Dachau when they were selected for the Dora factory, as we shall see in the next chapter. To illustrate the complexity of things, which was not new in that part of Europe, it should be mentioned that the former Slovenian prisoners of Dora include two Slovenians from the western part of the country who were at the time Italian prisoners of war and two Slovenians from northern Slovenia, who had refused to be incorporated into the German army. The Slovenians, who are necessarily multilingual, were often assigned to acceptable positions.

Other Nationalities

When we examine the head count statement regularly drawn up by the SS, we find various nationalities. They were often foreigners arrested in another country, like the two Hungarian students; Peter Gáti and Boehm, who were arrested in France.

One may note that there were few Spaniards. There were, however, many Spanish Republicans in the first convoy from Compiègne in January 1944. Like Jorge Semprun, who arrived with the third convoy, they remained at Buchenwald.

The Hungarian Jews

The Hungarian Jews were the last European Jews to be the subject of systematic deportation after the occupation of Hungary by German troops in March 1944. At the time they were supposed to be assigned to armaments factories, after "selection" at Auschwitz.

From 1938 to 1941, Hungary recovered part of the territories it had lost in 1920 through the Trianon Treaty. It added on the southern part of what is now Slovakia, sub-Carpathian Ruthenia, northern Transylvania, and Vojvodina. In these territories there was a large population of Jews who had been Czech, Romanian, or Yugoslav nationals since 1920 and were henceforth considered Hungarian Jews.

The characteristic of the Jews belonging to the Hungarian realm of the nineteenth century was their desire to be assimilated both linguistically and culturally. They spoke Hungarian, except in the northern zones where the rural population was Ukrainian; the Jews in these areas were very religious and spoke Yiddish. This was the case of Elie Wiesel's family, who came from Sighet, a small town on the northern edge of Transylvania. In the rest of Transylvania, which was Romanian from 1920 to 1940, the Jews belonged to the Hungarian-speaking minority.

It appears that the Jews who arrived at Dora in May–June 1944 were originally from Transylvania. Deportation began in that region because it was the most threatened by the advance of Soviet troops. Others came from sub-Carpathian Ruthenia, such as Theodor Braun, who was arrested in Uzhorod and spoke Czech. During his quarantine in Buchenwald he managed to get himself recognized as a Czech Jew by the camp bureaucracy. At Dora he was a sort of Hungarian-Czech Jew.[15]

Initially the first Hungarian Jews to arrive at Dora were put to work equipping the camp: carrying barracks components and finishing the roll-call yard. They were brutalized by the SS and the German Greens. They also had their own *Kapos,* as Mialet and many others have noted. Special harassment was invented for them. François Heumann gave the following account:[16] "Inside the camp, the Jewish barracks was specially surrounded by barbed wire; we walked beside them when we came back from work at night. One courtyard was surrounded by barbed wire; in the middle of the courtyard was a post; the courtyard sloped downward. After a day's labor, the Jews were required to go around this post. The farther they were from the post, the faster they had to walk. One had only to see them to realize that some of them would not come through the ordeal alive." Spitz also recalled:[17] "They were used to clear the camp to allow the construction of new barracks. Most of the time, they had no tools and we saw them dig with their hands around trees to extricate the roots." After a short stay at Dora these Jews were assigned to Harzungen and Ellrich. That is where the children were eliminated under the conditions we shall see in chapter 12.

Other Hungarian Jews arrived next at Dora from Volkswagen factories in Fallersleben, where they were working to produce V1s. They continued this activity in the Dora Tunnel. Lucien Fayman found survivors from this group in Israel who still spoke Hungarian.[18] The other "Hungarian" Jews who remained at Dora, such as Theodor Braun, were assigned to unload trains. Braun, who was still an adolescent and German-speaking, was then employed in the shoe warehouse.

The Hungarian Jews were apparently the only Jews who were sent to Dora to work. Other Jews of various nationalities arrived later in January–February 1945 due to the evacuation of Auschwitz, along with non-Jews, as we shall see in chapter 14.

A small number of French Jews, arrested as Resistance fighters, were not recognized as Jews. Some had false identity papers, which was no doubt the case of a few Jews of other nationalities.

The Gypsies

Several hundred Gypsies *(Zigeuner)* arrived at Dora in 1944 from Auschwitz via Buchenwald. Of German origin, there were many in Block 130. Spitz was *Schreiber* there, and he liked them.[19]

"Like everyone, I had certain prejudices about the 'Roms' and their reputation as thieves made me somewhat wary of them, but I soon changed my mind. They were a very friendly group. At night, no matter how long the roll call went on, they never went to bed without giving themselves the pleasure of a quick concert. Before going into the Block, they would sit in a circle and sing strange chants in their guttural tongue, using their overturned mess tins as tambourines.

"One day, they all left in a transport to Ellrich." Others were taken to Harzungen, where they made up 12 percent of the prisoner population in December 1944. In both Harzungen and Ellrich they took advantage of their knowledge of German to become frequently associated with the Greens, and they were not always judged favorably by prisoners of other nationalities.

[[9]]

THE TUNNEL FACTORY AND
ITS WORKERS

The assembly of V2s began in the Dora Tunnel factory in December 1943, since the first three rockets are known to have been rolled out in a symbolic gesture on the night of December 31. There is no information concerning the quality of the three rockets, which must have been mediocre. Indeed, the factory itself was not completely fitted out until a few weeks later.

A further complication arose in April 1944. The Mittelwerk company had to abandon the northern part of the tunnel as far as Hall 20 to Nordwerk Niedersachswerfen, a subsidiary of the firm Junkers. The decision was made by Kammler, who was in charge of putting German aircraft construction underground at the time. Thus Mittelwerk had to move part of its activity back to the area it retained. In July 1944, V1 assembly was transferred to the tunnel, but this time it had no effect on Mittelwerk, as it was carried out in the halls corresponding to the former dormitories and the southern end of tunnel A, which had already been dug out.

Mittelwerk was isolated from Nordwerk, which used foreign civilians and to which prisoners did not have access. Conversely, the latter were the only ones to assemble the V1s and V2s, and there was no need to separate *Werk I* (V2 construction) from *Werk II* (V1 construction). Yet, since all movement inside the tunnel was, in any case, strictly controlled, those who worked on V2s did not see the V1s, and vice versa.

All the tunnel workers were housed at the Dora camp as of May 1944. Every day at 11 A.M., the day shift (*Tageschicht*) took over from the night shift (*Nachtschicht*) which, in turn, started its shift at 11 P.M. The distance separating the camp from the tunnel was relatively short and the prisoners went on foot. Each Kommando was accompanied by its *Kapo*. The prisoners were counted at the beginning and end of their shift at the camp entrance.

Every four weeks the teams were switched, and each one did eighteen consecutive hours rather than the usual twelve. In May–June 1944, Sunday was indeed a day of rest, but that did not last long. Working hours were identical for German civilians, and each Kommando had the same *Meister* every day (except when he was ill or on leave). Starting in 1944 all the prisoners working in the Dora Tunnel were housed outside the camp. For this purpose a real camp had to be built.

The Construction of the Camp and Coming Out of the Tunnel

For the first six months of Dora's existence, between the arrival of the first prisoners from Buchenwald in late August 1943 and early March 1944, construction work on the camp itself was carried out only very partially and intermittently. The original camp, made up of marabou tents (some documents say they were "Finnish," but in any case they were round), grouped together near the southern exit of tunnel B at Kohnstein, was replaced by various isolated barracks located in the valley farther to the west that had been chosen as the final site, on land bought by the WIFO. Here, administrative departments and general departments such as the kitchen were housed, whereas several blocks were set aside to house the *Prominente,* Italian prisoners of war, and the sick from the *Revier* and the *Schonung.* Then a few blocks were assigned to prisoners in the Kommandos working outside the tunnel. From March to June 1944, however, a genuine camp was built in an orderly fashion, and it soon took on its more or less definitive form. The thousands of prisoners that filled the tunnel dormitories were moved to the camp in April and May. Many of them were to live there until the evacuation of April 1945.

CONSTRUCTION OF THE CAMP. The methodical construction of the camp started with the arrival in March 1944 of French prisoners who had come to Buchenwald in January by the third train from Compiègne. Unlike their predecessors, most of them did not go directly to the tunnel. This was also true, of course, for prisoners of other nationalities, such as Czechs. What it meant was that, from this point on, the tunnel factory ceased to be the priority for employing newcomers. It is therefore not surprising that the participants at the meeting with Rickhey on May 6, 1944, decided to ask Kammler for an additional eighteen hundred prisoners to meet the needs of Mittelwerk.

The construction of the Dora camp was not makeshift. It was built like any ordinary housing development. First the wooded areas to be used were cleared. Then the roads were marked out and the "roll-call" yard was delimited. Water and wastewater pipes were laid. A sedimentation tank was even installed south of the SS camp. During the same period there were serious water and sewage problems at Buchenwald. Finally, after leveling the sites, barracks were built using components and accessories delivered at the marshaling yard south of the tunnel. Since it was a concentration camp, all of the workforce and supervisors were prisoners. There were also Kommandos for the sizable amount of "excavation work," and a Kommando for assembling barracks known as the *Barackenbau.* At the same time it worked on housing for German civilians in

Krimderode, north of Nordhausen. Chérif Ben Hassen was a member of that Kommando.[1]

There are three firsthand accounts by prisoners in the aforementioned train who were put to work on "excavation": Alfred Untereiner (43652),[2] Paul Rassinier (44364),[3] and Marcel Petit (44448),[4] each of whom achieved a certain degree of notoriety, though in different ways. Alfred Untereiner, born in 1906, was a priest from Lorraine who taught in Épernay. He was known primarily as "Brother Birin, of the Christian Schools" (and will be referred to in those terms hereafter). Paul Rassinier, also born in 1906, was a schoolteacher from Belfort who had first been a communist and then a socialist activist. Marcel Petit, born in 1888, was much older than the other two. He was the head of the veterinary school of Toulouse.

Their digging activities were interrupted, as will be seen later on, under a variety of circumstances. Birin joined the Arbeitsstatistik, thanks to his knowledge of German. Petit finally found an important job in "Labor" at the *Revier.* Rassinier was admitted to the *Revier* as a patient and remained there. Their comrades pulled through more or less successfully. The young Fernand, a former pupil and companion of Rassinier, subsequently died in Ellrich.

There are still other eyewitness accounts from former members of the *Barackenbau:* Yves Béon, Louis Coutaud, Alain de Lapoyade, François Latappy, Marcel Leprêtre, and Pierre Meunier. With the exception of Meunier (a "21,000"), they were all sent by the same train as Birin, Rassinier, and Petit. It seems that the Czechs played an important role in this Kommando. Béon recounts that one of them, a highly qualified carpenter, built a portico with great care that turned out to be a gallows for the roll-call yard.[5]

The camp had to be built, of course, but it also had to be closed in by an electric fence. First, electric poles had to be put up and covered with insulators, and the Zaunbau Kommando (*Zaun* is the German word for "fence") was in charge of that task. It comprised a number of Frenchmen, again from the same train, such as Pierre Breton, Jacques Chamboissier, Maurice Clergue, Michel Delaval, Gustave Estadès, Louis Garnier, and Edmond Mallet.[6] These *Zaunbau* and *Barackenbau* veterans would subsequently be found in the tunnel factory Kommandos, who were generally far luckier than their comrades assigned to excavation work.

Within a few months the camp had become a small city with more than fifty blocks for housing, nine blocks for the *Revier,* and some twenty blocks and various buildings for administration and joint facilities, including a cinema, a library, a canteen, a whorehouse, and a fire station. It will be seen, further on, how these joint facilities might be viewed. The blocks and the other buildings (including the transformers) were numbered, but the numbering, which went up to 150, was deceptive, since there was nothing in the camp corresponding to the figures between 43 and 100. Rassinier, who wrote "We're now assembling

Block 144," was fooled by it, but that is only one of the errors with which his text is riddled.[7]

THE ROLE OF ALBERT SPEER AND ALBERT KUNTZ. There has been a great deal of discussion about the positive role played by Albert Speer and Albert Kuntz in the construction of the camp, each in his own field and without any direct connection between them. These roles have been, however, vigorously contested by some authors. The judgments that were made were no doubt considerably influenced by what happened to the two men afterward. Speer, sentenced at Nuremberg and then released after twenty years in prison, was to enjoy widespread recognition at the time due to his writings. Kuntz received only posthumous glory: he was eliminated at Dora before the Liberation and treated as a hero by East Germany. It is perfectly possible, nevertheless, to determine what was undoubtedly each one's decisive role, without taking later events into account.

At the time, building barracks from prefabricated components was one of the major problems facing German industry, over which Speer had full control. It was necessary to house workers of varying status as well as factories and work sites involved in war production that were being increasingly damaged by Allied bombing. Very strict priorities were laid down, and Speer delivered the authorizations.

He visited Mittelwerk on December 10, 1943, to find out what the firm needed and make the required decisions. According to his later statements, that was when he signed the papers authorizing barracks construction.[8] There is every reason to believe that this included the construction of both the concentration and SS camps, along with the pipes and various facilities, as well as housing for German civilians on other sites. All of this was in any case included in the summary drafted on December 31, 1943, by Neu, who was head of the WIFO.

Once missile production was declared an absolute priority, it was difficult to refuse the authorizations for workforce housing. It is puzzling that, subsequently, Speer linked his decisions to his observation of the prisoners' situation. It does seem logical, however, that these decisions were made at the time of his visit on December 10. Nevertheless, why the directors of the Sonderausschuss A4 and Mittelwerk, whom Speer had appointed, waited three months before requesting the necessary authorization remains an open question. The consequences of the delay were tragic.

No one knows who prepared the decisions on-site. Clearly, the camp was built according to a strict plan. Did the Mittelwerk company or the WIFO call upon an outside firm to draw up the plans? It is difficult to determine, except with regard to AEG, the amount of outside intervention in the construction of Dora. It is now known, however, that an important role was played by the Schlempp construction group[9] (linked to Speer) at Peenemünde, and Philipp

Holzmann AG at the bunker in Wizernes, for the Todt Organization, not only in building but also in designing the works.

Three months elapsed between the date the authorizations were granted on December 10, 1943, and the beginning of construction in March 1944. There is no way of determining whether the delay was due to insufficient prisoner man-power, which was monopolized by the requirements of Mittelwerk, or to delays in delivering barracks components. It was not until March that Albert Kuntz was actually in a position to begin directing the works, as *Bautechniker* or *Bauleiter* (according to the sources, both designations were used).

Kuntz was a longtime prisoner and had been interned since 1933. At the time of his arrest he was a communist deputy in the Prussian Landtag. Born in 1896, he was a war veteran who had been wounded in 1918. He had been at Buchen-wald since the beginning of the camp and was transferred to an outside Kom-mando in Kassel in 1943. From there he was brought to Dora in September and placed in charge of camp construction. Two other "Reds" or communists were sent from Buchenwald to be *Lagerältester,* but they were not of the same caliber as Kuntz, who was immediately considered by the prisoners to hold a central po-sition.

Such a situation would have been impossible without the approval not only of Förschner, the commander of Dora, but also of Pister, the commander of Buchenwald, both of whom knew about Kuntz's previous activities. No doubt they thought it would be good to be able to count on a man known for his orga-nizational abilities when an especially important camp was being set up. Later there was a great deal of speculation about the relationship between Förschner and Kuntz, but it was no doubt in vain. Each one found advantages in their de facto partnership.

It is not exactly known what Kuntz did during the first months. He undoubt-edly insisted that Förschner speed up camp construction, and he was probably consulted by those who drew up the plans and decided on the materials to be or-dered. Kuntz was not an architect or an engineer, however, and his *Baubüro* was necessarily rudimentary. He was surrounded by a certain Fritz Lehmann in the *Baubüro,* August Kroneberg, the *Kapo* of *Zimmerei* (carpentry), and Ludwig Leineweber. Kroneberg was said to be a social democrat, and the others were communists. Apparently (as there are no explicit documents), this was the team in charge of camp construction starting in March 1944.

Whatever may have been the exact role played by the various participants in the construction process, by June 1944 a real Dora camp and a real factory in the tunnel had been completed, each one perfectly distinct yet related to each other, with the camp operating as a sort of dormitory town for the workers at the factory.

COMING OUT OF THE TUNNEL. For prisoners confined inside the tunnel, coming outside was a major event. Paul Bolteau describes the experience very simply: "The wonderful memory of seeing the sun again in April 1944 after spending six months underground. The tears of joy at seeing the sun that were shed by an old Russian in my Kommando, who nevertheless died a few days later."[10]

Charles Spitz has also given an account: "On 1 May, work stopped at 1 p.m. and we were free after a relatively short roll-call. Free to walk about the camp. We were so surprised that we didn't know what to do. Obviously, we could have slept, but the idea of wasting our only chance to see friendly faces was unthinkable. So, like Sunday strollers in provincial sub-prefectures, we walked all around the camp. We set off from the roll-call yard by the widest road which went in front of Blocks 27 and 22 and on to Block 13, which we called De Gaulle Avenue. We went all the way to the end, to Block 132 and then came back to the roll-call yard, passing behind the kitchens. In the distance, we could see the church steeples of Nordhausen, the only town in the area of which we could get a glimpse."[11]

The site itself had been advantageously developed: the barracks were not in rows, as they are in most camps. Sadron goes even further in his observations: "In front of the Blocks, grassy yards and little gardens displayed their greenery. In front of the Italian barracks, one could even admire a statue and a white stone fountain of surprisingly sober elegance."[12]

Another surprise awaited those who had just left behind the tunnel dormitories, with their filth and their latrines, "our revolting underground lairs" as Sadron[13] called them. The blocks were brand-new and spotlessly clean, with bedsteads and straw mattresses intact. Above all there was water, with sinks for washing and real toilets with earthenware seats. It should be remembered that, in the everyday lives of many people in 1944, none of this was commonplace.

Rassinier who, despite his profession, is very poor at "writing," has provided the following recollection in his memoirs of the camp at that time: "A central swimming pool with a diving board, a sports field, cool shade within reach, a veritable holiday camp, and anyone passing by who would be allowed to visit while the prisoners were absent would have gone away convinced that people led a pleasant life and particularly enviable life, filled with sylvan poetry, in any case, a life that had nothing in common with the unforeseeable events of the war which were the lot of free men."[14]

This description is completely ridiculous, and the so-called swimming pool was a reservoir in case of fire. Yet behind this emotionalism lies the trace of a genuine impression, as a number of former Dora prisoners were to realize when a survey on the subject was carried out a few years ago.

One of them, Gustave Estadès, added the following testimony: "In the summer of 1944, an extraordinary convoy came to Dora, made up of numerous convertible cars flying the flag of each country. A few days earlier, some of the Blocks had been repainted and trees replanted. [. . .] Sheets and blankets had been placed in the first Block on the left. The camp was completely emptied of its prisoners, except for us, who were forgotten on the hill, from which we watched the farce. The visit lasted twenty minutes. The Red Cross Commission was forced to say it was a very good camp."[15]

The SS selected a few camps for such "masquerades." This was the case, for example, of the Jewish camp of Theresienstadt in northern Bohemia. Speer himself was treated to a visit of this type at Mauthausen on March 30, 1943, where he was photographed in the company of clean, well-fed prisoners.[16] At Dora the prisoners were at least kept out of sight and were no doubt supposed to be working in the factory.

There is also an outside account of Dora in June 1944 by Serge Miller, who belonged to the Ellrich Kommando that laid electric cable in the upper part of Kohnstein: "Our cable went through the woods on the mountain, and from there we had a panorama of the camp. It was, indeed, set in a magnificent spot and it made all of us think irresistibly of a sanitarium or a rest home."[17] It was springtime, the weather was fine, and the camp was new. Miller stayed at Ellrich from beginning to end, and he saw Dora only this once, from afar.

Factory Operations

RECRUITING SPECIALISTS. There were two categories of prisoners working in the tunnel: the most unfortunate ones had to carry often cumbersome V2 components to the assembly sites from outside. These prisoners belonged to the *Transportkolonnen,* which will be discussed later. The situation was the same for V1s.

All the others were considered "specialists," a convenient umbrella term covering a complex reality. If it had been a well-organized assembly line, such as the lines of civilian workers building automobiles, airplanes, or tanks at the time, they might be referred to as skilled workers. This was not, however, quite accurate. It was not until July 1944, on the eve of the launchings, that the missiles ceased undergoing modifications and could finally be mass-produced. The workstations, moreover, were highly varied. Thus, by convention, the term "specialist" was used to refer to all those who worked in a specific place on each shift *(Schicht),* whether as a warehouseman, painter, or gyroscope inspector.

Most of the specialists were recruited between December 1943 and March 1944, as noted in chapter 5. This was the period during which the arrival of new prisoners from Buchenwald could barely offset the number of prisoner deaths and departures in "transports." There are no German documents concerning the conditions under which recruitment was conducted. There was a prisoner-employment office called the Häftlingsarbeitseinsatz, which is known to have been run by a certain Dr. Simon. All our information comes from the firsthand accounts of a number of prisoners.

Dr. Simon is mentioned in the account given by René Croze, who joined the Kontrolle Scherer in early January 1944 and followed his *Meister* to carry out inspections on missiles (coming from Peenemünde). Dr. Simon sometimes accompanied them. Later, Croze no longer saw him. He described him as follows: "He was always dressed in a dark suit, with a white shirt, a tie and cufflinks. He knew our language perfectly but seldom spoke to me, except to say, for example: 'It is 12:15; you are going to have lunch. Would it be possible for you to come back at one o'clock?'

"I tried to tell him about our living conditions, but he turned a deaf ear. Dr. Simon pretended not to know what was happening at Dora."[18] He took part in the May 6, 1944, meeting with Rickhey, like von Braun and Steinhoff, in his HAP 11 capacity. Later on, von Braun reported in a letter to Sawatzski, dated August 15, 1944, that he "went to see capable prisoners at Buchenwald [...] in the company of Dr. Simon." One has the impression that, at least at a certain level, recruitment of prisoners for the factory was carried out by Peenemünde engineers who had been transferred to Mittelwerk and were working with Dr. Simon.[19]

Recruitment procedures varied. When prisoners were already working with a *Meister,* they followed him to the new organization. This was the case for some of those transferred from Peenemünde or Wiener Neustadt as well as those who belonged to small Kommandos already set up on the site.

Prisoners were usually brought before a small commission in charge of assessing their skills. Various accounts exist on this topic, such as the one about the ohmmeter by Paul Butet:[20] "In the tunnel gallery, there was a small wooden house like a shop manager's office. Inside, there were four civilians in charge of recruiting and assigning 'qualified' manpower. They examined the prisoners, asked questions about what they had done in France, their apprenticeships, jobs, etc.

"When it was my turn to go before them, no one asked me any questions. I was shown a comparator and told: 'This is a voltmeter.' I replied, 'Nein, it is a comparator which is used in precision mechanics to measure the size of parts.' I was then shown an ohmmeter. I knew what it was; I explained that it was a device used to measure the resistance to the flow of electric current from one point to another. Since I didn't have enough knowledge or practice in German to explain, I asked for a pencil and paper and wrote: R=U/I, which is the basic formula of Ohm's law."

Butet thus managed to pass himself off as an engineer: "I was given a paper bearing my number (38007) and the words: Ko Scherer, hall 28." Further details concerning the various Kommandos in the tunnel factory—particularly regarding the Ko Scherer—will be discussed later. Another account comes from André Gérard.[21] He was arrested by the Gestapo while a law student at the University of Strasbourg, which had moved to Clermont-Ferrand. He finally arrived at

Dora at the same time as the physics professor, Charles Sadron. They went before a small commission together. Sadron pretended he did not understand German and Gérard, who was from Colmar, served as his translator. As they had previously agreed, Gérard pretended to be one of Sadron's laboratory assistants. Both of them were assigned to Ko Scherer, Hall 28.

The accounts concern prisoners who were not in the same situation. For some time, Butet had been assigned to "stones" in the tunnel, and his account is mentioned in chapters 5 and 6. Sadron and Gérard were deported by the second train from Compiègne in January 1944 and were part of the last major reinforcement of personnel that the tunnel factory was to be given.

It was customary practice to test prisoners' skills upon their arrival or within a few weeks thereafter. There were, however, cases of quarantined individuals at Dachau and Buchenwald who were directly recruited under rather surprising conditions. Milan Filipcic,[22] a Slovenian, recalls that in November 1943, Albin Sawatzski went to Dachau to select a hundred intellectual prisoners from among those being held in quarantine. They were immediately separated from the others and formed a "Dora Kommando," which arrived in its entirety at Dora in late December after passing through Buchenwald. They were almost all assigned to the Kontrolle Scherer Kommando. The prisoners involved included a number of Slovenes as well as Czechs and Italians.

The author's account is the same:[23] "I arrived at Buchenwald in the first convoy of January 1944, and, like others, was summoned to meet someone who, I learned, was from the Dora factory. He was young and rather kindly and he spoke French. He asked me what my profession was. I told him I was a professor of history and geography, and that seemed to satisfy him. He was disappointed by my ignorance of German. He told me that he had classified me as an 'electrician,' insisting on the word. A few days later, I arrived at Dora, and the electricians were called to assemble. I presented myself, along with others. That is how I became a member of the Kontrolle Scherer Kommando where, like Filipcic, who was a young schoolteacher, I was to remain. In the list of the transport from Buchenwald to Dora on 11 February, my profession was marked 'Elektromonteur-lehrer,' teacher-electricity installer." A few months later von Braun and Dr. Simon went in person to make their selection among the prisoners in Buchenwald.

There were also those who improvised a specialty, like young Christian Desseaux,[24] who declared he was a fitter, tried out as a lathe operator, and ended up working on an automatic lathe thanks to the indulgence of an old *Meister.*

After March 1944, French prisoners were no longer systematically assigned as specialists to the tunnel factory of Dora. Only a few hardly significant groups were recorded: former workers from the *Barackenbau* and the *Zaunbau*, once camp construction was completed; a fraction of the "77,000"s who were thereby able to escape from Ellrich; a few prisoners from Buchenwald, after the Gustloff factory was destroyed. Some of the newcomers were assigned to *Werk I* (V2s) and the rest to *Werk II* (V1s). There is no clear-cut information about the assignments of prisoners of other nationalities, but everything leads us to believe that their situation was identical to that of the French.

Not only were there few new specialists, but those who joined a Kommando usually stayed in it until the evacuation in April 1945. They returned to it after stays at the *Revier.* The link was not broken unless an incident occurred, as in the case of Paul Butet. This permanent situation had one positive consequence: in the context of the time, the tunnel factory represented a relatively protected segment for the specialists. Nevertheless, they had previously been subjected to the tunnel dormitories for a more or less long period of time.

Due to a combination of circumstances, these men are now considered to have been relatively privileged. Assignments to the factory were not made by camp leaders, whether SS or prisoners, as they were not qualified, nor were they influenced by nonexistent political or national "organizations." They were decided by the factory managers on the basis of their own criteria, which no doubt were not very complicated.

ASSEMBLY ORGANIZATION IN THE FACTORY AND THE MAIN KOMMANDOS. No information about factory operations circulated among prisoners in the tunnel factory, nor, in all likelihood, among mere *Meister.* It must be admitted that the prisoners' primary concern was not to understand how the factory worked. For the main aspects, however, various survivors' accounts allow us to reconstruct an overall picture, with some inevitable lacunae.

Factory work involved, first and foremost, assembling quite varied prefabricated components from all over Germany. The missiles were assembled on specially designed rail trucks, pushed along tracks from north to south in tunnel B, from the boundary of Nordwerk to the exit. This route was the *Taktstrasse*, where the rate of assembly set the pace for all the work in the factory. Halls perpendicular to tunnel B, numbering from 23 to 42, were used to machine additional parts or for partial assembly. They also housed storerooms and offices.

The missiles were made up of three parts, which were assembled in succession. The center section *(Mittelteil)* was a rather cylindrical shell *(Schale)*, a tail *(Heck)* was fitted to the back, and a nose cone *(Spitze)* was placed on the front. The propulsion apparatus, by far the most cumbersome part, along with the engine and fuel tanks, was attached to the central part, next to the fuel tanks. The engine went into the tail, behind which there was an outlet for the nozzle. All the directional instruments were placed in the nose cone; explosives, which were located in the tip of the cone, were added in field installations. Just before launch, the fuel tanks were filled.

The main Kommandos grouped together those working on the central portion. Those in the Firnrohr Kommando took care of the shell, which arrived in the form of two half-shells *(Halbschale)* from the Saulgau workshop mentioned in chapter 2. According to Robert Roulard's account,[25] the Firnrohr Kommando included a sizable percentage of Russians and Ukrainians. Two Frenchmen, François Schwertz[26] and François Heumann,[27] worked at a joiner's bench. They were kept busy to the very end drilling spars that were part of a device covering the shell openings at the level of the fuel tanks. Their fellow prisoner Claude de Chanteloup was put to work cutting the sheet metal.

The Haukohl Kommando was the largest in the factory, with a majority of Russians and Poles, as Albert Amate[28] has indicated, but there were also a number of Frenchmen and a young Armenian (from France) named Agop (Jacques) Dayan. The engine and tanks had to be installed in the missile and were joined by a tubular frame. This required a good deal of welding: Pierre Lucas[29] and François Garault[30] continued the welding work they had begun at Wiener Neustadt, with the same *Meister.* This Kommando included a large amount of handling, under the supervision of *Kapos* and *Vorarbeiter.* The *Superkapo* was Georg Finkenzeller, who had already dealt ruthlessly with prisoners at Wiener Neustadt. Unfortunately, as will be seen further on, he once again made himself infamous in the tunnel.

In the early months the Kommandos working for Mittelwerk were "Sawatzski" Kommandos, who were differentiated by their numbers. André Gérard was thus assigned to Sawatzski 185, which became the Scherer Kommando. The names of their heads, Firnrohr and Haukohl as well as Bünemann and Scherer, for example, replaced that of Sawatzski. Other Kommandos were known from then on by their activity, such as the one in charge of producing the missile tail—the Heckbau Kommando—and its joining to the central portion— the Heckmontage Kommando.

Bernard Ramillon[31] has provided an exceptionally detailed description of the finishing work carried out by the Heckbau: "The tails were placed vertically on moving conveyers, the cylindrical body downwards. A landing stage was erected on the side to allow us to work high up. Various tasks were performed in hall 35, such as reinforcing body discs by soldering or explosive rivets, welding a few plates with a blow torch, assembling the 'ring,' which was a very important, ring-shaped part made of an alloy set at the tail exit, assembling the jetvane servomotors, etc." The majority of prisoners working in the Kommando were French, including Jean Cormont,[32] André Cardon,[33] Élie Korenfeld[34] (who was then called Roland Thibault), Robert Golfier, and André Guichard, a fine arts student who had become the "painter of the torpedo tail."[35]

Guy Raoul-Duval has described the task of the Heckmontage Kommando as follows: "The tail, carried by a sort of hoist, was brought out of hall 35 and placed on a small conveyer. Then we fitted it to the rear of the central portion in a victorious rush, and screwed it in place."[36] Raoul-Duval, a history student at the time, used a much less technical vocabulary than Ramillon's.

Another important Kommando was the Bünemann Kommando, which, according to Bignon,[37] was in charge of "electrical cabling of the V2 control devices which were housed in the front of the engine." For this purpose, in Hall 28, there were "long joiner benches and porticos equipped with Hauptverteiler which 'distributed' current to the devices in the missile 'head.'" This Kommando was made up of Belgians, Dutchmen, and numerous Frenchmen, such as Paul Priser, Jean Rieg, the Ecole Centrale engineering graduate Jacques Noël,[38] the young electrician Léon Navaro-Mora, and Jacques Maupoint, a former prisoner from Wiener Neustadt. Prisoners from the *Zaunbau* were assigned to it in August 1944 when they had finished putting the electric fence up first around the Dora camp and then around Harzungen: Breton, Garnier, and their friends suddenly found themselves to be qualified electricians! But they were made to work on reinforcing the latches of the doors on the truncated cone at the head of the rocket.

There were other Kommandos of varying sizes whose members also worked on missile assembly. It is impossible (and out of the question here) to list them all. There exists only limited information from certain accounts, such as the one by Louis Coutaud[39] concerning the large press in Hall 32. Francis Dunouau[40] has talked about the Lorentz mechanics' Kommando, and he described Lorentz himself as "blond, not very tall, light-colored trousers and riding boots." Henry Mas[41] belonged to the Tischlerei carpentry Kommando, Guy Tartinville[42] to the "painter-galvanizers," and Jean Gouvenaux[43] to the Askania Kommando.

It is interesting to note that work in the tunnel factory was very fragmented but the pace always remained moderate. Ramillon and Raoul-Duval talk of twenty to twenty-five missiles a day, which meant a dozen per shift *(Schicht)*, at best. There were, however, frequent interruptions of the assembly line.

INSPECTORS, TECHNICIANS, SECRETARIES. Operations in the tunnel factory were dominated by the inspection function—called *Kontrolle* in German. Checks were carried out at every step in assembly, on every aspect, as well as prior to assembly, on components such as gyroscopes provided by subcontractors.

In the Mittelwerk organization chart, Abteilung Kontrolle is shown separately, with its fifteen engineers and its own acronym Ko, which was reproduced on metal plates that the prisoners in the corresponding Kommando wore on their sleeves. As already mentioned, for more than half a year, until July 1944, the missiles that left the tunnel factory were intended for test firing in Blizna or Peenemünde, and determining which defects had to be corrected made no sense unless they were rigorously checked. The final inspection was carried out on the missile while it was standing in a vertical position in a hall dug out especially for this purpose. The final verification, called *Prüfung,* was performed by officers of the Wehrmacht, artillerymen under Dornberger who were in charge of accepting delivery of the missiles. Among the prisoners who helped them for several months were Claude Fisher[44] and Michel Bedel. The verifications continued, of course, after the first firings on September 8, 1944.

Ko engineers, who were headed up by a certain Scherer, were assisted by a number of specialized *Meister* and by prisoners from the Scherer Kommando. The latter were primarily recruited among the French (or their Belgian or Dutch counterparts) or Yugoslavians, Slovenes, and others, under the aforementioned conditions.

There is precise information on this Kommando thanks to Charles Sadron's firsthand account, published under the title "A l'usine de Dora" ("At the Dora Factory") in *Témoignages strasbourgeois,* an anthology concerning the concentration camps. He talks mainly about the small group in Hall 28 in charge of checking the gyroscopes prior to assembly (the *Vertikant* and the *Horizont*) and the *Mischgeräte,* the "mixing devices." As already mentioned, in von Braun's letter to Sawatzski, Sadron took care of the *Mischgeräte.* The author, along with several fellow prisoners, was concerned with the *Vertikant* right up to the last day. Sadron knew what the *Mischgeräte* were, whereas the author had no idea how the *Vertikant* were made. This did not matter, however, as there was no need to know. The head of the section was an engineer named Wellner, an Austrian, who is described by Sadron,[45] along with his various deputies Neumann, Jansch, Wells, and finally Krüger, whose name will come up again.

All sorts of verifications took place: Germain Roche[46] was in Heckmontage, Marcel Coulardot[47] checked gauges in Hall 20, and Claude Douay[48] the electromagnets used for rear-aileron control. Aside from the Scherer Kommando, factory organization offered a few relatively quiet jobs. Marcel Baillon,[49] one of the leaders of *Résistance-Fer,* arrived at Dora after being imprisoned for a long time, and ended up as a *Feinschlosser* in a remarkably well-equipped precision tool workshop. Robert Berthelot was in a precision mechanics Kommando.

In the same hall was a Kommando of draftsmen set up on a wooden floor which made up the Techniches Büro. While the camp was being fitted out, there was the Vermessung, a surveyor Kommando. The *Kapo* of that Kommando was a Frenchman named Robert Deglane, who arrived at Dora wearing a green triangle; he had been sentenced as a common-law criminal in Germany. Gustave Leroy, an aviation officer in the first train from Compiègne in January, was an early member of the Kommando, along with Henri Calès.[50] They were later joined by well-known Resistance fighters due to the intervention of Birin, who had become a part of the Arbeitsstatistik in the spring of 1943. This was especially true of Dejussieu-Pontcarral, one of the "77,000"s, who had succeeded General Delestraint (who was deported to Dachau) at the head of the Secret Army.

On the eve of the evacuation, the group also included Gabriel Lacoste, René Cogny, and Pierre Julitte. With Leroy's support, another aviator, Jean Demuyter,[51] was able to join the team in February 1945. He was a longtime prisoner whose account has already been quoted in chapter 5. He came by way of the Haukohl Kommando. He really was a draftsman, and he proved it.

André Ribault[52] found himself in an unusual situation. He arrived at Dora in February 1944 and was immediately assigned to the central drafting office, the Zeichnungsverwaltung, where all the missile drawings were kept that had to be updated throughout the modification process, copies of which had to be made on request. On carefully sealed-off premises, four prisoners—one Latvian, one Slovak, one Pole, and Ribault—worked with a few German civilians. As Ribault drew the plans, he was thus the only Frenchman to have seen the whole missile.

A number of secretarial tasks entrusted to prisoners required knowledge of German and were at first carried out by the Greens. They often proved incompetent, however, in sensitive areas such as the factory's civilian payroll. In early 1944, two Czechs, Otakar Litomisky[53] and Vlada Hlavac, became accountants after an examination on a calculating machine. They managed to gain the upper hand, bringing in other Czechs and gradually eliminating the Germans. At the same time, Jiri Beneš[54] was in charge of secretarial tasks for the military commission that carried out acceptance procedures on the missiles and noted the particular characteristics of each one that affected their firing.

Due to their knowledge of German, Czechs and Dutchmen were more often successful than the French in getting this type of work. Jacques-Christian Bailly,[55] an eighteen-year-old high school student, recounts how he managed to obtain one of the two available secretarial positions during an interview at the Arbeitseinsatz. He was asked if he knew how to write German, and he replied by writing Goethe's famous poem, *Erlkönig,* in Gothic script. The other position went to a consultant at the Dutch embassy "who was responsible for physical inventory at a spare parts warehouse." Bailly joined Jean-Paul (Father Renard), who was performing a similar task.

From then on he belonged to the Schreiber Kommando and wore the corresponding armband. This Kommando, whose members were scattered throughout the factory, was very cosmopolite, with a majority of Germans, many prisoners from Czechoslovakia and Poland as well as from the Netherlands, Belgium, Luxembourg, and a few from France.

THE *TRANSPORTKOLONNEN.* In a factory like Mittelwerk there was room for a minority of privileged employees and a mass of specialized workers. There was also room for an indeterminate number of unskilled workers in charge of transporting various loads from exterior warehouses into the factory. They formed a miserable, ill-treated lumpen proletariat mainly made up of Russians and Ukrainians. They willingly took it out on the French, Belgians, or Italians who were unlucky enough to find themselves in these same *Transportkolonnen* Kommandos.

There are no consistent accounts from former members of these Kommandos, as they have not written their memoirs, nor are there any texts by Soviet prisoners, for reasons that will be explained in the final part of the book. The Kommandos were designated by various codes: Dunouau[56] mentions BAU 5. Alfred Lacour[57] has provided the code TU and Paul Pagnier[58] TO 1 and TO 2. Marcel Pierrel,[59] who spoke German, was in TU 185. Albert Vuillermoz[60] and Raymond Zilliox[61] did not specify their codes.

The best account on the subject comes from Charles Sadron, who was in contact with the *Transportkolonnen* only occasionally. During the time when the prisoners came out of the tunnel in May–June 1944, those working in the factory were allowed to rest on Sundays. One Sunday, however, they were conscripted for transport into the tunnel in place of the usual Kommandos. The Ko Scherer, like the others, was forced to do this chore, which explains the following text by Charles Sadron:[62] "At seven o'clock, we were on the work site, in the network of railway tracks in front of the entrance to Tunnel A. Our job was simple: we had to transport large tanks into the factory which, when filled with liquid or alcohol, formed the body of the torpedoes. The tanks were made of sheet duralumin, and, when empty, weighed nearly three hundred pounds apiece. They were cylinders measuring nearly ten feet long and about five feet wide. It took six of us to carry one, which meant fifty pounds per person. The weight was not excessive, but we didn't know how to get hold of it. Three of us stood on either side, spread out along the length of the cylinder. Each man on the left side reached out with his right hand and took hold of the left hand of the man facing him on the other side. The load lay on these three pairs of extended arms. And off we went. We had to cover more than fifty feet. In the beginning, it worked, but very soon, it became unbearable. The grip of the hands clutching each other loosened. The sweat made our hands slippery. If someone lost his grip, the tank would fall, and that would mean brute punishment for us. Our shoulders were aching and the hearts of all of us undernourished men were beating fast. There was no question of slowing down. We marched in front of the SS who yelled and drubbed us.

"There were also civilians, but it was not the same as in the workshops, for they abused and hit us. One of the men in front tripped and dropped to his knees. The others continued holding up the enormous load, which gradually slipped and fell, making a huge racket. An SS was there in a second, laying into the man with kicks and blows from his club as he stood up slowly and shakily, with the look of torture victim on his face.

"We quickly speeded up our pace. Finally, we reached the goal and handed our load to the warehousemen. It was too hard; we slipped away in the halls. The SS ran after us, striking us with the butts of their guns or their clubs and brought us back to the work site. I don't know how many trips I made. We were dazed from weariness and blows."

Andrès Pontoizeau[63] has also given a very vivid account of the transport of half-shells, and, above all, tanks. There is no information available on the mortality rate of prisoners in the *Transportkolonnen,* but it must have been high. The activity of these Kommandos continued right up to the end, under the same detestable conditions. Fifty years later Michel Depierre,[64] who arrived late in the tunnel and was assigned to transport V1 components, is still cursing the Polish *Kapos* and *Vorarbeiter* he had to deal with at the time.

Relations Inside the Tunnel

ENGINEERS AND *MEISTER*. The prisoners who were assigned to secretarial work or to relatively delicate operations such as checking gyroscopes were put in barracks inside the tunnel along with their *Meister* and often with engineers. Their relations were usually acceptable and sometimes became cordial. That was the case for Ribault, Baillon, Jean-Paul Renard, and Bailly. It was also the case for the Czech Benès with Major Dutzmann of the Wehrmacht.

Krüger, whom Sadron[65] talks about, was less refined. "He was a brutal Pomeranian and a long-standing member of the party whose insignia he wore. He had been an SA member. The SS were his friends, and he had been wounded in June 1940 on the French front. He didn't hate us. He behaved without any wickedness towards us, like a good master towards his slaves. He saved a Belgian comrade from probable hanging who was convicted of having put together a portable stove from the pieces of an old radiator. He certainly spared me more than ten blows on the buttocks with a club, when I was caught warming my coffee with my soldering iron. On the other hand, he did accept small gifts. He liked French and Belgian tobacco, which induced him to close his eyes to our small pranks. He also helped himself generously to radio equipment in the repair cupboard; he would wink at us and we kept silent."

Raoul-Duval[66] describes the relationship with German workers in the Heckmontage: "Some of them were swine, some were good men, but most often they were stupid bastards, not really malicious but fierce, worn out by an interminable war, often devastated, always cut off from their families and reduced to living a communal life, terrorized by the police and the engineers, profoundly weary, and convinced of the inevitability of the Reich's defeat, yet not resigned to believing the disaster was imminent, and thus continuing, out of habit, the pace they had acquired." Raoul-Duval shows more esteem for the *Obermeister,* a certain Holz, a distinguished and kindly man, and for the noncommissioned officers and soldiers of the Wehrmacht, either wounded or ill, who carried out various inspections in the factory.

Some witnesses were eager to pay a tribute to certain *Meister*: in the case of Croze[67] it was to Hahn and Heusner; in the case of Amate[68] it was to Aschenbach; in the case of Bignon[69] it was to Seifert and Sebroot; in the case of Jazbinsek[70] it was to Hamm and Jancke. They had either intervened just in time to prevent punishment or they discreetly provided food. This was only possible within small groups. In the large Kommandos and especially the *Transport-kolonnen* the civilians hit out just like the others.

The prisoners did not know the names of the real camp directors, whom they saw only occasionally. The only name they really knew was Sawatzski, the eponym of a number of Kommandos, at least at the beginning.

From time to time a large group of personalities would come through the tunnel. Marcel Berthet and Joannès Méfret,[71] who belonged to the AEG Kommando, were required to supply maximum lighting one day to allow photographs of the V2s by the army cinema department. The general whom they noticed on that occasion had to be Dornberger, and not von Braun, who was a civilian. Another time, as already pointed out in chapter 7, both of them visited the factory in the company of the participants at the May 6, 1944, meetings.

Two French prisoners, Guy Morand[72] and Georges Jouanin,[73] were convinced they had dealt personally with von Braun under unpleasant circumstances. Morand had received twenty-five blows for damage (made by someone from the other shift to a chronometer used for a verification). Jouanin was violently slapped for having pressed his wooden-soled shoe a against servomotor while installing cabling in the tail of a missile.

SS AND KAPOS. Behavior within the hierarchy of prisoners also varied, depending on the Kommando. The *Kapo* of one of the two Ko Scherer shifts, Peter Sommer, never struck a single prisoner in fifteen months. They saw him only on the trips back and forth between the camp and the factory. The same was true of the *Kapo* of the other shift. They seem to have been designated personally to play that role. The *Schreiber* armband worn by Finelli and Sadron's *Vorarbeiter* were, under the circumstances, purely tokens. Nor was the Heckmontage Kapo particularly present, but Raoul-Duval[74] thinks that in this case it was the *Obermeister* who did not want him around.

The situation was altogether different in the Haukohl Kommando, whose *Oberkapo* was Georg Finkenzeller, a Green and, incidentally, a veteran of the French Foreign Legion. He was first interned in Mauthausen before being sent to the Wiener Neustadt Kommando, which he ruled by terror. When he was transferred to Buchenwald at the end of November 1943 he did not come to Dora with the other prisoners. At the time the prisoners thought that those in charge of Buchenwald would have him eliminated due to his behavior, but he turned up again a few months later at Dora, having been promoted after who knows what sort of scheming.

He was the "Big George" who went through the tunnel looking for prisoners to thrash. Amate[75] has given us this description of him: "He strolled through the halls where the prisoners were working under his authority, his tall silhouette stooped, his eyes on the look-out, his mouth hanging open, a truncheon hidden behind his back; ready to spring into action at the slightest escapade. The Russians were his *bête noire*; he would not let them get away with anything." He was the "Kapo," the central character in Dominique Gaussen's account.[76] A remarkable drawing by Léon Delarbre[77] dating from December 1944 shows him with his club behind his back in search of another victim. The caption reads: "One of the biggest brutes in the service of the SS."

And yet it was not even Finkenzeller but rather SS-Hauptscharführer Erwin Busta who was the principal terror in the tunnel. Beneš[78] describes him as being almost six-foot-six: "His head was so elongated at the top and the bottom that it looked like a horse's head [Pferdekopf]—which was his nickname in every language. He was the most vile of all the SS. He beat whomever he could. Tirelessly. No one knew when he slept. He was in the Tunnel first thing in the morning, at noon and in the evening, and never absent during the night. He prowled from one tunnel gallery to another, poking his nose everywhere, beating people on the spot, as well as writing reports to bring further punishment upon them."

One scene reported by Bailly[79] shows the terror he inspired in a secretarial office. "Two Poles were discussing their homeland, and the German engineers were bored. Suddenly the door opened. A Polish professor, who held the neighboring Schreiber position, rushed in with a terrified look on his face: 'Pferdekopf, Pferdekopf,' he cried.

"Usually, a prisoner preceded the SS man Busta, one of the most dreaded torturers of Dora, whom we nicknamed 'Horse Head,' due to the peculiar shape of his face. He made regular inspection rounds inside the factory and a prisoner was assigned strictly to him to warn the workshops when he was coming. Busta had no doubt fooled his guide. He went through the halls and offices, sowing panic along the way. The civilians quickly returned to their secret dossiers. Jean-Paul hid on his person the poem he had been writing.

"Busta entered. We feigned indifference, absorbed in our work. The SS came closer and Jean-Paul sunk further into his seat. Busta knew that he wrote poetry, having once discovered some harmless verses. Since then, he scornfully called him 'der Dichter.' The SS came prowling up behind us. He grabbed my lexicon: 'What is this?'—'I'm improving my German vocabulary.'

"He put down the paper, and the silence in the office grew heavy. Busta circled around us, encompassing both the civilians and prisoners in the same mistrust, smelling sabotage without being able to detect the source. He didn't dare indulge in any excesses in front of the engineers. He looked around the room one last time, his eyes filled with hatred, and walked out, clicking his heels. Our bodies, on edge from the tension of waiting, relaxed."

Busta's name will come up again in part 5, which deals with hangings in the tunnel.

AN INCOHERENT SITUATION. The preceding eyewitness accounts, all of them significant, show how inconsistent the situation in the factory tunnel was.

A considerable part of the leadership, both civilians and military, wished to see the factory operate under ordinary conditions and the prisoners treated normally as long as the work was done. This could not go smoothly, obviously, with a missile that took months to perfect, and an improvised setup that was not always efficient. Indeed, the German civilians themselves were far from being all competent and dedicated. Under such conditions, the ongoing threat of SS forays weighed on everyone, thereby adding to the general gloom.

Busta and the other SS could not help but sense the hostility they generated. According to Raoul-Duval,[80] the Wehrmacht soldiers in his segment were the ones who warned the prisoners of the arrival of the SS. On the pretext of *Geheimnis,* or secrets, Ribault's[81] *Meister* continually locked the premises that contained plans and forbid access to the SS. At least they were visible, whereas everyone knew that the SD and the Gestapo had their own agents in the factory.

There is no information about the personal reaction of Mittelwerk authorities such as Sawatski, Rickhey, Rudolph, Haukohl, and others. Apparently they decided to play the card of kindness. The company distributed cigarettes to good specialists (Makhorkowe cigarettes made in Bialystok) and above all bonuses in the form of duly numbered camp marks *(Werkmarke)* in the name of the Mittelbau *Arbeitslager,* which were supposed to be honored at the camp canteen. The canteen will be dealt with in the next chapter.

From the beginning, however, as mentioned in chapter 4, one of the directors of Mittelwerk was Otto Förschner, the Dora camp commander. He was in charge of security and was the immediate superior of Busta and the other SS in the tunnel. What game did he personally play as head of the camp? That question will be examined in the next chapter. In any case he was well aware of Kammler's position concerning security in the *Mittelraum,* particularly at Dora. The natural tendency was to increase the constraints rather than relax them, as will be seen later regarding the final months.

SABOTAGE. One of the plainly obvious concerns of those responsible for factory security was preventing sabotage (the Germans used the French word *sabotage*). A circular went around Mittelwerk on January 8, 1944, drawing attention to this point. Their fears were justified, for prisoners of all nationalities, except for the German Greens, loathed working for the Reich war industry.

Literature on this subject has amassed over the years, tending first to attribute the frequent missile failures to sabotage, and second, to suggest that sabotage was carried out on instructions from clandestine organizations. It is therefore important to look at firsthand accounts for mention of any acts of sabotage committed and of instructions given with regard to missile production.

Spontaneous accounts, whether published or not, were supplemented in 1988–89 by a survey taken among the members of the Association of Former Dora-Ellrich Prisoners. The observations that follow are based on these documents. The first observation concerns the entirely individual and spontaneous nature of the acts that were reported. Witnesses had no knowledge of any organization whatsoever that could have launched a watchword from one moment to the next. With very few exceptions, no one sought complicity or revealed anything, even to their closest comrades. The topic was never discussed; it was far too dangerous for everyone.

The second observation concerns the absence of any spectacular actions resulting in the deterioration of a missile or of equipment. Whatever attempts that were made had to be discreet; they had to go unnoticed at the time and have an impact only at a later stage. The third observation concerns the generally unprofessional nature of such acts. The prisoners were often not sufficiently qualified to realize how far-reaching their intervention could actually be.

There is good reason to question how much prisoners knew at the time about V2 missiles and how they worked. They would have had to be in a position to examine one, at least in its essential features, and possess the scientific and technical expertise required to understand what they saw. As noted earlier, André Ribault,[82] who handled and reproduced the plans, was the best placed Frenchman to know what V2s were all about.

Another person in the know was Serge Foiret,[83] an aviation construction technician, who was able to make a critical assessment about production conditions. There is also a 1952 document from René Davesne[84] regarding the various verifications he carried out. Finally, there were a few scientists in the factory such as Charles Sadron, the *Mischgeräte* inspector, and Louis Gentil, who was immediately assigned to the V1s upon his arrival. Working at their side, however, were some highly incompetent fellow prisoners, including the author himself.

There are few detailed accounts of sabotage that was successfully carried out, and it is difficult to outline the various types, given the few cases involved. The most subtle category consisted in taking advantage of a certain amount of negligence on the part of German civilians to increase already existing administrative disorder. Two examples of this have been provided by the Czech Beneš,[85] one by himself and the other by his fellow Czech Jelinek. Ribault[86] and Bailly[87] have given similar accounts. A subsequent attempt was unthinkable at the time. Beneš, who explained what he did in detail, played for high stakes and was very much afraid.

A relatively simple form of sabotage was to be overzealous in checking materials brought in from outside, once it was acknowledged that the quality of the material varied enormously. Deliberately clumsy handling could easily increase the number of rejects.

Most of the sabotage mentioned, however, corresponded to producing slight defects, the consequences of which could be serious, particularly when they involved weld seams. Of course, the defects had to escape final verification. Two accounts, one by Bernard Ramillon and the other by Joseph Béninger, situate the problems clearly, although they did not involve the same types of weld seams.

According to Ramillon,[88] "One of the early problems with the missile must have been the quality of the seams made by multiple spot welding that held the outside plates to the reinforcement discs I mentioned earlier. This was remedied either by rivets or by electrode spot welding all around the discs inside the tail body. Thus, quite a number of our reinforcement welding spots were sabotaged, since metal was not always deposited, and holes were often hidden by the slag from the electrode."

Béninger[89] has given an account of a later stage: "I was checking under the supervision of a Hauptverteiler Meister. It was a metal box about two feet wide, three feet high and four inches deep. On the top and the bottom of the box were two or three rows of small electromagnetic relays. Four or five terminals were positioned vertically between the relays. A myriad of electric wires were soldered to the relays and terminals with pewter.

"At one point, I noticed that a few seams were cold junctions. A few technical details: when a pewter seam is done properly, the surface is smooth and shiny; the wire is incorporated into the terminal or relay to which it is attached. On the other hand, a cold junction looks gray and dull, and the surface is not smooth. The person who had done this cold junction had not allowed the pewter to heat up sufficiently and the conducting wire was not incorporated in the terminal or relay. The wire might become detached under the effects of vibration and interrupt the circuit. It was clearly an act of sabotage. I did not inform my Meister who, by the way, knew nothing about weld seams, and the continuity tests were good.

"Some time later, the Meister gave me an electric soldering iron, some pewter and flat long-nosed pliers. I was ordered to re-solder any seams that looked suspect and use the flat pliers to draw all the conductors to the spot where the weld seams were made. Not a word was said about why a further verification had to be carried out. Moreover, I was given self-sticking diamond-shaped papers (with 4- or 5-centimeter sides), carrying the official stamp of the Reich. I had to write my identity number on the paper. It was a sort of seal, which had to be glued across the structure and cover of the Hauptverteiler once the verification was completed. I no longer carried out my inspections with the same couldn't-give-a-damn attitude. Our relations with the Meister were no longer the same. There were three or four prisoners doing this job. Needless to say, we all had a few strange thoughts."

That is the real story about attempted sabotage and how the Germans kept an eye out for it. Certain heroic acts did not have the impact they were alleged to have had on the outside.

DAILY LIFE IN THE TUNNEL FACTORY. For more than ten months the majority of the thousands of prisoners spent most of their time in the tunnel factory. For them the camp was literally a dormitory. There was no question of sleeping at the factory, even when there was nothing to do. Prisoners were there to work without stopping—or to appear that way when an SS came prowling around. There were places of refuge, at least for the specialists, in some barracks and corners, but the SS knew where they were and a lookout was always necessary.

A lookout was also required during slack periods, the time being used to make small crafts. Raoul-Duval,[90] who was not good with his hands, recalls: "More than once, I found myself facing a difficult problem and every time a comrade would help me out with touching kindness. The same was true for objects we needed: a knife, a spoon or a margarine box which I would make very crudely and then regularly lose. I can't remember how many times one of my comrades would spontaneously offer me something pretty he had made himself."

Prisoners sometimes took their crafts a bit far. Butet mentions his "electrolysis system" and the risks he took. The same was true for Bignon[91] and Herrou.[92] He also made "cigar lighters" that he supplied to civilians in Hall 28.

Along with talking, these occupations were used to kill time, which seemed endless. Raoul-Duval[93] recalls a genuine obsession with the time for the toilet break, just to be able to go in front of a clock. Lingering there was out of the question, however.

The various accounts show that small, quite stable groups were formed. Raoul-Duval belonged to the Heckmontage group. Amate[94] mentions his comrades who were employed in assembling engines in the Haukohl Kommando, with their Belgian *Vorarbeiter*. There was another group in the Heckbau, led by André Guichard, and the Breton-Clergue-Belaval-Garnier group, which went from the Zaunbau to the Bünemann (to which Herrou also belonged).

A solid group formed around Charles Sadron, the "Old Man" (he was born in 1902), including Guy Boisot, René Bordet, Francis Finelli, André Fortané, Pierre Gáti, André Gérard, Marcel Gouju, Bernard Gross, Pierre Hémery, Raymond de Miribel, Yvon Navet, André Sellier, and René Souquet. With the exception of Hémery and Miribel, who were "21,000"s, they all arrived at Buchenwald by the first two trains in January 1944 and were more or less quickly assigned to the Ko Scherer in Hall 28. Mathieu Anfriani, Michel Bedel, Jean Guyon des Diguères, and René Fourquet, a "14,000" who had gone through Peenemünde, were in the vicinity.

There was also an outstanding character in the Ko Scherer named François Le Lionnais, a scientific writer who belonged to the Oulipo group, who used to give lectures on the most varied topics to his neighbors such as Pouzet[95] and Béninger. He was an "absent-minded professor," always lost in his thoughts and bringing blows upon himself.

These examples are taken from French accounts. Naturally there were also

Slovene groups (Milan Filipcic, Emil Cucek, Franc Svetic, Anton Peskar, and Aleksander Kump, all of them from Dachau), Czechs, and others. Language was the basis for these groups, but friendships also grew between Frenchmen and Soviets in the Ko Scherer, such as Béninger, a Russian from Leningrad and a young Bachkir, who has already been mentioned. The harder the Kommando, however, the stronger the national antagonisms.

WAITING FOR THE "LIBERATION." The big thing for everyone was the likely date of the "Liberation," and the ups and downs in the news about the war that reached the tunnel generated alternating highs and lows of rash excitement and despair, which took their toll on the weakest prisoners.

Our main source of information was necessarily German news broadcast on the radio (called the "wireless" at the time) or printed in the newspapers. Some German civilians in the tunnel listened to the radio. In the Ko Scherer this was particularly true of Krüger, who shared an office in a Hall 28 barracks with numerous prisoners, including Gérard, who was fluent in German and took note of everything he heard. The members of the Schreiber Kommando were often placed in similar situations. The only accessible press was usually the big Nazi daily, *Völkischer Beobachter.*

The problem, of course, was to determine the veracity of the information being disseminated. One has to acknowledge that German news releases were seldom inaccurate, which is confirmed by reading the press of the period after the fact. The difficulty lay in interpreting the information, which required paying careful attention to the geographical names mentioned, especially the cities and rivers. If a German counteroffensive on the Eastern Front was said to be taking place west of a large city, it meant that the city had been recaptured, or was at least surrounded by Soviet troops, which may not have been clearly stated beforehand.

These comments are quite banal, and anyone who has ever put flags on maps in a game of Kriegspiel has had the same experience. Yet it must not be forgotten that the tunnel prisoners had neither flags nor maps available at the time, and they could not be sure they had heard all the news releases.

Sadron[96] discusses the problem in these terms: "A map was pinned to the wall above Neumann's desk. From where I was sitting, I could see it clearly and I followed the progress of the Allied armies. Moreover, one of the prisoners had taken his degree in geography, and he was amazingly knowledgeable. He had a collection of maps he had drawn from memory on the back of verification sheets."

Indeed, the author himself had useful knowledge concerning the Dnieper, the Dniester, the Pripet, and the Berezina rivers. He also knew how to locate Tschernigow and Czernowitz with their German spelling. He did not, however, have a collection of maps—which would have been crazily imprudent. He had to improvise every time. Whenever new information became available, his chief problem was to remember what point had been reached the previous time, for there was no way of referring to notes. Long afterward, while reading the memoirs of his colleague and friend Raoul-Duval,[97] he realized that he had played the same role in his own Kommando.

It is easy to reconstruct the stages by which the morale of French prisoners at Dora gradually improved. The first event was the Allied landing, which took place on June 6, 1944, and was immediately known by the shift in the tunnel who announced it to those taking over in the new shift. There was considerable excitement, and some comrades, such as Edmond Caussin,[98] manifested their joy too openly and were punished for it. Our excitement gradually diminished as the battle of Normandy raged on while the civilians in the factory (Krüger, for example) exulted at the announcement of the launching of the first V1s on London. After the breakthrough at Avranches the news kept coming, and each piece of information was more extraordinary than the last: the Americans were in Brittany, the Allies had landed in Provence, Paris had been liberated, then Brussels and finally Luxembourg. At that pace nearly everyone thought they would be home for Christmas at the latest.

The landing in Normandy and the gradual liberation of France had one unexpected consequence: France's prestige rose in the eyes of the Czechs and Poles. On July 14 the French sang *La Marseillaise* on their way down into the tunnel, and the SS did not react until the Russians took over with their own songs. There were no regrettable repercussions. Behind the euphoria there was still evident anxiety.

After the failed assassination attempt against Hitler it was clear that the Nazi regime would fight to the finish. There was also fear that those who were working on secret weapons would ultimately be eliminated. In October, illusions of being home for Christmas began to disappear. German propaganda emphasized two events: the first firings of V2s on September 8, and the British failure at Arnhem at the end of September. Once again the situation appeared to be at a standstill. In truth it was not easy to follow the battles being fought for control of the port of Antwerp and the Allies' progress in Lorraine and Alsace.

Those who were able to follow simultaneously what was happening as of June 1944 on the Eastern Front, in the Balkans, and in Italy from German news releases were able to put the importance of what was taking place in the West into perspective. They knew that continuous progress was impossible anywhere, and also that the German armies were everywhere on the defensive.

That is not entirely true, for on the eve of Christmas a German offensive (the last one) was continuing in the Ardennes. For the Dora prisoners as for many others at the time, the year drew to a close in painful disillusionment.

The Other Mittelwerk Kommandos

THE KOMMANDOS OF NIEDERSACHSWERFEN, ROSSLA, AND KELBRA. At the Mittelwerk factory in the Dora Tunnel, V2s were assembled from components shipped by railway from suppliers located throughout Germany. The factory had a large stock of these components, which was particularly necessary as the Allied bombing of factories and communication routes might interrupt the supply at any moment. There was only limited warehouse space in the factory itself, and only the most fragile things were stored there, such as instruments and gyroscopes. The rest included very cumbersome objects such as engines, tanks, and half-shells as well as sheet metal, crates of metal parts, packages of glass wool, and so on.

Warehouses belonging to Mittelwerk were set up outside the factory at various points in the surrounding area. Three of them are known to us through first-hand accounts from the corresponding Kommandos. No doubt there were others. The first warehouse was connected to an open-air warehouse *(Freilager)* located at the northern exit of tunnel A of the Kohnstein, hence on the territory of Niedersachswerfen. The Kommando that took care of loading on this site came on foot from the Dora camp. It was primarily made up of Czechs, with *Kapos* and *Vorarbeiter* who were also Czech. One Frenchman, Émile Nérot,[99] belonged to it.

The second warehouse was in Rossla, thirteen miles east of Nordhausen on the railway line leading to Halle. There was an old building on the site flanked by a former lime oven or *Kalkofen,* which gave its name to the entire storage area. Only tanks covered by camouflage nets were left outside. The corresponding Kommando is well known from the account of Max Dutillieux,[100] which is particularly suggestive. This was the Kommando that had been assigned to loading in the tunnel, whose *Kapo* was Willy Schmidt mentioned earlier in chapter 6. With Willy Schmidt still in authority, it was put in charge of the Rossla warehouse. Starting on August 1, the prisoners, about a hundred strong, were taken there by train every day from Dora. In September they were put into a minicamp set up specifically for them, where they remained isolated until the evacuation in April 1945.

Life in the Kommando for the Poles, Czechs, a few Frenchmen, and many Russians, under mild German supervision, was peaceful, and the *Unterschar-führer* in command of the SS was not overzealous. Few prisoners fell ill. Two of them were operated on at the *Revier* in Dora and came back. As Max Dutillieux has observed: "Willy Schmidt's Kommando spent eight months in Rossla without any loss of life, either among the French or among the others. [. . .] Not a single death! Rossla was really a sort of intermission." Afterward, Dutillieux learned that there had been one death.

A third warehouse was located a few miles to the south, in Kelbra according to the account provided by Edmond Caussin,[101] with an equally peaceful Kommando. Caussin was the victim of a real work-related accident due to a broken hoist cable. He was operated on at the *Revier* in Dora by Dr. Jacques Poupault for a fractured hip, recovered, and was assigned to Hall 28 in the tunnel.

Conditions there were unusually favorable, whereas at that very same time tragic situations were developing in Ellrich, Nordhausen, and Blankenburg. Similarly, again at the same time, the Mülhausen Kommando, under the authority of Buchenwald, was spared in the north the hellish conditions of Ohrdruf. In the same vein, Langbein[102] has mentioned the Brieg camp on the Oder River, operating under the authority of Gross Rosen, which only had one death out of a thousand prisoners over a period of two months.

The fact that such situations existed demonstrates that the slaughter could have been avoided. The death of prisoners was the result of a deliberate attitude at one level or another of the hierarchy.

THE KLEINBODUNGEN KOMMANDO. A sizable number of V2s were destroyed simply by a successful firing. Others disintegrated in the air without reaching their target. In the case of other missiles, however, particularly during the final testing period in Blizna and Peenemünde, the firing aborted, leaving the engines in a more or less damaged state. Lastly, the missiles had to be transported by railway over long distances, the trips marked by various vicissitudes, accidents, or bombings. As a result, by the middle of 1944 the Wehrmacht had acquired a stock of V2s that was useless except for salvage.

In the summer of 1944, Mittelwerk decided to set up a site for dismantling damaged missiles that was served by a branch line and located at a former potassium mine in Kleinbodungen, near Bleicherode. A Kommando from Dora (with Charles Spitz)[103] first had to remove all traces of former activity in the buildings, as it had been a munitions factory with a powder magazine in the former galleries two thousand feet underground.

At the same time, a camp going by the code name of "Emmi" was being set up for a new Mittelwerk Kommando, which operated until April 1945. The Kommando sent components that could be recycled to the tunnel factory warehouses as fast as they could be salvaged. Since many parts were numbered, those who had access to the files could see how long it took before they came back.

The prisoners who were sent from Dora came from various countries. As far as the Frenchmen were concerned, Fernand Rousseau, a "14,000" from Buchenwald, had already been at Peenemünde and the Dora Tunnel, Marcel Gouju had been in the Ko Scherer, Raoul Giquel[104] and Jean Voisin had come via Wieda (see chapter 11).

THE CONSTRUCTION OF VIS BY MITTELWERK. Production of VIs in the tunnel by Dora prisoners employed by Mittelwerk did not begin until September 1944. Until then production had been carried out by various Reich mechanics firms, particularly Volkswagen. Whereas the A4/V2s had been developed by the army Weapons Office on its own premises, particularly at Peenemünde East, the Fieseler firm (Gerhard Fieseler Werke) in Kassel turned out Fi 103s, baptized "Richard" and later known as V1s, for the Luftwaffe. The Luftwaffe base in Peenemünde West was used only for testing.

The V1s that were fired on London from France, starting on June 13, 1944, were mounted either by Fieseler in Kassel or in Cham (in Bavaria northeast of Regensburg), or by Volkswagen in Fallersleben (Wolfsburg) or in Burg (north-east of Magdeburg), or by Opel in Rüsselsheim (near Frankfurt), or even in France in Thil-Villerupt, in the northern Meurthe-et-Moselle.

At some point Hitler's headquarters decided that V1s should henceforth be assembled in an underground factory, and Paul Figge, one of the directors of the Sonderausschuss A4, was put in charge of transferring the equipment and personnel from Fallersleben to the Dora Tunnel. That set off a violent conflict with Anton Piëch, managing director of Volkswagen, who had no choice but to comply.

As noted earlier, the Mittelwerk *Werk II* factory, in charge of V1s, was set up in the southern tip of tunnel A and in the halls corresponding to the former dormitories. Until the new factory was commissioned, production was concentrated in Burg and Cham, and was gradually transferred until, by February 1945, Dora was the only factory, producing 2,275 V1s.

As mentioned, a team of Hungarian Jews came from Fallersleben to Dora. The other *Werk II* prisoners came partly from *Werk I,* such as Jacques Chamboissier, Claude Lauth, and Xavier de Lisle. Didier Bourget, who had come back from Bergen-Belsen via Buchenwald, found a job there painting V1s. Edmond Debeaumarché and Louis Gentil were in the "77,000" train. Olivier Richet and Marcel Ranchain, who had been in a verification Kommando in a bombed-out Buchenwald factory, were again given jobs checking V1s. They did not belong to the Ko Scherer, however, for *Werk I* and *Werk II* Kommandos were totally separate. Thus, *Werk II* also had its own *Transportkolonnen,* which were just as dreadful as those of *Werk I.*

V1 missile inspection and acceptance continued to be carried out by Luftwaffe officers, whereas the army was responsible for the V2s.

[[10]]

THE CAMP AT DORA IN 1944

As has already been indicated, it was not until April–May of 1944 that a real, properly organized camp came into being in the valley of Dora. It was, however, primarily a sort of small dormitory city for the prisoners working in the nearby tunnel factory and the corresponding maintenance departments. At the same time the Sonderstab Kammler (see chapter 11) launched a series of work sites in the surrounding area and opened new camps. The workforce generally came from Buchenwald and sometimes passed through the Dora camp, where some prisoners stayed for a while. Sick patients received care at Dora, where there was also a crematorium. The entire group remained, however, under the authority of Buchenwald.

This confusing situation came to an end in the autumn of 1944. The decision was made to grant autonomy to the new Dora-Mittelbau camp on September 28, and it took effect on November 1. In addition to the Dora camp itself, the new entity included a specific number of camps and Kommandos. The details of the new structure that was set up at the time will be presented in chapter 15. A few weeks later, in early 1945, the arrival of trains evacuating the camps in Eastern Europe disrupted the balance in this system.

The present chapter deals only with the Dora camp, taken in the strict sense, until the end of 1944.

Camp Administration

BETWEEN THE REDS AND THE GREENS. As in all camps of a certain size, internal administration was left to prisoners—in other words, practically speaking, to German prisoners. At Dora like everywhere else, the SS had to choose between the Reds and the Greens, i.e., between political prisoners and common criminals, first of all for the position of *Lagerältester*, or senior member of the camp.

During the first months the LÄ1 and 2 were communists named Georg Thomas and Ludwig Sczymczak, who arrived at Buchenwald after the first convoy. They were relieved of their functions in February 1944 for refusing to carry out hangings, and camp management was placed in the hands of Willy Zwiener, a Green. It would appear, however, that the second most influential person after Förschner, the camp commander, was another Red, Albert Kuntz, the *Bautechniker,* who was in charge of camp construction.

It seems that he was the one who persuaded Förschner and Pister, the Buchenwald commander who came to inspect Dora, to designate two communist leaders, Joseph Gamisch and Christian Beham, who were sent from Buchenwald to become LÄ1 and 2. These men were of higher caliber than Thomas and Sczymczak. Later accounts by Czechs and Poles were favorable to them. Apparently the objective was to put the Dora camp under an authority comparable to the one imposed at Buchenwald. It would seem that in order to ensure the smooth running of the factory, the workers were to be properly treated in the camp. Another communist leader, Fritz Pröll, simultaneously arrived from Buchenwald at the Dora *Revier.*

It is difficult to determine the exact date on which Gamisch and Beham assumed their functions, but it appears to have been sometime in July. Certainly the months that followed were the least unpleasant in the Dora camp for those lucky enough to remain there. The communist leaders at Dora were arrested in late 1944 and early 1945, which will be discussed later, and camp management was again placed in the hands of a Green, Roman Drung, who remained the LÄ to the end.

Aside from the top leadership of the camp, in the summer of 1944 Reds played the main roles in camp administration at the *Revier,* kitchen, etc., but there were not enough of them to exert real control over the entire base—that is, to manage the blocks.

BLOCK ORGANIZATION. Each concentration camp in Nazi Germany contained a number of blocks. Some were permanent structures and others were made of wood. At Buchenwald some blocks had two floors. When the prisoners were housed in preexisting buildings that were not always suitable, such as those at Ellrich, the buildings were called blocks. The tunnel "dormitories" were supposed to be blocks.

In the Dora camp, which was methodically constructed, the blocks were all built on the same model, out of wood and assembled using prefabricated components, with their sanitary and other facilities. The entrance was in the middle of the façade, and each building had two wings, called *Flügel.* In each wing were two succeeding rooms; the first was used as a dining hall with tables and benches, and the second was the dormitory, with bedsteads. Each wing was heated by a stove in the refectory. In the center of the block was the *Waschraum,* a sort of shower room with basins and toilets.

The block hierarchy was composed of a *Blockältester*—or block elder—and his two deputies the *Stubendienst,* each one in charge of a wing. The *Blockältester* was the "senior member of the block," but, in French, he was almost always called the block chief, which generated a certain amount of confusion with the *Blockführer,* who will be discussed shortly. The other important person in the block was the *Schreiber* or secretary, who kept track of the number of people in the workforce. In one block there was also a *Friseur,* who was a hairdresser, along with various other aides who had a more or less permanent status, such as a night watchman. In each wing a corner was set aside in the rear of the first room for the *Blockältester,* the *Schreiber,* etc.

Each block was under the authority of an SS man, the *Blockführer,* who could intervene at any time but was usually content to make regular inspection visits and sign the papers kept by the *Schreiber.* The personal relationship between the *Blockführer* and the *Blockältester* was important.

LIFE IN THE BLOCKS. Many of the blocks at Dora were occupied by tunnel specialists working in shifts in Kommandos that had almost unvarying head counts, which ensured a great deal of stability. The two shifts of the Ko Scherer relieved each other in Block 104 from May 1944 to April 1945, and the prisoners such as Guy Boisot and André Fortané, René Souquet and André Sellier, Joseph Béninger and Aurélien Féliziani, and many others got used to sleeping head to foot on the same straw mattress day after day. The Bünemann Kommando, as Breton notes, was in Block 102.

The block was first and foremost a dormitory, and the role of the *Blockältester* and the *Stubendienst* was to enforce discipline and cleanliness. Some of them took advantage of their authority in the long-standing concentration camp tradition to become overzealous regarding muddy shoes or the alignment of blankets. This was one of the ways prisoners were terrorized at the Breendonck fort in Belgium; but at Dora, the authorities rarely went that far.

The block was also the place where soup was served and rations distributed. Strict rationing was a characteristic feature of most of the Buchenwald blocks, but that was seldom the case at Dora. The *Blockältester* and the people around him tended with more or less discretion to put some aside for themselves. The very limited rations also encouraged stealing, especially of bread, among prisoners. In the camp blocks there was no longer any organized looting like that in the tunnel dormitories. Yet the temptation remained strong, and theft was often severely punished.

Packages and letters were another major problem, because of the address. When new prisoners arrived at Buchenwald in quarantine, they were allowed to write to their families (unless they were classified NN) and give them the number of a Buchenwald block. After their transfer to Dora their address remained Weimar-Buchenwald; Block 17 meant Dora. Then the number of the block at Dora was added, and the address became, for example, 17/14. Later, Weimar-Buchenwald disappeared and was replaced by Sangerhausen, a town in Prussian Saxony twenty-five miles from Nordhausen. The same address was used for packages. Hence it was important not to change camps and consequently identity numbers.

Packages arrived intact at Buchenwald. At Dora they were more or less looted even before they reached the block. It was therefore generally a good idea to be generous with the *Blockältester,* if what was left in the package was worth anything. The most extraordinary experience in this regard is recounted by Rassinier, who arrived at Dora in March 1944.

According to Rassinier's account[1] he was saved by his packages and the way he made use of them. First, he earned the protection of his block chief, who wore a black triangle, by sharing a "huge piece of bacon" with him. As a result the packages addressed to his identity number were no longer looted. He thus had the advantage of a "precious exchange currency" allowing him to go to the *Revier* and stay there. He claims that he received a package every day. By comparison Birin[2] was at a severe disadvantage. "Out of the 219 packages sent by my family, colleagues and friends from Épernay," he writes, "no more than twenty actually reached me, and they were usually looted."

The vast majority of French deportees, aware of the problems of getting fresh supplies and of the cost of living in France in 1944, were naturally impressed by the volume of Rassinier's packages. They received fewer, more modestly sized packages, which indicates how precious sharing among small groups of comrades in the same Kommando actually was.

Daily life in Dora depended in large part on the atmosphere of the block and the *Blockältester*'s personality. Sadron[3] talks about Block 104: "Naturally, our Block chief was a German. He was very dignified, with a dark, impassive, odd-looking face. Apparently, he was a highly esteemed crook, and therefore enjoyed the esteem of the SS who gave him small gifts. He lived in a small enclosure in a corner of the refectory, decorated with lace and paintings.

"The Stubendienst maintained this holy place with fearful enthusiasm. The Stubendienst, who was also German, was merely a petty criminal without any stature. Prognathous, with a low forehead, short nose and outsized arms and legs, he was nicknamed the 'Pithecanthropus.' For a few quarts of soup, he became totally enslaved to the Block chief. He, in turn, supported a small circle of friends, mostly Russians, who did the work he was supposed to do. He compensated them by giving them food stolen from our rations.

"Upon entering the 'dining hall,' one had a favorable impression. The walls were decorated artistically in apple green and brown. They were covered by a number of paintings, some of which were not bad. It is hard to say where they came from. I think our Block chief, in keeping with a long tradition, was the patron of a few artists who were spared drudgery and were given a bit of our food.

"The light wooden tables were covered with multicolored tablecloths. These came from our packages: handkerchiefs, shawls and scarves, imprudently sent by our families. There were also vases filled with artificial flowers. I have no idea where they came from. They lent a rather funereal air to the place, which was rather unfortunate, but we couldn't expect too much. . . ."

Block 9 was just below Block 104. Georges Soubirous[4] remembers his block chief, named Karl, a communist mason who ran his block without any brutality. He pretended not to know about the religious activities of the abbot, Jean-Paul Renard, who, in exchange, was careful to remain discreet.

Block 9 and Block 104 were located in the city center, so to speak, unlike Block 130, which was at the far end of the camp, filled with Gypsies who had only just arrived when Spitz[5] assumed his position as *Schreiber*. Paul, the block chief, another communist, was then transferred to Block 12 and replaced by a half-Polish Green from Upper Silesia named Eric Wyglendatz, who was known as Anna. He engaged in bootlegging alcohol along with the other members of his team. "Folette," referred to as "the infamous" by Pierre Gabrion,[6] who, like Bailly, had to deal with him in Block 24, was also in the area. He was then let loose as the chief of Block 132. Spitz claims to have seen him wearing first a pink, then a red, and finally, a green triangle. How he met his end at Bergen-Belsen will be discussed later.

Anna managed to persuade Maurice de la Pintière,[7] a friend of Spitz, to paint a fresco in his block. He had already decorated the canteen and Spitz notes: "I remember, among other things, a village feast where all the people were given the masks of Kapos, Lagerschutz and even familiar SS members, and everyone admired their resemblance."

CAMP BUREAUCRACY. Administering a German concentration camp always involved a great deal of paperwork. A list of prisoners had to be kept up to date, indicating their current whereabouts (in a block, at the *Revier,* etc.) and their assignment to a Kommando. Statistics were kept by nationality or by prisoner status, especially in the case of Germans. Even cause of death was recorded.

This meant finding bureaucrats among the prisoners. At Buchenwald the bureaucracy in 1944 was entirely in the hands of German political prisoners and their friends from Czechoslovakia, Poland, the Netherlands, etc. At Dora the situation was more confusing: there were few German Reds and the Greens were often mediocre, which meant there were possibilities open to prisoners from other countries who had some knowledge of German. This was also the case for administrative positions in the tunnel.

The basic component of the camp bureaucracy was the *Schreibstube,* the secretariat, which was associated with the block *Schreiber.* One witness, Charles Spitz,[8] has provided a definition of their work. He became the *Schreiber* for Block 120 in October 1944 and remained in that position until the evacuation.

"In short, I was in charge of keeping the Block's 'accounts.' I was given a Blockbuch for this purpose, in which the prisoners' family names, first names, identity numbers and nationalities were written, along with the Kommando to which they were assigned. When I arrived, the Appellbuch listed 239 occupants. The number varied, however, because whenever anyone changed Kommandos, he automatically went to a different Block. There were also hospitalized prison-

ers who were required to show a paper with their identity number and date of release as soon as they left the Revier. When only the paper arrived, bearing a
Saint-Andrew's cross, it meant that the prisoner had been released via the crematorium. All I had to do was put a similar cross in the Blockbuch, along with
the date, and reduce the unit's headcount.

"At night, we had to prepare for roll-call. It was a big deal. The Appellbuch
was divided into two parts. On the left-hand side were the identity numbers of
incoming and outgoing prisoners, those who were ill in the Block and those who
were in the Bunker. The right-hand side was used for three days. First, the theoretical headcount was entered, then the actual headcount, with an adequate justi-
fication for the difference between the two. We were not released until the SS
Blockführer had signed his name in the box reserved for the day at the bottom of
the page. Roll-call did not end until all of the Blocks had received their final release."

Spitz's experience has allowed us to determine how the head count evolved
in a block. In Block 120 there were 239 occupants when he arrived; the number
rose to 313 and then to 345 on April 1, on the eve of the evacuation.

On the basis of information received from the blocks, the *Schreibstube* kept
his file—the *Kartei*—up to date. On October 15, 1944, Butet[9] was taken on as a
typist after a short stay at the *Revier*. He had to retype some thirty-two thousand
Kartei data sheets onto new forms as a consequence of the autonomy that was to
be granted Dora-Mittelbau.

The other mainstay of the camp bureaucracy was the Arbeitsstatistik, which
kept up-to-date figures on jobs that were filled and jobs that went vacant. As the
Kommandos worked for Mittelwerk, there was an Arbeitseinsatz man in the tunnel who noted the needs of the personnel director and presented candidates to
him when the position called for a specific skill. The Arbeitsstatistik would
search for specialists in the camp by questioning the *Schreiber* and making an-
nouncements on the camp radio. Thus those who worked could find out about
vacant jobs and tell their friends about them.

That is what Alfred Birin,[10] a fluent German-speaking native of Lorraine, actually did on numerous occasions. When he was working on an excavation he
heard on the radio in his block that the Arbeitsstatistik was looking for a
Schreiber. He presented himself and was taken on along with another Frenchman, Pierre Ziller. First he worked as an interpreter, then he drew up Kommando lists. Later on, for example, he was the one who had Spitz appointed as
Schreiber for Block 130.

A third institution, the Politische Abteilung, did not concern itself with the
internal operations of the camp. It kept the political and criminal files that followed the prisoners on their peregrinations between the prisons and the camps.
By chance Albert Besançon,[11] who went through the small camp of Rechlin-
Retzow (in Mecklenburg) before arriving in Ellrich at a late date, was able to get

a glimpse of his file, which had accompanied him from Fresnes to Sachsenhausen via Neuenbremme, Trier, Cologne, and Berlin. The prisoners who worked at the Politische Abteilung managed the data sheets but did not have access to the files.

Prisoners were not only tracked by their files but also by their personal "belongings," as Guido Schreve, a Dutchman arrested in France under the false French identity of André Bérard,[12] was to observe. After several weeks at the Lagerkommando, he was assigned as a bureaucrat to the *Häftlingskleidungskammer,* the storehouse where the personal "belongings" of camp prisoners were kept in order. The block was especially fitted out with a big hall and offices. There was a data sheet for each prisoner with an inventory of his stored belongings; clothes were kept separately from valuables. In an envelope bearing his identity number, Bérard found his wallet, his watch, his rings, and a pen, which had been taken away from him when he was imprisoned at Fresnes. The objects had followed him to Buchenwald. When the Dora camp became independent from Buchenwald, the belongings of the prisoners who were transferred to Dora went along with them.

Two other examples may be given to show the care with which these belongings were stored. Michel[13] recounts that one day Pierre Rozan was called to the gate of the camp to be given his watch, which had been sent from Buchenwald, for reasons that will soon be explained. André Rogerie[14] found himself in Auschwitz after passing through Buchenwald and Dora and being sent in a "transport" to Maïdanek; one day he was summoned to an office to identify his belongings, which had been transferred from Buchenwald.

Death notices were sent to the *Kammer.* Only then did the prisoners' belongings become the property of the Reich. In the context, such legalism never ceased to be a source of amazement for those who encountered it.

THE ROLE OF THE BUREAUCRATS. It was important for each of the national communities to have well-placed representatives in positions where they could gather information and help their comrades.

Among the French, as luck would have it, the German-language skills of Pierre Rozan (a "21,000") were discovered within the first few weeks by the SS-*Lagerführer,* who made him his *Schwung*—that is, a sort of orderly. As a result of this position he was to be precious witness later on. Since it was necessary to know the time in his department, he was able to recover his watch under the aforementioned conditions. Similarly, it was important for the French to have the influence of Birin and Zeller in the Arbeitsstatistik.

Czechs obtained most of the administrative positions (half of them, according to Krokowski),[15] especially in the *Schreibstube* and as *Schreiber* in the blocks. The others were Polish or French, such as Reverend Heuzé, Barbaud, and Baillon in addition to Spitz, who remembers that the *Schreiber* of Block 116 was Belgian, a secretary at the town hall of Malines.[16]

The Polish were well represented in the Politische Abteilung, which was jokingly referred to as the Polnische Abteilung. Above all the Poles succeeded, together with a group of students, in monopolizing the firemen's Kommando, which was sometimes called outside the camp to intervene after bombing raids. The sampling of nationalities sometimes seems to have been systematic. In the *Kleiderkammer,* the pseudo-Frenchman Bérard found himself in the company of a Pole, a Czech, and a Belgian.

Largely thanks to Birin, a few odd Frenchmen found relatively peaceful positions. Georges Pescadère, an artist and painter, was called back to Ellrich to become *Schriftmaler* (letter painter) in a studio for making armbands, where three Czechs were already working. In the final weeks Bramoullé became *Schriftmaler* at the Politische Abteilung.[17] Arsène Doumeau, on the other hand, a former prisoner in Wiener Neustadt, after many vicissitudes, was made *Lagerbuchbinder* (camp bookbinder).

Even in subordinate positions, camp bureaucrats were privileged. After joining the Arbeitsstatistik, Birin[18] slept in a block divided into separate rooms, with eight individual beds in each. "The food, moreover, was not as bad. We were given our rations in the office itself, and there were often extras which we were able to share with many of our comrades."

Butet,[19] who became a typist, was assigned to Block 27, a peaceful block with Marien Leschi and his team who were in charge of the camp radio, and Georges Schmidt, the Alsatian polyglot who worked as an interpreter. Bollaert was also there in his capacity as night watchman. "I could have almost as much soup and bread as I wanted." He was also given a new, clean uniform in keeping with his role.

A FEW ANCILLARY FACILITIES. When the prisoners left the tunnel dormitories to occupy the camp blocks in May 1944, they found not only an administration already set up but a number of facilities typical of large traditional camps: a canteen, a cinema, a library, a whorehouse, and a special block for young prisoners. No documents are available on this topic, but it is not unreasonable to suppose that Kuntz as well as Förschner considered that all of this was necessary in a camp of a certain level. Naturally, appearances had little in common with reality.

In theory the canteen was linked to bonuses for specialists that were given out by Mittelwerk in the form of camp marks—supposedly to allow them to improve on their ordinary fare. When they went to the canteen, they saw that there was almost nothing to buy, which is hardly surprising. Sadron[20] mentions red beets and mustard, whereas the author found nothing but cumin seed. Everyone was thus reduced to hoarding. The canteen building mainly served as a meeting place for block chiefs, *Kapos* and *Lagerschutz,* which explains why La Pintière's frescoes met with such success.

The *Kino* was hardly ever frequented by anyone besides the German "functionaries" in the camp. Some Frenchmen such as Soubirous[21] remember going there once out of curiosity and never going back. The building was used for another purpose, which will be discussed later: it was there that people arriving by trains, such as the convoy from Gross Rosen in February 1945, were crammed together.

There really was a library—run by Emile, an Austrian communist—though it was remarkably second-rate. Once, out of curiosity, the author borrowed a treatise on geopolitics by Hausenhofer, a classic of the Nazi period. Garnier[22] read a work that was, interestingly enough, highly critical of the USSR and its work camps. Eckert[23] took out two books, including a Maigret detective story in French, which was, incidentally, confiscated by an SS man. It certainly did not encourage cultural activity in the camp, which no one cared about anyway. The Puff—that is, the *Bordell*—operated, as in Buchenwald, only for a minority. The euphemism used for this gathering of interested individuals was *Sonderbau*, the "special building." The rest of the camp had nothing to do with it.

The young prisoners' block was number 115 (Bailly says 31). It housed the *Jugendliche,* i.e., prisoners under the age of eighteen who were neither Jews nor Gypsies. They wore a white armband with a J surrounded by a black circle. Two Frenchmen who stayed there have each given an account: Jean Gouvenaux[24] and above all Jacques-Christian Bailly.[25] Most of the occupants were Ukrainians, who were easily given to violence.

Kommandos in charge of various excavation, road, and construction-work projects remained in the Dora camp until August 1944. This included, in particular, the Schachtkommando to which Mialet[26] belonged. He describes himself as a "sleepwalker," digging a trench, building brick walls, and taking part in pouring the concrete for the tunnel halls where the dormitories were located, which were to be used for assembling V1s. Bailly belonged to the Gawabau Kommando, which dug trenches and unloaded freight cars.

These Kommandos disappeared in mid-August and their members were sent to Harzungen (e.g., Mialet) or more often to Ellrich. The AEG Kommando, which had until then been a privileged Kommando, was also sent to Ellrich. They will appear once again in the next chapter.

THE LAGERKOMMANDO. Thus no one was left in the Dora camp except the tunnel workers who came and slept there, shift after shift, and a hodgepodge of prisoners assigned to maintenance services and grouped together under the convenient umbrella term of Lagerkommando. Subsequently there would again be Kommandos working outside the camp and further Mittelwerk sites.

Some Lagerkommando activities were ongoing and organized, such as running the kitchen, the laundry, and disinfecting. Prisoners of all nationalities were assigned to them. Marcel Martin[27] was in the kitchen at Dora before changing to the one in Harzungen. Sermot[28] worked in the laundry. The Russians and the Poles seemed solidly entrenched there and they fiercely defended their positions.

Two ancillary activities were partly reserved for prisoners released from the *Revier* with written recommendations. In February 1944, instead of going back to the Maurer Wifo, Mialet[29] was assigned for a time to the *Kartoffelschäler,* the potato peelers. Joseph Jourdren[30] remained there from February 5, 1945, until the evacuation. Others patched up striped uniforms. These activities were precarious, however. New candidates were constantly arriving and had to be put someplace. Above all, when new "transports" of sick prisoners were being organized, there was always the danger of being added on to fill the specified head count.

The Lagerkommando was also responsible for the cleanliness of the camp. The roll-call yard had to be swept, for example, which Martin[31] did for a while. Delarbre[32] did a remarkable drawing representing the "sweeper of the roll-call yard" seen from behind. The SS camp had to be maintained, and for a time Pierre Géhard[33] was a member of that team. Le Puillandre[34] belonged to a Kommando that tidied up the Nordwerk workshops at night in the northern part of the tunnel.

THE CREMATORIUM. Lagerkommando members lived in dread of being conscripted into the Sonderkommando, the "Special Kommando" that unloaded trucks of corpses from exterior camps such as Ellrich and transported them to the crematorium. There are eyewitness accounts: one by Sermot[35] and one by Bérard/Schreve,[36] before he joined the *Kleiderkammer.*

The crematorium was not a priority at Dora. As has already been noted, until March 1944 corpses were transported to Buchenwald for incineration. A temporary crematorium was then built, which Sadron[37] has described: "It was a single oven, inside a miserable shed made of planks, surmounted by a long, sheet-metal pipe topped by a cone-shaped cap. It looked like a hovel in a slum. It was quite visible in the center of the camp. Day and night smoke came out of the pipe. First, when the oven was still empty, a curtain of warm air escaped, rippling transparently. Then, suddenly, black, greasy smoke poured out. The smell of burnt flesh seeped into our nostrils; we never could get used to it. After a few minutes, the smoke became bluish and transparent, like cigarette smoke. A body had been consumed."

According to Maurice Gérard,[38] this "country crematorium" was located "high up on the right, a little above Block 109." Gérard Pichot remembered it as being close by: when he had no news of his father, Léonce, who had gone to the *Revier,* he dreaded finding him there on a pile of corpses waiting to be burned.[39]

In late September 1944 a permanent crematorium, which is still in place today, was started up on the northern hillside near the block of tubercular patients from the *Revier.*

THE NEW KOMMANDOS AT DORA. In the autumn of 1943 the Dora camp was initially planned to house only the prisoners working for Mittelwerk or its own personnel, which was, in fact, the situation until mid-1944. The industrial ambitions of the SS, particularly of Kammler, led to the creation of new Kommandos and the arrival of new prisoners in the camp.

Whereas the specialists working in the tunnel factory were housed in the blocks nearest the roll-call yard, newcomers were sent to the most recently built blocks in the rear of the camp. This was the case, as noted earlier, for the Hungarian Jews and Gypsies arriving from Auschwitz before they were transferred to Ellrich or Harzungen. The specialists hardly had the chance or the free time to loiter about the area. Personally, the author preferred to walk up the hill behind Block 104, where one could have an unobstructed view.

Some of the new Kommandos were made available to firms in Nordhausen, where they went to work every day. Thus one morning, Roger Combarel[40] and Martial Bel were put into a group that was being taken up in two trailers hitched to two tractors. Their destination was the Schmit und Kraus tractor factory. Combarel's job consisted in trimming parts that were cut out with a blow torch. The *Meister* was very unpleasant but the *Kapo* was a distinguished, very polite German. The factory workforce was made up mainly of French and Russian civilians with whom it was difficult to communicate, since any contact was forbidden. In early 1945 the SS transferred the Kommandos that were employed in Nordhausen to the Boelcke Kaserne, which was still acceptable.

Those Kommandos were relatively privileged. The situation was totally different, however, for those working on the B 11 underground site at Niedersachswerfen. A description of the "new Kammler work sites," including B 11, will be provided in the next chapter. Here the workers were for the most part housed in Ellrich or Harzungen, but some were at Dora, at least for a while. One of them was Leopold Claessens,[41] a Belgian from the "54,000" convoy who "was to dig underground passages in the Kohnstein for Ammoniakwerke of Niedersachswerfen." Later on, Pierre Maho[42] after working on the assembly of V1s, was sent to Kommando 32, which was doing excavation work in Niedersachswerfen.

Claessens and his comrades would later join up with their fellow Belgians in Harzungen. Kommando 32 was transferred to the Boelcke Kaserne of Nordhausen in January 1945. At Dora there was still a whole population about whom very little is known, for it would seem to have been composed mainly of Russians and Poles sent in as reinforcements when deportees stopped arriving from the West, except for a few transfers from Buchenwald. Neander[43] has shown that from October 1944 to March 1945 the population of Dora grew perceptibly, whereas it was stable at Ellrich and Harzungen. This increase was used to maintain the head count among workers at the B 11 site and in the tunnel *Transportkolonnen*.

The Revier

THE WORKINGS OF THE *REVIER*. In the camp as it appeared in the summer of 1944, a number of blocks—nine in all—were reserved for the *Revier,* forming a unit that was closed off from the rest of the camp by a fence. Only *Revier* personnel were allowed to go back and forth between the *Revier* and the rest of the camp. The sole SS who were allowed inside were those who belonged to the SS medical department; others were not allowed access in order to avoid contagion.

As Rassinier has noted,[44] the blocks were gradually divided into special units for general medicine, surgery, pneumonia, pleurisy, and tuberculosis. The information he has provided does not quite coincide with the available camp map, which itself is subject to caution. In any case, the witnesses who refer to their stay at the *Revier* never specify the number of the block they were in, which they may never have known.

Two blocks are well known thanks to the plans drawn by André Lobstein.[45] The oldest one, number 16, near the roll-call yard, was used for consultations and administration, and the last one to be built, number 129, housed tubercular patients up at the top of the camp near the new crematorium. He has called it 39A in his contribution to *Témoignages strasbourgeois.*

Other camps were built near Dora in Wieda, Ellrich, Harzungen, Blankenburg, and Rottleberode, which will be discussed in the following chapters, each with its own *Revier,* which varied widely in operating standards. Sometimes patients were sent to the *Revier* at Dora.

The extremely difficult conditions under which the *Revier* at Dora began operating in the last few months of 1943 have already been described in chapter 6. Later the situation gradually improved for three reasons: the premises were considerably expanded, new personnel were brought in, and, from April 1944 until the autumn, there was a sharp drop in patient mortality. The situation once again grew worse during the final months of the year, which will be discussed in part 5.

One of the primary concerns of those in charge of the *Revier* was the extreme shortage of medicines. There were, it is true, those famous, strikingly colored ointments used in the "outside ambulance." The black one contained ichthyol and was used to disinfect and heal wounds. The whitish one was zinc oxide, which had a soothing effect. The greenish one was a mercury-based ointment used as an antiseptic. The yellowish one contained sulfur and was used to treat scabies. The only available material for bandages was crepe paper.

THE *REVIER* STAFF. During the year 1944 the SS doctor—or *Lagerarzt*—was Dr. Karl Kahr, a distinguished, distant man who had been seriously wounded on the Eastern Front. He was competent and supported improvements in his ward. On the prisoners' side, authority in the *Revier* was given to two German Reds, both communists, Fritz Pröll and Schneider. They have both been described as

Kapos, according to the sources, but it would seem that Pröll was actually the *Schreiber.* Whatever may have been the case, it appears that Pröll was sent specially to Buchenwald in April 1944 to take over the *Revier,* with the consent of the commanders of Buchenwald and Dora. Despite his youth, Pröll had ten years of camp life behind him and was an important figure in the communist hierarchy along with Kuntz, Gamisch, and Beham. When Lobstein[46] arrived on September 28 he carried a message for Pröll from the *Kapo* of the Buchenwald *Revier.* Pröll was highly intelligent and proved to be a remarkable organizer, according to Rassinier's account,[47] which can hardly be suspected of indulgence toward communists. Furthermore, everyone held him in esteem.

The prisoner personnel was gradually increased. In February 1944, Jan Cespiva, a Czech surgeon, arrived from Auschwitz via Buchenwald. It seems that Dr. Louis Girard also joined the *Revier* staff in February. The team was further strengthened in March–April by two veterinarians, René Morel and Marcel Petit, director of the veterinary school of Toulouse, and in May by Dr. Jacques Poupault, who became head surgeon of the *Revier* with Cespiva as his deputy. In September the Belgian radiologist Frans Canivet arrived from Buchenwald and took charge of tuberculosis screening.

Aside from the doctors, scientists such as the bacteriologist Jean-Pierre Ebel and the pharmacist Albert Graf from the University of Strasbourg also played an important role. Ebel and Petit saw to it that the *Labor,* a test laboratory that was always snowed under with work, operated efficiently. Two medical students, André Lobstein and Jean Doucet, arrived at Dora in September and October 1944. They worked as nurses in the tubercular patients' block, which will be discussed at length in a later chapter. The Gaillot brothers, Pierre and Jean-Louis, reinforced the team of dentists.

The importance of the *Revier* in the life of the camp was twofold, from the hospital as well as the political point of view. Despite inadequate resources the doctors managed to save lives. Poupault carried out a successful operation on Edmond Caussin. Paul Rassinier was to return to France after six long stays in the *Revier,* thanks to special protection.

At the same time the *Revier* was the only place in the highly fragmented concentration camp that was open. Patients arrived bringing with them information and hearsay of all sorts. The *Revier* was the place where rumors were disseminated, and Rassinier's text, when examined closely, is the worst possible document on Dora, for the information it reports is more or less seriously distorted. The *Revier* staff members were in the best position to make contact inside the camp. The "resistance" in the camp that will be discussed later on, whether on the part of the Germans, the French, or the Czechs, was usually started by staff members from the *Revier.*

"PAPA" GIRARD. Dr. Jean-Louis Girard, born into a family of modest farmers in 1881 in Haut-Doubs, managed to get through medical school and in 1919, after three years of military service and five years of war and occupation, was appointed an ear-nose-and-throat doctor at Saint Joseph's Hospital in Paris. He soon became a renowned specialist, particularly for mastoid operations.

He was arrested in August 1942, went through Fresnes, Romainville, and Neuenbremme, and finally arrived in Buchenwald in October 1943, where he was assigned the identity number 30088. He was quickly sent to Dora and put on the tunnel excavation crew. He managed to hold up through sheer willpower as well as the protection of a group of young Ukrainians who were filled with respect for "Stari" (the old man). He was then sixty-two and had been unable to get himself recognized as a doctor.

One day he was summoned to report by the loudspeaker in the camp. He arrived before an SS man, his shovel resting on his shoulder and clothes covered with dust. The SS man asked him if he could operate on the mastoid of a ten-year-old child (who may have been his own son). "Doctor Girard said nothing. He put down his shovel, calmly took off his work clothes and donned a white coat. After he washed his hands and face at length, he put a gauze mask over his nose and mouth, took the trephine and hammer that were handed to him, and began striking the hammer with the extreme precision for which he was famous."

The child survived and the skilled doctor was given a little storeroom in the *Revier* where, for more than a year, he was able to attend to his comrades until the end. Known as "Papa" Girard, who was "always even-tempered and efficient" according to Groeneveld, he performed fifty-two more mastoid operations. He remained at the Dora *Revier* during the evacuation.

He died in 1947. His daughter, Anise Postel-Vinay, who was arrested with him, managed to come back alive from Ravensbrück.

Buchenwald and Dora: Two Different Worlds

A COMPARISON. In the summer of 1944 the Buchenwald and Dora camps appear to have operated in roughly the same way. The newly completed Dora camp was organized along the lines of Buchenwald. At Dora, just as at Buchenwald, the Reds held positions of authority in the internal camp administration, and the most important ones were experienced communist activists.

There is nothing surprising about their similarity. Despite its unusual size, Dora continued to be an exterior Kommando of Buchenwald. All the prisoners at Dora had come through Buchenwald and their identity numbers were Buchenwald numbers. There were only a few weeks when the corpses from Dora were not incinerated at Buchenwald.

The vast majority of prisoners, as has already been pointed out, was composed of newcomers to the concentration camp system, but the supervisory staff, the *Prominente,* were all veterans of Buchenwald who knew the rules and customary practices of the system. They were mainly Germans, both Reds and Greens, and in order to be selected on high by the authorities, at least tacit agreement on the part of the SS commanders of both the camps and the political authorities of the Buchenwald camp was necessary.

The balance of power was not, however, the same in both camps. At Buchenwald the Reds enjoyed unquestioned control. At Dora there were few Reds who were politically aware and hence their situation was precarious. There were more Greens, but they did not seem to form a coherent political group. The eyewitness accounts of prisoners of other nationalities suggest that different clans organized the looting of rations and packages.

Rassinier,[48] who claimed to have explained the workings of the camp from his own limited experience, gave a great deal of importance to the *Häftlingsführung,* or government by the prisoners. He neglected to underscore the fact that, in reality, he himself was connected to a sort of internal camp Mafia, which ensured that his packages were safeguarded and that he was able to enjoy repeated stays at the *Revier,* as mentioned earlier.

Gamisch and Beham, the two *Lagerältester* from Buchenwald, assumed their role for a short time—only a few months—which was not long enough for them to develop certain moral practices that had been possible at Buchenwald. Some eyewitness accounts of Buchenwald seem unreal to former prisoners of Dora. The author himself was struck, for example, by the following lines from an account written by Paul Le Goupil:[49] "From the corridors, we could enter the common-room where there were cupboards with pigeonholes and several large tables and benches where everyone had a place—even though we could not all sit down at the same time. My soup tin together with my bread and margarine ration were at place 14 on the right-hand side of the first table, located on the left upon entering. If someone was late due to working hours, his rations remained there, all day long if necessary, and no one touched them." That was in Block 40. Le Goupil was then transferred to Langenstein, where he found the conditions at the new camp altogether different.

In fact, the vast majority of Dora prisoners had no knowledge of Buchenwald beyond the quarantine, often accompanied with latrine and quarry duty, and hence held a poor opinion of daily life in the camp. Those who came from Buchenwald to Dora at the end of 1944, after a more or less long stay interrupted by the destruction of the factories in August, were in the best position to compare the two camps.

One of these prisoners was Olivier Richet,[50] who remained at Buchenwald from January 24 to September 22, 1944. He made one point that seemed to him essential: "The great difference between Buchenwald and Dora was that social life at Buchenwald was very wide-reaching. People from one Block visited those in another Block, they could walk around and talk to one another, especially on night duty, when they had much more free time. At Dora, night duty was much harder, and the Blockältester did not encourage walking around at all. Going into another Block to try and talk to friends was definitely not appreciated. Very often, 'definitely not appreciated' actually meant that it was prohibited. As a matter of fact, we had very, very little contact with each other at Dora."

Olivier Richet's text helps us understand how it was possible at Buchenwald to have a real cultural life in addition to a social life, with a real library and even, discreetly, a jazz band. It should be noted that neither Olivier Richet nor Paul Le Goupil belonged to the camp "functionaries." They both worked in camp factories (Gustloff, Mibau), which they were forced to leave after their destruction by bombing on August 24. They enjoyed the same status as the tunnel "specialists" at Dora who belonged to the Scherer or Bünemann Kommandos. Richet was then sent to work in the tunnel in a Kommando inspecting V1s.

The most important difference between Buchenwald and Dora was the compartmentalized social life that was restricted to the Kommandos, whose members tended to remain the same and were all housed together in the same blocks. As a result, some found themselves in a privileged environment, which was exactly how our young Bachkir viewed his situation.

POLITICAL LIFE. At the time there was a genuine political life at Buchenwald. The Reds who administered the camp were committed German communists, with an efficient clandestine leadership. Close, well-organized contact was maintained among Czech, Polish, and Dutch communists in the camp. The situation was not as clear-cut among French communists until the arrival of Marcel Paul in May 1944. The German communists also had relationships with other German Reds identified as social democrats or Catholics. The convoys from Compiègne, starting at the end of 1943, brought noncommunist parliamentary representatives and trade union activists who had friends among the French prisoners.

There was no equivalent to this at Dora, where the most outstanding personalities were either military or civil servants involved in the Resistance, as shown on the lists of those who would later become *compagnons de la Libération* or presidents of the Dora-Ellrich Association. Among the future presidents, Gustave Leroy, Marien Leschi, and Gabriel Lacoste were graduates of Ecole Polytechnique, along with the *compagnons* Jacques Brunschwig-Bordier and Louis Gentil.

General Pierre Dejussieu, a graduate of Saint-Cyr officers' academy, head of the Secret Army in July 1944 after the arrest of General Delestraint (who was executed at Dachau at the very end), and then head of the national FFI headquarters, was arrested in May 1944. He was at Dora in August with the "77,000"s and would later be named a *compagnon de la Libération* and president of the association. With him arrived Émile Bollaert, prefect of the Rhône, who had been removed from office by the Vichy government and appointed in

September 1943 to succeed Jean Moulin as the general delegate to the French National Liberation Committee. He was arrested in February 1944 at the same time as Pierre Brossolette. He, too, was to be named a *compagnon de la Libération.*

The same distinction was given to Edmond Debeaumarché, an important Resistance fighter in the French post office, who was also a "77,000," Pierre Julitte, a "14,000" who arrived late at Dora after a long stay at Buchenwald, André Schock, who will be encountered later in connection with Harzungen, and, posthumously, André Boyer. The latter, a comrade of Brunschwig-Bordier, was killed during the bombing of Nordhausen under conditions that will be described in chapter 16.

The first former Mittelbau prisoner later to have a political career was Dr. Pierre Ségelle, who experienced not Dora but rather Ellrich, along with the evacuation to Oranienburg and Schwerin. After 1945 he was elected Socialist representative from the Loiret, then mayor of Orléans, and later appointed minister of health and minister of labor. He was also the first president of the Dora-Ellrich Association until his death in 1960. After 1958, two former Dora prisoners were elected Gaullist deputies to the National Assembly: Pierre Ziller in the Alpes-Maritimes riding and Paul Boudon in the Maine-et-Loire riding.

LOUIS GENTIL. Like Dejussieu and Bollaert, Louis Gentil was a World War I veteran. He was nearly fifty years old when he arrived at Dora and was assigned to V1 construction. He was an artillery colonel and up to date on the modest level of French rocket development. He obtained a leave in the spring of 1943 and was the assistant of Henry Gorce-Franklin, head of the Gallia network, which specialized in military intelligence. He then founded the Darius network in Paris and was called to London, but he was arrested a few days before his departure on May 24, 1944, and was deported in the convoy of the "77,000"s and sent to Dora. He became acquainted with V1s in Hall 45 of the tunnel factory, which he was able to evaluate as a connoisseur. He belonged more or less to the same profession as Dornberger.

He was arrested at Dora on November 3, 1944, having been denounced along with Debeaumarché and Latry by Naegelé, as we shall see in Chapter 15. He was subjected to very rough interrogation and imprisoned in Nordhausen, where, in a weakened condition, he suffered an attack of boils that went untreated. "He had a high fever. His body was covered with lesions. [. . .] On his right leg, he had a deep wound that looked like it was festering." Doctor Poupault, who was in the same cell, got hold of sulfides and bandages, but the wounds suppurated and his fever continued unabated. He was finally transferred to the *Revier* at Dora, but it was too late and he died of septicemia in March 1945.[51]

POETRY AND RELIGION. The availability of paper and pencils was a decisive factor not only in drawing maps of the military situation but also for writing poems. Jean-Paul Renard's reputation as the *Dichter* has already been mentioned. Upon his return to France he published a book of poems called *Chaînes et Lumières (Chains and Light),*[52] containing the following line, which has often been reproduced: *"J'ai vu, j'ai vu et j'ai vécu"* [I saw, I saw and I lived]. Gustave Leroy published another text bearing the title *À chacun son dû.*[53] When the author returned to France in 1945 he was able to bring back the writings of his friend André Fortané.

In the summer of 1944, having left the tunnel dormitories, Jean Maupoint once again took up his role as camp cabaret artist. Linotypist at the printer of the local Clermont-Ferrand newspaper in 1943, it was above all as a cabaret artist that he had been known in the city—and certain texts with a double meaning had led, in part, to his being arrested. In the course of going through Compiègne he had continued to compose songs, one of which began with "In Compiègne, in Compiègne, in this camp entirely surrounded by barbed wire"; it was known by all the prisoners who passed through. The lyrics, which were written and sung by him in Dora between August and October 1944, have been preserved. Other songs were written by Gustave Leroy, who relates in the preface to his own collection his collaboration with Jean Maupoint. Both traveled home sick from Dora in May 1945; Maupoint died in Clermont-Ferrand on August 21, 1945. What took place at that time was exceptional; yet the author, present in the camp during that same period, knew nothing about it. But he may have belonged to a different shift than Maupoint.

Jean-Paul Renard was one of the camp poets, but above all he was a priest who played a very important role. In his memoirs, Birin[54] recounts the early celebration of the mass at Dora: "I was overjoyed to find some flour and some raisins in my package. The most difficult part was to make the hosts. Later on, it was easy for me to cook the dough in a sardine tin in the Arbeitsstatistik, producing hosts the size of lentils that were consecrated during particularly moving masses following a ritual even more primitive than in the Catacombs."

Birin gave the names of three priests who left Dora: the Abbot Bourgeois, Father Renard, a Trappist and homonym of Jean-Paul, and Abbot Amyot d'Inville. Louis Coutaud[55] recounts that Abbot Bourgeois was taken in a transport to Bergen-Belsen and Abbot Amyot was transferred to Wieda. He was brought back to Senlis in 1945, where he died shortly afterward. In the end Abbot Renard was the only one able to continue his priestly vocation in the camp. François Heumann[56] recalls that his Firnrohr Kommando companion, the seminarian François Schwertz, took communion with hosts he provided. It would seem that the celebration of Mass under the conditions prevailing at Dora took on greater importance than at Buchenwald.

JEAN-PAUL RENARD. Jean-Paul Renard, born in 1902, was the parish priest of Miraumont in the Somme when he was arrested by the Gestapo on November

11, 1942. For a long time he continued to go by his Resistance name, Jean-Pol. He was interned for a long time at Fresnes, then in Compiègne, and finally deported to Buchenwald by the first train in January 1944. He was transferred to Dora in early February. He stayed in the tunnel dormitories until May 1944.

With his knowledge of German he was able to become a *Schreiber* in the Mittelwerk factory, as mentioned earlier. He enjoyed considerable prestige, both in the tunnel and in the camp, both for the calm courage with which he exercised his priestly vocation and for his open-mindedness toward fellow prisoners who were not Catholics. He succeeded in gaining the collusion of both his *Kapo* and his block chief, who were grateful for his discretion. On April 1, 1945, he celebrated Easter Mass under conditions that will be described in chapter 16.

Eudes de Galzain,[57] a fervent Catholic, describes him in the following terms: "Jean-Paul drew people to him. He was cheerful, impulsive, poetic and priestly. As secretary to the civil engineer of Hall 15, he spent his time working in a shed made of planks. By evading the surveillance of the Kapos, we could come and see him on short visits.

"The snatches of traditional teaching he communicated to us during these brief breakaways ceased being dogmatic and became almost subversive. Subjects such as the Trinity, original sin and the Redemption that, under normal circumstances, seemed abstract and timeless, took on an air of bravado as Jean-Paul explained them in the Tunnel, under the nose of the SS. *Menschen,* fallen human beings, we went against the prohibitions to do our dangerous theology."

Resistance and Arrests

RESISTANCE AT DORA. Discussing the "Resistance" at Buchenwald and at Dora is a delicate task for two reasons. First, because there have been sharp controversies on the topic with respect to Buchenwald, which have resurfaced on occasion. Second, because some witnesses have occasionally lacked restraint in narrating certain events, which antagonized some of their comrades.

As far as the French are concerned, the most recent statement issued by Pierre Durand in 1991 might well serve as the basis for several observations concerning Dora. It is obvious that in late 1943 and early 1944 certain practices enabled certain Frenchmen to avoid the "transports" from Buchenwald to Dora because they were recognized as communists. Conversely, others were classified in such a way as to make their transfer unavoidable. A single quotation from Durand[58] will suffice here, for it is characteristic: "Marcel Petit knew one of those false Communists who played a harmful role in the relations between French and German prisoners. He was one of those people who was ready to play any card to his own advantage. I am not confusing these people with the Communists I knew later on, under difficult circumstances. [. . .] The fellow I am talking about—we'll call him 'Maufaix'—had succeeded in gaining the trust of the Block chief, Erich, in the quarantine camp where we had been since our arrival by the third convoy from Compiègne in January 1944. He claimed to be a Communist and had acquired a privileged position in the Block. He 'helped' Erich determine the political opinions of each person. Only later did I learn that he had categorized me as a rather suspect 'bourgeois reactionary.' I tried to let Erich know that his trust had been misplaced, but was unable to do so. The individual in question was not unmasked until later on, but by then, he had already done a great deal of harm." Louis Garnier,[59] who was in the same convoy and had talked with Petit, knew the name that "Maufaix" was using at the time and that he was suspected of having denounced his comrades in Toulouse. It was impossible to locate him after 1945. Garnier also knew that the same character appears in the account given by Rassinier,[60] who was also in the same convoy, under the name of the "little gimp" who claimed to have identified Thälmann and Breitscheid at Buchenwald. Petit, as was stated earlier, went to Dora and was assigned to the *Revier.* He saw Rassinier there and later agreed, out of indulgence, to serve as a moral witness for him in a trial.

In his account, Rassinier reveals the low opinion he had of the other members of his convoy, which also included David Rousset and Jorge Semprun—who, of course, were not yet famous. He mentions only the writer Benjamin Crémieux, who was Jewish.

Durand furthermore shows how the leaders of the French Resistance who belonged to the three convoys in January were able to be identified and kept at Buchenwald. Pineau, who was there under the false identity of Grimaux and knew too many secrets to disclose his real identity, allowed Colonel Manhès (whom he calls Manevy) a free hand. Courtaud[61] says in his memoirs that he met Manhès. He preferred to remain with his companions and ended up being sent in a transport not to Dora but to the Laura Kommando, which will be discussed in chapter 11.

The French prisoners at Buchenwald entered a new phase with the virtually simultaneous arrival of two trains in May 1944, the second of which had made a detour via Auschwitz. Among the prisoners was Marcel Paul, who managed to establish ties with the German communists and with the noncommunist leaders of the French Resistance.

In an article published in 1997 in the magazine *Le Serment,* Paul Le Goupil[62] was eager to specify the conditions under which the "transport" lists were drawn up and sometimes modified at Buchenwald. This topic, as will be seen later, generated serious debate after the war between German and Soviet communists. Le Goupil thought that Marcel Paul had played a positive role under delicate conditions. Le Goupil belonged to the "tattooed" convoy that went through Auschwitz on its way to Buchenwald in May 1944, along with Marcel Paul and the author's father, Louis Sellier, who was one of the noncommunist trade union activists (among them Christian Pineau) who had founded the Libé-Nord resistance movement.

Everything that has just been said concerns Frenchmen about whom information is available, even if it is confusing and does not rule out controversy. Regrettably, there is nothing comparable concerning the Czech, Polish, or Dutch prisoners.

At Dora itself no real ties between prisoners, outside of very small groups, were conceivable before June 1944, when a real camp finally came into existence. The French began having a certain amount of influence only when their numbers increased at the *Revier* and two Frenchmen arrived in the Arbeitsstatistik. Young prisoners working in the tunnel, Claude Lauth and Pierre Hémery, had contacts in the camp. Lauth was a comrade of Jean Michel, who had been at the *Revier* a long time. Hémery became friends with Marcel Petit. He worked in the Ko Scherer, in Hall 28, where the French members of the Bünemann Kommando also worked.

The French community at Dora did not begin to become organized until the arrival of personalities such as Dejussieu-Pontcarral, Bollaert, and Debeaumarché with the convoy of "77,000"s. Birin in particular was able to keep them in positions in the Dora camp or in the tunnel when most of their companions were transferred to Ellrich. The scope of this development should not be exaggerated. The author himself was vaguely aware of it through Hémery, who was one of his work mates. As Richet notes, however, there was so little contact among prisoner groups that such information, which was necessarily highly confidential, did not get around.

POLICE CONTROL. It should be added that Dora was not only a concentration camp but was located in the heart of the *Mittelraum,* which was kept under tight police control. Control was exercised first on the Germans themselves, both civilians and military. One civilian named Victor worked with prisoner Marcel Baillon[63] in the tunnel tooling workshop. On one occasion he went into the camp without an authorization to do a repair job. When he went home to Erfurt on permission, he talked about the camp to his wife and daughter, who did not hold their tongues. He was arrested, tried, and hanged. Baillon had confirmation on this from his widow after the war.

Two SS men, overcome with drink in a Nordhausen cabaret, threatened to send the boss, who was trying to calm them down, to the Dora camp to teach him a lesson about life. They were tried and shot. The officers who made up the court martial were then asked to a reception given by the camp commander, who had Gypsy prisoners brought in to play music. Pierre Rozan witnessed the scene, which Michel has recounted.[64]

Two prisoners were convinced that there were other SS executions. Chamboissier[65] recalls: "One morning, in the bottom of the hole, we found a sort of smooth tree trunk, stuck in the ground, which turned out to be an execution post, for it was bullet-ridden (I tried in vain to extract one), blood-stained and a rather heavy rope was lying at its foot. As soon as we arrived, we were told to remove the post."

Maurice Gérard[66] recounts: "I remember seeing an SS transporting the body of a comrade who had just been shot. [. . .] It was not yet mid-September 1944. The weather was still very warm and the SS man who was pushing the wheelbarrow in which the bloody body lay was completely white."

Numerous testimonies from Dora as well as the other camps mention prisoners being hanged in public following a well-known, unvarying ritual. According to information contained in the Wincenty Hein report,[67] there were forty-nine executions during the year 1944. The victims seem to have been Germans (apparently not executed in public), Poles, and Russians. No French prisoners were executed. The massive numbers of executions at Dora, particularly in the tunnel, did not take place until the early months of 1945, a topic that will be discussed in part 5.

ESCAPES AND THE BUNKER. A few prisoners managed to escape, and there is an account of five Frenchmen who were caught. Gaston Pernot[68] escaped on March 15 with three comrades by hiding in a freight car. They were caught in the region of Fulda and brought back to Dora on April 21. On March 16, Luc Clairin[69] escaped, again in a wagon train with three comrades. They did not get beyond Halle and were back in Dora by March 26. On July 1, Pierre Jacquin[70] tried to escape from an exterior Kommando, under the authority of Wieda, with André Moutel, but he was soon caught and Moutel a bit later. On July 8, Auguste Henner[71] escaped (he does not say how); he was arrested two days later in the region of Kassel. On July 27, Roger Couëtdic[72] took off from the Nüxei work site and was finally caught on the 29th near Rhumspringe. He was taken to Duderstadt, then to Erfurt, and then to Dora after more than two weeks.

Upon their return, they were locked up in the bunker and thoroughly beaten up, to the point where Henner's jaw was broken. The length of the investigation and the number of execution threats were proportionate to how long the prisoners had been gone and how far away they had managed to get. Ultimately all these prisoners found themselves in the Schachtkommando wearing a *Fluchtpunkt,* "a white cloth circle, with a red dot in the middle, that we had to sew beneath our identity number, in the middle of the back and on the right pant leg."

The most accurate description of the bunker comes from Jacquin. Originally it was merely a room in a shed at the camp entrance, adjacent to the SS command post. The final bunker, which opened at the end of July, "was a permanent one-floor building, containing some thirty cells divided into two wings separated by the entrance door and the SS guard post. The building was surrounded by a high wall with a door that was opened by remote control from the SS guard post. Cell number 7 where I was put measured about six square feet. Inside, there were boards which served as a seat and a latrine. A mesh-covered window, twelve by fifteen inches wide, opened onto the outer wall door. It had wooden shutters that could only be operated from the outside."

THE SCHACHTKOMMANDO. All the escapees from all the camps in the region were assigned to the Schachtkommando, among them Stéphane Hessel and Robert Lemoine, who escaped from Rottleberode, which will be discussed in chapter 13. The prisoners were of every ethnic origin, with more Russians and Poles than Western Europeans such as Frenchmen, Czechs, Belgians, and Yugoslavians. They were housed in Block 135 in the upper part of the camp. Couëtdic describes at length life in the "SK II" to which he belonged from October 13, 1944, to early April 1945.

The Kommando's work was not part of the Arbeitsstatistik agenda. It was performed outdoors and included various excavation and unloading tasks in the camp. One of them involved building pyres, whose importance will be discussed later on, which were needed to eliminate corpses upon the arrival of the evacuation transports from Auschwitz and Gross Rosen. Special tasks were often requested by block chiefs who knew the SK II *Kapo* and the *Vorarbeiter,* particularly the supplying of wood. Henner and Couëtdic thus became the suppliers of the whorehouse where they were fed a floury soup.

Life outside the camp was very hard due to the mud and cold. Couëtdic comments, however: "The Fluchtpunkt did not lose a single one of their sick patients during those harsh winter weeks." That was the period when the mortality rate shot up so terribly at Ellrich. But the constraints were far more constant and negligence was widespread, as will be described later.

THE "PLOT." Until November 1944, life inside Dora appeared rather humdrum. Starting in November, on the contrary, there were more arrests, affecting Czechs, Frenchmen, Russians, and Red Germans. It is not easy to provide a consistent account of these events because the relationship among the events themselves is not always clear-cut. No doubt the story should begin with the French and the Czechs on the basis of four documents: Marcel Petit's account, which was quoted at length in Durand's book, Birin's account, Jean Michel's book, and Langbein's statement concerning Cespiva.

The fundamental problem raised at Dora, undoubtedly more than elsewhere, obviously concerned the attitude of the SS as the Allied troops neared the camp. Would they try and exterminate the prisoners? How could the prisoners cope with such a situation? How could it be avoided? Birin[73] has summarized the predicament in this way: "As Geheimnisträger (carriers of V1 and V2 secrets), we knew we would be sentenced to death and executed when the Allies drew near. One SS gave us a brutal warning, in confidence: 'If things should go wrong for us, none of you will come out alive.' [...] Perhaps the time had come to try and devise a plan to save ourselves from the massacre. If we had to die [...] should we let them cut our throats without reacting?" That was the logic Birin claims to have expressed "around mid-October 1944" to his young comrade from the Arbeitsstatistik, the Russian Nicholaï Petrenko, when he asked him to recruit reliable comrades.

Petit[74] gives a somewhat different description when he recounts his conversations with Cespiva, who came to see him at the "Labor" *Revier* set up in Block 16. His account is quite vehement and worth quoting, despite its length, in view of later developments. "Thus, I learned from Cespiva, in bits and pieces, that the matter was already well under way. Nicholaï from the Arbeitsstatistik would answer for the Russians, and he would do so for the Czechs. As for the French, I was to continue on the path I had taken. He did not want to know anyone else. In the event of a serious setback, it would be easier to defend ourselves. The goal was to preserve ties of solidarity between the best members of each nationality, organize small groups familiar with the use of automatic weapons, with practice in explosives, able to group themselves together upon call at a location designated by the chief. [. . .]

"Next, we might have to take the initiative. No weapons yet, but that would come. The locations of SS munitions dumps and the tank in front of the Tunnel had already been noted; they would be the first objective, the hardest part would be to get started. Two Russian volunteers—those people were not bothered by metaphysical questions—would be in charge of battering a Posten (a sentinel) to death by surprise. With a uniform and weapons, it would be possible to approach an officer and grab whatever he had, naturally not without risk. There was not a single sentinel up on a watchtower who would not rush to carry out the orders of an officer in uniform.

"The specialists were in charge of short-circuiting the electric current in the fences. Finally, we were in contact with anti-Nazi civilians who would get hold of a munitions dump near Nordhausen and join us. There was a war treasure in civilian marks."

In his account, Birin talks of a "plot." The word seems rather weak to describe the plan put together by Cespiva, according to Petit. The same Petit, according to Michel, explained that it was necessary to note exactly which tools would be required to cut down trees. At the chosen moment, the cut trees would crush the barbed wire in their fall. After 1945, works published in Czechoslovakia, East Germany, and Poland gave more scope to the uprising planned for December 24, 1944. "The rebels proposed, after massacring the SS at the garrison in Dora, to come and liberate Buchenwald. Then, by tens of thousands, the prisoners were supposed to go to Czechoslovakia to join the Soviet partisans." The altogether extraordinary excesses of such a plan widely contributed to dismissing, after the fact, the already rather mad schemes of the 1944 plotters.

At the Essen trial there was a great deal of speculation about the reality of the transmitter built at the *Revier* by the Czech Jan Chaloupka (or Halupka), a radio mechanic, who had already assembled a receiver. Langbein[75] says: "We don't know whether or not the radio was used before its components, along with those of the receiver, had to be destroyed in the crematorium. The German court, which questioned the witnesses it was able to contact on this point in Essen in 1968, concluded that it was impossible to get to the bottom of the question concerning the existence and operation of a transmitter."

When recapitulating the statements it can be noted that Cespiva knew Nicholaï from the beginning, whereas Birin said he contacted him much later. Jean Michel[76] on the other hand claims that he came in contact with Cespiva through Cimek, without telling him that he already knew Petrenko. Whatever the case may have been, and lacking any way of establishing the order in which they met, there was indeed a network of "plotters" comprising Czechs and Frenchmen from the *Revier* as well as a Frenchman and a Russian from the Arbeitsstatistik.

In addition to Cespiva, the Czechs at the *Revier* included the dentist Otto Cimek and Jan Halupka, the radio mechanic. Among the Frenchmen at the *Revier,* the one with the most seniority was Jean Michel, and the others included Petit, Poupault, and his friend André Boyer (his network chief), who was hired as a *Kalfaktor* (waiter). Birin had his own connections, particularly from Épernay, such as Paul Chandon-Moët, whom he knew well enough to entrust him with keeping hosts. The names of Petrenko's accomplices are not known.

THE ARRESTS. The existence of the plot, if not its strength, was known to the SD since most of the plotters mentioned were arrested at the same time during the night of November 3 and 4. The informer could only have been a certain Grozdoff, who appeared as chief of Block 15 when Cogny was *Schreiber* there. Perhaps careless words were spoken in the first block, whose *Blockältester* was French and seemed trustworthy. Perhaps Grozdoff had staged a provocation.

Another informer took simultaneous action in another area. This was a Frenchman named Maurice Naegelé, who became tunnel *Kapo* overseeing the manufacture of V1s and who deceived Debeaumarché and Lauth. Lauth, who had begun committing acts of sabotage, was arrested as early as October 20 (or 28?), and on November 4, Debeaumarché and Colonel Gentil, who were also working on V1s, were in turn arrested with the others. As will be seen, Grozdoff was a very mysterious character, which was not true of Naegelé, who was an agent of the Gestapo in France before he was caught for embezzlement and deported. At Dora he went back to work for the Gestapo. As he had experience with the French Resistance, he was able to gain the trust of Debeaumarché.

The outcome of this affair will be described in part 5, with an approximate indication of the identity of the prisoners involved. A few comments are not out of order here, however. The first concerns the lack of precise information concerning the grounds for making arrests. Some of the leaders who were heavily involved, like Petit, were forgotten, but Petit had been especially prudent. Puppo was arrested at the same time as Poupault, just in case. The second comment concerns the officers who were not arrested, i.e., neither Dejussieu, nor Cogny (even though he was *Schreiber* of Block 15 at the time), nor Leroy, nor Cazin d'Honincthun. The action was not directed at them. The third remark concerns the absence of Belgians, who, incidentally, were very few in number at Dora itself. Joseph Woussen[77] has explained this quite clearly. He was contracted by the Russians and the French. "In fact, the General refused to embark on this adventure, because he suspected there were informers, thought that the conspirators did not have any weapons, and above all, considered their plans unnecessarily foolhardy. The tragic outcome of the matter confirmed, as it turned out, some of his fears."

Surprisingly, the outcome was not tragic either for the Czechs or for the French, but it was dreadful for the Russians and for the communist leaders at Dora. Pröll committed suicide before they could arrest him. Kuntz died on January 25 (or 23?), 1945, in the hands of the Gestapo. The others, who were arrested one after another, were almost all executed on April 4, 1945.

These events will be discussed again. It has never been possible to establish a link between the French-Czech affair and the elimination of the German communists. No doubt the history of the Resistance at Dora cannot really be understood by mixing up stories that took place at different levels.

MEANWHILE, AT PEENEMÜNDE. As has already been noted in chapter 4, the Buchenwald prisoners who had been transferred to Karlshagen (i.e, Peenemünde) in June and July 1943 came back to Buchenwald in October and were quickly assigned to Dora. Contrary to what is generally assumed, prisoners still remained at Peenemünde. In fact, the Karlshagen camp was immediately reconstructed, and was to be evacuated only in March 1945 to Ellrich. It appears that the first prisoners concerned, especially the German Greens, Russians, and Poles, came from Sachsenhausen.

They were joined in mid-November 1943 by prisoners from a convoy train from Struthof, which arrived directly at Karlshagen from Schirmeck. One of them was Roger Predi,[78] who was incarcerated at the central prison of Metz while awaiting trial. Similarly, within two weeks 350 prisoners found themselves on the island of Usedom. They occupied the last of the four blocks of a camp which would ultimately contain five. Predi says there were various Kommandos. Some prisoners worked in mechanics workshops or at boilermaking, including on V2s, the "cigars."

Others were put on work sites to repair buildings or extend the airfield. Others unloaded boats. Some could therefore be found both at Peenemünde West, under the Luftwaffe, and in Peenemünde East, where von Braun continued to run his development unit.

A group of 500 prisoners was sent from Sachsenhausen to Karlshagen on October 17, 1944. Among them were 150 Frenchmen, 4 of whom have written up eyewitness accounts. Three of them had arrived directly from France only a short time earlier: Jean Duale,[79] Pierre Pinault,[80] and Pierre Pujol.[81] The other,

Jean Fournier,[82] was in the "Loos train" (a prison near Lille). Sent from Tourcoing on August 31, just before the Allies arrived, he made a detour by Utrecht and Groningen before finding himself in Cologne, then Magdeburg, and finally arriving in Sachsenhausen. The newcomers were all employed in outside Kommandos and suffered considerably from the cold, especially due to the wind. The mortality rate was high.

Each account recalls an unusual event that occurred on February 8, 1945. A Kommando of ten Russians was put in charge of camouflaging planes. On the aforementioned day they attacked two members of the crew of a Heinkel 111 that had just landed, killed one of them, and forced the other to go back on board along with them. One of the Russians, a certain Deviataev, was a lieutenant pilot who managed to take off. He landed near Warsaw after escaping German fighter planes and was lucky enough to avoid being shot down by his compatriots. To everyone's surprise, the camp was not punished after this adventure. Deviataev became a "hero of the Soviet Union."

FROM ONE HELL TO ANOTHER. Chapters 9 and 10 have recounted the ordinary operation of a concentration camp closely connected to a secret weapons factory in the Reich in 1944, covering the period from May to December. In May, German troops still dominated Europe, from Hendaye to Vitebsk and from the North Pole to Greece. By the end of December the Americans were in Aachen and the Soviets at the gates of East Prussia, and a German army was under siege in Budapest. The downfall of Nazi Germany was near.

The Dora prisoners who survived the hellish conditions of the early months, thanks to this period of relative respite, were to be sorely tried during the first three months of 1945 and again during the evacuation. Parts 5 and 6 of the book will be devoted to those periods. Part 4, which follows under the title "Renewed Hell," recounts what took place in 1944–45 on the work sites and in the open camps in the area surrounding Dora, at Wieda, Blankenburg, and Harzungen, and above all at Ellrich.

PART FOUR

Renewed Hell

[[11   ]]

KAMMLER'S NEW WORK SITES

In the spring of 1944, Kammler, who had just finished the underground construction for the rocket-building program, both in the Dora Tunnel and at Lehesten and Redl-Zipf, embarked upon new underground and surface work sites, making use of an abundant concentration camp labor force. These work sites opened throughout what was then the territory of the Reich except on the north German plain. Some were located in the area around the Harz Mountains, particularly in the Dora area.

The largest work sites were placed under the control of a new SS operation known as the Sonderstab Kammler. Elsewhere it provided prisoners for work being done for the Todt Organization. It also used *Baubrigaden* made up of prisoners, directly administered by WVHA departments in Oranienburg.

In any case it was these departments that decided on the use of the newly arrived prisoners and on the redeployment of a portion of veteran prisoners. All that remained for the big camps' Arbeitsstatistik offices to do was to draw up lists for the "transports" to the exterior Kommandos, forced upon them by Oranienburg. Kammler ran no risk of difficulty on that front either, given that he was himself the head of Department C of the WVHA. His powers were thus very extensive.

The structure that came progressively into place was thus made up of two networks: that of the work sites and that of the camps. The network of work sites depended on the work to be done: digging tunnel galleries or building railways, roads, bridges, and so on. These work sites were thus more or less mobile. The camp network was partially distinct from that of the work sites in that the same camp could provide prisoners for several different work sites, and the same work site could use prisoners from different camps—as shall be seen with regard to Mittelbau as a whole.

To house the prisoners, existing buildings were sometimes used—industrial or farm buildings, more or less adapted for the purpose. New barracks were also built, in some cases added on to existing structures, in others making up entire camps. The prisoners' fate varied considerably depending both on housing conditions and on conditions of getting from the camps to the work sites. One last characteristic of the new setup was the extensive mobility of many of the prisoners. The individual "trajectories" of some of them, as will be seen further along, were quite complicated.

The three chapters of this particularly dramatic fourth section seek to make a complex situation more intelligible. However, only that overall group that ended up being known as Mittelbau—along with several other neighboring Kommandos—will be dealt with in a thoroughgoing fashion. Similar indications could have been given for other areas of the Reich.

Aside from more general characteristics, this chapter deals above all with the Helmetalbahn railway work site, the corresponding Wieda and Ellrich-Theater camps, along with their Kommandos. Chapter 12 is devoted to the Ellrich and Harzungen camps and those work sites known as B 3, B 11, B 12, B 13, and B 17. Chapter 13 brings together a variety of data on Rottleberode, Blankenburg, Langenstein, and various other camps in the Harz area.

The Sonderstab Kammler and Its Work Sites

THE SONDERSTAB KAMMLER'S ORGANIZATION. As was shown in chapter 7, the Sonderstab Kammler was created in March 1944 when, on Hitler's instructions, Göring put Kammler in charge of getting the aeronautical industry set up underground. This special staff—which is the translation of *Sonderstab*—was divided in terms of geography into four *Sonderinspektionen*.[1]

Sonderinspektion I was based in Porta Westfalica, near Minden, in the north of Westphalia, on the border of Lower Saxony. In principle, Sonderinspektion II's headquarters was in Halle, on the Saale, but was actually in Bischofferode, near Woffleben.[2] This location will be discussed in the next chapter. Sonderinspektion III had its headquarters in Bad Wimpfen on the Neckar River near Heilbronn. Sonderinspektion IV's headquarters was ostensibly in Vienna, for the work sites located in Austria. Which of the known Kommandos were actually concerned by each of these inspectorates will be examined later.

Each of these inspectorates was in charge of a certain number of projects. A *Führungsstab*—or management team—was at the head of each project. All the projects were coded by a letter, A, B, or S, followed by a number. The letter A seems to have been applied to the modification of existing underground structures, including caves, mines, or railway tunnels: thus, A 5 designates the *Heimkehle* cave at Rottleberode. The letter B apparently concerned underground structures that were to be dug—such as B 3, B 11, and B 12, which will be mentioned. The letter S seems to have been reserved for special work sites, S III designating, for instance, the command post built for Hitler at Ohrdruf.

Emphasis was laid in chapter 4 on the systematization of coding that distinguished codes based upon mineral names from those based upon animal names, both of which were used by Speer's services. The mineral code names apparently referred to underground installations; in addition to *Zement* and *Schlier,* mentioned above, there were also, for instance, *Kaolin* for B 12, *Zinnstein* (cassiterite) for B 11, *Malachit* for the Langenstein work site, and *Porphyr* and *Turmalin* for the work sites at Blankenburg. The animal names refer more to programs, such as *Kitz* (kid) for Peenemünde, or *Kuckuck* (cuckoo), *Eber* (boar), *Schildkröte* (tortoise) for the subsequent work done by B 11, or *Reh* (deer) for Neu Stassfurt and *Gazelle* (also a German word) for Weferlingen. Chronologically, the last of these programs seems to have been *Kalb* (calf) for the restructuring of a salt mine at Springen, in Thuringia, on the Hesse border. Marcel Colignon arrived there in January 1945 with a Kommando coming from Buchenwald.[3]

To these sites and programs correspond—or do not correspond as the case may be—camps that are themselves designated by codes. The danger of using such indications without adequate precaution is to overlook the fact that many of them, in one way or another, had more than one use. Caution will thus be shown in this regard in the following chapters.

LOCATIONS OF THE WORK SITES. One finds a certain number of underground installations in the foothill region in the north of the Harz Mountains, especially to the east of Helmstedt. These correspond to the code A 3, because they had to do with transforming old mines. They were dependent on Porta Westfalica, where the A 2 work site was also to be found. The corresponding Kommandos, created by Buchenwald, were subsequently linked to Neuengamme.

Other work sites were situated to the east of the Harz Mountains, first Langenstein (B 2), then Neu Stassfurt and Wansleben, whose Kommandos remained linked to Buchenwald. By way of exception, the Blankenburg work site was operated by the Todt Organization. The Heimkehle work site, to the east of Nordhausen, given the code A 5, was dependent on Porta Westfalica, as was Stempeda (B 4); the neighboring Kommando of Rottleberode was transferred in late 1944 from Buchenwald to Mittelbau. But the *Mittelraum's* largest group was at the Kohnstein and Himmelberg work sites, which will later be examined in greater detail.

More to the south, two large Kommandos dependent on the Flossenbürg camp provided manpower for work sites B 5 (at Leitmeritz, in the Sudetenland) and B 7 (at Hersbruck, in Franconia). The Leitmeritz work site depended on Porta Westfalica. The corresponding camp will come up again in the chapters dealing with evacuations. The Kommandos in the Neckar valley, dependent on the Struthof camp, supplied those work sites dependent on the Bad Wimpfen inspectorate. The Kommandos of the B 8 work sites, in Linz, and the B 9 work sites, in Melk, in Austria, were Mauthausen-based Kommandos as were those in Gusen and Ebensee.

In late 1944 there was an S III work site at Ohrdruf on a military site in Thuringia building a command post for Hitler. That Kommando was dependent on Buchenwald.

THE NEW WORK SITES AT KOHNSTEIN AND HIMMELBERG. The existence of the Dora Tunnel, capable of sheltering three large factories, clearly shows the interest in using the layer of anhydrite located to the south of the Harz Mountains for digging out new underground spaces. The layer was thick and regular, the rock required no retaining structure, and the tunnels could emerge straight onto the nearby plains and easily be hooked up to the railway network. The Zorge River had cleared a wide valley from Woffleben to Niedersachswerfen through the bed of anhydrite, separating Kohnstein in the south from Himmelberg and Mühlberg to the north. Three of the principal projects of Kammler's[4] Sonderinspektion II were located in this context: B 3, B 11, and B 12.

Project B 12, alias *Kaolin*, had to do with digging out the Kohnstein to the west of the Dora Tunnel starting at Woffleben. It was a large-scale project in that the overall usable surface was to be some 1.73 million square feet, as opposed to 1.325 million for the Dora Tunnel. The blueprints show several tunnels, C, D, E, and F, running parallel to tunnels A and B and joined together by halls. The south end of the envisaged underground complex was to be situated (but without any way out) underneath the hill located to the north of the Dora camp, by the crematorium. It seems that the purpose of this complex was to house two aircraft factories.

Project B 11, alias *Zinnstein*, was also located beneath the Kohnstein, to the east of the Dora Tunnel on the Niedersachswerfen side. It was there that the open-pit mine was located (still being exploited some fifty years later) as well as the entrance to the two galleries whose other ends opened into tunnel A: the *Notstollen* to the north at the level of Hall 17 and the *Grenzstollen* to the south at the level of Hall 43. The blueprint is a diamond-shaped plan, between these two galleries, with a usable surface of 860,000 square feet. Responsibility for carrying out the work was given primarily to the Ammoniakwerk Merseburg company, the subsidiary of IG Farben supplying the Leuna factory, former partner of the WIFO. It continued to use anhydrite for its needs. Three factories were subsequently planned on the site: *Kuckuck* was to produce fuels, *Eber* liquid oxygen, and *Schildkröte* was to be an aircraft factory. As will be seen further on, a B 17 project also existed further to the west, associated with B 11.

The B 3 project—alias *Anhydrit*—concerned the west part of the Himmelberg toward Bischofferode. It had a diamond-shaped layout with twenty-eight east-west tunnels hooked together by perpendicular halls. It was more irregular to the south because of the shape of the hill. The planned usable surface was 1.4 million square feet and the factory—known as *Hydra*—was to have been an aircraft factory. This work site was generally known as project B 3a, in that there had also been a project B 3b, which was abandoned in favor of Ohrdruf. It was located further to the east, toward Appenrode.

Finishing all these work sites meant establishing major rail and other links, which led to an upheaval on the Zorge plain because of the multitude of earthworks underway. The plain was moreover cluttered with stockpiles, such as the Mittelwerk's *Freilager* in Niedersachswerfen, mentioned above. The civilian workers—whether German or foreign—from the neighboring factories and work sites such as the Junkers Nordwerk also had to be housed. A camp was built for them at Woffleben. It was even envisaged to move the inhabitants out of the village. The execution of all these infrastructures was sometimes referred to as project B 13. It was apparently because of superstition that the number 13 was not given to any underground project.

The next chapter is entirely devoted to the life of the prisoners on these work sites and in the corresponding camps.

PASSING THROUGH THE LAURA CAMP. It is not possible to speak of Dora and the attached Kommandos without making some reference to the Laura camp. Indeed, three of the principal witnesses, Aimé Bonifas, Jacques Courtaud, and Jean-Henry Tauzin, passed through this camp after their quarantine period at Buchenwald before getting to Ellrich or Wieda. But contrary to what is often held—and has sometimes been written—the Laura camp never depended on Dora. It was and remained until the end a Buchenwald Kommando.

As noted in chapter 4, after the bombing of Peenemünde the decision was made to scatter the sites involved in V2 production. At the same time the Kohnstein Tunnel was being adapted for assembly, propulsion-system test centers were being installed both at Lehesten, in a slate quarry in the south of Thuringia, and in Redl-Zipf, in Upper Austria. The camp set up near Lehesten for prisoners sent from Buchenwald was given the name Laura at the same time the camp near Kohnstein was named Dora.

Aimé Bonifas,[5] whose identity number was 20801, arrived there on October 1, 1943, with the second transport. The housing was "an immense hangar full of drafts" with a rudimentary *Revier* in "a kind of low cellar." There were the same nationalities as at Dora, including the Italian prisoners of war, who soon fell victim to the Ukrainians. Within a couple of weeks the camp came to hold a thousand prisoners. On November 1 it was installed in three blocks set up in farm buildings and outfitted with an electric fence.

The work site was very harsh. The prisoners had to dig the underground galleries, which made up a "veritable molehill," and construct outside access points, including a railway link. It was bitterly cold, "a terrible winter." There were many sick, the *Revier* was overrun, and a *Schonung* was set up in conditions similar to those at Dora. "Twice a week, a truck packed the cadavers away to the crematory oven at Buchenwald."

When the digging was finished the machines were installed. "The beginning of spring coincided with the end of the terrible period at Laura." The mortality rate dropped quickly, but on May 26 a transport of sick prisoners left for Bergen-Belsen. Bonifas and several French and Belgian friends were in Block 2—the best one—with a block leader who was a German communist for whom Bonifas had "profound esteem." The rest of the supervision, including the position of *Lagerältester,* was in the hands of Greens.

Jean-Henry Tauzin,[6] part of the first convoy of 1944, left Buchenwald for Laura on March 28 (or 24?) along with René André,[7] Jacques Courtaud,[8] and his friends Olaf, Poussin, and Lefauve, who were in the third convoy. They remained there until May 9. The work was often very hard, in particular the loading and transport of iron bars, camouflage nets, cement, and sand, with Kommandos working round the clock.

On the other hand, Tauzin and Courtaud found that camp life was tolerable because roll call was brief, the blocks were clean, there were weekly hot showers, and care packages arrived intact. There was a—fairly impoverished—canteen and even a movie theater: Bonifas points out that on Sundays the SS would sometimes chase the prisoners out and pack into the theater themselves.

Bonifas explains the purpose of the Lehesten factory: "The underground factory was finished after a work project on a gigantic scale. It was used for fine tuning and as a test stand for the V2's propulsion device. [. . .] The compressor rooms were used to produce liquid oxygen. The device's ignition took place in the two blockhouse-shaped test stands overlooking the quarry's enormous theater. [. . .] Every day, twenty-five or thirty tests were carried out. Each time, the siren would sound the alert and everyone had to run for cover. The effect it produced was just incredible; out of these blockhouses there would come a roar and a 160-foot-high column of fire would shoot out, which would send all the stones flying with an infernal racket." Bonifas adds that many of the tests backfired.[9] Tauzin gives an identical description of the explosion, without knowing what it was, putting forth the hypothesis of tests on underwater mines (though why underwater he doesn't say). At the time Courtaud also believed them to be mines.

Tauzin and André as well as Courtaud and his friends left Laura on May 9 and ended up at Ellrich, as did Pierre Inchauspé,[10] who arrived with Bonifas. Bonifas left Laura on August 31, 1944, and ended up at Wieda, as did Georges Jougier, who arrived with Tauzin. Many others remained at Laura; they would be evacuated by train in the direction of Dachau in April 1945.

The Helmetalbahn Work Site and the Wieda and Ellrich Baubrigaden

THE HELMETALBAHN WORK SITE. A whole series of railway branch lines— both those that already existed, such as the Dora line to the south of the Kohnstein or the Nordwerk line to the north, or those that were just being put in for the future factories at Kohnstein and Himmelberg—hooked into one and the same line that ran through the Zorge valley from Herzberg, through a tunnel between Walkenried and Ellrich, all the way to Nordhausen via Woffleben and Niedersachswerfen. In order to reserve the line for industrial traffic and personnel transports, long-distance trains were to be routed along a new line between Herzberg and Nordhausen to be built farther to the south. It was a project of long standing for which plans already existed. Because part of the route ran from west to east through the valley of the Helme—a tributary of the Zorge—the planned line was known as the Helmetalbahn, or Helme valley line. It was to go through the towns of Osterhagen, Nüxei, Mackenrode, and Günzerode before reaching Nordhausen station by means of several civil engineering structures.[11]

THE SS-BAUBRIGADEN AND THE EARLY DAYS AT WIEDA. In order to build the Helmetalbahn, it was decided in 1944 to call upon SS-Baubrigaden. These construction brigades were special Kommandos of prisoners used for building roads and railways. They were used in particular in the north of France. But they were also deployed in German cities that had been bombed, and the two brigades that were brought into the *Mittelraum* were BB 3—then based in Duisburg and Cologne—and BB 4, based in Wuppertal. They arrived in May.[12]

BB 3 set up in Wieda, a village located in a valley in the south of the Harz Mountains, while BB 4 set up in Ellrich itself, in the buildings of the Bürgergarten Restaurant in the Spiegelgasse—which came to be known as Ellrich-Theater, or the "little camp," as opposed to Ellrich-Station, or the "big camp," which will be discussed in the next chapter.

The prisoners who arrived on May 11 in Wieda, followed by the camp equipment, were Russians and Poles under the supervision of Germans. On June 6 these prisoners of long standing were joined by French prisoners who arrived by train from Buchenwald at the Walkenried station. They belonged to the convoy that had left Compiègne on May 12, 1944, and their identity numbers ran from the "49,000"s to the "53,000"s. Among them were Jacques-Christian Bailly, who wrote a detailed account of this period, Paul Chandon-Moët, René Cogny, Roger Couëtdic, Raoul Giquel, Bernard Girardin, Roger Jourdain, André Laroche, Maurice Leteuil, Marc Maire, Max Oesch, Jean de Sesmaisons, Louis Vallier, and Jean Voisin.

Bailly[13] notes that the camp commander greeted them in French with a surprising speech, informing them of the landing and asking them simply to remain calm. The camp was comprised of farm buildings with a courtyard, all of which was surrounded by simple wire mesh. Barracks were adjoined to the camp for the troops, made up principally of soldiers from the Luftwaffe. As Bailly continues:

"German prisoners left the camp to go to the village unescorted. Certain SS men chatted with the Polish prisoners. Everything seemed strange in this Kommando—so different from the Buchenwald camp. Rumors spread. The former prisoners from Wieda came back from Cologne where they had taken part in the cleanup work in the bombed-out city. In the ruins, they had discovered the riches which the SS had expropriated for themselves. An agreement had been concluded: war booty for the wardens, lives spared until the end of the fighting for the prisoners." On Sunday afternoons, villagers who were out walking came to see the prisoners behind their fence. The Russians would dance to the sound of the harmonica of a prisoner named Ivan, and the villagers would toss them cigarettes. In June 1963 a woman from Wieda, Emilie Denecke, gave Manfred Bornemann[14] the following—and perhaps somewhat embellished—account:

"The sentries belonged to the air force. They treated the prisoners decently and we even had the impression that the prisoners were not subjected to the sort of abuse which was often talked about. The relations between the troops and the prisoners struck us as being fairly good at Wieda. [. . .] An example comes to my mind to illustrate this feeling: it happened that the soldiers would play football against the prisoners, on the Wieda sporting club's field. After the match, the prisoners, accompanied by the soldiers, would come through the village singing, followed by the children and the inhabitants. [. . .] The camp's existence and the sight of prisoners dressed in black-and-white stripes was initially very unusual for the villagers, and the camp was something of a pole of attraction. It sometimes resembled a veritable fairground. The prisoners, after work, grouped together in the roll-call area and played music."

The newly arrived were first of all put to work helping the village peasants with hay-making. The French were asked to sing the *Madelon* as they went along. Then they were sent in Kommandos to Osterhagen, Nüxei, and Mackenrode for clearing and deforestation work along the route of the future railway. Provisional camps had to be set up along the way. In 1972 a Nüxei farmer, Wilhelm Walter, told how an enormous barn had been requisitioned from him in which an entire level was added by laying floorboards. The problem quickly became one of water supply, as is confirmed by Sesmaisons's diary.[15] In Osterhagen, Bailly refers to an isolated barracks out in the country where there was only a single tap with ice-cold water.

Wieda remained the central camp from where the daily food supplies were sent out to the three Kommandos. It also housed a rudimentary *Revier.* A certain laxity prevailed, as Walter suggests: "From time to time, the German prisoners obtained permission to go have a drink in the village café. [. . .] On Sundays, the prisoners helped me clean up, cut wood, or put up a new chicken coop. I had them served a hot lunch as recompense for their work."[16] Through the camp, the farmer got hold of various items such as nails.

This situation could not go on forever. One morning in July, Bailly, who was at Wieda, heard gunfire. He gives the following account: "A group of prisoners were assembled at the barn entrance. [. . .] Through the door, I saw helmeted SS, arms in hand, going into the courtyard. The SS commander came out of his office, pale, bare-headed, his face worn, and his uniform undone. An SS man, a defiant smile on his lips, was pushing him with violent shoves in the back, a revolver pointed between his shoulders. They left the camp and got into a black Volkswagen which sped off with a squeal of its tires. [. . .] When they arrived, the SS (sent from Buchenwald) had found the camp open, German prisoners unsupervised in the village, and the commander asleep in his office."

The very next day, in Wieda and in the Kommandos, everyone—both wardens and prisoners—had to leave. The prisoners reached the Dora camp on foot. It is not known what became of the wardens and prisoners who made up the Wieda administration. It seems that in the end the consequences were not too serious for them. The French prisoners were spread out between the various Kommandos. Most of them remained assigned to Dora, especially to the tunnel. Others were subsequently sent to Harzungen (such as Sesmaisons), Ellrich (such as Oesch), or Kleinbodungen (such as Giquel and Voisin). On July 30 a thousand prisoners from Dora, some of whom had been there several months already, such as Lucien Colonel, Alain de Lapoyade, Marcel Patte, and Bernard Perrot or the Dutchman Van Dijk were sent to replace them at Wieda and in the Kommandos. They were joined by others, including Bonifas, Ego, and Jougier coming from Laura. The Wieda incident thus changed the destiny of a great many prisoners—for better or for worse.

A quote from Rassinier[17] gives some idea of how the events can be quickly "doctored up" by hearsay: "I had seen next to me [in the *Revier*] a prisoner who had spent a month at Wieda and who had told me that the camp's 1500 occupants were not too badly off. Of course, there was work and not much to eat, but it was a family-style life: on Sunday afternoons, the villagers would come dance at the edge of the camp to the prisoners' accordions, exchange a few friendly words with them, and even bring them things to eat. It seems that it didn't last, that the SS got word of what was going on and that within two months Wieda had become as harsh and inhuman as Dora."

THE BAUBRIGADE 3 KOMMANDOS IN OSTERHAGEN, NÜXEI, AND MACKENRODE. By the summer of 1944 the preliminary clearing and deforestation work was finished, and leveling and filling-in work got under way—without the adequate equipment. The fate of the prisoners on the work sites worsened with the coming of the rains in late September.

Bonifas,[18] at Mackenrode at the time, observed: "The camp organization was always extremely precarious and, with the coming of the bad weather, a life of misery began once again. We had to go out in the morning for roll-call in the driving rain, head off to work in the rain, work twelve hours outside in the rain, and return to camp soaked to the skin. Our poor clothes were heavily soaked with water, and we had nothing to change into and not even the slightest fire to dry ourselves out. Fortunately, we had a blanket for every two persons for sleeping, which enabled me to get partially undressed. But just try and imagine the moment when the blow of the whistle rustles you out of bed before dawn when you have to put that wet poultice back on. [. . .] The camp turned into a swamp, and roll-call, where we wallowed up to our calves in the sticky clay, was a dreaded chore. [. . .]

"The filth invaded us. [. . .] Our clothes, in a pitiful state from working in the forest, had not been replaced. No change of clothes was to be found in the camp. For three months, we had been wearing the same shirt, without a sweater or a coat. The snow flurries pierced right through us. The water was so cold that even the bravest could no longer wash themselves. Vermin appeared and we scratched ourselves raw. I walked along in the snow and mud in shoes without soles. The whole day long, my feet were in an ice bath that ensured that I had a perpetual head-cold. I fortunately learned how to blow my nose proficiently without a handkerchief, because of course we lacked absolutely everything, and every last bit of cloth I could get my hands on I used to wrap around my poor feet, which was far more essential."

There was a French doctor at Mackenrode, René C., whom the SS commander had appointed camp doctor. When Bonifas had a very serious carbuncle, he had him evacuated to the *Revier* at Wieda.[19] Bonifas relates: "Because in the infirmary I wouldn't be needing clothes, I was forced to leave my jacket and pants for another prisoner." At Wieda at that time there were "a hundred or so occupants dispatched between the kitchens, the infirmary, the clothing store and the administration offices of the three other camps." Bonifas was entitled to a hot bath and clean bedclothes. A French doctor, Dr. René A., from Gap, operated on his carbuncle. He stayed at Wieda from December 6 to 25, 1944, at which time he was transferred to the infamous *Straflager* at Osterhagen,[20] "the disciplinary camp of foul reputation" where, on Christmas Day, he ran into Abbot Amyot d'Inville.

As work on the Helmetalbahn was interrupted because of the frost, the Osterhagen prisoners were taken daily by train to work sites near Woffleben, from January 2 to February 15, 1945. This period was all the more arduous as the camp had been invaded by lice. Moreover, food diminished and "everyone could be seen growing thinner as you watched."

The return to the railway work site, eliminating as it did the fatigue of the daily trips, along with a general disinfecting on February 20, which got rid of the lice, enabled Bonifas and his friends to overcome the trials of the final weeks.

"And then a sort of generalized sluggishness overtook the work site. Not only did the prisoners lack the strength to lift their picks and began to pace their every movement, but the Kapos themselves no longer had the strength to yell at them; both Meister and SS also seemed resigned to no longer being able to push us on. The masters' morale was burnt out; the German people were inexorably marching toward the greatest disillusion of their history. Thus, our objective was to do as little as possible, to work 'with our eyes,' that is, to pretend to be working when we were being looked at. There was no other solution. Some days, I scarcely moved more than three or four wheelbarrow loads of dirt in the course of the whole day."[21]

Bonifas's account, providing a continuous picture of what took place on the Helmetalbahn work sites from September 1944 to April 1945, is the only overall document published on the subject. Manfred Bornemann's *Chronicle of the Ellrich Camp*—several pages of which are devoted to the *Baubrigaden*—makes reference to no other text of this kind. It contains indications as to the number of prisoners concerned.[22] At the end of October 1944 the BB 3 in Wieda with its three Kommandos had 996 prisoners. This number had reached 1,102 by January 15, 1945, at which time it was administratively linked to the camp at Sachsenhausen.

THE BAUBRIGADE 4 KOMMANDO IN GÜNZERODE. The BB 4 was made up of 826 prisoners at the end of October 1944, a third of whom were at Ellrich-Theater while the rest were part of the Günzerode Kommando. The *Lagerältester* from Ellrich-Theater was a German communist who made sure there was a fair distribution of foodstuffs, even among the prisoners in the *Revier* and the *Schonung,* who were ever more numerous in the Bürgergarten in the early months of 1945.

Denis Guillon[23] has described the Günzerode camp as follows: "We were housed in a large abandoned sheep barn, requisitioned for that purpose. There were almost a thousand of us all told, crammed in like animals. Bunks five levels high entirely filled the first floor. Down below as well, a large part of the space had been transformed into a five-story dormitory.

"We were put behind the central buildings of a beautiful farm. The little camp was surrounded by posts and barbed wire, with a watchtower at each corner, and large lights on the top of each post. A guard post was set up at the entrance. A house located outside of the barbed-wire compound housed the sentries. [. . .] Whole families passed by in front of the barbed-wire fences and our passing by 'in ranks of five,' solidly guarded by the SS, was always followed by an attentive crowd which turned up to look at their slaves."

Guillon's highly evocative account—who was there with his friend Lucien Clot—tallies with Bonifas's: the obsession with the mud, the soaking-wet clothes that never dried at night and that had to be put on again in the morning: "The work site was more waterlogged than ever. We sunk in past our ankles into the freezing-cold water and the snow which would melt during the day and freeze up once again the following night. The backfill was a pothole against which we fought for the ragged remains of our Russian socks, what was left of our clogs, which were forever threatening to stay stuck in the sickeningly glacial and viscous muck. The landscape was squalid—as if you were looking at it through swampy water. The sky was dirty and the heavy clouds hung low in the sky, clinging to the hills where they fizzled out, driven by a violent wind that ran through us."

There was a kind of *Revier* with a French doctor, Dr. Jean Berthéol. On March 23, 1945, the survivors of Günzerode were removed to Ellrich-Theater. On April 6 the sick and the invalid were evacuated by train. In chapter 20, Guillon will be found evacuating on foot in the Harz Mountains.

[[12   ]]

HARZUNGEN, ELLRICH,
AND WOFFLEBEN

It is difficult to dissociate the study of the Harzungen camp from that of the Ellrich camp for a number of reasons. The first is that the two camps' labor forces were involved on the same series of work sites; the second is that the camps developed simultaneously during the first months, beginning with the first convoys coming from Buchenwald; lastly because there were exchanges of prisoners between the two camps. The Woffleben camp came only later, functioning during the final months to house a portion of the prisoners from Ellrich working on digging out B 12.

The prisoners of the three camps all suffered on the underground-digging sites, where they were placed under similar conditions. But life in the camp was harder for those at Ellrich than for those at Harzungen and, in the end, at Woffleben, who were put into new buildings.

As will be shown, the worst-off prisoners seem to have been those from Ellrich, who traveled back and forth on a daily basis to work site B 13, where they were employed out of doors, whatever the weather, on earthwork projects or backbreaking handling work. They actually ended up, as will be pointed out, envying the miners' jobs.

The Beginnings of Harzungen and Ellrich

It was in March 1944 that Kammler was put in charge of setting up the aircraft industry underground and created Sonderstab Kammler, which was established at Bischofferode at the foot of the Himmelberg. The prisoners were then brought in to get the work sites started, in utterly improvised fashion. To dig out the underground spaces of B 3, B 11, and B 12, and to build the outside infrastructures for B 13, manpower was brought from the Buchenwald camp, which, between March and June 1944, gave priority to sending the newly arrived prisoners, in particular those from the last convoys coming from France and Belgium.

There was not enough room for everyone at Dora. It was the period when construction was finishing up on the camp intended for prisoners employed by the Mittelwerk, where the last inhabitants of the tunnel "dormitories" were to be transferred. Most of the time, those just arriving did not go to Dora or merely passed through. New camps therefore had to be built, and, at the same time, the civilian workers—such as those from the Junkers factory being set up in the north part of the Dora Tunnel—had to be housed. New prisoners' camps were established at Harzungen to the east of the work zone and next to the Ellrich-Station to the west of the zone.

Building a *Barackenlager* at Harzungen had been envisaged for several months, as indicated in the recapitulation drawn up on December 31, 1943, by Neu, director of the WIFO's Ni Agency. In late March 1944, Kammler seems to have envisaged sending the Green Mittelwerk personnel there for reasons of security. Dr. Kettler then refused to allow his personnel to be shut up behind barbed wire; or at any rate, that is what he claimed in a testimony quoted by Bornemann.[1] The entirely new camp was henceforth free to take in prisoners. It was at the edge of the village, several miles to the east of Niedersachswerfen.

The site selected at Ellrich for the establishment of the concentration camp was of an entirely different nature. At the beginning it was made up of the abandoned buildings of a plaster factory with a vast tract of uncultivated land to the south of the railway line running from Herzberg to Nordhausen, near the station of the small town of Ellrich.

The chronology of the beginnings of Harzungen and Ellrich is murky, as will be seen from the fragmentary testimonies available. Prior to the camp's opening, many prisoners coming from Buchenwald were taken to Bischofferode to a former farming operation located between the villages of Woffleben and Appenrode. As mentioned above, it was the real headquarters of the Sonderstab Kammler's Sonderinspektion B, set up in the old main farm building. The prisoners were temporarily installed in the other building of the "Woffleben farm"—so-called because the operation was located on that district's territory.

The first testimony is that of Joseph Jourdren,[2] who left Buchenwald on March 17, 1944, along with several other French and a number of Polish prisoners and who ended up as the only Frenchman in an uncomfortable camp situated, it would appear, at Niedersachswerfen. He was put to work digging trenches under the supervision of Greens and guarded by soldiers of the Luftwaffe. On April 3 these prisoners were transferred into the new Harzungen camp. "It's Byzantium!" exclaimed Jourdren. But on April 10 they were again transferred and arrived at the Woffleben farm. There Jourdren met René Gilbert and Roland Coty, who was at the time the camp commander's *Friseur.* On May 13, 1944, he was once again transferred—this time to Ellrich.

Gilbert,[3] who got to Dora on March 13, 1944, was employed for only a short while in the tunnel and was then transported daily by truck to Woffleben to work on a railway line. He was then transferred to the Woffleben farm and ended up at Ellrich on May 1 along with Paul Fournial—the day the camp was founded.

Lucien Fayman[4] was transferred directly from Buchenwald to Woffleben on April 1, 1944, where he met up with Wolf Wexler and Coty. They were moved to Harzungen in mid-April. Guy Marty, who arrived at Harzungen from Buchenwald on April 26, was at Ellrich from May 2 on. As far as the French were concerned, it was thus above all the deportees from the third convoy of January who were the first to arrive at Harzungen and at Ellrich. Other deportees from this same convoy, as seen in chapter 9, then worked on building the Dora camp.

Bornemann[5] assesses the number of prisoners as follows: on April 2 there were 617 prisoners at Harzungen and 300 at Bischofferode/Woffleben. On May 9 the Bischofferode camp was disbanded and the prisoners were transferred to Ellrich, then comprised of 724 internees. There were many Poles and Russians, alongside the French.

New arrivals of prisoners took place throughout May and June 1944. First of all, on May 11 there were the 200 who left the Laura camp for Ellrich. Among the French prisoners—as shown in the preceding chapter—were Courtaud, Tauzin, and Inchauspé. At the same time a convoy of 600 prisoners coming from Buchenwald—and made up above all of Gypsies—arrived at Harzungen after a short stop at Dora. Then came the transports of Poles and Russians, amidst whom was the odd Frenchman, such as Serge Miller. At the end of May the Hungarian Jews arrived at Dora. Many of them were quickly sent to Ellrich.

On June 6 a transport from Buchenwald brought French prisoners from the May 12 convoy from Compiègne—including Maxime Cottet and Albert Bannes—to Dora. They were dispatched between Harzungen and Ellrich. Other deportees from the same convoy left the same day for Wieda, as was seen in the preceding chapter. At the same time the Belgian deportees from the convoys of May 12 and 23, who arrived in large numbers, were also spread out for the most part between Harzungen and Ellrich. Lastly, on June 14 the transport coming from Buchenwald was above all made up of Russians and Poles.

It was in this way that Harzungen and Ellrich's multiethnic groups progressively came together. Exchanges of prisoners, for no apparent reason, took place frequently between the two camps. Moreover, the Harzungen *Revier,* the first to be set up, was used for some time for the sick from Ellrich.

Harzungen: The Camp, the Work Sites, the Revier

THE HARZUNGEN CAMP. In June 1944, construction of the Harzungen camp came to an end. There was no possibility of expanding the site. The camp was first of all surrounded by barbed wire, and then an electric fence was put in by the Zaunbau Kommando, which had just finished the fence around the Dora camp. Garnier and his friends then returned to Dora and were assigned to the tunnel.[6]

The camp had a quadrilateral shape, along the south side of the Niedersachs-werfen road on the western edge of the village next to the church. "It was a pretty little village, with brick houses whose wooden frameworks could be seen, all spruce and fresh," remembers Mialet.[7] The camp was made up of fourteen barracks, ten blocks of which were for housing and prisoners while two others were for the *Revier* in the southwest angle. A brook ran through the northwest part and a pit was dug in its bed in August 1944. It was subsequently covered over. The camp was planned for a population of some four thousand prisoners. The wardens were initially SS, soon replaced by soldiers from the Luftwaffe. Their two barracks were on the other side of the road.

From June 1944 on the convoys coming from Buchenwald were no longer directed toward Harzungen but toward Dora, and especially toward Ellrich or Blankenburg. This was the case of the Belgian convoys of June 19 and August 10, and the French "77,000"s. In July and August, it is true, prisoners from several Dora Kommandos were transferred to Harzungen, but many of them remained there only a short while. This was the case for Pierre Auchabie, who arrived on August 15 only to leave again on August 30 for Ellrich. Thanks to an "accident on the job" (injured by a stone falling on a work site), Jean Mialet avoided this transfer.[8] Those who also remained at Harzungen—such as Raymond Jacob, Joannès Méfret, Lucien Maronneau, Pierre Pointe, and Jean de Sesmaisons—consider themselves lucky.

The testimonies of the Harzungen survivors are very contrasting. They describe their working conditions on the outside work sites as especially difficult, but feel that if they made it through at all it was because of the "acceptable" conditions of life in the camp. They generally avoided brutalities and interminable roll calls. The blocks remained clean, without the proliferation of lice (except toward the end). Food was provided on a more or less regular basis. The notion of "acceptable" is entirely relative. It was above all those such as Jean Mialet, who had experienced Dora's beginnings, who expressed this opinion. The newcomers, not unjustifiably, did not feel inclined to paint an excessively pleasant picture of Harzungen.

The camp atmosphere made relations between friends possible during free time. In his book of memoirs, Jean Mialet emphasized the comfort that he drew from his contacts with Jean de Sesmaisons and René Haentjens, his classmates from the Saint-Cyr[9] officers' school. Relations remained close between prisoners from the Jura region, victims of various roundups during the month of April. But Maxime Cottet, who kept a diary, recorded the death of several friends who were transferred to Ellrich.

For nine months Cottet was able to keep a small diary and a minuscule pencil and jot down the odd word from time to time in secret. As he says: "I had to keep the booklet hidden; my friends advised me to throw it away, because I ran the risk of death if it were discovered. It made it through maybe thirty or forty frisks. In the end, it was stolen from me by a prisoner. I was sad to lose it, but almost relieved. It was after my return, in September 1945, that it was sent to me by a repatriated Belgian, who had found it in the clothes of a dead prisoner, after the liberation of Harzungen, and who wanted to send it to the family of the supposed 'dead man.' I immediately recopied it, because it had become almost indecipherable."

Right until the end, the Harzungen prisoners' wardens were soldiers from the Luftwaffe, "no longer young men, who, in general, were not nasty," observes Mialet,[10] who on one occasion was able to chat with one of them about the Gaillac region, where he had been a prisoner of war during World War I. The camp commander was himself fairly liberal. He authorized a Mass in the camp on Christmas Day, 1944. Boxing matches were even held (for the better fed). On December 25 a talent contest was held in Block 7—Cottet's block: he sang and won two hundred grams of bread.[11]

There was a more or less equivalent number of Russians, Poles, French, and Belgians in the camp, whose influence balanced itself out. But the Germans, generally Greens, made up most of the supervision, along with certain Gypsies, who were German-speaking themselves.

A Belgian priest, François Poiré,[12] after three months' work in the tunnel, nevertheless became *Schreiber* of Block 8 and then Block 5. It was he who asked the camp commander for authorization to celebrate Mass on December 25, and a noncommissioned officer was sent to Nordhausen to get what was required, including the hosts. One of the three Belgian priests in the camp, the others serving as acolytes, thus officiated in the presence of the commander and a certain number of noncommissioned officers.

Marcel Martin went from the kitchen at Dora to the kitchen at Harzungen. "Thanks to an astonishing gift for languages and a lively intelligence, he had become one of the important figures in the camp." Mialet, who was delighted by this, claims to owe him a great deal.[13] But far and away the most noteworthy institution in the camp was the *Revier,* which will be mentioned shortly.

USING THE HARZUNGEN LABOR FORCE. Testimonies, though nuanced with regard to the camp's relatively human character, as opposed to Ellrich, are unanimous regarding the harsh work conditions. All the prisoners who did not have a job in the camp were occupied on outside work sites, especially on underground digging operations. Several accounts, including Mialet's, spoke of a tunnel at Niedersachswerfen, which may have been B 11.

But it seems that the teams coming from Harzungen mostly worked on B 3 at the same time as the teams coming from Ellrich. It was at any rate strictly the same work, in the same rock, digging out identical galleries. Bannes[14] noted that the Ellrich prisoners were in worse shape than those from Harzungen. What was characteristic about work site B 3 was that the hill (Himmelberg) was attacked simultaneously at the base through different galleries bearing numbers, with corresponding Kommandos. Nicola[15] was thus in 2, Bannes in 27 and then 5, Cottet in 14 and then in 21 and 23.

The "miners"—that is, the borers *(die Bohrer)*—made up a particular category, and their *Meister* were themselves veritable miners. Nicola explains the role of the borer: "We worked in teams of two. On a long plank about twenty-five feet long by fifteen inches wide, the borer sits behind the compressed-air drill, fitted out with a bit twelve feet long and at least two or two and a half inches in diameter, and pushes the machine with his feet. His teammate sits behind him, back to back. His job is to press very hard against his buddy's back to help him drive the bit into the rock face. The work requires a very good level of understanding between teammates. There were eight teams of us braced up against eight drills, boring eight holes spread out over the width of the upper tunnel. Below us, other forced laborers, using jackhammers, brought down the back fill so that we borers could bore out another line of holes, and so on right to the bottom of the tunnel. It goes without saying that the scaffolding that held us up was not very stable and accidents were frequent."

Mialet,[16] who learned the work from an experienced French fellow prisoner, Raymond—a pharmacist's assistant from Saint-Claude—describes it as follows; "The work consisted of using a drill which turned long steel bits to bore eighteen-foot-deep holes into the rock face, which were then packed with dynamite intended to pulverize the rock. It was a far less disagreeable task than the slow torture of shoveling. It did not require as violent and continuous a physical effort, but required, mentally, sustained concentration. While the drill was boring the hole, the bit had to be watched carefully, the compressed air checked on, and, between drillings, the bits chosen and the machine greased."

The testimony of the Belgian Raymond Wautrecht[17] makes it possible to complete the picture, for he notes that the miners were "positioned at different heights on the scaffolding or on the rock piles." The blast then had to be set off, giving off thick smoke while everyone ducked under cover in a cloud of gray dust. Cottet noted various accidents in his diary: collapsing scaffolding or falling rocks.

Cottet[18] also emphasized the effects of the dust: "It was full of toxic gases of powder coming from the simultaneous explosion of twenty or thirty mines. This, moreover, led to lung problems: tuberculosis, silicosis, pleurisy, and blood poisoning which led to furonculosis, carbuncles, edema. There was also what was referred to as 'purple-lip disease,' with blue all round the eyes, indicating the disappearance of the blood's hemoglobin, arrested by the toxic gases. It led to death within three days."

Other prisoners, still more disadvantaged, filled the carts for the evacuation of the backfill. Conditions were the same as during the digging of tunnel A in the Kohnstein, mentioned in chapter 5, when Butet and the others were in the "stones." But the work seems to have been better organized this time round, and accounts are less devastating in this respect. Before becoming a miner, Mialet[19] had been a well-digger. He had been part of the Schachtbau Kommando, digging vertical ventilation shafts straight down from the hill's summit into the new underground galleries. Fayman[20] on the other hand recalls building a bridge over a stream for trucks to pass over.

The digging operations required few "specialists" such as those who were then working in the Dora Tunnel. There were nevertheless jobs for carpenters, and electricians for the gallery lighting. An important member of the French *Résistance,* André Schock (under the code name André Chevalier) was the *Kapo* of a small Kommando made up above all of the Frenchmen André Clavé, René Haentjens, Raymond Jacob, and Jean de Sesmaisons.[21] Fayman pointed out that "they moved about constantly in the perimeter of the neighboring work sites, supervised by two or three sentries, to check on the electrical and other mains."

The galleries were dug in three eight-hour shifts: from six o'clock in the morning until two o'clock in the afternoon *(Morgenschicht)*; from two o'clock in the afternoon until ten o'clock in the evening *(Nachmittagschicht)*; and from ten o'clock in the evening until six o'clock in the morning *(Nachtschicht).* The teams changed shift every week.

To get from the Harzungen camp to the work sites, military trucks were used at first, then tractors with trailers, and then a train starting in August 1944. A line had indeed been built from Harzungen to Niedersachswerfen by prisoners from the Harzungen camp. It was the most extensive "earthwork" mentioned in the testimonies.

Once they had arrived at Niedersachswerfen, the prisoners had to go to the far end of a narrow-gauge railway that circled around Mühlberg and Himmelberg by the north to reach the entranceways to the B 3 galleries. The route was especially cruel in bad weather, as Raymond Wautrecht pointed out:[22] "A further short march was required to get to the other narrow-gauge railway; after having been counted once again, we had to climb into little carts where we were sometimes as many as twenty-five, jammed in next to one another, our feet in water or on ice, without being able to avoid the biting wind or the pelting rain. A little locomotive hauled this long line of carts freighted with miserable human hulks: it would stop and start, with sudden lurches, which would hurl us against one another. A good half-hour of veritable torture in order to get to the work site." This line continued as far as Cleysingen, where the anhydrite extracted from B 3 formed a slag heap.

In February 1945, as Cottet pointed out, when coal was in short supply, the train from Harzungen to Niedersachswerfen was stopped and the prisoners had to do the six miles on foot to reach the work sites.

To appreciate just how tiring the work conditions were for the prisoners of

Harzungen, it must be borne in mind how long this drudgery went on. Cottet went from camp to work site from June 11, 1944, to March 2, 1945, with a single one-week interruption at the *Revier* in February. On March 3 he was transferred to Ellrich along with Wautrecht. The same misadventure had befallen Bannes at the end of January.

The elimination took place progressively, and Cottet recorded the deaths of his fellow prisoners in his diary beginning at the end of December. Some died and others were evacuated to Nordhausen on February 28. The camp's more or less acceptable conditions simply prevented things from getting any worse, and the *Revier* could not do anything about exhaustion. Those who found work in the camp doing masonry work such as Jean Marillier,[23] or who became butchers in the kitchen like Lucien Maronneau,[24] were of course privileged—however, they were but a tiny minority.

THE HARZUNGEN *REVIER*. The Harzungen *Revier* functioned throughout the entire duration of the camp in very particular conditions, under the de facto direction of two French "doctors"—who were not doctors at all but who played a highly positive role. The structure of this *Revier* is exceptionally well known through a document that has often been reproduced: the so-called Dienstplan dating from December 12, 1944, initialed by the *Lagerarzt*—the camp doctor—who was a military doctor with the Luftwaffe.[25] It provides a complete table of the medical and paramedical personnel chosen by the prisoners.

The *Kapo* was a German, Heinz Jessen, and the *Schreiber,* a Belgian, Louis Clukkers. The surgical ward *(Chirurgische Abteilung)* was run by Dr. Jacques Desprez, who was the surgeon, and Dr. Paul Lagey. The internal medicine ward was under Dr. Georges Desprez's authority. Jacques and Georges Desprez were brothers, but had not arrived at Buchenwald by the same convoy, were not arrested together, and by all accounts scarcely had anything to do with each other—not even in the camp.

In fact, Jacques Desprez was a dentist in the French department of the Aisne and spoke German. He had arrived at Dora in September 1943 and was a doctor in the *Revier* until February 1944. Jean Michel, who had introduced him into the dentistry ward and who knew him well for several months, described him as cyclothymic: highly jovial one minute, gloomy the next.[26] Sidelined at Dora, he resurfaced in the *Revier* at Harzungen right from the beginnings of the camp and held onto his position until the evacuation to Bergen-Belsen.

His older brother Georges was neither a doctor nor a dentist. According to Lucien Fayman[27] he had "a certain amount of embryonic and fragmentary medical knowledge, but commanding a level of nerve beyond anything that can be imagined, and possessing a very lively intelligence, and highly developed powers of observation, boundless loquacity and an optimal quality of human contact, he had acquired a level of authority to which the Luftwaffe Stabsarzt himself, as supervisor of the Revier, would acquiesce." It will be seen in chapter

20 what he managed to obtain during the evacuation. Paul Lagey, who really was a doctor, arrived in the last months of 1944 as indicated by his identity number 89622. The team of eighteen male nurses—the *Pfleger*—seems to have been put together quickly, either at the Woffleben farm or very early on at Harzungen. It was comprised of four French (Roland Coty, Rémy Chevalier, Georges Daubèze, and Georges Gos), three Belgians (Jean Dumont, Jean Rémy, and Jean Petit), two Dutch (Job Franssen and Jack Sänger), a Swiss arrested in France (Gottlieb Fuchs), a German, four Poles, and three Russians. Fayman, who had been a borer and was sent to the *Revier*, stayed on there as a masseur in October 1944. He was a privileged witness who paid particular homage to his friend Georges Mazellier, who until November 1944 was in charge of supplies at the *Revier*.

This team was a great help to a certain number of prisoners in difficulty, by giving them notes for the *Schonung*, switching them from one Kommando to another, assigning them to the camp, and so on. Mialet for instance was able to relax for a week by going, along with a Russian who was even more myopic than himself, to get glasses at Dora which, as it turned out, they never got. But these initiatives quickly reached their limit in a concentration camp dependent upon Kammler.

Description of Ellrich

THE ELLRICH CAMP: THE SITE. There is only one usable map of the Ellrich camp. It was drawn up in 1987 by Manfred Bornemann[28] on the basis of indications provided by former inhabitants of the area and former prisoners, whose names he gives. All traces of the camp had indeed disappeared in circumstances after 1945, which will be pointed out later. The site included a more or less flat section where the building occupied by the prisoners and by the SS was located. It was dominated to the south by a hill that was a distant prolongation of the Kohnstein to the west. The plans mention the site of the quarries *(Steinbruch)* and the galleries *(Stollen)* corresponding to the former anhydrite mines.

Superimposed upon these natural relief lines runs a very old and important political border. Part of the plain is on the Ellrich District's territory; the rest of the plain and the hill are on the territory of the Walkenried District. Ellrich was part of the Hohnstein, a territory attached in 1648—by the treaties of Westphalia—to Brandenburg, which subsequently became the kingdom of Prussia. For centuries Walkenried belonged to the duchy of Brunswick. It so happens that in this region, this same border that would be used in 1945 to distinguish the Soviet and British zones of occupation would subsequently separate the GDR (German Democratic Republic, or East Germany) from the FRG (Federal Republic of Germany, or West Germany). Since the reunification of Germany it has been the limit between the *Länder* of Thuringia and Lower Saxony. The prisoners' camp was situated at Ellrich. The SS were established in the neighboring hamlet of Juliushütte, further to the west and dependent on Walkenried.

In 1944, to the south of the Ellrich-Station, at the foot of the hill, the abandoned buildings of the former Kohlmann plaster works *(Gipswerk)* were still standing. A first building, in half-timber and brick, two or three stories high, was occupied on May 1, 1944, and divided into three blocks, 1, 2, and 3, with separate entranceways. The prisoners slept initially on the ground; bunks were later installed. Upstairs in Block 1, accessible by an exterior wooden staircase, there was a sort of *Revier.* There was no washroom; a mere pit served as a latrine. At the end of May, Block 3's stairway, overloaded, collapsed—leading to injuries.

It was at this period that a second industrial brick building, located behind the first one, began to be used, and became Block 4. The *Mémorial* contains an evocation of this block at its origins, no doubt due to Louis-Clément Terral, who was the *Friseur* there.[29] "From the outside, Block 4 does not look anything like the Blocks at Buchenwald or even at Dora, which are painted green. The Ellrich camp was organized in an old abandoned plaster works, and Block 4 was nothing but a miserable transformed hangar, two hundred feet long, sixty feet wide, forty feet high.

"A shed, put up by the Häftling, extended the building a further forty or so feet. Gray and dirty, facing directly north, its façade was ominous looking with its large gate, its two doors and six high windows that never a sunbeam would cross.

"On the inside, three partitions reaching the roof divided the Block into four rooms of unequal size. The big gate opened first of all into a large unadorned room, sixty-five feet by fifty, which served as a place for regrouping, handing out food, a Friseur's stool, a theater of corporal punishment. The ground was made up of great stone slabs, the roof itself served as a ceiling. Not long before, ten or so wobbly tables, twenty wooden stools and a wood stove had been brought in as the only furnishings.

"In front, a door opened onto the Stube, the Block larder where rations were prepared. It was also the door leading to the room of the Stubendienst and the Schreiber, and to that of the Block chief. That was everyone's focal point, for it was from within that terror in person could emerge, truncheon in hand. And that was also where the much-awaited soup came from.

"To the left, three low doors opened onto the dormitory. 105 feet long and sixty feet wide, it was the largest room in the Block—and it was also the coldest and most sordid; it had an uneven earthen floor; the walls were made of uncovered stone, which, saltpetered by humidity, reached some thirty-five feet up to the roof, which was covered in clouds of cobwebs.

"A twilight fell from the excessively high windows and the dust reduced visibility still further. In this half-darkness, men are like ghosts, bumping into the shivering shapes which stagger along past the beds. These were arranged in squares three stories high and made up small boxes along three rows in extension of the three doors. 150 men could fit in without much comfort; up to 845 were often piled in."

One of the first barracks to be built was the guard post at the camp entrance, which was located to the north, near the station where a special platform had been set up for the prisoners. Another barracks housed the kitchen. A barracks was then built for the *Revier,* transferred to Block 1, in August. A certain number of others followed, but not all the blocks could be identified on the plan. They were normal, with washrooms and toilets. But, as Jacques Courtaud has written,[30] "Ellrich's major characteristic was the virtually perpetual lack of water." The result was inevitable: "The latrines became a veritable cesspool: you literally walked about in shit."

A sort of swamp with reeds was located in the western part of the camp, at the foot of the hill. It was known as the *Kleiner Pontel*; there was also a *Grosser Pontel* on the other side of Juliushütte. The SS having decided to fill in the *Kleiner Pontel,* the reeds first had to be gotten rid of—under conditions described below. It then had to be filled in with stones that the prisoners had to bring with them when they returned from their work sites.

The SS barracks were concentrated at Juliushütte. Villas were requisitioned for the officers and barracks built for the soldiers. A factory—the Trinks factory—continued to function in this area and certain prisoners worked there, including René Ardouin and Henri Barat.

The last building put up in the Ellrich camp was the crematorium, built on the hill (thus at Walkenried), which would only be used in March 1945.

THE ELLRICH CAMP: THE PEOPLE. The camp was guarded by the SS, though some of the wardens came from the Luftwaffe. It was thus that Bornemann[31] obtained (from his daughter) letters that Stefan Pauler—a *Gefreiter* (corporal) in the Luftwaffe, assigned to Ellrich on September 19, 1944, as SS-*Rottenführer*— had sent to his family. He quotes—often highly disabused—passages from them in his *Chronique du camp d'Ellrich* that he published in 1987. The last letter was dated February 4, 1945. Pauler was subsequently reported missing.

Regarding the original SS the language was unequivocal, as shown by Serge Miller[32] in describing how the newcomers of May 20, 1944, were received: "We saw an SS officer, or rather a puppet, a lanky looking fellow, moving toward us. He crossed his arms on his chest, threw his head back, and jeered at us: 'So! That's how you remove your forage caps, is it? You must think you're still at Buchenwald! In the Sanatorium! With the Bolsheviks! Well, that's all over now, I'm in charge here and to start with, you bunch of louts are going to do a half-hour of exercise.' On paper, that may not have the same effect, but, I swear, it had one on us. He didn't speak, he bellowed, gesticulated, and frothed at the mouth as if he had been bitten by a rabid dog. And those who didn't speak German must have wondered if it was the devil himself in front of us. All the soldiers and noncommissioned officers who supervised us were from the Luftwaffe, but the commander—which is who he was—was with the SS."

The man in question was no doubt Ritz, who subsequently became *Lagerführer* when Karl Fritzsch was appointed *Lagerkommandant* on September 10, 1944. The latter, after having been at Dachau, was the assistant to Höss at Auschwitz, where he carried out gassings. At some point, perhaps in October, Stötzler—the *Lagerführer* at Dora—became *Lagerkommandant* at Ellrich, replacing Fritzsch, whose subsequent fate remains unknown. Meanwhile, Otto Brinkmann—*Rapportführer* at Dora—became *Lagerführer* at Ellrich. Both seem to have kept their positions right to the end.

The Greens, or Blacks, held the principal positions in the camp administration. They were all the more fearsome that they had already been banished first from Buchenwald and then from Dora. They were the SS's zealous assistants. It was observed that they were often accompanied by an entourage of young Gypsies, who could also be extremely fearsome. Richard Walenta, *Blockältester* since May 1944, became *Lagerältester* in the course of the summer. He was then transferred to Dora. He was replaced by someone by the name of Arthur Schimmeck. Courtaud recalls three successive LÄ, all Greens, all detestable, but does not know their names.

As indicated above, beginning in the months of May and June 1944 there were prisoners of every nationality at Ellrich, who had transited through Bischofferode/Woffleben or Harzungen, and then arrived from Buchenwald, in some cases via Dora. There were Poles and Russians as well as Czechs, French and Belgians, Hungarian Jews, and German Gypsies. The population at the end of May was 1,696 persons—and by the end of June had reached 2,880.

From July to September, with the transfers from Dora and Harzungen and the arrival of new convoys arriving particularly from France and Belgium—whose deportees were largely assigned to Ellrich (or Blankenburg for the Belgians)—the camp grew in size. The population went from 4,104 persons in late July to 6,187 at the end of August, and to 8,189 by the end of September. It had dropped to 7,957 by the end of October. There would only be 6,571 by the end of January 1945.

It is difficult from this point on to appreciate the development of the total population because of the arrival of prisoners evacuated from the camps in the East. At the same time the mortality rate rose steeply, in particular among the newcomers. Lastly, there were large transfers between Ellrich, Harzungen, and Dora. At the beginning of March 1945 there was an overall population of 8,000 prisoners, including those in Camp B 12 at Woffleben. But many of them were invalids.

During the month of March the structure of the population continued to change. Many people disappeared because of deaths and above all because of the "convoy of March 3," which will be mentioned below. A subsequent and very large transfer from Harzungen to Ellrich did not suffice to bring the population back up. The last count, on March 31, gave a total of 7,259 prisoners.

THE FATE OF THE YOUNG HUNGARIAN JEWS. The Hungarian Jews were not spared—a fact testified to by a number of French prisoners. They speak above all of the children. Jean-Pierre Couture relates the following:[33] "In Block 5, the ground floor of Block 6, every night, some twenty children grouped together in a corner of the large room. The adult prisoners refrained from taking over this space—though the Block was overcrowded to such an extent that, at night, only a pathway through the center aisle remained free to enable people to get to the toilet. Everywhere else, jammed up against one another on the bricks on the ground, prisoners of every nationality pressed together. There were even people under the bunk beds which were themselves overcrowded. In the space that remained free, there were several blankets and sawdust. That was where the little Hungarian Jews—from about eleven to fifteen years old—slept. Slept is a figure of speech. Throughout the blackout (from around eleven o'clock at night until five o'clock in the morning), the voices of these children could be heard whimpering, and, so it seemed, calling out for their parents who would never come. Moreover, as it was supposed that they had smaller appetites because they were only children, these poor kids sometimes only got reduced rations—even though they were integrated into the adult work Kommandos. The whimpers of those children are my most distressing memory, and are the origin—or rather the confirmation—of my tenacious hatred of their tormentors."

"Toward the end of May 1944," Gilbert[34] witnessed the arrival "of young Hungarian Jews between ten and fifteen years old. Under the whip of the Kapos and the SS, they worked without a break at clearing away the dilapidated buildings of the former plaster works. They were all decimated in a very short time."

Jourdren[35] remained at Ellrich from May 13 until July 16. He was then sent to the Dora *Revier* because of a foot injury. One day in May he was put to work tearing out the rhizomes of the reeds from the *Kleiner Pontel,* which was to be filled in. "The water was very muddy and came halfway up our thighs. With our bare hands, and with our stomach, shoulders, even our chins as well as our hands in the muck, we ripped out those horrible roots until nightfall. [. . .] When we got back to the camp, there was obviously no way for us to wash ourselves, and still less to dry ourselves off. On top of which, we reeked." The following day the task was assigned to a group of almost two hundred young Hungarian Jews. They were all dead within three days.

Lafond[36] recalls having seen a convoy of Jewish children, this time in November 1944: "It was very late in the evening because we had come back from Woffleben. Coming out of Block 3 by the back stairway, I saw all along the fence which bordered the rails a whole group of young Jews, their heads covered with dark-green-colored woolen caps. I never saw these children in the camp again."

Using the Ellrich Labor Force

THE LESSONS OF THE *ARBEITSEINTEILUNG.* Between May and September 1944, thousands of prisoners were thus piled into Ellrich, in generally detestable material circumstances. As in all the camps, a *Lagerkommando* was set up. A small number of prisoners were employed in general services and upkeep of the camp. Those who in the first weeks managed to get themselves appointed to these positions endeavored to maintain their privilege. Thus the newcomers had ever less chance to avoid the outside Kommandos. This was what virtually all the French prisoners—whose identity numbers were in the "77,000"s—noticed upon their arrival. Of course, the existent industrial buildings had to be turned into blocks, and then new barracks had to be put up for the prisoners and the SS, and the camp had to be fenced in—but that was all finished within a few months. Pierre Goasguen,[37] who was involved with metal work, nevertheless remained employed in his field right to the end.

From the first day on, a maximum number of prisoners were required for the work sites dependent on the Sonderstab Kammler, whether for digging out underground galleries or for any number of civil engineering projects on the surface, enabling the outfitting and servicing of the vast industrial complex that was to be set up in these galleries.

A document dated January 29, 1945, gives the *Arbeitseinteilung*—the "distribution of work"—for that particular day and for all the prisoners at Ellrich.[38] The detailed descriptions are not always intelligible because there are proper nouns corresponding to various companies. There were 333 prisoners employed in the camp out of a total of 4,280 at work—in other words, 7.8 percent. This figure includes both the two LÄ, fourteen *Friseur,* and twenty *Kartoffelschäler.*

The rest of the population was supposed to be at the work sites, more or less removed from Ellrich. The closest-by were the B 3, underground, at Bischofferode, with 669 prisoners, and the B 13, outside, nearby, with 599 prisoners. Further afield, at Woffleben, was the B 12, with 668 employees in a twelve-hour-long day shift, and 721 spread out more or less equally in three eight-hour shifts, for a total of 1,389 prisoners. The work site furthest away was B 11, at Niedersachswerfen, with 576 prisoners.

Moreover, 309 prisoners were employed at B 17, the most recent work site, which will be mentioned further on. Another 336 were spread out between a wide variety of Kommandos, which are difficult to define and to locate. Lastly, seventy prisoners worked for the Sonderinspektion II of the Sonderstab Kammler, which was set up at Bischofferode, as mentioned in chapter 11.

The Ellrich survivors' testimonies as to the work they were made to do on these work sites is often not very explicit. Many of them were indeed considered mere slaves, indifferently forced to do earthworks or handling tasks. This was confirmed by Max Oesch:[39] "At Ellrich, we were very often shifted from one Kommando to another, for no apparent reason." The "miners," working in three teams like their fellow prisoners living at Harzungen, ended up by appearing, in the work sites taken as a whole, to be privileged. An illustration of this will be seen further along with regard to the B 12 camp at Woffleben.

Jules Bouvet[40]—a schoolteacher from a village in the Orne region—did nothing but moving work "with buckets, spades, and carts" at the Buchenwald quarry from December 1943 to March 1944, at Dora from March to August 1944, and at Ellrich from August 1944 until March 1945. Exhausted, he was in the Harzungen *Revier* at the time of the evacuation in April.

TOILING ON THE OUTSIDE WORK SITES. The few testimonies that exist regarding the outside work sites provide only a very partial view of what took place for months on end somewhere between Bischofferode and Niedersachswerfen. Tauzin was at Ellrich on May 11, having come from Laura. As he writes:[41] "When we got there, Woffleben was a vast plain of fertile fields, located at the foot of a sort of steep-banked hill; three months later, it was an immense work site, crisscrossed with railway lines. I was put to work on an earthworks project with a pick and a pail, then on building the wooden barracks, and then on carrying cement and all kinds of other materials. It was exhausting. And packing it on our already very gaunt shoulders—which by now were already sore, and becoming ever sorer as the days went by until the skin was utterly raw and scabs began to form! And then what torture it was to have to bear the weight of a rail or the corner of a cement block! We had to clench our fists and teeth with pain, and nevertheless do the job—under threat of death.

"And our feet in wooden clogs without soles or completely worn out on one side, or even split right down the middle and cobbled back together with a piece of wire. And when you had to walk miles on end with shoes like that, every single step was an indescribable torment, which nevertheless had to be overcome in order to move forward one way or another."

Serge Miller[42] had to unload the carts. As he writes: "That was really the most useless and the most painful way to die. And with each shovel-full of coal, and with every plank on my shoulder, I saw death looming. After eight days unloading the carts, I was nothing but skin and bones."

One of Miller's friends explained to him what had been going on since the beginning of the camp: "A whole area had been planted with wheat. There were 500 of us, at the beginning, and we formed the Ellrich camp. We were brought here by truck. It was in April, Easter Monday. Our first job was to spread out over the immense field and to stamp down the wheat as much as possible with our feet. Tractors were brought in to help us out and finish the destruction—and that scene was, for me anyway, the best illustration of the times of sheer madness in which we were living. In the Woffleben station, trains of material were waiting. Since then, as you have noticed, we've never stopped. Roads were cut, and the stream, which wound its way past the mountain, and would have caused problems for opening the tunnels, was diverted, and a picturesque little spot was turned into hell on earth."

One of the anonymous witnesses of the *Mémorial*[43] mentioned the work-site latrines: "When you went to the latrines, you would always try and stay there for a while; but you didn't just go when you felt like it. You needed the Vorarbeiter's permission, because he had to be able to account for his men at every moment.

"In the four corners of the vast work site stood three or four green shacks— the latrines. They were, just as in the Ellrich camp, highly frequented places. It was there that we went to relieve ourselves, and it was there that we went to get away from the exhausting work for a moment or two. And because, quite apart from real needs, everyone tried to pass by the latrines unnecessarily, you were almost always sure to come upon a friend to chat with.

"And so everyone prolonged each visit to these smelly places as long as he could; and next to the Häftling squatting down, there were always a bunch of others, who, their pants pulled back up, made the time last. You were better off there than down by the rails, lugging the cement or doing earthwork, and when the bad wind blew on the work site or the rain fell, there was a veritable pile-up at the latrines. From time to time, the facilities would be cleared out from one second to the next in the frenzy of a headlong rush, when a Kapo came to evacuate the area."

DIGGING THE TUNNELS. The Ellrich prisoners were to dig tunnels B 3, B 11, and B 12. Only their testimonies regarding the B 12 have been preserved. In the *Mémorial* under the title "The Woffleben Tunnel" is a description of the digging of the tunnel.

B 12 may have been better organized than the other digging sites. Jean Gineston[44] indicates how the stones were evacuated. "When you came out of the tunnel, there was a Decauville-type train. The numerous carts were typical pivoting-bin affairs and were filled up with stones. The Decauville hauled along quite a line-up of carts without any trouble." The fact that the B 12 miners were entitled to their own camp from January 1945 on—as will be seen—shows the particular attention devoted to this particular work site.

Alongside the miners digging the galleries, there were specialized Kommandos, and in particular Kommandos of electricians. This was the case at Dora for the AEG Kommando (which will be mentioned further along), or at Harzungen for the Kommando of which Schock was the *Kapo*. The Kommando of electricians based at Ellrich and that worked on B 3 depended on Siemens. It so happens that two of the principal witnesses of what went on at Ellrich, Serge Miller[45] and Jacques Courtaud,[46] were both members, after other more disagreeable experiences, of this Kommando.

Miller, who spoke German, was a sort of interpreter in a group made up for the most part of French and Belgians. Courtaud joined up with three members of his network—and they were the Three Musketeers to whom Miller makes reference. Courtaud and Miller designated a certain number of their friends, either by their first names or nicknames, or by pseudonyms—which makes crosschecking tricky. It can nevertheless be established that Courtaud's Lefauve, who died on March 2, is Miller's Lucien: in both cases he left a widow and orphans at Lyons-la-Forêt. It is more or less certain that Miller's Paco is Courtaud himself, but it is not sure that Courtaud's Mahler is truly Miller. In any case the *Kapo* was a German, Rudolph, a noncommunist anti-Nazi who had been a naval officer and then an engineer—with Siemens.

Another specialized Kommando was that of the forge where Jacques Grandcoin[47] worked. As he points out, "Amongst other jobs I was assigned, there was one tempering jumpers for the mine. The jumpers would wear out and would have to be forged once again. There were tilt hammers; we would reforge the jumpers on the tilt hammers, and then temper them." But the workshop engaged in other activities as well, for instance making pots and pans for civilians in exchange for bread. In the same way, as Abel[48] explains, "the woodworking Kommando had a Spanish Kapo who spoke French, by the name of Emilio. Before Christmas 1944, we made toys for the Luftwaffe sentries, who paid for them with bread."

There was also the painters' Kommando, which Jacques Vern[49] had already been part of at Dora. "Our job consisted of camouflaging stones and other rubble that had been hauled out by carts from the tunnels being dug by the prisoners. [. . .] To make the camouflage, powder of all colors had to be mixed with water and a liquid fixer." Vern remained at Ellrich from July 1944 up until the evacuation. Claude Marchand,[50] a professional painter, was engaged in the same activity.

There was also a Kommando of "surveyors" as at Dora, made up above all of more or less qualified Belgians.

ON THE TRAIN BETWEEN ELLRICH AND THE WORK SITES. The trip from the Ellrich station to the work sites was made by train in the morning, leaving at around five o'clock, and left more or less on time. There was a stop when it got to Bischofferode, another at Woffleben, and yet another at Niedersachswerfen. But the return trip was always delayed, and all the testimonies confirm that it was a very painful ordeal.

Tauzin[51] provides the following account: "When the workday was over, at around six p.m., we had to wait until eleven p.m. and sometimes even until midnight for the train which had to take us back to the camp. This wait in the Niedersachswerfen roll-call area, after an exhausting day of prolonged work, and beyond our forces and our physical resistance, was perhaps for me personally the most terribly sad thing I have ever lived through, the most extreme point, not of suffering, but of human distress. [. . .] And as this waiting went on for hours and hours, and often in the driving rain, with our clothes utterly soaked, we were overcome by an immense weariness and nevertheless we still reacted."

He continues, a little further on: "When the train finally arrived [. . .] we were crammed into the cars, and then there was the sickly, and actually sickening smell of wet flesh, soaked clothes and, then, of course, we had to get back out, still in the pouring rain, which fell long and hard. Then came the roll call and, finally, the return to the Lager."

THE AEG KOMMANDO'S EXILE AT ELLRICH. In the first months of the Dora Tunnel, as seen in chapter 5, the AEG Kommando, in charge of the electrical installation, had appeared as a privileged Kommando. It was the last one, on the day of Pentecost 1944, to leave the tunnel dormitories for a block (first Block 113, then another, headed up by a Czech) in the recently established Dora camp. There was then a relatively fruitful period that came to an end one Sunday at the end of July. The Kommando was transferred to Harzungen on foot, and then a week later to Ellrich. It was not, however, assigned to the Sonderstab Kammler's work sites, but continued to work in the Dora Tunnel. Every day its members went back and forth by train from Ellrich to Niedersachswerfen with the others before making their way to the tunnel on foot. There is in *Témoignages strasbourgeois* an account by Eugène Greff[52] entitled "A Ellrich, près Dora" on this episode of the Kommando's history, which came to an end on November 10, 1944. That day most of its members returned to the Dora camp, to Block 24, according to Bronchart.[53] Others remained at Ellrich and many of them were never to return.

Bronchart, Greff, and Walter's[54] accounts—along with those of several other prisoners—of the hundred days they spent at Ellrich do not add any original information on living conditions in the camp or the daily transports. They tally with other testimonies. One may question the reasons for this sort of exile, which appears to have been something of a sanction. Bronchart believes it had to do with trafficking, the silver from the high-tension fuses having been melted down by some people to make rings. But Bernard d'Astorg[55] has doubts about this. Bronchart also thinks that the sanction was lifted following a very direct discussion he had with an engineer from AEG, after having been caught along with other prisoners hiding in a transformer to relax.

THE B12 CAMP AT WOFFLEBEN. In early January 1945, certain prisoners from Ellrich working on work site B 12 stopped going back and forth every day by train between Ellrich and Woffleben and were housed in a new camp that was built on location. They were some of the prisoners working on the digging operations, on eight-hour shifts. The first prisoners concerned were those on the night shift, joined in the following weeks by those from the afternoon shift.

It was made up initially of 242 prisoners on January 3. There were 375 on February 20, 905 on March 1, and 840 on March 31. They were "miners" who were advantaged in comparison to the others because they avoided the fatigue of the transports and the roll calls. This is the very illustration of the situation mentioned above. This inequality of treatment was painfully felt by the other workers, as shown in the following passage from an account by Étienne Lafond: "I talked about the tunnel workers; they were the only ones to curry the SS's favor—in ridiculous and revolting fashion. Cost what it may, the tunnel had to move forward and only those workers had the privilege of eating, of living."

A testimony from the *Mémorial*[56] entitled "Lager Woffleben" gives some idea of the inside of the blocks: "The Blocks were new barracks with two floors of wooden partitions. The Häftling slept not on straw mattresses but on a bed of wood shavings, and everyone's greatest concern when they arrived was to try and recover the shavings that the neighbors on one side or the other might have stolen and slid underneath themselves.

"Space was very reduced—so reduced that instead of being able to sleep on our backs, we had to sleep on our sides, closely hemmed in by two neighbors. Our emaciated sides, which had a hard time bearing any weight, obliged us to change sides fairly often, which could only be done at the same time as all those in the same row. But however reduced the space may have been, at least we were sure of finding a place every day. And everyone infinitely appreciated, three-quarters of an hour after leaving the tunnel, already being 'back home' lying down.

"Then we had a table in the barracks where we were served soup and bread; there was scarcely any room on the bench for both buttocks at the same time and we had to wait our turns outside to come and sit down, but when we did sit down we no longer had to worry about finding a tin dish from which two or three others had already swallowed their soup." According to Gineston, before the evacuation there were seven or eight blocks, and one of them had still not been occupied.

At Woffleben the improvement of material conditions in comparison to Ellrich went hand in hand with more humane overseers. One witness in the *Mémorial*[57] points out that the C Shift *Kapos* had changed. Instead of two Greens there was a German Red, Walter, and a Pole from Silesia, Stachek. "He was a sturdy fellow with pale skin, a direct gaze, always clean-shaven amongst the dirty and hairy Häftling; he was there, it was alleged, for having been a lieutenant in the international brigades in Spain." Above all, the two *Schreiber* were two Belgians (who spoke German), Ernest Abel and Émile Delaunois. There was a (very insignificant) *Revier* with a French doctor, for several weeks at any rate, and Belgian or French male nurses.

The sick, however, were numerous, because work in the tunnel was harsh and the conditions over the past months had been grueling. The seriously sick were evacuated to Ellrich, and the dead were transported in boxes. On April 1 some seven hundred prisoners evacuated from Auschwitz and Gross Rosen arrived at Woffleben. They were in very bad shape, but it was claimed they were to be made to work at B 12. The evacuation from Woffleben to Bergen-Belsen took place several days later.

A new SS camp commander, Kleemann, also arrived from Auschwitz along with a new *Lagerältester,* Bruno Brodniewicz, former LÄ at Auschwitz I, who would supervise the evacuation. Abel[58] felt it important to pay homage to a noncommissioned SS officer at Woffleben, Sepp Zwerger, who was the B 12 *Arbeitseinsatzführer.* In his office Abel was able to listen to the news broadcasts from Luxembourg, freed by the Americans. He adds: "In March 1945, Zwerger deserted with other Austrians by stealing an armed vehicle and took refuge in the mountains of his country. I went and visited him in 1950 to thank him for everything he had done for us as far as he was able."

Surviving in the Ellrich Camp

THE *OHNE KLEIDER.* Thanks to the creation of the Woffleben camp, the miners in B 12 avoided for the most part during the final months the consequences of the dramatic negligence that characterized from beginning to end how the Ellrich camp was run. It was caused as much by the SS as by the prisoners they put into positions of responsibility.

There were from time to time individual initiatives that were striking because they were the exception, such as those of Theo.[59] "Theo, the big Kapo, was named Block chief, and that nonpolitical prisoner turned out to be a good chief. A mason by trade, energetic and hardworking, he transformed Block 4 from top to bottom. He had the scaffolding demolished and improved sleeping conditions very measurably by dividing the dormitory into little boxes for eighteen men. He had the latrines fixed up. He got the showers working—and that was a genuine feat, because if there was coal, there was no water, and when the water was running there was no coal. But Theo 'organized' things—in other words, he stole. Every evening, the prisoners brought back a bit of wood, a bit of coal from their Kommandos."

In the jargon of the camps, the verb *organisieren* meant procuring what was lacking by more or less licit means. As in the quotation, the term did not necessarily have a pejorative connotation. An example of negligence was the lack of tin dishes for the soup at a certain point. Abel[60] drew attention to this: "At noon, the soup was distributed on work site B 12 by the Kapos. There were neither tin dishes, nor spoons. We had to take rusty tin cans—thrown on a garbage pile by the civilian workers—without being able to clean them. It was only in the days to come that we managed to make ourselves spoons, by carving out pieces of wood."

Far and away the most serious problem was the lack of clothes and shoes, mentioned to the fullest extent in the text entitled "Histoire d'un Block" in the *Mémorial.*[61] Reference is to Block 4: "Everyone who left for the work sites [at the beginning of the cold period] was dressed in rags, jackets with only one arm, pants which left bums exposed, forty shirts for a hundred men, scarcely a single sweater, sixty pairs of socks for a hundred workers!

"During the first days of November [. . .] the Blocks were still cluttered with the sick and the SS declared: 'Those who do not work must be naked.' So the sick had to remove their clothes and give all they had to those on the work sites. [. . .] Those who had had their clothes and shoes stolen ended up every morning almost naked in the roll-call area. The SS sent them back to the Block, declaring them to be 'Ohne Kleider' (unclad). Considered to be sick, they didn't work, but were absolutely naked.

"A disinfecting brought this sad story to a head. We had to bundle up our clothes indicating our identity number, but we didn't have any pencils. Moreover, 'putting those rags through an overheated machine ended up destroying what was still hanging together.' The next day, many of the prisoners were Ohne Kleider. The number of prisoners unfit for work became enormous. [. . .] A nudist's situation was doubtless more enviable than that of his friends who left in a Kommando. But the SS decided to class the weaker amongst the Ohne Kleider in the 'Transport' category.

"Of the 600 men in his Block, Theo had 250 nudists. [. . .] He kept the nudists busy with trifling work. [. . .] With a blanket around the waist, they came and went, and they were known as the 'Peplum.' As the rhythm of death accelerated, the SS no longer dared to carry out a roll call of the naked men in the glacial field and allowed it to take place inside the Block, but with all the windows open." Theo blocked the windows.

In the month of January 1945, clothing arrived; the *Ohne Kleider* were dressed again and sent off to the work sites where most of them soon died. Roger Agnès[62] made it through but lost his buddy Jean Grignola. At the end of the same month the sick left Block 4 for the *Schonung,* recently set up in Block 10.

The account given by Miller[63] ties in with that in the *Mémorial* but allows it to be clarified on two points. The disinfecting, which multiplied the number of *Ohne Kleider,* took place in September 1944, and the situation apparently lasted three months. Especially "for those who were out of work involuntarily, the commander decided to give them only a half-ration of bread and margarine."

Those prisoners affected by this measure found themselves terribly weakened as a consequence and were unable to withstand being reclothed and sent back out on the work sites.

Even apart from the cases of the *Ohne Kleider,* testimonies as to the lack of clothes and absence of hygiene abound. René André[64] writes: "I spent eight months at Ellrich without taking a single shower, without changing my clothes, without getting undressed." Lafond[65] notes: "I wore the same shirt for eight months. No underwear, no sweater, no socks, no overcoat. Just a jacket, canvas trousers and wooden shoes that wore out in a month."

FAMINE AT ELLRICH. In mid-February 1945 a new and dramatic situation developed with the food. Miller[66] describes the situation as follows: "The bread factory which supplied us was destroyed sometime in mid-February and the only food that had prevented us from collapsing was taken away. The soup, for months, had been nothing but turnip and rutabaga water; it became our sole and unique food. A quart at four o'clock in the morning to replace the bread, and our usual quart when we got home in the evening. An average of seventeen hours without eating went by between the two rations. Panic set in, because it was famine in the truest sense of the word. The soup could no longer be felt a half-hour after we had swallowed it. It was nothing but a mere enema, which obliged us to urinate more than usual.

"On the work site, during the midday break, groups of men, like famished wolves around a village, would linger near the civilian canteen, attracted by the odor of the cooking. Vegetable refuse in the garbage, the stalks of cabbages, potato peels were all the object of fierce battles. Those who got their hands on them, after washing them, put them all in a pot and made a soup on a wood fire. It was nothing but water and peelings, without salt or fat, but when they swallowed it down, you would have thought they were eating roast goose."

Miller continues: "On the fourth evening without bread, the kitchen was attacked on the side where the rutabaga stock was kept. Some fifty prisoners, under cover of darkness, and in spite of the fact that it was forbidden to move about, smashed the window that gave onto the kitchen and a full-scale pillage began. A violent wind covered all the noise, but the sound of disputes and yells attracted the attention of a sentry who was in a nearby watchtower. The soldier opened fire with a machine gun in the direction the noise was coming from, and at dawn, the prisoners who went off for KP duty found two dead prisoners stiff from the cold and several others wounded, who were half frozen.

"The sixth evening the undertakers who undressed the corpses in front of one of the sheds of the Revier caught sight of a Gypsy in the throes of cutting himself a beefsteak from the buttocks of a dead prisoner. The camp commander, informed by the Kapo of the Revier about this first case of cannibalism, brought his wife and his entire staff out to watch the scene. I was informed in time to get there myself, and the Gypsy did not hesitate, following a sign from the commander who had brought a piece of bread and salt with him, to continue again in public what he had begun in secret. The sight of the bread whet his appetite, and after having carved another slice from the corpse, and salted it well, made himself a sandwich which he devoured in several minutes. I was well placed to see the color of the human flesh, which was dark red, as well as the commander who smiled at his wife, as if to say: 'My dear, I am offering you a rare spectacle.' Late that night, the Gypsy was executed by prisoners of all different nationalities."

There are varying accounts of this event, but they do not come from eyewitnesses. Already in 1945, Lafond[67] reported a camp rumor: "A Russian partially ate the calves of four corpses. He was discovered and he had to repeat his horrible act in the presence of two prisoner doctors and the German Lagerarzt— which he did without hesitation, asking for bread and salt. To punish him, he was handed over to his compatriots who stoned him to death." The account put together by Bornemann[68] in 1987 goes much further: "On the sixth day without bread, the undertakers noticed that the corpses had been cut into in order to remove flesh. Looking at the wounds, a doctor from the Revier came to the conclusion that it had been the work of an expert. The Revier Kapo informed the SS. Everyone was on their guard, and indeed, a Russian medical student was arrested early in the morning. The camp commander and his aides carried out an interrogation and decided to put on a show for the Prominente: the prisoner had to castrate a dead body, was given a slice of bread, salt and pepper, and was ordered to eat it all. That evening, after roll call, the Russian was lynched."

On March 8, Courtaud[69] noted the following in his diary: "Yesterday, a quarter of a bread: general rejoicing." The food shortage had lasted three weeks. Bread delivery also came to a halt during the same period at Dora and Harzungen. But the consequences were less serious than at Ellrich. Potatoes compensated to some extent, and the shortage was shorter lived. The disorder that reigned at Ellrich made all problems worse.

THE ELLRICH *REVIER*. Information on the Ellrich *Revier* is fragmentary. The fundamental text is anonymous and was published in the *Mémorial,* entitled "Le Revier."[70] Further indications are provided by the typewritten memoirs of Max Oesch,[71] and by short testimonies. The *Revier* was initially installed in the main building of the former plaster works. Oesch notes that it occupied the first and second floors. "On the first floor was the room for surgical patients. [. . .] On the second were the patients from the medical ward, contagious for the most part."

As at Dora in the autumn of 1943, the *Revier*'s functioning had disquieting aspects: "The surgeon saved for himself those operations which consisted almost entirely in opening abscesses. Until October 1944, this surgeon was Jupp, a Belgian from Saint-Vith who refused to be anything but German and who pretended to understand neither French nor Flemish. He was, by trade, a porter at the Cologne railway station."

The doctors and male nurses with the medical ambulance, run by a good Polish doctor from Warsaw, did what they could. "They handed out a quarter of an aspirin tablet to those with a fever; to those with dysentery, a spoonful of kaolin or coal diluted in dirty water, hard to swallow because there wasn't much water, and the sick person suffocated on this overly dry paste. When a prisoner had a fever of more than 40°C, he was allowed to rest in his Block where he had to put up with every imaginable rebuff if not actually do duties. Those who seemed in danger of dying were admitted into the Revier if space was available, corresponding to the number of deaths the day before."

Greff,[72] in the AEG Kommando, confirms this picture: "In what was known as the Revier, the sick were accepted if they were already half dead. The doctors abstained, moreover, from giving them any care. They were left alone to finish dying." Miller's account is similar:[73] "Every day, several prisoners from the Block left for the Revier and were never seen again. Some died directly in their berths without any sickness; they just flickered out like burned-down candles."

Several prisoners were saved by being transferred to the Dora *Revier* in rather unusual conditions, such as Stéphane Hessel's two liaison agents, Jacques Brun and Jean-Pierre Couture. Brun responded as follows to a recent questionnaire:[74] "Ellrich. Was admitted into the Revier in late October 1944 with dysentery, pleurisy, bronchitis, 40°C of fever under the arm. At that time, there was no medication, no doctors or nurses worthy of the name. Was evacuated to Dora with the transport of corpses to be burned in the crematorium, on a day that their number was insufficient, my survival being considered a matter of mere days, if not hours. Arrived late at night, after the lights had been put out." It was then that the Dutch doctor looked after him. Brun remained in the Dora *Revier* until the camp was evacuated.

Couture's account[75] is not very different: "I was evacuated from Ellrich to Dora in a small truck, which, twice a week, carried corpses to the Dora crematorium. Because I wasn't dead when we got there, I was put into waiting in the Revier, then sent to Nordhausen as a Muselmann." He remained in the Dora *Revier* from December 20, 1944, to March 10, 1945. Gilbert,[76] the victim of a serious accident, was transported unconscious to the Dora *Revier* in early October and was treated by Dr. Poupault. He subsequently managed to stay in the Altverwertung (recovery) Kommando until the evacuation.

For Tauzin[77] things were more complicated: "Personally, my condition was growing severely worse. My limbs were sometimes completely paralyzed. It was then decided to transfer me to the Dora Revier, where I would apparently be better cared for. In an ambulance car, eight of us left for Dora. By special favor, I was allowed to stay on a stretcher.

"We were only seven miles from the Dora camp, and yet, having left Ellrich at six in the evening, we only got there toward midnight: we were stranded for more than five hours because of a serious breakdown, and as the driver, totally drunk, was never able to put on the spare tire, all seven sick prisoners had to get out—they were all extremely sick, all shivering with fever—and, lying in the snow, underneath the car, were forced to help with the repairs. I should add that I never saw any of them again. Luckily a truck came along, hitched us up, and pulled us to the Dora camp." Tauzin remained in the Dora *Revier* from December 1944 until the liberation of the camp.

Conversely, things were much simpler for Mandelbaum,[78] alias Lambert, who was transported from Ellrich to Dora in an SS ambulance with the Czech Wodruzeck on December 29, 1944. Fifty years later he still does not know what motivated this favor. Leaving the *Revier* in February, he became night watchman in Block 108 at Dora.

New barracks were finally built for the *Revier* and the *Schonung,* on the other side of the roll-call grounds. The transfer took place in late December 1944 or early January 1945. "The supreme discovery was how the Schonung Block had been organized, divided into three rooms, one for the convalescents, the other for the surgical patients, the third occupied by those who, beyond recovery, were to die as quickly as possible. Almost without any food, in dreadful filth, they were indeed very quickly eliminated."

For a long time the *Kapo* of the *Revier* was Alfred Gutzkow, whom Oesch[79] knew from Wieda. It was thanks to Gutzkow that Oesch had got into the *Revier* as *Schreiber* and then as *Kalfaktor* before being dismissed, then reintegrated and becoming a nurse. These vicissitudes corresponded to the varying success of the intrigues carried out by the head nurse of the surgery, Gerhart Erler, a Red who had been imprisoned for a long time who was violently anti-French, as opposed to Gutzkow (who died of tuberculosis several months after the liberation). Gutzkow was transferred to Dora at his request at the end of February 1945. He was replaced, according to Grand,[80] by a *Volksdeutsch* from Romania "who was only interested in the quart of burning alcohol which I received on two occasions and which he made off with to drink."

With regard to the SS command, Gutzkow enjoyed the support of the camp's German doctor, Captain Schneeman, who was a member of the Luftwaffe, as well as that of his counterpart at Harzungen. Among the *Revier* personnel there were French such as Dr. Pierre Ségelle from Orléans, Dr. Henri Duflot from the Pas-de-Calais area (who arrived from Gross Rosen in February), and Dr. Albert Dubois, a Parisian dentist.

One of the very serious problems was the lack of medicines—which is what Raymond Grand ran up against. He was a pharmacist from Paris, whom Gutzkow had recruited as *Apotheker* for the *Revier* on Oesch's recommendation. Highly competent and efficient, he exerted a great influence.

He was helped by Georges Virondeau[81] in exceptional circumstances. The latter, who remained at Buchenwald until June 1944, was admitted into the Ellrich *Revier* where he found his network leader, Dr. Dubois (known as "Teddy"). By chance Dubois spoke of Virondeau to Captain Schneeman, mentioning to him that he did magic tricks, which was of personal interest to Schneeman. He then hired Virondeau as *Kalfaktor* in the soldiers' *Revier,* located five hundred yards outside the camp.

From October 1944 to April 1945, Virondeau held onto his position and was able, in particular, to provide Grand and Dubois with medications stolen from the soldiers' pharmacy. He relates: "Every day, a sentry took me there and brought me back. They had me wear very decent-looking civilian clothing because we had to pass by some thirty homes. I had a black armband emblazoned with a red cross and the word 'Truppenrevier' in white letters." Thanks to the complicity of two German soldier-nurses he was able to steal medicines, particularly sulfa drugs, and bring them back to the camp along with cigarettes. He could also listen to the BBC. He thus took major risks, but both he and his correspondents remained discreet right to the end. The only hitch came on January 1, 1945: "The sentry and I came back completely 'plastered' (from Rhine wine). When I started to want to sing the Marseillaise in front of my Block, a friend knocked me out and put me to bed."

Albert Besançon,[82] who, having come from Oranienburg, was *Schreiber* and pharmacist at the Rechlin-Retzow camp *Revier* in Mecklenburg, got to Ellrich on February 12, 1945, with identity number 114977 and then began working with Grand. (Paul von Gunten[83] had arrived on January 4, coming from Alt Ruppin after having passed through Buchenwald and Sachsenhausen. He ended up at Woffleben.)

MORTALITY AT ELLRICH. All the surviving witnesses of Ellrich, whenever they may have written their accounts, whatever the differences in the form and the style of what they wrote, present a remarkably homogeneous picture both of the working conditions in the tunnels and the outside Kommandos and of the conditions of life in the camp, in the blocks, and in the *Revier.*

A certain number of these witnesses had the good fortune to escape death through a transfer to Dora, including Couture, Pescadère, Tauzin, and Greff. Others were ultimately assigned to other, less exposed positions, such as Oesch, Goasguen, Grand, Virondeau, and Terral, or such as Abel, Miller, Courtaud, and Grandcoin. A knowledge of German was a precious advantage for Abel and Miller. Only very few witnesses, such as Auchabie and Lafond, remained exposed right to the end. Later chapters will show what they had to deal with at the last moment and why Lafond entitled his book of memories *Survie (Survival).*

It is not easy, on the statistical level, to appreciate the extent of the mortality due to Ellrich's particular conditions. Until August 1944 the number of deaths registered at Ellrich remained remarkably low—seventeen in all—because those prisoners acknowledged to be sick—that is, several hundred—were transferred to the Dora and Harzungen *Reviers,* where care was available, however limited. There is thus no way whatsoever of knowing how many of those sick prisoners died.

The death rate at Ellrich grew in September (29), in October (107), and in November (144), although the transfer of the sick continued. Beginning in December the mortality rate grew dramatically: 381 deaths were registered in that month, 498 in January 1945, 541 in February, 331 in the first ten days of March, 371 in the second ten days, and 319 in the last ten days.

But these figures underestimate the extent of the losses because there was a simultaneous transfer of Muselmänner to Dora. It was thus that at the beginning of February 1945, Guy Marty[84] left his block with a whole group of invalids who had just been dressed. They took the train as far as Woffleben, then made their way to Dora on foot, by way of the Kohnstein route.

The Ellrich camp in the first weeks of 1945 was cluttered with "inactive" prisoners. The *Arbeitseinteilung* of January 29, 1945, already quoted above, indicated indeed that, of a total of 6,571 *Häftling,* there were 467 in the *Revier,* 983 in the *Blockschonung,* and 203 in *Krankentransport* and thus ready to be transferred elsewhere as sick. The sum total of these unusable prisoners—some 1,653 of them—represented a quarter of the overall population. It was a considerable percentage, because those actually at the work sites were themselves very often in bad health.

THE CONVOY OF MARCH 3, 1945, AND THE FINAL WEEKS AT ELLRICH. It was in these conditions that a convoy was organized on March 3, 1945, to evacuate 1,602 prisoners of all nationalities from Ellrich. The convoy ended up at Nordhausen's Boelcke Kaserne. On March 6 a convoy left Nordhausen for an unknown destination with 1,184 of the 1,602 prisoners who had arrived on March 3. Another 346 prisoners died in between times at Nordhausen, or were already dead on arrival. The remaining 76 prisoners managed to stay at the Boelcke Kaserne and later shared the fate of the other camp occupants, in circumstances that will be mentioned in chapter 15. Pierre Auchabie[85] was among them.

In all likelihood the March 6 convoy was sent toward Bergen-Belsen, and practically all the prisoners died either during the journey or once they arrived.

Lafond[86] lost a good many of his friends in that transport. "That day I was at work and if I had known the departure time, I had the possibility to join up with my friends. I missed the chance." But he entered the *Blockschonung* himself on March 15 and only got out on April 5 to get onto an evacuation train.

In the last weeks at Ellrich death was present everywhere in the camp, just as it had been a year before in the Dora Tunnel. Lafond, when he entered Flügel C of the *Blockschonung,* observed: "Right when you arrive, they take away all your clothes, once and for all, they write your number in ink on your chests and count your gold teeth. The exit is by way of the crematory oven."

Outside the corpses piled up, as Max Oesch[87] writes: "They were dying in the Revier, dying in the Blocks, dying in the work Kommandos, dying during roll call. All these scrawny corpses were stacked up outside, exactly four steps from the window of my room." (There was no more gas for the truck that took the cadavers to the Dora crematorium.) "When there got to be about three hundred in the stack, all the bodies were taken to the pyre on the roll-call grounds. It was first of all a pile of straw, on which wooden crosspieces that had been soaked with tar were aligned. The cadavers were placed next to one another, top-to-tail, along two rows. Up above, other crosspieces were placed and then two more rows added. And so on. The next day, in the early morning, someone would set fire to the straw. A thick, acrid smoke would inundate the camp, all day long. In the evening, whatever was still burning was covered over with earth, because of the Anglo-American aircraft."

Oesch continues: "Along would come an SS holding a box, paper and pencil, and a dentist with tools: they were recuperating the gold teeth. A Kalfaktor pulled the cadavers up one by one, by the feet. Every mouth was inspected. If a gold tooth was found, the dentist pulled it out. An ink stamp on the corresponding stomach. The SS took the tooth, made note of it on his paper, and put it into the box. The Kalfaktors then took the corpse and threw it onto the heap."

In the month of March 1945, on the hill above the camp, the brand-new crematorium was put into operation.

THREE DRAMATIC TOLLS. At Ellrich, groups of prisoners had disappeared. It was indicated above, at the end of chapter 6, how André Rogerie and Pierre Auchabie had lost their closest companions in the hellish first months at Dora. Similar tolls can be established for the hell of the last months at Ellrich.

The first of these tolls[88] concerns the fourteen prisoners from Île-Tudy, a small fishing port in the Finistère region of Brittany, where they were arrested on June 20, 1944. They all arrived at Ellrich with the other "77,000"s. Their names were Joseph Cluyou (77784), François Coupa (77742), Grégoire Coupa (77738), Eugène Cratès (77743), Pierre Diquelou (77787), Georges Goasdoué (77737), Pierre Goasdoué (77739), Aimé Guégen (77801), Edgar-Félix Guinvarch (77757), François Guinvarch (77776), Jean Guinvarch (77741), Gilbert Le Bris (77740), Marcel Perrin (?), and Maurice Voland (77744). All were fishermen or petty officers in the navy on armistice leave. In 1945 there was only one survivor among them, Pierre Goasdoué.

They were young men, born between 1909 and 1924. The hostages taken on August 16, 1944, in the town of Puiseaux, in the Loiret,[89] were on the whole much older: the mayor, Émile Tinet (born in 1878) and his son Étienne, veterinarian (1912), the secretary of the town hall Marcel Lange (1883), the priests

Henri Retaureau (1881) and Jacques Baranton (1903), the chief of the gendarmerie Georges Detoux (1900) and the gendarme Edmond Marienne (1905), the garage owner Germain Berthier (1893), and the mechanics Lucien Piétrois (1901) and Georges Berthier (1923), confectioner Louis Maris (1902), the potato merchant Maurice Foiry (1899), and the fertilizer merchant Henri Masure (1913). The grocer Raymond Bourdois (1910) was also arrested.

Taken to Fresnes, they were deported from Pantin to Buchenwald and assigned identity numbers between 77398 (Detoux) and 77459 (Lange). Bourdois was given the number 76857. They were all transferred to Dora, and half of them went from there to Ellrich. Out of fourteen deportees, only three came back in 1945, the elder priest Retaureau, Bourdois, and Georges Berthier.

A third toll can be taken from the list of the dead companions to whom Étienne Lafond[90] dedicated his book of memoirs. It has to do with those with aristocratic names: the marquis René de Roye (77722), Francis de Buigne (31083), Ivan de Colombel (77040), Christian de Dancourt (53257), Philippe d'Elbée (77538), Richard de la Falaise (77200), to which the name of Robert de Renty (77096) must also be added, as he also died at Ellrich. A detailed knowledge of the list of prisoners—French and Belgian in particular—would make it possible to see how groups of deportees with close ties between them were thus affected by their common belonging to bad Kommandos.

Those who were not actually witnesses have a hard time imagining the terrible circumstances under which some of the Ellrich prisoners died. There is information gathered in 1945 on the death of one of the hostages from Puiseaux, the chief of the gendarmerie, Georges Detoux.[91] "Detoux was suffering from dysentery. He was extremely weak, his body was incontinent and gave off a nauseating odor, which provoked the fury of the Block wardens and other prisoners. They jumped on him, beat him up and violently hurled him down the steep stairway from the third floor. Having regained his balance on the floor below, he managed to use his remaining strength to make his way back up. Then he was knocked out with a bed board. It was eight o'clock in the evening, and it was the month of December 1944. His fellow prisoners found him the next morning on the first-floor landing, lying on his back, his mouth open. He had stopped living."

Overall it seems that, proportionally, the prisoners who arrived later suffered the most. This conclusion was reached after a detailed examination of the lists dealing with the Langenstein camp, which will be seen in the next chapter. At Ellrich it was the prisoners who had been there the longest, such as Serge Miller, Jacques Courtaud, Michel Debeauvais, Rémy Vincent, and Max Oesch, who were able to provide an overall view of the camp's history.

THE END OF THE KOHNSTEIN AND HIMMELBERG WORK SITES. During the holiday season in late 1944 the work sites were suspended to enable the German civilians to take leave and spend time with their families in a Reich that was still more or less intact, except for Aachen and a fringe of East Prussia. One civilian remained, however, who perhaps no longer had a house or family. He took advantage of the situation to requisition the prisoners and have them transport rails.

Right from the beginning of January work started up again, but the lack of concentration camp manpower was ever more obvious. It was no longer possible to call upon Buchenwald, upon which Ellrich, as will soon be shown, no longer depended. In any case, Buchenwald no longer received convoys of new deportees and had to draw upon the camp population to provide prisoners for the dreadful Ohrdruf Kommando. Ever more precarious, the local labor force had to suffice. Four initiatives were taken in the course of the first quarter of 1945—a particularly harsh winter quarter. In January, as seen above, a delivery of striped uniforms made it possible to reclothe the *Ohne Kleider* at Ellrich and to send them back out onto the work sites. In December 1944 a Kommando 32 was set up at Dora, which was sent to work on the Niedersachswerfen work sites. Pierre Maho[92] was part of that Kommando, which was ultimately established in the unoccupied buildings of the Boelcke Kaserne at Nordhausen.

When frost halted the work on the Helmetalbahn, the prisoners from the *Baubrigaden* were used from January 2 to February 15. Those from Osterhagen, as already mentioned, came to Woffleben every day by train. Finally, the evacuation of the Auschwitz and Gross Rosen camps having brought a flood of prisoners to Dora, seven hundred of them were transferred on April 1 to the Woffleben camp to be put to work on B 12. The results of these initiatives were practically null because of the newcomers' physical deficiency. Generally speaking, the only effect was to precipitate their end without speeding up the work.

The information Bornemann[93] put together makes it possible to appreciate the situation on the various work sites at the time of the evacuation. The usable surface opened up by the digging, in B 12, over a span of 350 yards in the principal galleries, with between eight and ten transversal galleries, was then 325,000 square feet, as opposed to 1.3 million square feet in the Dora Tunnel and the 1.73 million square feet planned. Its use for aircraft construction had not yet been able to get under way.

The digging of B 3 was further advanced, given that the usable surface was 486,000 square meters as opposed to the 1.4 million initially planned. But the aircraft factory was still not set up. The evolution of project B 11 was different. Not only did the usable surface resulting from the digging reach 572,000 square feet as opposed to the 864,000 planned for, but arrangements were made for the production of jet-aircraft fuel in the framework of the *Kuckuck* program. The early project was moreover modified and the *Kuckuck* program was broken down into *Kuckuck I* and *Kuckick II. Kuckuck I* remained beneath the Kohnstein for production itself, but another site further to the west, beneath the Kammerforst, was chosen for the refining station, where the refrigeration towers on the outside were easier to camouflage. The two sites were linked by mains laid on concrete platforms hidden by the forest. The second site thus housed *Kuckuck II,* which was built in the framework of a new project referred to as B 17, through the use of prisoners from Ellrich.

The prisoners in B 17 were above all miners. But Robert Lançon,[94] a cabinetmaker by trade, was one of the six members of the Sägewerk (sawmill) Kommando Schmidt up until the evacuation. As already mentioned, work on B 11 and B 17 in particular had been put in the hands of the Ammoniakwerk Merseburg, a company long since established in Niedersachswerfen. It employed in fact more civilian workers—both German and foreign—than prisoners, and work site B 11 is rarely mentioned in the prisoners' testimonies. What left a mark on people's minds were work sites B 3 and B 12, and above all the earthworks and carrying jobs on the Woffleben plain, whether or not in the framework of the B 13 work site.

Those who ran the Harzungen, Ellrich, and Woffleben camps between May 1944 and April 1945 were merely following orders. Those who belonged to the Luftwaffe, such as the commander of Harzungen or the doctors at Harzungen and Ellrich, behaved fairly well—given the circumstances of the time. The SS on the other hand were all in all a somber bunch of brutes, and they bear a heavy responsibility in the prisoners' sufferings.

But it should not be forgotten that the essential responsibility was Kammler's—for it was he who ran both the work sites and the camps. It is extraordinary that a project as insane as the digging of 4 million square feet of galleries was carried out with such obstinacy, even in the final weeks, and that nothing was done in this regard to protect the existence of an increasingly scarce labor force. Right to the very end there were still leaders and business executives who were willing accomplices in a massacre that, in the apocalypse of the end of Nazism, appeared premeditated.

ROTTLEBERODE, BLANKENBURG, LANGENSTEIN, AND OTHER NEARBY CAMPS

The Dora camp and tunnel, the Helmetalbahn Kommandos and work sites, the Harzungen, Ellrich, and Woffleben camps along with the new Kohnstein and Himmelberg work sites made up a coherent geographical whole, with numerous exchanges of both healthy and ailing prisoners. But beginning in the spring of 1944 other Kommandos were set up in the area, all round the Harz Mountains, out of Buchenwald. Some of them were later brought under the dependency of Neuengamme. In the autumn of 1944 still others were linked to Dora, Ellrich, and Harzungen, making up Mittelbau. The rest continued to depend on Buchenwald.

Part 6 will show the common destiny of all these camps and Kommandos at the time of their evacuation. The successive study of these neighboring camps will bring to light the names of some very well-known prisoners: Serge Balachowsky, Stéphane Hessel, David Rousset, Robert Antelme, and Robert Desnos.

Rottleberode: The Factory and the Camp

The transfer of aviation assembly plants into underground installations, which came about in the spring of 1944, was, in the *Mittelraum,* above all of interest to the Junkers-Betriebe company, whose traditional sites were immediately to the east in Anhalt (Dessau, Bernburg, Köthen) and nearby (Leipzig, Magdeburg).

The workshops transferred to the north part of the Dora Tunnel, evacuated by Mittelwerk on Kammler's orders, were known as Nordwerk Niedersachswerfen. They did not use concentration camp manpower but rather a largely foreign labor force (5,000 workers as opposed to 500 German civilians) with whom the Mittelwerk prisoners were not supposed to have any contact.

At the same time the Sonderstab Kammler proceeded with setting up a factory in a natural cave at Heimkehle, to the east of Nordhausen, as part of the A 5 operation. At the Schönebeck factory south of Magdeburg there was a large Buchenwald Kommando with skilled workers who had been selected upon the convoys' arrival. A large number of the Schönebeck personnel was transferred to the Heimkehle cave. Another Kommando of this kind was found in Halberstadt. The new factory, called Thyrawerke Rottleberode, built landing gear.

It was thus that Victor Letourneux,[1] from the "20,000"s convoy—which got to Buchenwald in September 1943—arrived from Schönebeck in the Rottleberode camp. Jean Rougier[2] came directly from Buchenwald on June 15, 1944. later, Stéphane Hessel would pass only briefly through Schönebeck before getting to Rottleberode on November 4, 1944. The corresponding camp[3] was established to the north of the village in the Max Schuck porcelain factory. It was given the code name of Heinrich. There were 903 prisoners on December 31, 1944; their number had grown to 1,700 on the eve of the evacuation. The *Revier* doctor as of July 1944 was a Belgian, Dr. Fernand Maistriaux,[4] from Beauraing.

The French male nurse was the Alsatian student Robert Gandar.[5] Rougier and Letourneux have both paid homage to these men's devotion. Gandar gave Maistriaux medication when he was "afflicted with serious pleurisy in the left lung" prior to the evacuation. There was also the black male nurse named Johnny, who deserves special mention. It is noteworthy that people as different as Stéphane Hessel and Johnny ended up at the same time in Rottleberode.

A little further to the north, at Stempeda, the Sonderstab Kammler opened an underground work site, the B 4, of the same kind as the B 3, B 11, and B 12 already mentioned above. The corresponding Kommando seems to have been made up above all of Hungarian Jews.

STÉPHANE HESSEL AND ALFRED BALACHOWSKY. At the end of March 1944, Stéphane Hessel arrived in France from London in a Lysander, sent by the BCRA on a mission to reorganize radio contacts between the different networks. For this mission, known as Cobra, two young men acted as his agents, Jacques Brun and Jean-Pierre Couture. Hessel and Couture were arrested on July 10, and Brun on July 11.[6] (Brun and Couture have already appeared in the preceding chapter in relation to the Ellrich camp and their transfer to the Dora *Revier*.)

Hessel was of German origin and like Semprun spoke excellent German, which was a significant advantage under certain circumstances at the time. On August 8 he joined a group of thirty-seven Resistance fighters arrested in France, comprised above all of French, several Belgians, three Englishmen, an American, and a Canadian who were transferred from Paris to Buchenwald,[7] where they arrived on August 12 and were grouped in Block 17. The newcomers had contacts with the Buchenwald prisoners. Hessel met Pineau, whom he had known in London; Henri Frager met Semprun, who had been a member of his network. They were visited by Alfred (also Serge) Balachowsky, who worked in Block 50, where a vaccination against typhus was being prepared.

Balachowsky, a Frenchman of Russian origin who had arrived in Buchenwald with the first convoy of January 1944, was quickly sent to Dora, where he did spray-painting on the *Spitze* of the V2s. As he was a well-known scientist at the Pasteur Institute, he was brought back from Dora to Buchenwald following a high-level decision because prisoners could not leave Dora (not at that time at any rate).[8]

At Buchenwald he was first sent to the bunker, until it was noticed that he kept coming back on a regular basis. He was then assigned to the Block 50 Kommando, which was made up of sixty-five prisoners of all origins, including seven Jews. There were many scholars as well as politicians, in particular the Austrian Eugen Kogon, who had a powerful influence on the SS doctor, Dr. Ding-Schuler. The latter was the head of both Block 50 and Block 46, where medical experiments were carried out on prisoners, in particular against exanthematic typhus, and where prisoners who were (often terminally) ill with typhus were also hospitalized. Blocks 46 and 50 were isolated from the rest of the camp, and the SS in particular never went in.

On September 8, sixteen of the thirty-seven resistance fighters were "called to the tower" (at the camp entrance) and executed by hanging. The others knew that their turn would come. And it was then that a rescue operation was organized for three among them, through Balachowsky. Kogon gained the complicity of Dr. Ding-Schuler and Dietzsch, the *Kapo* of Block 46, for an identity swap with the French prisoners dying of typhus. It was in this way that the Englishmen Yeo Thomas and Peuleve and the Frenchman Stéphane Hessel were saved. A detailed account of this operation—dramatic in more ways than one—is given by Kogon in *L'État SS (The SS State)* and by Hessel in *Danse avec le siècle*[9] *(Dance with the Century)*. Almost all the others, including Frager, were executed.

Hessel,[10] assuming the identity of the cutter Michel Boitel, and with identity number 81626, was assigned to Rottleberode via Schönebeck. His knowledge of German enabled him to become a *Buchführer*—that is, an accountant. He then remained in the camp before returning to the factory, thanks to two *Prominente,* the *Kapo* Walter and the *Schreiber* Ulbricht, politicians who explained the rules of concentration camp life to him.

When he got back to the factory, he and a friend, Robert Lemoine, decided to escape. They slipped away in the course of the walk from the camp to the factory in early February 1945. Quickly caught, they were sent off to Dora and locked up in the bunker. Once again Hessel's knowledge of German allowed him to minimize the damage. Lemoine and he were sent to the Strafkommando with the *Fluchtpunkt* of escapees. He had to do earthwork. He was also assigned the task of undressing the corpses from the evacuation convoys coming from the camps to the east.

JOHNNY. The "Negro Johnny" as Rassinier calls him, and as he was known at the time, was already a notable in Buchenwald, where he arrived with one of the January 1944 convoys and passed himself off as a black American. He obtained a position as a doctor in the *Revier,* where he was quickly recognized for his incompetence and boasting—but also for his generosity. From there he went to the Dora *Revier*, where Rassinier met up with him.[11] Then he became a nurse at the Rottleberode *Revier,* where Gandar was in charge of his initiatives. He was finally liberated in Mecklenburg after having left the column (in the course of the evacuation of Ravensbrück, which will be dealt with in chapter 21) in the company of the interpreter Georges Schmidt.

After the war, research was done on "Johnny Nicolas," the results of which are as follows:

"Johnny was not American, but French. His real name was Jean Marcel Nicolas. He was born in 1918 in Haiti. His parents came from Guadeloupe and were French citizens. He had learned American English from the Marines based in Haiti. Jean did a part of his studies in France and served for a time in the French Navy. He was living in France when the war broke out. During the German occupation, he claimed he was a pilot with the US Air Force and called himself Johnny Nicolas. He did intelligence work for the Allies, but was denounced in Paris by his 'girlfriend.' He was sent to Buchenwald, then to Dora. He survived the war, but died in France in September 1945. According to Dr. Groeneveld, Johnny was a boy with a character, who knew German well, which allowed him to survive and help out his fellow prisoners in the camp." Johnny was a phenomenon who fascinated a good many prisoners, especially the young Russians who had never seen a black man before.

The Blankenburg Camps

Blankenburg is a small town located in the northeast part of the Harz Mountains, on the opposite side from Nordhausen. Like most everywhere else in the Harz area there are mines and quarries nearby, some abandoned, some not. The Todt Organization decided in mid-1944 to open a work site in the area, defined by the testimony of Justin Gruat. He mentions "miners and frame-workers working in an abandoned mine, in order to enlarge the galleries and turn them into an underground factory."

The camp, called Klosterwerke, was located in Oesig, a town to the west of Blankenburg. Thanks to Belgian testimonies, in particular Albert Van Hoey's[12] and Narcisse Dufrane's, its history is known. It was opened on August 23, 1944, by a group of 500 prisoners who had arrived by train directly from Buchenwald. Among them there were 369 Belgians belonging to the August 10 convoy and several Frenchmen arrested either in Belgium, such as Hubert Tumerelle, or in the north of France such as Boleslas Leciejewski, from Lens.[13] The other prisoners were Greens involved in supervising the blocks, the Kommandos, the Poles and Russians, and so on.

The prisoners were first housed in a camp of tents. Some of them, including Van Hoey, were assigned to constructing a camp of barracks for which the plans exist, drawn up by Van Hoey and Maurice Bouchez. It was occupied on October 1. The other prisoners were sent off for digging and stone removal work or transporting bags of cement and iron reinforcing bars in the same conditions as those on the Sonderstab Kammler work sites. The French doctor from the *Revier,* Dr. Georges Ropers, who came from Ellrich, did what he could, but he too lacked medicines. The mortality rate was high. The corpses, stripped of their clothes, were thrown into mass graves.

Another camp was set up at the end of January 1945 in Regenstein, a hill located to the north of Blankenburg. Its code name was Turmalin. The prisoners were Jews evacuated from the Fürstengrübe Kommando, dependent on Auschwitz.[14]

Work remained unfinished when Turmalin and Klosterwerke were evacuated, both on the same day.

The Osterode Camps

A camp at Osterode is known to have existed because of the decision taken at the end of 1944 to link it to Dora, at the same time as Rottleberode and Blankenburg. It was known as Heber and had 286 prisoners at the time. It was set up at Freiheit in August–September and manufactured aeronautical equipment.[15]

A second camp, at Osterode-Petershütte, corresponded to the Dachs IV project and had to do with underground work carried out by the Todt Organization for refining mineral oil. It is known about through Hofstein's testimony. In January 1945, Dr. Jules Hofstein,[16] a French Jew, found himself at Dora following an evacuation from Auschwitz. He came from the Bismarckshütte annex Kommando, where he had been the doctor. He was transferred to Osterode, also as a doctor.

He provides some highly valuable details: "The camp was just in the process of being finished. There were, at the time, 800 prisoners, who, in three teams, were digging galleries into the mountain, where underground factories were to be installed. As if this heavy work were not enough, there was also camp-setup duty." Hofstein managed to have prisoners who were in the *Schonung* exempted from these duties. He was backed up by the LÄ, an old Bavarian communist.

He adds the following surprising fact: "Strange detail, but, during burials, a doctor was supposed to accompany the duty and make sure the service was properly carried out. I thus had the occasion to take part in the burial of Jewish prisoners in the Jewish cemetery—which had been neither destroyed nor ravaged by the Nazis, as was usually the case. I point this unusual fact out in passing as it is doubtless unique in Hitler's Germany.

"Around the 15 March 1945, we had to leave Osterode to make room for Russian prisoners of war. We were divided into three convoys. Mine landed in the Nordhausen camp." What then happened to Hofstein between his stay in the Boelcke Kaserne and his liberation at Theresienstadt will be seen later.

The Langenstein Camp

In Langenstein, halfway between the cities of Halberstadt and Blankenburg, there was a large concentration camp in 1944–45. It was located less than six miles from the Blankenburg-Oesig camp. However, there was no connection between the two camps or between their corresponding work sites. The Langenstein work site was the Sonderstab Kammler's B 2 work site. Until October 1944 the two camps were Buchenwald Kommandos. At that time Blankenburg was linked to Dora and Langenstein still depended on Buchenwald. In April 1945 the evacuations took place under very different circumstances. The Langenstein camp, unknown for a long time, was studied in exemplary fashion by Paul Le Goupil, who in 1996 put together a "Mémorial des Français" ("Memorial to the French")[17] who had passed through—of which he was one. The document includes a history of the camp from which the principal facts can be drawn. The camp was also known by the name of Zwieberge. Indeed it was set up at the foot of a clay hill that bears the name because of its two crowning summits.

The first prisoners arrived from Buchenwald on April 21, 1944, and the second group from Neuengamme on April 27. All the other convoys up until February 1945 came from Buchenwald with the exception of the October 15, 1944, convoy, which brought five hundred prisoners directly from Sachsenhausen. Every nationality was represented: Germans of course, but also many French, Poles, Russians, and Czechs, for instance. The arrival of Latvians on August 8, 1944, from a camp near Riga via Buchenwald was noted. There were no convoys of Hungarian Jews such as there were at Dora. The Jews coming from Auschwitz in February 1945 via Buchenwald were of all different nationalities.

As was generally the case, the prisoners in the first convoys were housed in temporary buildings, and some of them built the permanent camp blocks while the others were sent directly to the earthwork, digging, and handling work sites.

It was in August 1944 that the Zwieberge camp was occupied by some 2,000 prisoners. Their number reached 3,590 by early January 1945 and attained its maximum on February 18 of 5,160, after the arrival of convoys of 1,000 each; it was only 4,191 in April because of the number of deaths. But an annex camp known as the "Junkers camp" or "little camp" also has to be taken into account, for it was there that the prisoners (885 in all) arrived from the Junkers' factory Kommandos in Halberstadt, Aschersleben, and Niederorschel. Le Goupil's toll is as follows, taking account of the Junkers camp: in all, 7,013 prisoners passed through Langenstein, and, on April 3, 1945, there were only 5,089 left. Because 295 had been sent back to Buchenwald, 1,629 died in the camp. Until March 16, 1945, the dead were incinerated at the Quedlinburg crematorium, then thrown into a mass grave. There were also at this same date 483 prisoners in the *Revier* and 1,251 in the *Schonung.* That is, a total of 1,734—in other words, 34.1 percent of the surviving prisoner population, which is not negligible. It was the work in the tunnel, beneath the Thekenberge, which was essentially responsible for the mortality of some and the exhaustion of others.

The Langenstein "Mémorial" includes a chapter entitled "Extermination Through Work and Life in the Camp," which is an excellent synthesis of the testimonies the author brought together. Hélie de Saint-Marc's text[18] should also be mentioned, and is included as a conclusion to the book *Leçons de ténèbres (Lessons of Darkness)* under the title "The Place of People's Absolute Truth." He owes his survival at Langenstein to a Latvian miner who took him under his protection. Georges Petit[19] has also recently published, in the journal *Vingtième Siècle,* his thoughts on his concentration camp experience, in particular at Langenstein.

Further along, in chapter 20, mention will be made of the camp's liberation and of the tragic circumstances of its evacuation. At that time the work was not sufficiently advanced to allow the underground galleries to be used.

The Neu Stassfurt Kommando

On September 14, 1944, a Kommando of five hundred prisoners that had arrived from France by the Rethondes convoy of August 18 left Buchenwald. It arrived at Neu Stassfurt, in Germany's large potash-salt production region. There were two mine shafts, shaft 6 and shaft 7, and the plan was to transform the mines, located at a depth of between 1,300 and 1,500 feet, into underground factories. This fell into the framework of the Sonderstab Kammler's A-type projects. The work got under way at the same time as did the work at Blankenburg, whereas Langenstein was contemporary with Ellrich and Harzungen.

The Kommando arrived in an already existing camp that had four barracks. Some workers were assigned to surface Kommandos to build roads, lay water mains, and so on. Another camp was also constructed, which would never be used. And holes were dug underground to install test stands for airplane engines. The mine Kommandos had to clear out the rooms and galleries by extracting blocks of salt and pouring concrete in certain areas. That meant, on the surface as well as underground, getting rid of the rubble and handling sacks of cement, reinforcing bars, and so on. Then the machines had to be installed. Once again it was the Siemens Kommando—the electricians' Kommando—that appears to have been privileged. The work was carried out by companies employing not only prisoners but also civilians, above all Dutch workers, and Soviet prisoners of war. In February 1945, three hundred Russian and Polish prisoners joined the French, but contacts were rare.

An excellent collection of testimonies has been put together by the Amicale des anciens déportés à Neu Stassfurt (Association of Former [French] Deportees to Neu Stassfurt). It was published in 1996 under the title *Un pas, encore un pas . . . pour survivre*[20] *(One Step, Another Step . . . to Survive).* The title refers to the long and murderous evacuation from Neu Stassfurt all the way to the Erzgebirge, which will be looked at in greater detail in chapter 20. Some 20 percent of the French in the Kommando died in the camp (97 out of 493), above all in the final months. They were incinerated in the Magdeburg crematorium until late February 1945. The crematorium having been destroyed in a bombing raid, the final victims were buried in a mass grave.

In early April 1945 the mines were ready for the installation of an underground factory for producing tank parts, according to the Kommandos' list of March 25, 1945, found at Buchenwald.

To the south of Neu Stassfurt, another Kommando from Wansleben (Wansleben a. See, to the west of Halle) was working under identical conditions. André Cozette[21] was employed getting rid of the stones from the digging of the new galleries. He witnessed the arrival in the new factory of various equipment, including machine tools that he recognized as being French made.

Porta Westfalica and Helmstedt

David Rousset[22] arrived at Buchenwald in the third convoy from Compiègne in January 1944. One day in March he was part of the Max Eins transport; at the same time the Hannah transport left for Dora. Rousset and his friends were sent to inaugurate a camp at Porta Westfalica, a small town on the Weser River. The account of Rousset's trajectory, up until his time at Wöbbelin in Mecklenburg in April–May 1945, is incorporated in the "novel" he published in 1947 entitled *Les Jours de notre mort (The Days of Our Death).* Indications already figured in his *L'Univers concentrationnaire,* written in 1945. As already seen in chapter 11, the headquarters of the Sonderstab Kammler's Sonderinspektion I was established in Porta Westfalica. It was also the location of work site A 2, which was dependent on it. Rousset does not give any details about it because he did not stay long at Porta.

Pierre Bleton,[23] who also arrived in March from Neuenbremme and Buchenwald, remained there until the beginning of September. He worked digging underground galleries. Then as an NN he was targeted for regrouping in Neuengamme. Later, along with other NN, he would go to Gross Rosen and Dora.

Polish prisoner Wieslaw Kielar[24] was at Porta in November 1944, coming from Auschwitz through Sachsenhausen. Digging continued at the foot of the Bremsberg hill while a cog railway made it possible to accede to the nine levels of an abandoned mine occupied by the workshops of the Philips factories.

Meanwhile, Rousset was assigned to Neuengamme, which had just replaced Buchenwald as the main camp, which involved changing identity numbers. It must not be forgotten that at this time the convoys coming from Compiègne began to be directed toward Neuengamme. From Neuengamme, Rousset was sent to Helmstedt,[25] where he remained until the evacuation. It was also a camp created by a Buchenwald Kommando and was put under Neuengamme's jurisdiction.

The corresponding work site was given code A 3. The camp was not in Helmstedt itself but further to the east, in Beendorf. There were two work sites corresponding to two salt mines. One, situated at Bartensleben, had to be transformed for the Askania Company. The other, known as the Schacht Marie (Maria tunnel), was intended for a Siemens factory.[26]

As Helmstedt belonged, historically speaking, to the duchy of Brunswick, the city was attached in 1945 to the British occupation zone, then to the province of Lower Saxony in West Germany. It was for decades one of the rare road and rail border crossings with East Germany. But it was on the other side of the line that Beendorf and Bartensleben were to be found, because they had been Brandenburg and subsequently Prussian since the seventeenth century.

It was in the Helmstedt camp that David Rousset became very close to the *Kapo* Emil Künder, a German communist to whom he dedicated *Les Jours de notre mort*. Chapter 21 will once again deal with the prisoners from Porta Westfalica and Helmstedt who were evacuated to Wöbbelin such as David Rousset, Emil Künder, Alfred Rohmer, and Wieslaw Kielar.

While jurisdiction over Helmstedt passed from Buchenwald to Neuengamme, Buchenwald set up a new Kommando in August 1944 at Weferlingen, six or so miles to the north of Bartensleben. Its mission was to transform a fifteen-hundred-foot-deep salt mine, and the Kommando was called Gazelle. It is known about thanks to André Chicaud's testimony.[27]

The Gandersheim Kommando

This was a Kommando dependent on Buchenwald but was actually quite far away, given that the small town of [Bad] Gandersheim is located some seven miles west of the edge of the Harz Mountains. It is thus not far from Seesen and Münchehof, which will be mentioned in chapter 19 with regard to evacuations.

The Kommando was sent there in September 1944 to supply a factory that manufactured cabins for Heinkel airplanes with a concentration camp labor force. It was equivalent to those then assigned to aircraft construction in Rottleberode, Halberstadt, Aschersleben, Niederorschel, and Langensalza, to mention only the nearest. When it left Buchenwald the Kommando was made up of five hundred men, most of them French, along with some Belgians, Russians, Poles, and of course Germans—Greens, who looked after supervision. Some of the prisoners in the Kommando were more or less qualified workers.

Others were not qualified at all, and their fate was precarious. One of the latter, Robert Antelme, became very well known when he published his memoirs in 1957 under the title *L'Espèce humaine*[28] *(The Human Race)*. It is certainly a great literary work, but the historian is above all grateful to him for having provided a testimony of exceptional quality, remarkably accurate in terms of expression. Antelme devoted some two hundred very dense pages to evoking life in a camp and factory in which no really exceptional event ever took place until the evacuation which, little by little, took on tragic proportions.

It is a text that has to be taken as a whole, without isolating its anecdotal aspects, which are frequent, and without reducing it to its general considerations on the human race, which are deep. Some great works simply cannot be dissected—and *The Human Race* is one such work. Such is the reaction of a former deportee who can only identify with the work by considering it as a whole, in other words, by taking account both of the title and the first sentence which deliberately reads: "I went off for a pee." Antelme and the Gandersheim Kommando will be mentioned again in chapter 20 with regard to the evacuations.

Other Kommandos Further to the East

For the historian, the temptation is always great to extend the investigation still further. With regard to the Kommandos that existed in March 1945, he could take an even closer look at the entire Reich. He would thus end up at the Loibl Pass[29] underground work site, intended to establish a road tunnel between Carinthia and the Carniole, in other words between Austria and what is today Slovenia.

Let it suffice to mention the existence in the same geographical zone as Stassfurt and Wansleben of various Kommandos on Buchenwald, which will come up once again at the time of the evacuations. It is the case in particular of the Schönebeck Kommando south of Magdeburg, which remained sizable in spite of the transfers to Rottleberode. It was also the case for Flöha,[30] near Chemnitz, where the poet Robert Desnos was prisoner and which depended on Flossenbürg.

PART FIVE

The Final Months

[[14   ]]

THE END OF AUSCHWITZ
AND PEENEMÜNDE

At the beginning of January 1945 the Deutsches Reich could still sustain a certain illusion of power. In the west, around Aachen, a small part of what was traditionally German territory fell under Allied control; German troops, however, still clung to the last pocket of Colmar in Alsace. In the east the Soviets were still only on the fringes of East Prussia and on the Vistula facing Warsaw. They had already taken over part of the General Government of Poland, along with Lvov and Lublin; but Posen and Silesia remained entirely German. In the southeast, fighting continued in the western part of Hungary, protecting Austria, as German and Hungarian troops held out in Budapest. In Italy the Allies were halted between Ravenna and Bologna.

The concentration camp system was still largely intact. The prisoners from Struthof in Alsace had been transferred to Dachau or into Kommandos in southern Germany. Those prisoners from Maïdanek close to Lublin went toward the west. The Soviets had reached Sobibor, Treblinka, and Belzec, but these "killing centers" for Jews had been carefully destroyed after use.

Some three hundred miles still separated the Peenemünde base from the Soviet troops. Three months later, however, at the beginning of April, Peenemünde no longer existed. It had been evacuated and then destroyed—anticipating the Soviet arrival. And, as the Americans were making rapid advances, the factory in the Dora Tunnel had then to be abandoned. This chapter recounts the different stages in this collapse.

The Evacuation of the Camps in the East

THE SOVIET OFFENSIVE FROM THE VISTULA TO THE ODER. On January 12, 1945, Soviet troops launched an offensive all along the front line from East Prussia to the Carpathians. It was toward the center that the most rapid advances were made. Warsaw fell on January 17, Lodz (then known as Litzmannstadt) on January 19, and Gniezno (then known as Gnesen) on January 22. Poznan (then known as Posen) was surrounded and fell on February 22. The Oder, to the northeast of Berlin, was reached on January 31. Further to the north the Soviets seized Olsztyn (then known as Allenstein) on the 22nd and Bydgoszcz (then known as Bromberg) on the 26th. They quickly reached and surrounded Pila (then known as Schneidemühl)—the city that was home to Krüger, *Meister* of Ko Scherer from the Mittelwerk who was in charge of the gyroscopes. From this central axis the offensives directed toward the Baltic isolated Königsberg, Danzig, and the other Prussian and East Pomeranian ports.

The advance in the south of Poland and Silesia was just as rapid. The Soviets took Czestochowa on January 17 and Krakow on January 19. The Upper Silesian basin was conquered between January 24 and 28—before the Germans were able to destroy the industrial installations. Moving down the Oder, they surrounded Breslau on February 16; the Soviets applied pressure in the direction of Moravia but did not attempt to penetrate into Bohemia from Silesia. This decision was to have consequences on the fate of a certain number of convoys and columns of evacuated prisoners in the following months.

The entrance of Soviet troops into the regions of Prussia, Pomerania, and Silesia, which had German populations, resulted in a considerable exodus of the civilian population, affecting in total several million people. A significant number of them were transported by sea to Mecklenburg and Holstein.

THE EVACUATION OF STUTTHOF. Three principal concentration camps— along with their camp annexes and Kommandos—were then threatened by Soviet troops: Stutthof, Auschwitz, and Gross Rosen.

The Stutthof camp was in West Prussia, near the Baltic and east of Danzig. The prisoners, both men and women, were above all Polish, Baltic, Russian, and Jewish. Very few prisoners came from Western countries and there are few accounts available, other than the joint account of Alphonse Kientzler and Paul Weil, in *Témoignages strasbourgeois (Strasbourg Testimonies).*[1] The two men were doctors there who were sent from Dachau in September 1944. On January 25, 1945, the evacuation toward Pomerania in the west was decided. It took place in snow and mud. After a six-week stop in a work camp, the exodus continued on. The survivors were liberated in Putzig by Soviet troops on March 12, 1945. The evacuation of Stutthof was a significant event. It was in fact the only one for which an explicit SS document is available and in which the camp commander, Sturmbannführer Hoppe, explains how the evacuation was to take place.[2] The reality reported by Kientzler and Weil was far more tragic.

THE EVACUATION OF AUSCHWITZ. The Auschwitz camp was in Upper Silesia, in a part of Poland that was directly incorporated into the Reich in 1939. (The Polish name of the small nearby town is Oswiecim.) The camp was opened in June 1940 by the Polish under the supervision of Greens from Sachsenhausen.[3] The Czech, Russian, and other prisoners came next, but the Polish— still numerous—were in the end the most influential, alongside the Germans.

The camp was for a long time particularly harsh; the 1942 convoys of French hostages, men (the "45,000"s) and women (the "31,000"s) experienced considerable losses.[4] Afterward the situation improved for the survivors, and André Rogerie—who came to Dora via Maïdanek in 1944—considered he had seen worse. He was close at hand during the "selections" of Hungarian Jews and was one of the first to make mention of it in his memoirs published in 1946.[5]

While still remaining a concentration camp in keeping with the norms for all camps as defined by Eicke in 1942, the camp at Auschwitz actually became an extermination camp for Jews of various origins: first from Slovakia, then France, Belgium, the Netherlands, Italy, Greece (particularly from Salonica), and also—to some extent—from Poland. The final large convoys came from Hungary in the spring of 1944, sent by Eichmann. In the Auschwitz compound—which comprised in fact three camps—Jewish men and women who had escaped the gas chambers during the selections were put to work under often severe conditions. A special camp for Gypsies was also established at Auschwitz.

In 1943 and 1944, as noted in the preceding chapters, Auschwitz had a large labor pool to draw upon made up of Polish, Czech, and Russian as well as Hungarian Jewish and Gypsy prisoners who went from there to Dora via Buchenwald.

During the last months of 1944 a number of the non-Jewish prisoners from Auschwitz—often the more senior prisoners—were dispersed between the various other camps. In this way Hermann Langbein—an influential Austrian Red—found himself in August at Neuengamme;[6] Wieslaw Kielar—who arrived at Auschwitz in the first convoy of Poles—was transferred to Porta Westfalica;[7] and the majority of French survivors from the convoy of the "45,000"s were sent on to Flossenbürg, Sachsenhausen, or Gross Rosen.[8] The objective of these departures—so it seems—was to disorganize the (clandestine) political structures of prisoner groups set up for the purposes of escape during evacuation.

On the other hand, Himmler decided on November 26, 1944, to eliminate all of the death camp installations, as had already been done at Sobibor, Treblinka, and Belzec. The gas chambers were destroyed and the pits, where the corpses of Hungarian Jews were burned, camouflaged.

With the advance of Soviet troops—they seized Krakow the very next day, some thirty miles to the east—the evacuation, by foot, began on the morning of January 18, 1945. The purpose of this forced march was to reach an annex camp in Gleiwitz to the west of the mineral basin of Upper Silesia. It was very cold, many of the prisoners were quickly exhausted, and those who could no longer keep up were shot. It was one of the worst "death marches" in the history of the evacuations. Concerning this episode there are numerous testimonies available. One account was made by André Rogerie, who spoke of a three-hour rest period after a twenty-hour march, most of it at night, and of being forced to leave again just as a violent gale started up.[9] A similar account is given by Marc Klein in *Témoignages strasbourgeois.*[10]

The prisoners, men and women, Jewish and non-Jewish, came from the major camps or outside Kommandos; such as Simone Jacob (Simone Weil), who arrived with her mother and sister from the Bobreck Kommando;[11] or like Jules Hofstein, who arrived from the Bismarckshütte Kommando.[12] As the next chapter will show, they ended up at Dora.

In the end there remained the sick, who, considered contagious, were abandoned at Auschwitz, including the Italian Jew Primo Levi[13] and the Slovenian Porocevalec, who, like Rogerie, had arrived there from Dora via Maïdanek. In the end the camp was liberated only on January 27, at the moment of the final battles in the region—marked by the takeover of Katowice.

Economic activity in the large industrial zone of Upper Silesia having come to a halt, empty railway cars were not lacking in Gleiwitz and elsewhere, especially the open-top cars for transporting coal; the SS had the prisoners climb into them as soon as they arrived. The trains left one after the other as the Soviet troops drew closer. The Soviets took Gleiwitz on January 24—isolating Upper Silesia.

The itinerary followed by these trains is not well known, as those on the trains were hardly in a state to identify their whereabouts. They appeared to be heading to Moravia before going through Austria or Bohemia to reach one of the large German camps such as Buchenwald or Dora, or even Bergen-Belsen. Roger Climaud, a French Jewish Resistance fighter from Monowitz, arrived directly at Dora.[14] But certain trains, where Rogerie[15] and Marc Klein[16] ended up, headed toward the Gross Rosen camp.

The Gross Rosen camp—like the Stutthof camp—is not well known in Western countries because it did not receive large convoys, either directly like Buchenwald or Dachau or indirectly like Flossenbürg.

THE EVACUATION OF GROSS ROSEN. Gross Rosen was set up in May 1941 on the edge of the Lower Silesian mountains to the west of Breslau. The small neighboring town is now called Rogosnica in Polish. Like Mauthausen and Flossenbürg, Gross Rosen was established in connection with the exploitation—for the SS—of a large quarry. It was considered a particularly inhospitable camp, even by the "45,000"s who came from Auschwitz[17] like Roger Abada. The core of the population was made up of Poles, quite unwelcoming to the Western prisoners.

On October 31, 1944, numerous Belgian prisoners were sent there—NN who had been at the Gross Strehlitz prison in Upper Silesia, such as Léon-E. Halkin.[18] A number of French prisoners came with them, like Michel Poiteau, who came from the Loos-lez-Lille prison in May.[19] On January 5, 1945, the

French NNs—Ernest Gaillard, Charles Vedel,[20] and Pierre Bleton[21]—arrived from Neuengamme.

After having conquered Upper Silesia, the Soviet troops moved down the Oder toward Berlin. As previously noted, they ended up surrounding Breslau on February 16, 1945. The SS made the decision to evacuate the Gross Rosen camp, and railway convoys were formed, which, beginning on February 8, made their way toward various camps, in particular to Dora, but also to Hersbruck and Leitmeritz, two Kommandos dependent on Flossenbürg. Klein's convoy, which wound up in Buchenwald, was one of the least dependable.[22] It was one of the last great evacuations of this period, before the major series at the beginning of April. Some of the prisoners who left had only just suffered evacuation from Auschwitz.

The Soviets did not actually attempt to occupy the mountainous border of Upper Silesia right away; they were satisfied to protect their left flank during the advance on Berlin. The Gross Rosen camp, after its evacuation, would only be "liberated" on May 5, 1945.

The conditions in which these evacuations took place—as with the many that followed—make it difficult to assess how many people were actually involved. Concerning Auschwitz it is estimated that there was still a population of some 67,000 prisoners in the concentration camp complex in mid-January 1945, 58,000 of whom were evacuated. What is important is the sheer magnitude. In the same manner it is impossible to evaluate the ethnic or national composition of the various convoys. The only certain element was the large proportion of Jews in the overall number. Indeed, the transports at the end of 1944 from Auschwitz to other camps especially affected the non-Jewish prisoners—German, Polish, French, and so on.

Part of the next chapter will be devoted to the dramatic conditions that awaited the trains coming from Auschwitz and Gross Rosen, in January and February 1945, upon their arrival in Dora, Ellrich, and Nordhausen.

The End of Peenemünde

THE MOVING OF PEENEMÜNDE. At the beginning of January 1945, as seen at the end of chapter 7, the rocket-development unit of Wernher von Braun was still at the Peenemünde base under the auspices of a company known as EW, meaning Elektromechanische Werke GmbH. Like Mittelwerk it was dependent on the Armaments Ministry, which appointed Paul Storch as its executive director. The base itself remained military, under the command of General Rossmann. General Dornberger meanwhile was in Schwedt on the Oder, south of Stettin.

The transfer of the Peenemünde installation to an underground site in the

Austrian Alps had been planned for the end of 1943 (see chapter 4), but von Braun had not been very cooperative in this regard, and the tunnels dug at Ebensee were ultimately used for another purpose.[23] When it appeared necessary in January 1945 to carry out the evacuation of Peenemünde, nothing had been planned, and it had to be improvised.

Indeed, the situation deteriorated rapidly. By the eve of the January 12, 1945, offensive the Soviets were three hundred miles as the crow flies from Peenemünde. On January 31 they were on the Oder close to Küstrin, 105 miles from Peenemünde and 34 miles from Schwedt. The refugees from East Pomerania crossed the island of Usedom, and German civilians had to participate in Volkssturm exercises.[24]

It was Kammler who on January 31 gave the order to transfer the Peenemünde installation and personnel to the *Mittelraum*.[25] His powers were greater still, Göring having on January 26 given him command of the VI launching performed by the Luftwaffe; he was thus the head of a program known as Brechung des Lufterrors, or "breaking airborne terror." He set up an Armeekorps zur Vergeltung—a "retaliatory army corps"—bringing together the VIs and the V2s. As Neufeld puts it, "He was becoming the ruler of a shadow empire of skeleton organizations, false hopes, and self-delusion."[26] In April after the Dora evacuation, Hitler, from his Berlin bunker, would even give him "full control over jet-propulsion aircraft."

The order to evacuate Peenemünde was, of course, approved by General Leeb, Rossmann's hierarchical superior. It was followed as well by Dornberger. No one in any case was in a position to oppose Kammler; as Neufeld has emphasized, not even the *Gauleiter* of Pomerania, whom von Braun mentions in his subsequent writings. The actual transfer from Peenemünde to *Mittelraum* lasted three weeks. The first train arrived in Thuringia on February 17 and von Braun supervised its unloading. The operation was a success thanks to the organizational ability of the official in charge, Erich Nimwegen, who used the trains, trucks, and barges that were available to their best advantage. Certainly the SS knew how to impose its priorities, as will be seen at the time of the April evacuations. Later von Braun himself acknowledged that he had on this occasion made use of his status as an SS officer. He went to Peenemünde for the last time on February 27. The move was finished at the beginning of March.[27]

SETTING UP IN THE *MITTELRAUM*. The EW company headquarters was transferred from Karlshagen to Bleicherode, where von Braun set himself up. The material was divided between various nearby depots, particularly in the potash mines at Sollstedt and Obergebra, and at Bischofferode. A *Taifun* rocket manufacturing workshop was operating in the Dora Tunnel.[28] Von Braun proved himself to be very energetic, traveling all over the region looking for sites to get the research work going again.

He was especially interested—or so it would appear—in the transformation of the Leuchtenburg fortress near Jena, and traveled to Berlin to ask for the credit necessary. In the early morning of March 16—when it was still dark outside—he was in a car accident, his chauffeur having fallen asleep at the wheel. His arm was broken and put in a cast—as seen in the well-known photos of him from this period. He left the hospital on March 21 and returned to Bleicherode.[29] Dornberger and his entourage had meanwhile left Schwedt to set up south of Harz, in Bad Sachsa—not far from Wieda. In the west the Dernau factory was also transferred to Artern, northeast of Thuringia. The corresponding Kommando—dependent on Mittelbau—had the code name Adorf.

During the month of March following the Berlin bombings it was Speer's assistant Saur and his department who came to take refuge in the Dora Tunnel. Sadron has drawn attention to this episode: "Several of the north halls sheltered an evacuated ministry. And my friends who were there on installation duty still laugh when describing the picturesque sight of the men and women in their pajamas sleeping in those sinister galleries. Very well-to-do people it seems—they gave out bread and cigarettes to the prisoners and told them that all was lost."[30]

Raoul-Duval witnessed the situation himself: "An Austrian SS man was in charge of a group of four prisoners of which I was one. [. . .] We went to clean and set up some rooms for the Armaments Ministry which was moving into the Tunnel. [. . .] The SS spent the day looking for food for us. They brought us into the canteen for the ministry civilians where an old Werkschutz man served us soup." Having moved some furniture, the four prisoners came back with two packs of cigarettes.[31] This easing up in the last hours was altogether exceptional, as will be seen in the next chapter.

Saur's department was dispersed throughout the region, particularly in the town of Blankenburg.

THE END OF THE KARLSHAGEN CAMP. As mentioned at the end of chapter 10, in early 1945 not only was there the rocket development factory with its technicians on the Peenemünde site, but also a concentration camp where the prisoners suffered from the cold, with a high mortality rate.[32] The French survivors of this camp, Roger Predi, Pierre Pinault, and Jean Fournier, indicate that two transports of three hundred sick were sent to "rest camps," the first on January 20 and the second a month later, without knowing their destination, which was no doubt Bergen-Belsen. The final days, in March, were taken up with dismantling of barracks and equipment, which was evacuated by sea. Fournier makes particular mention of a crane.

The evacuation of the camp itself finally took place on March 28: at six in the morning, six hundred prisoners boarded three large metal barges. Fournier noted: "The [Baltic] sea was rough, it was cold, the wind was blowing in gusts, we were huddled up in the back of our boat. The three barges bound together were pulled by a tugboat; with the light load, they bobbed up and down." The voyage lasted forty-eight hours, arriving in the early morning of Friday, March

30, at Warnemünde—Rostock's outer harbor—where they disembarked. Pinault noted "a mournful crowd of men and women who watched us in silence."

The prisoners were immediately loaded onto cattle cars. The train passed by Wismar, Schwerin, Stendal, Magdeburg, and Halle before getting to Ellrich on April 1—Easter Day. The Elbe was crossed—from north to south—by the Wittenberge railway bridge, which will be mentioned again in chapter 19.

THE AMERICAN OFFENSIVE TOWARD THE ELBE. Predi, Duale, Fournier, Pinault, and their friends who had just arrived from Peenemünde/Karlshagen made only a brief stop at Ellrich. Three days later it was no longer the Soviets who would threaten their camp but rather the Americans, and they had to get back onto the trains for a new evacuation.

The final offensive against the Germans in the west at the beginning of 1945 was carried out in the north by the British (as well as the Canadians and the Polish), in the center by the Americans, and in the south by the French. It was the Americans who liberated the *Mittelraum* camps, generally emptied of the majority of their occupants. At the beginning of March, three American armies occupied the left bank of the Rhine between Wesel and Mainz. Simpson's Ninth Army crossed the Rhine at Wesel and continued to the north of the Ruhr. Hodges's First Army seized the bridge at Remagen on March 7 and made its way to the south of the Ruhr. Patton's Third Army headed from Mainz toward Fulda.

Kammler himself was among the generals who in March 1945 sought to contain the American advance. A document dated March 20 shows his position to be Rietberg southeast of Wiedenbrück, twelve miles north of Lippstadt. His full title was then SS-Gruppenführer und Generalleutnant der Waffen-SS Dr Ing. Kammler.

It was in Lippstadt that Simpson and Hodges hooked up on April 2, trapping Model's Army Group B in the Ruhr valley—where he surrendered on April 17. From there each continued to advance. Simpson had to go to the north and Hodges to the south of the Harz range. Patton headed in a more southerly direction. Their common objective was to reach the Elbe at Magdeburg and to seize the major cities west of Saxony such as Halle, Leipzig, and Chemnitz.

Helmstedt was in Simpson's path, Dora was in Hodges's, and Buchenwald in Patton's. On April 4, Simpson was at Hameln, Hodges at Kassel, and Patton at Gotha. The evacuation operations of the threatened camps began. They were the first camps to be evacuated in the west.

Illustrations

There exists no coherent iconography dealing with any particular concentration camp. Of course a certain number of photographs taken here and there in the camps were subsequently discovered, but they were never representative of a whole, whether of the prisoners at work on the work sites or in the factories, or of daily life in the camps themselves. The photographs that illustrate books dealing with the camps are most often those taken by Allied troops at the time of the camp's liberation. Thus they show either the prisoners' joy as they acclaimed their liberators or dramatic scenes of emaciated prisoners or cadavers.

Similarly, the drawings by the prisoners, whether done secretly in the camps or upon their return, are necessarily disparate. They provide a powerful idea of the concentration camp world in a general sense but are rarely characteristic of any one camp in particular. The author found himself in this very predicament with regard to Dora as he was writing his book. It was the fortuitous discovery in 1998 of a remarkable series of color photographs taken in 1944 in the Dora Tunnel which made it possible to envisage a public exhibition in 1999 on the theme of "Images of Dora" and to publish the corresponding catalog. The twenty-eight illustrations that make up the illustrations section in the English edition of *A History of the Dora Camp* are all taken (with one exception) from this exhibition.

It should be noted that they concern only the Dora Tunnel and the main camp at Dora but not such sub-camps as Ellrich nor the work sites of the Sonderstab Kammler or Helmetalbahn. An important—and tragic—part of the history of the Mittelbau complex is thus only known through rare accounts.

There exist very few documents making it possible to evoke the hell that was Dora in the early months. Five have been selected to characterize this period. They are all drawings. The following four documents (illustrations 6 through 9) show the camp as well as the prisoners assembling to go to work in the tunnel.

The Mittelwerk company factory in the tunnel with its prisoners can be seen in nine documents (illustrations 10–18), six of which are photographs taken by Walter Frentz, discovered in 1998. They make up only part of a veritable photographic report of more than thirty photos of the rocket factory, which was made in early July 1944 by Walter Frentz, an official photographer and filmmaker who was close to Leni Riefenstahl. Everything suggests that the photographs were commissioned by Arms Minister Albert Speer and that Hitler himself was the recipient. The point indeed was to convince Hitler in the wake of the Normandy landing that after a long period of trials the mass production of the V2 would be able to get under way under the best conditions.

Certain photographs bring out the factory's size and prevailing order; this can be seen in illustrations 10 through 12. Others show the prisoners at work (illustrations 13 through 15), as Hitler himself had demanded, barring foreign civilians from those tasks. But the prisoners appear as qualified workers—as befits a weapon of such importance. These photographs were not intended for propaganda, because their subject was both a concentration camp and a secret factory, which could not be shown. They ought to have been destroyed, but as it happens Walter Frentz held on to a certain number of them, hidden in a suitcase, which were discovered by his son, Hanns-Peter Frentz, when Walter Frentz moved into a retirement home. They provide a one-of-a-kind testimony.

Though the authenticity of these documents is undeniable, they were nevertheless staged. In fact, the technical necessities of lighting and exposure time required that the factory be shut down while the photographs were being taken. All one sees are a minimum of prisoners, some of whom are still alive and have recognized themselves in the pictures. Some German civilians may also be seen, but no uniform—whether of the Wehrmacht or of the SS—is to be seen. And among the prisoners, no *Kapo* is to be seen. In order to show the other side of the picture, a drawing (illustration 16) was selected, showing one of the many *Transportkolonnen* involved in carrying engines, fuel tanks, fuselages, and so on. The portraits of two redoubtable individuals from the tunnel have been added (illustrations 17 and 18): the *Kapo* known as "Big George" and the SS man Busta known as "Horse Head."

Contrasting with these images of Dora's industrial aspect, illustrations 19 through 23 show the constant presence of death in the camp during the final months, including the unloading of cadavers from Ellrich as well as the pyre that was put up after the arrival of the evacuation convoys from the camps in the east, and the hangings. Illustration 24, a photograph taken by the Americans upon their arrival at the Boelcke Kaserne in Nordhausen, is emblematic of the barbarism at the end of the camps, as is the drawing of the evacuation convoy heading for Bergen-Belsen and the photograph of the barn at Gardelegen (illustrations 25 and 26).

The photograph (illustration 27) showing the American officials contemplating the rocket, and the photograph (illustration 28) of the blowing up of the tunnel by the Soviets brings the history of Dora to a close.

1. This drawing by Guy Boisot (identity number 42188) shows the excavation work done by the prisoners at the far south of tunnel A under constant blows in the dust and din, not far from the "dormitories."

2. This drawing by the German civilian Werner Brähne is the only one showing the prisoners installing machines in the underground factory.

3. The French artist Maurice de La Pintière (31115) here evokes the earth-moving work at the outside entrances to the factory during the winter of 1943–44, which was especially murderous.

4. This charcoal drawing by René Souquet (39627) shows how the pallet beds were crammed into the dead-end galleries, thus making up the tunnel "dormitories" where for months on end thousands of prisoners covered in vermin succeeded one another.

5. In this drawing by La Pintière, one sees a line of sick prisoners who have just left the tunnel for the *Revier* in hope of receiving care.

6. and 7. Twice a day beginning in May 1944 the prisoners working in the tunnel left their blocks and assembled in Kommandos in the roll-call area on the orders of their *Kapos*. They then left the camp and went to the underground factory for a twelve-hour shift, either the day shift or the night shift. These drawings were done at Dora by Léon Delarbre (53083), curator at the Belfort Museum.

8. A general view of the eastern part of the camp taken by the Americans in April 1945. The eighty-odd blocks in this small town were spread out along a valley at the foot of the Kohnstein.

9. This drawing by Guy Boisot shows a number of blocks among the trees.

10. The first of the six successive photographs taken by Walter Frentz shows the enormous hall for storing fuel tanks, all perfectly lined up and awaiting assembly.

11. The fuel tanks are on the assembly line set up in tunnel B, which moves from north to south.

12. At the far end of the line, the finished rocket is lifted into vertical position for a last check, just before the Army—in charge of launching operations—would take possession of it.

13. The French prisoner Jean Maupoint, whose identity number 31851 can be seen, is doing electrical cabling with the Bünemann Kommando. Deported in April 1943, he died after his return in August 1945.

14. The person to the left is Claude de Chanteloup (43928). He is working on cutting sheet metal in the Firnrohr Kommando.

15. Certain components of the rocket were partially assembled in the halls perpendicular to tunnel B. Such was the case for the tail, which the prisoners then attached to the main body.

16. The other side of the picture consisted of above all the *Transportkolonnen*, which Walter Frentz was asked not to photograph. Delarbre's drawing shows half the fuselage of a V2 being moved.

17. The *SS-Hauptscharführer* Erwin Busta, known as "Horse Head," terrorized everyone in the factory, including the *Meister*. Missing in 1945, he was tried only later.

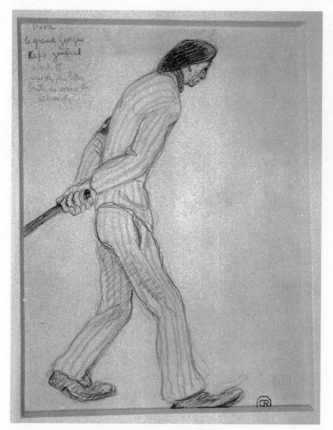

18. The German criminal prisoner Georg Finkenzeller, known as "Big George," was the *Oberkapo* of the Haukohl Kommando. He would be tried in 1947. Delarbre's drawing captures his disquieting silhouette.

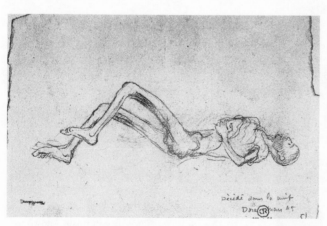

19. Léon Delarbre's drawing shows the corpse of a prisoner in front of the entrance to a block before being carried to the crematorium. He had "died during the night."

20. The mortality rate grew steadily higher at Ellrich during the winter of 1944–45. Cadavers were regularly transported to Dora, where they were incinerated. Delarbre bears witness.

21. Delarbre did several drawings of the hangings organized by the SS in March 1945. The victims were generally Soviet prisoners.

22. A photograph taken in late April 1945 shows the pile of human ashes in front of the Dora crematorium.

23. The evacuation convoys from the Auschwitz and Gross Rosen camps arrived at Dora with numerous corpses of prisoners who had not withstood the cold and hunger. The crematorium's capacity was not adequate, and the bodies were burned on pyres set up in the camp. This drawing done by La Pintière upon his return bears witness to this appalling spectacle.

24. American troops who arrived in Nordhausen on April 11, 1945, discovered an unbearable spectacle at the Boelcke Kaserne. The corpses were subsequently arranged in rows before being buried in communal graves by the city's inhabitants.

25. Delarbre's drawing is the only testimony of its kind to the conditions of the evacuation of the Dora camp and the other Mittelbau camps in April 1945. It shows a convoy between Dora and Bergen-Belsen, which wandered for five days.

26. The prisoners of the two evacuation convoys blocked in Gardelegen were locked into a barn and burned on the orders of a local Nazi official on April 13, 1945. This photograph taken by an American soldier on April 15 shows one of the 1,016 victims.

27. The discovery of the underground factory by American troops was followed by a series of official visits. This photograph shows congressmen contemplating components of the rocket.

28. In 1948 the Soviets blew up the factory tunnels after having emptied them out.

[[15]]

THE FINAL MONTHS AT DORA AND
THE BOELCKE KASERNE
IN NORDHAUSEN

The last months at Dora were a period of confusion. Everyone was fully aware—the prisoners as well as the SS and the German civilians in the tunnel—that the end was near. For this reason there was at once an easing and a tightening up. The prisoners waited impatiently to be liberated, but some of them—not without reason—wondered if they could hold on until then. And the last phase seemed threatening indeed for the "specialists" working on manufacturing secret weapons.

As time passed and deprivations intensified, winter 1944–45 was hard to endure. The number of sick in the *Revier* and *Schonung* was growing, and the arrival of the evacuation convoys from the camps in the east further worsened the situation. A new camp was built in the Boelcke Kaserne in Nordhausen, taking in those judged undesirable in Dora, and in Harzungen and the various Kommandos.

A New Setup at Dora

THE AUTONOMY OF THE DORA-MITTELBAU CAMP. In the autumn of 1944, Dora ceased being an outside camp dependent on Buchenwald to become an autonomous camp. More precisely, a decision dated September 30 transformed Arbeitslager Dora into Konzentrationslager Mittelbau. It went into effect on November 1, instead of October 1 as initially planned.

From that date on, the KZ Mittelbau was made up of three camps: Dora (same code name), Erich (code name for Ellrich) and Hans (code name for Harzungen). From the beginning the two outside Kommandos (Aussenkommando) of Rossla and Kleinbodungen were included and connected to Dora. Other decisions integrated into Mittelbau three Kommandos, those of Rottleberode, Klosterwerke (that is, Blankenburg), and Osterode-Harz as well as three *Baubrigaden* and three *Eisenbahnbaubrigaden*.

There was on this occasion a prisoner count of 25,944 for the main group and 5,931 for those integrated later. The 25,944 prisoners were divided up: 13,441 for Dora, 7,870 for Ellrich, 4,009 for Harzungen, 112 for Rossla, and 512 for Kleinbodungen. The 5,931 others were divided as follows: 819 for Rottleberode, 499 for Blankenburg, 286 for Osterode, and 2,863 for the *Baubrigaden* and 1,464 for the *Eisenbahnbaubrigaden.*

Knowledge of such structures and code names is indispensable for the interpretation of German documents from this period, but for the sake of standard usage the terms Ellrich and Harzungen instead of Erich and Hans will continue to be used. As for the vicissitudes in the joining up of various *Baubrigaden* and *Eisenbahnbaubrigaden,* only the hierarchy of the SS was really concerned. It is sufficient to know that the prisoners from Wieda, Ellrich-Theater, and the Kommandos of the Helmetalbahn work sites were dependent on Erich—to a certain point.

Normally, Mittelbau being set up as an autonomous camp would have meant a reregistering of all the prisoners thus transferred under a new series of numbers. This solution was dismissed and the prisoners maintained their numbers, which were all from Buchenwald. Only the newcomers from November 1944 on received six-digit numbers above 100,000. This was the case for the survivors of the evacuation convoys from the camps in the east. It must, however, be recalled that Butet at the *Schreibstube* had to undertake the typing up of some 32,000 new files for the *Kartei,* and that a new *Häftlingskleidungskammer* put together the Mittelbau prisoners' personal "effects," which were transferred from Buchenwald.

At the time the average prisoner himself knew nothing about this, even those who belonged to the Kommandos least exposed in the tunnel factory. Moreover, this had no direct consequences on their lot. The decision to make "Dora-Mittelbau" (according to the established wording) into an autonomous concentration camp served only to convey a powerful reality—that is, the concentration of the major underground secret weapons factory and the largest work-site complex of the Sonderstab Kammler, in the same geographical zone of the *Mittelraum.*

AN EVOLUTION OF A POLITICAL NATURE. However, such a change was in no way devoid of political significance, and the breakoff with Buchenwald may have revealed a certain evolution. It is undeniable that the internal functioning of that camp rested on a tacit agreement between the SS command and the "Red" prisoners—both Germans and those so defined—to the mutual advantage of the two parties. As will be seen later, the prisoners taking charge of the administration did raise some questions after the war. The fact remains nonetheless that the most fanatical of the SS did not view favorably such an important delegation of powers left to political opponents.

There was a "hard core" among the SS and, in chapter 12, Serge Miller's account of the welcome for new arrivals at Ellrich by the camp commander on May 20, 1944, was cited. On another theme, the talk given by the Osterhagen commander on Christmas Day, 1944, is equally significant. Bonifas made the following summary: "You are our enemies, but we will force you to work with us to destroy your homelands, and to destroy even yourselves. We have only one leader, Adolf Hitler, who came providentially to save Europe."[1]

On another level it was noticed during the last months—in Dora as well as in many other camps—a more and more obvious tendency of numerous SS to establish a real complicity with the German prisoners—and especially with the Greens, the common-law criminals—who were often themselves fiercely xenophobic. This was to be illustrated during the evacuations.

THE SECURITY ORGANS. From 1943 to 1945 the *Mittelraum* was closed off by a security network of great administrative complexity. But they were still the services dependent on Himmler via the SS, the SD, or the Gestapo. There existed, however, Abwehr agents for military security. The complexity of the system put into place corresponded to the multiplicity of security problems to be resolved.

One of these problems—a banal one—had to do with the existence of a large prisoner population spread out over several sites. These prisoners—whether political or criminal—had dossiers that went with them and were kept up to date by the camp's Politische Abteilung. Moreover, the SS and the Gestapo inspected the internal workings of the camp to prevent the prisoners from organizing among themselves in any way that could become worrisome. Informers were one of the realities of concentration camp life, and their "accidental" elimination was sometimes a necessity for the "political" leaders in charge. On top of which, at Dora, prisoners who were working on the manufacture of secret weapons and could engage in sabotage were kept under strict surveillance. The SS commander of the camp was—as has been shown—on the board of directors of the Mittelwerk Company, where he was in charge of security.

But otherwise it was necessary to keep an eye on the German civilian workers employed at Mittelwerk, at Junkers, or in other neighboring factories as well as on sites dependent on the Sonderstab Kammler. In the factories and on the work sites—except at Mittelwerk—there was also a large number of foreign workers who were more or less "free." And also prisoners of war. In fact, it was necessary to watch over the entire population, and the SS themselves. As shown above, they were not exempt either.

The security services were spread out between Ilfeld, Niedersachswerfen, and Nordhausen. It was noted in several previous chapters the wealth of codes used. The address of Sangerhausen was not totally fictive however, for it was the town where the central files of the prisoners kept by the Politische Abteilung and the camp post office—and censor's office—could be found.

Until the autumn of 1944 the commander of Dora, SS-Sturmbannführer (major) Otto Förschner, formerly of Buchenwald and supported by SS-Oberführer (colonel) Pister, commander of Buchenwald, seemed to have the situation under control. But little by little—under unknown circumstances—SS-Obersturmbannführer (lieutenant colonel) Helmut Bischoff came to exert greater and greater influence. He belonged to Kammler's staff and was given the responsibility—at the end of 1943—of protecting the secret of the V2 program. His office was in Ilfeld in the Napola buildings, next to those of the Sonderausschuss A4. Since February 1944 all the services—SD, Gestapo, and so on—of the *Mittelraum* off-limits zone were under his control. It was he who was in charge of the various police and repression operations, which increased toward the end of 1944.

This was not an isolated phenomenon. More or less everywhere over the second half of 1944 the SS were preoccupied with the clandestine organizations that potentially existed in the camps. At Auschwitz, as has been shown, they transferred German, Polish, and French prisoners to various other camps. At Buchenwald the arrests of German communists followed a (clandestine) funeral service in honor of Thälmann.[2] On September 11, twenty-seven prisoners from Sachsenhausen (twenty-four Germans and three French) were shot for communist activities.[3]

THE ARRESTS AT DORA-MITTELBAU. Directly in charge of surveillance at the Dora-Mittelbau camp was Kriminal-Assistent and SS-Oberscharführer (warrant officer) Sander, who belonged to the Niedersachswerfen SD. He dealt at the same time with the German Reds, Czechs, Poles, Russians, and French.

As previously mentioned, there was an overzealous auxiliary by the name of Maurice Naegelé: a French prisoner who had been an agent actively working for the Gestapo in France before he himself was deported for embezzlement and who wanted in a certain way to "redeem himself" by serving Sander. He was made tunnel *Kapo* in the VI assembly section, where he earned the trust of Debeaumarché and Lauth through his knowledge of the Resistance movement in France. Michel described him as a "big, strong, good-looking kid."

Lauth having been taken away after a sabotage, Naegelé denounced Debeaumarché as well as Col. Louis Gentil, another major Resistance fighter working on the VIs. They were all among the victims of a roundup that took place the night of November 3–4, 1944, under surprising conditions in more than one respect. The arrests were aimed at only certain Frenchmen in the *Revier*—Poupault, Boyer, Michel—and no others. There was some uncertainty as to the names, and Joseph Puppo (a communist railway worker from Miramas, according to Michel) was arrested—by accident—at the same time as his namesake Dr. Jacques Poupault, a surgeon from Dieppe.[4] The information at Sander's disposal was therefore uncertain.

What was certain, though, was that the rumors of "conspiracy" had reached him because he had two Czechs from the *Revier,* Cespiva and Halupka, arrested at the same time along with the Frenchman Alfred Birin and the Russian Nicolas Petrenko, both from the Arbeitsstatistik. In this matter we are inclined to incriminate a Frenchman who had recently become the head of Block 15, where everyone would meet up and express themselves, no doubt incautiously. His name was Grozdoff, at once White Russian and Alsatian and a polyglot. But, René Cogny—then block *Schreiber*—was not bothered.

From the detailed account of the events given by Jean Michel,[5] following his personal experience and the information he got from Claude Lauth and Jacques Poupault, an approximate chronology can be drawn: The prisoners arrested in the roundup, which included Naegelé and Grozdoff, were taken to Niedersachswerfen to be interrogated. It was then that Naegelé revealed himself and began to beat the others to extort their confessions. Debeaumarché, Lauth, and Poupault were especially mistreated, as was Nicolas Petrenko. Grozdoff served as translator because other Russians were interrogated as well.

Some of the prisoners were then sent to the Dora bunker and others went to the Nordhausen prison not far from the Boelcke Kaserne—which will be discussed shortly. It was in fact an ordinary prison, with prisoners of both sexes, German and especially foreign, of all nationalities. It was in this prison that the French in particular would finally remain locked up until March or April 1945 in several collective cells. Several other names must be added to those already cited—names that Michel also quoted in his 1986 dedication: Gabriel Alliens, Jacques Bordier-Brunschwig, the cousins André and Pierre Caruana, Paul Chandon-Moët, and Roger Latry.

The interrogations went on in Niedersachswerfen until December for some of them—including Poupault—and then came to an end. From that moment on they all remained unsure, but very worried, about what fate had in store for them. Naegelé himself remained imprisoned, by himself, in the same prison. Sander seems to have considered him a very mediocre informer and no longer turned to him. As for Grozdoff, he came and went and kept up his role as translator because of the numerous arrests of Russians. At the same time, according to Michel's account—he refers to him as "D"—Grozdoff claimed that he was plotting to save the French. But, as various testimonies show, the fate of the French was no different from that of the Czechs. Through Michel it is known that the Poles were also arrested, including someone called Hronstein from the Arbeitsstatistik, who for a time was his cellmate.

The story of the Russians was somewhat unusual. A mass arrest at the Dora camp took place in mid-December 1944. D gave the details to Michel: "All the Russians were assembled in the Dora roll-call area. Petrenko went through the rows designating the Soviets who were part of the camp organization. More than a hundred men were arrested. I served as translator. I was convinced that Nicolas had the poor buggers arrested—who, just because they had been deported weren't necessarily members of the Bolshevik party. It was monstrous!

But, Petrenko acted calmly. I'm sure he thought he was doing the right thing. He did his duty: the innocent sent to the gallows, the guilty saved; in this way, the latter could continue to sabotage. The Russian organization was safe. Petrenko would be hanged with the others, but he allowed the Soviets to continue the struggle. You had to see the faces on those unfortunate enough to be falsely accused! If they denied guilt and managed to convince the SS by giving out names of real resistance fighters, the latter would kill them in the Tunnel. If they went along with it and gave up, the noose awaited them."[6]

Nothing can be confirmed nor, on the other hand, denied in D's interpretation of events thus reported. But it is true that Petrenko pointed out a large number of his compatriots in the roll-call area, where other prisoners—not only Russians—were also lined up. The author has kept a precise and horrified memory of the scene.

Conversely, what happened to the camp leaders at the end of 1944—Reds, generally communist—remained unknown to almost all the other prisoners. The first to be arrested was Heinz Schneider, *Kapo* of the *Revier,* in the November 3–4 night roundup. The prisoners who made up the personnel were threatened, and Fritz Pröll, when he learned that he was next to be arrested, committed suicide on November 29, poisoning himself with cyanide.

In December it was Albert Kuntz who was led to the bunker. Tortured, he died the night of January 22–23, 1945. Krokowski believed he died from a heart attack. Others were arrested on various dates in December and January 1945. In particular this concerned the two practicing LÄ, Gamisch and Beham, and two former LÄ from the early days of Dora, Thomas and Sczymczak.

There is no way of knowing if there was a link between these arrests and those of the French, Czech, Polish, and Soviet prisoners. It may have been a purely repressive operation of a political nature carried out by a fraction of the SS deliberately hostile to the Reds and to the authority they were allowed in the camp's internal administration.

THE EARLY DAYS OF THE BOELCKE KASERNE. At the end of 1944 a certain number of Kommandos from the Dora camp were assigned by the SS to various companies in the town of Nordhausen. At the same time a large Kommando was put together at Dora, Kommando 32 (see chapter 10), which was sent daily to work in Niedersachswerfen in the underground digging sites of the Sonderstab Kammler. It was then decided to use the vacant premises in Nordhausen, in the Boelcke Kaserne, to build a camp annex and house everyone.

This all seems to have begun on January 2, 1945. As Pierre Maho—a member of Kommando 32—noted in a passage from his memoirs dated January 4: "Yesterday, disinfected, re-clothed in stripes, 1,800 of us were assembled at the roll-call area in Dora, and led to Nordhausen, five or six miles away. We entered a vast courtyard framed by elegant buildings to be used as offices and barracks. Each one was surrounded by lawn and clumps of greenery. Passing those buildings by, we were led into an empty garage on top of which there was, on each side, a central corridor with something like dormitories. That was where we were penned in the day of our arrival."[7]

The description of the area given here is a compilation of testimonies from Jean-Pierre Couture,[8] Léon-E. Halkin,[9] and Clément-Robert Nicola,[10] who arrived there in March and who will be mentioned later. The complex was in the south part of Nordhausen, not far from the Zorge, on the right bank. The train station was not far to the southwest. The countryside in the east could be reached quickly.

It was a disused tank barracks. The buildings surrounding the courtyard had served as lodgings for the noncommissioned officers and administration. They seemed to be occupied by foreign civilian workers. Between these and the Zorge, what was transformed into a concentration camp—with walls and watch-towers—were two enormous concrete garages with large metal doors opening southward. Traces of their normal functions were still visible: a grease pit with writing on the walls such as: "Don't leave your motor running" or "Use caution when backing up!" Halkin added: "I have never forgotten the words of Frederick II that easily covered the ten square meters: 'It matters little that I die, if at least I did my duty.' Nice motto which applied to us as well as to the tank drivers on the eastern front." The garages were divided into blocks. Above these blocks, between a concrete vault and a flimsy roof, beds were also set up—particularly for the *Revier.*

Life in Nordhausen was more or less tolerable for those working in companies in the city, like the Schmidt und Kranz tractor factory, mentioned above. But it quickly became difficult—as at Ellrich and for the same reasons—for the members of Kommando 32. Thus, as Maho stated on January 15 concerning the *Schonung:* "The sick temporarily unable to work were stripped of their shoes and clothes. They had to spend the day in shirtsleeves and underwear in that cold and damp building, and attend to internal chores that were allotted to them in spite of their swollen legs or their arms in slings."[11]

On January 30, Maho himself fell seriously ill and was admitted to the *Revier.* "I had a serious case of water on the knee, the thigh completely covered in bruises, the ankle hard and swollen. It was definitely an abscess forming. There was talk of sending me to Dora to the surgery ward for an operation. That would have been unexpected good fortune to escape Kommando 32 in such a way. In any case, the infirmary there was practically nonexistent, the medicine cabinets empty. No wounds could be dressed, there was only toilet paper for bandages which tore off every six inches.

"The filth was indescribable, we were jammed onto vile bunks with three levels, which being overburdened, collapsed and were patched up with loud hammering—preventing any rest. Dysentery and its pitiful consequences abounded, the latrines were of course outside the room, and there was a line to get in—during which time the inevitable accidents occurred which soiled the floor and the blankets and rendered the atmosphere abominable.

"Last night I was given a place on the bottom bunk of the beds. I slipped in between two emaciated Hungarian Jews, then the alarm sounded and everything was turned off. One or two hours later, I felt that my bedfellow on the right— against whom I had pressed for warmth—was freezing cold. I pulled the blanket off him; he didn't move, he was dead. I turned to the other side where, in the half-light, I saw his stare fixed on me. I motioned for him to push over a bit; he didn't budge, he too was dead. [. . .] I spent the night between them and I was gripped by fever—impossible for me to move or get out of my spot. It was only in the early morning that I pointed out their deaths; in fact, I managed to hide the death of the one on my right until after the bread was distributed, and I took half his ration."[12]

On January 31, he was taken in a truck heading for Dora. "The inside of the truck was loaded with crates of cadavers heading for the crematorium."

The Arrival of the Convoys from Auschwitz and Gross Rosen

THE CONDITIONS OF THE "TRANSPORT." The account given by Jules Hofstein on this subject is the last in the collection entitled *Témoignages strasbourgeois*. He tells of the transport from Gleiwitz to Dora of evacuated prisoners from Auschwitz and its Kommandos between January 20 and February 2: "Around midnight we were rounded up and packed into iron railway cars meant for transporting coal, open to the wind. We started off toward morning. [. . .]

"In the course of the journey—which lasted thirteen days—on only one occasion did we receive a half loaf of bread with a bit of rancid butter. If it hadn't been for the snow, we all would have died of thirst. All day long, we ate all the snow we were able to gather. The nights were horrible. In these jam-packed cars, there wasn't enough room for everyone to lie down or even to squat. Fights broke out all the time. The weaker were beaten to death or strangled by the stronger. In the mornings, it wasn't unusual to have between ten and twenty corpses, either victims of the fights brought on by sudden madness, or dead of the cold, hunger or despair. From time to time, a volley of machine gun fire rang out. The SS fired at those who tried to escape by jumping over the sides. At the next stop, the corpses were removed from the railway cars they were in. We thought that we'd therefore have more space, but that was without reckoning with the Machiavellism of our guards. They would simply empty an entire car, where they would stack the dead bodies, putting those still alive in the cars on a pro-rata basis of places available. On one occasion, they left an empty car at a station. Seen from this angle, evacuation was a form of extermination. [. . .]

"The cold, hunger and thirst made us lose all notion of time. And like that, we crossed Bohemia, Austria, Bavaria, to get to the Harz Mountains. Along the way we saw many cities that had been given a working over by the bombings, like the inner suburbs of Vienna, Linz, Plauen, and many others. Everywhere, passersby and passengers watched indifferently as we rolled by. The arrival at the Dora camp—after a long stop at the Nordhausen station—was almost greeted with relief. We mustered up the last bit of strength we had to walk the mile and a half in to the camp. Oh, how many weren't able to cover this distance! I don't know what happened to them, or rather I know only too well."[13]

Léon-E. Halkin provided similar information on the trip from Gross Rosen to Dora: "We got into open-topped, metal railway cars in densely-packed groups of one hundred men. We had no coats, no sweaters, no canvas covers, no blankets. It was cold, the wind blew over the low barriers. [. . .] No one could guess where we were going. I had the impression that not even the guards themselves knew. [. . .] The train made frequent and lengthy stops to let troop and ammunition convoys go by. [. . .] As the speed of the train increased, so did the cold. We rubbed our backs together, but tiredness replaced the cold, then the cold came back and tiredness remained. [. . .]

"It was getting dark, and the trip showed no sign of coming to an end. To render escapes more difficult, the SS made us sit down, crushing us up against each other. There wasn't enough space to lie down; in any case, squeezed together we were less cold. Sleeping was difficult; the train went faster at night; the wind bit into our faces; we dozed. The monotonous noise of the train was punctuated by gunfire from time to time as the SS shot at fellow-prisoners who—already practically unconscious—defied the ban on standing up in the railway car before daybreak."

There were those who died in the cars from sheer exhaustion. "Hunger gradually put us into a state of stupor. Some went mad. The others were amazed to still be alive. Sensations became less and less sharp. It seemed that we were engulfed in a sinister haze. My memories of that period are blurred, fleeting and incomplete. [. . .] Nightmares and memories are inextricably mixed together. [. . .]

"The final morning, Sunday 11 February, the SS once again ordered the corpses to be thrown on the tracks, no doubt to prevent us from devouring that fetid flesh. We hardly noticed the thinning out of our numbers. Total prostration took over our exhausted bodies, our beaten down spirits. The rain froze us to the bone. Each of us calculated the chance he had left, the number of hours he could hope to stay alive. The train lumbered through the countryside—unhurried."

When they arrived at Dora, Halkin—hanging on to two friends—dragged himself toward the camp roll-call area, where he met up with the other survivors. "My railway car started out with ninety men; when we got there, only sixty-two were left." He was led to a *Schonung* block.[14] Not all the convoys

coming from Gross Rosen went to Dora. Rogerie's convoy stopped at the Nordhausen train station and the survivors reached Boelcke Kaserne on foot—an
episode that will be dealt with later.

Six Witnesses of the Arrival

There are several testimonies of prisoners who were at Dora when the
convoys arrived from Auschwitz and Gross Rosen. They generally made no distinction between them. No commentary is necessary to accompany these texts.

CHARLES SADRON. "One night, coming back up from the factory into a
snowstorm, we made out on the roll-call grounds, a black, immobile mass in the
semi-darkness. It looked like men. At the Block, we were told it was forbidden
to go out. What was going on? We were soon informed by fellow prisoners who
were above ground during the day, and who were returning worn out and
somber. The Germans had evacuated the camp at Auschwitz, and thousands of
prisoners had arrived. These poor souls had spent two weeks on a train, in open-
topped railway cars, and they had arrived in a pathetic state. Our fellow prisoners had seen their columns emerge onto the roll-call grounds—clusters of dying
men collapsing in the snow. They had been rounded up by the Lagerschutz to
get rid of the corpses which followed behind in the trucks. They carted them off,
nauseated, for hours. Many of the corpses had been shot in the head."[15]

RENÉ CHAPUY. "During the final months, I was recruited into a 'cleaning'
Kommando of the Revier, and was very often obliged to transport the survivors
and the dead. [. . .] I will always carry that living image within me of the convoy arriving at dusk. Open railway cars loaded with tangled bodies heaped one
on top of the other with a terrible stench of death. Almost all of these poor souls
were incapable of moving, their extremities being frozen and gangrenous. We
carried and dragged all those showing some signs of life, to the Revier barracks.
A vision out of Dante—indescribable because unbelievable.

"I needed all of my eighteen years and experience of the Tunnel to bear that
night. Walking corpses transporting the living dead. The rest of the convoy was
taken charge of by the Totenträger Kommando. Just a few days later, those who
were able to find shelter and some medical care and perhaps nourish a fleeting
hope, had to be transported by us once again to the mound of corpses waiting in
front of the crematorium door."[16]

MICHEL THOMAS. "Sometime in January or the beginning of February 1945,
we were called upon to unload the corpses from the railway cars of a convoy
coming from the eastern camps. Most were tattooed. The hundreds of skeletons,
we stacked to the side, alongside the crematorium (the side facing the camp),
and in many piles. The crematorium—even operating day and night—wasn't
able to keep up, so a pit was dug out behind it. Next, the prisoners of another
Kommando, made up of many Russians, stacked wood and corpses; once every-

thing was set well ablaze, the prisoners continued to throw on the bodies—for an entire day."[17]

STÉPHANE HESSEL. "There are intense periods, atrocious ones; unforgettable ones. The breaking through of the Red Army forced the Germans to repatriate the prisoners from the eastern camps. Those from Gross Rosen had been evacuated to Dora in February. The living as well as the dead. Our crematorium was saturated, so pyres had to be built on which to stack the corpses. But, they had to be undressed first. A Kapo promised two slices of sausage to those who volunteered for this duty, without telling what it was. Two slices couldn't be refused. I accepted with another young guy. We spent the day yanking off clothes covered in blood and excrement, feeling flesh gone cold. Pure and absolute horror."[18]

PIERRE GABRION. "With another young Frenchman my age—the poor guy never recovered from it, he died in Nordhausen—we were picked out to work on the infamous pyres, as the crematorium could no longer keep up with the excessive supply of dead. We were therefore employed to stoke the fire—if I may say—with the bodies.

"The job was horrible. We were almost always obliged to drag the dead by the feet, through the snow, or the mud. The second day, I managed to get out of being put back on the job."[19]

ROBERT ROULARD. "I was hospitalized in the Revier at Dora, in the tuberculosis Block, for the first half of February. This was the Block closest to the building with the crematorium oven. In this way, I saw the crematorium oven in action as well as the pyre that had been set up just beside it, a layer of wood logs, a layer of corpses. At night, the pyre under our windows lit up the room of our barracks. We were sometimes present for the turning over of the corpses with the help of long forks—which at night was Dantesque—probably done to stoke the combustion of the corpses. Personally, I think that the decision to set up the pyres was taken because of the Gross Rosen camp evacuation transport arriving at Dora. The crematorium could not alone suffice before such an influx of corpses." Henri Barbier's[20] account confirms that of Robert Roulard.[21]

A DEATH COUNT MADE IMPOSSIBLE. Given the conditions of the transport and the arrival, it is impossible to know the number of deaths that resulted from the evacuations of Auschwitz and Gross Rosen and that ended up at Dora itself or at other points in the Mittelbau complex. The fact that a convoy turned up there rather than at Buchenwald, Bergen-Belsen, or at another camp was in no way premeditated, and convoy trajectories were not taken into account, contrary to the steadfast tradition of the concentration camp universe.

But the bureaucratic tradition reasserted itself for the survivors, who were duly registered with a new series of identity numbers for the Dora-Mittelbau camp. Halkin recalled as well going into the *Revier:* "It wasn't men that were treated there, but identity numbers. [. . .] Brought naked into a room, they were heaved up naked onto a bunk they couldn't choose. [. . .] They were nothing but a pretext for statistics; their medical files were more real than they themselves! That file was the reason for being at the Revier, the basis of its organization. [. . .] It would be all that was left of them in the camp, after their death."[22]

Along with not knowing the number of prisoners in the eastern camps who died before they could be registered at Dora, it is also not known to which group they mainly belonged. Everything points to the Jews from Auschwitz as being essentially the ones whose bodies were burned on the pyres. Overall they were in a state to put up the least resistance, except for those coming from less trying Kommandos—like Jules Hofstein, the doctor from Bismarckshütte. The Jewish women had only a stopover at Dora before leaving again for Bergen-Belsen. Simone Weil was one of them.[23]

In the evacuation the Belgians suffered major losses. As NN, the majority of them had already had to endure the severe prison of Gross Strehlitz since May 10, 1944, and then the Gross Rosen camp from October 31. The French NN like Ernest Gaillard and Charles Vedel had a long stay in Neuengamme (from August 31, 1943, for Vedel) before arriving in Gross Rosen on January 5, 1945. Their time spent in the latter camp was thus shorter.

Certain old concentration camp prisoners handled the shock more easily. Such was the case of André Rogerie, or the surviving hostages of convoy "45,000" from Auschwitz. Was there, for certain individuals, a sort of adaptation to the vicissitudes of concentration camp life? It is a question that can be posed, though it remains ultimately unanswerable.

But others didn't get through so well. On the occasion of the recent death of a very elderly lady, it was recalled that her son, Count Hubert de Bazelaire de Lesseux, died "in the Gleiwitz-Dora transport, on 28 January 1945." His father, Florent, died just afterward in Mauthausen, on February 5.[24]

The Revier's Last Months

JEAN-RENÉ DURAND AND THE "PATHOLOGY" OF DORA. On February 1, 1945, a prisoner came to Dora as a "pathologist." It was a German-speaking French doctor, Jean-René Durand, who came from Mauthausen. His story is interesting on several accounts.[25] "On 13 January, a French or Italian doctor was required to carry out pathology work. I applied and was accepted. That was how I left Mauthausen for Dora on 29 January. I left around three in the afternoon—alone with an SS, on foot in the melting snow, carrying a box of clothes—for the Mauthausen train station. Around five o'clock, we boarded a train packed with civilians who were surprised at my presence and at the revolver in the right hand of the SS aimed at me, ready to shoot. In the tunnels, he put the mouth of the revolver to my stomach. After a few hours, there was a stop in a bombed-out train station which I couldn't identify. I ate the meager cold meal that had been given to me. I spent the night in a cubbyhole of the train station, where I dried out my clothes, which were wet from the rain.

"We got back to the train the next day, arriving at night in another train station, also demolished by a bomb and which I could not identify either. We went out into the city to a sort of hostel for soldiers where the SS man ate; around midnight, he brought me some soup. We returned to a cubbyhole at the train station where I spent the night.

"In the morning, I left with an SS man who was more polite, who conversed with the German passengers, and who was taken aside by two soldiers of the Wehrmacht and one from the Luftwaffe. They led him into the corridor, giving me three cigarettes so I wouldn't understand the heated discussion taking place on my account. The night of the 31st, we arrived at the Nordhausen train station. The SS entrusted me to some military men, who were waiting in a room reserved for them, and went off to eat.

"When he came back around midnight, he spoke to me of his family and assured me that, thanks to my good behavior, he was going to enjoy an eight-day leave which would be authenticated by the signature of the SS man who was going to come and get me. I responded to him by speaking of my own family, which I hoped to see again. Out came the sentence which ended everything: 'Nur durch Kamin,' 'Only through the chimney' (of the crematorium). Around five in the morning, he put me under the watch of military men no doubt waiting for a train, and went to clean himself up—taking his time. The SS men of the Dora camp arrived at that moment, around seven o'clock, and moving towards me called out: 'Du bist schon weggelaufen' ("You're already on your way'). I acted like I hadn't understood, knowing that all attempts at escape were punished with death. The first SS man came back: exchange of papers, signatures, then depart on foot for the Dora camp. After some hundred yards, seeing I was exhausted, he gave me his bike to carry my box of clothes on. After two and a half miles on foot, we arrived at the camp.

"Stopped at the Schreibstube, questioning-interrogation, then on to Block 13. I met the first Häftlingsarzt, a Dutch doctor who seemed very nice. I was introduced to the Standortsarzt, who ordered me: 'autopsy tomorrow at nine o'clock.' The next day, I performed my first 'Sektion' (dissection), after having taken a thrashing from a German green Kapo who had carried out autopsies before me and had the autopsy instrument case under his guard. The camp commander and the Standortarzt watched me at work and after an hour, seemed satisfied. One said 'Stimmt' and they disappeared. I never saw them again at the crematorium.

"I continued to perform a daily autopsy, but the most difficult thing was filling out the final report. The first five ended with 'Todesursache: allgemeine Körperschwäche' (cause of death: generalized physiological exhaustion), which was the truth. I was called before the Standortarzt after the fifth autopsy. He said to me: 'Todesursache, das geht nicht mehr. Nächste mal, sofort' (that cause of death won't do anymore. The next time, right away) [...] gesturing being hanged, all the while looking me straight in the eye. I understood immediately, and afterwards I generally mentioned other causes of death. The advantage of my position as 'Patholog' was no one ever hit me again."

The arrival of Durand as pathologist at Dora was totally unimportant, as he well knew. His account is only interesting for the aspects it revealed of how the concentration camp system functioned. First, it had to do with the great number of small "transports" from one camp to the other. Researchers seeking to learn more about the destiny of the members of a convoy recognize that they will inevitably come across convoys without understanding why they took place. The example of Durand shows that this absence of necessity was not unusual. Evacuated from Struthof to Allach and Dachau, then transferred to Mauthausen, he ended up at Dora without actually being needed—and without this transfer having anything to do with his arrest.

Someone decided at the beginning of January that from then on a real pathologist would be required to do autopsies at Dora, and an administrative process of finding one was then set into motion, stretching from Durand to Mauthausen. It therefore got under way on the 29th. The fact that in the meantime the evacuation of the eastern camps had begun—which would emphasize the laughable nature of the autopsy rite—didn't cause anyone concern. Three SS were successively put in charge of carrying it out, and one even received leave for doing so. Germany was invaded from all sides, soldiers were lacking, and the SS went on with its petty routines as if nothing was happening.

Many years previously—when Eicke was there—it was decided that deaths in the camp would be followed by autopsies, and that death notices would be sent to the families indicating the cause of death. It was necessary then to continue the autopsies, even if the notices were no longer sent. And a pathologist was put in charge of the ritual to lend it more credibility. But of course he was not to take himself to be credible. It was up to him to see to it that he respected a certain "plausibility" in his findings. All of this was in no way rational; but the world of the SS was not rational and made no particular pretense of being so.

All during the transfer, each SS man behaved properly with the prisoner under his guard. The second SS man even spoke to him of his own family but considered it obvious that Durand was destined—sooner or later—to go up in chimney smoke. It was a simple fact. This conviction of an average SS member aids in understanding what was to happen in the following weeks, at the time of the evacuations.

THE LAST MONTHS OF THE *REVIER* AND THE *SCHONUNG*. The functioning of the Dora *Revier*—described previously in chapter 15—remained the same, as for structure, right to the end. But various events affected the personnel. First was the intervention of the Gestapo. As noted earlier, the arrests the Gestapo carried out during the night of November 3–4, 1944, were aimed particularly at two surgeons, the Frenchman Poupault and the Czech Cespiva. Other members of the *Revier* personnel were taken away as well, including the German *Kapo* Schneider, the Frenchmen Boyer and Michel, and the Czech Halupka. The threat bearing on Fritz Pröll—the uncontested leader of the *Revier*—was so great that he poisoned himself on November 29. After some time had elapsed, the *Schreiber* Ackermann—a very much admired Red—accepted the job of interim *Kapo*. The *Revier* then became removed from the political vicissitudes of the camp, as pointed out in the memoirs of Marcel Petit.[26]

At the beginning of December a new SS doctor arrived, Dr. Kurzke, an *Oberjunker,* exceptionally humane according to all accounts. He had a positive effect right to the end. New arrivals bolstered the staff.[27] A medical team with three doctors and ten nurses arrived in Dachau on January 21. The archaeologist Jean Lassus was one of the nurses, and Boris Pahor—a Slovenian from Trieste—was assigned to the Harzungen *Revier.*[28] Among those evacuated from Auschwitz via Gross Rosen was André Chabaud, an important scientist from the Pasteur Institute who joined Ebel and Petit in the laboratory.

The number of sick rose at the end of 1944. They came from the Dora camp, but also—as has been shown—from Ellrich, Harzungen, from Blankenburg or from Wieda, at least for a certain period. Next to the prisoners working in harsh Kommandos, the Ko Scherer inspectors arrived, like René Bordet,[29] who suffered from the aftereffects of the first months in the tunnel. Tuberculosis, in particular, spread in a frightening manner. Those who had been infected crowded into Block 39 A, recalled by André Lobstein in *Témoignages strasbourgeois.*[30] Bordet met up with his friend Henri Dondon, who died at the end of March.

Among the sick, two Belgian brothers, Count Guillaume de Liedekerke and Count Baudouin de Liedekerke, made a lasting impression. At first, as prisoners at Blankenburg, they were especially mistreated by the *Kapos* and the SS. Becoming sick, they were sent to the Dora *Revier* where Mialet,[31] just passing through, remembers having met them. But René Morel is above all the person behind keeping their memory alive, dedicating his book, *Perliris,* to them when it was published in Oyonnax in 1993.[32] He never forgot their dignity and kindness. They died in April 1945.

AFTER THE ARRIVAL OF THE CONVOYS. The arrival of the convoys from Auschwitz and Gross Rosen modified the facts of the problem, both quantitatively and qualitatively. The weakest newcomers, like Halkin and Bleton, after a period in the *Schonung*, were admitted into the *Revier* as dysenteric or tubercular. The blocks of the *Revier* became more and more overcrowded. The most courageous newcomers, after a few days of being crammed into the *Kino,* were divided between the blocks and the Kommandos. Hofstein was sent as a doctor to Osterode.[33] Chabaud went to the *Revier* laboratory. Vedel was assigned to the tunnel as a metalworker on the V2 tanks,[34] and Gabriel Ramet (coming from Monowitz) as a metal turner. Climaud and Poiteau also worked in the tunnel until the evacuation.

But a great number never recovered from the transport and withered away little by little. Sadron spoke in this regard of a "general roll call": "Lined up on my right were the prisoners that had been isolated in the barracks where a cinema was proposed to be set up. They were the poor souls evacuated from Auschwitz or the eastern camps and who, exhausted by dysentery, were no longer able to work. As there was no gas chamber at Dora and the transports to the Bergen-Belsen death camp could no longer be provided following the bombings, they were just left to die in the immense barracks where they were jammed in together, without medical care, in abominable filth.

"They arrived at the central area, at the same time we did, in a staggering procession. Clinging on to each other in clusters, the dying moved forward in fits and starts. Sometimes they stumbled and collapsed, many of them never to rise again. The most solid transported the dead, in fours, one at each leg, one at each arm. The body was thus dragged along like a sack, the head tipped, lolling back. The corpses were placed in the central area, nicely arranged, as if they were hunters' tally. The survivors tried to keep themselves standing up. But, after two hours, almost half were on the ground."[35]

As in the early period at Dora and Ellrich, a prison population that couldn't be redeemed came into being, one that the camp authorities wished to get rid of while waiting for a transport to be organized to a Bergen-Belsen-style "rest camp." So it was decided to round them up at the Boelcke Kaserne in Nordhausen.

The sick that turned up at the Dora *Revier* in mid-March 1945 had three different fates. The first ones were transferred in the second half of the month to the Boelcke Kaserne. Among those who remained at the *Revier,* a large number were integrated into the last evacuation convoy of April 5. The others were left where they were. Each of the groups suffered great losses under various circumstances that will be described later. The survivors of the first and third group were liberated at Dora or Nordhausen. Those of the second group were liberated at Münchehof.

THE UNFIT AT THE BOELCKE KASERNE. When Rogerie arrived at Nordhausen from Gross Rosen in February 1945 the Boelcke Kaserne camp still housed two prison populations: the "factory workers" who had a banal fate, and those of Kommando 32, which Maho had just escaped by going to the Dora *Revier.* Rogerie in the following weeks saw the situation worsen: "Every day, the newly evacuated arrived. The camp doubled, tripled, then quadrupled its number. Food was insufficient and, what was more, it was said that the bread factory had been bombed. And indeed, by the third day, we weren't given any more bread. During the following twelve days, we received no more than a half liter of soup, then bread only twice, and again a bit of soup for another ten days. During all the month of February, we managed to survive on a total of four pounds of bread. We were extremely weak and the outdoor roll calls were exhausting. Never had I imagined until then just how essential bread was to our lives."[36]

At the beginning of March, Rogerie was transferred to Dora. It seems this was at the same period the factory workers abandoned Nordhausen for Dora or Harzungen. Kommando 32 ceased to exist. At the Boelcke Kaserne there remained those unable to work who came from either Kommando 32, the evacuation convoys, or the Dora and Harzungen camps.

Meanwhile, on March 3, a convoy arrived there with 1,602 prisoners of all different nationalities, which had left from the Ellrich camp as was pointed out in chapter 12. Pierre Auchabie was part of it and has shed some light on the circumstances: "We were meticulously searched; and after having exchanged our perfectly good clothes for old unusable rags, inscribed our identity numbers on our chests with an aniline pencil, we were crammed together in a railway car heading to an unknown destination.

"After having rolled along a few miles, the train stopped, the door opened, and on the order to get out I jumped onto the ballast. I then saw the ultimate in horror: rail cars already opened, full of corpses and the dying that the SS pushed out of the rail car with their feet. Others jumped out, but having no more strength to get to their feet, were shot by the SS." From the train to the camp the route was strewn with the dead and the dying that fellow prisoners no longer had the strength to support and who collapsed into the snow forever. The column, quite reduced, finally arrived at the building. "I was assigned Block 6, and we received neither food nor drink that day. We slept sardine-like, on the cement with a bit of straw—quickly reduced to dust."[37]

On March 6 a convoy left again from Nordhausen with 1,184 of the 1,602 prisoners that had arrived on March 3. Another 342 had arrived already dead or died thereafter. Therefore 76 prisoners remained at Nordhausen, including Auchabie, as well as Henri Maubert, whose account, reiterated by Michel, confirms that of Auchabie.[38] Besides the 1,184 prisoners who came from Ellrich, the convoy that left from Nordhausen on March 6 was made up of 1,068 prisoners who were already there. This convoy finally reached Bergen-Belsen—under the worst conditions. Traces of almost all the prisoners concerned have in any case been lost.

Having rid Ellrich and Nordhausen of a large portion of those unable to work, it seems that the SS wished to repeat the operation with those from the Dora camp thanks to their transit through the Boelcke Kaserne. It was—at a one-year interval—to renew the purges made by the two "transports" to Maïdanek and the transport to Bergen-Belsen between January and March 1944.

FROM DORA TO NORDHAUSEN IN MARCH 1945. In March 1945 there had been several transfers from Dora to Nordhausen. Those known are: March 1 with François Alcaras and Michel Thomas, March 10 with Jean-Pierre Couture coming from Ellrich, March 15 with Clément-Robert Nicola coming from Harzungen (like Xavier Delogne), March 18 with Pierre Bleton coming from Gross Rosen, March 22 with Pierre Maho coming from Nordhausen and who went back, March 26 with Roger Agnès coming from Ellrich, March 29 with Léon-E. Halkin, and March 30 with Ernest Gaillard—both evacuated from Gross Rosen in the same railway car.[39] Given such a high death rate, a sort of shuttle service was established between Dora and Nordhausen. Dora supplied the sick and recovered the corpses for incineration.

Maho's account is detailed and confirms Auchabie's earlier statements about the arrival: the identity number was put on the chest and left arm in aniline pencil, followed by an indefinite wait without food. Maho added: "It seems we are going to be sent off to a rest camp to recuperate a bit." On March 24 he said: "Yesterday morning was the disinfecting." Dr. Jacques Normand, who arrived with the convoy from Gross Rosen, was more specific on the subject: "The disinfecting machine was brought into a garage and, one after the other, the sick received a freezing cold shower mixed with oil."[40]

Maho[41] continued: "We remained standing and naked in those unheated halls from five in the morning until six at night—an hour it was decided we could have our old rags back. We had spent the day squeezed one against the other. And, of course, since the paper bandages had melted away, the worst possible contact between the healthy and the sick had occurred. At bedtime, fifteen centimeters of wood fiber had been spread out evenly on the ground, and it was on top of this that we slept without blankets. To keep warm, we slept in groups of six to eight, stuck one against the other on the same side, fit together like spoons in a silverware case, collecting our jackets over us with the sleeves knotted together. But, the ground was damp, and many already had pleurisy. Three times per night, we changed sides on command!

"In a corner of the hall, a tiny room for the seriously ill was fitted out behind the wire fencing. They had the right to a blanket, and fifteen or so died the first night—about as many as in the morning. The convoy will be smaller to go 'to rest.' [. . .] This morning the roll call had been disproportionately long. It was to discover the identity of a dead man whose number had been erased. That was why six hundred sick men remained standing for four hours." On March 27 and then on March 30 he added: "Last night, we took the corpse of a Pole who had just died to sleep on, to isolate the thorax from the ground. A bit repugnant at first, but necessity won out over scruples.

"The cubicles reserved for the sick are horrible in their filth and stink. We call them the 'death box.' The only way out is to be dragged by the feet, and in the morning the corpses are lined up in disturbing numbers. At least twenty fellow prisoners die each day, and it's a miracle if we escape the epidemics. For seven days we haven't been able to wash for lack of water; no bandaging is done; sickness and blood poisoning have a field day on our debilitated bodies." Maho was admitted into the infirmary and more or less acted as nurse to Dr. Normand.

Around March 15, Dr. Jules Hofstein came from Osterode with the prisoners from there. He pointed out: "The death rate became such that it was necessary to set up a special Kommando responsible solely for transporting and piling up the dead in a tiny room termed the morgue. The men of this Leichenträger Kommando received a part of the dead man's ration."[42]

During all this period, the testimonies give little information regarding the supervision of the camp. A Belgian *Schreiber* and a French member of the Arbeitsstatistik, Yves Pétré, tried hard to limit the damage. There was also a Polish *Schreiber,* Wincenty Hein, the future special adviser for the American authorities. Dr. Normand had to put up with the *Kapo* of the *Revier,* Otto Skodas, a Viennese police commissioner imprisoned for homosexuality.

The worst was in the blocks.[43] Maho pointed out: "We were 'supervised.' A Gypsy head of the Block, three Polish Stubendienst, a German tailor, a Czech barber, two Polish male nurses; except for the nurses, they were all 'Greens,' who had already been demoted several times, and had every intention of being overzealous in order to keep their jobs. The cudgel never left their hands, and they really took advantage of their right to be cruel."[44]

The Last Months in the Tunnel and in the Camp

THE LAST MONTHS IN THE TUNNEL. Right up until the last day the factory functioned and produced V2s and V1s. It occurred more and more frequently that the assembly line stopped because it lacked a part—deliveries being irregular because of bombed-out communication lines. The SS still made their rounds and the problem—for the prisoners as well as for the German civilians—was often to give a semblance of working by taking apart something to put it back together or uselessly sorting the spare parts.

The war became more and more present. Loudspeakers broadcast *Luftlagemeldungen* in the factory, announcing the position of enemy bombers. Sadron added: "We were continuously flown over top of by waves of high-altitude bombers which got no rise from either artillery or fighter planes. Once in a while, fighting occurred above the clouds and two or three Messerschmitts could be seen taking a dive, in a hurry to land on Nordhausen territory. When the sky was clear, up high it was always possible to see the white slipstream left by a plane, droning unseen far above.

"The siren sounded all day long; rather by accident, it seemed. An alarm signal indicating a faraway or impending alert was no longer easy to distinguish. Added to that was the immediate-danger signal which was made—like our morning wake-up call in the past—by banging an iron bar against suspended scrap iron."[45] Off and on a plane would dive-bomb a locomotive in the distance. In the factory, "We barely had any light. We spent our time chatting under our breath. That half-light made an impression on us. It was through this we sensed Germany had been beaten."

Sadron continued: "However, in our dismal workshop, laughter and singing broke out and resonated all day long. The women were beside themselves. They sang at the top of their lungs and their laughter mixed with the jokes of the foremen and engineers who spent their time flirting with them. Wellner himself abandoned his work and got involved in the hullabaloo. Krüger was in great form and gesticulated as the loudspeaker made a racket. It was really festive!

"We were disgusted. We couldn't figure how these people could welcome, in our presence, the downfall of their own country. We had more esteem for the little guy Wells who watched our boisterous corner in a rage, taking us as witnesses to the scandal. As for Jansch—who had only just got back—he was shattered. The Volkssturm exercises infuriated him, and his wife and daughter, who had been evacuated too close to Breslau, were in the hands of the Russians [. . .].

"During this time, the wife of the Kommando's head engineer sang—in front of our friends in the offices—American songs and was learning to type in English. We were stupefied. [. . .] It was true that we couldn't yet understand."[46] Indeed, these people were totally disoriented. The author recalls a conversation where they speculated on the good or ill fortune of becoming respectively Russian, English, or American. Even as he continued to wear the Nazi insignia, another considered himself once again to be purely Austrian—and expected because of this some indulgence.[47]

THE LAST MONTHS AT THE DORA CAMP. The evacuation of the eastern camps in January–February 1945 not only brought new prisoners to Dora-Mittelbau. It freed the SS officials for new duties. This was the case for Richard Baer and Eduard Wirths. The SS-Sturmbannführer (major) Richard Baer had been the Auschwitz camp commander since June 1944, when he was in charge of the evacuation. In February 1945 he replaced, as commander of Dora-Mittelbau, Förschner, who was made commander of the Kaufering camp—dependent on Dachau. The SS-Hauptsturmführer (captain) Eduard Wirths was the chief doctor (*Lagerarzt*) at Auschwitz—where he arrived in September 1942. He was also appointed to Dora, where he was Kurzke's superior.

It was pointed out in chapter 12 that the new commander of the Woffleben camp, Kleemann, also came from Auschwitz. More precisely, he was the commander of the camp annex Bismarckshütte, where Hofstein was doctor. The prisoners were not aware of the changes that had occurred in the command of Dora. It was for them of no consequence. Henceforth the dreaded character was Sander—from the Gestapo. Nor were the prisoners aware of the name Roman Drung, the new LÄ, a Green.

During the entire month of March 1945 one of the major preoccupations of the SS was to rid the Dora camp of everyone they considered useless, newcomers from the eastern camps, or the sick of any origin—and to send them to Nordhausen. This policy came up against the passive resistance of the *Revier* doctors as well as the *Schreiber* of numerous blocks, who had allowed those fellow prisoners they wanted to save to benefit from the *Schonung*. This was the case of Charles Spitz in Block 130, and for some young "51,000"s from the Jura. Sander decided to crush this resistance, and as pointed out earlier the arrival of several of the witnesses of this period at the Boelcke Kaserne was registered in late March. As already noted, on April 1, seven hundred prisoners arrived at Woffleben in a very bad state and meant to work in B 12.

Sander's spite manifested itself on March 29 when he decided to bring together the *Schreiber* of all the blocks. Extracts from Spitz's account set the scene: "Sander arrived, surrounded by a group of SS. He began to bawl us out as only those wearing German uniforms know how and are able to. Among other reproaches, we were accused of having bribed the Schonung-Kontrolle who was then in the Bunker, in order to shield our dirty friends from work. Sabotage! The word cropped up at the end of each litany of alleged misdeeds. You're all going to pay and die like dogs.

"Assembled five by five, step in time, march. And we had to sing! Fortunately, there were the Germans and Poles who knew love songs. [. . .] That lasted a good hour. All of a sudden, change of course, direction Krematorium. [. . .] We continued toward Block 116 behind which stretched a steep hill. [. . .] Sander said we were going to have a race and that the last ten would be executed. [. . .] After an hour, he made the 'old ones' come up from the ranks.

"As each group got to the top, the winner had the right to withdraw from the competition. [. . .] This infernal race lasted until midday. By hobbling along, Barbaud and I had no trouble coming last in front of Sander who held his weapon aimed at us. When he saw our triangles and noticed we were French, he shook with a booming laugh. An avalanche of inanities punctuated with slaps followed and, in conclusion, [. . .] he put his weapon back and declared that two heaps of filth like us were not worth the tenth of the price of a German bullet."[48] It was in this manner that Sander filled up the morning of March 29, 1945. Earlier in the month he had engaged in far more criminal activities.

THE HANGING OF THE SOVIETS. As noted, the Gestapo had in November 1944 proceeded to arrest certain French, Czech, Russian, and Polish prisoners. Then, in December in the roll-call area, a very large number of Russians were apprehended. Finally, at different dates, the same fate befell several German political prisoners who occupied top positions in the camp.

The French—who were assembled at the Nordhausen prison—were separated into two groups on March 15—as Michel has noted. Poupault, Boyer, and Bordier stayed at the prison as did three others, Donnier, Ruskon, and Denais, whom Michel quotes and who were arrested under different circumstances.[49] The others returned to the bunker at Dora. The criteria for this separation are unknown, and no one knew what their fate was likely to be.

Things took a tragic turn for the Russians, who were sent to be hanged either in the camp or the tunnel. Eyewitness accounts exist in both cases, though it remains to be determined—if possible—in which order the events happened.

Concerning the hangings in the camp, Spitz's testimony is situated between March 9 and 14. According to him the rumor spread in the camp on March 9 that a mutiny had taken place in the bunker. Around twenty Russians had escaped after having knocked out an SS guard. After a search with dogs, they were recovered. They were executed a few days later in front of Spitz.

"When I got to the roll-call grounds, a cordon of armed SS obliged all those who passed by to head toward the gallows. A bunch of Russians, hands tied behind their backs and gags in their mouths, waited stoically. In groups of five, they stepped onto the stools, the Kapo of the Bunker put the noose over their heads and booted the stools out from under them. Grabbing the hanged men by the feet, he yanked violently on the body and undid the ropes. Stretched out on the ground, the hanged men were still moving. So the Kapo grabbed hold of one of the heavy stools and struck at their heads until they burst. [. . .] After some time, Sander was himself disgusted with the Kapo's hysterical fury. He drew his revolver and he finished the last ones off with a bullet in the head. When the gallows were taken down, we were requisitioned to clean the area."[50]

The following account is taken from Charles Sadron's description of the hangings in the tunnel. Once again the Russians were the victims: "Normally it happened at the far end of Tunnel B, not far from the exit facing hall 41. The condemned were taken, during the break, to the execution site. They had their hands tied behind their backs and heads uncovered. A piece of rough wood, like a bit, was shoved between their jaws and kept in place by an iron wire quickly twisted behind their necks. That day there were nine of them, lined up slightly below us, because the precaution was taken to have them go down into the excavation—a foot deep—where a rail switch was located. Hanging above their heads were nine steel ropes, carefully parallel, ending in slipknots while the upper ends were attached to a long horizontal rod used to handle the torpedoes [rockets]. The rod was held up in the center by a cable that would—high above beneath the vault—coil around the drum of an electric winch. A high-ranking prisoner was there to put the noose carefully around the necks of his impassive fellow prisoners. A group of SS, presided over by Oberscharführer Busta— 'Horse Head'—supervised the operation. Next, the executioner went to his post and grasped the motor's control gears. Busta motioned. The motor droned. Gently the strangled men rose as they spun slowly around. The motor stopped when they were a foot above ground. So their feet were at the same level as ours. A few spasms barely shook their bodies in which we could imagine the terrible rigidity. But that was not the end: it required more than a minute to die in that way. The young German secretaries who came to watch this ignominious spectacle got their money's worth.

"We, on the other hand, had to parade past the skewer looking straight into the faces with their eyes rolled back—at the same height as our own. A fellow prisoner, who took his hat off in respect—received a serious thrashing."[51]

According to the information given by Wincenty Hein, in March 1945 there were 162 executions—of which 133 were Russian and 24 Polish, the others were three Czechs, one Lithuanian, and a Gypsy.[52]

Two aspects of these executions are worth a closer look. The first is the high proportion of Soviets. Concerning the executions in March 1945, they were not linked to sabotage, though the Russians had previously been hanged for this reason. The victims of the last executions were Soviets arrested in December 1944, and many of them did not work on the V2 assembly. The Soviets seemed to have been eliminated for being Soviets, through racism, as had been a considerable number of prisoners of war as early as 1941. It was, it seems, what also happened to a group of Poles.

The second noteworthy aspect of the executions was the decision to use the tunnel for carrying out a certain number of them. This choice was not necessary if the point were to make an impression on the prisoners. The gallows at the roll call were more appropriate. It seems that the desire was also to make an impression on the German civilians, whose loyalty to the regime was no longer assured.

It should be borne in mind that a *Führerbefehl*—an order from the führer on March 19—imposed a scorched-earth policy in all regions just before they fell into enemy hands—including in the west. That meant the systematic destruction of the industrial infrastructure of the Ruhr and the Saar, for example. Speer and his section along with numerous generals made sure the orders were not carried out.

But in the final months there were among the Nazis a certain number of fanatics ready to draw the maximum number of victims into their own destruction, and the concentration camp prisoners were ideal candidates to be the first of these victims. The account of the "evacuations" of April–May 1945, which make up the sixth part of this book, will show to what extent the danger was real.

[[16]]

A CHRONICLE OF THE LAST DAYS

The last days of Dora-Mittelbau fell between April 1 and April 11—the day the Americans arrived in Nordhausen. It was a brief period marked by various—often highly significant—events that should not be disassociated if their full importance is to be grasped. The best solution seems to be to proceed in chronological order, moving from one place to another according to circumstances—in particular the Dora camp and tunnel to Bleicherode, the Boelcke Kaserne, and Ellrich.

An Easter Service

In 1945, Easter fell on April 1. All the witnesses who belonged to the Catholic Church have made special reference to this exceptional day. Jacques-Christian Bailly's account is revealing. The Schreiber Kommando was in the tunnel. "At noon, we gathered together in front of our offices to go back to the camp. Lined up in rows of five, facing the Kapo, we waited for the rest of the Kommando. Jean-Paul [Renard] being tall, towered above the group. He stared, keeping a close eye on the gallery. As usual, Paul, the Protestant minister, was at his side. Everything was calm. Jean-Paul took from his pocket the little shoe-polish box he used as a ciborium and took communion. He gave the box to the minister who held it out religiously to Bernard. Passing through, the French, Belgian, or Polish Catholics took a small host, rediscovering the simple gestures of their faith. The others, Protestant or agnostic, passed the precious viaticum around with caution and respect for the convictions of their fellow prisoners. The green Kapo watched the scene. He understood the significance of it and knew his complicity exposed him to retaliations. Prudent, he kept an eye out for any SS. The ciborium went back to Jean-Paul. The Kapo looked at him inquisitively, then gave the order to leave. In silence, lost in my thoughts, I walked through the deserted halls where the rockets made a strange backdrop for this Easter service."[1]

The End of Mittelwerk

HIDING THE ARCHIVES. On April 1, information reached von Braun about the advance of the Americans—moreover premature—making him worry about the damage that would ensue if Hitler's "scorched earth" policy were carried out. He wanted at least—suspecting they might one day be useful—to save the rocket construction archives. With the agreement of Dornberger he decided to hide them. Two trustworthy collaborators, Dieter Huzel and Bernard Tessmann, were put in charge of a triple mission—for which they were given the requisite means.

First, they were to bring together, classify, and pack each element found either in Mittelwerk's departments at Dora or at Bleicherode, having originally come from Peenemünde. When the work was completed on April 3, it represented fourteen tons of paper. Next, an underground site had to be found that was unoccupied and relatively accessible. After a good deal of searching, a former explosives warehouse of an abandoned mine was chosen somewhat to the north of the Harz Mountains at Dörnten, between Goslar and Salzgitter.

A convoy of three trucks—of which two had trailers—was involved in this search, laden with the fourteen tons. They were then unloaded and the crates carted into the cache. The access to the gallery was then blown up. On April 7, Huzel and Tessman left the region to join up again with von Braun, who had left for Bavaria—as will be seen later. McGovern's book gives the details of this operation and the precautions taken to avoid identification of the depot's whereabouts.[2]

SHUTTING DOWN THE TUNNEL FACTORY. André Ribault, who worked—as seen earlier—on drafting the plans, noted what happened in the tunnel on April 1 and 2. "1 April 1945—Easter Sunday. Down into the Tunnel at seven in the morning. Hall 41 off limits to Häftlings. Why? Pass through A. Einsatz. Return to the camp. 2nd April—seven in the morning down in the Tunnel. Get to the offices where all documents have been burned. Looks completely destroyed. Not a single 'cigar' left on the assembly line. Return to the camp around nine in the morning."[3]

Charles Sadron made the same observations:[4] "At the factory this morning (on 1 April), we did a sort of inventory. Active, we were full of good intentions. The civilians busied themselves with mysterious work. We were made to rip down notices and signs. We had to hand over written material we had on our persons. It was not the moment to compromise our lives for a folly committed in extremis: like my fellow prisoners, I handed over—with a heavy heart—all I possessed. There was a paper on the social role of scientific research, four lines of a sonnet I would never finish, and some technical notes. The value of these writings was uneven. [. . .] Wellner was lost in a mountain of paperwork. We had no time to get lost in thought: the Kapo came to get us and take us back up to the camp, even though it was only eleven in the morning. [. . .] Orders and counterorders came one after the other all throughout the day.

"The next morning (2 April) we went down to the factory at the regular time. We found our work benches destroyed, the verification apparatuses ripped out, the warehouse emptied of its gyroscopes and Mischgeräte. During the night, the civilians had carried out all this work. Everything to do with the V2 telemechanics installation had become unrecognizable. There was hardly anyone except for ourselves—and the engineers—who could bear witness to what had been there. This idea worried us a little. [. . .] The factory was silent. The motors were turned off. All that remained was the vague hubbub of people milling about in the tunnels. Our workshop was calm. The women were gone. We waited rather anxiously. Our useless presence, in this dead factory, worried me. Finally, we went back up. Apparently for the last time."

The destruction was not as thoroughgoing as one might have expected. Part of the paperwork sorted by Wellner was carted off with the archives. Only copies of documents or documents of no interest were actually burned. The machines stayed where they were. The electricity, ventilation, and telephone continued working. No information is available as to what happened to the aircraft engine factory of Nordwerk in the north part of the tunnel.

THE DEPARTURE OF FIVE HUNDRED SCIENTISTS AND ENGINEERS. On April I it was Kammler who decided to evacuate—by himself and under his supervision—five hundred selected specialists to the Bavarian Alps. He had a special train in the area at his disposal. His headquarters as of March 20—as mentioned in chapter 14—was in the region north of Lippstadt. The train was ironically baptized Vergeltungs-Express—the "retaliation express"—and allowed him to move between Peenemünde, Nordhausen, Blizna, The Hague, and other sites connected with the V2s.

The five hundred specialists—scientists and engineers—left for Oberammergau on the night of April 2 with one hundred guards from the SD. Von Braun traveled by car because of his injury and arrived there on April 4. Kammler escorted the convoy, then left. Dornberger, who had left Bad Sachsa, set up nearby. Some forty-five hundred specialists stayed in the area in the villages around Nordhausen and Bleicherode.[5]

It was around the same time as von Braun's people got onto Kammler's train that another train—as was seen in chapter 14—took the surviving prisoners from Peenemünde/Karlshagen to Ellrich after a difficult evacuation.

The Bombing of Nordhausen

THE AIR STRIKES AS SEEN FROM DORA. From the Dora camp—climbing the hill behind the bunker—a plain was visible, while to the southeast were the church towers of Nordhausen. At the beginning of April many of those prisoners who were not in the tunnel saw the city being bombed. Ribault[6] provides a detailed account.

"1 April, 10 a.m. Air raid on Nordhausen and surrounding area by single-engined fighter planes. Dive bombings, as well as bomb, cannon, and machine-gun attacks. Duration: at least an hour.

"3 April, 4 p.m. sharp. The bombing of Nordhausen during overcast sky, low cloud-cover. The planes that 'purr heavily' fly through the cotton-batting. First some explosive bombs over the city, then a raining down of fire bombs, and once again explosives. No antiaircraft fire. Five well lined-up bombs fell on the factory's sorting platforms. Bombs were also falling on Salza. A half hour later—during a sunny break in the clouds—another air raid by the single-engine fighter planes. Antiaircraft fire.

"4 April. During the night, a long stream of planes fly over. At nine in the morning, half overcast with threatening cloud cover, numerous four-engined planes, flying quite low over us in every direction. A few minutes later the bombs began to fall. At first a few explosions over Nordhausen, then the fire bombs began raining down, followed once again by explosives. During the fire bombing, a four-engine plane in flames plummeted over Nordhausen. No anti-aircraft fire. After the strikes, yet another attack by fighter planes. That night, Nordhausen seemed like nothing more than an immense inferno reddening the sky. During the night, many planes flying over."

Unbeknownst to those at Dora, their fellow prisoners in the Boelcke Kaserne in Nordhausen were under the bombings. The accounts made by those of them who survived were, of course, very personal and not always mutually consistent—depending on where they were at the time. The following extracts show the extent of the damage and losses, and just how widespread the disorganization was.

THE APRIL 3 BOMBING. The accounts refer first of all to the Tuesday, April 3 bombing: "Right from the first blast, I took shelter under the concrete staircase of the Revier. A bomb hit the Block and the staircase was demolished. I ran to the middle of the camp, to a shelter dug right into the ground, where there were already a dozen civilians, women, children, and also an SS man—as green from fear as his uniform—who could only stammer: 'Schrecklich! Schrecklich!' (Horrible! Horrible!) And indeed, it was not a pretty sight; corpses every five or six yards, headless or their innards ripped open. [. . .] The barbed-wire enclosure had been blown to smithereens. The watch towers were gone. Some of the SS had disappeared.

"We were tempted to escape—but where to? I hadn't even had breakfast! I had spent the evening collecting up the corpses. In all, there were around two-hundred dead. Two horses had been killed, that the cooks had already skinned for the next day. The Revier was full. Three per bed and no medicine." (Pierre Maho.)[7]

"The first day of bombing was enough to blast out the large metallic doors which collapsed on top of the prisoners. One flew through the hall and crashed into the lean-to where the corpses were piled together. There was an enormous puncture in the floor upstairs, and thus up above in the roof's concrete arch as well. Having spent time on the main floor a few days earlier, I had noticed the concrete roof's sturdiness reinforced by enormous doubling. It hadn't been enough to stop the bombs." (Jean-Pierre Couture—who notes that the horses killed were pulling a cart passing behind the camp.)[8]

That night the SS took things back into hand, and Delogne even spoke of an "evening roll call."[9] But, everyone thought the bombing would start up again the next day. The night was calm, and in the morning pears and marmalade were handed out.

The Nordhausen prison was also hit. The doors to the cells were open and there was an opening leading outside; but, because it was guarded, no one attempted to escape.[10]

THE APRIL 4 BOMBING. The bombing of Wednesday, April 4 was more fierce and dismantled the whole organization. The majority of the prisoners withstood it inside the camp.

Xavier Delogne was in a block when the bombing began. "The string of bombs began falling. Terrified, I lay down flat on my stomach in the center of the garage, right in the midst of the bombing; others preferred running away, but as soon as they stood up they were flattened by the shrapnel. All of a sudden there was a horrifying blast. Nothing could be made out, the place was filled with fumes, powder and dust. A few yards from me, one of the immense iron doors collapsed, crushing several poor souls under its weight. The roof was ripped off."[11]

Halkin's account was no different: "This time the bombing was fast, brutal and massive. I went back to my spot at the back of the garage, under a main beam. [. . .] I heard the carpet bombing going on over my head from left to right with an implacable regularity. [. . .] The bombing grew in intensity. I protected my chest with my knees, my face with my hands. [. . .] Through the gash opened up in front of us, shrapnel flew into the garage. Blocks of cement broke off from the ceiling. [. . .] A terrible blow plowed into my chest. I lost consciousness. [. . .] When I came to, I was lying among the dead, covered in dust and blood. [. . .] My wrists were bleeding, but they had saved my eyes from the bomb's shrapnel."[12]

Jean-Pierre Couture found shelter—as he had the night before—in the lubricating pit. Auchabie was in a block during the bombing, was injured in the left foot, and crawled out of the building, which collapsed behind him. He dragged himself into a bomb crater where five injured French were already huddled.[13]

As soon as the bombing began, escapes from the prison multiplied. Poupault and Boyer left, followed by Bordier, Donnier, and Denais. The bombs fell, Poupault was injured and fainted, and Boyer died from a direct hit. The other were in shock.[14]

Maho,[15] however, left the camp with other prisoners before the bombing began and reached the nearby countryside: "We rushed toward a small bridge already congested with runaways, civilian workers, Germans, prisoners, soldiers. A plane at two thousand meters veered around to the camp we had left behind us, and dropped two star rockets. This time it meant business. After crossing the bridge we took off into the countryside and looked for some sort of shelter. A streambed with high, sheer banks offered us relative safety. We were half a mile from the camp. There they were, the squadrons were right above us. They let the bombs go and we watched them fall. In the din of chains and whistling, we heard the bombs strike our Blocks. That was it; nothing more could be seen of the camp, now consumed by smoke and flames. For twenty minutes, the hurricane was unleashed and spread out over Nordhausen.

"Moreover, the bombers neutralized a zone infinitely more vast than the city and the air-force camp alone. Even being a ways from the camp, the bombs fell close behind us. One of them landed ten yards away. The earth reeled like the deck of a ship in mid-ocean; in an inky black cloud, my jacket caught fire then was put out by the ten or so square feet of earth that came down on me. The water's course had been diverted. I ended up with three gudgeons in my hand. [. . .]! Swamped in mud, earth and soot, de Poortère, Dutois and I ran off into the countryside—in the opposite direction from Nordhausen. Every fifty yards a crater, every twenty yards an opened or abandoned suitcase, a throbbing member or a body.

"The bombing had ceased, but the Spitfires and Hurricanes with their machine guns gave chase to isolated individuals. Because, from a distance, they didn't know who we were, it was best to remain wary. We'd fix a far-off rallying point, a farm we would go to individually. To travel in groups would have been dangerous. Twice a plane spotted me and I had to duck for cover behind the apple trees. Unfortunately, they shot in a dive and there was no dead angle for protection. A remarkable thing was that I no longer felt my injured foot, though I had been walking for two hours on churned up earth and shell holes.

"At eleven o'clock I got to the farm. We talked the situation over. What to do? Go back to the camp? It no longer existed. The SS had left; the barbed wire obliterated, the Blocks destroyed. We were without direction, without shelter. We decided to wait in the barn."

Roger Abada,[16] a "45,000" from Auschwitz—having arrived at Dora from Gross Rosen in February—gave a very similar account: "I hid in a sort of irrigation canal. After the bombing, came the machine gunning in a dive. I got through it, I don't know how." Everyone reacted as best he could. Gaillard ran off into the countryside looking for haystacks and woods in which to hide.[17] As did Hofstein and four friends[18] as well as Poupault and Bordier, after having given up on finding Boyer.

Xavier Delogne first left the camp and made his way "through the field plowed up by bombs, toward a house in flames." He met two Frenchmen and crawled into a shell crater with them, where they sat eating margarine. Then they went back to see what was happening at the camp.

"The inside and surrounding area were covered in corpses. From the collapsed ceilings legs and arms were hanging, bodies horribly mutilated. The poor souls who remained on the first floor were for the most part reduced to ashes." He stayed the night with friends, among the block ruins, in the midst of the wounded.[19]

Nicola and six friends spent the night in a shell crater in front of a block.[20]

Normand stayed with the sick in a *Revier* that was partially spared. Couture, out of his lubricating pit, was called upon by two SS. "Devastated, in the loose stones of the broken up road, they pulled along a four-wheeled cart on which they had laid their kits and a pile of belongings. I had to pull this vehicle right up to the camp exit, to the bridge over the small river where I managed to clear off, little concerned with escorting them in their retreat." Later, he and his friend Marcel Brière did their best to minister to the injured. He pointed out—as did Delogne—the danger of bombs that had timing devices, which continued to blow up for more than twenty-four hours.[21]

The horrible accounts of April 3 and 4 are mixed with colorful accounts about food provisions. Although there was no longer soup and bread distribution, the bombing in the surrounding area of the camp gave the prisoners access to various food reserves—in addition to horse meat. Delogne spoke of jam, margarine, and potatoes.[22] Maho, after having to make do with sugar beets close to the barn, found butter, blood sausage, canned asparagus, and grape juice.[23]

All that was left for the prisoners was to wait—wherever they were—for the Americans to arrive. This proved to be, as will be seen, a long and painful wait.

The End of Dora-Mittelbau

DISORDER AT DORA. Between April 2 and 5 the entire administrative structure of the Dora camp was progressively dismantled. Two factors contributed to the disorder. The first was the shutting down of the tunnel factory, which employed a large part of the camp population. All that remained was an immense mass of people with nothing to do. And the second was the absence of real authority and the incompetence of the gang of Greens who were the block leaders, the *Kapos,* and so on.

In any case, on April 2 and 3, the SS carried out major transfers between the Mittelbau camps. The first operation was the sending of a thousand prisoners from Dora to Harzungen. On April 2, as Yves Béon[24] related, not all the workers went down into the tunnel. Many of them were kept at the far end of the roll-call area. "The Lagerschutz began to surround the prisoners. It was the end, we couldn't do anything anymore. But in fact, yes, something could always be done. The revolt, the turning upside down, that unthinkable, unimaginable thing happened. Michel screamed to Charles: 'Let's get out!' The moment he yelled that the movement leapt up like a spark and reached instantly the thousands of men separated from the rest of the camp. It was a mad rush, in all senses, in all directions. The Lagerschutz charged with their truncheons out, but it was too late. They were powerless against this horde of madmen scattering to the left and right, and racing toward the hills, looking to conceal themselves amid the Blocks."

Little by little, however—the camp remaining closed in any case—the prisoners with armbands managed to group their people together at the roll-call area. The idea was to lead some of the prisoners to the disinfecting block in preparation for a "transport." This was not—not yet—the beginning of the evacuation, but a simple transfer from Dora to Harzungen. It was the next morning, Tuesday, April 3, that the group got under way. Upon arrival at Harzungen the newcomers were brought together to be told that the work Kommandos would be made up the next day. Then the alert was given: it was the beginning of Nordhausen's first bombing—a few miles away.

A supplementary operation took place the same day: a thousand prisoners returned to Dora who had been in Nordhausen, considered as more or less able-bodied. It is not known why the transfer from Dora to Harzungen took place. Perhaps it had already been planned, combined with a transfer of the sick from Harzungen to the Boelcke Kaserne, and a "transport" from Nordhausen to Bergen-Belsen. That transport was ready: after the bombing, Couture—wandering in the area—saw a train of cattle cars on a garage track with new wire meshing on the windows.

The prisoners who remained at Dora—the majority—were moving about in the camp on the morning of Tuesday the 3rd and Wednesday the 4th when the bombings—for which Ribault was present—took place. The bombings on April 4 were just coming to an end when at around half past ten the camp loudspeakers summoned "everyone, without exception, to the roll-call area with two blankets, for a departure." At the same time the papers in the Arbeitsstatistik and in the other offices had begun to be burned.

Initially this announcement resulted in indescribable disorder. The food and clothing storehouses were pounced on. "The Russians and the Poles exhibited thoroughgoing knowledge of the science of pillaging," as Ribault[25] as well as Hagenmuller[26] pointed out. The Germans were not to be outdone. The blocks themselves were devastated.

It seemed that there were at a certain moment measures taken to organize the departures that were more or less thwarted by the initiatives of someone or other. Everyone—as Ribault explained—sought to stay in the camp as long as possible. Concerning the Ko Scherer group—if Sadron is to be believed—things even took a rather surprising twist: "The Kapos busily arrived: they were given orders to separate those who were—among the French mostly—the best workers. It appeared to be a measure of preference. What did it mean? We jostled each other to be chosen. Thank God, almost all our good friends were there, together. The clan stayed intact, except for the dead, of course."[27]

In any case it was the Russians at whom the departure orders were first aimed. Four thousand were brought together and led on foot to Woffleben and Ellrich, passing along the Kohnstein road—north of the camp. Thus they were involved in several separated evacuation convoys except for the "last" convoy from Dora—that in which the prisoners would turn up at Ravensbrück.

The last evening in the blocks reflected the general disorder. Sadron described the situation of Block 104: "The Block was overwhelmed. The artificial flowers, the shawl-carpets, the paintings on the walls, all the things we had considered as sacred before had disappeared or were lying trampled on the floor. The Pithecanthrope could not be seen. A pity! The Block chief has disappeared. In the evening, under cover of darkness, he came back to sleep in his devastated cubicle with two women from the brothel."[28] Ribault mentioned Block 113: "Scene with the Block chief, who had gone completely crazy. Jean-Paul Renard was given a flogging and chased from the Block, but managed to find asylum at 122, where the majority of the Kommando were."[29]

THE EVACUATIONS GET UNDER WAY. The decision to begin evacuating the Dora camp along with the neighboring camps seems to have been taken the morning of Wednesday, April 4, at the time of the second bombing of Nordhausen. Essentially what was arranged was an evacuation by railway convoys to the north—with an important constraint. That constraint was imposed by the contours of the region. There was no normal track going across the Harz Mountains, a medium-sized range—but making up a very compact whole—with deep valleys. Therefore it was necessary to go around the Harz by the west and then return back to the plain of northern Germany—which would mean, in a certain manner, meeting up with the Americans.

Four loading points were possible: the Dora Tunnel marshaling yard, which was in a cul-de-sac, followed by the train stations of Niedersachswerfen, Woffleben, and Ellrich, before the small tunnel between Ellrich and Walkenried. There is no document making it possible to establish with certitude how many convoys left and in what order. Eight can be clearly identified.

Among the first, two convoys left from Ellrich, one with the prisoners who had arrived from Karlshagen a few days earlier, the other with the prisoners from Ellrich—among the most able-bodied. Fournier noted that the prisoners from Karlshagen traveled in "very, very old passenger cars, entirely in wood—

even the seats—without compartments and a passageway up the middle."[30] All the other convoys were made up of railway cars alone—cattle cars and uncovered flatbed cars.

Also among the first convoys, one left from Woffleben with the prisoners from the neighboring camp as well as some railway cars of prisoners from Harzungen, and another from Niedersachswerfen with prisoners from Harzungen—particularly the sick. Two other large convoys left from Dora. The common characteristic of all these convoys was that they finally ended up at Bergen-Belsen with varied unanticipated itineraries to be examined in chapter 18.

The next three convoys went in other directions, also unanticipated at the outset. One, with the prisoners from Rottleberode and Ellrich-Theater, was stopped at Mieste. The second, leaving from Ellrich, largely made up of the sick, turned up at Oranienburg. The prisoners from the third—and last—convoy went to Ravensbrück in three stages—the second one on foot. These three convoys will be dealt with in chapter 19.

As for the other prisoners in the Dora-Mittelbau complex, they left on foot in columns of various numbers. On April 4 the columns from Kleinbodungen headed to the north, while that of Gandersheim—dependent on Buchenwald—went east. At the same time the prisoners from the Osterhagen, Nüxei, and Mackenrode Kommandos left to regroup in Wieda. A large column from Harzungen set out on April 4 as well; and those from Rottleberode, Rossla, and Kelbra on April 5. Their destinies proved very different.

Thus in two days almost the entire population of Dora-Mittelbau was dispersed.[31] It will be seen under what very particular circumstances a small number of prisoners still in the camp would be "liberated" on location.

THE LIQUIDATION OF DORA'S *PROMINENTE*. The evacuation of Dora was accompanied by another heinous event, the liquidation of the principal German communist leaders, who had held the highest functions in the camp before being arrested in the last months. Michel, who was with other prisoners in the bunker, reported the following facts: "On the evening of 4 April, motorcycle backfiring. With caution, we watched the small door to the entrance, just facing our dormer window. We saw Sander enter. [. . .] Suddenly the voice of an SS: he called out identity numbers in German. Bare feet slipped in the hallway, a door opened in the courtyard. Impossible to see. The shutters of the dormer window had been shut. [. . .] Seven shots broke the silence. We heard the bodies fall, the sound of wheels, the impact of bodies being loaded into a cart, then once again the racket of the wheels and the footsteps of the two prisoners pulling the load."[32]

The victims were Gamisch, Beham, Thomas, Sczymczak, Schneider, Luzius, and Runki. With Fritz Pröll—who committed suicide on November 29, 1944—and Albert Kuntz—who died on January 22 at the hands of the Gestapo—practically all the camp's political leadership during its period of normal functioning was dead. Those who survived, like Ludwig Leineweber and August Kroneberg, had played a less important role.

Such executions in extremis of political adversaries were not at that time exceptional. On April 4, Admiral Canaris and the Protestant minister Bonhoeffer were hanged at Flossenbürg. On April 19, General Delestraint was executed at Dachau. Instructions came from Berlin, along with the lists—like that from Buchenwald—which included numerous communist prisoners but also a Catholic like Kogon.[33] This ultimate ferocity of the Nazi regime was coherent with its scorched-earth policy.

And yet at the same time French and Czech prisoners—among others—were spared. Louis Gentil was transported to the *Revier* seriously ill, where he died on April 7. The others joined with the first evacuation convoy from Dora: eighty prisoners from the bunker climbed into an open railway car. This clemency has never been explained. Perhaps at a certain level of the SS, bargaining had actually occurred. Perhaps the information given by Michel—with caution—on Grozdoff's role was in keeping with reality.

THE LAST DESCENT OF THE "SPECIALISTS" INTO THE TUNNEL. Thursday, April 5 was the last day at Dora. A convoy left that very morning. Those remaining in the camp experienced a surprising day, because they went back down into the tunnel without knowing why. Ribault relates that in his Kommando, which assembled in Hall 41, lists of prisoners were drawn up, then canceled, to be replaced by other lists, which were canceled as well. At half past two in the afternoon, groups of a hundred were formed, of which the Germans were taken out, then the groups of a hundred were re-formed.[34] Sadron was more explicit: "We went back down again into the Tunnel. We were afraid of some sort of dirty trick. But, the presence of all those civilians—men and women—who were milling around in the halls reassured us. They wouldn't slaughter us in front of all those witnesses.

"There were some two thousand of us down there. We were jammed into a deserted hall and we waited. An order came: 'In fives!' We lined up, docile, and off we went. An SS man came and bellowed. It seems there was an error: we stopped. All through the morning, orders and counter-orders followed one another with surprising regularity. We fully realized that things were going poorly between the SS and the engineers.

"Around noontime, we were put back into tunnel A. There was unrest in the air. Groups of engineers formed and they argued violently. The SS vanished and gathered at the far south end of the Tunnel—close to the exit. Wehrmacht soldiers came running out of a hall, grenades in hand; others rolled along machine guns. We asked ourselves with curiosity what was going to happen. But, everything calmed down. After an hour a command rang out: it was our turn to go out.

"We walked in silence, not too reassured. I thought, here we were, brought together, all of us who had worked on the most secret aspects of the torpedoes. I thought, machine guns and crates of cartridges had just preceded us. So, in spite of myself, when I saw the rows of heads go through the door I listened hard, expecting to be overcome by the rattling of automatic guns mowing down our lines.

"But nothing. [...] I was stunned. We went peaceably back up to the camp."[35]

The prisoners met up at the roll-call area in groups of five and a hundred. They waited for more than an hour. It was only then, Sadron points out, that a section of German prisoners—former *Kapos* or *Lagerschutz*—with guns on their shoulders, white armbands of the Volkssturm on their arms, went down to the factory singing. The author can still picture them, the *Kapo* of the Ko Scherer in the first row on the right.

The evacuation column went through the camp door for the last time between four and five in the afternoon. Ribault pointed out that in the equipment warehouse, "something was burning, with great puffs of black smoke." Sadron clarified: "A bit farther along three trucks were burning that were loaded with the secret equipment over which we had been bent for so many hours." But can he be certain? A train of cars, some flat-wagons, was lined along the shunting tracks. The prisoners got on, a hundred per car; at the same time three SS got on with their chairs. Ribault, with imperturbable precision, noticed that it was from the French National Railways, of the TT series, and measured fifty-six square feet.[36]

What happened in the tunnel has never been elucidated. It is certain, however, that the prisoners there belonged essentially to Schreiber and verification Kommandos, or were the "specialists" from Bünemann, Heckbau, and so on. Was the plan to get rid of them as *Geheimnisträger*? This is merely a possibility and is not certain.

THE DEPARTURE OF THE "LAST CONVOY" FROM DORA. Making up part of the convoy with the specialists were the prisoners having to do with the camp administration, like Rozan and Bérard-Schreve. There was also, in other railway cars, a portion of the sick from the *Revier* taken *manu militari* from their blocks, like Robert Roulard, Jacques Brun, and Claude Douay. The other sick prisoners who could not be transported remained, however, at the *Revier*. This was the case of Bordet, Tauzin, Depierre, Georges Lenoir, and also Gaston Pernot suffering from erysipelas, and Gustave Leroy, suffering with typhus. In addition to the sick, Jacques Maillard was hidden in the *Revier*, referred to as "Thum" because of his height (four-foot-nine).[37]

The SS doctor Kurzke gave the doctors and nurses the freedom to join the evacuation convoys or to stay—the personal risk being real in either of the two hypotheses.[38] Groeneveld, Petit, Lobstein, Doucet, Chabaud, and Lassus, among others, chose to leave. Lemière, Girard, Morel, Croizat, Ebel, Canivet, and also Durand stayed at Dora. Lobstein remembers all the Jews being summoned by loudspeaker to the roll-call area, to which Hermann Scharf—a gynecologist from Temesvar assigned to the *Revier* after the evacuation of Auschwitz—responded. His fellow prisoners wanted to hide him, but he refused by saying: "I must share the fate of my people." No one ever saw him again.

Waiting for the Americans at Nordhausen and Dora

THE WAIT AT NORDHAUSEN. On the morning of April 6 there remained in the Dora-Mittelbau area—which the Americans would not reach until Wednesday, April 11—three types of prisoners: those who had not left the Dora *Revier;* those who had remained at the Boelcke Kaserne in Nordhausen—voluntarily or not—and those who spread out into the neighboring area.

Among the latter was Pierre Maho. The group he was part of turned up on the night of Wednesday the 4th, in a barn not far from Nordhausen to the east. There too were other prisoners and civilian workers of various nationalities as well as Germans who had escaped from prison—including a dwarf. On Friday the 6th, Maho and his fellow prisoners went right to the ruins of the camp and returned with fresh supplies.

At night the barn was taken over by the SS, and no one was to leave anymore. At daybreak, Sunday the 8th, an evacuation column was formed and left in an eastward direction. It quickly became a march to death: those lagging behind were executed—including the dwarf.

In the course of the morning the prisoners were conscripted to clear away the streets of a bombed-out village. At eleven in the morning they noticed that their guards had changed. The SS had left and been replaced by the very peaceable "old men" of the Luftwaffe. The Luftwaffe made them turn around and escorted them—guns unloaded—to the west, taking breaks along the way. Thus they went through Nordhausen's ruins and arrived at six in the evening at the Dora camp, which was empty except for the blocks of the *Revier*—where they were taken. The camp was guarded by German soldiers along with an officer from the Wehrmacht. The former—questioned Monday the 9th by the head nurse—swore on his honor as an officer he would do no harm to the prisoners before the arrival of the Americans. During the night of Monday, April 9 to Tuesday the 10th, the guards disappeared.[39]

Things did not turn out the same way for Hofstein:[40] "Taking advantage of the general confusion, I took off through the woods with four fellow prisoners, to wait out the arrival of the Americans—said to be six or so miles away. We didn't have the good fortune we had dreamed of. We were recaptured by the Volkssturm, which had been scouring the vicinity. It wouldn't have taken much for us to have been shot. We were handed back to the police force and taken from prison to prison—from Sangerhausen, Eisleben, Halle. That was how we arrived at the Gestapo reeducation camp of Zöschen (east of Merseburg)." In chapter 20 the surprising end to Hofstein's peregrinations will be outlined.

This is the way Gaillard recounts his experience: "Run away into the fields, get to Berga, its stacks of straw, its woods, suffer from hunger and thirst until Sunday the 8th, get recaptured. Watched those in hiding being killed and finally escaped to curse and demand justice, thanks to a courageous man—a German— Otto Lamster, for whom man remained a brother and who, seeing me in distress had me come into his home, gave me medical care and fed me." Gaillard returned to the Dora camp after the SS left.[41]

Roger Abada[42] dressed in civilian clothes he found in a house. He took a large hat to hide his shaved head—knowing the SS were hunting down prisoners and executing them. He joined up with various survivors in the basement of a building and served as nurse, "having lasted around eight days" until the arrival of the Americans.

In his book on Dora, Michel devotes a long chapter on Poupault and his three friends' march to the west after their escape from prison. They were able to dress as civilians and blend in with the refugees who were heading in all different directions. In the end they met up with the Americans. But Michel's account is totally lacking in geographical and chronological indications.[43]

Nicola and his friends, after a night in their bomb crater, remained from the morning of Thursday the 5th to the morning of Monday the 9th hidden in the trucks at the back of the Boelcke Kaserne garages, only leaving in search of food (canned food, sweetened condensed milk, drinks) in a basement. Then "sometime Monday morning, seeming to come out of the waters of the Zorge, twenty or so Schupos swooped on top of us like birds of prey. Hitting with their rifle butts, they dislodged us from our trucks and took us back to the large yard of the garage. There—still hitting with their rifle butts—they searched the rubble to make all those who could still stand up—for better or for worse—come out. That was how the sixty-five of us wound up traveling the six miles that separated us from Dora."[44]

When they got there, all sixty-five of them were locked into a barracks after having learned that the next day they would be hanged for pillaging. Nicola added the following passage: "In the middle of the night, we heard bursts of machine-gun fire very close to us, then moving away. And once again, silence. The next morning, a fellow prisoner told us that he saw from his window the SDs getting ready to burn us with flamethrowers and a group of soldiers from the Wehrmacht attacked them with machine-guns, making them run away."

Michel Thomas seems to have been led the night before from Nordhausen to Dora with another group, some members of which were shot on the way.

Halkin and six others found refuge in the basements of the SS building, from which they left only to fetch water, wood, and potatoes.[45] In the end Delogne set up in a corner of the garage with a Luxembourgeois (a pastry chef in Esch) and an old, injured Frenchman; they had straw mattresses and blankets and something to eat; Delogne fetched the water,[46] Pierre Bleton and some friends hid on the second floor of the *Revier* behind the blankets. They had provisions, but Bleton had to go in search of water without being caught. Agnès and Alcaras remained where they were, in equally precarious conditions.

Auchabie, injured, remained for five days in his bomb crater, where his five fellow prisoners died one after the other. In the end he got out and was given medical treatment in the rubble by a fellow prisoner, Marcel Mathieu. When the Americans arrived two days later he was unconscious.[47]

Doctor Normand and Jean-Pierre Couture did their best to save those sick and injured left in the camp. They were under the threat of the *Schupos* and members of the Volkssturm patrolling the neighboring area; but the stench from the heaps of corpses kept these patrols at a distance. The two men managed to move themselves to an antiaircraft shelter where they awaited the American military doctors.

Couture recalled a terrible image: "Two days after the bombing, to find the blankets meant for the few injured men I was keeping fed, I climbed what was left of the crumbled staircase to the first floor. The gallery—collapsed at the two ends and from place to place—was a path of corpses. The three-level bunk beds were knocked over and there was no one left alive, no doubt because of the blast of the explosion. And yet there was a cry for help: a Frenchman with a leg injury. I was able to bring him down—with the help of Marcel Brière—by creeping along in the rubble. He hadn't had food or water for four days."[48]

In Nordhausen the Americans ended up appearing unexpectedly among the ruins.

THE WAIT AT DORA. What happened at Dora between the time of the departure of the last convoy on the night of April 5 and the arrival of the Americans on April 11 is unclear. It was a genuine little town that had suddenly been almost totally emptied of its people, and the relationship between the different parts of the whole was nonexistent.

According to Doctor Lemière's testimony, the SS left the premises after the last convoy and the Wehrmacht soldiers took over from them at the entrance and watchtowers. Their commander announced to the doctors: "You have nothing to fear. The gangsters have left." The city of Nordhausen could be seen still burning from the camp. The inhabitants, it seems, sought refuge in the tunnel.

One of the sick men who remained in the tuberculosis block was René Bordet, on whom two male nurses, Lobstein and Georges Van der Meer, performed a pulmonary puncture which relieved him greatly. He nevertheless avoided being evacuated. "We remained barely thirty or so, including some corpses." From his bunk he could see down to the roll-call area. Bordet spoke of what he saw, without being in a position to determine an exact chronology of events.[49]

One day an unknown vehicle drove up to the roll-call area. It was a jeep with Americans who were heading toward the *Revier.* "Certain fellow prisoners went down to meet them and brought them back to us; we spoke through gestures and a little French. We asked them for submachine guns. They still needed them to finish going around the camp. Coming back down again they gave us two and left with the promise that the rest of the army was soon to arrive. It was a small reconnaissance mission."

The next day "two SS went back up to the roll-call area. Certain prisoners were fighting over the submachine guns; two of them were probably the one-legged Russians with the rudimentary crutches. The two SS men went toward the Wäscherei, below the kitchens, and entered it. A moment after, two 'Häftlings' emerged. Some gunfire broke out, close by. Nothing like the sporadic shooting in the distance. I got up and went out to look from the gable across from the Block. A small group was coming back with the submachine guns. One of the one-legged men said to me: 'Zwei kaputt.' I went back up to bed, looking forward to the rest of the troops."

Two days later in the morning "there arrived a ration of potato soup and big chunks of meat. Racked with hunger—my temperature having gone below 38° C—I found the soup excellent. I took a second liter of it which I ate more slowly. I kept the meat for the afternoon, but I fell asleep." When he woke up it was a day later and the Americans were in the camp. He was left to sleep, sated.

The very succinct account by Doctor Lemière[50] made no mention of this episode. But neither does he make mention of the successive arrival—under differing conditions—of various groups of prisoners from the Boelcke Kaserne, like that of Maho, Michel Thomas, and Nicola. It is impossible to reconcile the accounts with each other. But, all of the witnesses were sick. The morning of Tuesday, April 10, the guards left, and it was Maho who thus noted an exceptional moment: "The camp was absolutely free. We could have gone out if we had wanted to, but where would we go? The weather was splendid, the heavy gunfire had ceased, reigning over the camp and the countryside was a prodigious silence. No more planes. Everything seemed to be quiet as if in expectation of something enormous and wonderful. We cocked our ears to the slightest sound."[51]

On Wednesday the 11th at three o'clock in the afternoon a jeep arrived with American soldiers, who were greeted with shouts and tears of joy. They were guided to the camp by a former German *Kapo* in civilian clothes. The soldiers went around the camp, machine guns in hand. Then they came upon the *Revier* barracks. The jeep took off again at high speed in search of indispensable medical assistance.

ROGER COUËTDIC'S SECOND ESCAPE. As shown in chapter 10, a certain number of French prisoners had escaped, been recaptured and imprisoned in the bunker, then assigned to a disciplinary Kommando—the Schachtkommando. Among them were two friends, Roger Couëtdic[52] and Auguste Henner, who had decided to escape the evacuation and leave the camp at the first opportunity. Like the other members of their Kommando, they now knew the camp perfectly and had spotted a closet under the stairs in the block of the *Kammer* that could be reached—by a ladder—through a door in the gable. The *Kammer* was the prisoners' clothing warehouse. Taking advantage of the unrest during the first days of April, they got into the understairs closet and found there "an enormous pile of new shoes" where they could conceal themselves, and ended up by hiding there on April 4 with some meager provisions.

On April 6 a discreet visit to the neighboring barracks of the Eigentum Verwaltung—already pillaged—allowed them to get their hands on civilian clothes; but they were interrupted by some SS who had come to find some as well, and thus became separated. Henner was able to take refuge in the *Revier.* Couëtdic hid in an empty block.

During the night he managed—the electrical network no longer working—to walk through the SS camp where there was a fire and to move away from the marshaling yard to reach a road. He then went through the countryside, noticed some soldiers without weapons, deserters from the Wehrmacht, and finally moved around more tranquilly by pretending to be a Dutch worker who had had his belongings stolen.

He walked along the outskirts of Niedersachswerfen, Ilfeld, and Ellrich, went to see his former camp of Nüxei, got something to eat in a neighboring inn, and then in a house in Bartolfelde. He ended up—without incident—by reaching the Americans at Duderstadt on April 10. He met no organized German resistance. Couëtdic then went back, quite tired, to a regrouping camp where he was repatriated. He arrived in Arras on April 25.

PART SIX

Evacuation, Liberation, Return

[[17   ]]

THE GREAT DISPERSION OF
APRIL 1945 AND THE
"LIBERATION" OF DORA

By early April 1945 what was left of Germany between the Rhine and Oder
rivers, including Austria and Bohemia-Moravia, was to be conquered within six
weeks until the capitulation on May 8. The entire surviving concentration camp
population was still located in this restricted territory, either in the camps (in
descending order from north to south) of Neuengamme, Ravensbrück, Sachsenhausen, Bergen-Belsen, Dora-Mittelbau, Buchenwald, Flossenbürg, Mauthausen, and Dachau, or in their innumerable Kommandos.

What happened to the concentration camp population during those few
weeks is generally described as the "liberation of the camps." This is a convenient expression, but it does not convey an accurate picture of events. In most
cases the prisoners were liberated outside of what had been their camps at the
outset. Before being "liberated" they were "evacuated" under extremely varying, more or less tragic conditions. Evacuations usually took place in the form of
railway convoys, although barges were sometimes used. When neither trains nor
barges were available, the prisoners were sent off in columns on foot, a procedure that has since come to be known as a "death march," which was sometimes
very long and very deadly. The term "death march" is not appropriate, however,
to describe all the evacuations.

With regard to the Dora-Mittelbau complex, virtually all of the prisoners
were evacuated one way or another, and the story of their evacuations will be
told in the following chapters. On their way they crossed paths with various
prisoners from Neuengamme, Buchenwald, Ravensbrück, and Sachsenhausen,
which will also be included in the story. It will therefore be possible to assess
what happened throughout the whole of northern Germany regardless of
whether the liberators were Americans, British, or Soviets.

It is impossible to discuss the evacuations without simultaneously taking
into account military operations. The advancing Western and Soviet armies
gradually triggered the evacuation process. The pace and orientation of the suc-

cessive offensives either speeded or delayed the liberation of prisoners in the highly varied places where they found themselves.

Characteristics of the Evacuations

THE "TRANSPORT" TRADITION IN THE CONCENTRATION CAMP WORLD. The German word *Transport,* which is the same in English, was one of the most common words in the concentration camp vocabulary as well as one of the most dreaded. It was never good to "leave in a transport," as the unknown would no doubt be worse than the known. A look at the various circumstances in which the word was used will make this attitude understandable.

The first type of transport experienced by foreign prisoners in the Reich was their "deportation." In the case of French prisoners (and other nationals arrested in France) the point of departure was usually the Compiègne train station near the Royallieu camp where prisoners were grouped together. The Drancy camp was used to group together Jews. The destination was one of the large Reich camps. Another type of transport, which did not become known until later on, took numerous Jews to extermination camps such as Treblinka, where the survivors of the Warsaw ghetto were eliminated.

Inside the Reich, transports between the major camps played an important role, as the previous chapters have shown. Buchenwald continued to receive Polish, Czech, Russian, and Hungarian Jewish prisoners from Auschwitz, but other prisoners left Buchenwald for Mauthausen or Flossenbürg. In such cases the convoys carried hundreds of prisoners, but there are also examples of smaller transports, such as sending "medical" personnel from Dachau to Stutthof (Kientzler and Weil) or to Dora (Lassus and Pahor). The individual transfer of Durand from Mauthausen to Dora was an extreme case but by no means exceptional.

Regardless of the size of the transport there was constant movement of prisoners from one camp to another up to the very end. A typical example was the transfer of twenty-six female Jehovah's Witnesses from Bergen-Belsen to Dora on March 5, 1945. They replaced the prisoners who were in charge of maintaining the SS camp, such as Rassinier, who was then the dogmaster's *"Schwung."*

In addition to these movements between camps, which had always existed, starting in 1943 there were also all the transports from main camps to ancillary camps or Kommandos, e.g., from Buchenwald to Dora, Laura, Wieda, or Blankenburg, or yet again, Gandersheim, Langenstein, or Neu Stassfurt. Finally, the transports to "rest" camps such as Maïdanek or Bergen-Belsen must not be forgotten. This long tradition must be borne in mind in examining the 1945 evacuation transports, both those from the Eastern European camps in January and February and those from the other camps in April and May.

EVACUATION PROCEDURES. The most important common feature was the total predominance of railway transport. Raul Hilberg has clearly demonstrated the close cooperation between the SS and the Reichsbahn regarding the transport of Jews to Auschwitz and the death camps. As far as transporting "travelers" was concerned, the SS were regular, influential customers of the German railways who duly paid their fares. They were entitled to requisitions of equipment and personnel until the very end, which will be discussed later.

The use of railways naturally involved special constraints. The tracks had to be clear and intact, which is seldom the case when enemy airpower dominates in wartime. Access to railway bridges, which were few and far between, was necessary to cross rivers such as the Elbe. It is therefore not surprising that train routes were highly complicated and it took a very long time to cover limited distances.

Ordinarily, military trucks were seldom used to transport prisoners. They were used to bring prisoners from Buchenwald to Dora during the first few months, but only because of the considerable manpower requirements at the time. That was not the case for the evacuations. Transport by barges or marches in columns on foot were only stopgap solutions for want of railway transport. On a number of occasions prisoners who were marching on foot were put onto trains to finish the journey.

The SS rules regarding transports were simple and had not changed for a long time. Transports involved conveying a number of prisoners from one spot under their control to another spot under their control, and delivering the prisoners in exchange for a receipt. As the next few chapters will show, those in charge of the April 1945 railway convoys from Dora-Mittelbau tried so hard to follow the routine that the transports proved to be almost a caricature. If they failed to reach Neuengamme, they succeeded in delivering their prisoners to Bergen-Belsen, Oranienburg, and Ravensbrück. Similarly, convoys from other camps ended up at Dachau.

THE "DEATH MARCHES" AND THEIR ACTUAL SIZES. On several occasions since 1945 and again recently, some authors have separated the "death marches" from the rest of the evacuations in an attempt to show that the SS deliberately used them to eliminate prisoners, or at least certain categories among them. The position adopted by these writers was not the result of a careful analysis of the facts, which were well known, but rather involved a thesis for which they selected firsthand accounts that were the most likely to support their views.[1]

In fact, as many witnesses observed, the SS preferred railway evacuations for obvious reasons. In addition to freight cars of one type or another (closed cars or platforms) where run-of-the-mill prisoners were crammed together, there were cars and compartments for the SS as well as for prisoner-supervisors wearing armbands so they could travel comfortably. Turns of duty could be easily ensured and food supplies normally divided up. Quite often female staff took part in the evacuation. Each person was allowed to take along a minimum of baggage.

The situation was altogether different for the SS who had to accompany, either on foot or sometimes by bicycle, columns of prisoners being evacuated by road. These prisoners often had great difficulty keeping up with the pace imposed on them. Eager to avoid delays, the SS eliminated any prisoners who fainted, as leaving behind prisoners who were still alive was ruled out. Those were the "death marches."

The next few chapters will describe the variety of actual situations, ranging from the march from Kleinbodungen to Bergen-Belsen, conducted quickly over a predetermined route, to the lengthy wandering of evacuees from Neu Stassfurt, who still had not reached any destination on the day the Germans capitulated. In northern Germany, compared to railway convoys, marches at first concerned only a minority of prisoners, the most unlucky ones. With the evacuation of Sachsenhausen at the end of April, the proportion changed, but there was no longer any question of using trains to move away from Berlin.

MILITARY OPERATIONS AND EVACUATIONS. The evacuations will be described in the next few chapters, together with information on concomitant military operations, but first, here is a brief overview of the operations in northern Germany.

1. The decisive importance of the simultaneous advance of three American armies that had crossed the Rhine, i.e., Simpson's Ninth Army, Hodges's First Army, and Patton's Third Army, has already been mentioned. Simpson and Hodges joined forces at Lippstadt on April 2, 1945, closing in on Model's group of German armies in the Ruhr. Next they went on toward the Elbe, with Simpson moving north of the Harz Mountains and Hodges to the south. Simpson's troops crossed the Weser River on April 6, first taking Hanover on the 10th, then Brunswick, and a vanguard following the highway reached the Elbe near Magdeburg on April 11. At the same time, once a breakthrough of the German front was achieved northeast of Hanover, other troops moved north toward the Elbe through Salzwedel and Gardelegen.

Hodges's troops also crossed the Weser, farther south, on April 6, took Osterode and Nordhausen on the 11th, and joined up again with Simpson's troops in the Magdeburg region on April 13. By then the German Eleventh Army was trapped in the Harz Mountains. The Germans gradually gave ground until the last troops surrendered in Blankenburg on April 20. This double offensive brought on what was virtually a total evacuation of the Dora-Mittelbau complex between April 4 and April 11 along with the other Kommandos of the region, particularly Gandersheim, Helmstedt, Langenstein, and Neu Stassfurt. Farther to the south, Patton's troops, which had reached Ohrdruf by April 5, liberated Buchenwald on the 11th and crossed the Saale on the 12th. The offensive continued until Halle and Leipzig were taken on April 19, followed by Chemnitz and Dessau.

The Americans, however, did not push farther into Saxony. Patton's troops, who controlled Plauen and Hof, did not go into Bohemia but turned instead toward the south in the direction of Bayreuth. In the past this had been Bohemian territory, but the northwestern part, including Karlsbad and Aussig, had been annexed by the Reich in 1938 with the rest of the *Gau* of Sudetenland. To the north of Magdeburg, Simpson's troops gradually occupied Altmark but did not cross the Elbe toward Brandenburg.

2. While the Americans were advancing east toward the Elbe, the British, who were on their left, were moving from the Rhine toward the North Sea and the Baltic. They arrived in Osnabrück on April 6, Soltau and Uelzen on April 18, and reached the Elbe near Lauenburg on the 19th. They liberated Bergen-Belsen on April 15. Bremen was taken on April 25 and Hamburg on May 3. The Neuengamme camp was evacuated on April 19 in the direction of Lübeck.

3. The Soviets began their offensive in the direction of Berlin on April 16 by crossing the Oder, and by April 25 their troops had surrounded it. The Sachsenhausen camp together with the Heinkel Kommando from Oranienburg were evacuated toward Schwerin on April 21.

Farther to the north the Soviets crossed the Oder on April 18 between Stettin and Schwedt to conquer western Pomerania and Mecklenburg. The French women prisoners left Ravensbrück for Sweden on April 23. The Ravensbrück camp was evacuated starting on April 26. On May 3 the Soviets coming from the east and the Americans who had crossed the lower Elbe joined up in the region of Parchim. It was then that the prisoners on the march from Sachsenhausen and Ravensbrück were liberated.

Hitler committed suicide on April 30, and all German resistance in Berlin came to an end on May 2.

4. Between May 2 and 8 the Soviets completed their conquest of Mecklenburg, Brandenburg, and part of Saxony.

The Americans crossed the Böhmerwald and occupied the western part of Bohemia. The Germans resisted the Russians in Moravia. When the Germans capitulated, a large portion of Bohemia and a small part of Saxony were still under German control. In these regions prisoners had not yet been liberated, and many of them perished.

As a very general rule, during the final weeks the German authorities made no attempt to force the prisoners of war and foreign civilian workers in the regions threatened by the advancing Allied armies to go elsewhere. Some were taken, along with German civilians, to escape from combat zones, for example, but there was no systematic organization of their evacuation.

On the contrary, to the very end the SS observed the rule that no surviving concentration camp prisoners were to fall into the hands of the Allied troops. Fortunately, as will be explained in detail, the rule could not be applied everywhere nor right up to the end. The evacuation of Bergen-Belsen, for example, where a typhus epidemic had broken out, proved to be impossible. Columns of prisoners on foot met up with the Allied advance, as in the region south of Magdeburg or around Parchim. Nevertheless, all the political, racial, and other prisoners lived under the threat of death to the very end.

The most striking and no doubt most disconcerting fact was that the determination of the SS continued unabated until the very last moment, even though the defeat of the Germans was inevitable. Once the machine had been switched on there was no way of stopping it, and it carried along in its wake the SS auxiliaries—prisoners wearing *Kapo* and *Blockältester* armbands who were almost always Germans with green triangles. The latter thus helped convey the other prisoners to Bergen-Belsen, where many of them were subsequently massacred. They helped hunt down survivors of the Boelcke Kaserne and shut the other prisoners into the barn in Gardelegen.

This ultimate barbarity, which was widespread, indiscriminate, and total, has to be taken into account in evoking the final weeks of the German concentration camp system. Here and there the Wehrmacht or the Luftwaffe intervened to save a few prisoners who were abandoned by the SS, but the latter never ceased to inspire fear in everyone.

The Liberation at Dora and Nordhausen

On April 11, 1945, the Americans in Hodges's First Army discovered, more or less simultaneously, the Boelcke Kaserne at Nordhausen, the tunnel factory at Dora, and the Dora camp with its *Revier.* It was important for them to see in the heaps of corpses left by the Nazis the true meaning of the fight in which they were engaged. It was also important for them to take control of the site at which an extraordinary device was being built. Whatever may have been the relative weight of these two discoveries, the matter of utmost urgency involved saving the survivors and burying the dead.

THE AMERICANS AT NORDHAUSEN. The American officers drew up reports at various levels on the situation they had found at Nordhausen and the measures they had taken to cope with it. Raymond Wautrecht has grouped together and translated these documents.

The Third Armored Division, called the "Lucky Spearhead," was the first to arrive at Nordhausen. On March 25 it had established a bridgehead in Remagen. The following paragraphs are taken from the history of the division.

Although the taking of Nordhausen did not constitute the heaviest fighting of April 11, that city will live forever in the memories of 3rd Armored Division soldiers as a place of horror. The Americans couldn't believe their eyes. . . . No written word can properly convey the atmosphere of such a charnel house, the unbearable stench of decomposing bodies, the sight of live human beings, starved to pallid skeletons, lying cheek by jowl with the ten-day dead. [. . .] It was a fabric of moans and whimpers, of delirium and outright madness. Here and there, a single shape tottered about, walking slowly, like a man dreaming."[2]

On the morning of April 12 the tank crews took up their offensive again in the direction of Sangerhausen. They were relayed by the soldiers of the 104th Infantry Division, called "Timberwolf," who regularly followed them. The history of this division contains the following account of the intervention of the American authorities. "All medical personnel that could be spared in the Division were rushed to the scene to give medical aid [. . .]. A temporary hospital was set up in a row of apartment buildings in the Steinstrasse. Seven hundred camp occupants were evacuated first. [. . .] Four hundred of them were then transferred to the 51st Field Hospital due to their critical condition.

"The burgomeister of Nordhausen having fled, his assistant was contacted by the Military Government and given explicit instructions regarding laws and ordnances and the responsibility placed on him. . . . Hundreds of the male citizens of the town were ordered to the camp, where under guard, they worked several days carrying litter cases and collecting corpses by hand. They dug mass graves on a prominent hill near the camp and carried the corpses through the town to the graves. [. . .]

"On the first day, 1,200 bodies were taken out of the buildings. By Saturday night, 14 April, all the bodies had been removed from the camp and 1,958 had been buried. [. . .] On 15 April at 2 p.m., 2,017 bodies had been interred, which includes those of 59 prisoners who died at the hospital."[3] A film was made of these operations, extracts of which can be seen at La Coupole Museum in Wizernes.

THE AMERICANS AT THE DORA TUNNEL. The last able-bodied Dora prisoners left the tunnel, and then the Dora camp, on April 5. It appears that the German civilians also abandoned their factory on the same day and scattered to their places of residence in the region. They will be encountered once again. For six days the tunnel was no longer guarded, and part of the population of Nordhausen took refuge there after losing their homes in the bombing raids. It was thus possible to recover electrical equipment in particular.

On April 11 in the late afternoon, American officers patrolling near Niedersachswerfen met up with prisoners in striped clothes who guided them to one of the tunnel entrances, which was still lit up. After a quick inspection of the site, the unit's commander, William Castille, the division information officer, informed the army intelligence service headquarters in Paris of the discovery of a factory for manufacturing V1s and V2s (and aircraft engines). It was decided that access to the tunnel should be prohibited, and specialists were sent to take possession of the factory equipment, the rockets, and their components. First, however, the north of Thuringia had to cease being in the zone of military operations.

The intelligence service was not, in fact, surprised at the discovery of the Dora factory, for it was first brought to their attention by the report of an informer working at the Technische Hochschule in Berlin who managed to reach London on October 3, 1944. In November, Mittelwerk (by that time its code name was perfectly familiar to the Allies) was the object of a special air sortie. The interpretive plan resulting from the sorties, which was drawn up by the Allied Central Intelligence Unit in Medmenham, was very precise, showing the topography of the Kohnstein, the Dora camp, the tunnel entrances, the railway tracks, the electric power cables, etc. The Allied pilots gave up the idea of bombing the site due to the thickness of the rocky layer which, they decided in advance, would prevent the strikes from having any effect.

THE AMERICANS AT THE DORA CAMP. On April 11, 1945, as noted, an American jeep arrived at the Dora camp. The soldiers toured the camp, found the *Revier,* and went off in search of help, which arrived the following morning at daybreak, according to Maho.[4] Military trucks came, "loaded with medicines, bandages, anesthetics and sterile instruments." Then "in perfect order, a column of German health workers arrived in the camp. They had come to do our chores, change our bandages and clean our Blocks. [. . .] The first graves were dug." The crematorium was no longer in operation.

Bordet[5] gives his assessment of the change of regime: "I presented myself and a few hours later I was put in a Block located higher up in the camp, in a room with two bedsteads. I was showered and given a clean shirt, and put on a bed between clean sheets with blankets, while waiting for my jacket and pants to come back cleaned. Good soup, white bread, cold meat, cheese. The next day, coffee with milk, white bread, butter and jam, plus a day's army ration 'to nibble on slowly to calm the hunger.' We were served by German soldier-prisoners. It's like living in a palace. I'm eating!"

The *Revier* occupants were either the seriously ill who were not evacuated by the last convoy on April 5 or survivors of the Boelcke Kaserne. They were a sight, and people came to look at them, as Tauzin has recalled:[6] "We were visited by the Americans who came by the truckload to see us. [. . .] We sang unrestrainedly, first the *Madelon,* then the *Marseillaise,* every time we saw new Americans arriving."

The Americans were "dumbstruck when they saw the small contingent of remaining prisoners come out, gaunt, emaciated and unbelievably thin, since some of them, who were of average height, weighed less than 60 pounds. Those of us who were able, literally dragged ourselves, for we had spent six days alone with almost nothing to eat. Naturally, the doctors and nurses, who were almost all Americans, worked wonders to give us good soup every day and they did not let a day go by without coming to see us." These visits to Dora by American soldiers were organized systematically on orders from General Eisenhower.

The Dora *Revier* was used to group together the prisoners from the surrounding area, except for Auchabie, who remained under treatment at the American military hospital. Delogne[7] found himself back in Block 36A, which he had left a month earlier. Brière again met up with Doctor Lemière, who had treated him earlier, and gave him a small microscope "organized" in the ruins of Nordhausen as a gift. The health of some of the survivors of the Boelcke Kaserne deteriorated again, including Delogne, who had pleurisy, and Nicola,[8] who was suffering from congestion of the lungs and then came down with typhus.

During the first few days after the Liberation the camp barracks was occupied by new arrivals whose attitude shocked Couture and Maho,[9] who recalls: "Huge numbers of French, Italian and Polish STO workers rushed in from all around, after being driven out by military operations, and moved into the empty Blocks." Couture[10] describes them as "loud-mouths" and "lively lasses": "Disorder settled in with their arrival; no one wanted to do any more chores, clean or help in the kitchens. They all grabbed blankets and straw mattresses; no one exercised any control. There were fights, filth and a real threat of famine." The American commander quickly and vigorously put an end to the situation. Thereafter the camp was used to group together foreigners in the area for repatriation. One of them, a Frenchman named H. D.—he did not wish his name to be mentioned—has provided the following account of his stay there. He worked in Nordhausen at the firm of Schmidt und Kranz, where a Dora Kommando was assigned.

"A few days after our arrival at Dora, one of my comrades met up again with a deportee he had worked with at Schmidt und Kranz. We decided to go with him to the Tunnel to see this underground factory. Alas, American sentinels were guarding the entrance and told us to go back the way we had come. The presence of our comrade in striped clothes had no effect on the determination of the sentinels to comply with the orders they had received. We were very disappointed.

"Within the next few days, again with a few comrades, we went to the Revier to greet the French deportees who were still there. We could not imagine human beings in such a physical condition. Our comrades asked us questions: What are you doing in Germany? Which region do you come from? Were you badly treated, too? [. . .] We were overwhelmed by what we saw, and our conversation did not last long. On the other hand, an overly lengthy visit and too many questions would have worn out these men who longed to enjoy a bit of rest."

On April 17 a Belgian unit, the Sixth Riflemen Battalion attached to the

American army, arrived in Nordhausen. It was made up of volunteers who joined up after the liberation of Belgium. Thus Halkin,[11] a university professor from Liège, saw former students arrive, and Delogne members of maquis in the Ardennes. During their stay the Belgian soldiers were able to help their countrymen and take care of correspondence between the survivors and their families while they awaited repatriation.

Several firsthand accounts, from Maho and H. D., mention Masses celebrated by priests, first a Belgian, then a Pole. Delogne mentions, however, that plans for a political demonstration on May 1 were ultimately canceled by the commander.

REPATRIATION. Prisoners were repatriated by plane once the Nordhausen airfield was back in operating condition. C-47 Dakotas that flew in to supply American troops flew back out to Le Bourget (Paris) with deportees, prisoners of war, and civilian workers. These departures appear to have begun on April 20. Depierre, Lenoir, Gaillard, Tauzin, and Maho have mentioned that date. Couture[12] and Brière requisitioned carts to be taken to the Nordhausen airfield with invalid comrades they had been caring for since the bombing on April 4. Prisoners of war allowed them to be given priority.

The final departures, mostly sick prisoners on stretchers, took place on May 7. Thus Bordet, Delogne, and Nicola left Dora on May 4 in ambulances, but they had to wait for three days in huge tents for the weather to clear. Auchabie[13] left with them. He recounts that at the American hospital, they removed shrapnel from his left foot and cared for him energetically. He was considered ready for repatriation on May 7, but "as a few of my comrades and I were at the end of our rope, a military chaplain at the American hospital gave us the last sacraments."

When Delogne arrived at Le Bourget Airport, he was taken to Neuilly Hospital and then to Lariboisière where he was treated for pulmonary disease. He left for Brussels on May 11 by hospital train and arrived home in Bertrix on June 25. Bordet, Nicola, and Auchabie were taken to Bichat Hospital.

Auchabie, who was five-foot-eight, weighed eighty-five pounds at the time. He was considered unable to be moved and spent four months at Bichat. He was not sent on to the hospital in Brive until August 1. He finally arrived home on May 31, 1946. As has already been mentioned in chapter 6, he was the sole survivor of a group of twenty-two deportees from the regions of Corrèze, Dordogne, and Haute-Vienne. After the worst period at Dora he was then sent to Ellrich, put in the transport of May 3, 1945, and survived the bombing of the Boelcke Kaserne. He died in 1997.

Among the repatriated prisoners from Dora in May 1945 was Jacques Can.[14] He was an NN, arrested in December 1942 at the age of sixteen, who was sent first to the camp at Hinzert, then to Wittlich, Breslau, and Schweidnitz before arriving at Gross Rosen a month before the evacuation. The evacuation took him to Nordhausen at the same time as Rogerie, and like him, he was transferred to Dora and then came back to the Boelcke Kaserne, which was promptly bombed, and finally returned to the *Revier* at Dora to be repatriated. He was nineteen years old.

THE LIBERATION "OF" DORA. Strictly speaking, there was no liberation "of" Dora in the sense that there was a liberation "of" Buchenwald or Bergen-Belsen. When the Americans arrived on the site, all the able-bodied prisoners had already been evacuated and only the seriously ill remained at Dora (with a few doctors and nurses) and the survivors of the Boelcke Kaserne in Nordhausen. Hence it is only possible to speak of the liberation of prisoners "at" Dora and "at" Nordhausen. As there was nothing left to suggest how the camp had once operated, what was first engraved in the collective memory was the image of the masses of corpses at Boelcke Kaserne and the name of Nordhausen, whether connected to Dora or not.

The documents of the period do not refer to the liberation of the large camp of Ellrich, which was empty on the evening of April 5, 1945, except for the last corpses. Virondeau[15] explains why: "On 5 April 1945, in the late afternoon, when the last prisoners had climbed into the freight cars (except the seriously ill, who could not stand up and were left lying on the ground in front of the camp), the SS lieutenant (the only one remaining, as the others were air force military) took his gun and put a bullet in their heads to finish them off. From the visual memory I have, there were about twelve of them. I was the last one to come out of the camp and the SS closed the gate."

In Harzungen, when the *Revier* was evacuated a small number of the most seriously ill were left there with some supplies, but they were massacred by a retreating SS unit a few hours before the arrival of the Americans.

After taking Osterode and Nordhausen the Americans took control of Bad Lauterberg, Bad Sachsa, Wieda, Walkenried, Ellrich, and Ilfeld at the edge of the Harz Mountains. The Germans, who had retrenched in the foothills, resisted for a few days.

Neither the Americans nor the Soviets afterward were particularly interested in the concentration camps they found that had been emptied of their prisoners, in the midst of all the camps in the region that still housed thousands of German civilians and foreign workers. Only the firsthand accounts of the survivors of these camps have preserved the memory of their existence.

FOUR CHAPTERS RECOUNTING THE EVACUATIONS AND THEIR CONSEQUENCES. As all of the evacuations of the Dora-Mittelbau complex and the other Kommandos of the *Mittelraum* and their consequences could not be dealt with in a single chapter, this account has been divided somewhat arbitrarily into four chapters. An attempt has been made to group together events that show similarities in terms of geography and operations. At the same time the narrative follows a roughly chronological order with the evacuations starting up one after another as the Allied armies drew closer. In a certain way this simultaneously involved moving from west to east.

Chapter 18 discusses the evacuations ending at Bergen-Belsen for prisoners from Dora, Ellrich, Woffleben, Harzungen, and Kleinbodungen.

Chapter 19 evokes the contrasting fate of five convoys running in the Altmark. Three of them crossed the Elbe, and the prisoners managed to reach Oranienburg, Ravensbrück, and Wöbbelin. Two were blocked en route, and most of the prisoners died in Gardelegen.

Chapter 20 groups together the "death marches" toward the east of prisoners from Harzungen, Langenstein, Neu Stassfurt, and a number of other Kommandos, who were fated to cross paths in Saxony and the neighboring regions. The special "odyssey" of the Blankenburg Kommando is included in this chapter.

Chapter 21 shows the consequences of the Soviet offensive on the prisoners in Sachsenhausen and Ravensbrück.

FROM DORA, ELLRICH, AND HARZUNGEN TO BERGEN-BELSEN

The evacuation of the Dora, Ellrich (and Woffleben), and Harzungen camps, as noted, took place on April 4 and 5, 1945. It took place mainly by railway convoys that left from the Ellrich, Woffleben, Niedersachswerfen, and Dora stations.

Nine convoys have been perfectly identified, six of which finally arrived at Bergen-Belsen, which does not, however, appear to have been their original destination.

The vicissitudes encountered by these convoys on their way to Bergen-Belsen will be discussed first, then the situation in the camp until it was liberated and the prisoners left, and finally the circumstances surrounding their repatriation.

The Evacuations to Bergen-Belsen

THE SIX CONVOYS. The first convoy to leave Ellrich on Wednesday, April 4, was apparently the convoy that evacuated the prisoners who had arrived three days earlier from Karlshagen. These prisoners had not been given new identity numbers and were kept separate from the rest of the prisoners in the camp. It was easy to round them up. Fournier took note of the convoy itinerary. After going around the Harz Mountains through Osterode and Seesen, the train went to Hamburg via Goslar, Braunschweig (Brunswick), Peine, and Hanover. Then it came back toward the south by Lüneburg and Uelzen to Celle and finally went back through Uelzen to reach Bergen-Belsen. The convoy arrived on Sunday, April 8, in the morning. The prisoners were led directly into the barracks near the main camp.

A second convoy left Ellrich, also on April 4 in the morning, with the camp prisoners who were still more or less able-bodied, including Jacques Courtaud, who noted that the convoy was in Hamburg on April 7 and then went south, arriving in Bergen-Belsen on Monday, April 9, at "around 4 o'clock."

Next, two more convoys left the Ellrich station, one that had been formed in

Niedersachswerfen, but they never arrived at Bergen-Belsen. They will be discussed in the next chapter.

Information on the evacuation from the Woffleben station is given in an article in *Mémorial*.[1] A train arrived there with a few freight cars already occupied by prisoners from Harzungen guarded by Luftwaffe soldiers. The train took on prisoners from the Woffleben camp on April 4 under the supervision of Kleemann, who was the camp commander, and his SS. After Osterode and Seesen the train went to Hamburg through Hildesheim and Hanover. It then continued on to Brunsbüttel at the far end of the Elbe estuary in Holstein, where it stopped before turning around and going back to Hamburg. It then went south and arrived at Bergen-Belsen on April 10. Other accounts give April 11 as the arrival date.

A map has long been available showing the itinerary of the convoy that left from Niedersachswerfen on April 4 with prisoners from Harzungen. Neither the map nor the excessive commentary that has accompanied it are reliable. What is clear from the various firsthand accounts is that the convoy also went to Hamburg before reaching Bergen-Belsen on April 10. This evacuation of Harzungen involved the prisoners who arrived at Dora on April 3 and the patients from the *Revier* and the *Schonung*. The other evacuation left at the same time going east on foot, which will be discussed in chapter 20.

The first of the three convoys used to evacuate the Dora camp itself along with some of the prisoners employed in the camp and in the tunnel left on the afternoon of April 4 from the Dora train station. The route followed by the convoy, which was noted by Charles Vedel,[2] was similar to the itinerary of the other convoys that reached Bergen-Belsen. After Osterode and Seesen, the train went through Hildesheim, Lehrte, Celle, Uelzen, and Lüneburg to Bergedorf, in the eastern suburb of Hamburg near the Neuengamme camp. Then it went south through Soltau to Bergen-Belsen where it arrived on April 10.

The second convoy from the Dora camp left on April 5 in the afternoon and arrived at Bergen-Belsen on April 10 in the afternoon, after following an unspecified route. The third evacuation convoy, which left Dora in the late afternoon on April 5, never reached Bergen-Belsen. That convoy will be encountered again in the next chapter.

The distance between Dora and Bergen-Belsen is 94 miles as the crow flies, which corresponds roughly to 106 miles by train. The fact that it took between four and six days to cover that distance shows that the situation was by no means simple. First, all the convoys made a detour via Hamburg, which shows what their original destination must have been. It was quite specifically the Neuengamme camp, which was supposed to receive all the prisoners evacuated from Dora-Mittelbau. Similarly, the camp at Flossenbürg, and then Dachau, were supposed to accommodate all the prisoners from Buchenwald, which will be discussed later.

The destination at the outset was thus Hamburg, once the convoys arrived in the plains after going around the Harz Mountains. This was a sensitive area from a military standpoint, bordering on the areas controlled by the American and British armies. The German headquarters would attempt a counteroffensive with the "Clausewitz" Panzer Division, which, incidentally, would be completely crushed. The circulation of convoys of prisoners behind the German front was particularly problematic at that spot.

A FEW STRIKING EPISODES. The convoys were also exposed to bombing raids, such as the one that took place at an unidentified station, recounted by Yves Béon:[3] "On Saturday, the train pulled into a large station. It seemed huge to prisoners whose weak condition had deprived them of any sense of proportion but, even so, it was certainly very large. Rows of platforms and tracks were cluttered with an enormous amount of military gear. There were trains filled with troops, equipment and munitions. There were tanks mounted on platforms, with their guns pointed downward, and machine guns grouped together by twos. There were mortars carefully lined up on flat wagons. Through the wide-open doors of the covered cars, we could see boxes of ammunition. The troop trains were overflowing with armed soldiers, looking tired and edgy. Everywhere there were antiaircraft machine guns and rapid-fire guns trained on the sky. On the platforms, worked-up officers shouted orders. The sun flooded the entire setting. It was unusually warm for the season.

"The train from Harzungen pulled up along a platform slightly isolated from the others. A little farther on, between the prisoners and the row of overloaded platforms, there was a convoy topped with a machine gun pointing at the sky. The servers looked at the convicts with astonishment. They were standing about twenty yards away. Charles was opposite a machine gunner who appeared to be the same age as he, about twenty, yet one of them was the master and the other a wretched slave. Tired of the hubbub of the station, the German gazed with interest at the strange creatures. Perhaps he had seen some before, perhaps not; but he had certainly never met men in that condition.

"Suddenly, the sirens started wailing and turmoil descended on the station, like panic in the anthill. [. . .] SS and prisoners immediately found themselves packed together between the wagon axles. [. . .] Beneath his wagon, Charles spotted a German soldier. He had secured his helmet and aimed his gun. It was a double-barreled machine gun. [. . .] Charles looked at the soldier; he couldn't take his eyes off of him. The soldier kept shooting like a madman, until he couldn't find anything else to shoot at. Suddenly, he straightened up, surrounded by flames and explosions. His uniform shriveled up and frayed like burnt paper. His face was covered with blisters and began to melt. He collapsed onto his weapon, with its guns pointing straight up at the sky. [. . .]

"The planes disappeared, but the station rang out with explosions and fires were burning everywhere. There was nothing left of the trains that had been standing there a few minutes earlier but a heap of twisted metal. The prisoners' convoy was spared. [. . .] Even the track leaving the station was intact. The convicts started off on their journey again."

This dramatic episode, which has been evoked by several witnesses, was of course only one example of the aerial attacks to which the convoys were subjected during their travels.

Many prisoners were also struck by the sight of Hamburg in ruins. Fournier[4] writes: "Most of the maneuvering we did was in the city of Hamburg. All I could see was a ghost town that had been practically destroyed, with the carcasses of buildings still standing but completely burnt out." He also says: "Through the windows of our car, we saw roads jammed with refugees, women, children, soldiers, on foot, on bicycle, in vehicles of all sorts, some pulled by horses, going in every direction."

At the Hamburg station, during the night of Sunday, April 8, to Monday, April 9, according to the account by Yves Béon,[5] the convoy from Harzungen was turned back at Bergen-Belsen.

"During the night from Sunday to Monday, the train arrived at a railway hub. The number of tracks increased until there were dozens of them crisscrossing and interfering with each other. Huge pylons holding darkened projectors stood like dead trees. Water cranes with their canvas arms and control cabins were scattered about the mineral landscape. From one area to the next, a lighted lamp made the landscape look surreal. The convoy jumped on the junctions and seemed to hesitate between the tracks. It stopped for a few minutes in front of a red light, then started up again and then went to a deserted platform off to the side, where it came to a stop. On a dimly lit neighboring building the name HAMBURG was written in large letters. [. . .]

"The convoy leaders leaped onto the platform and did stretching exercises. Military and station officers appeared in uniform. There was a fascist salute and the clicking of heels. They all got into the covered car. Would the train reach its final destination, were they going to unload the prisoners? [. . .] The summit conference was over. Once again, there was a fascist salute, a clicking of heels, and the welcoming committee went away. Time passed and nothing happened. The prisoners went back to sleep and all life seemed to cease on the platform. Then the locomotive sent up a spray of steam and the convoy slowly moved off."

There is no information regarding the circumstances under which the convoys that reached Hamburg were then redirected to Bergen-Belsen. Some of them were sent through Lüneburg, others through Buchholz. Former deportees have reconstructed an itinerary of the period starting from Buchholz and reaching Soltau via Wintermoor, Schneverdingen, and Wolterdingen, and then Münster before moving onto a secondary line. There was still a long distance to Bergen-Belsen to cover on foot from the place where the prisoners got off.

LIFE AND DEATH IN THE CONVOYS. Prisoners bore up under the long journey between the Dora-Mittelbau camps and Bergen-Belsen in very different ways, depending on their state of health at the outset. Some accounts came from survivors who were able to be extremely active in the days following the liberation of Bergen-Belsen. Yet they also witnessed the death of many of their comrades. The composition of the convoys varied according to the camp from which it departed.

Some German Greens did not take part in the evacuations because they had enlisted in the Volkssturm. When Pinault[6] arrived at Ellrich from Karlshagen, he watched them sign up. Sadron and the author remember having seen those from Dora parading with a white armband before our convoy left. The criteria for their selection remain unknown. Those who were in the convoys did not seem to be the most suitable. One of them did not embark, however. It was Anna, the chief of Block 130, described by Spitz (in chapter 10). He tried to escape and was shot, which did not sadden Spitz.[7]

The convoy from Harzungen included the ill who had been brought out of the *Revier* and the *Schonung*. Mialet explains how the operation took place: "As the patients were all in hospital gowns, the clothes in the dressing room were thrown pell-mell into the Revier room. The sick prisoners fought like savages for the least appalling clothes. I soon found myself more or less dressed and equipped with a blanket which I kept attached around my body." As a consequence, the clothes that each one was wearing carried identity numbers which were not theirs. This explains the problems involved in identifying the numerous bodies found later. The situation was the same for the last convoys that left Dora and Ellrich with sick prisoners.

The rations distributed at both Dora and Ellrich when the convoy was about to depart included a large loaf of bread and a tin, which was supposed to cover the prisoners' needs for a three-day journey. They were not given anything else. Hunger only made the seriously ill prisoners even weaker. Dysentery and pulmonary problems ravaged the group. Whenever the train stopped, corpses were removed from the freight cars and stretcher bearers carried them to a freight car at the rear.

Mialet[8] recounts: "The train stopped for a long time near a farm. The harvest of corpses during this halt was particularly fruitful. Bodies fell out of all the cars. [. . .] The dead were buried at that site. A hundred and fifty-seven. They were interred near a pond that had given the village its name: Grossmore. We stayed there all night." It was in fact Wintermoor where Lucien Fayman[9] remembers digging a mass grave in which all the corpses from the convoy were thrown without being identified. That was where the young Polish nurse Yanouk was murdered by an SS, as Jacques Desprez later told Jean Michel.[10]

For many prisoners the march from the train stop to Bergen-Belsen was a painful ordeal, which is how Courtaud[11] remembers it: "I can still see myself getting off at I don't know which station, on a platform that seemed endless. We went off in rows of five, of course, in the direction of the camp, which was located a few miles away. [. . .] Several of those who formed the convoy did not reach their destination. Woe betide anyone whose strength gave out, for they were shot without any pity by the SS, who continued to terrorize us until the very end. There was nothing we could hope for from them."

Courtaud's account is not quite accurate. He and his comrade went in the direction not of the Bergen-Belsen camp but of a neighboring camp made up of barracks. All the prisoners from five of the six convoys were led to these barracks. Many of those from the Woffleben convoy then went into the Bergen-Belsen camp itself.

It appears that the place where most of the convoys unloaded prisoners was a sort of "halt" which is still used today for troops on maneuvers who are housed in the barracks. The convoy from Harzungen stopped at the Bergen-Sülze station, located five mile from the barracks.

TWO ESCAPES. There are two accounts of successful escapes from these convoys. One of them has been told at length by Serge Miller,[12] who left the convoy from Ellrich somewhere near Lüneburg together with three French comrades and a Russian. They got their chance as a result of a night attack on the train by a passing plane. After hiding for several days, they saw the Americans arrive on their way toward the Elbe.

The second account is that of Stéphane Hessel,[13] who was in a convoy coming from Dora. "The train stopped at nightfall, after going through the Lüneburg station. A childhood memory: Lüneburger Heide, it sounded familiar, a Nordic landscape somewhere in the direction of Lübeck. It was time to jump off. The board operation went off well. The Russians didn't see anything, nor did the Germans. I slid under the train first. Someone fired shots. The four others, thinking the shots were aimed at me, decided not to jump. I stayed alone at the edge of the ballast. The darkness welcomed me. Once again, I was free.

"At this point, my memory wavers. How could I have covered the ninety-four miles from Lüneburg to Hanover, walking at night and sleeping by day in abandoned barns? How did I find sympathetic Poles and French compulsory workers who gave me clothes and money? By 12 April, I was at the gates of the city. Hanover had been evacuated by the army. Helpless civilians wandered in the streets. What was everyone waiting for? I started up a conversation. Does anyone know where the American troops are? 'They bombed the barracks. The shooting was coming from over there [. . .].' My guardian angel had not left me: at the bend of the road, I could see tanks with the US star on them."

THE DEATH MARCH FROM KLEINBODUNGEN TO BERGEN-BELSEN. Shortly after the convoys a column of prisoners from the Kleinbodungen Kommando arrived at Bergen-Belsen on foot. They had walked out on April 4 and Jean Voisin,[14] one of the survivors, has recalled the various stages with the corresponding dates: Osterode on the 5th, Seesen the 6th, Salzgitter the 7th, Rüningen (in the suburb of Brunswick) the 8th, Ohof the 9th, Husted (north of Celle) the 10th, and Bergen-Belsen the 11th. The column was then sent to the barracks.

During the march they walked very quickly, covering twelve to eighteen miles a day. It was a real "death march," with stragglers being shot along the way. The evacuation of Kleinbodungen was supposed to have been ensured by railway convoy, but a bombing raid prevented them from leaving at Herzberg.

A small group of prisoners from the last convoy out of Dora joined the column en route. They were coming from Oker after crossing the Harz Mountains. Most of their comrades, as the next chapter will explain, had got onto a train that took them to Ravensbrück.

The Evacuees and Others at Bergen-Belsen

THE BERGEN-BELSEN CAMP IN EARLY APRIL 1945. A brief glance at the history of Bergen-Belsen is necessary to understand what transpired at the camp in April and May 1945 and the complexity of its concentration camp population. Bergen-Belsen was located in the center of Lower Saxony just west of the road from Hanover to Hamburg that crosses the Lüneburger Heide, the Lüneburg moor. It was a poor region that had always been used to house military training camps, and even today one of the largest in Germany is located there, in the area west of the small town of Bergen. Belsen is a village situated slightly to the south, which belongs to the town of Bergen. Barracks were built there to house troops on maneuvers.

The Bergen-Belsen camp itself was located south of the barracks. The camp was first renovated by French prisoners of war and was then initially occupied in 1941 by Soviet prisoners of war, fifty thousand of whom are believed to have died in this "Stalag 311." The corresponding cemetery is still there, and a memorial has been put up in their honor.

In April 1943 the Wehrmacht transferred the running of the camp to the SS WVHA, led by Pohl. On April 27 it once again became a concentration camp, under the command of Adolf Haas. Prisoners from various other camps were sent there to prepare the site. The plan was to make it a camp for Jews who could be exchanged or used as hostages.

From the very beginning therefore Bergen-Belsen was different from all the other large camps. Four separate sections were set up in succession for groups of Jews subject to special regulations. First there was the "star camp" *(Sternlager)*, which was the largest, then the "neutral" camp, the Polish camp, and finally the Hungarian camp. Some of the Jews were indeed sent to Switzerland following negotiations or exchanges. Others on the contrary were sent to their deaths at Auschwitz. It was a complicated business involving a total of nearly ten thousand people, both men and women. The camp for ordinary prisoners working on the site was smaller than the special camps and separate from them. Its survivors were transferred to Sachsenhausen in February 1944.

In early 1944 the camp was assigned a new use. In addition to the sections reserved for Jews, Bergen-Belsen was transformed into a "rest camp" where other camps sent their sick prisoners. The first "transport" of 1,000 prisoners, already discussed in chapter 6, arrived from Dora on March 27, 1944. Most of the ill died at Bergen-Belsen, some of them very quickly, such as Colonel d'Astorg. Some came back to Dora via Buchenwald. Others survived until the camp was liberated, such as Michel Fliecx and Aimé Blanc.

After Dora, other camps organized transports for their sick prisoners including Laura, Sachsenhausen, Dachau, Neuengamme, and Buchenwald. Dr. Fréjafon,[15] who devoted himself to caring for his comrades, has recounted in particular the "last days of Georges Valois," who was transferred from Neuengamme in December 1944 and died in February 1945. Louis Martin-Chauffier also arrived from Neuengamme. At the last moment, on March 6, 1945, another transport, mentioned in chapter 15, left the Boelcke Kaserne at Nordhausen for Bergen-Belsen.

In the final months of 1944 the SS transferred numerous prisoners from Auschwitz to more centrally located camps, examples of which—concerning non-Jews—were given in chapter 14. At the same time Jews, especially women, arrived at Bergen-Belsen. Anne Frank was part of a transport in December. She died in March 1945. The largest influx, however, took place in January and February 1945, due to the evacuation of Auschwitz and the other eastern camps. Simone Jacob (Simone Weil)[16] arrived at Bergen-Belsen at that time, after a very short stopover in Dora.

The arrival of transports of sick and evacuated prisoners during the final weeks reached such a pace that the camp became incredibly overcrowded. According to some estimates the head count is believed to have risen from 15,250 prisoners on December 2, 1944, to nearly 22,300 on January 15, 1945, and more than 45,000 by March 31 (14,700 men and 30,400 women).

Hygiene conditions were appalling, typhus appeared, and by March, 800 to 1,000 prisoners were dying every day. There were corpses everywhere, as the crematorium ovens could not burn them all. By mid-March bonfires were lit, but the experiment was stopped partly because of complaints from the residents of Bergen who found the smoke unpleasant and partly because their glowing was visible from the air at night. Mass graves had to be dug.

On March 31, 1945, Jean-Pierre Renouard[17] was still with his friend Jean Mattéoli near Hanover in the Misburg Kommando, which was attached to Neuengamme. The next day he arrived at Bergen-Belsen. He described his activity on April 2: "On the road, there was an SS guard next to a handcart and a few camp prisoners who were standing there waiting. He shouted at me to come and we left, hitched to the empty handcart. He opened a barbed wire gate and we went into the women's camp. The road was winding, and the huts were set back from it, surrounded by young trees. Lying at various spots along the edge of the road were corpses of naked women piled up like logs, as in the men's camp. We loaded them into the handcart, and when it was full we came back by the central road toward the rear of the camp, pulling and pushing. The SS guard told us to stop, and we came up to a large mass grave, about nine yards deep, half filled with corpses that had been tossed in pell-mell. There were already quite a large number of them. I no longer paid any attention to the all-pervasive stench of death. Once the handcart was emptied, we went back to the women's camp to fill it up again, and I made the same trip back and forth all day long, without stopping, without drinking or eating."

On December 2, 1944, Haas was replaced as camp commander by the *Hauptsturmführer* Joseph Kramer, who had been commander of Birkenau. There was no longer any real administration or internal hierarchy in the camp. The SS were afraid of typhus and hardly strayed from the main roads that went through the camp.

Yet instructions continued to arrive from Oranienburg, and Kramer carried them out. They concerned in particular the departure of Jewish prisoners from the special camps, which the historian Eberhard Kolb[18] recalls in his monograph on Bergen-Belsen: "Three trains left Bergen-Belsen carrying prisoners from the 'Star camp,' the Hungarian camp, the special camp and those who were still left in the 'neutral' camps, 7,000 people in all. One of the trains arrived on 21 April in Theresienstadt with 1,712 prisoners. The two other trains, which were also en route to Theresienstadt, went along for days across northern Germany, prey to aerial attacks, and finally stopped, one near Magdeburg, on 14 April and the other in the village of Tröbitz, in Lower Lusace (southeast of Berlin) on 23 April. The sentinels fled, and the Russian soldiers in Tröbitz and the other American soldiers in Magdeburg took care of the prisoners who were liberated at last." Chapter 20 will deal with Theresienstadt and the grouping of Jewish prisoners in that camp during the final weeks.

THE DORA-MITTELBAU PRISONERS IN THE BERGEN-BELSEN BARRACKS. When prisoners in the convoys from Dora-Mittelbau (except some of those from Woffleben) arrived at Bergen-Belsen on April 9 and 10, as explained earlier, they were not taken to the concentration camp by the SS but rather to the barracks. In all likelihood when the train halted in Hamburg, those in charge of the convoy were given instructions to go there with their prisoners. Perhaps Kleemann, who went with his convoy from Woffleben to Brunsbüttel, did not receive these instructions in time.

A *Kasernenlager* or "barracks-camp" was formed "outside" the Bergen-Belsen camp. It had its own commander, the *Obersturmführer* Franz Hössler, who had just been the *Transportführer* of the first convoy from Dora on April 4. Formerly at Auschwitz, he had then become the *Schutzhaftlagerführer* at Dora.

When the prisoners arrived, most of them were at the end of their rope, particularly due to the conditions under which they had marched from the train stop. The firsthand accounts on the subject are telling. Bronchart[19] recalls: "We no longer had any control over our actions or gestures; we were completely exhausted. People fell wherever they stopped, out of neither desire nor choice, and they were lost. How long did it take? I never worried about that."

According to Courtaud,[20] "We had turned into amorphous, nonexistent creatures." Raoul-Duval[21] indicates: "We collapsed onto the sandy ground where I slept for several hours, in spite of a sharp wind." They occupied the buildings in a disorderly fashion, grouping themselves together on the basis of affinities. Blocs were formed by ethnic groups: the Russians, who were especially numerous, the Poles, the Czechs, and the Hungarian Jews. Minority groups such as the Belgians, the Dutch, etc., went with the French, who were numerous.

Among the arrivals was the team from the Harzungen *Revier,* with Jacques Desprez, Roland Coty, Lucien Fayman, etc. They moved the ill into barracks rooms. They looked after Brother Birin and Jean Michel in particular, who were weak after their stay in the Dora bunker. The *Revier* teams from Dora and Ellrich were not included in the convoys that reached Bergen-Belsen.

The prisoners were left to their own devices except for roll calls, which took place right up to the very last day. Spitz and Mialet have emphasized that the roll calls were always accompanied by the ritual cry "Mützen ab! Mützen auf!" The primary problem was lack of food. Once a day, a clear soup was provided by the kitchen of the neighboring camp. Raoul-Duval also talks of "a very small amount of tinned meat and sometimes a slice of black bread." A rumor subsequently went around that an attempt had been made to eliminate the prisoners by giving them poisoned bread (cf. Birin, Spitz, La Pintière, Mialet, Raoul-Duval). It appears that this was suggested to some of the prisoners by the SS doctor, Dr. Karl Kahr, Dr. Kurzke's predecessor at Dora. A supplement could be had by looting silos of rutabaga, but then prisoners ran the risk of being killed by the SS. Sharing the spoils afterward generated fights as well, in which the Russians especially distinguished themselves.

The Liberation of Bergen-Belsen

THE ANGLO-GERMAN CONVENTION ON THE SURRENDER OF BERGEN-BELSEN. The "liberation" of Bergen-Belsen took place on April 15 under very special conditions, and the prisoners' accounts mention surprising scenes. To help the reader understand what happened there is a remarkable account entitled *The First Four Days in Belsen,* written by William E. Roach[22] in 1946, one of the British officers who took part in the operation.

It all began on the morning of April 12, 1945, in Celle, where portions of General Roberts's Eleventh Armored Division were stationed. Their position was located to the extreme east opposite the British positions, close to the Americans who had taken Hanover and were moving through the Altmark toward the Elbe. The Germans were to the north beyond the Aller River. The English in Celle saw a vehicle from the German headquarters arrive, flying a white flag. It was coming from Winsen with two officers from the health service who had been instructed to warn the division of the existence of a camp with a large population in the region. A typhus epidemic had broken out there, and they asked that the area around the camp be declared a neutral zone.

Discussions got under way with the division headquarters to delimit the area involved. Finally it was decided that a small detachment of British forces equipped with a safe-conduct would cross the German lines and take charge of the camp, which would be accessible on April 14 at 10 A.M. The detachment was formed on the morning of the 14th with sixty men from two antiaircraft batteries, one headed by Major Chapman, the detachment commander, and the other by Roach, who was operating as a captain. Everything took place according to plan. The crossing of the Aller was delayed owing to the destruction of a bridge. The safe-conduct had become useless as the Germans had withdrawn beyond the camp. The detachment arrived at Bergen-Belsen in midmorning on April 15.

On April 11, Himmler had agreed to not conduct the evacuation of Bergen-Belsen. The *Standartenführer,* Kurt Becher, had therefore sent his order allowing the camp to surrender to the British without delay. Between April 11 and 15 most of the SS withdrew toward Neuengamme, and Hungarian soldiers in khaki uniforms with white armbands were placed on guard outside the camp. Kramer and Hössler stayed on the site with some fifty SS and SS supervisors, including Irma Greese. They also wore white armbands and were in charge of handing over both parts of the camp to the British detachment. The transfer took place on April 15 at about 3 P.M. There were witnesses to the scene.

THE ARRIVAL OF THE BRITISH AT BERGEN-BELSEN. The camp and the barracks were liberated simultaneously, though separately, on April 15. Late in the morning, barracks prisoners saw tanks going by at great speed on a neighboring road but were unable to identify them. At 3 P.M. a British jeep entered their camp. Fliecx,[23] who had been at Bergen-Belsen for a year, recounts what was going on in the main camp at the time. An hour after seeing the tanks go by, "a loud noise drew us out of the barracks: a British army radio-car, bearing the badge of Saint George, was going by and repeating through its double loudspeaker in every language the blessed words: 'You are free! You are free!'

"Kramer, still arrogant, was on the running board of the car, wearing a white armband, with his gun still in his belt. [. . .] When the car arrived at our section, the crowd of the living dead, gaunt, filthy, ragged and scrawny broke like a tidal wave through the fences and rushed towards the barrels of soup placed in front of the entrance to the section. The prisoners all tried to plunge their bowls in at the same time and the barrel overturned. Most of them, however, rushed in a cloud of dust towards the kitchens and the last pile of rutabagas. There were 2,000 or 3,000 of these ghosts swarming in the small space between the huts and the kitchen.

"Overtaken by the flow, I was carried along to the spot where the English car had stopped. There I saw a scene that has enshrined forever the murderous madness of the SS. Kramer got down, took his gun and took a few steps forward. He shot straight ahead, without aiming, knowing he would kill someone in the crowd. At the kitchen door, the chef, still in his white apron, was shooting his gun like a lunatic, killing prisoners at point-blank. Farther on, sentinels were also shooting. Men were rolling in the dust.

"One of the Englishmen got out of the car. He was out of his depth and did not know what to do. From behind, I saw him draw his Colt, wanting to fire into the air, hesitate and then drop his gun. I could understand his stupefaction quite easily. He was one person who would certainly remember Belsen. The crowd surged back from the kitchen to avoid the murderous shooting of the chef. Several bodies were lying on the ground. [. . .]

"The Englishman got back into the car and Kramer onto the running board. They went back to the rear of the camp. When they came back, Kramer no longer had his gun or the look of an animal of prey out hunting, but rather the look of a filthy wild beast caught in a trap. [. . .] By then, the English had seen the mass graves and understood the terrible tragedy of Belsen."

As soon as the British tanks had gone by on the road through the camp, the Russian prisoners went in search of the block chiefs, *Kapos, Vorarbeiter, Lagerschutz,* etc. "They were simply murdered on the spot, either by being thrown out windows, or by having their heads smashed in with paving stones." One of the most well-known victims was Folette, the chief of Block 132. A drawing by Léon Delarbre[24] depicts his corpse.

Between the Liberation and Going Home

BERGEN-BELSEN AFTER THE LIBERATION. The British were aghast by what they discovered, as indicated in reports on the subject by various officers, such as Gen. Glyn Hughes of the Health Service. Reporters soon came to take pictures and films. Maurice Druon[25] was a member of the Interallied Information Commission in April 1945, which had to "view" the filmed images of Bergen-Belsen. He remembers: "Three hours of projection of tapes made by several cameramen, hence, necessarily repetitive images, whether silent or not. The raw 'material,' as one says so atrociously. [. . .] I can still feel the physical sensation of sickness that overwhelmed everyone in that small room, or, as we say more exactly in Italian, of *malessere* or ill-being. Officers who had distinguished themselves in the war during rough fighting, couldn't stand it and left. We had the impression we were holding onto our souls with our teeth. It was truly an unbearable sight."

In the meantime Chapman, Roach, and their sixty men had few resources to cope with the situation while waiting to be relayed by other sections of their division. As there were two camps to administer, Chapman took charge of the most difficult, the main camp, which became the women's camp, although there were still some men in it. Roach took over the barracks camp, which became the men's camp. A reading of Roach's account gives an idea of the problems Chapman was facing. He explained the situation in these terms:

"At division headquarters, they thought it would be enough to change the guard of the camp. Everyone presumed that the concentration camp had an orderly administration and that the Germans would continue to take care of it, along with supplying food, medicine and medical care, until the arrival of a duly equipped detachment a few days later. No one in the hierarchy, from the general down to the lowest-ranking soldier, had any idea of what a German concentration camp was like, particularly Bergen-Belsen in the state in which we found it."

One of the first steps Roach took was to isolate the SS along with all the German prisoners from the rest of the camp population in order to put a stop to the vengeance being wrought. An arrangement was reached with the Hungarian soldiers who continued to guard the outside.

With information provided by an SS, an inventory of the food reserves (including those of the SS) was conducted, which revealed an amount sufficient to cover several days of mediocre food. Among the British soldiers were a mechanic and an electrician who got a pump and a generator running again.

To administer the camp, in view of the total insufficiency of the SS, it was necessary to ensure the cooperation of the prisoners, who numbered more than fifteen thousand in the men's camp alone. They had divided themselves into barracks, as mentioned earlier, by ethnic group. According to Roach: "The French, Czech, Belgian and Dutch groups were well-organized and disciplined. The Russians were neither, and the Poles were not much better."

The main problem was distributing food from seven centers, at which Roach noted the head count on the second day. There were two centers for the Russians (2,528 and 2,010 men), one for the Poles (2,463), one for the Russians and the Poles (2,319), one for the French, Belgians, Dutch, and various other nationalities (2,616), one for the Czechs, Germans and Gypsies (1,806), and one for the Jews, mostly Hungarians (1,473).

The circumstances had brought to Bergen-Belsen important leaders of the French Resistance. Coming from Dora, they included most of those who had been arrested in November and released from the bunker shortly before their departure, such as Debeaumarché, Lauth, Birin, Michel, Caruana, and Latry. Poupault, Boyer, and Bordier, as mentioned in chapter 16, were at the prison of Nordhausen.

A large percentage of the tunnel prisoners were also left from Dora, including members of the drawing Kommando: Dejussieu, Cogny, Julitte, and the

AEG Kommando including Brochart. Others had positions in the camp such as Bollaert the night watchman, Spitz the *Schreiber,* or Leschi. A French committee was set up with Bollaert as chairman. He took a census of all the French prisoners with the help of comrades from various convoys such as Butet from Dora, Schock from Harzungen, Goasguen from Ellrich, and Duale, a former prisoner at Karlshagen.

The French and Belgians from the Harzungen *Revier* set up a sort of hospital in the camp. Roland Coty, who spoke English and German, was extremely helpful to Roach as an interpreter and intermediary with other national committees. Latry, son of the owner of a French restaurant in London, was also a precious interpreter. The other nationalities besides the French also set up their committees. Unfortunately we do not know how things went for the Soviets.

Another step had been taken toward forming a central camp committee. Bollaert was elected chairman of the board officers on a proposal by the Russian and Dutch delegates. Lauth, who spoke English, was to assist him. Subcommissions studied proposals that would be transmitted to the British authorities. Roach notes: "I spent most of my time receiving delegations, listening to all sorts of complaints and suggestions that in most cases I could not accept, since I did not have the resources they called for. [. . .] I was constantly being asked for authorization to leave Belsen on the spot. [. . .] They had no idea of the situation outside the camp, nor of the problems involved in moving about a region where combat had just taken place."

Roach received Chapman in his camp and then went to visit the former camp with Chapman. "He had not been exaggerating. What was happening there was so horrible, much worse because it involved [mainly] women and children, that I was relieved to return to the men's camp."

Chapman, Roach, and their men arrived at Bergen-Belsen on April 15. On the 16th, Chapman went to headquarters to stress the catastrophic proportions of the situation. On the 17th the physician from headquarters (Glyn Hughes) and his assistant came to inspect the site. On April 19 in the middle of the morning, new troops arrived with food and sanitary equipment. Chapman's detachment went back to combat. Roach concluded: "We have spent exactly ninety-six hours in Belsen, the most terrible ninety-six hours of my life." The Hungarian soldiers left with them to cross the German lines on the Elbe with a safe-conduct.

The British remained in charge of the camp until the end. Prisoners continued to die with the development of the typhus epidemic. No one thought of anything except leaving the camp and going home.

REPATRIATING THE WESTERNERS. The problem of repatriation first arose for prisoners from Western countries that had already been liberated, i.e., the French, the Belgians, and the Dutch (in part). First, means of transport had to be found.

The first departure of French prisoners was organized for April 24 and the second for April 25. The prisoners were divided up more or less according to alphabetical order. First, the groups were taken by truck to Rheine, site of a large camp where deportees, prisoners of war, and compulsory workers were assembled.

Those who left Bergen-Belsen on the 24th went from Rheine to Brussels on April 26 in two departures. Upon their arrival they were given "a warm, extraordinary, unforgettable welcome."[26] Among them were Barbier, Bronchart, Clairin, Doumeau, Goasguen, Mialet, and Michel. The next leg of the journey was by train to Lille and then Paris. They arrived in Paris on April 29 in the morning.

The others left Rheine by truck via Bocholt to Kevelaer. The next part of the journey took place by train to Paris, through Tilburg, Brussels, and Lille. This group included Spitz and his friend La Pintière, Pageot, Vedel, and Butet. They arrived in Paris on the morning of May 1. It was snowing huge snowflakes when the deportees boarded city buses that took them to the Lutétia Hotel. According to Butet, Bollaert, Dejussieu, and Debeaumarché were flown directly to Brussels by a British liaison plane.

After describing the welcome at the Lutétia, Butet[27] recounts the rest of the 1st of May: "After lunch, at about 2 p.m., city buses came to take us to the Champs-Elysées, where we were met by Bollaert, Dejussieu and Debeaumarché who had put on their striped clothes. They headed up a procession in which, no doubt from concentration camp reflex, we lined up by five, and walked up the avenue to the Etoile.

"There were big crowds on the sidewalks. An astonished crowd, moved to tears, at watching these camp 'survivors' go by. I am sure that no one of us weighed more than 110 pounds. I was six feet tall, and weighed eighty-eight pounds. [. . .] At the Arc de Triomphe, we were received by General de Gaulle. Bollaert, Debeaumarché and Dejussieu placed a wreath on the tomb of the Unknown Soldier. The *Aux Morts* was sounded and the *Marseillaise* played. Then we went back to the Lutétia." A photograph of that parade was on the cover of number 500 of *Déporté* magazine.[28]

Not all the Western deportees were well enough to be able to stand repatriation by trucks or ordinary trains. There were still some left at the camp "hospital," as the word *Revier* was now banished. Little by little some were repatriated by car and then by hospital train to Roubaix, where a hospitalization center was located. That is how Defiliquier, Duvernois, Foiret, and Fournier came back. Birin left Bergen-Belsen with the last convoy in early May. After varying lengths of time, they went home.

There are, however, firsthand accounts that are not always very clear of seriously ill deportees who remained even longer in Germany. This was the case of Courtaud,[29] who was immobilized in a hospital in Sulingen on April 25 after leaving Bergen-Belsen in the morning along with Dupuy, Cottet, and others. He was finally repatriated to Le Bourget Airport from Quakenbrück (south of Cloppenburg) on June 5. This was also the case for Renouard,[30] who stayed behind in Bergen-Belsen. He was repatriated from Celle at an unspecified date. He said he was visited by Henri François-Poncet, who also went to the women's camp. Dupuy mentions his visit to Sulingen.

Annette Wieviorka[31] talks of "different repatriation" with regard to Bergen-Belsen based on the memoirs of Dr. Fréjafon, who remained at Bergen-Belsen and took care of the women, especially Jewish ones, who in May had still not yet been repatriated. Simone Jacob did not arrive in Paris with her sister until May 23.[32] Next, Dr. Waitz, a former prisoner at Monowitz and Buchenwald, went on assignment to organize the repatriation in early June of the 121 French prisoners still hospitalized in Bergen-Belsen and Sulingen. Even today it is impossible to say who was responsible, but there is no doubt that there was a certain amount of negligence at the time.

THE END OF BERGEN-BELSEN. It would naturally be helpful to have clear information on a number of points. An attempt could be made to calculate, however approximately, the number of prisoners, both men and women, Jews, and others, who died at Bergen-Belsen, which was undoubtedly considerable. Yet, as has already been mentioned, most of them were not "originally from" the camp but were rather sick prisoners that other camps wished to be rid of and prisoners evacuated from other camps under harsh conditions. The latter may, by the way, have been patients taken out of their *Revier* to be included in an evacuation convoy. The conditions at Bergen-Belsen itself, including undernourishment, overcrowding, and the typhus epidemic, made the situation distinctly worse. If information were available it might be possible to classify the victims according to their origin, but such gruesome accounting is no doubt impossible.

It is a fact that prisoners from Dora-Mittelbau died between their arrival at Bergen-Belsen in April and the repatriation operations, either before or after the liberation of the camp and the barracks. Survivors' accounts have mentioned names, but the total count is apparently not available. Most of the Western prisoners in the last convoys stayed at Bergen-Belsen only a short time. They arrived between April 9 and 11, were liberated on April 15, and left on April 24 or 25 to be repatriated. They did nothing during this period except for some members of the Woffleben convoy, among them Jean Gineston,[33] who had to transport corpses into mass graves.

The other prisoners remained for a longer time, waiting until they could be repatriated. This group included Russians and other Soviets, Poles, Czechs, and Yugoslavians. Little is known about what happened to these groups. The young Czech Jew named Theodor Braun joined the other Czechs in a repatriation center in Celle before returning to Prague.[34] Not all of them necessarily wanted to go home, and that included the vast majority of Jews. Those who had been arrested in Western countries were repatriated to them. Most of the others went to camps for "displaced persons" before being given the possibility of emigrating.

The camp itself was completely evacuated on May 6 and finally destroyed by the British army with flamethrowers due to the typhus epidemic on May 22. "There is nothing left of the camp but its graves." The barracks continued to house displaced persons until September 6, 1950.

A commemorative obelisk was erected on the site of the mass graves, where the remains of some 23,200 victims, both men and women, from the main camp lie. A cemetery near the barracks camp received the bodies of several thousand prisoners who died in the camp or after the liberation of the camps.

THE FIVE CONVOYS IN ALTMARK, AND THE GARDELEGEN TRAGEDY

On April 4 and 5, nine railway convoys left the Dora-Mittelbau camps moving toward the northwest. As explained in the preceding chapter, only six of them finally brought their prisoners to Bergen-Belsen after first going to Hamburg. At the moment they reached their final destination the three others arrived in Altmark and tried to cross the Elbe. This was also the case of two other convoys: one formed in Wernigerode with prisoners who left on foot from Wieda, and the other in Helmstedt where there was a Kommando attached to Neuengamme that was noted earlier. Altmark is a part of the plains region of northern Germany, west of the Elbe and north of Magdeburg. It is the northern part of what is now the land of Saxony-Anhalt. The main centers of this region are Stendal, Salzwedel, and Gardelegen.

As Simpson's Ninth American Army advanced, it caught the center of Altmark in a stranglehold in the area of Gardelegen. In the south it reached the Elbe near Magdeburg on April 11. In the north, leaving from Hanover, it arrived at the Elbe north of Tangermünde a little later.

Of the five convoys from Altmark, three managed to cross the Elbe. After a number of vicissitudes, the Ellrich prisoners finally ended up at Oranienburg, those from Dora at Ravensbrück, those from Helmstedt at Wöbbelin. The other convoys were stopped near Gardelegen, and only a minority of the prisoners escaped the massacre.

The Convoy from Ellrich to Oranienburg

According to Virondeau's account in chapter 17, the last surviving prisoners of Ellrich set off in a convoy of freight cars on April 5 late in the afternoon. Many of them had come out of the *Revier* and the *Schonung*. The *Revier* staff was also there, including the French prisoners Ségelle, Oesch, Grand, and Besançon. The convoy continued on the track used for evacuating the third and last convoy from Dora, which will be discussed later.

The route they followed can be established on the basis of information provided by the Belgian prisoners Gabriel Sprung,[1] Roland Bossue, and Joseph Uyttenhoef and by the French prisoner Albert Besançon.[2] The first part of this itinerary, which went through Osterode, Seesen, Salzgitter, and Brunswick, was the same one followed by the previous convoys. Next the train went eastward to Helmstedt, then it turned north and went through Oebisfelde, Buchhorst (April 9), Gifhorn, and Wittingen before arriving in Uelzen on April 11. As it was no longer possible to reach Bergen-Belsen in place of Neuengamme, orders arrived to go toward Sachsenhausen. The convoy went past Salzwedel and prepared to cross the Elbe at Dömitz the same day.

Once it had crossed the Elbe it went toward the Sachsenhausen camp north of Berlin, taking a detour via Ludwigslust and Wittenberge. On April 13 at 5 P.M. the convoy was close to the radio station in Nauen, sixteen miles from Spandau. At the time the Nauen wireless station was well known in Europe. At that point the convoy was bombed, as Besançon reported: "Bombing of our convoy by heavy machine guns and light bombs from English Mosquitoes. The SS took cover on the sides of the railway track, and, their guns against their cheeks, forbid us to take cover under the freight cars, most of which were open. [. . .] After the bombing, an SS requisitioned me to review the freight cars and take official note of the damage. I was to present the wounded and the dying to him. He finished off those who were the worst hit with his revolver. All the dead were loaded into a freight car."

The convoy went back to Neustadt, some forty-seven miles from Berlin. A mass grave was dug near the tracks, at a town called Segeletz, for 186 victims who had died of exhaustion or the bombing. On April 15 the convoy again went to Nauen and came back to Neustadt. Finally "on 16 April, at 6 A.M., imagine my surprise to observe that our train was parked in front of Heinkel at Oranienburg, which I had left nine months earlier," writes Besançon. Bergen-Belsen had been liberated the previous day.

The train went along for ten days and eleven nights. The distance between Nordhausen and Oranienburg is 134 miles as the crow flies. Upon arrival the prisoners had to dig another mass grave for the corpses from the train.

Of all the railway evacuations from Dora-Mittelbau, the one from Ellrich to Oranienburg was the most deadly due to the number of sick prisoners at the outset and the length of the journey. There are few accounts of the trip. A few remarks can be found in Étienne Lafond's account:[3] "Finally the trip began which was to last twelve days, nine of them without anything to eat or drink. It was terrible and I still have trouble recalling that part of my adventure. [. . .] We watched each other die with a calmness and an apparent indifference that were frightening. Friends would say to you at night: 'I will be dead by morning.' They went to sleep never to wake again. [. . .] The dead, by the way, were anonymous. Naked at the outset; we donned whatever clothes we could find. As a result, none of us was wearing his own identity number." When the train arrived in Oranienburg, Lafond weighed seventy pounds.

In *Mémorial*[4] there is an anonymous account of this convoy. Xavier Delogne has indicated that the author is Paul Caton, who had known his brother Yves well. The following passages are taken from his account: "When the Häftling emerged from their blankets in the morning, Roger's face [he had been knocked out by a *Kapo*] was so battered and swollen that he was almost unrecognizable. He told his neighbors that it didn't hurt too much, and indeed, he did not seem to be suffering. In the afternoon, however, leaning against the wall, his head fell onto his chest and, without a word, he died.

"Once again, we were all amazed at how simple, how calm, almost gentle death was. No doubt our suffering was the result of the struggle put up by our physical forces, and when, beyond a certain point of weakness and exhaustion, the forces of life no longer struggled, the suffering stopped and life simply went out.

"Seeing so many dead around them, the living were worried at every stop that they would find their closest comrades, the ones they did not want to be separated from, the ones with whom they had suffered so much, the ones they wanted so much to be with at the moment of their return they had talked so much about."

Caton continues further on in his account: "At each stop, everyone could tell merely by taking a few steps how much weaker they had become, how much heavier the dead were to carry, and some, whose legs refused to carry them, wondered if they could make it back to their freight car. [. . .] Each day, the traces of the ordeal were more visible in the faces, where ordinary daily filth was mixed with coal dust and a growing beard, and each man could follow his own degeneration on the features of his neighbor."

Yves Delogne, "the Belgian child of 20, had spent his night sitting on top of the five dead bodies" in the freight car when the train arrived in Oranienburg on April 16. At the time his brother Xavier, who had come from the Boelcke Kaserne, was waiting at the Dora *Revier* to be repatriated.

Chapter 21 will describe what happened to the survivors of the convoy.

The Last Convoy from Dora

The conditions under which the last evacuation convoy from Dora started out on the evening of Thursday, April 5, 1945, have already been mentioned in chapter 16. Most of the prisoners involved finally ended up at Ravensbrück on Saturday, April 14. Others, who remained in Osterode, were liberated on April 9 west of the Harz Mountains. Still others died en route under various circumstances.

FROM DORA TO OSTERODE. The itinerary of most of the prisoners, which has been well defined thanks to observations made by three members of the convoy, will be examined first. The earliest report known to the French research services comes from Yves Aleste.[5] The Belgian prisoner Joseph Woussen[6] made a similar report. Finally, André Ribault[7] has also discussed the topic.

During the first few days the convoy moved extremely slowly. It stopped first at Niedersachswerfen, then at Ellrich. By April 7 it had only reached Osterhagen, and arrived on Sunday, April 8, in the morning at Osterode. The train was considerably delayed given the fact that, by then, convoys that had left on April 4 were already in Hamburg. The major delay was due to serious problems with the preceding convoy, which will be discussed later on. It was no longer possible to go around the Harz Mountains: of the nine convoys, this was the only one that was unable to do so.

The SS had the prisoners get out of the train. Those unable to walk were killed. Quite a large group was formed by those who were ready to cover sixteen miles on foot; more than three thousand prisoners set out in a column. They crossed the Harz range from south to north. A number of them had overestimated their strength. In reality the journey involved twenty-four miles.

The rest (there were several hundred of them) were lined up on a dirt road. That group included survivors who were ill as well as those who feared a forced march, such as Mathieu Anfriani, François Le Lionnais, and Andrès Pontoizeau. What happened to them will be seen subsequently. The prisoners who left to cross the Harz Mountains were convinced they would never again see them alive.

CROSSING THE HARZ MOUNTAINS. The author remembers the first part of the journey up to the town of Clausthal-Zellerfeld, walking at a normal pace in radiant spring weather. The prisoners in the column who for the most part had not left the camp or the tunnel for more than a year gazed at the landscape. Soubirous[8] recalls: "A little farther up, on the left, ducks were swimming in a pond in front of a little house, not far from the road."

Then he recounts a murder that still moves him deeply fifty years later: "We had stopped and were standing in rows of five, arm in arm. I was third in the row. Behind me stood a young Dutchman, about twenty years of age. In the camp, he wore the armband of a Dolmetscher (interpreter)."

"A noncommissioned SS officer came up slowly behind us. I had noticed him at the factory when he did his rounds, because of the dark navy blue scarf with white polka dots he wore around his neck. After saluting the SS, the young Dutchman, who spoke perfect German, asked the noncommissioned officer for permission to drink from the stream that was flowing close by. Permission granted. Our comrade knelt down and leaned over to drink right from the river.

"The SS man calmly took two steps and stood between my neighbor on the right and me. With his legs spread and his arm held out straight, holding his gun, he carefully took aim three or four yards below, and put a bullet through the neck of the wretched lad as he was carrying water to his mouth with his hand. He fell headfirst into the water. An order was given not to touch him. We moved on slowly. Another stop. The same SS man, who was decidedly feeling his oats, shot a duck in the pond. A few minutes later, the SS adjutant, no doubt alerted by the owner of the duck, came up to reprimand his subordinate for killing a duck."

Louis Coutaud and Eugène Laurent have also given accounts of the murder.

Next the convoy stopped in a square in Clausthal. The author noticed agitation at the SS headquarters, with emissaries going back and forth on motorcycles. He did not learn until much later[9] that the *Obersturmführer* Sell (who was *Arbeitseinsatzführer* at Dora), in charge of coordinating the evacuation of Mittelbau, was there with the *Transportführer* Hans Möser. The former finally found a solution, and the column set off again.

It went in the direction of Oker, through Zellerfeld, Schulenberg, and Romkerhalle. "The road went down into a valley hemmed in by a mountain torrent that we could hear flowing. The hillsides were wooded and when night came, it was pitch black. Each prisoner followed the one in front of him, trying not to stumble. We marched in silence, and aside from the noise of the torrent, the only sounds we heard were gun shots whenever a straggler was killed, which happened frequently."

At about 9 P.M. the head of the column arrived at the Oker station. A train of cattle wagons was waiting, and the prisoners got in one after another as they arrived. Oker belongs to the town of Goslar, with a station situated at the end of the road on which the column was. It is remarkable that the SS were able to obtain the formation of a sizable train so quickly from the Reichsbahn. Its last stop was in Ravensbrück.

FROM GOSLAR TO RAVENSBRÜCK. The train left at daybreak on April 9. The destination was still Neuengamme, but traffic on the lines led the convoy eastward. The train went around Brunswick by the south to reach Helmstedt, and then Magdeburg, where violent bombing at the end of the day caused a withdrawal to Barleben, slightly to the north. On April 10 the convoy tried twice to get to Magdeburg in order to cross the Elbe, but both times it was forced to return to Wolmirstedt.

Since it was impossible to cross at Magdeburg, another solution had to be found. The train set off across the Altmark on the morning of April 11 and went through Haldensleben and Calvörde before arriving at Oebisfelde. There Möser learned that Bergen-Belsen would be abandoned to the British and that his convoy was to go to Sachsenhausen. It set off again in the direction of Salzwedel and Arendsee to cross the Elbe at Wittenberge by night. This was the same day the convoy from Ellrich crossed the Elbe at Dömitz, some thirty-two miles downstream.

The Dora evacuation convoy crossed by the Wittenberge bridge[10] from south to north. Twelve days earlier the same bridge had been crossed from north to south by the Karlshagen evacuation convoy on its way to Ellrich, as described in chapter 14. Those prisoners then arrived at Bergen-Belsen.

Once the convoy had crossed the Elbe it immediately went toward Sachsenhausen. It reached Nauen, continued on to Flatow and Kremmen, and had to come back to Nauen on April 12. It made another attempt as far as Döberitz, a station located south of Falkensee, in vain. The train departed again on April 13 and got as far as Nauen, Kremmen, and Oranienburg, which was then bombed. After a long stop, access to the Heinkel Kommando in Oranienburg proved to be impossible. The convoy left again and this time managed to reach Ravensbrück via Gransee and Fürstenberg on April 14 at 1:30 P.M. Two days later the Ellrich convoy was admitted to Oranienburg. It had been delayed by two days, perhaps due to crossing the Elbe farther downstream than the Dora convoy.

The reports made by Aleste and Woussen note mass graves dug for corpses in Wolmirstedt, Calvörde, and Döberitz, but there were far fewer losses than in the convoy from Ellrich. Indeed, the ill who had survived were left in Osterode, and those who crossed the Harz Mountains were mainly tunnel specialists who were in relatively good health.

The journey was nevertheless trying due to hunger. The prisoners were given no further food supplies from the time of departure from Dora all the way to Ravensbrück. They grew weaker and, on arrival, Abbot Renard had to hold up Reverend Heuzé and Pierre Gáti had to hold up Pierre Hémery. In addition, some prisoners died of erysipelas, which the author contracted during the last days of the journey. He was given medicine by the Red Cross at Ravensbrück, which will be discussed in chapter 21.

LIBERATION AT MÜNCHEHOF. The Dora prisoners who were "lined up on a dirt road" in Osterode on Sunday morning, April 8, watched their comrades leave to cross the Harz Mountains, and then they got back on the train. It continued on to Münchehof, where they were liberated. On the basis of extracts from Pontoizeau's[11] account, it is possible to reconstruct the subsequent events.

"There were about 300 of us left, the ill, the disabled, except for about twenty of us, including me, who were considered healthy. Just as we, too, were about to start off on foot, we had to hurry and get back into the wagons. We thought it was an air raid and we tore down the embankment. It took us a while to get back into the wagons, because we had to help the sick climb up, pushing them from below and pulling from above; somehow, they all managed to get in. The doors were closed and the train pulled out in the direction of Nordhausen. We reached another station, but it was obvious that no one wanted us. [. . .] By evening, we were back within a mile of Osterode.

"Before night fell, we started off again: the Osterode station had been seriously damaged; the tracks were gashed, wagons lay ripped open across the tracks, buildings had collapsed under the explosions or from direct hits. This was war, the real thing. We kept going and the landscape changed. The train was now running along fields where farmers were still plowing the last furrows. [...]

"At daybreak, we were stopped in the little station of Münchehof. From the wagon we got a glimpse of a few isolated houses and a rather large village. We got down from the wagon. As we had presumed, there were only a few Kapos left. We got ready to leave [with a few comrades]. We looked for blankets, and once we were equipped, we tried to get out of the station. Immediately, however, we ran into an SS man, quite fat and old, who despite his gun, did not look the least bit fierce. Next to him stood two adolescents from the Hitlerjugend, who were infinitely more dangerous with their automatic pistols.

"Once again, we were promised food supplies and we began to line up by five for the distribution. First, we had to bring down the dead from the wagons and the corpses were piled up on the grass at the edge of the stream. The distribution began; everything got in line in a more or less orderly fashion. Once the supplies had been given out, we were directed toward a Lager abandoned by the Arbeitsfront, less than half a mile from the village. We walked there, conversing with each other. [...] Late in the morning, we heard the gun. [...]

"At 3 p.m., perhaps a hundred German soldiers—Volkssturm and Hitlerjugend—stole by the edge of the woods along the Lager. [...] Shells began falling. [...]. It was 5 o'clock in the afternoon. I had been assigned to peel potatoes at the sink near the door. Suddenly, at the far end of the square, I saw the silhouettes of soldiers creeping along the Blocks. My heart stopped. I heard a sound nearby and turned around. An American officer was looking at me in surprise. I fell into his arms and said, stupidly 'What are you doing here?'* and he answered 'The war.'* [...] We were free at last!" This occurred on April 9 in the evening. They were the first prisoners from Dora-Mittelbau to be liberated.

An account by Robert Roulard[12] helps complete the one by Pontoizeau. He says that it was Dr. Groeneveld ("in his legendary white coat") who talked the noncommissioned SS officer into ordering us back into the wagons. He gives April 10 as the date on which the Americans arrived at the *Arbeitsfront Lager* in Münchehof, where the prisoners had been housed and found food.

Groeneveld,[13] who escaped with a few nurses, was finally liberated by the Americans after three years in captivity. He asked to have some means to get home as quickly as possible, and for want of a car he was given a bicycle, "yellow with red tires" along with "a document stating, for your information, I was a doctor who has been liberated from the Dora concentration camp." Thus he set off to cover between 250 and 312 miles, sleeping in barns. One day he finally arrived home in Nijmegen.

*In English in the original text.

There is another account of the escape by Rassinier[14] which makes up the final chapter in the book *Passage de la ligne*. The style is very different from the rest of the book, and no doubt the chapter was written separately. On the basis of a few details it would seem that Rassinier jumped from a train and was liberated by the Americans near Seesen.

MEDICAL ATTENTION AND REPATRIATION. Pontoizeau and Roulard recall that several days elapsed between the arrival of American vanguard, who quickly went off again to prevent the German troops from regrouping, and the moment a system capable of taking charge of the ill and a few prisoners wounded during the fighting was actually set up. There was widespread disorder throughout the region.

With the help of some countrymen (prisoners of war "transformed" into civilian workers), Roulard[15] was able to "requisition" a hotel in a town very close to Seesen, where his comrades who had stayed behind in Münchehof were transferred by carts. He was aided by the new anti-Nazi burgermeister of the town and by a group of young Russian and Polish women awaiting repatriation. Some of the sick were in dire condition. Douay had to help Brun reach the place where he was to have the fluid drained from his lungs. The two of them had gone to school together. Fifty years later they discovered they had not recognized each other at the time.[16]

On April 30 the French Secours Catholique team arrived in Seesen, found the deportees, and transferred them that very day by truck or ambulance to Eisenach. The next day Roulard[17] and many of his comrades, such as Guy Marquet[18] and Léonce and Gérard Pichot,[19] were taken by truck to Saint Avold, then to Metz, where they arrived in a snowstorm on May 1. Others were later repatriated from Eisenach by train via Kaiserslautern and Saint Avold. Brun was back in Paris at Bichat Hospital by May 7. In his highly detailed account, Roulard was very critical of the conditions of repatriation, which ties up with observations made concerning Bergen-Belsen in the previous chapter.

Pontoizeau[20] reached Seesen, then Münden (near Kassel) where he directed the regrouping of Frenchmen for repatriation in early May, which was not without problems.

The Convoy from Helmstedt to Wöbbelin

Of the Kommandos attached to the Sonderstab Kammler, the one located farthest west was at Porta Westfalica near Minden on the Weser River. It was directly threatened by the American offensive at the end of March 1945. The Polish prisoner Wieslaw Kielar,[21] in *Anus Mundi,* recounts his evacuation on April 2 by train toward the east. It was the day on which the two American armies joined up at Lippstadt forty-four miles away. The prisoners were told to get down from the train near Brunswick and were led to the Schandelah camp east of Brunswick. Others went as far as Helmstedt, where David Rousset saw comrades arrive from Porta Westfalica.[22]

On the evening of April 10 they were all put on another train that arrived the next day in the Magdeburg station, almost at the same time as the convoy of Dora prisoners coming from Goslar. The train was unable to go straight on and turned instead toward the north through Altmark, stopping at the station in Stendal and crossing the Elbe in Wittenberge on an unspecified date. Its destination was close at hand: the Wöbbelin camp south of Schwerin, which housed a Kommando attached to Neuengamme.

The evacuation of Porta Westfalica to the sister camp of Helmstedt and the delivery of other prisoners from Neuengamme to Wöbbelin went normally. It was impossible, however, to go any farther, which led to consequences that will be discussed in chapter 21.

The Gardelegen Tragedy

THE CONVOY FROM ELLRICH TO MIESTE. It has already been noted that, of the five convoys in the Altmark, three crossed the Elbe at almost the same moment going north before arriving at Oranienburg, Ravensbrück, and Wöbbelin respectively. The other two convoys were stopped en route and, except for a small number who escaped under various circumstances, these prisoners were victims of the Gardelegen tragedy. Before looking at what happened at Gardelegen, it is first necessary to explain how some of them went from Niedersachswerfen to Mieste and the others from Wernigerode to Letzlingen.

The convoy that left Niedersachswerfen has often been called the "Brauny convoy" from the name of its *Transportführer*, Hauptscharführer Erhard Brauny, who was commander of the Rottleberode camp at the time. The convoy left the camp on April 4 in the evening with a column of four hundred prisoners. The only consistent, though brief, account on this subject is by Dr. Fernand Maistriaux,[23] who was the *Revier* physician mentioned in chapter 13. He says that some prisoners went on foot or in carts through Buchholz and Harzungen to the station at Niedersachswerfen, where freight cars were waiting, including a cattle wagon in which he put his patients.

Another column of some eleven hundred men led by Brauny's deputy Unterscharführer Lamp set off later, but it was caught in an aerial attack and withdrew to the camp before leaving again for an evacuation on foot toward the north, which will be discussed in the next chapter.

The Brauny convoy went from Niedersachswerfen to Ellrich on April 6, taking on other prisoners, particularly the ill from the Ellrich-Theater camp. The train started up and at one point passed the last convoy from Dora. During a stop in Osterode, prisoners from the Ilfeld Kommando who had arrived on foot were taken aboard. As the convoy was going around the Harz range at Badenhausen it was blocked by an aerial attack. A period of great confusion followed, which gave prisoners a chance to escape, some of them successfully, such as Robert Gandar,[24] a nurse from the Rottleberode *Revier*. A new locomotive had to be brought, which delayed the trains following behind. On April 8 the last Dora convoy, thus waiting in vain to go through Osterode and Möser, decided to cross the Harz Mountains on foot.

When the Brauny convoy started up, it went through Salzgitter and Brunswick on its way north until it reached Gifhorn, where orders were received to go to Sachsenhausen. At that point a bombing raid exploded an ammunition train in the station of Solpke, west of Gardelegen, making the tracks impossible to use. On April 10 the Brauny convoy was forced to stop at the station in Mieste. The Ilfeld Kommando had already set out on foot from Oebisfelde. Another convoy then arrived in Mieste. It was coming from the camp in Stöcken in the western suburbs of Hanover, with three to four hundred sick prisoners accompanied by two French doctors. "Living skeletons" said Doctor Maistriaux.[25]

On April 11 a column was formed that set off toward Wiepke, six miles north of Gardelegen. No doubt the idea was to get to the bridge over the Elbe on foot, as it was impossible to do so by train. Many of the ill prisoners were abandoned in the train. Others who could not keep up were executed along the way by the SS. Very quickly it turned into a genuine "death march" with numerous victims.

A young Frenchman, René Morel,[26] succeeded in escaping during the night after getting to Breitenfeld and reached a wooded hillside east of the road where he was to hide for four nights and three days. The column stayed parked in Wiepke during the night from April 11 to 12. Then it reached Gardelegen after going through Estedt and arriving from the north.

THE CONVOY FROM WERNIGERODE TO LETZLINGEN. At the beginning of April the prisoners in the *Baubrigaden* were still on their work sites at Osterhagen, Nüxei, and Mackenrode. Bonifas recounts that work did not stop until April 4. On April 6 they were regrouped at the base camp in Wieda, where other comrades such as Lucien Colonel, who was at the *Revier*, were located. Next they had to leave Wieda toward the north, crossing the Harz Mountains. Two columns went through Braunlage and ended up on April 9 at Wernigerode, where a convoy of cattle wagons was waiting. Those who were ill took the narrow track railway that crossed the Harz range.

As the *Baubrigaden* were in the end attached to Sachsenhausen, the convoy set off in the direction of Magdeburg via Heudeber, Jerxheim, Schöningen, and Eisleben. Since it was too late to cross the Elbe at Magdeburg or go directly to Stendal, the convoy went instead to Haldensleben where it took a secondary line (which is gone today) through Roxförde and Letzlingen. At Letzlingen the train was immobilized by an aerial attack at noon on April 11.

The double American offensive in the south and the north, as mentioned earlier, had turned the Gardelegen Kreis (circle) into a veritable "cauldron" under fire from Allied planes. Three of the five convoys from the Altmark were fortunate to get out, but the two others in the region were totally blocked.

The train that had stopped at Letzlingen was momentarily abandoned by its guards following a hedgehopping attack by two Canadian fighter planes, according to Lucien Colonel's account.[27] Numerous escapes took place at that moment. Then the SS came back and hunted down the escapees. A number of them were killed. Aimé Bonifas[28] and his friend Amaro Castellevi were not caught, which was an exception to the rule. Lucien Colonel and André Girardi went back to the train and concealed themselves.

In the evening the prisoners were grouped together by the SS, and one column set off toward the east in the direction of Burgstall. The next morning those who had remained in the train—some fifty prisoners—were put into groups by Volkssturm members and taken by truck to join the others. That was the case of Colonel and Girardi as well as Alain de Lapoyade.[29] They were later able to escape, along with Pierre Garnavault, Deconninck, and Lhoste. Another column was formed, which went off in the direction of Gardelegen. Guy Chamaillard was in it.

WHO WAS RESPONSIBLE FOR THE EVENTS AT GARDELEGEN? In April 1945, Lucien Colonel was not yet twenty years old. After his return home he took up a career as a journalist and went to East Germany on several occasions to get information on the results of the investigation into the Gardelegen events. He later published an article in *Le Serment*[30] in which he determined who played what role in these events. The following account is based on his analysis.

From the moment the prisoners in the two convoys arrived in Gardelegen their fate depended on several authorities who acted in various capacities. First there were the SS who were supervising the prisoners: Erhard Brauny, commander of the convoy that had been stopped in Mieste, his deputy the noncommissioned officer Miel, and chief warrant officer Braun, who was at the head of the column coming from Letzlingen. Then there was the Luftwaffe colonel Walter Milz, commanding the town of Gardelegen, and the captain Joseph Kuhn, interim commander of the cavalry barracks in the center of town.

Finally and above all there was Gerhard Thiele, the *Kreisleiter* of Gardelegen. In the Nazi system there was a *Gauleiter* at the head of each *Gau,* and Gardelegen belonged to the *Gau* of Magdeburg-Anhalt, the northern part of what is now Saxony-Anhalt. Under him, at the level of the *Kreis* or circle, was the *Kreisleiter,* who was therefore an all-powerful figure at the local level.

According to events reconstructed by Colonel, Thiele noticed the arrival of the prisoners from Mieste on the morning of Thursday, April 12, and ordered Brauny to take them to the cavalry school, where Kuhn shut them in the ring. The prisoners led by Braun who were on their way from Letzlingen joined them later.

Thiele, who was very irritated, wanted them all shot immediately. He tried to convince Brauny and Kuhn of this, apparently without success. In the afternoon, Brauny and part of the SS disappeared. Thiele got no further with Milz but did not give up the idea of exterminating the prisoners. He ordered members of the Hitler Youth and the Volkssturm from Gardelegen and the neighboring villages to hunt down prisoners who had escaped into the woods.

On the evening of April 12, Mrs. Bloch von Blochwitz, the lady of the local manor, "organized a farewell party for the Nazi brass at her fancy residence on the Isenschnibbe estate. The local Nazi party officials gathered there with SA, SS and officers from the Wehrmacht. [. . .] They drank a great deal and were dazed by the time Thiele burst into the sitting room cursing: 'Here I am with a thousand criminals on my hands. The Yanks are down the road and will be here within a couple of days. I can't very well have all these criminals shot in the open country. What can I do?'

"At which point, Mrs. Bloch von Blochwitz instantly shot back: 'There is an old barn up there that belongs to me. Why don't you put them inside and set it on fire.' In a footnote, Colonel explains that this firsthand account was provided by Mrs. Rost, a former servant, on April 25, 1976, in Kloster Neuendorf near Isenschnibbe, when she was eighty years old. Mrs. Bloch von Blochwitz was no longer alive to answer the accusation. But the barn that was used was indeed located on her property a few miles east of the town. The next day, on Friday, April 13, Thiele went there with Miel. He decided that the building was suitable and told Miel to get everything ready, the straw and the gasoline. Meanwhile, the prisoners who were caught here and there in the surrounding area were brought to the barracks. Among them was Amaro Castellevi, who was taken by surprise a short distance from Bonifas, who went unseen.[31] Another was Dr. Maistriaux, who had stayed with comrades on a hill near Wiepke.[32]

When they arrived at the barracks, Maistriaux was recognized by an old Austrian noncommissioned officer whom he had treated in Rottleberode a few months earlier and who said to him: "Doctor, doctor, what are you doing here?" They were rushed into a stable and shut inside after being given something to eat. Then they heard a great deal of coming and going outside, then nothing more. The prisoners in the ring suspected nothing. They were given soup, and the *Kapos* behaved with their customary brutality.

Thiele's problem was to find people to supervise the column when the prisoners were taken up to the barn. There were only about thirty SS left since Brauny and his team had departed. Both Kuhn and Milz refused to allow their soldiers to be involved in the operation. Kuhn did, however, lend two carts pulled by horses to transport the ill, of whom there were many.

Thiele gathered the *Kapos* together and promised that they would be spared if they agreed to put on German uniforms and act as an armed escort of the column. About thirty of them accepted. One of the survivors would remember seeing *Kapos* from Osterhagen wearing SS uniforms. For the rest, they succeeded in mobilizing members of the Volkssturm, the Arbeitsfront, and the Hitler Youth with disparate uniforms and weapons. Thus the procession set out through the streets of the town.

THE BURNING OF THE GARDELEGEN BARN. What took place at the barn starting at 7 P.M. is known to us from the firsthand accounts of three French survivors, Amaro Castellevi[33] and Guy Chamaillard[34] from the Letzlingen convoy, and Georges Cretin[35]from the Mieste convoy. Chamaillard's account, which is the most frequently published, is considered the authoritative version. He was almost twenty-five years of age at the time.

The column had to climb a hill before it came in view of the barn, which was enormous. The group waited for the ill prisoners to arrive in the carts and be transported inside. Then the other prisoners entered. Inside was a pile of straw three feet high doused with gasoline. Three SS came into the barn with torches and set fire to the straw. According to Colonel, the first one was Miel.

Prisoners tried to get out by forcing the doors, particularly the Russians, but they were shot one after another with machine guns. Bodies piled up in front of the doors. Chamaillard took shelter behind the corpses, which protected him from the straw and burned less quickly. He escaped the flames by remaining vigilant for hours, then everything grew quiet. He recalls:

"Above the charred corpses that now formed a pile more than five feet high, I could see that day was dawning. [...] There was less smoke, and I could breathe more easily. The fire had practically died out, a few blazes were still burning, but almost nothing. I had not been wounded, but I was covered with blood. It was blood from my comrades who had been killed near me. [...] I crawled away from the door and went to lie down farther inside. I arranged two corpses and lay down between them, after carefully smearing myself with black in case the SS came back into the barn."

At daybreak the SS came back. With soldiers and inhabitants of Gardelegen they dug two mass graves to bury the corpses. Chamaillard was a witness: "I heard the noise of shovels and spades. They were digging holes. I raised my head a little and saw a pitchfork come in through the door, stick into a corpse and then pull it outside. [...] From time to time, they pulled bodies that were only wounded. I could hear the poor wretches screaming, then the laughter of the SS, an explosion, more SS laughter and then nothing more."

Around midday the sound of battle drew nearer. The gravediggers stopped and went away. Chamaillard was at least no longer in danger. He fell asleep, exhausted.

"When I woke up, I couldn't hear anything, there was silence everywhere. I was able to move around the barn, crawling as usual. I found a few potatoes half-cooked by the fire and I ate them. [...] After a moment, I got up and went from one door to the next. There was the same silence. I was cold; I went out and I saw a coat left behind by the SS. I took it and came back into the barn.

"In one corner, corpses were still burning; I went over there to warm up. Next to the fire, I saw a blanket and was surprised that it hadn't been burned. I pulled on it and underneath I spied two Russians, alive. They had escaped from the bullets by making a hole along the wall. [...] We sat near the fire and talked in a mixture of German and Russian. From time to time, one of us would go to the door to see if anyone was coming. The Russians had a little tobacco. We smoked.

"After a while, we saw several men coming toward the barn. We immediately hid, but when we heard nothing more, we went back near the fire. Another alert; we hid again. Fifteen minutes went by; my Russian comrades called to me. I came out in turn and saw three men with them. I could tell from their clothes that they were Russian prisoners [of war]. They spoke with my comrades and asked what had happened. After explaining in a few brief words, we went in search of the wounded."

They found two Frenchmen, Georges Cretin and Amaro Castellevi, two Poles, Wladimir Wognia and Eugene Sieradzki, and a Hungarian Jew, Boudi Gaza. "With my two Russian comrades, we went down on foot to the barracks, and the wounded were transported by a cart by the Russian prisoners. All eight of us were sent to the hospital." But not immediately.

THE AMERICANS INTERVENE IN GARDELEGEN. By now it was Saturday, April 14, in the afternoon. At about 3 P.M., according to the firsthand account of a neighbor, Thiele left by car dressed in civilian clothes after bidding farewell to his wife. He seemed to have completely disappeared until a recent investigation traced him, after his death, to Düsseldorf, where he had lived under a false identity.[36]

At around 5 P.M. a dozen escaped prisoners, including several Frenchmen, were in a cabin at the edge of a wood near Burgstall. They were watching the road in the distance. Colonel and his comrades saw two American jeeps arriving and went to meet them. They were taken care of; first they were given new clothes, and they burned their striped ones. Colonel adds: "An ambulance arrived, we were given food, some powder against vermin and were photographed. Those must have been sensational pictures, given the state we were in. On the scales, I weighed in at seventy-nine pounds." Alain de Lapoyade, who spoke English, contacted members of the Thirty-fifth Infantry Division in Burgstall and asked to enlist in the American army.

That night more troops entered Gardelegen without a fight, under the command of Maj. Gen. F. A. Keating. It was not until the next day that they saw what had happened. Dr. Maistriaux[37] and his comrades were freed from their stable by a German officer surrounded by two American soldiers. They met up with a French prisoner in the barracks courtyard, no doubt Georges Cretin, who had been wounded by gunshot in the left thigh. On April 18, Lapoyade was allowed to enlist in the counterespionage department, and he went for his medical exam on April 21 in Gardelegen. That is when he heard Cretin's account. Afterward he went twice in uniform to the barn. The Americans were horrified by what they discovered, and Major Keating seriously considered having the town bombed in retaliation. The (Protestant) religious authorities of the town managed to dissuade him. (They had not done anything to talk Thiele out of his scheme.)

Major Keating had all the able-bodied men of Gardelegen brought to the barn. Five hundred and seventy-four bodies were dug up and 442 were removed from the barn. In all, 1,016 victims were counted, four of whom were identified by name, 301 by their identity number, whereas the other 711 could not be identified. Many of the bodies showed traces of bullets. The entire population of the town, with the notables at the head, were made to walk in procession past the corpses.

During the days that followed, the Americans had the members of the Hitler Youth and the Volkssturm as well as townspeople dig individual graves. The women had to provide sheets to be used as shrouds, and 1,016 inhabitants of Gardelegen had to walk from the town to the barn in Isenschnibbe, each one carrying a cross. Once the burial was completed, on Wednesday, April 25, a religious ceremony was celebrated and military honors were given to the victims.

Another necropolis was to be established in Estedt in memory of the prisoners who died in the area, particularly during the forced march from Mieste to Wiepke. A veritable manhunt had taken place throughout the region, and many of the prisoners had been killed. The Ilfeld Kommando, which left Oebisfelde on foot, suffered severe losses.

The few survivors of the two convoys, the eight survivors of the barn, those of the barracks stable, and the prisoners who had escaped were sent home, rather quickly in the case of the French and the Belgians. It was not until Bonifas reached Paris, however, that he found his friend Amaro, who he thought had perished in the fire.

VAN DIJK BEYOND THE ELBE. On April 12, 1945, a column of a hundred prisoners left Leztlingen alone, walking eastward towards the Elbe. It was led by Hans Weber, a *Kapo* from Luxembourg with a black triangle. The Dutchman Van Dijk,[38] a veteran of the tunnel (cf. chapter 6) and later transferred to Nüxei, was part of the group.

Once the column crossed the Elbe it went toward Oranienburg via the city of Brandenburg. On about April 24 it arrived at a farm near Tremmen. Van Dijk escaped and was hidden by a Russian *Ostarbeiterin* who kept him for four days before placing him under the protection of a group of French prisoners of war when the Russians arrived. The Soviet troops met up on April 25 in Ketzin, four miles south of Tremmen, thereby surrounding Berlin. On May 28, Van Dijk was transferred to the British in Fallersleben and was repatriated to the Netherlands on June 2.

Tremmen is quite close to Nauen, where the townsfolk witnessed the passage of the convoys from Dora and Ellrich mentioned earlier in the chapter. This was also the region crossed by the prisoners from Rottleberode, Rossla, and Schönebeck, which will be discussed in the next chapter.

[[20   ]]

DEATH MARCHES TOWARD THE EAST, AND THE ODYSSEY OF THE BLANKENBURG KOMMANDO

The two preceding chapters recounted what happened to the railway convoys that evacuated the prisoners of Dora, Ellrich, Woffleben, and Wieda and some of the prisoners from Harzungen and Rottleberode in April 1945.

Due to the swift advance of the American forces in the north and south of the Harz the convoys could not be used everywhere, and columns of prisoners on foot set out marching eastward under varying conditions, often with tragic consequences. It is difficult to study these "death marches" in a systematic way, for the itineraries are not always well known, and they sometimes crossed paths or have been confused with each other. In addition, the marches were often relayed by trains or barges.

This chapter is devoted primarily to the evacuation on foot of prisoners from the Dora-Mittelbau complex, i.e., Harzungen, Rottleberode, Rossla, Kelbra, and Blankenburg. At the same time the fate of the satellite Kommandos of Buchenwald, which were marching under the same conditions in the same geographical area, will also be examined. These mainly include the Kommando of Gandersheim, located west of the Harz, and those of Langenstein and Neu Stassfurt to the east.

To simplify the account, this chapter will deal with the following topics in order:

- columns of prisoners that were joined and liberated by the American troops, particularly the last column to leave Harzungen;
- columns that crossed the Elbe going northeast, such as those of Rottleberode and Rossla;
- the odyssey of the Blankenburg Kommando, which took place in the same geographic region;
- the evacuation of Langenstein, ending up across the Elbe in the region of Wittenberg;
- columns, such as the one from Neu Stassfurt, which remained for several

weeks between the Americans and Soviets in the center and eastern part of Saxony, on both sides of the Elbe, and in the Sudeten. Sometimes the marches were relayed by trains (as in the case of the Gandersheim column) or barges. The prisoners in these columns were generally the ones who suffered most.

Liberations by the American Army

THE EVACUATION OF HARZUNGEN ON FOOT, AND THE LIBERATION OF THE LAST COLUMN. It was noted in chapter 18 that a railway convoy left Niedersachswerfen on April 5, 1945, with prisoners from Harzungen, particularly sick prisoners from the *Revier.* The day before, a long column of some two thousand men had left the camp on foot. Numerous firsthand accounts, especially from Belgians and Frenchmen, have been given of this evacuation. The departure took place on April 4 at about 3 P.M. The column left Harzungen going north and crossed the Harz by Hasselfelde. It arrived on the 6th at the Blankenburg camp, which had been evacuated except for twenty or so of the ill who stayed behind.

There were also prisoners in the rear of the column who could not keep up. Georges Desprez, who played the role of doctor at Harzungen, which was mentioned earlier, was widely accepted by the SS. As a Belgian witness[1] recalls: "He managed to isolate 116 sick prisoners from Harzungen and Blankenburg from the rest of the convoy. He had them transported first by carts, then by train. It was to take them four days, from 7 to 11 April to cover less than sixty-two miles. They ended up being housed at the Beendorf camp, near Helmstedt. They were finally liberated on 13 April and most of them were then treated at the Helmstedt hospital."

It was not until after Blankenburg that several columns were formed, the destinies of which were later to diverge. The following description concerns the last column, which was also the largest and the first to be liberated. According to the Belgian chroniclers,[2] "When we arrived in Langenstein, the column took a detour westward via Derenberg to Minsleben. In Minsleben, the prisoners were put onto a train that soon came under machine gun fire and was bombed. There were several escapes. The train wandered all night long in the direction of Magdeburg, then turned back. The next morning, the prisoners found themselves in the surroundings of their starting point. They got off the train and found the main road at Heudeber." The attempt to launch a sixth railway convoy across the Altmark had failed.

By the time the column was formed again, it was already far behind the previous ones. It went off toward Schönebeck, through Halberstadt, Oschersleben, Borne, and Biere, and was finally intercepted by the Americans. The liberation of the prisoners took place in great confusion, as shown in extracts from the account by André Rogerie,[3] once again a precious witness. A similar situation was to be encountered in early May west of Mecklenburg, which will be discussed in the next chapter.

Rogerie was paired up for the march with an older prisoner, a forty-five-year-old former miner who ran a bistro in Lens. His name was Daguin, and Rogerie calls him his "old man." "We walked and we walked. Eighteen miles a day without anything to eat. Sometimes in villages at night, we would be given boiled potatoes, three or four small ones. I was very thin. [. . .] It was difficult to keep going with my old man, who was making it hard for me. Unshaven, dirty and skinny, barefooted, dressed in pants that were too large held up by an electric wire and a jacket fastened in the same way, with a large rectangle of striped fabric on the back, I arrived on the night of Wednesday, 11 April, at about 5 p.m., at a farm in a small village located nine miles from Madgeburg. [. . .]"

Rogerie and Daguin considered escaping, but the column was formed again, with puzzled-looking SS. "Suddenly, there was a very violent explosion in the village. The SS thought they were surrounded. They got together and discussed the matter, and then suddenly started out again. Daguin and I, along with several others, stayed behind. No one paid any attention to us, and as soon as the column had disappeared, we found ourselves [. . .] 'free' on the road.

"Our freedom was precarious and our weariness great. We had been walking for eight days, and sustained only by the rattling of American machine guns, we went back to the village. There, as I have recounted, the guards ordered us to leave and then went off themselves. A woman gave us some soup. [. . .]

"Under cover of night, with our hunger somewhat abated, the two of us arrived at an old abandoned windmill on a hillock, where we decided to spend the night. The sky was clear, it was springtime. Feeling my way in the dark, I pushed aside a few stones on the floor of the mill with a roof that was half caved-in. Then I looked in the distance and could see fighting. We were between the lines, with the Americans on the right and the Germans on the left. With the rumbling of guns for a lullaby, we went to sleep. [. . .]

"It was daybreak. I had slept well, with a big stone for a pillow, and Daguin was still asleep. I got up and climbed against the wall up to a small window. [. . .] I woke up old Daguin and we went back down to the village. I did not feel safe; the Germans had fled, but the Americans were not there. I got some potatoes and matches from a woman. The people were terror-stricken, and no longer dared refuse us anything. I spotted a little girl who ran away as soon as she saw us. It is true that we did not look good.

"We met up with a French prisoner of war who was housed in the village, and he took us to his room where we were finally able to shave. [. . .] At about 3 p.m., we were in a village where an American tank and a tiny car went through. We were to learn subsequently that it was the famous Jeep. [. . .]

"We lay down outside, at the foot of a tree, and we slept until morning. We were awakened by the sound of disarmed German soldiers, looking sad and defeated, who did not know where to go to avoid being taken prisoner. [. . .] The two of us set off again toward the next village which was called Glöthe." It was Friday, April 13, and they were greeted by a large Kommando of French prisoners of war housed on a big farm. "As we were very dirty, we took a warm bath in a large vat."

Jean de Sesmaisons[4] was in the area at the time. On Wednesday, April 11, he had escaped with Maurice Berrod. Caught by people from the Volkssturm and locked in a barn, they were taken out the next day. They escaped once again, and from the marsh where they were hiding they could see the American tanks arriving. They went back to the village, which was Eickendorf. In the same area René Chapel[5] also managed to lose his guards, as did Marillier,[6] on the morning of the 12th in Klein Mühlingen. All these villages, which were close to one another, were located south of Schönebeck.

THE "TRUCE" BETWEEN SCHÖNEBECK AND STASSFURT. Sesmaisons, Berrod, and another prisoner decided to set off immediately in the other direction. They requisitioned three bicycles in Gross Mühlingen and rode toward Halberstadt, where they arrived on the 15th. Sesmaisons notes that fighting was still going on in the Harz south of Derenburg. He reached Wernigerode on the 16th, Bad Harzburg on the 17th, Northeim and then Göttingen on the 19th, where he was suffering from dysentery. He was repatriated by air on April 24 with Berrod.

Rogerie[7] left too. Daguin, who was exhausted, refused to go with him. He did not get far: "Thus, I walked for about nine miles, but I was tired. I stopped in the little town of Stassfurt. There I met up with a political deportee like myself. He told me that there were some thirty deportees living in the school and that they were well fed. According to the Americans, our departure was near. So, tempted by the easy life, I settled in with them in the school to wait for the repatriation convoys. I stayed there for a month. [. . .] In the school yard, I made crepes on a stove. [. . .] A month went by, during which I gained back 37 pounds and, one morning, the American trucks arrived." The return took place by train through Hanover, Maestricht, and Charleroi. Rogerie was back in France by May 17.

While Rogerie was putting on weight in Stassfurt, Wolf Wexler was busy in Biere. The following account[8] of his adventures has been considerably simplified. Wexler was a French prisoner who belonged to a Russian family that had arrived in France at the turn of the century. He spoke German, Russian, and English.

He was in Biere when the Americans arrived. He was not the only one. There were numerous prisoners, particularly Russians, who, like him, had just been liberated. There were foreign civilian workers. There were also French prisoners of war settled in with the local population. In all, some "two or three hundred displaced persons."

The village mayor, "an old, quite sickly man," hearing that Wexler spoke German and English, asked him to go with him to Schönebeck to present his problems to the American administration. Wexler translated the mayor's words and then spoke for himself and told them what had happened in the camps. He then told them what he thought about the village situation: the ill, the displaced persons, etc. The American lieutenant in charge of the area promised to go to Biere. Wexler recounts his visit:

"Indeed, a few days later, he arrived in the village by jeep. He had everyone—the inhabitants, the deportees, the prisoners, etc.—brought together in the town square, not far from the town hall and the church. He got up onto a bench, and, striking his two revolvers (it was a scene right out of the Far West), he said, pointing to me: 'This is the mayor. From now on, you do what he tells you.' I was translating, and, dumbfounded, I wound up mayor of Biere. He left promising to send me food, blankets, etc.

"So, I went into the town hall as mayor to organize the attribution of housing billets, food distribution, etc. I appointed a militia to keep order. Then, I went to see the school where I had a Revier set up, with the help of the schoolmaster, incidentally, who swore by all the gods—like everyone else—that he had never been a Nazi. Many women came and offered to work as nurses."

Wexler provides a savory description of various aspects of his term as mayor and concludes: "On 10 or 11 May, the Americans sent us trucks. We were told to assemble in front of the church—deportees, prisoners of war, STO workers. A hundred of us got into the trucks. Some of the German women were weeping!" Wexler was on the same repatriation train as Rogerie. He went to the Lutétia Hotel, whereas Rogerie went by himself from Jeumont to Angoulême. A month elapsed between the liberation and the return of Rogerie and Wexler, who were both in relatively good physical condition. This sort of decompression period was no doubt important from a psychological standpoint. We might call this period a "truce," which is the term used by Primo Levi.[9] In a book entitled *La Tregua,* he chose the word to describe the events that occurred between his departure from Auschwitz and his return to Turin. There was also a period of truce for some prisoners in Mecklenburg in May 1945, which will be described at the end of the next chapter.

THE OTHER LIBERATIONS SOUTH OF MAGDEBURG. The liberation of the last column from Harzungen by the American forces south of Magdeburg is best known from firsthand accounts in French, but others took place in the same region.

The Kommando of Wansleben am See, west of Halle, was evacuated on April 12 and went off in the direction of Dessau. In Könnern at the crossing of

the Saale, the column met up with other columns such as those from Neu Stassfurt and Aschersleben. On April 14 the Americans arrived in Hinsdorf, east of
Köthen, and the Wansleben prisoners were free. The Americans halted their offensive shortly thereafter, once they had gained control of the highway between
Berlin and Leipzig. The column of the Leau Kommando, which had started out
on April 12 from Bernburg-Plömnitz, was also liberated on the same day in
Hinsdorf. It had been caught earlier in a tank battle.

Farther south, one of the railway evacuation convoys from Buchenwald,
which had set out on April 10, was forced to stop on the 11th in Jena with its locomotive out of order. A column was formed and stragglers were shot. It
reached Gera on April 12. After violent fighting that caused numerous losses in
the column, it was liberated on the 13th.

Altogether, only a few columns were liberated in this fashion, and often the
survivors were gravely ill. André Cozette,[10] who was liberated in Hinsdorf with
the Wansleben column, was transferred with others by the Americans to the *Revier* at Dora before being repatriated by air from the Nordhausen airfield. Another exceptional situation occurred farther north, concerning a camp that was
liberated on April 12 without being evacuated by its commander, an officer of
the Wehrmacht. This was the Gazelle Kommando at Weferlingen.[11]

The departure of three convoys of Jews from Bergen-Belsen to Theresienstadt was noted in chapter 18. One of those convoys was abandoned by its
guards and liberated near Magdeburg.

LIBERATIONS NORTH OF MAGDEBURG. The swift advance of the American
forces, as mentioned earlier, made it possible for a number of prisoners to escape, thereby avoiding the massacre in the Gardelegen region. It was also favorable to members of the Osterode Heber Kommando,[12] which set out on foot on
April 5 and reached Gifhorn on the 8th. Three groups were formed. The first one
went in the direction of Celle and was liberated on the 9th in a woods near Ohof.
The Americans caught up with the second one, which had gone in the direction
of Salzwedel, in Ehra, northwest of Gifhorn, also on the 9th.

Going west from Hanover, the Americans reached the Elbe north of Tangermünde. Farther west beyond Celle the British were moving north. In between,
the Germans retained control for a while of an area on the left bank of the Elbe,
where the third group was finally liberated on April 18 in Tannenkrug.

LIBERATION OF THE SICK. The general rule governing evacuations was that
prisoners were not to fall alive into the hands of enemy troops. If they could not
be evacuated, they had to be killed. That is what happened in Ohrdruf, which led
to the first large macabre discovery made by the Americans in early April 1945.
In Gandersheim as well, those who were too ill to leave on foot were executed
on April 4, as Antelme explained.[13]

As described earlier, the SS put the sick prisoners from Ellrich, Harzungen,
Wieda, and Rottleberode and most of the patients from Dora into railway con-

voys. Only at Dora did the Americans find patients who had been spared in the *Revier.* They also found some at the Boelcke Kaserne in Nordhausen, but under very unusual conditions.

The situation in Langenstein[14] was also an exception to the rule, because no "transport" had been organized to Bergen-Belsen. On April 9, the day of evacuation, of a total of 4,900 prisoners, only 3,000 were able to set off on foot. The others were abandoned in the *Revier* (some 500), the *Schonung* (1,200), or in the camp. When the Americans discovered the camp on April 13, they found many corpses as well as survivors in very poor condition. Hélie de Saint-Marc, for example, was unconscious. They were transported to an American field hospital set up in a barracks in Halberstadt. In Langenstein, as in Nordhausen, the civilian population was requisitioned to bury the dead and had to provide food and clothing.

In numerous camps evacuated by marches, such as Neu Stassfurt, the sick were put in carts. Most of them quickly died. In these instances, when the Americans arrived, the camps were empty.

PRISONERS FROM GÜNZERODE WITH THE SS DURING FIGHTING IN THE HARZ. A number of prisoners were liberated in the very heart of the Harz, where they had been taken. As mentioned in Chapter 17, the advance of Simpson's army in the north of the Harz and Hodges's army in the south, followed by their junction on April 13 in the Magdeburg region, isolated an entire German army in the Harz. It took some time before this new pocket could be gradually reduced. When Sesmaisons went by bicycle to Derenburg on April 16, he heard the sound of fighting near Blankenburg.[15]

Some of the prisoners that had been grouped together at the Ellrich-Theater camp in early April left by convoy. They ended up in Gardelegen. Others set off in columns going eastward. There were 350 prisoners left, including 60 Frenchmen, among them Denis Guillon,[16] who has recounted their highly unusual evacuation. It began on Tuesday, April 10, at 8 P.M. The column was led by the usual guards "as well as an SS combat section, at the head of which the prisoners had the displeasure of recognizing the former commander of Günzerode, sitting stride a big motorcycle, with hand grenades in his boots and his machine gun slung from around his neck." The column went in the direction of Sülzhayn, then Benneckenstein. On April 11 a fighter plane destroyed two German tanks, which exploded at the head of the column.

After a relatively continuous march through Trautenstein, the column reached Hasselfelde on April 12 at the end of the afternoon. It was in Güntersberge by nighttime on Friday, April 13, where it stopped at a lumber mill. Women workers from Poland took charge of getting the guards drunk. Numerous escapes took place in the dead of night, including that of Guillon and six other Frenchmen. They scrambled out of the way, into the forest.

After several episodes they were caught by SS fighters and brought back to

Hasselfelde, where they had to help the soldiers consolidate their positions. They were fed properly. They managed to be out of view in a cellar when the SS pulled back. They heard the noise of shells and grenades and were brought out of the cellar *manu militari,* not by Germans but by American soldiers. That was on Tuesday, April 17.

Guillon and his friend Xavier Piguet stayed with the Americans and took part in mopping up operations. Four *Kapos* from Günzerode were caught and executed. On May 28 the two were repatriated by airplane from Hildesheim to Le Bourget.

Evacuations on Foot Toward the Northeast, and the Odyssey of the Blankenburg Kommando

Inasmuch as plans for the first evacuations were decided at SS headquarters in Oranienburg, it appears that the Dora-Mittelbau prisoners were to be taken to Neuengamme and those from Buchenwald to Flossenbürg. Broadly speaking, it was impossible to follow these instructions, but traces of them remained in some surprising routes, such as that of Gandersheim, which will be examined later.

THE EVACUATION OF ROSSLA. The prisoners from Rossla left in a column on the morning of April 5 to cross the Harz in the direction of Halberstadt. Max Dutillieux[17] has described that evacuation. He points out that the column was joined en route by others, with prisoners in even worse condition. They were probably prisoners who had left on foot from Rottleberode and Stempeda.

"The SS supervised the long column closely. Our SS from Rossla turned savage again. [...] At first, they were content to bark out orders from time to time, because the carts were moving along at a good pace. We were still far from exhaustion—at least those of us from Rossla—and as long as we had a few more sacks of potatoes, we could hold up. [...] At night, we slept in barns in farmyards. It seems that our guards always found enough potatoes or grain to make soup. [...]

"We crossed through forests, villages, towns, but only a few cities, including Halberstadt, where the inhabitants had disappeared, leaving everything there. [...] Our forced march took us on secondary routes. Stragglers were shot in cold blood. [...] We went on in this fashion to Oranienburg, without meeting a soul on our long route. It was as if we were the only people who were fleeing. The villages and cities we crossed seemed weirdly empty.

"Upon our arrival in Magdeburg, the SS speeded up the pace. We crossed the bridge and it was blown up half an hour later. The column continued quickly on its way along the highway toward Berlin. Then it turned off onto secondary roads. On the way, our column had grown considerably and by the time we arrived in Oranienburg-Sachsenhausen, it had swollen into a human river made up of numerous tributaries."

THE EVACUATION OF ROTTLEBERODE. Among the columns moving toward Oranienburg was the one formed by prisoners from Rottleberode and Stempeda who were unable to join Brauny's convoy at Niedersachswerfen. After crossing the Harz through Stolberg and Güntersberge, they reached Quedlinburg on April 8. They went northward to Oschersleben, Seehausen, and Haldensleben.

On April 9, north of Seehausen in Drackenstedt, young people from the RAD (the German Labor Service) massacred prisoners from this column who had hidden in a haystack in a barn. A young Alsatian named Jean Uhl witnessed the scene.[18]

After Haldensleben the column went eastward to cross the Elbe by ferry between Rogätz and Bittkau. In Genthin on April 12 a train took the surviving prisoners to Oranienburg, where they arrived on April 16 after going through Brandenburg and Potsdam.

THE EVACUATION OF SCHÖNEBECK. The prisoners from Rossla and Rottleberode were not the only ones to cross the Elbe in that area before the Americans arrived. Some of the prisoners of the Schönebeck Kommando were to cross upstream at Barby on April 12, whereas the others were liberated on the spot along with the last column from Harzungen.

The itineraries of the two columns from Schönebeck[19] starting from Barby are known. The first one went all the way to Oranienburg via Brandenburg. It is possible that this itinerary was ultimately confused with the one mentioned by Dutillieux. In any case, as will be seen in the next chapter, all the new arrivals were fated to leave Sachsenhausen quickly for a new evacuation to Schwerin. The second itinerary starting from Barby began farther south and went toward Berlin. It turned north at Potsdam, through Nauen and Fehrbellin, then northwest to Neustadt-Glewe, near Wöbbelin. The Helmstedt convoy in which David Rousset was traveling arrived at Wöbbelin as well as the small Kommando from Kelbra after crossing the Altmark and following an unspecified route. One way or another, those who were sent toward the northeast to flee the American forces arriving at the Elbe were sent on to the northwest to flee from the Soviets as they took over Berlin.

THE ODYSSEY OF THE BLANKENBURG KOMMANDO. Of all the *Mittelraum* Kommandos evacuated in April 1945 that started by a march, the route followed by the Blankenburg Kommando was the most varied. It began on April 6 north of the Harz, and the survivors returned from Sweden in mid-July.

Some of the prisoners in this Kommando did not take part in the march. On April 4 a group was transferred to Dora, and it followed the evacuation of that camp. A small group of sick prisoners was left behind. As previously mentioned, Georges Desprez, who was caring for the ill in a column arriving from Harzungen, took charge of the group two days later. He had them all transported to Beendorf.

The other prisoners from Blankenburg-Oesig (Klosterwerke), most of whom were Belgians,[20] and a few Frenchmen such as Gruat, Tumerelle, and Leciejewski were put together in a column that went through Halberstadt, Oschersleben, Egeln, and Langenweddingen. It reached Magdeburg on April 8. The pace was very fast, and prisoners who were too weak to keep up were killed en route. The itinerary taken by the Jews from the Blankenburg-Regenstein camp (Turmalin) is unknown, but they reached Magdeburg at the same time as the others.

In Magdeburg they were all put on a Dutch barge, the *Wilma,* which went down the Elbe toward Hamburg. There is a painting by Jean-Baptiste Deknibber of the embarkation. The inside of the barge was totally lacking in comfort. Nothing had been planned for sleeping. "The first ones to arrive, who thought they were ensuring themselves a good spot by leaning up against the walls, soon realized their mistake: they were penetrated by dampness and when they tried to move toward the center to take advantage of the warmth of the group, they were mercilessly shoved back against the damp shell." Everyone suffered from hunger and thirst. Neuengamme may have been the first destination the authorities had in mind, but at Lauenburg the barge left the Elbe and entered the Elbe-Lübeck canal. On April 12 in the evening it came alongside in Lübeck.

On April 13 the prisoners were once again put into columns, first the Jews, then the others. A seventeen-mile march took the Jews via Schwartau and Ahrensbök to Siblin in Holstein. The others went a few miles farther, to Sarau-Glasau. There were more victims along this route. Various firsthand accounts of the period that followed have been provided by Belgians. The prisoners arrived exhausted in a huge barn and began their wait, which turned out to be very long, as it lasted from April 13 to 30. The British did not arrive in this region until the Germans had surrendered.

"After three or four days, those who were put to work for private individuals were given a few potatoes, a piece of meat or an egg, but they were a minority." During this period, prisoners died from hunger in the barn, and their comrades barely had the strength to drag the corpses outside to a mass grave. The same situation was occurring in the Wöbbelin camp at the same time, which will be discussed in the next chapter.

On April 30, trucks belonging not to Allied troops but to the Swedish Red Cross arrived, combing the region in search of prisoners in need of emergency care. According to an arrangement between Count Folke Bernadotte and Himmler, the Swedes were allowed to take Western prisoners, not only from Scandinavia but also from France, Belgium, Luxembourg, and the Netherlands, out of Germany. The Blankenburg prisoners of these nationalities were taken to Lübeck. The others, both Jews and non-Jews, set out on foot in the direction of Neustadt. They stopped in Süsel, where the Swedish Red Cross again arrived on May 1 and carried out a similar selection of prisoners, this time including the Czechs.[21]

Those selected were put onto two Swedish Red Cross boats,[22] the *Mag-*

dalena and the *Lillie Matthiessen.* The others went to Neustadt and joined the prisoners crowded into two ships, the *Cap Arcona* and the *Athen.* A British bombing on May 3 left many of these prisoners dead.

After a perilous crossing, the two Swedish boats arrived on May 2 in the port of Trelleborg. The sick were immediately hospitalized. The prisoners were given new clothes. "Our striped rags were burned. We were only allowed to keep a piece of uniform with our identity number on it.

"After two weeks in quarantine, we were divided up into various groups and sent to places that were able to receive us. I arrived in Veinge, about 16 miles southeast of Halmstad," explains Albert Van Hoey. "Outside of mealtime, we went about in the town whose inhabitants were very kind, receiving us in their homes and offering us sweets."

The repatriation to Belgium and the other countries began in June (the 13th for Gruat) and continued in July. There were exceptions, however, such as Van Hoey, who fell seriously ill on June 4 and was hospitalized with the effects of typhus. He was not repatriated until August 11, when he was flown from Copenhagen to Brussels via Malmö. Soon afterward the village of Stekene got its schoolteacher back.

THE EVACUATION OF LANGENSTEIN. The circumstances surrounding this evacuation are among the best known, thanks to the work of Paul Le Goupil,[23] who has already been quoted in chapter 13. He himself was part of "Column no. 1," and he noted down the route it took. He gathered and analyzed various first-hand accounts, including a considerable one by the Pole Rudolf John. In his memoirs he discusses this period. The evacuation took place in two stages: first the SS fled from the American forces, then from the Soviets within a gradually shrinking area. After hesitating, the camp commander ordered the evacuation on Monday morning, April 9, 1945. The circumstances no longer permitted a withdrawal to the main camp of Buchenwald as the other Kommandos had done. This time the group had to go east. The camp head count was nearly 4,900 prisoners. Some 3,000 of them left that night on foot, in six columns of 500 prisoners. The rest of them, as already noted, would not see the Americans arrive until April 13.

Column no. 1 set off toward the east on a country path and crossed the city of Quedlinburg under the cloak of darkness. They spent the night of April 10 to 11 in Ermsleben, then went on to Wiederstedt, taking small roads. During the night of April 12 to 13 there was a forced march to cross the Saale at Könnern before the bridges were destroyed. That night the column reached Hinsdorf east of Köthen. The Americans were still very close. The prisoners had to go through Wolfen and Bitterfeld quickly. At that point on April 14 the Americans stopped their offensive.

At first the column camped in the Dübener Heide, then crossed the Elbe on the 16th by a bridge made of boats. It stayed until the evening of the 19th in a marshy field near Prettin. Then the SS, who learned that the Soviets had crossed the Oder on April 16, had to decide which direction to take. Those from Langenstein decided to set off quickly toward the north, going west of Berlin.

The column went from Prettin to Jessen during the night of April 19 to 20, then from Jessen to Wittenberg during the night of April 20 to 21 on dirt roads in the midst of the panic-stricken population and the routed German troops. On April 21 it crossed the city during the daytime and then split up in the countryside near Griebo. Until then the other columns had followed roughly the same itinerary as Le Goupil's column. The column whose story has been told by the Czech Josef Traxler had to march one more day, to Zieko.

The ordeal was much longer for the column to which the Pole Rudolf John belonged, which continued on its way northward. It managed to reach Wiesenburg in Brandenburg on April 22. Then, in order to escape the Russians, it drew close to the Elbe. It was in Ziesar on the 24th, Genthin on the 26th and Güsen on the 27th, just a few miles away from the Americans. John escaped on the 28th.

In his memoirs Le Goupil[24] recalls in detail what happened to him from the moment his column split up on April 21. First he hid with his friend Serge in the country until April 27, when they were caught by other German soldiers and put into the prison at Coswig. They were released the next day and went on to Buro. On April 30 they were liberated by the Americans coming from Rosslau, and then the Russians arrived. It was not until May 24 that the French were authorized to cross the Elbe into the American zone. On May 30, Le Goupil arrived in Thionville.

Stragglers were massacred from the very first day. There were many victims when the column set out from Prettin, and again from Jessen. Then, many died in Wittenberg. There were more than 120 men in John's column after Wittenberg, but when John himself escaped only 32 were left.

Le Goupil sought to find out what had happened to the 953 Frenchmen who had arrived in Langenstein by various convoys starting in April 1944. Four hundred and fifty-one of them returned to France and were alive on July 1, 1945. He found no trace of the other 48, who no doubt died in Germany. Of the 454 identified dead, 351 died in the camp or in hospitals prior to June 30, 1945. The 103 others died within a few days on the death march. No similar study has been carried out on the other nationalities, but the losses were probably of the same order.

Compared to others, the march of the columns from Langenstein was not unusual either in terms of distance or length, but it was particularly deadly for two reasons: the prisoners had already suffered a great deal physically, and on two occasions the SS forced them to go at a very rapid pace.

THE FATE OF PRISONERS EVACUATED FROM CENTRAL GERMANY IN SAXONY AND THE SUDETENLAND. As chapter 17 explained, once the American troops arrived in Magdeburg they settled in along the left bank of the Elbe in the

Altmark without crossing the river. Farther south, after gaining control of the major cities of Dessau, Halle, Leipzig, and Chemnitz, they halted their offensive eastward. The central and eastern part of Saxony therefore remained in the hands of German troops under Marshal Schörner, who still held all of Bohemia.

When the Soviets under Koniev began the maneuver to surround Berlin from the south, they were attacked on their left flank (to no effect) by Schörner's troops. The Soviets did not undertake the conquest of Saxony until after the fall of Berlin.

The prisoners who had not been liberated by the American advance thus found themselves east and south of two fronts that remained practically stable for several weeks. Evacuation could only proceed by the south, through Sudetenland and the protectorate of Bohemia-Moravia.

The term Sudetenland traditionally designates the mountainous area separating Bohemia from Silesia. It is also used for the population of the region, which was German-speaking at the time. In 1938, after Munich, the part of Czechoslovakia annexed by Germany was formed into a *Gau* called Sudetenland, enlarged beyond Sudetenland proper to include regions south of Erzgebirge and east of Böhmerwald. Here "Sudetenland" has been used in the latter, extended sense of the term.

The events that transpired in Saxony and Sudetenland in April–May 1945 were extremely complex. The information available also varies enormously from one column to another, and the inventory that follows is no doubt incomplete. The details of the routes are provided only to give an idea of the density of the itineraries followed within a restricted territory, some ninety-four miles from north to south and from west to east.

GANDERSHEIM AND ASCHERSLEBEN. The column that made the longest journey on foot before arriving at the border of Saxony was the one that left Gandersheim on April 4 and was unable to reach Buchenwald. The conditions of that evacuation have been described in detail in the book *L'Espèce humaine* by Robert Antelme,[25] mentioned earlier. It would be impossible to take extracts from this account, which runs from page 213 to page 306; the entire passage would have to be quoted.

At the outset the column comprised about 450 prisoners—Poles, Russians, Frenchmen, and Italians. After four days it reached Wernigerode on the northern border of the Harz. All stragglers were executed along the way. There were escapes, however. Except for a short five-mile interlude by railway, the march continued via Halle until it arrived in Bitterfeld on April 14, where a train was waiting. In the end the Americans did not catch up with the column, since they did not take Halle until the 19th.

There are more than ninety-four miles as the crow flies between Gandersheim and Bitterfeld, and the route was not direct. The survivors who boarded the train in Bitterfeld were therefore already exhausted before facing the journey by railway through Saxony, Sudetenland, Bohemia, and Bavaria, which proved to be horrendous until their arrival in Dachau on April 27, thirteen days later. This will be discussed later.

Another train convoy started out in the same direction from Freiberg on about April 21. It was made up of prisoners who had left Aschersleben,[26] west of Bernburg, on foot on April 11. They too crossed the Saale at Könnern, then spent ten days on small roads east of Leipzig before arriving in Freiberg. Their convoy will also be discussed later.

HARZUNGEN, SCHWARZHEIDE, HADMERSLEBEN, THEKLA. The first evacuation columns from Harzungen, composed of a few hundred prisoners that had not been liberated by the Americans south of Schönebeck, went farther east. Once they arrived in Schönebeck on April 12, some of them crossed the Elbe at Elbenau, went through Zerbst and skirted Wittenberg by the north. There were many escapes, including those of French prisoners René Haentjens[27] and Pierre Pointe. The others, still on foot, went eastward up the Elbe through Jessen, Mühlberg, and Grossenhain. By the time they reached Radeberg they were east of Dresden and entered Sudetenland by Hinterhermsdorf in Swiss Saxony.

The evacuation column from Schwarzheide,[28] which was a satellite camp of Sachsenhausen located north of Dresden, also ended up in the same region. It set out on April 19 after the Soviets had crossed the Oder. It went across southern Lusace and reached Warnsdorf west of Zittau in Sudetenland on April 24.

A few prisoners from Harzungen[29] joined a column, apparently coming from the Wernigerode Kommando in northern Harz. The column was put onto barges that went up the Elbe past Torgau and Dresden to Leitmeritz (Litomerice) on April 13.

The column that left from Hadmersleben[30] (between Halberstadt and Magdeburg) on April 10 reached the Elbe at Aken. On April 15 the prisoners embarked at Rosslau on barges going up the river to Bad Schandau before coming back to Pirna on April 20. It was not until May 7 that they went in the direction of Aussig (Usti) in Sudetenland, to be liberated on May 8 in Lobositz (Lovosice) slightly to the south.

The Kommando column from Thekla[31] north of Leipzig started out going eastward at a fast pace on April 13 and by April 17 had arrived in Glaubitz beyond the Elbe, where it paused for three days. The Soviet threat caused it to cross back over the Elbe and set off toward the south on April 24 from Strehla. How the liberation found the column on May 9 in Teplitz (Teplice) in Sudetenland at the foot of the Erzgebirge is not known.

ARTERN, COLDITZ, BERGA, FLÖHA. A column was formed in Artern[32] south of Sangerhausen on April 5 to evacuate the recent satellite camp of Dora. The column went through Nebra, Naumburg, and Zeitz and reached the Kommando in Tröglitz, east of Zeitz, on April 8. The members of this Buchenwald Kommando, mainly populated by Jews, were in very poor condition. During the night of April 11 to 12 a train came to pick up 2,200 prisoners, including those from Artern. The convoy passed through Chemnitz and Flöha before stopping for three days in Marienberg with its locomotive out of order. It started up again on April 16 but underwent an air attack in Reitzenhain, on the border of Saxony and Sudetenland. There were prisoners killed in the attack and prisoners who escaped, some of whom were caught and executed: in all, some 250 victims. The survivors set off on foot through Komotau (Chomutov), Postelberg (Postoloprty), and Lobositz, finally arriving in Leitmeritz on the evening of April 20.

Other columns were moving through Central Saxony. One of them started out from Colditz[33] on April 14, went through Döbeln and Freiberg, and ended up in Leitmeritz. Another started from Berga[34] (south of Gera) on April 11 and crossed Zwickau and Aue before arriving in Leitmeritz as well, after taking an unspecified route. A third column left from Flöha east of Chemnitz and arrived at Theresienstadt on May 9.

THE EVACUATION OF NEU STASSFURT. Finally, among the columns that have been identified, only two remained in Saxony until the end, under quite different circumstances. The first included part of the Junkers Kommando of Halberstadt,[35] which set out on April 9, crossed Bitterfeld on April 13, and arrived in Borstendorf east of Chemnitz where it stopped some twelve miles from the Americans. Prisoners died of exhaustion on the way but none were executed. On May 7 the SS commander gave passes to Western nationals, enabling them to join the American lines. They regained their freedom in Mittelbach, southwest of Chemnitz. The other column was from Neu Stassfurt, and its story was typical.

The evacuation of the Neu Stassfurt Kommando,[36] like that of Langenstein, is well known from a collection of firsthand accounts already quoted in chapter 13. It began in haste on April 11, for the Americans were advancing quickly. The column crossed the Saale north of Halle on April 12 and moved eastward. On April 14 it went through Delitzsch, south of Bitterfeld, arriving on the 15th in Kossa in the Dübener Heide. The Neu Stassfurt column then camped close by those from Langenstein.

When the Langenstein columns crossed the Elbe on April 16 and then went northward, the Neu Stassfurt column went south, remaining on the left bank of the river. The prisoners from Harzungen did the same thing on the right bank. The trailers transporting the ill were eliminated and the sick prisoners murdered.

Taking small roads, the column reached Oberaudenhain on the 16th, Bockwitz on the 17th, Raitzen on the 18th, and Riemsdorf on the 19th. Then it went by Dresden and on to Kurort Hartha on the 20th, Friedersdorf on the 21st, Nassau on the 22nd, and Clausnitz on the 23rd, where it stopped for two days. When it set off again snow was falling and many of the prisoners were walking barefoot. The survivors arrived at a farm in Dittersbach on April 26 and stayed there for ten days. On average they covered a distance of fourteen miles a day, and every day prisoners died either from weakness or being killed. Some prisoners did try to escape, at considerable risk.

During the first days of May the Soviet troops began their conquest of Saxony. As they drew closer, panic set in among the SS, who got their columns moving again. That was the case, mentioned earlier, of the prisoners from Hadmersleben, who left Pirna on May 7 for Aussig and then Lobositz. Similarly, on May 7, 1945, the Neu Stassfurt column set out again, once those who were too weak to walk had been eliminated. The column again covered twenty-five miles on the 7th and the 8th, crossing the Erzgebirge via Olbernhau, Marienberg, and Mildenau to Annaberg, which was nineteen miles from Chemnitz, where the American forces were located. The survivors were liberated by the Soviets, however, on the day the Germans capitulated.

It has been important to follow the chronicle of this evacuation day by day, for, in a certain sense, it was typical of all the others. The SS obstinately pursued this evacuation from April 16 to May 8 in a frantic headlong flight that served no other purpose than to obey the instructions not to allow the prisoners to be liberated, first by the Americans and later by the Soviets.

The death toll was established by the association of French deportees, of whom there were many in this Kommando: of 493 prisoners, 181 came back alive, 94 died in the camp, and 124 are known to have died en route during the evacuation. There was no trace of the remaining 94 prisoners, most of whom no doubt also died during the evacuation.

LEITMERITZ AND THERESIENSTADT. With two exceptions the columns that were in Saxony in April and May 1945 crossed the Erzgebirge and arrived in Sudetenland. At the time they were still in German territory, and there were Kommandos of various sizes in the *Gau,* which were usually satellites of the Flossenbürg camp in the Upper Palatinate.

The largest one, with some six thousand prisoners, was on the Elbe in Leitmeritz, which led the SS in charge of columns to "deliver" their prisoners there until the very last moment. As mentioned earlier in chapter 11, this Kommando corresponded to the B 5 underground work site of the Sonderstab Kammler. When they were liberated in Lobositz, the Hadmersleben prisoners coming from Pirna were in a sub-Kommando of Leitmeritz.

The area of the protectorate of Bohemia-Moravia began immediately to the south with the small fortified town of Theresienstadt (Terezin), which had been transformed into a ghetto for German and Czech Jews who lived there under "privileged" conditions until they were sent, like the others, to Auschwitz. This made it possible to a certain extent to fool visitors such as those from the International Red Cross. When the prisoners from Tröglitz and Artern arrived in Leitmeritz, the Jews were placed in a separate group and sent to Theresienstadt. A convoy was formed with the others and set off southward.

THE EVACUATION COLUMNS IN SUDETENLAND. The Harzungen prisoners[37] who arrived in Leitmeritz by the Elbe on April 13 left again by train on the 17th and then went on foot to Landeshut (today Kamienna Gora), where they arrived on April 19. Then they went into Silesia, to a satellite camp of Gross Rosen that still had not been "liberated." Its liberation took place on May 5, and the Soviets then arrived in Landeshut.

The prisoners in the other columns from Harzungen, who arrived on foot through Swiss Saxony, went through Hohen Leipa (Krasna Lipa) and continued on to Kamnitz (Ceska Kamenice) and finally reached Rabenstein (Rabstejn) on April 26. A satellite camp of Flossenbürg was located there, which was liberated by the Soviets on May 8. In the same region, the prisoners from Schwarzheide remained in Warnsdorf from April 24 to May 8, except for the Jews, who were evacuated by train to Theresienstadt on May 5. On May 8 the SS forced the column to make one more march via Haida (Novy Bor) to Langenau (Skalice). It was not until the morning of the 9th that they finally disappeared.

It would be interesting to learn the fate of all the Kommandos situated in Sudetenland during April and May of 1945, but that task would fall outside the limits of this study. It will have to suffice here to include some information about the two evacuation columns that set out from the women's camp of Zwodau (Svatava) east of Karlsbad (Karlovy Vary), which have been the subject of recent publications.

The first column was made up of Jewish women accompanied by German women prisoners. An account of that evacuation has been given in the controversial book by Daniel J. Goldhagen[38] entitled *Hitler's Willing Executioners.* The book contains a map showing the itinerary but does not indicate the dates of the various stages of the journey. The evacuation probably began on April 16 with the column moving east along the Böhmerwald, which was still German territory at the time. It was liberated on May 6 in Prachatice, after the Americans crossed the Böhmerwald and entered Bohemia. On April 16 a second column of non-Jewish women, including Brigitte Friang,[39] set out from Zwodau. She has recounted this evacuation in a book of memoirs entitled *Regarde-toi qui meurs,* which has just been republished. The column's peregrinations continued interminably in northern Bohemia and finally came to an end on May 8 with the arrival of the Soviets in Plochat. Brigitte Friang joined up with the Americans who had reached Karlsbad before being repatriated on May 18.

THE LAST LEG OF JULES HOFSTEIN'S MARCH. Whereas all the SS in charge of columns automatically directed their prisoners toward Leitmeritz, the Jews were often sent to Theresienstadt during the final weeks to be regrouped. As has already been mentioned in chapter 18, three trains filled with Jews with special status left Bergen-Belsen at the time heading for Theresienstadt, and one of them reached the camp on April 21. On the same date the Jews from Tröglitz were transferred from Leitmeritz to Theresienstadt. On May 5 the prisoners from Schwarzheide were transferred by train from Warnsdorf. Jules Hofstein has given a telling firsthand account of these last-minute transfers.

Hofstein[40] and four comrades, as mentioned in chapter 16, were in the Gestapo rehabilitation camp of Zöschen. There they met up with other escaped prisoners from Nordhausen. "Soon we were put into closed freight cars, along with several hundred prisoners of all types and of every nationality, seventy-five prisoners to a car. A new odyssey was about to begin, even more hallucinatory than the previous ones, which was to last twenty-one days." The convoy dragged on aimlessly in Saxony and Sudetenland.

"One day, we had stopped in a small station in Sudetenland, when a train of prisoners from Buchenwald arrived. The next day, the SS went through all the freight cars shouting 'Juden raus!' 'Jews get out!' I got out with some twenty comrades. We were expecting the worst. We were left standing in front of the freight car, in a single row, for an hour. Then, to our surprise, we were given bread to eat and even sausage, and told to go and join the convoy opposite us, where the same sorting process had been carried out. There, we were given half a liter of warm soup and we got into the freight cars.

"We left that night with the SS. The next morning, to our amazement, they had vanished. We were guarded by men from the Volkssturm wearing ill-assorted uniforms. At about 10 a.m., we arrived in Leitmeritz station and the Volkssturm handed us over to the Czech *gendarmerie* (i.e., of the "protectorate").

"Shortly afterward, around noontime, on 28 April, 1945, we entered Theresienstadt. We were saved. Indeed, all around the city there were big red posters proclaiming that it was under the protection of the International Red Cross. The Germans, who avoided entering, merely bypassed it during their withdrawal. Finally, on 8 May, we were definitively liberated by the Red Army."

After the liberation there was no reason to maintain the distinction between Jews and non-Jews, and various prisoners were housed at Theresienstadt. That is where Robert Desnos, who had come from Flöha, died of typhus on June 8.

THE CONVOYS THROUGH BOHEMIA. Two trains were formed to evacuate prisoners through Saxony, Sudeten, and Bohemia, one in Bitterfeld on April 14 for prisoners from Gandersheim, and the other in Freiberg on about April 21 for prisoners from Aschersleben.

The convoy from Gandersheim is well known from the highly evocative account provided by Robert Antelme.[41] After thirteen days the train arrived in Dachau on April 27, filled with dead and dying prisoners. There has been some discussion as to whether or not the train went through Dresden and Prague, but the details of the itinerary are unknown.

It is possible to get an idea of what the convoy went through by following the route of another convoy that arrived in Dachau on the same day. The information comes from a recently published book by François Bertrand,[42] *Notre de-*

voir de mémoire. Bertrand belonged to this convoy from Buchenwald, which left Weimar on April 7 in the evening with 5,080 prisoners from the small camp, many of whom were already very weak. Others, such as Bertrand, came from prisons or satellite Kommandos.

There can be no question in this book of studying the conditions under which the Buchenwald camp was partially—and only partially—evacuated in April 1945. Some information on certain points is required, however. At the time of the American offensive toward Thuringia, prisoners from a number of satellite Kommandos were brought back to the main camp. The withdrawal took place under tragic conditions for Springen and Ohrdruf, but far more normally for the prisoners of Mühlhausen, Niederorschel, Halberstadt, (including Henri Thomas), and Langensalza (including Michel Vidal). On the other hand, as was already mentioned, those from Gandersheim, Langenstein, and Neu Stassfurt, for example, left directly in evacuation columns.

Next the SS tried to conduct the evacuation of the Buchenwald camp itself. They succeeded in organizing a few convoys either with prisoners living in the camp or prisoners coming from satellite Kommandos or prisons. That was the case of the Kommando to which Bertrand belonged.

The above-mentioned convoy set off toward the east and took two days to arrive in Dresden via Leipzig on April 9, then two more days to arrive in Pilsen via Aussig on the 11th. The column was initially instructed to go to the Flossenbürg camp, but after the long detour it was assigned a new destination: Dachau. The train slowed down and took eight days, from April 11 to 19, to go through Bavaria to Bayerish-Eisenstein, arriving in Nammering north of Passau, where the convoy stopped until April 24. It set out again with a new locomotive, went through Passau, and finally arrived at Dachau during the night of April 27 to 28. It had taken twenty days to go from Buchenwald to Dachau, a distance of 187 miles as the crow flies. The thirteen-day train route of the Gandersheim convoy from Bitterfeld to Dachau was the quickest journey, but it came after ten days of forced march. The results were the same. Of the 5,080 prisoners who left Weimar, there were 816 survivors, many of them ill, upon arrival at Dachau. Of the 450 prisoners who left Gandersheim there were 122 survivors, as the sick prisoners had been killed prior to departure.

When Robert Antelme got down from the freight car he was in very poor condition. He was recognized in early May by a French mission visiting Dachau, which included François Mitterrand, who was the leader of Antelme's Resistance group. A veritable expedition was mounted by Dionys Mascolo and Georges Beauchamp on May 8, 1945, to hustle him out of Dachau despite the quarantine in force due to typhus.[43] Thus he was saved, as was young Michel Vidal, another new arrival at Buchenwald, through another example of devotion.

The other convoy that left Saxony was the Aschersleben Kommando,[44] which pulled out from Freiberg on April 21. The SS wanted to abandon their prisoners at the camp in Leitmeritz, but the stop lasted only one night and the convoy had to start back southward. The train went past Prague, stopped in the middle of the countryside from April 30 to May 7, and then set off again, fleeing from the Russians. On May 8 the SS refused to stop at Budweis (Budejovice), but the convoy was liberated a little farther on by Czech partisans. The same thing happened to the convoy that left Leitmeritz on April 21 with prisoners from Artern[45] and Tröglitz. The train went through Kralup a.d. Moldau (Kralupy nad Vltavou) and Prague, coming to a halt on April 30 in Beneschau (Benesov). It did not set out again until May 7, when it went through Tabor and Budweis and was stopped by Czech partisans on May 8 in Kaplitz (Kaplice).

Two other convoys can also be identified that crossed Saxony and Bohemia with prisoners from Buchenwald. One of them left Weimar on April 8, went through Chemnitz and then Karlsbad, and finally arrived in Bavaria via Eisenstein. Then it meandered through southern Bavaria until it was liberated on April 30 by the American forces in Landsham east of Munich.

The other convoy, which left on April 10, first went through Chemnitz, then Komotau, but did not reach Pilsen. It wandered endlessly in Sudeten between Saaz (Zatec) and Aussig in the same zone as Brigitte Friang's column. It was not until May 7 that the survivors were able to get off in Theresienstadt. It is possible that this Buchenwald convoy is the same one mentioned by Hofstein in his account of the last leg of his march.

THE GREAT JOURNEY OF THE TAIFUN EXPRESS. The evacuation conducted by a train nicknamed the "Taifun Express"[46] was a very special one. As already noted, one of the last activities at Peenemünde involved a request from the Luftwaffe to do a study on a small antiaircraft missile called the *Taifun* (typhoon). Manufacturing had begun in the workshops of the Dora Tunnel.

On April 5 at 7 P.M. a convoy left from the Dora station under the authority of Dr. Klaus Scheufelen, the *Taifun* specialist, who was an *Oberleutnant* in the Luftwaffe. The train was being used to move the missiles whether finished or not, along with documents and specialized equipment. Some fifty civilian workers from Mittelwerk as well as Luftwaffe soldiers took part in the convoy. Nearly four hundred prisoners, particularly Greens, also left in the convoy along with SS under the command of Erwin Busta, known as Pferdkopf. Wilhelm Simon, the head of the tunnel Arbeitseinsatz, came with them.

The train set out in the same direction as the evacuation convoys. At one stop in Herzberg freight cars were added on with a Kommando of young Jewish women who had been at Grosswerther for a month. The itinerary was comparable to that of all the principal evacuation convoys. The Taifun Express went through Seesen, Goslar, Magdeburg, Dresden, and Prague, and finally arrived in Linz during the night of April 14 to 15. Despite the special features of the convoy the journey took nearly ten days.

At that point the freight cars of the Grosswerther Kommando were taken on to the Mauthausen camp. It is possible that some Jewish prisoners were then evacuated to Switzerland. The train continued its route to Gmunden am Traun- see, and most of the Dora prisoners went to the Ebensee camp with Busta.

In the train there remained Scheufelen, his equipment and his specialists, and a few prisoners with the SS man Simon. Scheufelen wanted to join von Braun, Dornberger, and the others in the Bavarian Alps. The convoy made a sharp detour through Tyrol to reach Bavaria, but the train came to a halt defini- tively in Fischbach, south of Rosenheim, where the Americans arrived on May 2. Scheufelen managed to find his Peenemünde colleagues and go with them to the United States.

[[21]]

FROM SACHSENHAUSEN AND RAVENSBRÜCK TO THE SCHWERIN REGION

All of the numerous evacuations discussed in the previous chapter took place, with a few exceptions, particularly that of Blankenburg, in the regions located south of Berlin left untouched first by the offensive of the American forces and subsequently by the Soviets. Quite often the prisoners had to wait for the German surrender to recover their freedom.

The situation was different north of Berlin, in the northern part of Brandenburg and Mecklenburg. The SS conducted the evacuation of two large camps, Sachsenhausen and Ravensbrück, and the columns ended up together in the Schwerin region not far from the Wöbbelin camp in early May 1945.

The Soviet offensive from the Oder toward the Elbe and a final American advance beyond the Elbe put an end to any further movement of prisoners. Generally speaking, the survivors were set free "in the middle of countryside" after various episodes.

Germany in April and May 1945

MILITARY OPERATIONS BETWEEN THE ODER AND THE ELBE. The American armies stopped at the Elbe after their offensive on Magdeburg. At that time Soviet forces were stationed along the Oder River (with a bridgehead at the level of Küstrin) and the Neisse River to the north of Görlitz.

On the morning of April 16 the offensive in the direction of Berlin was launched, with Zhukov's armies emerging from the bridgehead and those of Koniev crossing the Neisse between Forst and Muskau. By April 19 the German front had been broken east of Berlin. By April 22 the Ninth German Army was surrounded between Berlin and Cottbus. Zhukov moved north from Berlin and took Oranienburg. Koniev advanced southward beyond Jüterbog. The two armies joined up on April 25 in Ketzin, between Potsdam and Brandenburg. The siege of Berlin had begun. It would end on May 2 with the surrender of the city's last defenders. Hitler committed suicide on April 30 in the afternoon. Farther south, Koniev's troops joined up with the American forces on the Elbe at Torgau on April 25.

In the north on April 18, Soviet troops under Rokossovsky began crossing the Oder between Schwedt and Stettin. They took Stettin on April the 26th, Prenzlau on the 27th, Anklam on the 29th, Neustrelitz on the 30th, and Stralsund on May 1. By May 3 the link-up with the Americans was in place north and south of Wittenberge. The American forces, on the right of the British, crossed the Elbe in the direction of the Baltic and took Schwerin and Wismar in early May.

THE REICH FROM HITLER TO DÖNITZ. There is a great deal of confusion concerning the events at the head of the Reich, especially during the final months. It is possible, however, to present the main ones, particularly those that took place in northern Germany, as some of their aspects directly affected the fate of concentration camp prisoners.

First, the role of the International Red Cross must be situated, especially the one played by Count Bernadotte. For a long time the IRC did not do much to help camp prisoners, and after 1945 a number of controversies arose concerning its role. Obviously the operations of the German Red Cross were entirely controlled by the Nazi Party, and the IRC never had a suitable relay organization inside the Reich. Visits to camps were few and far between, and always carefully prepared and supervised.

In early 1945 the IRC stepped up its activity with the support of its correspondents in two neutral countries, the Swiss Red Cross and the Swedish Red Cross. The president of the Swedish Red Cross, Count Folke Bernadotte, was led to play a leading role not only from a humanitarian standpoint but also from a political one. The Red Cross had two aims. The first was to obtain the liberation and transfer to neutral countries of as many prisoners as possible. Negotiations were restricted to certain groups, however, and proved to be complicated. Toward the end, for example, it was easier to intervene with certain authorities in favor of Jewish prisoners or Jehovah's Witnesses than on behalf of other categories of prisoners. The other aim was to deliver packages of food and medicine to the camps.

In order to achieve results, requests had to be addressed to those in control of the concentration camp system, namely the SS. Hence Count Bernadotte addressed himself to the leader of the SS, Reichsführer-SS Heinrich Himmler. These contacts appear to have been facilitated by Walter Schellenberg, a young SS general, on the occasion of two trips Bernadotte made to Berlin, one in February and one in April. It was only on April 23 that their relations took on a political dimension, with important consequences. First, everything had to be happening at once at the top level of the government.

Aside from negotiations with Bernadotte, Himmler had a meeting on April

21 at the office of his masseur, Kersten, with Dr. Norbert Masur, a Swedish Jew who was representing the World Jewish Congress. Himmler authorized the Jewish women at Ravensbrück to leave for Sweden and those at Theresienstadt to go to Switzerland.

The last important general meeting of Nazi dignitaries, which has been described by numerous authors,[1] took place in the bunker of the Reich Chancellery in Berlin on April 20, 1945, on Adolf Hitler's fifty-sixth birthday. To situate the event, a break in the German front east of Berlin had occurred the day before, and the next day the Sachsenhausen camp was to be evacuated. A hundred people were at the meeting, all of them leaders, including Göring, Goebbels, Ribbentrop, Himmler, Kaltenbrunner, Bormann, Ley, and Speer as well as Dönitz, Keitel, Jodl, and many others.

Hitler had already announced that he would not leave Berlin. All the others left with the exception of Goebbels and Bormann. Only Speer returned to Berlin on April 24 to say good-bye to Hitler.[2] He flew from Rechlin (near Mirow, in Mecklenburg) to Gatow and then back to Rechlin. Himmler and Keitel were in the vicinity.

Himmler was in Hohenlychen at the hospital of his friend, Dr. Gebhardt. He had been hospitalized there in March and had set up his headquarters there. Keitel and Jodl were in Fürstenberg, "with a skeleton OKW." Most of the Wehrmacht command had withdrawn to the Holstein between Kiel and Lübeck with Dönitz, who was in Plön. On April 25, Speer went to see Himmler[3] and found him in a hospital room transformed into an office. Speer himself had been in the same room when he first fell ill in January 1944 (cf. chapter 7). Keitel was the next to visit Himmler. Himmler told Speer he was planning to set up a government and asked him to be part of it. He talked about the negotiations he was conducting with Bernadotte to transfer the concentration camps to the International Red Cross.

Indeed, Bernadotte did achieve some success on behalf of certain prisoners, as mentioned earlier, and as will be discussed again later, but Himmler went even further in his proposals. He proposed the surrender of the German armies on the Western front. According to some accounts the meeting took place in the evening at the Swedish consulate in Lübeck on April 23. More specifically, it is said to have taken place in the cellar of the consulate during a bombing raid and by candlelight because the electric power was out. Schellenberg accompanied Himmler. Bernadotte went back to Stockholm and made the appropriate contacts. Naturally the Western Allies rejected Himmler's proposal for a separate peace, and Bernadotte came back on April 27 with their refusal.

On April 28, Hitler's bunker in Berlin picked up a BBC broadcast containing a dispatch from Reuters in Stockholm revealing Himmler's secret negotiations with Bernadotte. By all accounts Hitler was profoundly disturbed by the treachery of Himmler, who was known as "faithful Heinrich" *(der treue Heinrich).*

Then everything began happening at once in Berlin. On April 29, Hitler married Eva Braun. He dictated his "political testament" and appointed Admiral Dönitz "president of the Reich and supreme commander of the armed forces." He even went so far as to put together a government (which never came into being). Speer was not part of it; he was replaced by Saur.

On April 30 at 3 P.M., Hitler and Eva Braun committed suicide. On May 1, Goebbels and his family followed suit. Apparently, Bormann was killed trying to leave the city. On May 2 the last defenders of Berlin surrendered.

In Holstein, Dönitz formed his government on May 2. He set it up in Flensburg near the Danish border. Speer was named minister of the economy and of production.

On May 4 in Lüneburg, Adm. Hans von Friedeburg signed the official surrender of all the German forces currently in the northwestern section of the Reich and in Denmark and Holland. On May 5 he arrived in Reims to negotiate the surrender. Jodl joined him there on May 6. On May 7, Jodl signed the unconditional surrender. On May 8, Keitel signed it in Berlin.

The End of Sachsenhausen

ORANIENBURG AND SACHSENHAUSEN. Oranienburg is a city in the northern suburbs of Berlin in what is now Brandenburg state. It is located in a wooded region where between 1933 and 1945 the SS was able to broaden its hold to a considerable extent. The Sachsenhausen concentration camp, named after part of Oranienburg, was an important component of the complex that was gradually built up and can be described as it was in early 1945.

First of all, the SS administrative center, the WVHA under the command of Pohl, which was mentioned in chapter 1, was located in Oranienburg within an enormous complex of varied buildings. All decisions regarding the concentration camps, even those concerning the smallest details, were made there. Kammler was at home there. The complex also contained the barracks of the Brandenburg SS detachment, a major arsenal, motor fuel storage depots, and repair workshops for military vehicles and equipment hidden in the pine forest.

The history of this concentration camp has been written by Jean Bezaut,[4] who was a prisoner there. The name of his book is *Oranienburg 1933–1935, Sachsenhausen 1936–1945.* As the title indicates, as early as 1933 there was already a camp in Oranienburg in a former brewery where the Nazis, in this case the SA, interned their political opponents. The camp came under SS control in 1934 and was closed in 1935. Another one, called Sachsenhausen, was built on a new site starting in July 1936. It quickly grew into a large camp, and prisoners from Sachsenhausen were sent on to open the camps of Neuengamme, Gross Rosen, and Auschwitz.

The Sachsenhausen prisoners worked[5] for the SS in the arsenal, the warehouses, and the workshops. Beneath the pine trees there was also a plant where *Panzerfaust* (bazookas) were produced, and the Klinker brick factory was located near the Havel Canal. Annexed to the camp itself was a DAW armaments factory (as at Buchenwald).

Above all, beginning in August 1942 concentration camp manpower was made available to the large aircraft construction company Heinkel in a factory located in Oranienburg. The experiment was successful, and a Heinkel Kommando was housed at a camp inside the factory itself, which ended up reaching a total head count of 6,000 to 7,000 prisoners. It was so successful that Rudolph, who was chief engineer of the V2 factory at Peenemünde, paid a visit to the Heinkel factory on April 12, 1943, as has been mentioned in chapter 2. His report was favorable, and he too put in a request for a prisoner workforce for Peenemünde. As already indicated, this initiative was responsible for their being employed by Mittelwerk in the tunnel factory at Dora.

The Heinkel Kommando was not the only one working for the armaments industry. There was a "Speer Kommando" at Oranienburg that recycled nonferrous metals from old electricity and telephone cables and scrapped vehicles. A camp was also set up west of Berlin in Falkensee by the DEMAG factories. Degenkolb, head of the Sonderausschuss A4 (cf. chapter 2), and Rickhey, managing director of Mittelwerk as of April 1944 (cf. chapter 7) both came from the DEMAG company.

The Sachsenhausen camp and its Kommandos, of which there were many more than the ones just mentioned, have been described in the collection of firsthand accounts drawn up by the association of French deportees of the camp. The book is entitled *Sachso,* the familiar name used by these deportees. The camp head count, which was always sizable, reached 28,000 at the end of 1943 and 47,700 at the end of 1944. It grew considerably in early 1945 with the evacuations from the camps in the east.

As at the other large camps, transports left Sachsenhausen and went in various directions. In September 1943, French miners, including Léon Bronchart, were transferred to Dora via Buchenwald to finish digging out tunnel A (cf. chapter 5). When the prisoners who left Buchenwald for Peenemünde in June and July 1943 (cf. chapter 2) came back to Buchenwald to be assigned to Dora (cf. chapter 5), Sachsenhausen was the camp that acted as a relay until the end (cf. chapter 10). Reinforcements were sent in October 1944 to Langenstein (cf. chapter 13).

In April 1945 the strategic withdrawal of the exterior Kommandos to the main camp exacerbated its overcrowding. Newcomers who arrived from the west were comparatively few. It is a fact that the train from Ellrich ended directly at the Heinkel factory, but Dutillieux, who came on foot from Rossla, understood only that he had arrived at "Oranienburg-Sachsenhausen." He was given a six-figure identity number, which he "hastened to forget." Wautrecht,[6] who arrived from Ellrich, remembers that his was 138551. Lafond's was 138148.

THE EVACUATION OF SACHSENHAUSEN. The evacuation of the Sachsenhausen camp, which began on April 21, 1945, was the most important operation in the history of the evacuations, for it involved the entire population of a major camp all leaving together in a single direction on foot with no prospect of reaching any other camp by railway convoy.

Only one other previous evacuation was on a similar scale: that of the Auschwitz concentration camp. After an initial "death march," however, the prisoners had been transported by train to other camps. This time it was no longer possible to form trains, and there were no longer any camps able to receive the prisoners.

An evacuation column leaving Oranienburg on April 21 could go in only one direction: northeast to Schwerin in the western part of Mecklenburg, then to Lübeck, and beyond that to Holstein. Naturally, such a plan was based on the assumption that the Soviet and American forces would stay put, which they did not do. Inevitably the route ultimately turned into a dead-end. There has been a great deal of speculation, after the fact, about what the SS actually had in mind when they decided on the evacuation, which presupposes that they could have decided not to evacuate Sachsenhausen and Oranienburg with all that that implied. Once the decision to evacuate was made, there were no longer any other possibilities. When Keitel and Jodl went to set up headquarters in Fürstenberg and Plön, they were caught in the same geographical trap. In early May it was easy for them to avoid the dead-end route, but one week later it meant surrendering.

During the days preceding the evacuation the Sachsenhausen camp continued operating, since newcomers such as Dutillieux, Wautrecht, and Lafond were given identity numbers. At Ellrich, on the other hand, prisoners arriving from Karlshagen at the beginning of the month were not given identity numbers. The situation was not calm, however, for there were bombing raids, particularly one on March 15 of the Auer factories and the one on April 10 that hit Klinker as well as the SS factories in the pine forest.

The collapse of the front east of Berlin on April 19 set off the evacuation on April 21. Indeed, by Sunday, April 22 in the afternoon, Soviet troops had arrived in Oranienburg. The Falkensee camp west of Spandau could not be evacuated because it was caught when Berlin was surrounded.

It is impossible to say how many prisoners were involved in the evacuation of Sachsenhausen. In his book published in 1989, Bezaut,[7] who studied all the literature on the subject, wrote: "The headcount of those on the march varies from 30,000 to 42,000; the headcount of the survivors, between 18,000 and 28,000. That means there must have been between 12,000 and 15,000 poor wretches who were struck down by SS bullets or who died of hunger or exhaustion along the way, and many in the Below woods." In this mass of prisoners, there was nothing unusual about the fate of the prisoners from Ellrich and Rossla. At the time of the evacuation, prisoners who were too ill to move were left behind.

The departure was organized by nationality: first the Germans and the Czechs, then the Poles, the Russians and the Ukrainians, and finally the French and the Belgians, to mention only the most heavily represented nationalities. A group of twenty-seven natives of Luxembourg arrived in the front of the column in Schwerin. They are well known for having kept a precious diary of the march. The column was divided into "detachments" of five hundred prisoners under the supervision of SS and armed Green *Kapos*. This order was not strictly maintained throughout the evacuation.

THE STAGES OF THE EVACUATION. There were three periods in the evacuation. The first, from April 21 to 25, was the real death march to Wittstock. The itinerary, which varied depending on the detachment, was as follows: Sachsenhausen-Hohenbruch on April 21, Löwenberg-Herzberg-Neuruppin on April 22, Katerbow-Rägelin-Rossow-Herzsprung on April 23, Papenbruch on April 24, and Wittstock-Eichenfelde and the arrival at Below Woods on April 25. At that point they were on the border of Brandenburg and Mecklenburg.

Some thirty-seven miles to the east, Speer and Keitel were visiting Himmler at Hohenlychen on April 25.

The second phase took place in the Below Woods, where all of the columns were immobilized while awaiting no one knows what. Their stay in the cold and rain, without food, was fatal to many of the prisoners. Hundreds of corpses were abandoned at the site. On April 28, Red Cross trucks arrived carrying packages that were divided up after the SS and *Kapos* had first helped themselves. The firsthand accounts of the Red Cross delegates who brought the packages to the site are particularly valuable and coincide with those of the prisoners.

On April 26 the prisoners from Dora began evacuating Ravensbrück. Keitel and Himmler had to leave Fürstenberg and Hohenlychen. The third phase included four days of march: Freyenstein-Stepenitz on April 29, Redlin-Pankow-Siggelkow on April 30, Parchim-List-Neuruthenbeck on May 1, and Crivitz-Pinnow on May 2. A little farther on the group from Luxembourg spotted the first American tank, and the SS vanished. The other prisoners still marching behind them were left to their fate somewhere between Parchim and Schwerin, and gradually arrived in Schwerin. A large percentage of the prisoners had in fact been "liberated" during their sleep in the country.

The succinct accounts by former Ellrich and Rossla prisoners are part of this story. Dutillieux[8] says that when he and his companions awoke on May 2 after sleeping close to the fire, they noticed that the SS were gone. Besançon, Henri Ertlen, and Raymond Grand have the same memory. Rémy Vincent[9] was in

Parchim. He notes that it was the town of the famous von Moltke family. At some point he was able to flee and was given care and food by French POWs.

Pierre Choquenet,[10] a prisoner from Sachsenhausen, spent the night of May 1 to 2 with a hundred other prisoners in a barn filled with straw, guarded by SS. By morning the SS were gone. He had a fright in retrospect when he learned what had happened at Gardelegen.

There were few successful escapes during the journey. One example was Harry Paylon[11] and Louis Lévy, who left their column before Wittstock, hence on April 25, and hid in the vicinity of Blumenthal in Dannenwalde. The Russians arrived there on May 2.

THE "AWFUL WEEKS AT WÖBBELIN." On April 30, before moving in the direction of Schwerin, the American forces that had just crossed the Elbe liberated the Wöbbelin camp. This is the camp mentioned in chapter 19, a satellite of Neuengamme, where the convoy of prisoners from Helmstedt went after making a detour through Altmark. It arrived on about April 12. Two weeks then went by before the arrival of the Americans. David Rousset,[12] who was in that convoy, talked about the "awful weeks in Wöbbelin" in his book *L'Univers concentrationnaire:*

"The last weeks in Wöbbelin were rather blurred. Several transports found themselves gathered together in this encampment, and the men did not know each other well. A distance of about two hundred and eighteen yards separated the kitchens from the Revier, and a dozen armed men were needed to protect the soup cans that were brought to the sick. Every day, violent acts were committed on the wasteland surrounding the barracks. As soon as the distribution was completed, groups of about ten prisoners got together and attacked the weakest ones, isolating them in order to steal their food. There were three cases of cannibalism and the morgue had to be put under guard.

"There was not a drop of medicine; men were dying by the line. Soon, it became difficult to transport them. The stench of the mass graves was horrible. There were scenes of madness every night in the Schonung Block, a branch of the Revier, where the weak and the dying were crowded in together, and a few others lay low to avoid drudgery. Every night people were killed and the screams went on until dawn. From time to time, the Kapos would intervene, striking the prisoners with their clubs."

Wieslaw Kielar,[13] in *Anus mundi,* talks about the camp at length in identical terms. It suffices to quote a single paragraph: "There were countless corpses. In one barrack, the skeletons were piled up to the ceiling, and the rats had the run of the building. The authorities had absolutely no interest in what was going on in the camp. They left us to ourselves, and were content to keep watch over the walls to be sure we did not escape. [. . .] It only took us a few days to turn into 'Muselmänner' who were indistinguishable from the rest of the inhabitants of the camp."

The camp remained under surveillance until the last moment. The SS and the German *Kapos* departed shortly before American tanks came up along the fences. Kielar even says: "The sentry in the nearest watchtower came rushing down, abandoning his weapons and running as fast as he could into a thicket nearby." The fighting continued in the neighboring forest, but the army had already taken control of Ludwigslust to the south.

"The prisoners stormed the wagons loaded with food parked on a siding. They came back with their arms filled with bread, sugar, flour and tinned food." Kielar and his comrades went off on foot toward Ludwigslust.

The Evacuation of Ravensbrück

THE STAY OF DORA PRISONERS AT RAVENSBRÜCK. The third of the Altmark convoys that crossed the Elbe finally arrived in Ravensbrück, where the largest women's concentration camp of the Reich was located. The first prisoners arrived there in May 1939. The camp was situated north of Brandenburg a few miles from Mecklenburg, directly east of the small town of Fürstenberg. Hohenlychen was located seven miles farther east.

The same variety of origins and nationalities existing in the large men's camps was also found at Ravensbrück. There were many French prisoners, virtually all of whom were liberated in April 1945, even before the evacuation. The first ones, 299 in all, were taken out on April 3 by Swiss Red Cross trucks. The others were liberated on April 23 by the Swedish Red Cross following the negotiations between Bernadotte and Himmler and transferred to Sweden. Marie-Claude Vaillant-Couturier remained voluntarily at the camp, and she was still there when the Russians arrived.

When the Dora prisoners arrived on April 14 by the convoy that had come from Goslar via Magdeburg, Wittenberge, and Oranienburg, they were not sent to the main camp but rather to the *Jugendlager*, a satellite camp that had served as a sort of "little camp" for aged and invalid prisoners who were ultimately eliminated. Contrary to a widely held opinion, there was no correlation between their arrival and the liberation of the French women prisoners by the Swedish Red Cross, which took place later.

There was no communication between the two camps from April 14 to 26, the date on which the evacuation of the *Jugendlager* began. The Dora prisoners did not see the liberation of the French women prisoners nor did they know they were close neighbors of Keitel and Himmler.

Of the prisoners in the three Altmark convoys who arrived at Wöbbelin, Ravensbrück, and Oranienburg, those from Dora were better off than the others. They were alone in their new camp, and most of them had already cohabited for more than a year under generally peaceful terms, which reduced friction between them.

Furthermore, their existence was well known to the Red Cross. Benès[14] and Litomisky[15] noted the presence of six white IRC trucks on the site the day they arrived. They brought packages, which were distributed for the first time on the third day. Benès explains: "It was the first package of its kind I received. The contents were fantastic. There was even some chocolate, raisins, tinned meat, margarine, powdered milk and, imagine this, real (instant) coffee." Several accounts mention insomnia caused by the coffee. The packages also contained soap, toilet paper, and cigarettes. The packages were individual American army rations.

The Red Cross also brought medicine, which was used in the improvised *Revier.* The author, who arrived with erysipelas, swallowed something (no doubt sulfa drugs) and was back on his feet in a few days. He was able to join those among his comrades who went every day to dig antitank ditches in the surrounding sand with a total lack of enthusiasm and efficiency.

As has already been explained, the evacuation from Dora had been a terrible ordeal due to the long forced march through the Harz and the absence of any food distribution after the departure, in other words, between April 5 and 14. The rations distributed upon departure were supposed to last three days. The oldest prisoners appear to have suffered the most. Some died, including Reverend Heuzé, who was a forty-seven-year old "21,000."

THE EVACUATION FROM RAVENSBRÜCK TO MALCHOW AND PARCHIM. The evacuation of Dora had been triggered by the approach of the American forces, who were presumed to be in Kassel some fifty-six miles away. It ended at Ravensbrück, which was located about forty-seven miles from Schwedt on the left bank of the Oder River with Soviet troops already opposite them on the right bank.

After Zhukov and Koniev, it was Rokossovsky's turn to cross the Oder, which he did on April 18. First he had to take Stettin, which fell on April 26. From then on he was free to move through western Pomerania, northern Brandenburg, and Mecklenburg. There was nothing left for the Germans to do but evacuate Hohenlychen, Ravensbrück, and Fürstenberg.

The first phase of the evacuation, which began on April 26, took the columns from Ravensbrück to Malchow, where a second camp was set up. The sick prisoners stayed at the camp; they will be discussed later. Some prisoners who were still weak, such as Jean-Paul Renard, Raymond de Miribel, and Richard Pouzet, were transported directly to Malchow by four gas-generator trucks.

The others set out on foot in columns of a hundred men. The SS escorting them were no longer the same as those who had been on guard between Dora and Ravensbrück. The latter had presumably gone off at last to fight the war. Those who replaced them were rather older men, "reservists." They seemed peaceful but no one trusted them, for they were armed and wearing SS uniforms. While they proved to be harmless, no one could have foreseen that. At the time of departure each prisoner was given a Red Cross package, but there were none left for the last ones leaving. The SS must have helped themselves beforehand.

The itinerary noted by Woussen was as follows: Steinförde-Menow-Strasen-Wustrow on April 26, with an encampment in a small wood for the night; Wesenberg-Zirtow-Mirow on April 27; Lärz-Vipperow-Röbel on April 28, and again a small wood (after Lärz, the column was in the vicinity of Rechlin, where the airfield used by Speer was located); Sietow-Roez-Malchow on April 29. Ribault's column went farther north but also arrived in Malchow.

The author remembers two anecdotes. After the first night in the woods the SS wanted to form their columns of a hundred men again, but one of the prisoners had gone to join a friend in another column. The first SS counted his flock, once, twice, and found only 99. Stück said that there had been an escape and gave the signal to depart. The second SS counted his flock and found 101 several times, ended by shrugging his shoulders, and also gave the signal to depart, without comment. Later there was a pause in the center of the village. Prisoners exchanged a part of their packages, soap for potatoes, with some peasants. An SS came up and set some sort of exchange rate, to be sure "his" prisoners were not cheated.

The only concern of these old SS was to go west as quickly as possible and be taken prisoner by the American forces and not by the Soviets. They could lose a few prisoners en route without worrying about it. The main thing was that enough of them remain to justify their employment. The adventures of those who "escaped" before Malchow will be discussed later.

At the camp in Malchow a number of prisoners gave up trying to go any farther. One of them was Woussen. Again there were sick prisoners in need of care, and their fate also will be discussed later. The others set out again, going around Lake Plau. The columns had become totally slack, and a great many prisoners scattered in the countryside east of Parchim, hiding in small groups, since any armed detachment could still be dangerous even if they were not SS. There are a number of firsthand accounts in French. The interpreter Georges Schmidt[16] was in the company of Johnny.

In Lübz between Plau and Parchim, prisoners[17] who were there saw an American vanguard arrive on May 2 at 8:30 P.M. The next morning the American forces had withdrawn. The Russians arrived next, slightly delayed by rearguard fighting with German soldiers who were protecting the withdrawal of the mass of their comrades. The Russians finally joined up with the Americans, who had been in control of Parchim for some time.

The prisoners scattered in the vicinity were free. They mention Lübz, Parchim, Spornitz, and Stolpe as the places of their liberation. Most of them quickly went to the zone controlled by the American forces[18] at various points: Neustadt-Glewe, Ludwigslust, and Grabow. Ribault[19] has provided the chronology of a repatriation: by truck on May 6, Ludwigslust-Jessenitz (Americans);

May 11, Jessenitz-Celle (British camp); May 13, Celle-Sulingen; May 15 and 16, Sulingen-Rheine-Bocholt-Kevelaer; by train on May 17, Kevelaer-Brussels-Lille.

The Great Crossroads of Schwerin

In early May 1945 the American troops formed a sort of barrier between the Elbe and the Baltic in the western part of Mecklenburg around the capital city, Schwerin, where many columns converged. They had hardly finished liberating the prisoners at Wöbbelin when they found themselves on May 2 faced with the long column of prisoners from Sachsenhausen, which stretched along the road from Pinnow to Crivitz and Parchim and had just lost its guards. It was sixteen miles from Wöbbelin to Parchim.

Immediately to the east of Parchim, all around Lübz, the prisoners from Ravensbrück had just arrived. The Soviet troops were on their heels. The junction between the Americans and the Soviets was made during the day on May 3, and the war was over in that part of Germany.

The accounts of the prisoners from Wöbbelin, Sachsenhausen, and Ravensbrück mention that they met up with columns of women prisoners, but there is no consistent view of their movements. There are no accounts by French women deportees at Ravensbrück on this subject because they were transferred separately to Sweden.

That was when Milan Filipcic, one of the Slovenes in the Ko Scherer, met his sister, who unbeknownst to him had been deported to Ravensbrück. He himself had been arrested in the part of Slovenia annexed by Italy in 1941 and then occupied by the Germans in 1943. His elder sister, Zmagoslava Filipcic, had remained in Maribor (Marburg in German) in 1941, in the part annexed by the Reich. She was arrested there in April 1944 under the germanized name of Victoria Filiptschitsch and arrived at Ravensbrück in July.

Filipcic recalls:[20] "Towards evening, we arrived in Malchow. There was a small camp there with a few barracks. We went inside and fell on the ground, half-dead with fatigue. During the night we were awakened by the arrival of other prisoners. It was a transport of women. In the morning, in the general confusion, I spotted a young girl with a red triangle and the initial 'J.' I recognized her, for we had gone to the same school for a while. I called to her by her name and told her mine. She told me that my sister was there and went to fetch her. We had not seen each other for four years. We embraced on the camp road. A woman SS guard came running up to hit my sister. People cried out that we were brother and sister and she did not insist."

Filipcic's column and that of his sister then set out going west, not far from each other, and were liberated by American tanks. The Russians arrived next.

They were cavalrymen with accordions. Filipcic concludes: "For the first time in a long while, we danced."

A very special case was that of Margarete Buber-Neumann.[21] A German communist activist who had emigrated to the USSR, she was interned in a gulag and her companion, Heinz Neumann, was a victim of the 1937 purges. She was handed over to the Gestapo by the Soviets at Brest-Litovsk in 1940 and was a prisoner at Ravensbrück until 1945. She was part of a group of some sixty Czech and German women, all "veterans" of the camp, who were suddenly liberated on April 21 "with a certificate stating that we had been freed, but that we were to go and present ourselves within three days to our local Gestapo office." They left the camp in rows, walking toward Fürstenberg. "We didn't have any money or any ration tickets, and all we had to sustain ourselves were a few slices of bread."

She found a refugee train in Fürstenberg that went right past all the stations until Güstrow. People from the Volkssturm gave her money and tinned food. After many a fright, she ended up with the Americans in Bad Kleinen (to the north on the edge of Lake Schwerin). Given her past, she did not wish to be "liberated" by the Russians. She finally went home to her family in Franconia by bicycle.

Concentration camp prisoners, both men and women, accounted for only a small portion of the mass of people moving westward. Most of them were from what was left of the "Vistula" group of German armies, who were trying to avoid captivity in the Soviet Union. There are two accounts on this subject, one by the Czech prisoner Jiri Benès and one by the Pole Wieslaw Kielar.

Benès[22] had just arrived in Parchim: "Everywhere along the roads lay thousands, tens of thousands of weapons, silent guns frozen in their last firing position. On all sides, heaps of shells. On the way out of the village, the first German suicides. [. . .] And the roads were overrun with a crowd of frantic, terror-stricken people staggering westward. In the villages, hundreds of soldiers. A few of them shattered their weapons against boundary stones and telephone poles."

Kielar[23] was already farther west, in Ludwigslust: "We were in danger of being separated from each other in the crowd of Germans who were coming to give themselves up. We were fascinated by the sight of them. They were standing in rows on either side of the street, in which American soldiers were patrolling, and from time to time, shouting incomprehensible orders. On a wide avenue harshly lit up by floodlights arrived an uninterrupted flow of vehicles of all kinds, gigantic tanks, armored cars, guns of every caliber hitched to each other. Soldiers from all the armed forces were hanging onto these vehicles in bunches. The earth shook and the windowpanes of the abandoned houses vibrated as these monstrous vehicles rolled by."

Among the soldiers in German uniform who arrived in the region of

Schwerin were French SS.[24] They were the remains of the "Charlemagne Division," which had joined the fighting in Pomerania in February and March 1945 and suffered considerable losses. Those who were able to get away (about 1,100 men) regrouped on March 24 in Mecklenburg east of Neustrelitz. Their headquarters was in Carpin, twelve miles north of Ravensbrück. At the time their head count broke down into 400 workers and 700 combatants. Three hundred and fifty of the combatants went to Berlin on April 24 and were among the last defenders of the Reich Chancellery. The 350 other combatants and 400 workers were evacuated westward on foot along the Malchin-Teterow-Güstrow route. They surrendered to the British. The Dora prisoners who had escaped from their columns met up with isolated French SS moving southward under circumstances that will be described later.

There was also the pathetic exodus of civilians of all ages, reminiscent of other earlier ones in other places. Some had come from great distances with their carts from Pomerania or even East Prussia.

The "Escapees" of Mecklenburg

THE ESCAPES OF JOUANIN, BRETON, AND SCHREVE. During the first days of the evacuation of Ravensbrück, various escapes took place. All of them have not been the subject matter of a detailed account, but there are six which have been recounted in French. In short, this section will discuss the escapes of Baillon, Boisot, Breton, Jouanin, Schreve, and Thiercelin, with the understanding that each of these prisoners had, of course, excellent companions during their adventures, except for Jouanin who acted alone.

There is no connection among these escapes, which took place under different circumstances and ultimately took varied routes. They are presented in no particular order, except that Baillon's escape is described last, since the participants made the longest journey and were the last to return.

Jouanin's firsthand account[25] is short: "In Wesenberg, after the second night in the forest, taking advantage of the chaos when everyone got up, I remained hidden in a thicket of juniper bushes, which are really prickly! The column set off again, with the last ones walking close to my hiding place, and I didn't flinch. Quickly, keeping close to the ground, I took refuge in a changing cabin near the pond. On 30 April, I was liberated by the Red Army. I was given food and ordered to stay behind the line of fire." He returned to France on June 5.

Breton's escape[26] actually involved four comrades who had been together for more than a year: Pierre Breton, Maurice Clergue, Michel Deleval, and Louis Garnier. On the evening of April 29, with the column increasingly stretched out, they dropped out without attracting any attention and disappeared into the forest. Mecklenburg is a very wooded area. They slept and then wanted to make a fire. "All of a sudden," Garnier recalls, "we heard someone yelling behind us. It was an SS man who was limping, the little bastard. He must have had to let go of his unit because he couldn't keep up, but he was still trying to be useful."

The SS man pushed the four friends along in single file to a clearing where there was a Luftwaffe captain with several soldiers. There he took his automatic pistol and shot a single bullet (no one knows why), which wounded Garnier in the shoulder. The captain questioned them and then let them go. They were put in a barn and told to wait. There was a brief skirmish outside. The Russians arrived and sent them to the rear. That was on April 30, not far from Fürstenberg. They set off again toward Ravensbrück and were free in the country for a week. Then they were taken to a reassembly camp.

That was when Garnier had to be hospitalized in two consecutive hospitals, due rather to dysentery than to his gunshot wound, which was rather superficial. The second hospital was in Neuruppin, where Soviet noncommissioned officers and soldiers, a group of French prisoners of war, a Belgian deportee, and a few others had gathered. "It was quite an environment," Garnier recalls. One day the Frenchmen were transferred to Berlin. They were repatriated by airplane on June 21, 1945.

Schreve's escape[27] took place between Lärz and Vipperow, hence on the 28th, according to Woussen's chronology. There were several Dutchmen and the Frenchman Pierre Rozan. As in Breton's escape, it involved fleeing into the forest, "taking advantage of a turn in the road." The escapees heard a group of French SS go by. In Vietzen they went to a castle where they found "a well-dressed lady, with gray hair framing an aristocratic face with gorgeous blue-green eyes," a young blond girl, and two old servants. They were received very well and slept at the castle.

Dressed in civilian clothes, they mixed in with the refugees. They were in a barn in Rödel when the Russians arrived. From then on they went in the direction of Wittenberge via Stepenitz and Putlitz. All the bridges on the Elbe were down. Downstream in the vicinity of Schnakenburg they had trouble reaching the Americans on the other bank. Schreve, who spoke several languages, was authorized to cross over, after extensive negotiations, and came back with a "paper" allowing him to continue on his way with his companions.

THE ESCAPES OF BOISOT AND THIERCELIN. Boisot's escape[28] involved three closely knit comrades from the Ko Scherer: Guy Boisot, Francis Finelli, and André Fortané. José, another French prisoner, went with them; they never heard from him again after 1945. On April 27 they dropped out of their column, which had stretched out very far and set off across the fields. They found civilian clothes and food in abandoned houses. When they arrived in Mirow on April 30 they moved into the cellar of a house under construction. The Russians arrived on May 1 and threw grenades into the cellar. They came out alive.

From Mirow they went toward Wittenberge after "requisitioning" a carriage pulled by two horses. Fortané, who was a farmer at the time, took the reins. They made a French flag. "When we crossed a Russian cavalry detachment, the soldiers decided our horses were more beautiful than theirs, and without any further discussion, they proceeded to exchange animals."

They arrived in Wittenberge by the main road through Wittstock, Pritzwalk, and Perleberg, but the bridge was no longer standing and they had to take an American patrol boat to cross the Elbe. "To get to the patrol boat, you needed a Russian exit ticket. To get that ticket, you had to state your identity and the purpose of your trip." Finelli and Fortané, pretending to be polyglots, managed to have themselves taken on as *Schreiber* by the Russians, who were completely unable to cope and took a dinghy to reach the patrol boat "taking advantage of the change in the shift of the Russian functionaries."

Thiercelin[29] gave a remarkable account of his escape, which he started writing "on 9 or 10 May" during the period between the Liberation and repatriation. Unfortunately, it can only be summarized here. "On 29 April, taking advantage of a hesitation caused by a military convoy, I made my way to a haystack and hid inside, covering myself with a few bales. A little later, I sensed other movements in the haystack and a dialogue began among the escapees who did not know each other. It turned out there were six of us: Gabriel Lacoste, Henri Calès, Robert Thiercelin, Bernard Aubin, Marcel Minguet and a young man with whom we lost touch afterward." At the time they must have been near Malchow in Penkow.

The next morning Thiercelin discreetly called out to a French prisoner of war who was pushing a wheelbarrow nearby. He went to get work shifts from his Kommando, which was set up on a large farm. In their new guise the six companions went to the farm, where they ate and slept.

On the evening of May 1 the prisoners of war set off on foot to Lübeck. The six escapees started out accompanying them, but they did not have the strength to keep up. The next day they went toward Goldberg, beyond Karow, and then turned toward Lübz. They discovered two large Kommandos of prisoners, one French and the other Italian, on a big state farm. At that point the Russians arrived. They remained there from May 3 to 5.

The Russians looted shops and brought them food supplies. "Two sacks of sugar and cases of flour that, I seem to remember, was or merely looked like cornstarch. Following the advice of our doctor comrades when we left Ravensbrück, concerning how to readapt to food, the farm milk, sugar and cornstarch provided the makings for excellent dishes and a way to recover our strength during those few days."

Then, they decided it was time to leave. "We requisitioned a four-wheel wagon at the farm and mounted a wooden chassis which we covered with a big rug from the castle for shelter. A large flag on a wooden pole attached to the frame floated above the team of horses. Henri Calès, who said he had learned something about teams of horses in the artillery division, would be the coach-man. We loaded food onto the wagon and a sizable reserve of potatoes." They went to Parchim and were then allowed to go over to the American side on May 7. On May 8 they had to abandon their wagon and horses and get into American trucks. They were brought to a reassembly center and repatriated to France in stages.

The most important part of the entire account of this route was Thiercelin's finding of a saxophone. Abandoned on the road by a prisoner in very poor con-dition, Thiercelin had recovered it. Thus he was able to salute a passing German detachment by playing "Vieux Camarade," accompany the raising of the French and Italian flags for the two Kommandos at the farm, begin a recital for Soviet officers, and accompany the wagon with military music.

BAILLON'S ESCAPE. Baillon's escape[30] was barely an escape. It was rather the observation by a group of some ten prisoners that their column had become extremely slack and that they were no longer being guarded. No SS were in sight when they entered a village, and so they walked straight on and entered a cemetery instead of following the road, which turned off to the right. As they were discussing what to do they were overheard by prisoners of war, who went and got them civilian clothes in the abandoned houses in the neighborhood. The author was in this group, with René Souquet, his companion in the Ko Scherer, and Marcel Baillon, with whom he had been active politically in Amiens before the war. He did not know the others. A careful (and very recent) study of a de-tailed map has allowed him to situate the escape at Zirtow on April 27.

Disguised as Mecklenburg residents more or less in their Sunday best, the ten prisoners blended into the flow of refugees who were moving westward. As in any exodus, there was a mass of civilians on foot or in wagons and isolated soldiers who had become separated from their units. One of them was an SS wearing a "France" badge. Hearing French being spoken, he started up a con-versation with the author and explained how he had managed to get out of the "Kolberg pocket." From an historical point of view the conversation with this young man, who seemed personally rather sympathetic, would have been inter-esting, but they were not really in equal positions at the time, and the author broke off the surprising conversation after walking a mile at a good pace to wait for his companion, who had not taken any notice.

The group, still mixed in with civilians and prisoners of war (and others) of all nationalities, went past Mirow, Röbel, Malchow, and Karow and that night went to sleep in the loft of a barn, away from the road. They had a noisy awak-ening: on one side they could see Russian tanks shooting over the barn onto a German rearguard on the other side, which they watched as it finally picked up and left. They made contact with their liberators and were invited to a quick lunch at headquarters. The Russians went off to fight again but not for long, as it was by then May 2. The group did not know this and had to decide on a course of action. There were French prisoners of war throughout the region, from satellite Kommandos of a *Stalag* located in Neubrandenburg in eastern Mecklenburg. Their instructions were to go to the *Stalag*. The group of escapees decided to follow their example, in short stages.

Food supplies were not a problem, for abandoned houses were everywhere. The author, who did not have a big appetite, did not overeat. He found an eleven-pound bag of granulated sugar and ate it, bit by bit, with a small spoon. By the time they arrived in Neubrandenburg everyone was apparently in acceptable health. Their reception at the *Stalag* began with an inspection of their underarms, as the SS bore tattoos on that part of the body. Survivors of the Charlemagne Division were trying to get back to France without being recognized. Repatriation began shortly thereafter, and the oldest prisoner of the *Stalag* gave priority to the deportees, of whom there were few.

The firsthand accounts of French deportees often include their encounters with groups of prisoners of war. Sometimes they contain grievances that are vehemently expressed. Most of their judgments, however, are very favorable. The French prisoners (and their Belgian, Dutch, and Italian comrades) played an important role in 1945 in rural areas. This was especially obvious in regions that had large farms such as Mecklenburg. The "escapees" in this region owed them a great deal. That was true of Antoine Cirieco,[31] an Ellrich prisoner who had gone through Oranienburg and left the evacuation column with a comrade near Parchim. They were quickly camouflaged as French prisoners of war.

British trucks arrived from Schwerin carrying Soviets of every status, prisoners of war, former prisoners, and *Ostarbeiter* as well as Poles and citizens of other Eastern European countries. They went off with citizens of Western European countries. In Neubrandenburg these were mainly Frenchmen. It was apparent that the repatriation of Westerners to the west was in some way conditioned by the return of all Soviets to the east, some of whom had no desire to go.

It should be noted that British replaced American forces in Schwerin at the end of May 1945, before the transfer of the western part of Mecklenburg to Soviet control. From Schwerin the escapees were transported to Lüneburg, where they were sprayed with DDT and housed, and then sent to Sulingen. From there a train took them to Kevelaer, and the author made the following comments:

"The weather is sunny, it is Sunday, and the people are dressed up to go to Mass. The people of the area, Germans, in a lovely little town, intact. I'm here, like a simpleton, disguised as a Mecklenburg native over my striped uniform, with a rucksack containing a few books found here and there. I feel out of place. I come from another country, a country of madmen, governed by insane rules. It's true, I have escaped. Now, I am going to escape from any constraints. No one is going to dispose of me at will anymore."

The author was not quite right about what he wrote. He was minimizing the importance of the few weeks of wandering he had experienced between Zirtow and Neubrandenburg, without papers or money. Well, not exactly. In a piece of corrugated cardboard folded in half, he did have a few letters received at Dora with his name and identity number, including those from his father posted at Buchenwald and Wertmarke testifying to his enthusiasm as a *Vertikant* controller. This period of "truce," during which the prisoner was no longer a prisoner but not yet a civilian with family and professional responsibilities, was spent in different ways: Wexler spent it playing the role of burgermeister of Biere, Rogerie spent it making crepes in Stassfurt, and Dutillieux[32] spent three weeks in Schwerin doing nothing, for he had just walked nearly 375 miles. Fifty years later, whenever anecdotes come to mind, the first to be told are the ones about the Guy-Francis-André trio in the carriage and Thiercelin's saxophone.

THE LATE RETURN OF THE LAST SURVIVORS. As has been explained in the previous chapters, due to the vagaries of the evacuations, sick prisoners were more or less abandoned at Dora, Seesen, Bergen-Belsen, Sulingen, Beendorf, and Halberstadt. Doctors and other devoted comrades took care of them with the limited means available prior to the intervention of American or British military, who could not cope themselves when the problems reached the scale of Bergen-Belsen. Similar situations arose between the Elbe and the Oder Rivers, in Sachsenhausen, Schwerin, Malchow, and Ravensbrück.

THE LAST PRISONERS IN ORANIENBURG. When the Sachsenhausen camp was evacuated on Saturday, April 21 in the morning, there were still fifteen hundred patients in the *Revier,* including sick prisoners transferred by truck from the Heinkel Kommando. Six prisoner doctors stayed with them: two Frenchmen, Émile-Louis Coudert and Marcel Leboucher; two Belgians, Delaunnois and Jean Sommerhausen; and two Dutchmen, Justus Koch and Franz Bischoff. There had been some discussion of blowing up the five blocks of the *Revier,* but it did not occur.

On April 22 at the end of the afternoon, Russian soldiers appeared, but fighting continued in the vicinity. Those who could went to Bernau, nineteen miles farther east. Others stopped in Basdorf. Oesch,[33] after wandering through bombing attacks, joined other Frenchmen in Wandlitz.

Raymond Wautrecht[34] has given a highly personal account of what happened at the time in the area: "The Russian officers who came to take stock of the situation advised those of us who were able to walk to leave the camp, get away from the combat zone and take shelter on the other side of the Oder. Helped by other prisoners who were a little more able-bodied than I, I left the camp. [. . .] We walked through a forest on a road littered with the debris of military equipment, along with the bodies of German soldiers and horses that had been killed. I confess I felt more pity for the poor animals than for the Germans who had made us suffer so much.

"At the end of the day, we occupied a farm where a French comrade prepared our first meal as free men. A patrol of Russian soldiers brought us a bottle of vodka to celebrate our liberation. Unfortunately, the next day, we found one of our companions who had not been able to handle the feast, and had died during the night. That forced us to be more cautious. I stayed with the group for a few days, and once I had recovered some strength, I decided to go back in the direction of the camp, which I avoided like the plague, and reached the city of Oranienburg, largely empty of its inhabitants.

"As I wandered around the city, I had the pleasure of meeting up with Belgian and French prisoners of war who had left their Stalag with a cavalry horse hitched to a wagon loaded with packages intended for the prisoners but which proved to be impossible to distribute. Together, we settled in an unoccupied apartment building not far from a hospital where I could be treated for my dysentery. There, we began the wait for repatriation. Our group was composed of two French POWs, two Belgian POWs, an American political prisoner and myself. I spent my time walking the horse in the surrounding meadows; we became good friends. From time to time, I would go to the camp for news. I found comrades there who hoped that by staying in the Revier, they would be repatriated sooner. Two thirds of the sick prisoners were there, and the mortality rate was still high."

Only after two months, on June 24 and 25, did French airplanes transfer the 113 French survivors from Tempelhof to Le Bourget. Those from Bernau and Wandlitz left by truck in early June for the American zone in Dessau. As for Wautrecht, who was evicted along with his comrades from the apartment building and forbidden to remain in the town by order of the burgermeister of Oranienburg, he went through Leipzig to be repatriated. He arrived in Liège on July 5, and an ambulance took him home to his parents in Houdeng-Goegnies.

Some of the sick prisoners arrived in Oranienburg from Ellrich on April 16. One of them was Étienne Lafond.[35] First he was assigned to an ordinary block. "I had illusions about my strength. In the company of my comrades, I washed myself from head to toe and shaved. What a relief to become civilized again." The next day, however, he had to go to the *Revier,* where he was admitted.

"For the first time in many long months, I looked at myself in a mirror. My hair, which had started growing back, lay shaggy on my emaciated skull. My face was nothing but two sockets, a stretched nose and cheekbones sticking out. As for my body, it had been reduced to the state of a skeleton. I had lived off my buttocks, the way a camel lives off its hump."

After the Russians arrived, Lafond stayed for eight days with a few comrades in the abandoned Oranienburg camp. On April 30 a Polish ambulance drove him to Sachsenhausen. He was saved. Starting on May 5 he noted the improvements in his condition along with various comments about those around him, such as this one on May 14: "Two beds away from me, there is a Pole who has gone mad and will not take off his bowler hat or let go of his umbrella, which he guards jealously day and night."

On May 18 he observed, "Since yesterday, a very clear improvement in the food" and "I am fattening up by the minute." On May 22, "I am starting to devour books." Then the food declined. On June 3, "For the first time, I got up and went to take some air and sunshine on a garden bench." He left on June 24. He wrote an account of his deportation in May and June before being repatriated, which was published under the title *Survie.*

Yves Delogne, the brother of Xavier, finally died there on July 12, 1945.

THE LAST PRISONERS IN SCHWERIN, MALCHOW, AND RAVENSBRÜCK. After the long evacuation march from Sachsenhausen, "most of the survivors stopped in Schwerin,[36] which began to look like an unsavory area." They were housed in the arsenal, in town, or in the Adolf Hitler barracks on the outskirts. After many difficulties, repatriation began in the middle of May. It was carried out by train as far as Hagenow, then either directly by plane or by trucks to Lüneburg and Sulingen. From Sulingen there were trains. The last Frenchmen and Spanish Republicans went back by French planes from Lüneburg to Le Bourget on June 10.

A medical team was working in the barracks in Schwerin with Dr. Ségelle, who had been in the evacuation first from Ellrich to Oranienburg and then from Sachsenhausen to Schwerin. Grand and Besançon were with him.

At the camp in Malchow on April 30 were prisoners who had arrived the night before on foot. They had made the journey from Ravensbrück in several stages and did not have the strength to go back on the road with their comrades. There were also sick prisoners who had been transported by truck from Ravensbrück. There was also a women's camp, which refused to be dragged into an evacuation.

Finally the SS vanished and the Russians arrived. There was widespread disorder. The Polish took over the *Revier,* and the French-speaking prisoners set up their own separate organization in the SS infirmary, three hundred yards from the camp. Three French prisoners, Jean Cormont,[37] André Cardon, and Roland Filiatre, took charge of this little camp, with two woman prisoners, Lucie Brembéche and Mélanie Gaude. They were helped by Father Aubrun, chaplain of the POWs. After three weeks they succeeded in convincing the American authorities to come and get the Western prisoners from Malchow and bring them to Schwerin. They were repatriated along with the others. Cardon remained in Schwerin with the assignment to see the repatriation through to completion.

Richard Pouzet[38] was among the ill who were transported by truck from Ravensbrück to Malchow. He had a serious attack on May 1. He said: "I nearly gave up the fight." Then he regained consciousness: "After those days of incoherence, raving, delirium and evanescence, I recovered my lucidity, all my lucidity, total lucidity.

"What my eyes could not perceive for lack of light and a mirror, my hands revealed to me as they moved across my face. I had the 'mask.' The mask of death was on my face. One by one, I felt its marks: rigid, prominent jaws, angular cheekbones, wrinkled skin, ears sticking out, contorted features, sunken mouth, swollen lips." He remained for hours struggling in this fashion. He heard the SS leave and felt he was saved. His young friend from Touraine died near him. He did not know his name.

Jean Doucet,[39] a medical student and nurse at Buchenwald, then at Dora, was in Ravensbrück at the time of the camp evacuation. Two hundred sick prisoners could not be moved. He remained with them in the company of Dr. Ximenes and waited for the arrival of the Russian tanks.

Two months went by before the surviving Western prisoners were transferred by truck to Lübeck in the British zone. From there an airplane took them directly to Le Bourget on June 27, 1945. He was the last of the Frenchmen who have given firsthand accounts in this book to be repatriated from Germany.

[[22   ]]

THE DORA-MITTELBAU TOLL

The Death Toll

Chapter 6 presented an estimate of the loss of human lives in the Dora camp from its inception at the end of August 1943 to the end of March 1944. It is possible to estimate the overall death toll at the end of May 1945, just over a year later. The estimate must take into account not only the Dora camp as such but also the satellite camps and Kommandos added on to the Dora camp. It also must take into account the sizable loss of human life during the evacuations of April–May 1945.

There are a number of problems involved in establishing such an assessment, as will be seen, and they must be overcome one by one. The author has taken for his guides the Polish prisoner Wincenty Hein[1] and the German historian Joachim Neander.[2] The first played a leading role in the pretrial investigation of 1947, which will be discussed in chapter 23, by studying the various incomplete documents abandoned by the SS. The second has attempted in his recent thesis to measure the consequences of the evacuations in particular while taking the necessary precautions. To understand what happened it is best to proceed in chronological order.

THE DEATH TOLL AT DORA UNTIL MARCH 1944. Between August 1943 and March 1944 the Dora "camp" barely existed. Most of the prisoners, whether working inside the tunnel or digging out exterior access routes, were still housed in the tunnel itself. There were not yet any satellite camps. The mortality rate was high but there was no crematorium on the site, and corpses were transported to Buchenwald to be incinerated. The camp had a dreadful reputation, for good reason.

During this period, as explained in chapter 6, there were 2,882 Dora prisoners incinerated at Buchenwald. Hein's statements, based on Dora documents, show 2,844 deaths. The difference is insignificant given the conditions prevailing at the time. What is important is the percentage of deaths compared to the average head count during the four months from December 1943 to March 1944. In February it was 4.5 percent and in December and March it was 6.5 percent.

These figures, however, do not remotely account for the true gravity of the situation at the time. Indeed, the two convoys of sick prisoners sent to Maïdanek at the beginning of January and in early February and the convoy that left for Bergen-Belsen at the end of March also must be taken into consideration. Each of these convoys had a thousand prisoners, and, as is well known, only a very small number of them survived. The others died either during the "transport" or more or less quickly after their arrival at the destination camp. Presumably most of them would have died at Dora had they remained there. The above-mentioned statistics on deaths at Dora are therefore greatly underestimated if they are viewed in terms of loss of human life during this initial period.

A chart by Neander covering the period from September 1943 to April 1944, taking into account the transports, gives a cumulative figure of 5,987 deaths for a head count of 17,382, which corresponds to 34.4 percent.

THE MISLEADING RESPITE OF THE SUMMER OF 1944. The number of deaths recorded at Dora suddenly dropped from 766 in March 1944 to 149 in April and stayed at a relatively low rate until September. The lowest level was reached in July with 105 deaths, or 0.87 percent of the head count. Various factors can explain this respite. It is undeniable that the figures for April, and even for May, are somewhat fallacious due to the transport of sick prisoners at the end of March. Yet it cannot be denied that improved living conditions at Dora later played a role. The improvement mainly involved transferring prisoners from their "dormitories" in the tunnel galleries to the new barracks in the camp, an event that coincided with the arrival of spring. Furthermore, the factory was completed, and the work of the "specialists" was less exhausting than the digging and loading done earlier.

A second factor was the arrival of "fresh troops" in January to fill the vacancies left by the deaths of members of the first convoys. Finally, the new work sites, whether the underground sites of the Sonderstab Kammler or the Helmetalbahn railway sites, were still in their initial phase. The sudden rise in the mortality rate was to manifest itself particularly among workers in these areas.

THE TURNING POINT IN THE AUTUMN OF 1944. According to Neander's calculations, the total population of Dora and of the satellite camps was some 16,700 prisoners at the end of May 1944. By October 28 it had reached nearly 31,000. The population of the Dora camp itself remained virtually stable, rising only from 12,400 to 13,800. The increase was due to the satellite camps, above all Ellrich and Harzungen as well as Blankenburg, Rottleberode, Kleinbodungen, and the various camps of the *Baubrigaden*.

The number of prisoners who were unfit to work, *arbeitsunfähig*, whether in the *Revier* or the *Schonung*, estimated at 1,670 at the end of May, had reached 4,040 by October 28. Instead of 10 percent of the total, they now represented 12.9 percent. This marked the beginning of a deterioration that would only accelerate until March 31, 1945, the eve of evacuations.

THE TERRIBLE WINTER OF 1944–45. From the end of 1944 onward it is extremely difficult to keep close tabs on the evolution of the population of the entire complex, which had taken the name of Mittelbau. The prisoners tended to be scattered, with higher head counts at Blankenburg, Rottleberode, Kleinbodungen, and particularly at the Boelcke Kaserne in the new camp of Nordhausen. On the other hand the population at Ellrich and Harzungen as well as in the *Baubrigaden* remained more or less stable. The population rose, however, at the Dora camp itself.

Throughout the winter months there was constant movement between the camps. The evacuations of Auschwitz in January and Gross Rosen in February brought to the Mittelbau complex, along with numerous corpses, a mass of prisoners in increasingly poor condition that had to be housed, especially at Dora. As the *Revier* was overcrowded, some of the ill were transferred to the new camp at Nordhausen, which originally housed only workers employed in the area.

When the figures for October 28, 1944, are compared to those of March 31, 1945, it may be observed that the total head count rose from 31,000 to 41,300, and at the same time the number of those unfit to work doubled from 4,040 to 8,470. The percentage of the unfit compared to the total head count thus reached 20.6 percent by March, compared to 12.9 percent in October. As was seen earlier in chapter 19, the situation was exactly the same when the Langenstein camp was evacuated.

The number of prisoners unfit to work at the end of March is all the more startling as two factors must be taken into consideration that actually reduced these figures: the high mortality rate of the final weeks and the departure of a "transport" of sick prisoners to Bergen-Belsen. According to the figures collected by Hein, the number of recorded deaths was 6,757 from October 1944 to March 1945, including 2,341 in February and 2,542 in March. The transport that left the Boelcke Kaserne on March 6 carried 2,252 sick prisoners, about half of whom had been transferred from Ellrich three days earlier.

Thus a population that was largely in extremely poor health was about to be quickly dragged into evacuation operations.

THE DEATH TOLL OF THE EVACUATIONS. Joachim Neander has taken the risk of estimating the loss of human life that occurred during the evacuation period. He has taken every precaution, without claiming to achieve any sort of fallacious exactitude. After carefully examining all the evacuation processes himself, the author considers that these estimates, reported below, are quite plausible.

In early April 1945 there were about 40,000 prisoners still in the Mittelbau complex, and overall their ultimate fate is not a mystery. Some 3,500 among them were not affected by the evacuation: the prisoners at the Boelcke Kaserne, which was bombed on April 3 and 4, and those left behind at the Dora *Revier.*

Between the patients, who were often gravely ill and died during this period, and those who were killed in the bombing raids, Neander has estimated the loss of human life at 2,500, which leaves a thousand survivors. The 36,500 other prisoners at Mittelbau, i.e., more than 90 percent of the total, were evacuated in three days, either by railway convoys or on foot in columns.

The majority of them, about 20,000, were involved in evacuation operations that ended up at Bergen-Belsen. Their losses have been estimated at 2,500. Some died in transit, particularly the sick prisoners from Harzungen. Others were victims of the terrible conditions at the Bergen-Belsen camp, particularly members of the convoy from Woffleben.

Neander does not include (for good reason) the 3,000 or so prisoners who reached the Gardelegen Kreis. He estimates that 2,000 of them died either in the barn or as victims of the manhunt that took place in the surrounding area, or from exhaustion in the case of sick prisoners from Rottleberode, Ellrich-Theater, or Wieda. The figure of 1,000 survivors is necessarily only a very rough approximation.

Another group concerned the convoys or columns, many of which found themselves at Sachsenhausen or Ravensbrück before setting off toward the Schwerin region. This group also concerns the Blankenburg prisoners. Three thousand prisoners are believed to have died out of a total of 11,500. This significant proportion can be explained by the high number of sick prisoners from Ellrich and Dora at the start of the evacuation. It also takes into account the length of the train journey and of the march as well as the deadly character of the Sachsenhausen evacuation.

Finally, Neander groups isolated evacuations together, particularly those that ended in Saxony and Sudetenland, with 1,000 victims out of a total of 2,500 prisoners.

A recapitulation shows a total of 8,500 deaths out of 36,500 evacuated prisoners. Taking into account the losses at Nordhausen and Dora, the head count of 40,000 prisoners at the beginning of April translates, a few weeks later, into 11,000 dead and 29,000 survivors. The 11,000 figure should be compared to the figure of 8,470 corresponding to the unfit as of March 31. A number of those who were unfit at the time fortunately survived, but for most of them a further ordeal was simply more than they could bear.

THE OVERALL DEATH TOLL OF DORA-MITTELBAU. Based on the figures just presented, an overall death toll can be quickly estimated. For the whole concentration camp complex, which finally reached about 40,000 prisoners, the loss of human life during a period of slightly more than twenty months amounted to some 26,500 victims—15,500 in the camp and the "transports" and 11,000 at the time of the evacuations.

THE CONDITIONS OF THE SURVIVORS' RETURN. The conditions for the survivors' return differed widely depending on their nationality. Roughly speaking, returning prisoners were grouped into six categories: the Germans and Austrians, the Western Europeans, the Czechs and Yugoslavs, the Poles, the Soviets, and the non-Western Jews.

German and Austrian prisoners returned home under the same conditions as their compatriots at the time. It was impossible to return to the territories beyond the Oder-Neisse line, *Kapos* and others wearing armbands who could be held accountable were in danger of arrest, those captured from the ranks of the Volkssturm had POW status, etc. The account by Margarete Buber-Neumann gives a good idea of the problems facing a woman prisoner from Ravensbrück returning to her family in Franconia after twelve years of exile and imprisonment.

Western Europeans returned home by various routes. Collective repatriation, which was more or less well organized, concerned those from Buchenwald, those at Bergen-Belsen, and those more or less scattered throughout the Schwerin region. National groups for repatriation comprised people of varying status (prisoners of war, civilian workers) in various regions, e.g., in the area of Seesen, south of Schönebeck, and in the Gardelegen area. Hospital transports, often by air, brought patients hospitalized at Dora, Bergen-Belsen, Sulingen, Halberstadt, and Schwerin back to their home countries.

The main problem was to ensure the return of those who had been liberated by the Soviet troops in Mecklenburg, Brandenburg, Saxony, and the Sudeten. Delays were due to transport problems as well as to the determination of the Soviet authorities to recover those among their citizens who had been liberated in western Germany.

The prisoners who had been evacuated by the Red Cross, women from Ravensbrück and men from Blankenburg, went home from Sweden. Jews deported from France, Belgium, and the Netherlands were repatriated along with non-Jews. The same was true for Spanish Republican refugees in France, who were prisoners in the large camps such as Mauthausen, Buchenwald, and Sachsenhausen.

The return of the Czechs and Slovenes was delayed by the fact that their countries had remained under German control until the moment of the German surrender or thereabouts. There were also political delays for those among them who had been liberated by the Soviets. For example, the Slovenes who were liberated in Mecklenburg went home in one of two ways. Either they tried their luck individually, like Emil Cucek, or, like Filipcic, they remained with their women compatriots, were grouped together in Neubrandenburg, and returned home to Maribor on August 28, 1945, by train via Berlin, Prague, Budapest, Belgrade, and Zagreb.

Little is known about the conditions under which the Poles returned to a territory that had become very different from the one that existed in 1939, both in the east and the west. Some of them, incidentally, did not wish to go home, for political reasons. That was also the case for a large number of Soviets who did not expect to be well received, and their fears were justified. The American and British authorities nevertheless automatically sent camp prisoners home at the same time as prisoners of war and *Ostarbeiter.* The only exceptions were made for Balts, Estonians, Latvians, and Lithuanians, for the annexation of their countries by the USSR was not recognized by the Western governments.

Jews who came from Western countries were repatriated according to their wishes. The others, particularly Polish Jews, generally did not wish to return to their countries. They remained in Germany in camps for "displaced persons," often for several years, before they were allowed to emigrate to Israel or the United States or to another Western country.[3]

Images of Dora

In the immediate postwar period there were three dominant images of Dora, which did not coincide.

THE FIRST IMAGE: THE HELL OF 1943–44. The first images came from the veterans of Buchenwald who still remembered, long afterward, their fear of being sent in a "transport" to the Dora Kommando. The idea of death was not foreign to the Buchenwald prisoners at the end of 1943, but in November, when the trucks began returning from Dora loaded with corpses to be incinerated at the crematorium, this fear gradually penetrated the entire camp. For the trucks kept coming until the end of March 1944, when Dora was equipped with its own incineration system.

Christian Pineau (under the name of Jacques Grimaux) arrived at Buchenwald on December 16, 1943, and received the identity number 38418. Luckily he managed to avoid a transport and later learned that it was a transport to Dora. When he published an account in 1960 of his years in the French Resistance and deportation under the title *La Simple Vérité,* he gave one chapter the title "Kommando for Dora," as if to exorcise his fear in retrospect.[4]

Jorge Semprun, in *Quel beau dimanche!* published in 1980, talks about a dreaded transport being organized at Buchenwald with its destination as Dora.[5] He writes: "A terrible camp, Dora! It was a work site where they were digging the tunnels of an underground factory for manufacturing V1s and V2s." He came back to this topic in 1994 in *L'Écriture ou la vie:*[6] "Dora was the work site of an underground factory where V1 and V2 missiles were going to be produced. It was a hellish work site, where the prisoners were driven like slaves to perform exhausting work, in the dust of the tunnels, by the Sturmführer SS themselves, without any other intermediaries between themselves and the deportees than the common-law prisoners who added an extra dose of stupidity and brutality to consolidate their power. In short, avoiding Dora meant avoiding death. Or avoiding, at least, increased chances of dying." Semprun believes that the fact of being classified at the time as a stucco layer saved him from a transport to Dora. His identity number was 44904, and he had arrived at Buchenwald on January 29, 1944. Paul Le Goupil, 53354, was part of the convoy of the "tattooed" who went through Auschwitz on their way to Buchenwald on May 14, 1944. At the time "there were numerous rumors about our destination. There was talk of Dora, a name that everyone whispered with horror. It was an underground factory where the mortality rate was appalling." That is what he wrote[7] in *Un Normand dans . . .* , published in 1991.

Thus fear of Dora continued unabated in the middle of May, even though the truckloads of corpses had stopped coming at the end of March. It would appear that the prisoners at Buchenwald did not know about the three "transports" of sick prisoners that left Dora for Lublin-Maïdanek and Bergen-Belsen, as Pineau, Semprun, and Le Goupil do not mention them.

One may wonder about the causes of this fear. There were no doubt three main ones. The first was the pace at which the deaths occurred, even though the prisoners had just come out of quarantine at Buchenwald and therefore were not yet weakened by a long stay in the camps. The second was the high number of victims, which in fact appeared lower than the reality, however, because they did not know about the transports of sick prisoners. The third was the way the corpses looked, completely emaciated.

THE SECOND IMAGE: THE MASS GRAVE AT NORDHAUSEN. The second image resulted from the grisly discoveries made one after another that took the American forces completely by surprise at the time of their offensive toward the Elbe in April 1945. The first of these discoveries, on April 5, was Ohrdruf, where a Buchenwald Kommando, the sinister S III, had been ordered to dig out an underground command post for Hitler.

A few days later, on April 11, the Americans arrived in Nordhausen and found the corpses of the Boelcke Kaserne. There the SS had gathered together the weakest prisoners from Dora and the neighboring camps. The site, south of the city, was bombed, and the bombs often fell on the dead or the dying. A few miles away, in the Dora camp itself, the inhabitants of which had been "evacuated," the Americans saw nothing but abandoned, gravely ill prisoners and again, emaciated corpses.

Still later, on April 14, they were told about a burned-out barn in Gardelegen containing the remains of the prisoners who had been shut inside and perished in the fire. They belonged to two evacuation convoys of exterior Kommandos of Dora.

On April 12, Eisenhower visited Ohrdruf with Patton and Bradley, and he decided to alert American officials and journalists to the discoveries made in the camps. Everyone still remembers the photographs taken at the time at Nordhausen, Dora, and Gardelegen, like those at Ohrdruf and the "little camp" at Buchenwald, because for fifty years they have consistently been used to illustrate books and articles on the German concentration camps. Yet the dates and places are generally not indicated. When the names are shown, Nordhausen is necessarily mentioned more often than Dora.

THE THIRD IMAGE: THE TUNNEL FACTORY. The third image, a forceful yet indistinct one, is that of the underground factory devoted to producing "secret weapons," the V2s and, secondarily, V1s. For years what is now commonly called the "Dora Tunnel" was more a figment of the imagination than an object of knowledge, as the extravagant film entitled *Operation Crossbow* demonstrated. The Americans found the factory in April 1945 practically intact. It remained a secret under their control. Once it passed into Soviet hands with the rest of Thuringia on July 1, it again remained secret. Then it ceased to exist physically in 1948. The Soviets dismantled and carried off everything that could be removed, and then blew it up with explosives to cause some of the galleries to collapse and completely obstruct the four entrances. There is nothing left but the memory of what once was, or so it was said, the largest underground factory in existence at the time.

For a time the mass of prisoners who were dragged unwillingly into this historical adventure were ignored. Only gradually did the writers of these more or less scientific works realize that Dora, once a mere Kommando under the authority of Buchenwald, had in fact become one of the most dreaded concentration camps in Nazi Germany. The prisoners and their sufferings were mentioned in the accounts but only incidentally, as they were merely supernumeraries, which, by the way, they have remained. How the camp actually operated was never dealt with either.

A FOURTH IMAGE: THE ANTIFASCIST STRUGGLE. East German propaganda strove to popularize a fourth image: that of a camp controlled by a group of communist activists and their associates who led the resistance and sabotage. Naturally things were not that simple, if only due to the fact that very few of the Germans there could truly be considered political prisoners. Here again in a sense, the camp was being viewed from outside.

DORA SEEN FROM FRANCE: THE CEMETERY OF FRENCHMEN. *Dora: le cimetière des Français* is the title of a small book recently published by André Rogerie. The importance of this camp for French deportees has been brought to the fore in several documents, including the following two examples.

Annette Wieviorka, in an appendix to *Déportation et Génocide* in which she discusses her sources,[8] analyzes "firsthand accounts and books published prior to 1948" concerning deportation. The breakdown of the camps is not easy because prisoners were moved back and forth among them. The result is roughly as follows: seventeen texts on the Auschwitz complex and twenty on Ravensbrück and its Kommandos, twelve texts on Buchenwald alone, nine on various Buchenwald Kommandos, and seventeen on Dora as well as thirty-three on all the other camps put together, including twelve on Mauthausen, eight on Neuengamme, and seven on Dachau.

The other document is the list of the dead from the University of Strasbourg shown in *Témoignages strasbourgeois.*[9] Sixteen people died in France, either shot or killed under other circumstances. Eighteen died in Auschwitz, mainly Jews. Thirty-four died during deportation outside of Auschwitz, including twenty-five in identified camps: fourteen at Dora and eleven at all the other camps combined.

As mentioned earlier, the situation was the same for the Belgian deportees.

THE PRODUCTION AND USE OF V2S. Although the subject of this book is the history of the Dora camp and of its prisoners, and not the history of the missiles, it may be useful to give some information about V2 production, firing, and the number of its victims. Taking into account the conditions of the period, some of these statistics are only approximate.

According to Irving, who is quoted by Bornemann,[10] production is believed to have started in January 1944 with 50 units and was increased until May, with 86 in February, 170 in March, 253 in April, and 437 in May. It is then believed to have dropped sharply: 132 in June and 86 in July before starting up again with 374 units in August. It is noteworthy that firing operations did not begin until September. The V2s produced until July were thus used only for tests in Blizna and Peenemünde. Regardless of whether the firings were successful or failed, the V2s were destroyed except for those that were damaged in transport or before firing, which were brought back for dismantling and recycling in Kleinbodungen. Presumably the low point in June and July corresponded to the last fine-tuning and the first missiles that were supposed to be operational that were produced in August.

Starting in September 1944 until March 18, 1945, production remained more or less steady: 629 in September, 628 in October, 662 in November, 613 in December, 690 in January, 617 in February, and 362 in March. The total from August 1944 to March 1945 is therefore held to be 4,575 missiles.

According to another source[11] the total number of successful V2 firings is believed to have been 3,255, including 1,403 on the United Kingdom (1,359 on London), 1,696 on Belgium (1,610 on Antwerp and 86 on Liège), and 156 on other continental targets (19 on Paris). The difference is thought to correspond to failed firings and missiles destroyed before the firings under various circumstances. It is interesting to note that no stock of V2s was found waiting to be fired, which would have saved a lot of trouble at White Sands and Kapustin Yar.

In all there were more successful V1 firings (21,770) than V2 firings (3,255). The V1 firing campaign in June and July 1944 from France was effective before the British began destroying the missiles in flight. It should be noted that at the time the devices were not being produced in the Dora Tunnel. Subsequently a large percentage of the VIs fired on Holland were destroyed by Allied air defenses before reaching English or Belgian soil.

The total number of people killed by VIs and V2s was 8,938 in England (6,184 for the VIs and 2,754 for the V2s) and 6,448 in Belgium (no distinction made). For purposes of comparison, there were nearly 6,000 deaths among the Dora prisoners in September 1943 and in April 1944 alone.

EPILOGUE

Fifty Years After Dora

The history of Dora began in August 1943 and ended, taking account of the evacuations and returns, in June 1945. That is just under two years. Between the end of Dora and the writing of this book, more than fifty years passed. These fifty years can be divided, in necessarily very schematic fashion, into three periods, corresponding to the three chapters of the epilogue.

The first, lasting some ten years, was the direct follow-up of the devastating world war. Germany, in ruins, ceased to exist as a state. Trials of war criminals got under way. A whole concentration camp system, which had just been discovered, was examined and cross-examined. And each of the victors sought to appropriate the techniques of the vanquished—above all its "secret weapons." This is the subject of chapter 23.

The second period was long, given that it continued right up until the 1980s. The world was divided into two blocs competing for the mastery of space. Camp survivors divided their lives for the most part between their professional life and family life. Their associations were devoted to solidarity and commemoration. This will be looked at in chapter 24.

The third period began in the 1980s, initially without any major events. Historians drew up evaluations, and the last of the survivors concerned themselves, while there was still time to do so, with the maintenance of "memory." Retirement made it possible for them to devote themselves to doing so. Finally, the transformation of Europe and above all the reunification of Germany opened new perspectives. Chapter 25 opens onto the near future.

[[23]]

AFTER THE WAR:
BETWEEN MISSILES AND TRIALS

The capitulation of May 8, 1945, marked a brutal historical rupture. Not only did it put an end in Europe to a long and hard war, but at the same time it turned Germany into a country without a government, placed entirely under the control and responsibility of four victorious powers. It is in this framework that a certain number of events and debates that characterized the post-Dora period for several years must be situated.

The complexities of American politics and the ambiguities of Soviet politics were characteristic of this necessarily confused transition period, the detailed history of which goes beyond the scope of this book.[1]

Three realms deserve to be explored, in that they prolong the history of Dora itself. There was, first of all, beginning with the V2 experiment, rocket research that migrated from Germany to the United States and the USSR, and even France and Great Britain. The period of the Dora Tunnel was thus seen as a mere episode, left aside for many long years. There were the trials of the war criminals, especially those connected to the concentration camps, including Dora. And there were, lastly, the consequences for historians and public opinion of the discovery of the concentration camp system. The Buchenwald camp was at the heart of the debate—which meant that the Dora camp was also concerned.

The Partition of Germany in 1945 and Control over the Rockets

In mid-May 1945 there were no more prisoners from Dora-Mittelbau on location in the *Mittelraum*. The last of them, in need of medical repatriation, had left from the Nordhausen airfield. The others had either already gone home or were waiting to leave from the distant regions where the evacuations had taken them. Nor were there any more SS on location. The evacuations had dispersed them as well, and they were either prisoners of war or sometimes in hiding. The German communists who had been camp leaders had been liquidated by the SS—some of them at the very last moment. Tens of thousands of men who had, for the past twenty months, played a prominent role in the activity of the region had thus vanished. The concentration camp apparatus had entirely collapsed.

There remained around the abandoned factory idle work sites and deserted camps, several thousand unemployed German civilians—"specialists" of every level more or less dependent on the Americans who had occupied the region for a month. This American presence was not to last, however, because of the agreements with the Soviets regarding the demarcation of the zones of occupation.

Indeed, though Germany's capitulation on May 8, 1945, led to the de facto division of the Reich according to the positions the various Allied armies had reached by that date, what still remained was to move from that state of affairs to the division that had been agreed upon by the Allied governments regarding the zones of occupation in Germany as well as Austria. This exchange would be completed by the beginning of July 1945. As it turned out, on May 8 virtually everything to do with the V2s—sites, facilities, already constructed rockets and rocket parts, archives, personnel—was very largely under American control in the zones that had to be retroceded. The Americans therefore had only several weeks to take a certain number of initiatives if they were not to lose this control.

THE PARTITION OF GERMANY INTO OCCUPIED ZONES. The dividing-up of the various regions of Germany into the future Soviet, British, American, and French occupation zones was generally carried out along traditional border lines. The agreement arrived at can be described by looking at how the *Länder* in present-day Germany are divided.[2]

The city of Berlin had to be first of all isolated from the rest of Brandenburg in order to establish a quadripartite occupation with four "sectors." The rest of Brandenburg remained under Soviet occupation with the exception of the territories located to the east of the Oder-Neisse line, which were ceded to Poland. It was in this reduced Brandenburg that Sachsenhausen, Oranienburg, and Ravensbrück were located. With the exception of a small territory to the east of the Neisse, Saxony was located in the Soviet zone. It expanded into the part of Lower Silesia that was located to the west of the Neisse. Mecklenburg was included in the Soviet zone along with "Fore" Pomerania (Vorpommern) to the west of the Oder. It was in this part of Pomerania that Peenemünde was located. The Hanoverian territory located north of the Elbe was also attached to Mecklenburg.[3]

Saxony-Anhalt and Thuringia completed the Soviet zone. The traditional—and generally age-old—political borders were respected in the demarcation with Lower Saxony, Hesse, and Bavaria. Only a few enclaves of Brunswick and of Hesse were incorporated into Saxony-Anhalt and Thuringia. Buchenwald was included in the Soviet zone along with virtually all of its Kommandos such as Ohrdruf, Laura, and Langenstein. But Gandersheim was located in Lower Saxony.

The situation is more complex to describe with regard to the Dora-Mittelbau complex. The Dora camp and factory were in Thuringia, as were Nordhausen and Harzungen, Bleicherode and Kleinbodungen. This was also the case for the city of Ellrich, but the demarcation line actually ran right through the Ellrich-Station camp. The heights including the crematorium and the hamlet of Juliushütte with the SS camp were located in the district of Walkenried and were, for this reason, in Lower Saxony in the British zone whereas the prisoners' blocks were in Thuringia. In the same way, Wieda was located in Lower Saxony as were Osterhagen and Nüxei whereas Mackenrode and Günzerode were in Thuringia. Blankenburg, Rottleberode, Kelbra, Rossla, and Sangerhausen were all located in Saxony-Anhalt along with Langenstein and Stassfurt as well as Gardelegen.

The British-occupied zone was comprised of four *Länder*: Schleswig-Holstein with Lübeck, Hamburg (including the Neuengamme camp), Lower Saxony, and North Rhineland-Westphalia. The Land of Bremen with its port was later included in the American zone. Porta Westfalica was located in Westphalia, and Gandersheim, Osterode, Wieda, and Walkenried in Lower Saxony. The same went for Helmstedt, whereas the Beendorf and Weferlingen installations were in Saxony-Anhalt. The site of Bergen-Belsen was situated in the heart of the British zone, in Lower Saxony.

Americans and French divided up the southern part of Germany. Dachau and Flossenbürg remained under American control. Friedrichshafen ended up included in the French zone.

RETROCESSIONS BY THE AMERICANS. With regard to the limits agreed upon, the Americans made the greatest concessions. They had to retrocede to the Soviets the western part of Mecklenburg, with Schwerin, Wöbbelin, and Ludwigslust, the better part of Saxony-Anhalt including Magdeburg, Dessau, and Halle, the western part of Saxony including Leipzig and Chemnitz, and all of Thuringia. They also had to withdraw from the west of Bohemia including Karlsbad (Karlovy Vary). They also had to give the British a part of Lower Saxony and the better part of North Rhineland-Westphalia, but obtained Bremen in exchange.

They began their retreat by the north, leaving the British in control of the west of Mecklenburg until it was ceded to the Soviets. When Marcel Baillon and his friends left Neubrandenburg at the end of May 1945 it was in British military transport trucks that had come from Schwerin to get them. They had transported Soviet citizens returning home—willingly or unwillingly—in the other direction. The Americans then turned their position in the Altmark and Lower Saxony over to the British.

But it was the Americans themselves who gave Thuringia as well as those territories under their control to the east of Thuringia to the Soviets. These explanations are necessary if one is to understand what happened on the ground in May–June 1945.

THE FATE OF THE PEOPLE FROM PEENEMÜNDE. As shown in chapter 16, five hundred selected specialists from Peenemünde were evacuated by Kammler's special train in early April from the region of Nordhausen all the way to Oberammergau in the Bavarian Alps. Von Braun, due to his injury, made the trip by car. Dornberger and his entourage left Bad Sachsa at the same time to meet up with them. The other specialists waited where they were in the villages in the Nordhausen area for the arrival of the Americans. Leaders such as Sawatzki and Rickhey remained at Ilfeld.

At Oberammergau[4] those concerned first set up in a comfortable barracks, nevertheless surrounded by barbed wire and guarded by members of the SD. After several days, Kammler left for an unknown destination. He was never to be seen again. He is known to have pulled back from Halle to Dresden and then to Prague. He is thought to have been killed in last-minute fighting on May 9.

His replacement at Oberammergau, an SS officer named Kummer, allowed himself to be persuaded of the risk of an air raid on the barracks and accepted that the specialists be dispersed, still under guard, in the neighboring districts. Wernher von Braun first established himself more to the north, in Weilheim, then went to a hospital in Sonthofen south of Kempten to have his arm attended to by a surgeon. He remained there until April 25, when an ambulance sent by Dornberger came to get him, taking him to a hotel at Oberjoch near the Austrian border. A small group met there, including Dornberger and Magnus von Braun, Wernher's younger brother. It was on May 2, after the radio had announced Hitler's death, that Magnus von Braun, who spoke English, went down into the valley by bicycle to make contact with the American authorities.[5] He met an antitank company and was taken to explain himself to Reutte, in the neighboring Tyrol area. He obtained safe-conducts for seven people: his brother Wernher and himself, Dornberger and his assistant Axster, Lindenberg (a combustion chamber specialist), Bernhard Tessmann, and Dieter Huzel. The two latter men, after having hidden the V2 archives at Dörnten, as seen in chapter 16, reconnected with their colleagues by their own means.

Von Braun and his party traveled first to Reutte, and were from there taken to Garmisch-Partenkirchen, to a barracks where the Americans had gathered the specialists from Peenemünde whom they had come upon in the area. After willingly responding to the questioning of diversely qualified technicians, conducted by Dr. Richard Porter (of General Electric), who had arrived from London for the very purpose on May 8, von Braun wrote a report on May 15 and Dornberger another on May 17. It was then that the contact was established with the team that went into action in Thuringia.

SALVAGING ONE HUNDRED ROCKETS AND ARCHIVES. As shown in chapter 17, the Americans had discovered the entrance to the Dora Tunnel on April 11. But no experts could get there as long as the Nordhausen region remained a combat zone. The Eleventh German Army, encircled in the Harz Mountains, still had to be vanquished; the last units capitulated on April 20.

The V2 recovery operations were directed from Washington by Col. Gervais William Trichel, who since September 1943 had been the head of the rocket office.[6] He had signed a contract with the General Electric Company for the creation of a firing range at White Sands, New Mexico. He sent Maj. Robert Staver to London in February 1945; an artilleryman, Staver was responsible for identifying, with the help of the British services, both the sites of V2 production and the competent German technicians. The announcement of the discovery of Kohnstein came as no surprise to him. He still had to locate the corresponding documentation and get his hands on von Braun and the others.

Staver got to Nordhausen on May 3. He made various contacts in the region and ended up convincing Karl Otto Fleischer, the commercial director of Elektromechanische Werke, to start looking for the archives.[7] And indeed Huzel and Tessmann had confided in him on this matter before they left for Bavaria. On May 20, not without some difficulty, Fleischer and another former Peenemünde collaborator, Dr. Eberhard Rees, located the cache of the cases of archives in the Dörnten mine. The question remained as to how to transport them. This was all the more urgent as Dörnten happened to be in Lower Saxony in a zone that had to be retroceded to the British, whereas the Americans wanted to keep the treasure all for themselves.

Finally, the fourteen tons of documents were transferred by trucks to Nordhausen on May 27, then to Paris, and then shipped on to Aberdeen, Maryland—under heavy guard the whole way. The logistics of the operation were organized by the Paris representative of Ordnance—the U.S. Army's armaments office—Col. Holger Toftoy, whom Colonel Trichel had asked to have a hundred or so V2s delivered for trials at White Sands.[8]

There were practically no entirely assembled rockets on location. The corresponding pieces for that quantity of units had to be gathered together in the Dora factory, packed up, and loaded. For this task a unit of the 144th Motor Vehicle Assembly Company was brought in from Cherbourg and arrived on May 18; the first convoy was ready to leave on May 22. It was followed by eight convoys every day until May 31.

All in all the operation involved 340 freight cars carrying 450 tons of material. The coordination was ensured by Maj. James Hamill based in Fulda, assisted on location by Major Bromley and Dr. Louis Woodruff. They had to identify the elements to be shipped and then find the corresponding railway cars. The convoys arrived in Antwerp and the cases were loaded onto sixteen Liberty ships after the most fragile pieces had been repacked. The cases were unloaded in New Orleans at the end of June, then shipped by railroad to the White Sands base, where they awaited assembly.

THE ORIGINS OF OPERATION OVERCAST. The Allied troops moving across Germany were followed by groups of experts dealing with a wide variety of curiosities. In chapter 3 the Rosenberg team, from the Psychological Warfare Division, has already been mentioned; they arrived at Buchenwald on April 16, 1945, to study the functioning of a concentration camp. Other teams made up of technical officers and civilian scientists were preoccupied with the state of advancement of German research in such domains as aeronautics, nuclear development, rockets, and medicine. They reported to an American-British organization called the CIOS (Combined Intelligence Objectives Subcommittee). There was, in the nuclear field, a mission known as Alsos. Dr. Porter's Hermes group was in charge of the rockets.

Their goal was not merely to recover the equipment and the archives but to get their hands on the German experts and convince them to collaborate.[8] Above all they had to secure their services for a sufficiently long period to be sure to be able to take advantage of all their experience. With regard to the rockets, a significant group of German specialists had been gathered together at Garmisch, but the others had remained in Thuringia—a region that had to be retroceded to the Soviets. The Americans hoped that the experts would settle in their zone of occupation. They especially wanted to make sure that the families of the experts at Garmisch did not stay in the Soviet zone as potential hostages.

Staver had the department heads from Peenemünde who were at Garmisch return to Nordhausen to hook up with their principal collaborators and convince them to join the Americans. Steinhoff and others arrived on June 8, and von Braun himself arrived on June 19. Vehicles of every description were driving back and forth across the region and gathered some thousand people at the Nordhausen station. On June 20 a fifty-carriage train took them to Witzenhausen in Hesse, several miles from Thuringia.[9]

These sorts of evacuations were thought to be taking place in extremis as Soviet troops were expected the same day. It turned out to be a false alarm. In fact, Stalin had wanted to delay the western entrance into Berlin until July 1 and consequently postponed the arrival of the Soviets in Thuringia.

The grouping of the people from Peenemünde at Witzenhausen and in the neighboring town of Eschwege was a preservative measure, because the Americans were not yet in a position to make them precise offers. Some of the administration in Washington was hostile to allowing German citizens—civilians as much as military personnel—into the United States. But the American specialists, each in his field, felt it important that this opportunity to make technical progress in fields of key significance not be lost. They shored up their point of view with the need to strengthen their means to curtail the war against Japan.

It was only at the beginning of July 1945 that Operation Overcast, designed to bring German civilian scientists to the United States for a limited period, was decided upon. This secret decision took effect on July 17.

GERMANY AND THE CAPITULATION. The capitulation of Germany on May 7 and 8, 1945, was signed in Reims by Jodl, then in Berlin by Keitel on instructions from Dönitz, designated by Hitler as his successor. His government was established at Flensburg in the far north of the territory of the Reich in a zone that had not yet been occupied by the British army. The very act of capitulating stripped his government of its legitimacy, for there was no more German state even if there continued to be a Germany, whose fate was henceforth in the hands of the victorious powers. In the confusion of the moment Dönitz's government, as Speer reports in his memoirs,[10] nevertheless continued to sit until its "activity" was interrupted and its members finally arrested on May 23.

Already in October 1943, in the course of a meeting in Moscow, the EAC, or European Advisory Commission, had been created at the level of the American, British, and Soviet ministers of foreign affairs. It was this same commission that on September 12, 1944, in the London protocol, decided on the division of Germany into three zones of occupation and of Berlin into three sectors. At the Yalta summit in February 1945 a zone in Germany and a sector in Berlin were added for France by drawing upon the American and British zones and sectors. The following June 5 a "Berlin declaration" was published by the four Allied commanders in chief "exercising supreme control in Germany" who were at the time Eisenhower, Montgomery, Zhukov, and de Lattre de Tassigny. In this way an Allied Control Committee was set up for Germany, and for Berlin an Allied Berlin Command—the *Kommandatura*—which were in charge of the country's government.

The problem at the time was to know whether there would be common administrations for all of Germany under quadripartite control. The Soviet Union, wishing to extend its influence to the country as a whole, was favorable. France, wanting Germany to remain divided, stated its opposition in the course of a meeting in London in September–October 1945. France particularly wanted to isolate the Saarland from the rest of Germany, both politically and economically. This blocking action consequently led to the development of distinct policies in the four zones, the occupation's quadripartite aspect remaining expressed in concrete terms only in Berlin.

It is how the American zone functioned that most concerns the post-Dora phase. The key person was Gen. Lucius Clay, Eisenhower's assistant, and then his successor Gen. Joseph McNarney. The American government, caught up in internal problems and having to deal with the war against Japan and the fighting in the Pacific, left great freedom to Clay, who acted—effectively as it turned out—as a "proconsul." On October 1, 1945, he set up the OMGUS—the Office of the Military Government of the United States—in Frankfurt. In parallel, however, at least for several months, the activities of a certain number of organizations accompanying the advance of the American troops continued—and not necessarily in coordinated fashion.

Operation Overcast and the Future of the V2s

THE INQUIRY CARRIED OUT BY THE WESTERN POWERS. In 1945 in the Western countries and especially among Americans there was considerable curiosity about the state of German science and technology and interest in the Reich's economic performance. The manifestation of this is seen in the attention shown in what Speer had to say. He was questioned continuously for several months.[11]

The first to meet him were three important American special advisers, Paul Nitze, George Ball, and John Kenneth Galbraith, who had been President Roosevelt's advisers. They directed the USSBS—the United States Strategic Bombing Survey—responsible for analyzing the impact of the bombings on production and civilian morale. They came to see him especially in the Glücksburg castle near Flensburg, where he was being put up by the duke of Mecklenburg-Holstein.

Subsequently arrested along with the other ministers on May 23, Speer was taken with them to Mondorf in Luxembourg, where he found other Nazi dignitaries such as Göring. Two weeks later he was transferred for further interrogation by the British and the Americans to Versailles, where General Eisenhower had his headquarters. When they were moved to Frankfurt, Speer was taken back to Germany and interned at Kransberg in an outbuilding of one of Göring's castles. There he met up with several of his collaborators as well as such financiers as Hjalmar Schacht, leaders of industry such as Ernst Heinkel and Ferdinand Porsche, and a whole series of scientists and technicians. He was once again interrogated, then transferred to Nuremberg along with Schacht to stand trial beginning on November 20, 1945.

As seen above, a team of American technicians had gone to Bavaria as early as May 1945 to begin questioning von Braun and the other specialists from Peenemünde. Inquiries began very rapidly in other fields as well, as they had with Speer. It was only after several weeks that these investigations were brought together at Kransberg. There were exceptions however: the atomic physicists were questioned in England.

At Kransberg a whole inquiry apparatus was set up by a specialized organization known as FIAT, Field Information Agency, Technical. The interned Germans left there progressively, either to stand trial, to be hired on a contract basis, or merely to be released. The receptacle of competency came to be known by the rather unflattering code name "Dustbin." Among those hired were a good number involved in Operation Overcast, which will be mentioned shortly. Other camps took in the Reich's political and economic executives. Sawatzki, one of the directors of the Mittelwerk, seems to have disappeared from a camp in the Frankfurt region at the beginning of May 1945, but he had previously given the names of those in charge at Mittelwerk and of the SS officers at Dora. Extremely varied hypotheses have been advanced as to his fate.[12]

OPERATION OVERCAST AND THE RECRUITMENT OF THE ROCKET SPECIALISTS. Operation Overcast, providing for the hiring of German (or Austrian) specialists by the American authorities, was approved on July 6, 1945, by the interallied general staff[13] and took effect on July 17. One of the arguments put forward was the ongoing war against Japan. In the terms in which it was presented, its scope was limited. The Germans concerned had to have a particular specialization. They had to be grouped in precise zones. Their contracts had to be established for a limited period. It was in this general framework that the recruitment of the rocket specialists took place.

In Washington, Colonel Trichel having been assigned to the operation in the Pacific theater, Col. Holger Toftoy was named head of the rocket office in late June 1945.[14] Promoted to general, he remained in charge of this sector for several years. He traveled to Europe at the end of July, first to Paris, then to Hesse, where the rocket specialists were housed with their families, in precarious conditions, at Witzenhausen and at Eschwege.[15] Von Braun was in discussions with Staver and Porter to draw up a departure list for the United States. The number of specialists had already been reduced from 500 to 300 when Toftoy arrived with an offer of only 100 short-term contracts. He stretched the quota to 115 on his own authority. In awaiting their departure it was planned that they be put up in a barracks in Landshut in Bavaria with their families. The establishment of the list was thus based on purely technical considerations, without individual inquiries.

THE BRITISH EPISODE. The Americans' isolated initiatives did not satisfy the British. In June they had already tried to stop the crates containing the one hundred rockets from leaving Antwerp for New Orleans. They too sought to reconstitute a certain number of V2s in order to fire them from Cuxhaven over the North Sea, and the Americans lent them several specialists for this purpose. This was known as Operation Backfire.[16]

In August the British even managed to have von Braun, Dornberger, and four other experts come to England for questioning. They seized the opportunity to make them offers, but without success. Finally, von Braun and the four civilian experts returned to Germany, without Dornberger, who was considered a prisoner of war and interned in Wales with other high-ranking officers. The British wanted to put him on trial as responsible for the V2 bombings of London. The charge would ultimately be dropped. Dornberger was in command of the training of the specialized artillerymen but not of carrying out the firing itself. Above all, a trial regarding the firing of the V2s would have made it possible to bring up the massive bombings of German cities by the Royal Air Force.

Operation Backfire came to an end with three fruitless launches at Cuxhaven in September in the presence of Allied observers including the American Toftoy and the Soviet Serge Korolev. The British continued their tests in Australia, at Woomera, and then gave them up.

THE SOVIETS IN THURINGIA. The Soviet troops who arrived on May 5 at Peenemünde in Pomerania found nothing but ruins. Conversely, at Dora, on July 5, the Mittelwerk factory was intact except for certain machines such as the inspection devices, which had been destroyed by the German specialists in early April prior to their leaving. The Americans had contented themselves with getting their hands on the plans and packing away the components for the construction of one hundred rockets. The situation was identical in the Kleinbodungen workshops and at the engine test center at Lehesten.[17]

The Soviets' problem was the disappearance of the German specialists who had emigrated from Thuringia to Hesse or Lower Saxony. They sought to bring them back with tempting offers of salaries, housing, or food rations, which were broadcast widely, including by radio. Very few were seduced by these attempts. The most important among them was Helmut Gröttrup. He had been arrested by the Gestapo in early 1944 with von Braun and was considered left-wing. But his rallying to the Soviets does not seem to have been ideologically motivated. He did not like Toftoy's offers and seems to have been influenced by his seductive wife Irmgard, whose strong personality—already noticed at Peenemünde—would again stand out in the Soviet Union. Gröttrup was put at the head of a so-called Rabe Institut, the Raketenbetriebe Bleicherode, and the Mittelwerke became—somewhat uninspiredly—Zentralwerke. The German team was made up of some two hundred men of an average technical level.

Top-level Soviet experts came and set up in Thuringia. The most important among them, Serge Korolev, born in 1907, was already a great rocket specialist when he had been sent to the gulag in 1938 in the wave of purges at the time. He was released in 1944 but not rehabilitated. His identity remained secret. He moved to Bleicherode in the villa left vacant by von Braun.

THE ARRIVAL OF THE "PEENEMÜNDER" IN THE UNITED STATES. The V2 specialists were not the first Germans to arrive in the United States in the framework of Overcast. Nor were they the most numerous. In the end they would number 127, as opposed to 146 aeronautical specialists at the Army Air Force's Wright Field in Ohio. But they made up by far and away the most homogeneous group in terms of their origin and conditions of recruitment.

Von Braun, back from London, also ended up at Kransberg at the same time as Speer before leaving for the United States.[18] He left Frankfurt on September 12, 1945, with six of his former collaborators from Peenemünde. From France they crossed the Atlantic in a cargo plane with demobilized GIs. Upon their arrival in Boston on September 20 they were taken to Fort Strong, a fortress on an island in Boston Bay where they underwent a series of questionings before being transferred to the Aberdeen Proving Ground in Maryland. There, waiting to be sorted through, were the fourteen tons of documents recuperated at Dörnten. According to McGovern, they represented 310,000 drawings and 3,500 reports.

Von Braun alone was taken to the Pentagon, then made the journey to El Paso, Texas, by train with Maj. James Hamill, who had returned from Germany and was in charge of the rocket operation under orders from Toftoy. El Paso is a large city in the far west of Texas, separated from Mexico by the Rio Grande. It is in the northeast part of the city that the vast military camp of Fort Bliss begins, straddling the border between Texas and New Mexico. Farther to the north in New Mexico is the White Sands firing range—a gypsum desert 120 miles long and 40 miles wide. Von Braun was first of all joined by his six companions. On December 2, 1945, he was joined by fifty-five more specialists who had crossed the Atlantic by ship from Le Havre to New York. Forty-nine others arrived in February 1946 under the same conditions. Sixteen others came to complete the team of 127.

TESTING THE V2S AT WHITE SANDS. The German specialists from Peenemünde were not particularly well received by the base commander at Fort Bliss. And the task that awaited them was difficult and unrewarding.[19] When they set about to assemble the components of the V2s, they discovered that they were not in the best state of repair. They had been packed up at Dora in May 1945, transported by train to Antwerp, partially repacked, loaded onto Liberty ships, unloaded in New Orleans, and shipped by train to El Paso where they had been stocked for six months without any qualified personnel there to take delivery. To get them into workable condition they had to rely on the personnel from General Electric sent by Porter.

The first static test took place on March 14, 1946, and the first successful launch on June 28—that is, fifteen months after the last V2s were launched on London. But sixteen more months, it is true, passed before the first successful launch in the USSR. The firing then continued and was marked by a serious incident on May 29, 1947.[20] A rocket veered off course, crossed the Mexican border, and made a crater in a cemetery in the city of Ciudad Juarez, on the other side of the Rio Grande. There were no victims, but excuses had to be presented to the Mexican government. In all, seventy rockets were fired. The others were not fired, and, for the most part, not assembled.

THE PEENEMÜNDERS' SHADOWY STATUS. The conditions under which the German specialists were admitted were restrictive, but the planned time frames were not respected. Immigration rules were broken. Discreet measures were taken. A change of code was made on May 13, 1946, and Overcast turned into Paperclip.[21] It was then that the conditions were modified: an increase in the number of specialists recruited, an extension of the contracts' duration, admission of families. President Truman gave his consent, and the administration gave it a broad interpretation. The following information has to do with the Peenemünde people, but the treatment was identical for other German and Austrian specialists.

In October 1946 the contracts were extended for five years. In December 1946 the families began to arrive in Fort Bliss. In the summer of 1946, von Braun had his parents brought from Silesia, which had become Polish, to Landshut.[22] Through them in late 1946 he asked for the hand of his cousin Maria. The marriage took place at Landshut on March 1, 1947. Von Braun returned to the United States with his wife and his parents, who stayed five years.

The announcement of the presence of German technicians in the United States was made on December 3, 1946. It caused an outcry, but the onset of the Cold War inhibited the movement from developing further. The Germans remained illegal immigrants nevertheless. Later they were transported by bus from Fort Bliss to Ciudad Juarez, where they were able to obtain visas from the American consulate and legally enter the United States.

Beginning in the summer of 1947 the intelligence services, which had recruited German agents from among former Nazis, managed to block all inquiries into the specialists who had settled in the United States in spite of the State Department's efforts. It was known, for instance, that Rudolph, Steinhoff, Hermann, and von Braun had been members of the Nazi Party and that von Braun had been made an SS officer. But it became impossible to take any action on those grounds. Rickhey, who had arrived in the United States in different conditions, was, it is true, sent back to Germany in May 1947 to stand trial. His case was rather particular because charges had been laid against him personally, as will be seen, and his behavior in the United States had been disagreeable.[23] Conversely, Dornberger, released by the British, was recruited by the U.S. Air Force and sent to Wright Field. Rudolf Hermann, director of the Kochel wind tunnel, was hired by the air force. The wind tunnel itself was reconstructed by the navy at White Oak, Maryland, to the north of Washington.

In 1950 the Fort Bliss site appeared inadequate. Toftoy found a new location on the site of a former arsenal in Huntsville in northern Alabama. The transfer took place on April 1, 1950, under the supervision of Colonel Hamill and von Braun.

THE GERMAN TECHNICIANS FROM THURINGIA TO THE SOVIET UNION. An interallied agreement explicitly forbade the continuation of military research on German territory. That did not particularly bother the Russians, and it was not in order to respect this agreement that they one day decided to leave Thuringia, in entirely surprising conditions that were to be recounted only many years later.

On October 22, 1946, General Gaïdoukov, in charge of the rockets, held a work session with Gröttrup and his collaborators. It was followed by a lengthy dinner where drink flowed freely. After the dinner the German technicians could not go home. A complete moving operation was under way—for both them and their families. Two hundred rocket specialists were all affected. They had to get into the trains awaiting them in the Kleinbodungen station.[24] The same operation took place simultaneously throughout the Soviet-occupied zone. Some five thousand specialists in the aeronautical, optical, and mechanical fields all had to leave under the same conditions with their personal possessions. With their families, twenty thousand people all told were involved. The ninety-two-train convoy arrived in Moscow on October 27, 1946.

The Soviet services were well versed in such population transfers.[25] During the war they had sent into Central Asia or western Siberia all the "Germans of the Volga," men, women, and children, then all the Chechens and the Ingouchis, then all the Tatars from the Crimea, and several other peoples of the USSR.

THE GERMANS IN THE SOVIET UNION AND THEIR RETURN. Little is known about the German technicians' stay in the Soviet Union except that they were kept carefully away from the population and were less and less associated with work on the rockets.[26] They were first of all divided into two groups. One went to Gorodomlia, 180 miles northwest of Moscow. The other group remained in Moscow, along with Gröttrup.

Then a firing range was secretly set up at Kapustin Yar in the steppe 120 miles east of Stalingrad. In August 1947, Gröttrup was there with a certain number of Germans. The first successful launch of a V2 took place on October 29, 1947. Eleven reconstituted V2s were fired. Five reached their target.

From 1950 on, Gröttrup's role was reduced, as was his salary. The German technicians' return to Germany began in March 1951. The Gröttrups returned on December 28, 1953, and moved to West Germany. In 1958 they both published memoirs of their stay in the USSR.

FRANCE'S RECOURSE TO THE PEENEMÜNDE TECHNICIANS. Beginning in the summer of 1944, French specialists headed by Professor Moureu endeavored to glean information from the debris of the German missiles that had crashed in France—either V1s, a hundred of which had crashed because of the malfunctioning of their launch toward London, or the V2s fired on the Paris area in September–October 1944. Ties were established with American and British colleagues, who were also interested in the concrete structures at Watten and Wizernes.[27]

In May–June 1945, Moureu traveled to Oberradebach near Friedrichshafen and then to the factory in the Dora Tunnel, and to the engine test center at Lehesten. The Americans delivered four V1s and V2 parts. Another mission was at Kochel in September, just as the wind tunnel was being dismantled for its transfer to the United States. Finally, Moureu traveled to Cuxhaven in October for the launch of the V2s by the British. Right from the beginning, French specialists therefore took part in attempts to make use of German technology in this domain.

Thus the French DEFA—Direction des études et fabrications d'armement,

or Office for the Study and Manufacture of Armaments—decided on the creation, on November 14, 1945, of the CEPA—Centre d'études des projectiles autopropulsés, or Center for the Study of Self-Propelled Projectiles—directed by
Moureu. On May 17, 1946, the LRBA—Laboratoire de recherches balistiques et
aérodynamiques," or Ballistic and Aerodynamic Research Laboratory—was set
up in Vernon. A research department also existed at Emmendingen to the north
of Freiburg in the French-occupied zone.

It was there and in the neighboring towns of Riegel and Denzlingen that the
hundred German engineers and technicians hired by France were progressively
brought together with their families, some of them from Kochel, the others having formerly been at Peenemünde. Among them was Heinz Bringer, who many
years later would be the father of the Viking engine of the European launcher
Ariane. In the spring of 1947, those who had formerly been at Peenemünde were
transferred to France, above all to Vernon, and those from Kochel remained at
Emmendingen until the creation of the Franco-German Research Institute in
Saint-Louis in 1950.

Attempts to reconstitute a V2 were given up in 1947, and work began in
other directions. In the 1950s some of the engineers returned to work in Germany either in the university or in industry. Those who remained at Vernon were
integrated in 1971 into the SEP, the "European Propulsion Company." That was
the case for Heinz Bringer and his team.

AMERICANS, FRENCH, AND SOVIETS IN THE ROCKET RACE. Of the four
countries occupying Germany in 1945, one ended up by losing interest in rockets. As mentioned above, the British did not continue their research in this
domain.

The Americans on the other hand, led by Toftoy and Hamill, consistently
supported the coherent team chosen by von Braun, whose technical authority
never seems to have been contested. The team never disbanded—and in 1960
there were still eighty-nine former collaborators from Peenemünde at Huntsville. They generally lived on a wooded hill south of the city known as Monte
Santo and nicknamed Sauerkraut Hill.[28] In 1955 most of them became American
citizens, von Braun leading the way. And that same year Oberth came from
Germany to join them for three years. Some of them came to hold important
positions in American companies, such as Ernst Steinhoff with the Rand Corporation and Dieter Huzel with North American. Dornberger joined Bell Aircraft.

With the greatest discretion the French implemented an identical policy, and
the French army beginning in 1945, with the express consent of General de
Gaulle, hired specialists from Kochel and then from Peenemünde.

Soviet practices were different. The Russians had only second-rate German
specialists aside from Gröttrup and a handful of others. Above all as of 1945
they had their own team, ill-disposed to working in confidence with the Germans, whom they ended up sending back home.

Several remarks are in order regarding the attitude of the various parties. The first is that, in the first years after the war, the point was only to develop military devices, which explains at once the total secrecy and lack of curiosity as to the past history of the German collaborators. Everyone knew what the others were doing, but no one could point an accusing finger. The conspiracy of silence is the rule in such circumstances. It is possible that von Braun and Korolev had at the time already considered a space program, but that was not the decision-makers' objective.

The second remark is the separation that quickly came about in people's minds between technical research, such as it had been developed at Peenemünde, and the production conditions of the V2s by Mittelwerk at Dora and elsewhere. The only Mittelwerk director to have been bothered was Rickhey, and he was even taken from the United States to Germany to stand trial. But it will be shown later just what sort of trial it was, and how it turned out.

Trying the War Criminals

At the end of 1945 the office of the American military government was established in Frankfurt. It was near Frankfurt that the Kransberg camp was located, where the Americans and British gathered together the scientists, technicians, and economic and financial executives whom they wished to question. The American officers from the Psychological Warfare Division were there too, and, thanks to them, Eugen Kogon moved into the Frankfurt area to write his book on the camps. It was also nearby, in Wiesbaden, that the investigators of the War Crimes Investigating Team were working, preparing cases against the war criminals.

The Americans were not the only ones to pursue the war criminals, and especially those in charge of the concentration camps, but it was they who took on the brunt of the task in this domain. They had significant means at their disposal. Some of them, moreover, had a good knowledge of the German language because of their origins, Jewish or otherwise. They had liberated Buchenwald, Dora-Mittelbau, Flossenbürg, Dachau, and Mauthausen as well as the camps' Kommandos. They had discovered Ohrdruf, Nordhausen, Gardelegen, the little Buchenwald camp, typhus at Dachau, Ebensee, and Wöbbelin. In the Schwerin region they had taken in the prisoners evacuated from Sachsenhausen and Ravensbrück. They were not inclined to indulgence, as will be seen in the first trials.

Three phases can be distinguished in the trials. The first of them took place in late 1945, before Nuremberg. Then came the Nuremberg trial, which ended in 1946. Finally, other trials took place in 1946–47, such as the trial dealing with Dora.

THE TRIALS OF LATE 1945. In the American zone the trials took place at

Dachau, and the accused were imprisoned in the former concentration camp. Those condemned to prison sentences were sent to serve them in the Landsberg prison. The first two major trials had to do with the camps of Mauthausen and Dachau. The preparation of the prosecution for these trials was relatively quick. These had been the last camps to be liberated, and the SS had neither the time nor any place to hide. As an American historian put it, the first trials "concentrated on proving guilt by circumstance," which meant, for instance, that the camp commander was automatically held responsible for all the atrocities perpetrated in his camp. The death sentences and hangings were thus more numerous for Mauthausen and Dachau than they were to be subsequently for Buchenwald.

Among the SS executed was Förschner, commander of Dora when the camp was created and until the beginning of 1945. He had then been placed at the head of the Kaufering camp, one of the most terrible sub-camps of Dachau. His quick elimination would deprive the later Dora trial of a first-rank witness.

Another trial that finished up quickly, between September 17 and November 17, 1945, was that of Bergen-Belsen, in Lüneburg in the British zone. The principal SS leaders—and first and foremost Kramer—were sentenced to death and executed. Among them was Franz Hössler, who had been *Transportführer* of the first convoy from Dora to arrive at Bergen-Belsen and then, for several days, the commander of the "barracks camp" mentioned in chapter 18.

THE NUREMBERG TRIALS. The trial at Nuremberg of the principal dignitaries of the Nazi regime as war criminals was planned for by the "London charter" established by the representatives of the four occupying powers in June 1945. There were twenty-two defendants, one of whom, Martin Bormann, was judged in absentia. The trial opened on November 20, 1945, and the verdict was announced on October 2, 1946. Three of the accused were acquitted. Eleven were sentenced to death; Göring committed suicide and the others were executed.

Among the accused sentenced to prison was Albert Speer, who would serve his full twenty-year term. He was the only one on trial whose charge had an indirect link with the Dora camp.

THE BUCHENWALD AND DORA TRIALS IN 1947. The Buchenwald trial took place at Dachau from April to August 1947. The camp commander, Hermann Pister, was one of the accused. He was sentenced to death but died of a heart attack in the Landsberg prison in September 1948.

The Dora trial is not referred to as such in the archives. It is either designated as the Nordhausen War Crimes Case, or as the *United States of America v. Kurt Andrae et al.* Although the name of Nordhausen was emphasized to describe the trial, there is no equivocation. Aside from the title, the documents, starting with the bill of indictment, constantly refer to Dora. One can suppose that it was the discovery on April 11, 1945, of the Boelcke Kaserne in Nordhausen and the notoriety given to this discovery that determined the choice of title. The second formula is a commonplace of American case law: the name of the first of the accused is indicated, followed by "and others." With regard to the Buchenwald trial the title was *United States of America v. Prince Josias zu Waldeck et al.* In the absence of any prince at Dora, the first of the accused was taken in alphabetical order, though Kurt Andrae was not really the most important.

The trial opened in Dachau on August 7, 1947. The verdict was announced on December 30. Of the seventeen accused, fourteen were SS; three were acquitted. The only civilian, Rickhey, was acquitted. Three of the four incriminated prisoners were found guilty. The preparations carried out by the American prosecuting officers had been long. They had begun on April 27, 1945, some two years before the trial began. A particularly important role was played by Wincenty Hein, a young Polish lawyer who had been a prisoner at Dora and ended up as *Schreiber* in Nordhausen during the final weeks. He became the expert witness to the prosecuting officers and helped them exploit the camp documents, which had escaped destruction in the final days. They were found after the evacuation, particularly in the blocks of the SS camp and in the outside Kommandos such as the Boelcke Kaserne. Already in 1945, Hein put together a proposed bill of indictment with an overall description of the Dora-Mittelbau complex and its history. In 1967 he used his documentation for a study published in Polish in Warsaw. In 1969 this study was published in Warsaw in French under the title *Conditions de vie et de travail des prisonniers dans le camp de concentration Dora-Mittelbau (Living and Working Conditions in the Dora-Mittelbau Concentration Camp)*. The author, like many others, found this reference work extremely valuable.

The 1947 trial was not satisfying—but that was not due to any inadequacies in the prosecution. It lacked, both as defendants and witnesses, the main protagonists. The principal defendant should have been Kammler, as much for the tunnel in the first months as for the work sites subsequently under the control of his *Sonderstab*. He had disappeared in May 1945. The camp's first commander, Förschner, was not there either: he had been executed after the trial of the Dachau camp. Also missing was his successor, Baer, who was in hiding. He would later be arrested, charged with acts committed at Auschwitz, and would die in prison before coming to trial. Also absent was the SS Dr. Plaza, who was dead.

The two German civilians having played an important role when the tunnel was undergoing modification work were also absent: they were, above all, Sawatzki—who had died in May 1945 under unknown circumstances—and Rudolph, who had left for the United States with his colleagues from Peenemünde, as the role he had played prior to the transfer of the prisoners from Buchenwald to Peenemünde was unknown. It was not, however, impossible to have Germans who had left Germany in the framework of Overcast brought back to stand trial. This is what happened to Rickhey—but he was not involved in what went on in the first months of the tunnel.

Three German communists having occupied functions at the time—Kuntz, Thomas, and Sczymczak—would have been valuable witnesses as to the first months of the tunnel and camp. The SS had eliminated them along with others in 1945. Without Kammler and Förschner, without Sawatzki and Rudolph, without Kuntz and Thomas, the demarcation of fundamental responsibilities during Dora's crucial period was an impossible task for the judges.

The trials moreover were henceforth limited to determining the personal responsibility of each of the accused in precise circumstances such as hangings, cases of serious brutality, or the assassination of prisoners in the camp or in the outside Kommandos, or during the arrival of the "transports" or the evacuations. Other crimes were also targeted including the theft of packages destined for the prisoners. Rickhey was charged in connection with the tunnel hangings, but his personal guilt could not be established and he was acquitted.

Only one of the SS was condemned to death: Obersturmführer Hans Möser, who, as seen in chapter 19, had been *Transportführer* of the last evacuation convoy to leave Dora. He was hanged on November 26, 1948. Among the six SS sentenced to life imprisonment were Erhard Brauny, commander of Rottleberode and *Transportführer* of one of the convoys that arrived at Gardelegen; Otto Brinkmann, commander of Ellrich; and Wilhelm Simon, in charge of the tunnel Arbeitseinsatz.

Three prisoners—all Greens—were sentenced: Willy Zwiener, LÄ at Dora at the beginning of 1944, to twenty-five years' imprisonment; Richard Walenta, LÄ at Ellrich, and then the SD's assistant in the bunker, to twenty years' imprisonment; and Josef Kilian, executioner at Dora, to life imprisonment. Among the witnesses were two German prisoners—Greens—who had volunteered to help the Americans. Roman Drung, the last of the LÄ at Dora, had escaped at Oker from the last convoy along with SS concerned with getting rid of their uniforms. Willy Schmidt, well known to Max Dutillieux as the *Kapo* in the tunnel and then at Rossla, had also escaped from the evacuation column before passing over the Elbe.

At the same time the main trial was being held, several other annex trials took place with summary proceedings. The *Kapo* Georg Finkenzeller, "Big George" mentioned in chapter 9, convicted of abuse but not of murder, was thus sentenced in October 1947 to two years' imprisonment.

THE DORA TRIAL AT ESSEN. Though it took place much later, it is important to mention the trial of three SS from Dora, which was held at Essen between November 17, 1967, and May 8, 1970. On this occasion the trial was before a German court. The creation in 1958 of the special inquiry service on Nazi crimes indeed made it possible to gather evidence and prepare prosecution regarding those cases that had not been judged by the Allied courts.

The three accused in Essen were Obersturmbannführer Helmut Bischoff, head of the Mittelbau SD unit; his collaborator Oberscharführer Ernst Sander; and Hauptscharführer Erwin Busta, nicknamed "Horse Head" as mentioned in chapter 9. The three defendants were given prison sentences.

THE FRENCH TRIALS. Two French trials took place to judge French citizens in connection with Dora. One was aimed at Naegelé, already sentenced to death in absentia in Tours for his role as a Gestapo agent before the Liberation. He was arrested upon his return, judged once again, including for what he had done at Dora, sentenced to death on January 28, 1947, in Paris, and executed.

Charges were also laid before the French military tribunal in Rastatt against Grozdoff, who moreover did not seek to hide. Arrested on July 1, 1946, he was acquitted.[29]

The Debate over the Concentration Camps

Great confusion reigned for several years after 1945 with regard to judgments about the concentration camps—essentially because of Soviet policies at that time. The debate had to do with Buchenwald, and parenthetically, Dora. French opinion was affected only by the correlative revelations about the gulag. Things were far more serious in Eastern Europe.

THE VISION OF ROUSSET AND KOGON. At the beginning of May 1945, David Rousset was in Wöbbelin, the camp that had just been liberated by the Americans under the conditions mentioned in chapter 21. Suffering from pulmonary congestion and typhus, he managed to have himself repatriated quickly.[30] He had gone from 190 to 104 pounds, and when he got to Paris, Maurice Nadeau found him unrecognizable. He went to spend time recovering at Saint-Jean-de-Monts with his wife Sue, and his memory came back to him as he regained his health. In three weeks he dictated *L'Univers concentrationnaire (The Concentration Camp World)* to Sue, which was published in the *Revue internationale,* then published in mid-1946 and awarded the Renaudot Prize. His next book, *Les Jours de notre mort (The Days of Our Death),* demanded more research work and writing effort. It appeared in 1947. Immediately upon their publication, both books became classics on the Nazi concentration camps.

In writing the *Jours de notre mort,* Rousset acknowledges having used two German documents. The first, published in Weimar under the supervision of former communist prisoners and prefaced by Ernst Busse, was entitled *Konzentrationslager Buchenwald.* The other was the German manuscript of Eugen Kogon's work, *Der SS Staat.* As indicated in chapter 3, Kogon had first of all, at the request of the team from the American Psychological Warfare Division, written—in Buchenwald itself—a report subsequently known as *The Buchenwald Report.* He then set himself up near Frankfurt and wrote, on that basis, *Der SS Staat,* a book devoted to the camps in general but which is based especially on the example of Buchenwald. Finished in November 1945, the book was published in Germany in 1946. It was translated into French in 1947 and entitled *L'Enfer organisé,* then in English in 1950 as *The Theory and Practice of Hell.*

The dominant picture of the camps that appeared in the Western countries at the time was that of Buchenwald. This was especially true in France, where many former prisoners from Buchenwald would go on to hold notable positions in politics or journalism: Claude Bourdet, Guy Ducoloné, Pierre Durand, Albert Forcinal, Frédéric Manhès, André Marie, Marcel Paul, Christian Pineau, Rémy Roure, Pierre Sudreau, and Eugène Thomas, for instance. They returned at the end of April 1945, as did Louis Sellier, the author's father, and his friends from Amiens, Louis Despierres and Paul Gaillandre. Pineau became supplies minister in 1945, Marcel Paul became minister of industrial production, and Eugène Thomas became postmaster general.

Among the characteristics that stand out in Rousset's and Kogon's schema, the Reds' victorious struggle against the Greens for the control of the Buchenwald camp's internal administration is of primary importance—which contributed to the prestige of the communist leaders. This is all the more noteworthy as neither Kogon nor Rousset were communists themselves. Kogon was a Catholic activist and Rousset was a former member of the Socialist students who had turned to Trotskyism. Neither of them was a novice or gullible with regard to political issues. It is also noteworthy that the publication of Kogon's book was supported by the American officer Rosenberg and the future leader of the British Labour Party, Richard Crossman, as is the fact that it came out in the American-occupied zone.

RASSINIER'S DISSENT. Rousset's and Kogon's schema does not, however, reflect a unanimous opinion. In 1946 one of the few British prisoners at Buchenwald, Christopher Burney, published *The Dungeon Democracy* in which, among other bold assertions, he declared that the communists were nothing but "Nazis painted red." It should also be pointed out that two members of the Psychological Warfare Division, Egon W. Fleck and Edward A. Tenenbaum, had passed through Buchenwald before Rosenberg's team got there and that in a brief report they did not seem very convinced by the testimonies they had gathered. Their text was later exploited against the communists.

But it was in France itself that the most lively dissent arose, from the pen of Paul Rassinier, a French deportee at Dora who had passed his quarantine at Buchenwald in January–March 1944. In 1949 he first published, at his own expense, an account entitled *Passage de la ligne. Du vrai à l'humain (Crossing the Line: From the True to the Human)* dealing with his deportation. In 1950 he published *Le Mensonge d'Ulysse. Regard sur la littérature concentrationnaire*

(The Lie of Odysseus: Looking at Concentration Camp Writings) in which he criticized other authors of texts on the camps. In 1955 the two texts were collected under the common title *Le Mensonge d'Ulysse* in two parts: *L'Expérience vécue (Lived Experience)*, corresponding to the earlier *Passage de la ligne*, and *L'Expérience des autres (The Experience of Others)*, corresponding to the later *Mensonge d'Ulysse* of 1950.

The author has carefully examined Rassinier's testimony, just as he examined the testimonies of the other Dora prisoners, and refers to it in six different chapters. This analysis confirms that Rassinier only followed the common lot from January 30 to April 8, 1944: his arrival at Buchenwald, quarantine, transfer to Dora, and assignment to an earthworks Kommando. On April 8, 1944, he went into the Dora *Revier* and remained there under privileged conditions until April 1945. His stay in the *Revier* was interrupted only by brief returns to the camp and by a stint in the service of a noncommissioned SS officer between December 23, 1944, and March 10, 1945. He thus had no direct experience of the tunnel nor of any of the other Mittelbau camps. Most of the indications that he provides stem from conversations with fellow prisoners who arrived sick in the *Revier.* They were generally very approximate, and on several occasions entirely erroneous.

Rassinier's personality is disconcerting. He established no friendships in the camp and had only negative judgments with regard to the other prisoners, both at Buchenwald and at Dora. Entrenched in his solitude and his inaction in the *Revier,* he fabricated a schema for interpreting the concentration camp world that is at times banal and at others just plain aberrant. As he was naturally given to pontificating, he was known in the *Revier* as the "professor." (He has actually kept this title in certain bibliographies in German.)

His first work, in 1949, went unnoticed. The second, in 1950, in which he attacked nominally and successively Brother Birin, Abbot Jean-Paul Renard, Abbot Robert Ploton, Louis Martin-Chauffier, David Rousset, and Eugen Kogon, was necessarily better known—particularly as it was accompanied by a preface by Albert Paraz, casting doubt in passing on Edmond Michelet, a former deportee to Dachau (who also became a minister in 1945), which caused a scandal. In this book the first reservations regarding the gas chambers appeared. But negationism would only develop later on in other writings. At the time, Rassinier's key objective was to try and replace Rousset's and Kogon's schema regarding the camps with his own. He did not manage to do so, but the 1955 collection would be translated into German in 1960, into Spanish in 1961, and into Italian in 1966—as if it were an important reference book. Yet, both with regard to Buchenwald and Dora, it is a document to be treated with caution—to a far greater extent than the books of the authors Rassinier incriminates.

THE SOVIETS AND THE CAMPS IN GERMANY. Given the notoriety of the camps in Germany—and especially of Buchenwald—in the Western countries, one might normally have expected a generally positive attitude as well from the Soviet authorities, henceforth established in the east of Germany and particularly in Thuringia. There was nothing of the sort.

The point of difference in comparison to the Western countries was the reception of the former prisoners of the camps when they were repatriated to the Soviet Union. There was then, as is now known, no indulgence whatsoever with regard to the prisoners of war, generally accused of not having fought to the finish. There was still less indulgence for the *Ostarbeiter*—the men and women who had come to work in Germany, often in the arms factories, whether voluntarily or not. As the Soviets in the concentration camps were for the most part prisoners of war or *Ostarbeiter* who had turned into prisoners for real or alleged infractions, they were not entitled, generally speaking, to a warm welcome.

It was hoped that the opening of the Soviet archives would make it possible to gain a clearer perspective on this painful period. This would not appear to be the case—for the time being, at any rate.[31] There are only several rare testimonies, such as that of a Ukrainian from Dora, originally from Kremenchug, who was only eighteen years old when arrested in 1943. For this reason he got away with only ten years in the Soviet army, as a simple soldier.

The camps of Buchenwald, Sachsenhausen, and Ravensbrück were not then considered by the Soviets as centers that had to be preserved but as handy installations for whomever they had to intern. In their zone, they of course arrested the Nazi leaders, Gestapo agents, and so on. But they also went after social democratic activists who were hostile to their party joining up with the Communist Party to form the SED.

They above all went after landowners, business leaders, professionals—thereby carrying out a profound social revolution. Buchenwald from September 1945 up until 1950 was one of the indispensable internment centers for these operations.

The communist prisoners at Buchenwald, of whom there were still almost eight hundred in 1945, were entitled, because of the coherency of the bloc which they had constituted, to hope to play an important role in the new Germany liberated from Nazism.[32] This is indeed what initially occurred for a certain number of them, who happened to have links with Saxony and Thuringia.

Some of the principal leaders returned home to western Germany. Such was the case for Hans Eiden, who had been LÄ2 in 1943–44, then LÄI in 1944–45, and thus during the liberation of the camp; he settled in Trier, where he died in 1950. Paul Schreck, who remained LÄ3 from 1942 to 1945, returned home to Mannheim where he died in 1948. Emil Carlebach, a Jewish communist survivor, returned home to Frankfurt and founded the *Frankfurter Rundschau;* he would later move to the GDR.

The others started careers in the Soviet zone. Ernst Busse, former member of the Reichstag, had played a leading role in the camp from 1939 to 1945. He was

LÄ2 in 1939–40, LÄ1 in 1940–41, then *Kapo* of the *Revier* from 1942 to 1945. He was also from 1943 to 1945 one of the three clandestine leaders of the Communist Party. In 1945 he became minister of the interior and vice president of Thuringia. Erich Reschke, first of all *Kapo* of the *Baukommando,* was successively LÄ2 in 1940, LÄ3 in 1940–42, LÄ2 in 1942–43, and finally LÄ1 in 1943–44. In 1945 he became *Polizeichef* in Thuringia. Harry Kuhn, one of the three clandestine leaders of the Communist Party from 1943–45, became in 1945 Bezirksleiter des KPD in Leipzig.

The most important communist leader from Buchenwald was Walter Bartel, who was one of the three clandestine leaders from October 1939 until the liberation of the camp. In 1946 he was the secretary and the spokesman for relations with the press of Wilhelm Pieck, president of the SED, and subsequently president of the GDR.

But these activists who came out of Buchenwald were considered with suspicion by the German communists who returned from Moscow. In the autumn of 1946, in the course of a secret internal procedure, a commission of the SED's central committee examined the behavior of those who had exerted functions in the camp and questioned the role of Ernst Busse, as *Kapo* of the *Revier,* where the SS doctors had carried out mortal injections in certain blocks.[33] In the November 7 report the clandestine leadership finally obtained a general acquittal, but certain leaders, including Busse, were later reduced to subaltern functions. Nevertheless, as will be seen later, the issue, in which the Soviets did not get involved, was not closed. It was only the first episode.

DAVID ROUSSET AND THE DISCOVERY OF THE GULAG. In his two books, David Rousset did not hide his consideration for the communist leaders in the camps. He had dedicated *Les Jours de notre mort (The Days of Our Death)* "to Emil Künder, my German comrade in the concentration-camp universe." Künder was a *Kapo* he had known at Helmstedt and at Wöbbelin. This attitude, as seen above, was to earn him Rassinier's reprobation. In 1950 he nonetheless engaged in a court battle with a Communist-run publication, *Les Lettres françaises,* this time with regard to the gulag.[34]

The question as to the existence of concentration camps in the Soviet Union had been raised in 1947 by the publication in France of Kravtchenko's book, *I Chose Freedom*—with considerable success. Accused of lying by the communist press, Kravtchenko had summoned *Les Lettres françaises* to appear in court. The trial had taken place from January to April 1949, and Kravtchenko won his case.

Rousset looked into the subject. He knew Margarete Buber-Neumann's story, mentioned above in chapter 21. He also had testimonies of Poles who had left the USSR during the war to join the Anders army. Lastly, he came upon the Russian text of the "Code of Correctional Labor in the SSFRR"—the Soviet Socialist Federal Republic of Russia. He launched an appeal to former deportees in the *Figaro littéraire* of November 12, 1949, for the creation of a commission of inquiry into the matter. The text mentions the existence of a gulag. It was approved by such former deportees as Jean Cayrol, Michel Riquet, Louis Martin-Chauffier, and Rémy Roure.

After much debate, a "French commission of inquiry against the concentration-camp regime" was created on January 24, 1950, demanding the creation of an international commission to lead an inquiry in Spain, Greece, and Yugoslavia as well as in the USSR. The president of the French commission was a former deportee to Buchenwald, A. S. Balachowsky (who was mentioned in chapter 13).

On March 13, 1950, a text was published in *L'Humanité* entitled "David Rousset disowned by the former German deportees who saved his life." Among the signatories was Emil Künder, with his identity number (from Neuengamme) 21462. Pierre Daix, himself a former prisoner of Mauthausen, accused Rousset of fraud with regard to a detail of the translation of the Russian code; Rousset brought a lawsuit against *Les Lettres françaises*. The trial began on November 25, 1950, and concluded on January 12, 1951, with Pierre Daix's condemnation. Meanwhile, the situation had worsened in the GDR for the former prisoners of Buchenwald.

TRIALS AND INQUIRIES IN EAST GERMANY AND ELSEWHERE. On March 29, 1950, Ernst Busse was arrested by the SMAD, or Sowjetische Militäradministration, the Soviet military administration—the very organization that had interned so many Germans at Buchenwald.[35] Charges were laid against him as a *Kriegsverbrecher*—a war criminal. On June 8, 1950, Reschke was in turn arrested on the same charges. The details of their trials, which remained secret, are known only through anonymous testimony, gathered by Lutz Niethammer and published in *Der "gesäuberte" Antifaschismus* dealing with the "Roten Kapos von Buchenwald."

They were condemned in early 1951 to life imprisonment and the confiscation of their possessions. They were sent to the gulag—to the well-known Vorkouta camp. The end of their trial happened to coincide with the end of the Daix trial in France, initiated by Rousset, also regarding the gulag. Busse died at Vorkouta on August 31, 1952. Reschke, as will be seen, would be released in 1955 and would return to Germany. The Soviet involvement was limited to these two instances.

One might almost be tempted to consider that in Busse's and Reschke's cases it had to do with incriminations of a personal nature, were it not for the fact that suspicion cast on Walter Bartel in 1953 shows that it was actually the whole system of internal control of the camps by the communists that was being criticized. Bartel is indeed the only one to have been a member of the clandestine leadership, without interruption from 1939 to 1945, but without having at the same time had a notable function involving responsibility in the administration of a camp, such as LÄ, or the *Kapo* of a *Revier* or the Arbeitsstatistik.

In the spring of 1953 the supervisory commission of the SED therefore engaged proceedings against Bartel, who was still Pieck's secretary.[36] In this regard the minutes of his questioning on May 29, 1953, are available. In August 1953 he was informed orally that the case would not be pursued further, but he was stripped of all political responsibility and had to accept a position as a teaching assistant in modern history at Leipzig.

The documents gathered and published in extenso by Niethammer show the extent of the criticism leveled at the policies pursued in the camps. Overall the objection was to have agreed to collaborate with the SS to ensure the camps' functioning. More precisely, it had to do, for example, with having engaged in what was known as "victim swapping"—*der Opfertausch*. This expression refers to the replacement of threatened prisoners, whether communists or not, by other prisoners, whether known or unknown. This had been the case, in particular, at Buchenwald (as it also had, moreover, at Dachau), during the establishment of lists of transports to the more feared Kommandos such as Dora or Laura, Langenstein, or Ohrdruf. The Soviet—or Soviet-inspired—prosecutors set themselves on the same terrain as such critics as Rassinier. But one wonders whether they were truly acting in good faith.

Indeed, in late 1952 the trial of communist leaders, which would be known as the Slansky trial, took place in Prague. Among the eleven sentenced to death, and hanged on December 3, was Josef Frank, who had worked at the Buchenwald Arbeitsstatistik, where he represented the Czechs, just as Jorge Semprun had represented the Spanish and Daniel Anker the French. He "acknowledged" having, in that capacity, been responsible for the death of several fellow prisoners and having cooperated with the Gestapo. Semprun is utterly convinced of his innocence on this point. In the same trial, another former communist prisoner, from Mauthausen, Artur London, was condemned to life imprisonment, after *L'Aveu*.

It is possible, as Niethammer believes, that a German variant of the Slansky trial was cooked up.[37] In December 1952, Paul Merker, a Jewish leader of the SED, was arrested in connection with this trial. Slansky and London were also Jews. Merker was condemned in 1954 to eight years of forced labor following a secret trial. In May 1953, Franz Dahlem was excluded from the central committee of the SED; he was, like London, a former soldier with the International Brigades in Spain and a former prisoner from Mauthausen.

In Slovenia too, political prisoners who were not Titoists were after 1945 accused of collaboration with the SS and executed. Three remarks are called for at this point.

The first is that the succession of inquiries, trials, and rehabilitation does not

make it possible to state clearly if there were, for instance, liquidations of undesirable elements in the *Revier* or manifest abuses of authority of certain of those
wearing armbands. One is inclined to think that the conditions particular to concentration camps did not allow for total innocence.

The second remark concerns Willi Seifert, who had become, in 1941, at the
age of twenty-six, *Kapo* of the Arbeitsstatistik—a position he still held in 1945.
If ever a Red *Kapo* had his authority broadly contested after the fact, it was indeed the *Kapo* of the Arbeitsstatistik. Yet Seifert was never subsequently bothered for this—even though Frank was executed. Quite to the contrary, he was,
from 1957 to 1983, *Generalleutnant* of the Volkspolizei and took part in this capacity in putting up the Berlin Wall in 1961. Niethammer enumerates, on page
136, the impressive series of decorations he was awarded between 1950 and
1985.

The third concerns the communist officials at Dora, Albert Kuntz in particular. The latter had been one of the first clandestine leaders at Buchenwald, until
his imprisonment in the bunker and his being sent to an outside Kommando at
Kassel. He was later one of the first to arrive at Dora, where he played, as already noted, an important role. If he had not been eliminated by the Gestapo in
early 1945, would he too not have had to account for his actions in the atmosphere of suspicion that prevailed in the early 1950s?

BACK TO NORMAL. The preceding paragraphs have shown the exceptional
confusion that reigned with regard to the concentration camps between 1945
and 1953—that is, until Stalin's death. Subsequently they all came to take their
normal places, so to speak.

The Americans, who contributed by prompting the writing of the *Buchenwald Report* to popularizing through the works of Kogon and Rousset a certain
picture of the camps, consigned this report to oblivion because it was favorable
to the communists. Its text was made public, everything having by then calmed
down, only in 1995, thanks to Rosenberg, who brought out of his personal
archives the copy that he had held onto of the *Bericht über das Konzentrationslager Buchenwald bei Weimar*—the *Buchenwald Report*'s original German
title. An academic in El Paso, Texas (the very city of Fort Bliss), he allowed one
of his colleagues from the German department, David A. Hackett, to publish the
document.

Hackett translated the entire text into English and wrote a long introduction.
It was published by Frederick A. Praeger, whose father died in a camp after having been imprisoned at Buchenwald; in 1945, when he had arrived on location
as an American officer, he looked for him in vain before meeting Rosenberg and
Kogon in Frankfurt.

The German edition of the original text came out in 1996. It included a translation of Hackett's introduction and notes. These two publications are most appreciated, because the failure to publish an important text is always frustrating

for historians. They did not, however, really modify what was already known about the subject on the basis of Kogon's book. Until his death in 1987, the latter remained the authority on the subject, along with Hermann Langbein, who was, as a young communist, a prisoner at Dachau, Auschwitz, and Neuengamme. Rousset's works have lost none of their importance.

It was in East Germany that the situation evolved after 1953, at first progressively and then discreetly. The Soviets' abandoning the camp facilitated this development, but silence prevailed as to what the site had been used for between 1945 and 1950. In 1955, Reschke, freed from the gulag, returned to Germany and obtained a position in the police force. He was rehabilitated but refrained from any account of his trial and detention. Busse was also rehabilitated posthumously—and in secret. Paul Merker was freed in 1956. Dahlem, rehabilitated in 1956, returned to the central committee in 1957. In 1956, social democrats who remained in prison were still being freed. In Czechoslovakia, Artur London was freed in 1955 and rehabilitated in 1956. Other rehabilitations were subsequently announced, for instance in Czechoslovakia and in Yugoslavia.

It was Walter Bartel's newfound status that best translated the overall rehabilitation in the GDR of the Buchenwald communists and their leadership. In 1957 he became director in Berlin of the Institut für Zeitgeschichte, and then in 1962, Professor für Neuere und Neueste Geschichte (professor of modern and contemporary history) at the Humboldt University in Berlin. In 1959 he edited the camp's international committee's publication of *Buchenwald Mahnung und Verpflichtung*, which became a fundamental work on the subject. That very German title could be translated as: *Buchenwald: Admonition and Obligation*.

[[24]]

SOLIDARITY AND MEMORY

For more than fifty years now, associations of Dora survivors have existed in various countries. They maintain the memory of the Mittelbau complex with a certain amount of support from officials and historians. It may be useful for the contemporary reader to point out some of the more striking episodes of this long period.

Associations and "Amicales"

When a war comes to an end, the veterans are always concerned with the idea of getting back together in a great élan of unity. Among the French soldiers of World War I—the so-called *poilus*—the slogan "United as we were on the front" was on everyone's lips. But in the end, once they had returned to civilian life the veterans joined various associations based, generally speaking, on political cleavages. The author—son of a First World War veteran, involved in various forms of political activism—still has a clear memory of such a situation in the 1930s. What was striking to note at the time was the simultaneous pursuit of close ties at the level of former military units. The regiment associations, for instance, had no trouble bringing together men who, in a more general sense, belonged to different veterans' associations.

There is therefore nothing surprising in the fact that a similar evolution can be observed after 1945 in the movement of the former deportees. The subject has been addressed by Annette Wieviorka in *Déportation et Génocide,*[1] and its systematic study cannot be undertaken here. Several remarks on the French deportees will suffice.

The first is the heterogeneity of the concentration camp population. The Jews deported from Drancy and submitted to a selection upon their arrival at Auschwitz must first of all be distinguished from the mass of the deportees from Compiègne, themselves different from one another: *Résistants* or not, communists or "Gaullists," hostages or victims of roundups, even various small-time offenders.

Certain among them were staunch activists whose convictions were not dulled by their deportation. The major political vicissitudes of the postwar period, particularly in a country like France, later led to cleavages that culminated in schisms, as for instance in the trade union movement. But on closer inspection the consequences are not always very clear, particularly with regard to the French from Buchenwald.

The second remark has to do with the importance of the "camp associations" whose membership has very generally remained united. What also must be pointed out is the existence, alongside the camp associations, of a certain number of "Kommando associations" that have remained very active—such as those of Neu Stassfurt and Langenstein. This was pointed out in chapter 20. With regard to Dora, two arrangements were ultimately arrived at. According to one, because Dora was for a long time a Kommando of Buchenwald, an association for Buchenwald-Dora had to be set up, without discrimination. According to the other, the life of the prisoners at Dora had been dissociated to such an extent from that of the prisoners at Buchenwald that a separate association was necessary. Many of the prisoners from Dora chose to join both associations. Most of them had been members of the first convoys. Those who had spent time at Ellrich alone on the other hand generally lost interest in Buchenwald.

In Belgium the Dora and Kommandos Political Prisoners' Association was entirely distinct from the Buchenwald association.

The Dora-Ellrich Association and Orphans' Aid

The Association of Political and Resistance Deportees of Dora, Ellrich, Harzungen and Annex Kommandos was established on May 11, 1946,[2] by the fusion of two associations created on October 28, 1945: the "Dora Deportees" and the "Political and Resistance Deportees of Ellrich." The usual term used is the "Dora-Ellrich Association," which concerns the former prisoners from the whole Mittelbau complex such as it was defined in late 1944.

The association's first president, until the time of his death in 1960, was Pierre Ségelle. A doctor, he had treated his fellow prisoners in the Ellrich *Revier,* and at Schwerin following the evacuation of Sachsenhausen. After his return he collaborated on researching the illnesses of deportees and the possible causes of these illnesses.

In its first years the Dora-Ellrich Association, like the other former prisoners' associations, was mainly concerned with helping its members, informing families, doing research on missing persons, and denouncing war criminals. Its social service activities were especially important, under the direction of the widow of a deportee, Mrs. Sanchidrian, with the assistance of Olivier-Jacques Courtaud, whose memoirs were cited in chapters 11, 12, and 18. Georges Sanchidrian was at Ellrich, as were Courtaud and Ségelle. The problems that had to be dealt with were of such magnitude that Courtaud took the initiative of creating, in December 1949, a separate association, "Orphans' Aid," for the assistance of widows and their children. The association brought together the needs of the Dora-Ellrich Association and those of the *Résistance* network CND-Castille, of which Courtaud was a member. Its objective was to help the orphans in every respect—materially, but also through stipends for studies, summer camps, and so on, and finally through a personal link through godfathers and godmothers. In all, 83 families were involved, representing 183 orphans, 95 girls and 88 boys.

The resources came from members of the associations concerned but also from the very large number of outside members, recruited thanks to the activity of Courtaud, who, as a radio-navigator with Air France, mobilized an extensive network of relations in France and abroad. A publication, *Le Lien*[3] *(The Link),* kept members, families, and children informed. Fifty issues came out between 1950 and 1962. Courtaud devoted himself completely to the association, as did his wife. Their home served as headquarters. He was known as Jacot, the name he had used in the *Résistance,* and his wife was known as Jacotte.

They had practically accomplished their task by 1962. There were some fifteen young people to support for several more years. The association was disbanded on March 31 and the remaining funds divided between the two associations on a pro rata basis depending on the number of orphans they still had to support. The Dora-Ellrich Association took over the publication of the *Lien,* directed by Pierre Goasguen, until issue 65 in June 1970. Marien Leschi then replaced Pierre Ségelle as president. He died in 1971. He was succeeded by Gustave Leroy until 1978, Gabriel Lacoste until 1983, Pierre Dejussieu until 1984, Louis Garnier until 1993, and Jean Mialet until 1999. At that time the presidency was taken on by Yves Mével, son of the former prisoner Louis Mével.

The Memorial of the Dora-Ellrich Camps

At the same time they showed their solidarity with the families of their late fellow prisoners, the former Dora-Ellrich prisoners were concerned from 1949 on with preserving the memory of the trials they had undergone, by putting together a variety of testimonies in a single publication. A 142-page, large-format collection was thus established and entitled *Mémorial des camps de Dora-Ellrich (Memorial of the Dora-Ellrich Camps).* It was comprised of twenty-two accounts of various lengths, five poems, and eight drawings. The rule having been to maintain the anonymity of the contributions, the historian is somewhat frustrated, though various cross-checks make it possible to identify some of the authors.

Many of the texts are of great interest, and it is important that they be preserved in this way. As a whole, however, the collection lacks coherency, and the absence of notes does not allow moments and places to be situated with accuracy. It can be assumed that Abbot Jean-Paul Renard—who already in the tunnel was known as "der Dichter" (the poet)—played a determining role in putting the collection together, and that he was himself the author of a long text entitled "Death Tunnels and Living Tabernacles."[4]

In the preceding chapters the author quoted at length the various accounts in the *Mémorial* on Ellrich, which were especially relevant. With regard to Dora, other sources appeared more complete. There were no further collections of this kind, which are difficult to put together.

Buchenwald and Dora as Places of Memory in Germany

As seen above, the Buchenwald site was not available for a commemoration before 1950. The same went for the Dora site, for different reasons.

In Thuringia until October 1946 the Russian rocket specialists with the assistance of German technicians controlled all the sites connected with the V2s, such as the Dora Tunnel, Bleicherode and Kleinbodungen, and even Lehesten. Then in October 1946, as pointed out, the Soviets transferred the German rocket technicians along with the others they had recruited in other fields to the USSR; their own specialists went with them. Behind them, other teams systematically dismantled the corresponding material, which was shipped on behind them. The Russians proceeded everywhere in the same fashion—in the Junkers factory, for instance. The tunnel factory was thus stripped of all its equipment, including cables, piping, and so on.

The final liquidation operation took place during the summer of 1948: the Russians blew up the tunnel. More precisely, they blew up each of the four exits, at the north and south ends of tunnels A and B. They also caved in the interior at several points, in Halls 14 to 17, 25 to 28, and 35 to 38. They simultaneously obstructed other of Sonderstab Kammler's underground sites, including the former mines at Neu Stassfurt and Wansleben.

Near the tunnel the camp barracks were used until 1945–46, first as a place of internment and later to shelter the refugees from the Sudetenland. They were then abandoned and the materials were recovered by those nearby. This is true of the Dora, Harzungen, and Woffleben prisoners' camps, for instance, but also of the camps that housed the SS or the German and foreign civilian workers. The area was not far from the demarcation between the Soviet and the British zones, which was ever more closely controlled. And the population was confined in the surrounding area. The camp that held up least to the destruction was Ellrich, which was, as has been mentioned, divided between the two zones. The prisoners' blocks were in Thuringia but the various buildings of Juliushütte, where the SS were located, were in Lower Saxony along with the crematorium above the camp.

When the *Mémorial* was published in 1949, the foreword began as follows:

"In anticipation of the pilgrimage we all want to make some day to Dora and Ellrich . . ." In April 1950, pilgrimages began to Buchenwald, and a French group, which Jean-Pierre Couture[5] was part of, was authorized to travel by bus to Dora, to the crematorium, and to Nordhausen and the Boelcke Kaserne necropolis.

The Soviets having abandoned Buchenwald in early 1950, the GDR authorities were able to give some thought as to what to do with the site. Major work was carried out until 1958, culminating with today's commemorative and monumental complex that makes up the memorial, the Nationale Mahn- und Gedenkstätte, "national place of exhortation and memory"—the largest in the country. It was solemnly inaugurated on September 14, 1958,[6] by Otto Grotewohl, copresident of the SED (East German Communist Party) and head of the GDR government, in the presence of eighty thousand people. Investigations into the behavior of the "Roten Kapos" were over, and in 1959, Walter Bartel edited *Buchenwald Mahnung und Verpflichtung*.

At Dora the commemoration came later and was more discreet. A memorial was set up only in 1964 in the form of a sculpted group of five prisoners on a small square near the crematorium, which had been preserved. Only a few barracks remained; all that was left of the others were the foundations progressively grown over by the vegetation. That was already the case in 1950.

There is strictly no comparison between Buchenwald and Dora as far as the symbolism inspired by the commemoration is concerned. Buchenwald is near Weimar, making it possible to recall the memory of Schiller and Goethe. The latter had taken walks on the Ettersberg, and the burned-out remains (following the bombing of August 1944) of "Goethe's oak tree" can be seen in the camp. But no reference was made to the Weimar Republic.

Buchenwald was above all one of the large classical camps of the essentially German period of the concentration camp system, where a great many communist activists were interned. It was at Buchenwald, though not in the camp itself, that on August 18, 1944, the SS executed Ernst Thälmann, the great leader of the German Communist Party before 1933. The conditions of the liberation of the camp on April 11, 1945, were utterly exceptional. Nowhere else did the liberators find a camp of such magnitude (it still held more than twenty thousand people) still under the effective control of an international leadership of prisoners. At Buchenwald, however, there are no great heroes who stand out on the individual level. The period of suspicion left its mark.

It was at Dora that one finds heroes to be honored—Albert Kuntz foremost among them. He had been an important figure at Buchenwald, and along with Bartel was one of the three clandestine communist leaders from his arrival in 1937 until his departure for a Kommando at Kassel in 1943. As seen in chapter 9, he later ended up at Dora as a *Prominent* from the very beginnings of the camp. He was *Bauleiter* and seems to have been listened to by Förschner, who had also come from Buchenwald, where he had not left a bad memory. It is likely that Kuntz was thus behind two other communists sent from Buchenwald being appointed LÄ1 and 2 in the summer of 1944.

He was nevertheless arrested in December and died in January 1945 in the course of an interrogation session. The fact that he had been the head of the German communists at Dora was obvious, and the Gestapo right from the beginning could not have been unaware of the fact. That he also died in this capacity is just as obvious.

The execution just prior to the evacuation of seven of his comrades is an indication of the will to do away with this team of communist leaders. Pröll, in committing suicide, had anticipated such an outcome, mentioned in chapter 16. It was thus entirely normal that the GDR authorities make heroes of these nine victims—and of Kuntz in particular. It is perhaps inevitable that, on that basis, overzealous propagandists ended up producing sometimes outrageous hagiography. That these hagiographical excesses in turn led to reactions that are themselves no doubt excessive is also understandable.

The brochure *Geheimwaffen im Kohnstein* by Kurt Pelny and Manfred Weisshaupt, distributed at Dora in 1964, also accords a large place to the account of Dr. Cespiva, the Czech doctor in the *Revier.* It has been vigorously contested, particularly by the Pole Krokowski, in his correspondence with Hermann Langbein.[7] With regard to the history of Dora the most substantial contribution nevertheless remains that of Professor Dr. Walter Bartel of the Humboldt University in Berlin dating from September 1968. It was published in 1970 in Frankfurt-am-Main under the title *Wehrwirtschaftführer Geheimwaffen KZ. Gutachten über Rolle und Bedeutung des KZ Dora-Mittelbau und die Funktion der SS bei der A4 Produktion.* In the same year of 1970, two other works were published in German. One appeared in the GDR, at Nordhausen: *KZ Dora. Produktionsstätte des Todes* by Götz Dieckmann and Peter Hochmuth. The other appeared in the FRG, in Stuttgart: "Das KL Dora-Mittelbau," in *Studien zur Geschichte der Konzentrationslager* by Manfred Bornemann and Martin Broszat.

The Glorification of von Braun and the Concealment of the Dora Camp

While Dora was becoming a subject of historical study in Germany, its memory was occulted in the United States and Great Britain due to the considerable interest in von Braun. Indeed, there had been a shift from the development of rockets for strictly military purposes to the space race. The rivalry between the United States and the USSR was symbolized by a "duel for the conquest of space." It was *Von Braun contre Korolev,* as Pierre Kohler and Jean-René Germain put it in the title of their French book, one of the many publications of the subject.

This personalization was characterized by the number of biographies on von Braun. In his 1990 study "Le silence sur Dora: pourquoi?" ("What Is Behind the Silence Around Dora?") Jacques Delarue indicates no less than six titles between 1959 and 1969.[8] The period in question is in truth marked by a succession of noteworthy events: orbiting of the first satellite Explorer 1 on January 31, 1958, launch of the Apollo space program in 1961, first successful trial of Saturn V on November 9, 1967, and, finally, Armstrong and Aldrin's lunar landing on July 20, 1969. Von Braun, an American citizen since 1955, was covered in honors.

His fame reached France. In the spring of 1996, *Match* published a story on him, and the president of the Dora-Ellrich Association, General Leroy, protested vigorously. On March 15, 1967, von Braun was awarded the Galabert Prize for astronautics. The indignation of the former Dora prisoners was all the greater that the ceremony was held at the Lutétia Hotel, where the deportees were received upon their return from Germany in 1945. Maurice Rolland, president of the Association of Judges from the Resistance, wrote to General de Gaulle.[9] But Wernher von Braun's brother, Sigismund, a career diplomat, was the FRG's ambassador to Paris between 1968 and 1972. On December 12, 1969, the president (Leroy) and the vice presidents (Pouzet and Dejussieu) wrote to the editor of the journal *Historia* following an article on von Braun neglecting to mention the Dora Tunnel.[10]

Von Braun left the Huntsville space center in February 1970 and quit NASA on June 30, 1972, to join an aerospace firm. Operated on for cancer on August 6, 1975, he died on June 16, 1977, at the age of sixty-five. Sergei Korolev died on January 14, 1966, in the course of an operation, at the age of fifty-nine.

The books published on von Braun do not entirely overlook the Dora Tunnel. In the biography written by Bernd Ruland in 1969 and translated into French in 1970, he himself acknowledged having gone to the Dora factory (but not the camp) and having seen the fate of the prisoners. He of course disclaimed any personal responsibility. The biographies of von Braun are perhaps not the most revealing works of this period. The fact of wanting to minimize his possible responsibility and that of the other Germans at Peenemünde was one thing. But what was more important at the time was to glorify the action of the American and British intelligence services in "hunting down the secret German weapons," which contributed first to the victory and then enabled the United States to take part in the conquest of space. The phrase just quoted is how the title of James McGovern's book, *Crossbow and Overcast,* was so well translated into French. Published in 1964, it appeared in French in 1965. It is clear and well documented, and a certain number of facts were taken from it to illustrate the chapters of the current study.

McGovern's account begins with the 1943 discoveries that led to the bombing of Peenemünde and ended with the launch of the Saturn rocket in 1964. The

French edition of the book is 215 pages long. The only passage on Dora is the following, on page 71: "The handling work was reserved for non-Germans. Kammler had assigned 6,000 slave laborers to the Mittelwerke, taken from the neighboring concentration camps of Nordhausen and Dora, as well as Buchenwald, some thirty-five miles away."[11] Not only is it very little, but the information itself is extraordinarily mediocre. There would be further instances of such mediocrity in American publishing.

However surprising this text may be, it is positively banal in comparison with the screenplay of the film *Operation Crossbow,*[12] with which it is entirely contemporary in that it dates from 1965. The film has to do with an underground secret weapons factory that has to be destroyed. It is located, or so it would seem, at Peenemünde.

But the factory is something out of a science fiction or James Bond film, without the slightest hint of prisoners in striped uniforms. Secret agents sneak in as workers, communicate with the outside, and guide in an air raid of surprising accuracy. In spite of its mediocrity the film is still frequently rerun on television, in France and elsewhere. The fact that the indecency of the screenplay struck neither the producer at the time nor the broadcasters of today is mind-boggling.

Dora Catches Up with Arthur Rudolph

One of the repercussions of Watergate in the 1970s was to spark questions in Congress regarding the functioning of the American intelligence services in the past. It was thus that Elizabeth Holtzman, a representative from the State of New York, came to take an interest in 1974 in Nazi war criminals who were in the United States, and the conditions under which they had immigrated.[13] In 1978 she attached the "Holtzman amendment" to the law on immigration, which provided a legal basis for expelling Nazi war criminals and preventing their entry as either immigrants or visitors. She thus obtained the opening, at the Criminal Division of the Department of Justice, of the Office of Special Investigations, or OSI.

Among the investigators, Harvard law student Eli Rosenbaum came upon the trail of Dora when reading Jean Michel's recent book. In 1975, Jean Michel had published, along with Louis Nucera, a book entitled *Dora,* bearing the subtitle *In the Hell of the Concentration Camp Where the Nazi Scientists Prepared for the Conquest of Space.* It would have been hard to be more explicit. The subtitle reflected the emotion of the former Dora prisoners in 1966 and 1967, referred to above. The book was awarded the *Résistance* literary prize and was translated into English in 1979. It was well received in the United States.

A discreet inquiry was then carried out by the OSI into the case of Arthur Rudolph, who seemed to have had particular responsibilities in running the Mittelwerk factory.[14] The investigators discovered in particular an intervention in favor of Wilhelm Simon, sentenced to life imprisonment in 1947 for his role at the head of the tunnel Arbeitseinsatz. Rudolph, retired in California, was interrogated on October 13, 1982, then again on February 4, 1983. He could not deny the facts. Threatened with indictment, he chose to give up his American citizenship, which he had acquired in 1955, and leave the United States. He settled in Hamburg and later got back his German nationality. Later, in 1990, he sought to return to the United States through Canada, but had to leave Canada shortly thereafter. He died on January 1, 1996, in Hamburg at the age of eighty-nine.

It is noteworthy that Rudolph was forced to leave the United States for good even though the real extent of his responsibility was not yet known. In the notes provided by Linda Hunt regarding the questions he had been asked figures the following passage: "When Sher asked him directly if he had asked that more forced laborers be sent into this underground hell, he admitted it."[15] Reference is to the meeting of May 6, 1944, the minutes of which were analyzed in chapter 7. The request for supplementary manpower is a banal point on the meeting's agenda, and Sher seems to be unaware of two aspects of the situation. The first is that for almost a year Rudolph had been asking for prisoners from the SS, from Maurer and then from Kammler, for his factory, and he had obtained thousands of them, many of whom died there. The second aspect is Kammler's refusal in May 1944. He himself needed new prisoners for his underground work projects and felt that Mittelwerk had enough personnel as it was. It is indeed unfortunate for these new prisoners that they were not sent to the factory, where the risks had by then diminished.

What an American investigator in 1983 cannot of course even imagine is that, in the preoccupations of the people in charge of the rocket program, the prisoners' fate was of no concern whatsoever.

From Testimony to History

In the postwar years there was no dearth of testimony on Dora and its Kommandos. The publication of the *Mémorial* in 1949 is characteristic of this concern to testify. But these accounts are not, for the reader, clearly situated in time and space, and they do not really allow Dora to be characterized in relation to the other camps, which were, at the same time, the object of other no less dramatic accounts.

The image that dominated opinion was that of a vast and ill-defined concentration camp complex symbolized by several especially well-known names such as Buchenwald and Dachau, or even Sachsenhausen and Mauthausen. Nothing at the time, for instance, drew attention to the particular fate of the Jews at Auschwitz, and Bergen-Belsen seemed a usual sort of camp.

Putting together collections of testimony implies thematic classification.

This was Olga Wormser and Henri Michel's decision in their classic *Tragédie de la déportation*,[16] which dealt successively with the following subjects: the convoys, arrival in the camp and the quarantine, daily life, work, social categories, spiritual life and resistance, the *Revier,* death, evacuations. Their collection, like a certain number of others put together later following an identical schema, enables the description of the concentration camp system, but does not make it possible to see its evolution or to distinguish one situation from one another, though they were often very different from one moment or camp to another.

It had become necessary to introduce history in a serious way, with monographs by camp or by Kommando in chronological order. Studies of this type had certainly already been carried out, for instance on Mauthausen: the historian (medieval specialist) Michel de Bouard, a former prisoner of that camp, had described its development in a study in 1954.[17] The sociologist Germaine Tillion had done the same for Ravensbrück.[18] But these were isolated examples.

This approach became generalized from the 1970s on, generally at the initiative of the associations. The most notable example is that of the collective work entitled *Sachso,* which was mentioned in chapter 21. Put together by the French deportees to Sachsenhausen, it was published, with the success it deserved, in 1982.

Toward the History of Dora Sought by the Deportees

With regard to Dora and the various Mittelbau Kommandos, a conjunction of initiatives now enable a truly historical approach to the documents on the work sites and the camps. Within the Belgian Dora association, beginning in 1976, deportees' accounts were collected, which enabled a young historian, Christine Somerhausen, to write a study on the "Belgian deportees to Dora." Research was continued in 1985 by another historian, Brigitte d'Hainaut. Under their joint signature, in 1991, *Dora, 1943–1945* was finally published under the patronage of the association. The rule of the anonymity of the testimonies was respected. The Slovenian association proceeded differently. The book that came out in 1989 in Ljubljana entitled *Dora KL Mittelbau* is made up of a collection of thirty-four texts by thirty-one deportees. The collection is preceded by a long study by Milan Filipcic.[19]

In France a first synthesis was published in the second half of 1989 in the form of a brochure "put out in the framework of the Dora, Ellrich, Harzungen and Kommandos association."[20] It was comprised of eleven parts, representing the beginning of a plan for a monograph. This publication was followed on April 25, 1990, by a "historical symposium" in Vincennes, France, with various contributions, including that of the historian Jacques Delarue, who raised the question quoted above: "Le silence sur Dora: pourquoi?" and concluded by addressing the former Dora prisoners directly: "To you survivors of one of the most horrendous experiences ever lived by humans, allow me to give the friendly advice of an historian: if you do not want to be definitively forgotten, if you want to carry out the ultimate sacred duty of preserving the memory of your fellow prisoners assassinated at Dora, at Ellrich, or in one of the Kommandos, you shall have to testify while you are still able to do so. Write your testimonies, put together as complete, as precise and as thorough a dossier as your memory permits. Be careful of any imprecision, for our memory is fickle, it works unbeknownst to us and often betrays us."

A historical commission was set up within the association. It was run by Lucien Fayman and subsequently by Georges Soubirous. It managed to bring together a large number of testimonies in the widest variety of forms. The majority of the author's quotations are taken from that collection. At the same time, in the course of the past few years, testimonies that had long been out of print were republished, and new books of memoirs came out, which are often updated versions of older texts that had been abandoned by their authors. In France as elsewhere, retirement has often been used profitably for this return to the past, after a long active life. The author himself had this very experience, having written practically nothing on the subject previously.

The curiosity of two students has contributed to this effort of memory. The first is Florent Brayard, who became interested in Paul Rassinier—initially in his capacity as a prisoner at Buchenwald, then at Dora. Through the association, Brayard distributed a questionnaire in 1990, the answers to which are of a more general interest. Brayard, no doubt caught up with reverence for a former deportee, ended up giving Rassinier's testimony too much credit.[21] In 1991 the student Anne Le Turdu was placed in charge of analyzing a series of oral testimonies on Dora that she herself had collected, on the basis of which she produced a useful study on various aspects of the camp's history.[22]

Recent Fundamental Works

As the former Dora prisoners were preoccupied with putting together and publishing their memoirs, historians were doing important work focusing on various aspects of rocket production in the Reich. There was first of all the Canadian Michael J. Neufeld's book, published in 1995 and entitled *The Rocket and the Reich: Peenemünde and the Coming of the Ballistic Missile Era*. It made it possible to follow, on a technical level, all the stages in the invention of rockets, from the first attempts of the amateur enthusiasts in the 1920s until the collapse of the Reich in 1945. At the same time it made it possible to situate precisely the competencies and rivalries of the various people involved throughout this whole period: the Wehrmacht artillerymen, the scientists and engineers, the technocrats from the Arms Ministry and their counterparts in the big companies, and finally the SS, providing the concentration camp labor force and ultimately taking control over firing the V2s.

The German Manfred Bornemann situated his research in the north of Thuringia, where he was born. He put together a *Chronik des Lagers Ellrich 1944/45* on the basis of various documents. This chronicle, written in 1987, was published at Nordhausen in 1992. In 1994 it was appended to a broader study entitled *Geheimprojekt Mittelbau*, which traces the history of the Dora Tunnel from the WIFO depot right up to the destruction of the entranceways by the Russians, with indications on the work sites of the neighboring camps.

German academic Rainer Eisfeld devoted several successive studies to determining the responsibility of the people at Peenemünde in the use of camp prisoners in producing the rockets. He showed, in particular, the role played in this regard by Rudolph in the spring of 1943, long before the bombing of Peenemünde and the transfer of its rocket production unit beneath the Kohnstein. It is obvious that, already at this time, both military and civilian specialists—with von Braun leading the way—were aware of what was going on. Eisfeld's last book, published in 1996, is entitled *Mondsüchtig. Wernher von Braun und die Geburt der Raumfahrt aus dem Geist der Barbarei.*

These indications have blocked the inevitable attempts to glorify von Braun in Germany. Already in 1980 the West Berlin Senate had wanted to name the airport Tegel-von Braun. It is true that the airfield corresponds to the Reinickendorf Raketenflugplatz, where in 1930 the rocket enthusiasts carried out their tests mentioned in chapter 2. In the framework of Berlin's quadripartite regime, Tegel was then situated in the French sector, whose military governor opposed the initiative: Gen. Bernard d'Astorg happened to have been part of the first convoy of French deportees to arrive at Dora.[23] But it was above all at Peenemünde where there was a recent move to put up a sort of memorial to German aerospace technology. These sorts of projects have run up against strenuous opposition.

The most recent German historical study on Dora is Joachim Neander's thesis, *Das Konzentrationslager Mittelbau.* Neander defended it in Bremen on April 30, 1997, and published it in November of that year. It had to do with the Mittelbau concentration camp complex, and more particularly with the period of the evacuations.

DORA TODAY

In Europe the past decade has been marked by profound political change—one of the main aspects of which was the reunification of Germany, coming about at the end of a peaceful process. Its consequences are manifold, but one of them is to situate the "places of memory"—including the concentration camps—in a new environment. These changes can be measured with regard to Dora on two levels: the practical level (free movement of persons, modified administrative trusteeship, privatizing of businesses) and the ethical level—having to do with the very meaning of the commemoration.

Practical Consequences of German Reunification

The "fall of the Berlin Wall" occurred on November 9, 1989. The reunification treaty was signed on September 12, 1990, and came into effect on October 3. The first joint legislative elections to be held across Germany took place on December 2.

Chronologically speaking, the first consequences of these events in people's lives was the reestablishment of free circulation of persons between the two parts of Germany. What happened on November 9, 1989, at 6:57 P.M. was East Germany's decision to open all of the border points toward West Germany and West Berlin. The Berlin Wall was but one of the aspects—though admittedly a particularly spectacular aspect—of the "Iron Curtain," which had cut the country in two. In an article in the Belgian bulletin put out on Dora, Albert Van Hoey mentioned a telephone conversation he had on November 12 with Mrs. Monicke from Walkenried—whose name will reappear later. She told him that the border had been opened in various places in the Harz Mountains and that eight trains had passed through the railway tunnel between Walkenried and Ellrich. Locally this was quite an event, comparable to the fall of the Berlin Wall. It also culminated, as will be shown, in the regrouping of the components of the Ellrich camp.

One important political consequence of the reunification was the reappearance of *Länder* in eastern Germany. The division into *Länder,* bearing historical names, dating from 1945, had been replaced in 1952 by a division into smaller *Bezirke,* named according to their principal towns. Thuringia, for instance, had been divided into the *Bezirke* of Erfurt, Gera, and Suhl. The German Democratic Republic (GDR) was an authoritarian and centralized state. On October 14, 1990, however, elections were held in the reconstituted *Länder,* and the governments were given real decision-making power in the realm of culture—extending, for instance, to concentration camp memorials.

A third consequence was the planned privatization of the state-run companies, which was dealt with by a financial organization created for this purpose, known as the Treuhand Anstalt. It so happened that one of those state-run companies was still mining anhydrite at Kohnstein.

Germany and Its Memory

When German academic Peter Reichel's book—initially published in German in 1995 under the title *Politik mit der Erinnerung*—was published in French in March 1998, it was decided to entitle it *Germany and Its Memory.* Reichel emphasizes the fact that, for a period of fifty years, "commemoration" in East Germany and West Germany was utterly different; the question arises as to what should be celebrated—and in what way—in unified Germany, especially in reunified Berlin, once again the capital city. Much of his study was of course devoted to the concentration camps. In this respect, from a purely material point of view what was done in the GDR was far more impressive than in the FRG. Buchenwald and Sachsenhausen were made into large monument complexes, and Ravensbrück and Dora, with more modest means, were by no means overlooked. In the Federal Republic of Germany (FRG) on the other hand, Dachau and Bergen-Belsen had been dealt with discreetly while Neuengamme—and still more so Flossenbürg—had been neglected altogether.

In fact, memory had not played the same role in the East and in the West. In the GDR the objective was to magnify the antifascist struggle, both in the camps and elsewhere. The last brochure put out at Dora is explicit in this regard: it begins by asserting that "responsibility for the crimes against humanity committed in the Dora-Mittelbau camp lies with the triple alliance of monopoly capital, the governing and terrorist fascist apparatus with its generals and SS, all within a conjunction of monopoly state-capitalism." And it concludes that the "antifascist memorial brings back to life the terrifying and moving history of these camps along with the merciless and reasoned struggle of antifascists under the leadership of Communists against the malign enemy of German fascist imperialism."

This manner of writing history accounts for the characteristics of the Buchenwald monument. "It represents a child and ten men. But their faces are not emaciated; they bear none of the stigmata of death. The group's stance is that of fighters, brandishing flag and rifle, the hand clenched in a fist or raised as if to swear an oath: the victims are at once fighters and victors."[1]

For fifty years in the FRG these sorts of reassuring certainties did not exist. Memory was played out above all in the writings of historians. Joseph Rovan writes: "When one gets right down to it, it was history and its interpretation which, by far and away, dominated the culture of the Federal Republic. Historians in the GDR were obliged to be crafty with the orthodoxy. If they had any talent, it had to be sought out behind the ideological mumbo-jumbo. On the other side of the border, in the FRG, the situation was plethoric—a situation of abundance. For years and in a variety of forms, the debate on German history kept the intellectual world spellbound; that is also, in my opinion, how the literary qualities were best preserved."[2]

Reunifying German memory and commemoration will require, quite obviously, some considerable time. It is first of all the unity of the sites themselves that has to be recovered—and the example of Ellrich is especially striking.

THE REDISCOVERY OF ELLRICH. On the very grounds of the Ellrich prisoners' camp were placed the boundary markers separating the districts of Ellrich and Walkenried—that is, the Soviet and British zones of occupation. In 1945 the camp buildings were destroyed and the limit was materialized. A little further to the west the village of Juliushütte, where the SS camp had been set up, was abandoned. Though administratively dependent on Walkenried, its inhabitants were linked to Ellrich for their day-to-day life. It seems that, in the years to come, a good many Germans leaving the Soviet zone passed clandestinely from Ellrich to Juliushütte, whose houses served as relay points. In 1953 they were destroyed by fire, and the Brunswick (Lower Saxony) authorities subsequently had the ruins eliminated.

In any case, an electrified barricade henceforth prohibited passage. The whole border area, extending three miles back, was a prohibited zone, a *Sperrgebiet.* No border crossing was open to traffic between the GDR and the FRG between Helmstedt, well to the north of the Harz Mountains, all the way to Duderstadt far to the south. In June 1989, Van Hoey had to pass through Worbis and Duderstadt—in other words, a sixty-mile detour—to go from Ellrich to Walkenried.[3] The hill that overlooked the former camp, with its crematorium on the other side of the barricade, was overgrown with vegetation.

Interest in the Ellrich camp was relaunched by the German historian Manfred Bornemann, whose *Chronik des Lagers Ellrich* was written in 1987. He was in contact with former deportees, including the Belgian Ernest Abel. Through him, contact was established between a town councilor from Walkenried, Mrs. Ruth Monicke, and Van Hoey, the representative of the Belgian association of former Dora prisoners. The decision was made in June 1989 to erect a monument near the foundations of the crematorium, which were finally located.

When the stele was inaugurated on May 13, 1989, reunification had already taken place and those participating in the ceremony traveled freely from the east and the west.[4]

The day before, another stele had also been inaugurated at Blankenburg following contacts between the Belgian association and the local municipality. Van Hoey himself, as mentioned in chapter 13, had been a prisoner at Blankenburg.

The European Dora Committee

Until 1990 there was an "international committee" for Buchenwald-Dora but no committee for Dora per se. Its creation in the context of Germany's new situation resulted from an initiative taken in the summer of 1990 by the representatives of the former French and Belgian deportees, supported by their Dutch and Czech fellow prisoners. The constitutive meeting was held in Paris on October 18, and Jacques Brun, its founder, was placed in charge of the legal registration of its statutes in France. It was a nonprofit organization conforming to the French law of 1901 regarding associations with international objectives. It was officially registered under the name "European Dora, Ellrich, Harzungen and Ko Committee 'For Memory' " ("Comité européen de Dora, Ellrich, Harzungen et Ko 'Pour la mémoire' ").[5] Since then, the new committee and the International Buchenwald-Dora Committee have coordinated their activities without problems.

The committee's French president, Jean Mialet, is still in office. The Belgian Van Hoey is first vice president; along with the Dutchman Van Dijk, second vice president, who is in constant contact with the German officials in their language. The founder, Jacques Brun, gave up his position as general secretary in 1996 to Marie-Claire du Bois de Vroylande, the daughter of a Belgian deportee who died at Ellrich on December 15, 1944.

The European Committee's task is twofold. It represents all the former prisoners of Dora-Mittelbau and their families in their dealings with the competent authorities. It is part of the group of international Nazi concentration camp committees, of which there are nine in all: Auschwitz-Birkenau, Buchenwald-Dora, Dachau, Dora-Mittelbau, Mauthausen, Natzweiler-Struthof, Neuengamme, Ravensbrück, and Sachsenhausen. These groups meet informally to undertake actions of common interest. Their decisions are taken in unanimity. The group's presidency changes every year, following the alphabetical order of the camps.

The international committees have endeavored on a number of occasions to interest international authorities in the preservation of the camps and their archives. One of their initiatives was aimed at the CSCE—the Conference on Security and Cooperation in Europe—which had met for a symposium in Krakow in June 1991. The declaration adopted on June 6 declared: "The participating states will endeavor to preserve and to protect these monuments and places of memory, including, particularly, the extermination camps and the archives linked to them, which themselves bear witness to the tragic experience of the common past."

Another initiative took place in Strasbourg on December 15–16, 1992, in the presence of the presidents of the groups in the European Parliament. A common resolution drafted by the groups was adopted almost unanimously on February 10, 1993, by the Parliament. In particular, the resolution "asks member states, the Council and the Commission to provide support, including financial support, for any initiatives seeking to conserve the meaning of the Nazi concentration camps in their specificity and to place them under European and international protection."

Trusteeship of the Camps

Not all the camps concerned were located in Germany. Mauthausen was in Austria and Struthof in France. With regard to the Federal Republic of Germany—which henceforth corresponds to reunified Germany as a whole—there is no common policy on the subject; however, in early March 1994 the Bundestag's Foreign Affairs Commission organized a public hearing of experts on the "federal state's participation" in these places of memory. Until such time as any decisions are made in this regard, the *Länder* remain responsible for the camps located on their territory. The camps are Dachau and Flossenbürg in Bavaria, Bergen-Belsen in Lower Saxony, Neuengamme in Hamburg, Sachsenhausen and Ravensbrück in Brandenburg, Buchenwald and Dora in Thuringia. But Saxony-Anhalt, for instance, also has commemorative monuments and necropolises on its territory, including Blankenburg, Langenstein, and Gardelegen.

In April 1991, as noted by a delegation of the European Committee that traveled to Dora, a "Mahn- und Gedenkstätte" still exists, but its status is highly uncertain. It was only in August 1991 that the Nordhausen *Kreistag*—or district council—took things into hand and designated a *Kuratorium* to look after the functioning of the Gedenkstätte Mittelbau-Dora. This administrative body was comprised of representatives of the different religions and various political factions of the *Kreistag* as well as academics. It elected the Reverend Joachim Jaeger as president. The victims of Nazism are also represented: Jews, Gypsies, and former prisoners in the camp, including the Belgian Van Hoey and the Dutchman Van Dijk from the European Committee. Dr. Cornelia Klose, scientific adviser for the Gedenkstätte in May 1991, was appointed director on November 11, 1992, by the Nordhausen Landkreis.

This formula was only temporary because the Ministry of Science and Culture of the Land of Thuringia itself designated in September 1991 a commission of experts presided over by the historian Eberhard Jäckel. Its role was to consider the renovations of the land's commemorative sites—in other words,

Buchenwald and, incidentally, Dora. It filed its conclusions in early 1992. It recommended that the exhibition dealing with the history of the Buchenwald concentration camp put an end to the partiality imposed by East German historiography. It also suggested that everything to do with the Speziallager 2, set up at Buchenwald by the Soviets between 1945 and 1950, be dealt with by a special museum clearly separated from the one devoted to the Nazi camp. (The necessary renovation work has now been carried out.) The commission of experts also visited Dora, looked carefully at the conservation of the camp and tunnels, and adopted Dr. Klose's recommendations as laid out at a meeting of the European Committee on January 10, 1992, in Brussels.

It was in March 1994 on these bases that the new organizational setup was established, concretized by the creation of a "foundation" known as the Stiftung Gedenkstätte Buchenwald und Mittelbau-Dora. Its purpose was defined as follows: "The purpose of the Foundation is to preserve the memorials as places of mourning, where the memory of the crimes committed there are kept, to fit out these memorials on a scientific base and to make them accessible to the public in a suitable form, as well as promoting the study and transmission of the attendant historical processes. The Buchenwald memorial shall give priority to the study of the history of the concentration camp. The history of the Soviet internment camp shall be dealt with in scholarly publications and a museographical presentation in a suitable form. In the Mittelbau-Dora memorial, account will be taken of the particular problem of the exploitation of the prisoners in manufacturing weapons of extermination. Finally, the history and instrumentalization of the memorials during the time of the German Democratic Republic will be exhibited."

The Foundation is headed up by a council, the Stiftungsrat, with representatives of the Land of Thuringia, the federal state, the Nordhausen Landkreis, and the city of Weimar as well as the Central Council of the Jews of Germany. It is assisted by a *Kuratorium* (at the Land level) of qualified persons, historians, museum curators, and so on. This *Kuratorium* is itself assisted by three *Beiräte*, scientific councils of former prisoners, for each of the three camps: Buchenwald, Mittelbau-Dora, and the special Soviet camp. The Dora *Beirat* is comprised of a German Jew, a German Gypsy, an Italian, a Belgian (Van Hoey), a Dutchman (Van Dijk), and two Frenchmen (Garnier and Mialet). Mialet was elected president.

The Reopening of the Dora Tunnel

Commemorative monuments are located on the different Mittelbau sites. Ellrich and Blankenburg have already been mentioned. There is a monument in the Harzungen cemetery for the sick killed by the SS after the evacuation of the camp. Another is located at the bottom of the Heimkehle cave for the victims of the Rottleberode. Another is at Nordhausen near the Boelcke Kaserne, whose ruins have disappeared and been replaced by other buildings. Lastly a large necropolis at Nordhausen commemorates the dead of the Boelcke Kaserne and the last to die at Dora. A stele erected in 1986 must also be mentioned; it marks the location of the former synagogue, burned down in 1938 during Kristall-nacht. Interned in a camp, Raphael Katz is a survivor of the Jews who were deported at that time. The Gedenkstätte's principal activity remains the conser-vation and fitting out of the Dora camp itself, which are regularly examined dur-ing the *Beirat*'s meetings. But the essential modification of the Dora site was the reopening of the tunnel, which, though partial, is highly significant.

In 1945 the Kohnstein was dug in three different ways. In the middle was the Dora Tunnel with its A and B tunnels running from north to south and linked by the halls. It was entirely occupied by the three factories: Nordwerk (Junkers), Mittelwerk I (V2), and Mittelwerk II (V1). To the west near Woffleben what was undertaken on work site B 12 had made it possible to dig large galleries. This situation was the same near Niedersachswerfen to the east on work site B 11. On each side of the A and B tunnels, secondary galleries ensured connections with galleries B 12 and B 11.

After 1945, each of the three parts of the Kohnstein had a different history. The Soviets, when they abandoned the tunnel in the summer of 1948, blew up the north and south entrances to tunnels A and B and caved in parts of the under-ground complex. One of B 12's three access points—the closest to the north en-trance to tunnel B—was also blown up, but the others still offered access to those galleries that were still intact and used in part by a refrigeration ware-house, in part for a storehouse for potatoes, and so on.

Things evolved very differently regarding B 11. For a long time it was here that the Kohnstein anhydrite was extracted from a quarry on the east side of the hill, gradually cut away by the mining. It was used above all to supply the synthetic-fertilizer factory at Leuna near Merseburg controlled by IG Farben. After 1945 the company running the operation came to be known as Leuna Werke, and the use of the anhydrite remained unchanged. The mining operation over a period of fifty years, with its ups and downs, ended up destroying the B 11 galleries and by 1990 had reached almost all the way to tunnel A itself. The company exploiting the quarry was then known as the Harzer Anhydrit Werke GmbH.

Tunnels A and B seemed threatened, and in August 1991 a wave of concern was expressed in the local press. If the Kohnstein massif were to collapse, ecol-ogists predicted a considerable impact on the local microclimate. The Dora European Committee, the French and Belgian associations, and the International Buchenwald-Dora Committee made contact with the federal government, the Land of Thuringia, and the Nordhausen Landkreis.

Such was the situation when the commission of experts, designated by the

Land of Thuringia to write a report on the future of Buchenwald and Dora, came to visit the tunnel on November 15, 1991. Though he had not been invited, Van Hoey joined them. On November 16 in a press conference the commission declared, in particular, that tunnels A and B had to be conserved and that some portion of them had to be integrated into the Gedenkstätte and opened to the public. It would appear that the law of January 6, 1993, regarding the protection of historical monuments in the Land of Thuringia, also aimed at sites of cultural interest, made it possible to register tunnels A and B along with their lateral galleries as classified monuments in order to ensure their protection.

Contrary to what appeared to be the case, access into the tunnel by circuitous routes such as B 12 had been possible for some time; it was thus that the commission of experts was able to evaluate its sheer size. Souvenir hunters also knew about it. According to a 1994 inquiry, a London-based auctioneer actually proposed in his catalog pieces of missiles that had been abandoned by the Russians. But though it was possible to get inside, access was not authorized and entailed the risk of an accident.

Attention was thus given to putting in a new entranceway that would be more practical, based on the work undertaken in 1988; but this entranceway was abandoned for lack of money and sealed up. The plan had been to dig a gallery running from the south entrance to tunnel B just before the caved-in section, connecting diagonally with tunnel A beyond the collapsed section. Work started up again in late 1992 and had reached tunnel A by September 1993, which enabled a muddy and flashlit "inauguration." The entranceway was completely finished in June 1994, enabling people to go down tunnel A as far as Hall 46—one of the "dormitories" at the tunnel's beginnings. Today the heaps of fallen earth have largely been cleared out of tunnel A all the way to Halls 46 and 45 as well as those halls themselves. The arches have been consolidated and the whole complex lit up. Modifications to facilitate visits are under way. To go farther, tunnel A—obstructed at the level of Hall 44—would have to be cleared out.

Meanwhile, on September 30, 1992, the Treuhand, in charge of privatizing state-run companies, sold the Kohnstein open-pit anhydrite mine to a Bavarian company called Münchner Baustoff Werke Wildgrüber, the name of its owner.

As the Dora Tunnel itself reappeared, what was left of B 12 and B 3 remained accessible, though it continued to be used by companies. B 3 had been turned into a very large mushroom bed—very much like those in the former underground limestone quarries in the Paris area.

It is especially important that the renovations of the Dora Tunnel be continued. Indeed, the camps themselves in their current state provide a necessarily imperfect picture of concentration camp life. In Buchenwald the very monumentality of the commemoration and the disappearance of the blocks used for housing leave the visitor perplexed—above all if the visitor happens to be a former prisoner. At Dora the entirely charming natural setting tends to make one forget what the site, long ago and for a relatively short period of time—some twenty months overall—was used for. The author, on the basis of putting things together and examining what remains of the foundations, was able to find the site of his former block and to reconstruct it in his mind; the average visitor, however, cannot carry out such an exercise. In terms of its size and indestructible character, the Dora Tunnel is no doubt the place of memory most suited for the final phase of the Nazi concentration camp system—and the 1991 commission of experts made no mistake about that.

Jugend für Dora

As is customary for former deportees as well as veterans, pilgrimages to the sites are organized on a yearly basis by the various associations concerned. With regard to Dora, the European Committee, the International Buchenwald-Dora Committee, the Belgian and French associations (Dora-Ellrich and Buchenwald-Dora) were these past few years especially active.

But other initiatives have been undertaken by young people: high school students from Liffré in France (in the Ille-et-Vilaine), from Waremme in Belgium, from Luxembourg, and from many other places have traveled to Dora and elsewhere in Germany, with students from the Robert-Koch High School in Clausthal-Zellerfeld and their teacher Joachim Neander, and students from the Hamberg High School in Göttingen along with their teacher Renée Grihon, for instance.

Given the interest taken in the Dora-Mittelbau complex by various groups of young Germans, an organization known as "Jugend für Dora"—Youth for Dora—was created in 1995 in the course of a meeting between deportees and young people on the basis of a suggestion put forth by the European Committee. Its founder and president is Dorothea August, a young woman from Ellrich. Among its activities, every year Jugend für Dora organizes an international camp for youth. The 1998 program was devoted to Ellrich. Under the supervision of an archaeologist, the goal was to find and reveal the foundations of the former camp and write an account of the findings. Leisure time was devoted to visiting the Harz Mountains. The former prisoners' associations supported this initiative. It is encouraging that, just as he was concluding this book, this was the last piece of information to reach the author—as is the fact that it came from Germany. He felt it important to emphasize that.

Mittelbau-Dora in the System of Nazi Concentration Camps

Two points characterize the National Socialist concentration camp system in the final phase of Nazi rule in the years 1943–1945. First, it was not limited to the annihilation camps "somewhere in the East" or to the well-known, seemingly isolated "large" concentration camps, such as Buchenwald, Dachau, and Neuengamme, among others. Rather, the system formed a closely knit network of main and satellite camps in the German Reich and the occupied neighboring states, a net that could not remain hidden from the civilian population. Second, forced labor became the determining factor of annihilation, be it through work methods that killed human beings or through the selection and murder of those unable to work.

The history of the Mittelbau-Dora camp illustrates, in a paradigmatic sense, this last stage in the genesis of the camp system. At the beginning of Nazi rule the concentration camps were used as improvised sites to intern the opponents of the dictatorship. From 1936 on, within the general social and racial framework of restrictions, they were transformed into permanent detention centers. And finally, in 1942–1943, the concentration camps became sites of ruthless exploitation of the camps' forced laborers. Mittelbau-Dora was one of the first and, ultimately, the largest concentration camp founded with the exclusive goal of exploiting the labor potential of its inmates. From the start the murderous exhaustion of the inmates' strength was part of the calculation of production.

Those parts of the Kohnstein tunnel system, accessible since 1995, in which the camp inmates had to live and work give visitors to the memorial site (*Gedenkstätte*) a sense of what forced labor in the tunnels meant. They also point up a specific aspect of Mittelbau-Dora. The creation of the underground rocket factory with the designation "Mittelwerk" was the first project of the

Nazis' mad attempt to place the entire German armaments industry underground. For all other underground endeavors of the last year of war, Mittelwerk
was the reference point.

Finally, the forced labor of camp inmates in the production of rocket
weapons that, as "retaliatory weapons," caused extensive damage in England
and Belgium and the death of thousands, raises the question of responsibility of
the scientists, engineers, and technicians who contributed to the project. The history of Mittelbau-Dora shows the potential consequences of a technical, case-
oriented, nonpolitical attitude on the part of such individuals.

The importance of rocket production in Mittelbau-Dora should not be overestimated, however, even though the Mittelbau-Dora Camp in the public image
and in scientific research was long considered virtually the exclusive "production center of the V-weapons" (as reflected in the title of an East German
brochure that appeared in the 1970s).[1] The myth, created by Nazi propaganda,
about "retaliation" or "miracle" weapons, still lingers today and is carried forward and written about in books with mystifying titles such as *Secret Project
Mittelbau*.[2] Further, the emphasis on secrecy conforms to a contemporary apologetic German stereotype of perception. The camouflage—more a matter of
speech than reality—offered every observer and beneficiary the occasion to
evade personal responsibility. The common expression in postwar Germany
"We knew nothing" could thus evolve without a break from wartime perceptions.

But the pictures of the unique "Rocket Camp" and of the "Secret Project" do
not agree with historical reality, a fact already noted in the brilliant study by
André Sellier. To be sure, the history of Mittelbau-Dora began with the transfer
of rocket construction from Peenemünde to the underground Mittelwerk, built
by inmates from the Dora camp. Actually in the spring of 1944 only a minority
of inmates of the ever-expanding Mittelbau-Dora complex were engaged in
rocket construction. The far larger contingent of inmates had to work under catastrophic conditions at the numerous construction sites in the Nordhausen region, sites that were organized in light of the anticipated transfer of the aviation
armaments industry to underground facilities. The Mittelbau camp was, as its
name implied, purely a "construction camp." Nothing about that was changed
by the "Development Corporation Mittelbau" scheme, existing only on paper,
for a very large underground rocket research center in the Nordhausen region.
The project was conceived in connection with the February 1945 transfer of the
development facilities at Peenemünde, under Wernher von Braun's direction, to
the Harz area.

Mittelbau-Dora in the Research on Concentration Camps

For many years virtually only the survivors wrote about the Nazi concentration camps; along with the Allied photographic reports and the accounts of the major camp trials from 1945 to 1947, they shaped the public perception of the camp system. (In the course of this, not surprisingly, different perceptions emerged in various countries, and these ideas persist.) Toward the end of the 1940s several hundred, if not thousands, of memoirs of surviving camp inmates appeared. Many were both memoirs and scientific studies. Among the most important of these, the publications of Eugen Kogon, David Rousset, and Christopher Burney still shape the public image of concentration camps that is held in many countries.[3] André Sellier is part of this tradition because his book unites memoir with historical analysis.

Outside the circle of the survivors, historical research long remained aloof from the subject of Nazi concentration camps. All that changed, albeit slowly, in the 1960s. In 1962 Eberhard Kolb's study of Bergen-Belsen was the first German-language monograph about a single camp. A little later Enno Georg presented a study of the economic enterprises of the SS.[4] With the evidence developed for the Auschwitz trial, Martin Broszat in 1965 published his fundamental and comprehensive study entitled *Die nationalsozialistischen Konzentrationslager 1933–1945*. It was followed in 1968 in France by Olga Wormser-Migot's examination of the *"système concentrationnaire Nazi."*[5] The *Studien zur Geschichte der Konzentrationslager*, co-authored by Broszat, produced separate studies of six concentration camps, among them Mittelbau-Dora.[6] With the publication in French of Joseph Billig's study of the SS economy in the camps,[7] the first phase of the historiographical debate in the West about the concentration camps ended. Except for Falk Pingel's pioneering study of inmates under SS rule and a collective volume about some Natzweiler satellite camps in Württemberg, little followed these studies during the 1970s.[8]

With an emphasis on regional and everyday life, West German research on concentration camps in the mid-1980s took a new direction. The Hanover studies of Rainer Fröbe and others were soon followed by numerous and sometimes detailed studies of various satellite camps.[9] But most of these studies were devoted primarily to the history of a specific camp. Studies on camp complexes were found wanting.[10] A further shortcoming of the research at the time was the lack of examination of the linkage between the concentration camps and other types of camps, especially those for prisoners of war and foreign laborers.[11]

Many of these studies of the satellite camps grew out of the methodological discussion of *Alltagsgeschichte*. Surprisingly, they either ignored or limited their consideration of the relationship between the camps and their geographic environment. The same is true of recent monographs on specific camps or camp complexes.[12] Moreover, the fact that a few years ago a large collective volume published by Ulrich Herbert and others on the history of the concentration camps, organized into seven sections but without a separate section on the social surroundings of the camps, points to a far-reaching neglect of the theme in research to date.[13] Thus far the only studies that deal more fully with this subject, surprisingly, do not approach it from the perspective of the satellite camps but from that of the two main camps of Dachau and Buchenwald.[14] But in these two studies the reciprocal effects between different types of camps and forms of unfree labor remain unexamined, though this kind of analysis is a precondition for understanding the complex Nazi camp system and awareness of it by the perpetrating society. And while both studies analyze in depth the economic and social relations between the camps and the two cities of Weimar and Dachau, they scarcely address the question of the motivational structure of the participating criminal associates, that is, the broad spectrum between passive witnessing and active participation.

Mittelbau-Dora has largely been a "forgotten camp," indeed "one of the least known and researched Nazi concentration camps," as Joachim Neander notes in his dissertation on the history of Mittelbau-Dora.[15] This was also true of earlier West German publications.[16] Still, Mittelbau-Dora is one of the few camps that were presented in the 1970 *Studien zur Geschichte der Konzentrationlager*.[17] In 1967 an integral study of the camp, not by an historian but by former Dora prisoner and jurist Wincenty Hein, had appeared in Poland.[18] In the German Democratic Republic (on whose territory the "Mahn und Gedenkstätte" existed since 1963) a student research group, guided by Walter Bartel,[19] produced several detailed and scientific studies. They took the form of diploma theses or dissertations and were submitted to the East Berlin Humboldt University. Some of them were and still are difficult to find.[20] As a result, by the late 1960s the "little" Mittelbau-Dora camp was better researched than the major camps—Buchenwald, Sachsenhausen, and Ravensbrück—located in East Germany.

With the exception of two works,[21] the East Berlin studies were limited to aspects of the main Dora camp or treated the camp system and the Nazi armaments industry in a general manner. Hence the satellite camps of Dora played only a marginal role in the research of the East Berliners. All the pre-1991 East German publications bearing on the history of the Mittelbau camp were based on these early ones; little new data or analyses have been developed since the early 1970s. Indeed, many studies have not even matched the 1960s level.[22]

A similar pattern is discernible in West German research. Until the end of the 1980s, Manfred Bornemann was virtually alone in researching the history of Mittelbau-Dora. His book, published in 1970 with Martin Broszat,[23] as well as his comprehensive study[24] of a year later, were based to an important degree on the findings of East German researchers. To be sure, Bornemann was able to make use of the Arolsen International Tracing Service documentation (still accessible in the early 1970s) as well as other sources not available to the Berlin research group. His comprehensive 1971 study essentially reduced the history of the Mittelbau camp to the Mittelwerk and V-weapons production. A number of other Western works relative to V-weapons, either in a technical or a military-historical framework, touched on the theme of the Mittelbau-Dora complex. But the conditions of the inmates received virtually no attention.[25]

More recent studies on the history of the Mittelbau-Dora camp are centrally concerned with the responsibility of scientists in V-weapons production and the interdependence of progress and contempt for human beings.[26] The studies necessarily focus on the history of the main Dora camp and neglect the importance of the construction projects and the satellite camps of Mittelbau. Only in recent years do new studies, some still unpublished, address the camp *complex* Mittelbau-Dora[27] and the internal structure of the Mittelbau camp.[28] Still other more recent studies approach the history of Mittelbau-Dora in terms of the macrostructure. Walter Naasner, Michael Thad Allen, and Jan-Erik Schulte have in recent years presented detailed organizational-historical studies that illuminate the political and armaments-economic context of forced labor in the concentration camps.[29] With these, as well as with the Mittelbau-Dora monographs of Neander (1997), Sellier (1998), and Wagner (2001), a change in perspective has taken place since 1997. The focus has moved from Dora to the satellite camps, where inmates performed forced labor at the construction sites and in the excavation of new underground facilities. Mittelbau-Dora is now viewed less as a "rocket camp" than as a "construction camp." If a symbol for Mittelbau-Dora were needed, it would be—aside from the mountains of famished inmate corpses—the shovel and not the rocket.

Altogether it becomes clear that under no circumstances can Mittelbau-Dora be viewed today as a forgotten camp. Moreover it would seem that the strategy of the rocket technicians, who from the beginning sought to conceal their participation in the crimes at Mittelbau-Dora, stimulated rather than prevented a confrontation with the history of this camp. To be sure—in East and West—it is but a partial confrontation, an historiographical issue limited to Mittelbau-Dora, and, moreover, shaped largely by the mysterious V-weapons. That is true not only in regard to the technical-historical depictions that commonly evoke fascination with rocket weapons and the secret underground facilities. It is also true for critical studies such as Rainer Eisfeld's, which, though for opposite intentions, make use of the myth of the V-weapons.

The relationships between the Mittelbau camps and their environs were almost totally ignored in the earlier research. The sole exception is a small, unpublished diploma thesis that was presented at the Pädagogische Hochschule in Erfurt.[30] In terms of content and writing form this study is totally beholden to the typical GDR projection of the history of anti-fascist resistance, one that excludes the broad dimension of criminal complicity. Even in the title the author points to the "anti-fascist collaboration and help" of the people toward the inmates and concludes "that the German nation is not identical with the Germany . . . of the fascists" and that "the fascist propaganda did not succeed in extinguishing the humanistic sentiments of the largest part of the population."[31]

More recent studies on this theme[32] have shown that this was more wishful thinking than the result of empirical research. This was also obvious to the East German leadership. At the beginning of the 1970s the Office of Historical Remembrance Sites in the GDR Ministry of Culture abruptly canceled a planned exhibition titled "Ties with the Civilian Population"—to be mounted within the context of a refurbishing of the exhibition displays at the *Gedenkstätte* Mittelbau-Dora. The explanation offered stated that "regrettably almost all civilians had let themselves become the helpers of the Nazis."[33] That conclusion simply did not fit into the GDR picture of history, which depicted the German population as victims of the dictatorship of a "monopolists' " alliance with the Nazi Party and hence freed of any responsibility for Nazi crimes.[34]

Mittelbau-Dora as Paradigm of a New Type of Camp

André Sellier's remarkable study makes it forcefully clear: the camps of Mittelbau-Dora were located in the center of Nazi Germany, and by no means only in the topographical sense. Like the other concentration camps, Mittelbau-Dora did not exist on the edge of society but in the center. Its inmates did not live on "Planet Dora" (Yves Béon[35]), though they may have had that impression, but in camps that were integral parts of their social environs. The tight camp network was difficult to perceive in its composition, with its mixture of satellite camps and many forced labor camps of various categories. Because of the forced-labor inmates in the German armaments industry, the limits of the concentration camps had been expanded far into society by the end of the war. The interpenetration of society and the camp system eventually went so far as to end all considerations of a strict separation of the internal and external worlds of the concentration camps. For Mittelbau-Dora, which was created only in the final phase of the war, these observations are even more valid than for most of the other concentration camps.

In 1933 the concentration camps were not yet sites of mass murder. They became that only after the attack on the Soviet Union and the start of the systematic murder of the European Jews. In the occupied territories of Poland and the Soviet Union the Nazi annihilation policy became radicalized to the level of millions of murders, which for the time being were committed chiefly on the periphery of the German occupied territories. Only with the military turn of fortunes did a change take place. What had become apparent in 1942 and was already practiced to a limited extent by 1944 became the cruel reality of daily war in Nazi Germany. With the creation of the dense net of satellite camps and the steady enlargement of the categories for imprisonment, the criminal deed returned from the periphery to the place it had come from: the center of German society. There it exploded with brutal power and, with the crimes of the last phase of war, took on the character of a collective murderous frenzy of the culprit society. The death marches of 1945 were nothing other than the implosion of a collectively supported annihilation policy that already before 1941 had taken on an internal dynamic that precluded reconsideration or reversal.[36]

The indicator of this process was the appearance of structural dissolution, which forms a recurrent theme through the history of Mittelbau-Dora. The Mittelbau camps had been the result of steady improvisation and ideological concessions by the SS, mandated by the war economy, that spelled a step-by-step retreat from its erstwhile dogmas. In 1943 the creation of a minicamp of fifty inmates in a town was still thought impossible. There was the difficult problem of guarding such a facility and the concern over unfavorable reactions by the population in the face of all-too-clear evidence of Nazi crimes. The protocols of the "Jägerstab" (responsible for fighter-plane construction and in charge of advancing the construction projects of Mittelbau) show that in the spring of 1944 the SS opposed industry demands to "allocate" groups of five hundred to a thousand inmates to industrial facilities. At the same time the SS created ever-smaller new Mittelbau satellite camps, and these moved ever closer to towns. Lack of fuel and frequent air attacks made it difficult to transport labor from the large camps to workplaces dozens of kilometers away. Hence improvisation led to the creation of provisional minicamps each of which, at times, were occupied by only a dozen inmates. But as André Sellier graphically describes, inmates were often forced to cover the distance between camps and workplaces in murderous marches.

The steady enlargement of the main Dora camp also showed all the signs of improvisation. Indeed, its external appearance had already set it apart from all the earlier constructed main concentration camps. There was no "representative" entrance gate to the camp with typical SS slogans. Furthermore the SS passed up the construction of massive quarters for the guard units. Even more evidence of improvisation was furnished by a look at the construction projects of the Kammler and the Geilenberg staff. The mania for gigantic construction projects of "Enterprise Mittelbau" were reflexes linked to the desperate military situation. They were also projection screens for flights from reality, a tactic that many party officials, members of the military, and industrialists used to escape the realization of military defeat. Mass death in Mittelbau was mainly a consequence of the auto-suggestive dynamic of the power fantasies of architects, rocket engineers, and Nazi armaments planners. The plans for the subterranean transfer project were constantly altered. When target dates could not be met—which was almost always the case—still more ambitious plans were submitted. Gradually all sense of reality was lost in an ever-growing demand for labor. Workers were "borrowed"—according to the "Quellen-Begriff" of the Kammler staff—from the concentration camps at the construction sites. Given minimal food allocations, in a situation where the approaching end of war spelled little concern for maintaining reserves, the inmates at the construction sites had a life expectancy of a few weeks or, at most, a couple of months. André Sellier describes this form of killing in affecting words.

This extensive form of economic exploitation, which included calculations about the inmates' death rate, led to the creation in the Mittelbau complex of a camp system based on functional dimensions. Accordingly, in keeping with the demands of the SS-Führungsstäbe and the construction projects, new inmates arrived at the Dora camp in a steady flow from other concentration camps. They were assigned, on the basis of physical fitness and professional qualification, to the various camps of the Mittelbau complex. Prisoners who were professionally qualified and appeared to be still fit for production remained mostly in the main Dora camp or were sent to camps that housed work commandos assigned to the armaments industry. Exhausted inmates stood virtually no chance of escaping assignment to one of the notorious "construction" camps where the last ounce of labor energy was beaten out of them. Most of the inmates experienced a *via dolorosa* that, in ever-shorter time periods, took them from camp to camp and ended in death. This practice of mobile selection made it possible for the SS and the firms profiting from inmate labor to achieve maximum output with a minimum of food.

Inmate Groups in Mittelbau-Dora

The consequence of forced labor in the armaments industry was that the camp system with its satellites penetrated ever deeper into German and European society in the second half of the war. But the expansion beyond its parameters also became noticeable in other ways. Not only was the recruitment field for guards steadily enlarged, so especially was the circle of those potentially threatened with incarceration in these camps. The arrest categories were constantly enlarged; in Mittelbau-Dora there were inmate categories unknown in the earlier concentration camps.

One of these new incarceration groups were the "Wifo-inmates." They consisted mainly of former Polish and French workers of the *Wirtschaftliche Forschungsgesellschaft (Wifo)*, who since the early 1940s had been working on the excavation of the Kohnstein underground complex and who in 1943 were incarcerated as police prisoners in Dora. Another group were the "in transit" prisoners *(Zwischenhäftlinge)*. These were armed forces members who because of desertion or other infractions were transferred in winter 1944–1945 by the military courts via Buchenwald to Mittelbau-Dora.

To be sure, the prisoners of this incarceration category formed but a small minority in Mittelbau. The far largest group in the fall of 1944, with nearly a third of the inmates, were prisoners from the Soviet Union and included some prisoners of war. Also numerous were Poles, with approximately one-fourth of the prisoners, and Frenchmen, about 15 percent of the camp inmates.

Among the prisoners from the Soviet Union, Poland, and France there were no Jews. In fact, in the beginning there were no Jewish inmates in Mittelbau-Dora. But that changed at the end of May 1944, when one thousand Hungarian Jews arrived in Dora, many children and teenagers among them.[37] Most of them were immediately sent on to the *"Buna-Lager"* Ellrich-Juliushütte, where many suffered painful deaths because of the murderous working conditions. Only at the end of September did a second transport with Jewish prisoners arrive at Dora. These were three hundred Hungarian Jews who, as skilled workers, had to toil in V-1 production for the Volkswagen plant in Schönbeck on the Elbe, in France (camp Tiercelet), and on the Moselle (camp Rebstock). In Dora they were assigned as a forced-labor group to V-1 production.

Those two transports notwithstanding, Jews remained a minority in the Mittelbau camps until January 1945; in most of these camps there had been no Jews at all. All that changed in January 1945, when in the course of the abandonment of the forced-labor and concentration camps in the East, several thousand Jews were "evacuated" to Mittelbau, including more than a thousand inmates from Czestochowa.[38] In camp Harzungen at the beginning of April 1945, the number of Jews climbed to 10 percent of the inmates,[39] and that despite a mortality rate among Auschwitz and Gross-Rosen evacuees that exceeded the rate in the early phase of Dora. Most of the terribly weakened inmates from Auschwitz and Gross-Rosen were taken to the Boelcke Barracks. One may assume that in this camp the percentage of Jews was much greater than in Harzungen.

Differing from the usual practice of heterogeneous composition of blocks and work commandos, the SS camp administration stressed the rule that, as much as possible, Jewish inmates were to work and be housed separately from non-Jewish inmates. Furthermore they were to be assigned to as few camps as possible. Thus the November 1, 1944, Mittelbau roster listed Jewish inmates only for camps Dora, Ellrich, and Harzungen (except for two inmates in Klein-Bodung and one in the SS construction brigades).[40] Even after the arrival of the transports from Czestochowa (most prisoners of these transports arrived in camps Rottleberode and Stampeda, where many were murdered by SS personnel and Kapos or died of the effects of forced labor in the underground galleries of Bauvorhaben B 4), Auschwitz, and Gross-Rosen, the SS changed its practice little and sent its Jewish prisoners almost exclusively to the large camps. Most Jews were assigned to construction sites, and a few were assigned to the production commandos of the Mittelwerk. There they had to work in isolated commandos and were housed in Dora separately from the other production workers.

In the camps of the Mittelbau-Dora complex, in spite of the "economization"

of all inmate work, the annihilation pressure on the Jewish inmates had not sub-
sided, even though there were no gas chambers at Dora and its satellite camps.
The inmates who suffered in the most cruel fashion were those who had been
"evacuated" from the annihilation and concentration camps in the winter of
1944–1945 and who, besides their stigmatization as Jewish inmates, had an additional shortcoming. In the view of the SS and the profit-oriented firms, they
were *wertlos* (of no value) because they were completely exhausted and unable
to work. This was the consequence, one should remember, of their earlier treatment.

The main product of the Mittelbau-Dora project was death. Of the sixty
thousand inmates who were deported between August 1943 and April 1945 to
the camps of Mittelbau-Dora, careful estimates suggest that twenty thousand
and possibly many more did not live to see the end of the war.[41] Under the hor-
rific conditions, especially at the construction sites, nearly all inmates suffered
to the same extent, whether they were Jews, already facing annihilation, or
French inmates, who ranked higher in Nazi racial ideology. One consequence
was that the death rate of French and Belgian inmates, of whom many were deported to dreaded construction sites such as Ellrich-Juliushütte, reached catastrophic levels. In December 1944 nearly 40 percent of all Mittelbau-Dora dead
were non-Jewish French and Belgians.

In this matter there arises also the question of the number of victims among
Nacht und Nebel (NN) inmates, whom the SS often were predisposed to kill.
According to a December 7, 1941, OKW decree by Keitel, resistance suspects in
the occupied areas of Western Europe were not to be tried in their countries of
origin but were to be taken, in total isolation, "bei Nacht und Nebel" (by night
and fog), across the border to Germany.[42] By 1942, but especially in the last
year of war, nearly all NN inmates in prisons and in the "Sonderlager" Hinzert
were transferred to the concentration camps; most of them were sent to
Natzweiler and Gross-Rosen.[43] As *Verschwundene* (the "disappeared," as one
may call them today in reference to the Latin America term), they were always
under very immediate threat of death and could hardly hope ever to see their
families again.

In all likelihood a group of NN inmates were deported to Mittelbau-Dora.
One may assume that a large number of the 1,085, mainly French, inmates transferred in September 1944 from the Natzweiler-Cochem satellite camp to Dora
were category NN prisoners. In contrast to other concentration camps, NN inmates of Mittelbau were not identified as such, either by markings on their
prison garb or in statistics. It is therefore rather unlikely that as a group they suffered worse privations than other inmate groups. Some survivors' oft-advanced
claim to NN status seems hardly useful in trying to clarify the high number of
dead among West Europeans in the Mittelbau camps. Rather, numbers of such
claims seem indicative of a latter-day effort to rationalize one's own suffering

and the death of fellow inmates, this since the idea of senseless suffering often collides with the self-image former inmates have.

Work or Annihilation?

The tremendous wear and tear on the construction project inmates in the last months of war is repeatedly described in the literature as evidence of an ideologically motivated annihilation objective of the SS—an overriding goal that not only dominated economic considerations but virtually worked against them. For example, one of the principal proponents of this thesis, Herman Kaienburg, wrote in his 1981 case study of the Neuengamme camp that the cause of the inhuman conditions, in the last analysis, had not been the economic endeavors. "Rather, the intent was to annihilate the [camp] inmates. The ruthless work assignments were a method by which to realize these intentions."[44] Such stubborn insistence on perceiving an intentionalist and ultimately single-cause thesis of a long-planned annihilation program—except for some war-economy concessions—failed to comprehend the dynamics of a process that was shaped by the interactions of real and assumed political, economic, and military factors as well as by ideological imperatives. Racism, which Ulrich Herbert quite rightly identified as the top priority (*"Fixpunkt"*) of the system,[45] did not exclude utilitarian considerations that accorded with the disposition of the perpetrators. It was such a rationalization that, for example, brought about the death of French prisoners in the Mittelbau complex.

In the death of these originally less-threatened prisoners, one can discern the real nature of the "economization" of the camp system. Forced labor did not, in most cases, bring an improvement in the living conditions of inmate groups classified at the lowest levels of the SS racial hierarchy. Actually it produced a general lowering of the survival chances of inmate categories ranked higher in the chart and hence a greater exposure to the murderous conditions faced by the lower-ranking groups. Although with certain groups, such as the Jewish inmates, their death was actively pursued, with others death was "merely" a part of the death-assumption calculation. In both cases the consequence was the same: mass death.

Mittelbau-Dora and the Kammler-Staff

The Mittelbau camps, whether in their external appearance, changed interior structures, constant functional expansion, or organizational core, showed very little resemblance to the prewar concentration camps. Amtsgruppe D of the SS-WVHA, which had developed from Theodor Eicke's Inspectorate of Concentration Camps, in the end had a very small consultative role in Mittelbau. By the end of 1943 SS General Hans Kammler had succeeded in his step-by-step extraction of Mittelbau-Dora from the organizational mesh of Amtsgruppe D. Without the increasing manifestations of dissolution in the Nazis' governance structure, the formation of an independent Mittelbau-Dora complex would have been unthinkable. With the change in the military situation in the winter of 1941–1942 new centers of power established themselves in the eroding system of Nazi rule. One need cite only the expansion of Speer's armaments ministry as well as the creation of the SS-WVHA and of the office of the General Plenipotentiary for Labor Allocation. With the beginning of 1944 this development accelerated with the appointment of the diverse interministerial *Sonderstäbe*, or special staffs. The Kammler staff office was one of these new power centers that, in addition to its institutional and personnel "moorings" in the armaments ministry, the Reich Air Ministry, and the SS apparatus, also was able to create a territorial basis for itself with Mittelbau-Dora and the closed district "*Sperrkreis Mittelbau.*"

The fact that Kammler chose the southern Harz area to create his "own" camp complex, rather than other sites of his industrial relocation project, may have been due either to the spatial density of the southern Harz construction projects or to the specific armaments-economy designation of this complex. Indeed, the side-by-side location of the V-weapons manufacture and the construction projects of the fighter aircraft (*Jäger*) procurement staff, along with Kammler's extensive authority in both these matters, caused him to make the planned armaments center in the southern Harz the focal point of his ambitious plans. Given the approaching end of the war, these plans were little more than an escape—albeit a murderous one—from reality. Kammler's steadily enlarged authority was due only to the growing dissolution of the Nazi state. And because of this fact, doubts about the modernization paradigm are justified. Mittelbau-Dora was not the result of planning for the future but, instead, was a characteristic of the murderous dynamic of collapse.

Mittelbau-Dora and the German Population

The Mittelbau camps, even in their alternating social permutations, were hardly comparable to the camps of the prewar era. That is especially clear in the enlargement of the recruitment pool of guard personnel. The SS, under Eicke's leadership, had succeeded in 1933–1934 in annexing the concentration camps to its sphere of authority. But by spring 1944, because of pressing demands for personnel, ever more armed forces men assumed guard duties, especially in the satellite camps. Although the camps' authority remained to the end of the war in the hands of long-serving (*altgediente*) SS members, in satellites such as Mittelbau camp Harzungen, armed forces officers functioned as camp leaders. This put them in the exposed position of responsibility for the living conditions of the inmates. This development showed that SS control in matters of personnel also began to fracture. Living conditions in camps administered and/or guarded by the armed forces were in most cases no better than in camps under SS supervision, whose staff had been trained according to the "Dachau Model." Clearly the violence discharged in the last months of war did not stand in need of an SS annihilation program.

All this also pointed to the broad dimension of complicity manifested by the far-reaching acceptance of Mittelbau-Dora by the civilian population in the camp environs. Few were ready to assume the risk of helping the inmates. Many others participated in the crimes by requesting laborers from the camp administration or by tormenting or mistreating them on roads or at work sites. Most of these civilians trained themselves to ignore the situation. The presence of crime did not cause them to turn away from the regime. Rather, it led to complicit identification with the evildoers and often exceeded the "going-along-with-it" participation.[46] An important part of the readiness to collaborate was quite likely the fear, deliberately fanned by Nazi propaganda, of revenge by the victor. With the taboo broken, the individual had the feeling of being unreservedly tied to the regime and possibly perishing with it. Bernd Rusinek has vividly described the attitude of Cologne Gestapo members who believed that, before their own deaths, they must take "a few others with them."[47]

In a climate of intensified fear of revenge (or punishment?) by the victors and the liberated inmates, Nazi propaganda smoothly connected with the Manichean concept of order, which since the early 1930s had served to isolate *Gemeinschaftsfremde* outsiders and to give comradely *Volksgenossen* a feeling of material and emotional security. The prospect of murdering and plundering inmates cast a sense of impending danger emanating from the Mittelbau-Dora camps and collided with the sense of security that bound the population more closely to the regime, which promised to keep this self-made danger in check. Another reason for broad acquiescence and passivity was the years-long adjustment to the suppression and exclusion (*Ausgrenzung*) of those not considered acceptable by the community, those *Gemeinschaftsfremde*. All this prepared the ideological and emotional basis for an attitude by which only a few saw the abused inmates as having suffered an injustice. By the same token, that attitude demonstrated that little was left of earlier values of civilization. A contributing factor, no doubt, was that the camps and their inmates, in terms of perception and memory, were simply shelved by the local population under the category "war experiences."

Adjustment over the years to force and exclusion, the longing for "order" and "security," a world image polarized by war, and a deep fear of everything "alien" made possible an evolution of force and a readiness of the population to collaborate, energized by an ideological point of view. Without the passive or consensual collaboration of substantial sections of the population, the concentration camp system could not have lasted long. That no specific Nazi ideology was required is the most disquieting result of the study of the Mittelbau camps and their social environs. But had it "only" been, as Daniel J. Goldhagen asserts, the "eliminationist anti-Semitism" of the Germans that made nearly an entire society co-perpetrators of the mass murder, one would have to treat as only half-serious the warning of the French writer and camp survivor David Rousset that the camp crimes could happen again "in a new form."[48]

JENS-CHRISTIAN WAGNER

Biographical Glossary

RICHARD BAER. Commandant of Dora-Mittelbau from February 1, 1945, until the end of the war. Born 1911. Entered Nazi Party in 1931, the SS in 1932. Served in various capacities at Dachau, Oranienburg, Buchenwald, and Neuengamme, as well as on the Russian front, 1933–1942. Adjutant to Oswald Pohl, chief of the SS Business Administration Main Office, November 1942–May 1944. Commanded the Auschwitz I camp, May 1944 to February 1945. Went into hiding after the war. Captured near Hamburg, 1960; died while in custody, 1961.

HELMUT BISCHOFF. Counterintelligence and countersabotage officer for the V-2 rocket program, and SD commander. Born 1908. Entered Nazi Party in March 1930 and the SS in 1935; assigned to the Gestapo. Commanded various Staatspolizei units, 1935–1943; also led an Einsatzkommando in Poland in 1939. In December 1943 took over as the Armaments Ministry's representative on Hans Kammler's SS construction staff, in which he was responsible for counterintelligence and countersabotage within the V-2 production program. In February 1945 took over as commander of the Security Service (SD) within the Mittelbau reservation; responsible for spying on, torturing, and executing prisoners. Captured by the Soviets in 1946, held in Buchenwald, then sent to Siberia. Returned to Germany, 1955; arrested in 1967; declared unfit to stand trial and released in 1970.

WERNHER VON BRAUN. Rocket researcher, technical director of the Army Testing Facility at Peenemünde. Born 1912. During his studies became an employee of the Army Weapons Office, 1932. Became technical director at the rocket testing facility at Peenemünde and also joined the Nazi Party, 1937. Joined the SS, 1940. From August 1943 until the end of the war, worked closely within the project to manufacture V-2 rockets underground; promoted the use of prisoner labor. Taken to the United States, September 1945. Rose to senior rank in NASA. Died 1977, in Alexandria, Virginia.

ERHARD BRAUNY. Born 1913. A professional dyer, from September 1937 a member of camp SS in Buchenwald. Served in 1942–1943 with SS Construction Brigade III in Cologne and subsequently was for six months at Dachau. Became commander of

Source: Jens-Christian Wagner, *Das KZ Mittelbau-Dora: Katalog zur historischen Ausstellung in der KZ-Gedenkstätte Mittelbau-Dora*. Herausgegeben im Auftrage der Stiftung Gedenkstätten Buchenwald und Mittelbau-Dora (Göttingen, 2001).

the Buchenwald satellite camp Wernigerode and then returned as Rapportführer (in charge of daily reports) to Dora. From November 1944 to April 1945 led satellite camp Rottlebrode. After the Dachau Dora trial he was sentenced to life in prison. Died in prison in Landsberg in 1950.

ERWIN JULIUS BUSTA. Block leader in the tunnels and in the Dora camp. Born 1905. Entered Nazi Party in 1928 and the SS in 1930. Served in a variety of capacities in Dachau, Esterwegen, and Sachsenhausen. Transferred to Peenemünde in summer 1943, then to Mittelbau in the autumn. Was senior SS man within the tunnels and camp, where he developed a reputation for inventing cruelties and tortures. After the war, lived in Germany from 1952 on, under his real name. Arrested in 1968, sentenced in 1970 to eight years, six months in prison, but never began his sentence. Died 1982.

GERHARD DEGENKOLB. Engineer, head of the Special Committee A4 (V-2). Born 1892. Entered Nazi Party in 1930. Served in senior positions in various manufacturing firms and industrial committees, 1941–1945, including the Special Committee A4, which coordinated the process by which A4 (V-2) rockets were produced in series. He also served as chairman of the Mittelbau Advisory Council. Temporarily under arrest in 1947, then employed by various manufacturing firms. Died 1954.

WALTER DORNBERGER. Army rocket expert. Born 1895. Served in the Army Weapons Office from 1930 until the end of World War II; specialized in rockets and other special weapons. Named a member of the Mittelbau Advisory Council in September 1943. In British custody 1945–1947, while preparations were under way to prosecute him for V-2 attacks, but then resettled in the United States, where he worked for the U.S. air force. Later active in the American aircraft industry. Died 1980.

OTTO FÖRSCHNER. Commandant of Dora-Mittelbau from August 1943 until the end of January 1945. Born 1902. Transferred from the Reichswehr to the Waffen-SS in 1934. Served at the front for the first two years of the war, then transferred to Buchenwald. Transferred (apparently as a punishment) to command the Mittelbau camp in September 1943. Also named business manager of the Mittelwerk limited company in October 1943. Transferred to Kaufering, a subcamp of Dachau, February 1945. In December 1945 the Americans sentenced him to death for his role in Kaufering. Executed May 28, 1946.

FRANZ HÖSSLER. Born 1916. SS member from early 1933 and at the end was Obersturmführer; had a long career in camp administration. He trained first at Dachau in summer 1933. In June 1940 transferred to Auschwitz; by 1941 was on temporary assignments in the Waffen-SS. After his return to Dachau became commander of Auschwitz I and, as of February 1945, commander of Dora. Finally, in April 1945 became commandant of the Bergen-Belsen auxiliary camp (known as either "Nebenlager" or "Kasernenlager"). In consequence of the crimes he had committed there he was sentenced to death in the first Bergen-Belsen trial on November 17, 1945, and executed on December 13, 1945.

KARL KAHR. Born 1914 in Austria. From 1940 a member of the Waffen-SS. A medical doctor, in 1943 he was camp physician in Dachau, subsequently in Dora, especially Mittelbau. Early January 1945 transferred to Gross-Rosen, followed by several months in American custody, where he worked closely with U.S. investigation as witness for the prosecution in the Dachau Dora trial and in the Nürnberg Pohl trial. Later a physician in Graz.

HANS KAMMLER. Architect, chief of the SS construction office. Born 1901. Entered Nazi Party in 1931, SS in 1933. Served in a variety of administrative posts in the food and air ministries, 1933–1940, then joined Waffen-SS. Participated in the construction of the Majdanek camp, summer 1941. Named to head SS construction office, 1942; participated in planning and construction of Auschwitz-Birkenau. In August 1943, Heinrich Himmler and Albert Speer placed Kammler in charge of moving key production facilities underground. In August 1944, Himmler gave him responsibility for the deployment of the V-1 and V-2 weapons. Died May 1945, suspected suicide.

HANS MÖSER. Born 1906. Trained businessman, member of the Nazi Party from 1929, SS from 1931. In 1939 was a member of SS in camps Hinzert, Neuengamme, and Auschwitz. Transferred end of April 1944 as 2nd and later as 1st commandant of protective custody camp in Dora. Sentenced to death in 1947 Dachau Dora trial; executed in November 1948.

PAUL RASSINIER. Prisoner. Born 1906. Arrested by Gestapo for resistance activities, 1943, sent first to Buchenwald, then to Mittelbau. In the 1950s he began to publish works that questioned the existence of the Holocaust; in one work he asserted, for example, "with regard to gas chambers . . . never at any moment did the responsible authorities of the Third Reich intend to order—or in fact, order—the extermination of the Jews in this or any other manner" (from a collection of his writings, *The Holocaust Story and the Lies of Ulysses* [Costa Mesa, Calif., Institute for Historical Review, 1978], p. 270). He has been characterized as the father of the so-called revisionist school, whose representatives continue to refer to his works.

GEORG RICKHEY. Engineer, general director of the Mittelwerk limited company. Born 1898. Entered Nazi Party in 1931. Beginning in October 1942, occupied a senior position in the Ministry for Armaments and Munitions while also business manager for the DEMAG vehicle manufacturing works in Berlin-Falkensee. In autumn 1943 took over the firm that tested the V-2 rocket engines. In April 1944 named general director of the rocket works in the Mittelwerk limited company, in which role he was also responsible for the use of concentration camp prisoners as forced labor. Arrested by the U.S. army in May 1945, tried by a military court in 1947, but acquitted after placing the blame on the (already dead) V-2 production chief Albin Sawatzki. Died 1966.

ARTHUR RUDOLPH. Engineer, operations director for the Mittelwerk limited company. Born 1906. Entered Nazi Party in 1931. Hired by the Army Weapons Office, 1934. Entered into collaboration with Wernher von Braun at Peenemünde, 1937. By

June 1944, responsible for assembly and quality control of V-2 rockets as well as the employment of civilian and concentration camp laborers. In 1945 taken to the United States along with von Braun and other rocket specialists, where he eventually occupied senior positions in the space program. Questioned by U.S. Department of Justice, 1982–1983; left the United States voluntarily, 1984, rather than face a deportation hearing. Reissued German citizenship. Died 1995 in Hamburg.

ERNST SANDER. Member of the Gestapo in Mittelwerk and in the Mittelbau Camp. Born 1916. Entered the SS, 1933. Joined the Gestapo, 1939, and served in a variety of secret police positions. In January 1944 assigned to counterintelligence and countersabotage in the Mittelwerk and in the Mittelbau camp. Participated in torture and murder of prisoners. Interned by American troops in May 1945 but released to a hospital because of appendicitis, then took a false identity. Identified and placed on trial in Essen, 1968. Sentenced in 1970 to seven years and six months in prison, but never began the sentence. Died 1990.

KARL-OTTO SAUR. Born 1902. Engineer. Entered Nazi Party in 1931. Employed by the Thyssen-Combine until 1937, then in the Todt Office. In 1942 became director of the Technical Office, Speer Ministry, and became Speer's representative in the Jägerstab in 1944. Interned 1945–1948. Later technical adviser for sundry enterprises. Founder of publishing firm Dokumentation der Technik (now K.G. Saur Verlag). Died 1966.

ALBIN SAWATZKI. Engineer, V-2 production chief. Born 1909. Entered Nazi Party in 1933. In 1943 became director of the Henschel Works in Kassel, which produced Tiger tanks; he also became head of the "serial production" working committee under Special Committee A4. That year Albert Speer put him in charge of production; from September he was present in the camp. In February 1944 he became director of the planning department for Mittelwerk. Died May 1, 1945, as a result of injuries inflicted by former concentration camp prisoners.

WILHELM SIMON. Labor allocation manager in Mittelbau. Born 1900. Entered Nazi Party and SS in 1932. Held various bureaucratic posts, 1935–1941. Entered active SS duty as a guard at Buchenwald, 1941. Became an assistant to the labor allocation manager at Buchenwald, summer 1942. December 1, 1943, named labor allocation manager for Mittelbau. In May 1945 transferred to a Wehrmacht unit. Within days he was captured, then either released or escaped. In 1947 the Americans tried him for his crimes and sentenced him to life in prison, but he gained release in 1954.

EDUARD WIRTHS. Born 1909. April 1942 troop physician in Dachau and in July 1942 in Neuengamme. Later he was station physician in Auschwitz, and as of February 1945 in Mittelbau. He surrendered to British authorities in May 1945 and committed suicide in captivity.

Notes

Introduction

1. Known as the Amicale des déportés à Dora-Ellrich, Harzungen et Kommandos annexes, 55, quai Le Gallo, 92100 Boulogne.
2. Known as the Association française Buchenwald-Dora et Kommandos, 66, rue des Martyrs, 75009 Paris.
3. Known as the Amicale des déportés politiques de Dora et Kommandos, CNPPA, rue du Commerce 21, 1000 Brussels.

Chapter 1. The State of Germany in August 1943

1. Philippe Masson, *Histoire de l'armée allemande* (Paris: Perrin, 1994), pp. 247–57.
2. Ibid., pp. 267–73.
3. Ibid., p. 295.
4. Gitta Sereny, *Albert Speer: son combat avec la vérité* (Paris: Seuil, 1997), pp. 273–89.
5. Ibid., pp. 291–93.
6. Ibid., pp. 307–8.
7. Jacques Delarue, *Histoire de la Gestapo* (Paris: Fayard, 1962), pp. 55–56.
8. Ibid., p. 81.
9. Ibid., p. 181.
10. Marlis Steinert, "L'ordre noir de la SS," in *L'Histoire, L'Allemagne de Hitler* (Paris: Seuil, coll. "Points Histoire," 1991), p. 101.
11. Jean Bezaut, *Oranienburg, Sachsenhausen* (Hérault-Éditions, 1989), pp. 25–26.
12. Michel Fabréguet, "Une entreprise concentrationnaire de la SS," in *XXe siècle,* Dossier sur les camps de concentration du XXe siècle, no. 54, April–June 1997.
13. Ibid., p. 161.
14. Ibid.
15. Albert Speer, *L'Empire SS* (Paris: Laffont, 1982), pp. 32–33.
16. Bezaut, *Oranienburg, Sachsenhausen,* pp. 163–64.
17. Ibid., pp. 192–94.

Chapter 2. The Rocket Program Prior to Dora

1. Michael J. Neufeld, *The Rocket and the Reich* (New York: Free Press, 1995).
2. Ibid., pp. 19–22.
3. Ibid., p. 28.
4. Ibid., pp. 22–23.
5. Ibid., p. 37.
6. Ibid., p. 53.
7. Ibid., pp. 32–38.
8. Ibid., pp. 43–48.
9. Ibid., pp. 48–51.

10. Ibid., p. 63.
11. Ibid., pp. 68–70.
12. Ibid., pp. 73–109.
13. Ibid., pp. 114–15.
14. Ibid., pp. 178–79.
15. Ibid., pp. 51–53.
16. Ibid., p. 127.
17. Ibid., pp. 139–40.
18. Ibid., pp. 147–48.
19. Ibid., pp. 161–64.
20. Ibid., pp. 164–65.
21. Ibid., p. 171.
22. Ibid., p. 192.
23. Ibid., p. 174.
24. Ibid., p. 286.
25. Ibid., pp. 184–85.
26. Ibid., pp. 190–91.
27. Ibid., pp. 191–93.
28. Ibid., p. 194.
29. Ibid., pp. 180–83.
30. Ibid., pp. 183–84.
31. Ibid., p. 186.
32. Ibid., pp. 186–87.
33. Ibid., p. 188.
34. Ibid., p. 189.
35. Georg Metzler, *Geheime Kommandosache* (Bergatreute: Wilfried Eppe, 1996).
36. Neufeld, *The Rocket and the Reich,* p. 189.
37. Roger Berthereau, letter, AADE (from *Archives de l'Amicale Dora-Ellrich*; see "Sources: The Testimonies" at the back of this book for details).
38. André Cassier, letter, AADE.
39. Eugène Laurent, letter, AADE.
40. Michel Fliecx, *Pour délit d'espérance* (Nice: Récits de vie, 1989), pp. 27–40.
41. Ibid., pp. 27–28.
42. Ibid., pp. 28–29.
43. An overview of the major features of the concentration camp system, including camp commanders and senior-most prisoners in the camp, Reds and Greens, etc., is laid out in chapter 3 below on Buchenwald in 1943.
44. Neufeld, *The Rocket and the Reich,* p. 189.
45. Fliecx, *Pour délit d'espérance,* p. 37.
46. Louis Crotet, letter, AADE.
47. Pierre Lucas, letter, AADE.
48. Paul Bouchet, letter, AADE.
49. R. V. Jones, *La Guerre ultra-secrète, 1939–1945* (Paris: Plon, 1978), pp. 320–35.
50. James McGovern, *La Chasse aux armes secrètes allemandes* (Paris: Stock, 1965), pp. 15–22.
51. Neufeld, *The Rocket and the Reich,* p. 199.
52. McGovern, *La Chasse aux armes secrètes allemandes,* pp. 29–34.
53. Neufeld, *The Rocket and the Reich,* pp. 197–99.
54. Ibid., pp. 200–202.
55. Emmanuel de Martonne, *Europe centrale–Allemagne* (Paris: Armand Colin, 1930), pp. 275–77.
56. Manfred Bornemann, *Geheimprojekt Mittelbau* (Bonn: Bernard & Graefe, 1994), pp. 11–20.
57. Ibid., pp. 20–21.
58. Ibid., pp. 21–30.
59. The question of compatible terminology in English has been resolved as follows, in keeping with established usage. To designate the overall underground compound as of August 1943, the "Dora Tunnel" will be referred to in the singular and with a capital T, but "tunnel A" or "tunnel B" will be referred to without a capital. With regard to the galleries, the word "hall" will be used to translate the German *Halle*.

60. Jacques Delarue, *Trafics et Crimes sous l'Occupation* (Paris: Fayard, 1968), pp. 54–55.
61. Ibid., pp. 70–82.

Chapter 3. Buchenwald and the Concentration Camp System in 1943

1. Henri Amouroux, *La Page n'est pas encore tournée* (Paris: Laffont, 1993), pp. 102–10.
2. Annette Wieviorka, *Déportation et Génocide* (Paris: Plon, 1992), pp. 82–84.
3. Amouroux, *La Page n'est pas encore tournée,* pp. 97–98.
4. Interview with the author.
5. Jorge Semprun, *L'Écriture ou la vie* (Paris: Gallimard, 1994), p. 54.
6. Ibid., pp. 38–41, 47, 51–56.
7. Eugen Kogon, *L'État SS* (Paris: Seuil, 1993), p. 15.
8. Semprun, *L'Écriture ou la vie,* pp. 88–92, 107–9. Semprun spells his name Rosenfeld.
9. Kogon, *L'État SS,* p. 15–19.
10. Bezaut, *Oranienburg, Sachsenhausen,* pp. 37–38.
11. Daniel Chlique, in *Le Déporté,* July 1996.
12. Jean-Henry Tauzin, *Quatre Ans dans les bagnes hitlériens* (Corbeil, 1945), p. 44.
13. Paul Rassinier, *Passage de la ligne,* 6th ed. (La Vieille Taupe), p. 22.
14. Frère Birin, *Seize Mois de bagne* (Épernay: Dautelle, 1947), pp. 41–42.
15. Kogon, *L'État SS,* pp. 50–55.
16. Rassinier, *Passage de la ligne,* pp. 33–35.
17. Kogon, *L'État SS,* pp. 304–5.
18. Max Dutillieux, *Le Camp des armes secrètes* (Rennes: Éd. Ouest-France, 1993), p. 67.
19. Pierre Julitte, *L'Arbre de Goethe* (Paris: Presses de la Cité, 1965), pp. 172–73.
20. Semprun, *L'Écriture ou la vie,* p. 308.
21. Christian Pineau, *La Simple Vérité* (Paris: Julliard, 1960), p. 341.
22. Guy Raoul-Duval, *Témoignage de déportation,* pp. 24–28.
23. Jiri Benès, *Détenu en Allemagne.*
24. Otakar Litomisky, *Les Mémoires du prisonnier 113.359.* This number corresponds to an Auschwitz identity number, tattooed on the forearm.
25. Hermann Langbein, *La Résistance dans les camps de concentration* (Fayard: Paris, 1981), pp. 37–66.
26. Wolfgang Sofsky, *The Order of Terror* (Princeton: Princeton University Press, 1997), p. 41.
27. Ibid., p. 55.
28. Kogon, *L'État SS,* p. 171.
29. Sofsky, *L'Organisation de la terreur,* (Paris: Calmann, 1995), pp. 55–56.
30. Langbein, *La Résistance dans les camps de concentration,* pp. 29–30.

Chapter 4. The New Organization of Autumn 1943

1. Bornemann, *Geheimprojekt Mittelbau,* pp. 47–48.
2. The Napola, or Nationalpolitische Erziehungsanstalt, was school for the indoctrination of future National Socialist leaders.
3. Bornemann, *Geheimprojekt Mittelbau,* p. 21.
4. Ibid., pp. 50–53.
5. Roger Berthereau quotes Paul Blanchard, Marcel Choquet, Guy Dussud, Michel Fliecx, Jacques Gaudel.
6. Neufeld, *The Rocket and the Reich,* pp. 204–5.
7. Ibid., pp. 203–4.
8. Ibid., p. 204.
9. Ibid., p. 220.
10. Ibid., p. 205.
11. Ibid., p. 249.
12. Ibid., p. 207.
13. Ibid., p. 207. Also, Gordon J. Horwitz, *Mauthausen, ville d'Autriche* (Paris: Seuil, 1992), pp.

136–39; and Étienne and Paul Le Caër, *K.L. Mauthausen*, Heimdal, 1996, on the topic of Redl-Zipf.

14. The site is in the neighboring town of Helfaut, less well known. For the British pilots, it was Wizernes that served as a reference point.
15. Bornemann, *Geheimprojekt Mittelbau*, p. 42.
16. Ibid., pp. 47–48.
17. Ibid., p. 9.
18. Henry Bousson, letter, AADE.
19. Fliecx, *Pour délit d'espérance*, pp. 36–37.
20. Léon Bronchart, *Ouvrier et Soldat* (Vaison-la-Romaine: Meffre), p. 133.

Chapter 5. Nine Months of Ordeal

1. Bronchart, *Ouvrier et Soldat,* p. 136. Jiri Benès, *Détenu en Allemagne,* pp. 22–23. Jean Mialet, *Le Déporté* (Paris: Fayard, Paris), 1981, p. 70.
2. Émile Nérot, letter, AADE. Jean Rieg, letter, AADE.
3. Raymond Jacob, letter, AADE.
4. Benès, *Détenu en Allemagne,* p. 36.
5. Bornemann, *Geheimprojekt Mittelbau,* p. 65.
6. Neufeld, *The Rocket and the Reich,* pp. 211–12.
7. Paul Butet, *Cinquante Ans après!,* p. 47, AADE.
8. Charles Sadron, "A l'usine de Dora," *Témoignages strasbourgeois,* 3rd ed., 1989, pp. 201–2.
9. Marcel Pierrel, narrative account, AADE.
10. Dutillieux, *Le Camp des armes secrètes,* p. 91.
11. Fliecx, *Pour délit d'espérance,* p. 54.
12. Litomisky, *Les Mémoires du prisonnier 113.359,* p. 73.
13. Fliecx, *Pour délit d'espérance,* p. 54.
14. Litomisky, *Les Mémoires du prisonnier 113.359,* p. 74.
15. Raymond Jacob, letter, AADE. Fliecx, *Pour délit d'espérance,* pp. 54–55.
16. Fliecx, *Pour délit d'espérance,* p. 57.
17. Bornemann, *Geheimprojekt Mittelbau,* p. 28.
18. Ibid., pp. 60–62.
19. Francis Dunouau, letter, AADE. Émile Nérot, letter, AADE. Georges Soubirous, letter, AADE.
20. Francis Dunouau, letter, AADE. Serge Sermot, letter, AADE.
21. Bornemann, *Geheimprojekt Mittelbau,* p. 41.
22. Ibid., p. 40.
23. Neufeld, *The Rocket and the Reich,* p. 208.
24. Joachim Neander, *Das Konzentrationslager Mittelbau* (Clausthal-Zellerfeld, 1997).
25. Jean Demuyter, narrative account, AADE. Marcel Martin, letter, AADE. Benès, *Détenu en Allemagne,* pp. 52–53.
26. Dutillieux, *Le Camp des armes secrètes,* p. 82.
27. Bronchart, *Ouvrier et Soldat,* p. 171.
28. Ibid., p. 137.
29. Butet, *Cinquante Ans après!,* p. 42, AADE.
30. Fliecx, *Pour délit d'espérance,* pp. 46–47.
31. Bornemann, *Geheimprojekt Mittelbau,* p. 28.
32. Benès, *Détenu en Allemagne,* p. 48.
33. Pierre Auchabie, *Les Rayés,* p. 13, AADE. Marcel Alabert, letter, AADE.
34. Albert Amate, *Dora,* pp. 11–12, AADE.
35. Jean Michel, *Dora* (Paris: Lattès, 1975), pp. 119–23.
36. Neufeld, *The Rocket and the Reich,* p. 213.
37. Benès, *Détenu en Allemagne,* pp. 57–58.
38. Neufeld, *The Rocket and the Reich,* p. 212.
39. Speer, *L'Empire SS,* pp. 219–20.
40. Dutillieux, *Le Camp des armes secrètes,* p. 86.
41. André Rogerie, *Vivre, c'est vaincre* (Paris: Curial-Archereau, 1946), p. 48.
42. Claude Douay, letter, AADE.

43. Benès, *Détenu en Allemagne,* p. 52.
44. Bronchart, *Ouvrier et Soldat,* pp. 140–41.
45. Joannès Méfret, letter, AADE.
46. Raymond Jacob, letter, AADE.
47. Pierre Vagnon, letter, AADE.
48. Georges Soubirous, letter, AADE.
49. Roger Berthereau, letter, AADE.
50. The Ohrdruf military camp operated uninterrupted from the time of the German empire in the nineteenth century until the time of the Soviet troops.
51. Jacques Vern, letter, AADE.

Chapter 6. Death in Dora

1. Michel, *Dora,* p. 130.
2. Ibid., pp. 129–30.
3. Ibid., p. 127.
4. Fliecx, *Pour délit d'espérance,* p. 49.
5. Butet, *Cinquante Ans après!,* pp. 46–47, AADE.
6. Fliecx, *Pour délit d'espérance,* pp. 52–53.
7. Dutillieux, *Le Camp des armes secrètes,* pp. 114–15.
8. Jean Rieg, letter, AADE.
9. Fliecx, *Pour délit d'espérance,* p. 53.
10. Rogerie, *Vivre, c'est vaincre,* p. 52.
11. Fliecx, *Pour délit d'espérance,* p. 53.
12. Dutillieux, *Le Camp des armes secrètes,* pp. 115–17.
13. Fliecx, *Pour délit d'espérance,* p. 61.
14. Michel, *Dora,* p. 171.
15. Ibid., p. 171.
16. Ibid., pp. 173–74.
17. Rogerie, *Vivre, c'est vaincre,* pp. 55–61.
18. Michel Fliecx, *Pour délit d'espérance,* p. 86.
19. Jean Rieg, letter, AADE.
20. Rogerie, *Vivre, c'est vaincre,* pp. 54–55.
21. Bronchart, *Ouvrier et Soldat,* p. 149.
22. Fliecx, *Pour délit d'espérance,* p. 61.
23. Max Simonin, letter, AADE.
24. Rogerie, *Vivre, c'est vaincre,* p. 52.
25. Butet, *Cinquante Ans après!* p. 46.
26. Mialet, *Le Déporté,* p. 89.
27. Litomisky, *Les Mémoires du prisonnier 113.359,* pp. 79–81.
28. Albert Van Dijk, CV Fondation and appendix, pp. 10–11, AADE.
29. Bronchart, *Ouvrier et Soldat,* p. 147.
30. Fliecx, *Pour délit d'espérance,* p. 51.
31. Pierre Auchabie, *Les Rayés,* p. 13, AADE.
32. Fliecx, *Pour délit d'espérance,* p. 56.
33. Ibid., p. 56.
34. Bronchart, *Ouvrier et Soldat,* p. 171.
35. Liste Greffier, *Bulletin mensuel de l'Amicale Dora-Ellrich,* no. 6 and 7, June–July 1946.
36. Sorting carried out by the author.
37. Mialet, *Le Déporté,* pp. 79–80.
38. Bernard d' Astorg, letter, AADE.
39. Rogerie, *Vivre, c'est vaincre,* p. 50 sq.
40. Auchabie, *Les Rayés,* appendix, AADE.
41. Rassinier, *Passage de la ligne,* p. 70.
42. Antoine Belin, CV Fondation, AADE.
43. Auchabie, *Les Rayés,* p. 14, AADE.
44. Mialet, *Le Déporté,* p. 121.

45. Dutillieux, *Le Camp des armes secrètes*, p. 85.
46. Mialet, *Le Déporté*, pp. 72–74.
47. Dutillieux, *Le Camp des armes secrètes*, pp. 121–23.
48. Ibid., p. 89.
49. Ibid., p. 120.
50. Bronchart, *Ouvrier et Soldat*, p. 148.
51. Manfred Bornemann, *Aktiver und passiver Widerstand* (Bonn: Bernard & Graefe, 1994), p. 35.
52. Hermann Langbein, *La Résistance dans les camps de concentration* (Paris: Fayard, 1981), pp. 258–59.
53. Otakar Litomisky, *Les Mémoires du prisonnier 113.359*, p. 81.
54. Benès, *Détenu en Allemagne*, p. 33.
55. Ibid., chapters 12 to 14.
56. Rassinier, *Passage de la ligne*, pp. 44 sq.
57. Bronchart, *Ouvrier et Soldat*, p. 144.
58. Lucien Maronneau, letter, AADE.
59. Neufeld, *The Rocket and the Reich*, pp. 209–10.

Chapter 7. Speer, Kammler, Dornberger, and von Braun in 1944 Germany

1. Neander, *Das Konzentrationslager Mittelbau*, pp. 215–16 and 248–55.
2. Sereny, *Albert Speer: son combat avec la vérité*, p. 435.
3. Ibid., pp. 371–72.
4. Ibid., pp. 409–10.
5. Ibid., pp. 415–26.
6. Neufeld, *The Rocket and the Reich*, pp. 213–20.
7. Pierre Kohler and Jean-René Germain, *Von Braun contre Korolev* (Paris: Plon, 1994), p. 88.
8. Ibid., subtitle of the work.
9. Sereny, *Albert Speer: son combat avec la vérité*, pp. 426–30.
10. Speer, *L'Empire SS*, p. 237.
11. Sereny, *Albert Speer: son combat avec la vérité*, p. 420.
12. Bornemann, *Geheimprojekt Mittelbau*, p. 81.
13. Ibid., p. 86.
14. Ibid., pp. 82–84.
15. Ibid., p. 89.
16. Neufeld, *The Rocket and the Reich*, pp. 220–23.
17. Bornemann, *Gehimprojekt Mittelbau*, p. 71.
18. Neufeld, *The Rocket and the Reich*, p. 230.
19. Ibid., p. 221.
20. Ibid., p. 224.
21. Ibid., pp. 230–38.
22. Ibid., p. 236.
23. Ibid., p. 237.
24. McGovern, *La Chasse aux armes secrètes allemandes*, pp. 38–39.
25. In particular Michel Hollard's "Agir" network.
26. Dossier put together by Yves Le Maner.
27. McGovern, *La Chasse aux armes secrètes allemandes*, pp. 43 and 52.
28. Ibid., pp. 61–63.
29. Ibid., pp. 64–67.
30. Neufeld, *The Rocket and the Reich*, p. 239.
31. Ibid., p. 240.
32. Ibid., p. 240.
33. Ibid., p. 243.
34. Ibid., p. 240.
35. Ibid., p. 241.
36. Ibid., p. 245.
37. Ibid., p. 242.
38. Ibid., p. 243.

39. Ibid., p. 241.
40. Ibid., p. 241.
41. Ibid., p. 288.
42. Bornemann, *Geheimprojekt Mittelbau,* p. 79.
43. Neufeld, *The Rocket and the Reich,* pp. 247–48.
44. Ibid., pp. 251–54.
45. Ibid., pp. 248–51.
46. Ibid., pp. 254–55.
47. Ibid., p. 255.
48. Sadron, *A l'usine de Dora,* pp. 198–99.
49. Neufeld, *The Rocket and the Reich,* p. 223.
50. Ibid., p. 243.

Chapter 8. The Peoples of Dora

1. There is in fact no adequate English translation for Reich.
2. Kogon, *L'État SS,* p. 38.
3. Benès, *Détenu en Allemagne,* chapter 11.
4. Litomisky, *Les Mémoires du prisonnier 113.359.*
5. J. B. de Korwin-Krokowski, letter, AADE.
6. Kogon, *L'État SS,* pp. 417–18.
7. Joseph Béninger, letter, AADE.
8. Serge Miller, *Le Laminoir* (Paris: Calmann-Lévy, 1947), p. 129.
9. François Heumann, letter, AADE.
10. Maurice de La Pintière, letter, AADE.
11. Lists in Brigitte d'Hainaut and Christine Somerhausen, *Dora* (Brussels: Didier-Hatier, 1991), pp. 151–208.
12. Ibid., pp. 17–19.
13. Ernest O. Abel, letter, AADE.
14. Ernest O. Abel, narrative account, AADE.
15. Recent correspondence, in English, between Theodor Braun and Yves Béon, AADE.
16. François Heumann, letter, AADE.
17. Charles Spitz, *Cellule 114* (Cahors: Le soutien par le livre, 1988), p. 169.
18. Lucien Fayman, letter, AADE.
19. Spitz, *Cellule 114,* p. 185.

Chapter 9. The Tunnel Factory and Its Workers

1. Chérif Ben Hassen, letter, AADE.
2. Birin, *Seize Mois de bagne,* pp. 54–57.
3. Rassinier, *Passage de la ligne,* p. 78.
4. Marcel Petit, narrative account, pp. 5–29, AADE.
5. Yves Béon, *La Planète Dora* (Paris: Seuil, 1985), pp. 32–34.
6. Louis Garnier, narrative account, AADE.
7. Paul Rassinier, *Passage de la ligne.*
8. Sereny, *Albert Speer: son combat avec la vérité,* pp. 404–5.
9. Neufeld, *The Rocket and the Reich,* p. 129.
10. Paul Bolteau, CV Fondation and appendix, AADE.
11. Spitz, *Cellule 114,* p. 140.
12. Sadron, *A l'usine de Dora,* p. 209.
13. Ibid., p. 204.
14. Rassinier, *Passage de la ligne,* pp. 67–68.
15. Gustave Estadès, letter, AADE.
16. Sereny, *Albert Speer: son combat avec la vérité,* p. 382.
17. Miller, *Le Laminoir,* p. 140.
18. René Croze, CV Fondation and appendices, AADE.

19. By a coincidental homonym, Hauptscharführer Wilhelm Simon was, on the SS side, one of the officers in charge of the Häftlingsarbeitseinsatz.
20. Paul Butet, *Cinquante Ans après!,* p. 50, AADE.
21. André Gérard, *The Slaves That Built the Rockets,* narrative account, AADE.
22. Filipcic, correspondence with the author.
23. André Sellier, narrative account, AADE.
24. William Fourtot, *Perdu dans la tourmente, d'après l'histoire vécue de Christian Desseaux.*
25. Robert Roulard, letter, AADE.
26. François Schwertz, letter, AADE.
27. François Heumann, letter, AADE.
28. Amate, *Dora,* pp. 19–21, AADE.
29. Pierre Lucas, letter, AADE.
30. François Garault, letter, AADE.
31. Bernard Ramillon, letter, AADE.
32. Jean Cormont, letter, AADE.
33. André Cardon, letter, AADE.
34. Élie Korenfeld, letter, AADE.
35. André Guichard, letter, AADE.
36. Raoul-Duval, *Témoignage de déportation,* p. 50.
37. Claude Bignon, letter, AADE.
38. Jacques Noël, letter, AADE.
39. Louis Coutaud, letter, AADE.
40. Francis Dunouau, letter, AADE.
41. Henry Mas, CV Fondation, AADE.
42. Guy Tartinville, letter, AADE.
43. Jean Gouvenaux, letter, AADE.
44. Claude Fisher, letter, AADE.
45. Sadron, *A l'usine de Dora,* pp. 197–98.
46. Interview with the author.
47. Marcel Coulardot, letter, AADE.
48. Claude Douay, letter, AADE.
49. Marcel Baillon, interview with the author.
50. Henri Calès, letter, AADE.
51. Jean Demuyter, narrative account, AADE.
52. André Ribault, narrative account, AADE.
53. Litomisky, *Les Mémoires du prisonnier 113.359,* p. 87.
54. Benès, *Détenu en Allemagne,* p. 66.
55. Jacques-Christian Bailly, *Un lycéen à Buchenwald* (Paris: Ramsay, 1979), pp. 161–62.
56. Francis Dunouau, letter, AADE.
57. Alfred Lacour, letter, AADE.
58. Paul Pagnier, CV Fondation, AADE.
59. Marcel Pierrel, narrative account, AADE.
60. Albert Vuillermoz, CV Fondation, AADE.
61. Raymond Zilliox, CV Fondation, AADE.
62. Sadron, *A l'usine de Dora,* pp. 210–11.
63. Andrès Pontoizeau, *Dora-la-Mort* (Tours: COSOR, 1947), p. 77.
64. Michel Depierre, letter, AADE.
65. Sadron, *A l'usine de Dora,* p. 198.
66. Raoul-Duval, *Témoignage de déportation,* pp. 56–57, AADE.
67. René Croze, CV Fondation and appendices, AADE.
68. Amate, *Dora,* p. 26, AADE.
69. Claude Bignon, letter, AADE.
70. Joseph Jazbinsek, letter, AADE.
71. Joannès Méfret, letter, AADE.
72. Guy Morand, letter, AADE.
73. Georges Jouanin, letter, AADE.
74. Raoul-Duval, *Témoignage de déportation,* p. 58, AADE.

75. Amate, *Dora,* p. 19, AADE.
76. Dominique Gaussen, *Le Kapo* (Paris: France-Empire, 1966).
77. Léon Delarbre, *Dora, croquis clandestins* (Paris: Michel de Romilly, 1945).
78. Benès, *Détenu en Allemagne,* p. 89.
79. Bailly, *Un lycéen à Buchenwald,* pp. 177–78.
80. Raoul-Duval, *Témoignage de déportation,* p. 59.
81. André Ribault, narrative account, AADE.
82. Ibid.
83. Serge Foiret, articles in *Revue de la France libre,* no. 273, and the journal *Icare,* no. 148.
84. René Davesne, letter, AADE.
85. Benès, *Détenu en Allemagne,* pp. 95–96.
86. André Ribault, narrative account, AADE.
87. Bailly, *Un lycéen à Buchenwald,* pp. 178–79.
88. Bernard Ramillon, letter, AADE.
89. Joseph Béninger, letter, AADE.
90. Raoul-Duval, *Témoignage de déportation,* p. 53.
91. Claude Bignon, letter, AADE.
92. François Herrou, letter, AADE.
93. Raoul-Duval, *Témoignage de déportation,* p. 51.
94. Amate, *Dora,* pp. 20–21, AADE.
95. Richard Pouzet, *Dora* (Paris: Castet, 1946), pp. 136–37.
96. Sadron, *A l'usine de Dora,* p. 213.
97. Raoul-Duval, *Témoignage de déportation,* p. 153.
98. Edmond Caussin, letter, AADE.
99. Émile Nérot, letter, AADE.
100. Dutillieux, *Le Camp des armes secrètes,* pp. 127–46.
101. Edmond Caussin, letter, AADE.
102. Langbein, *La Résistance dans les camps de concentration,* p. 31.
103. Spitz, *Cellule 114,* pp. 154–56.
104. Raoul Giquel, *Le Prix de la liberté* (Nantes: Opéra, 1996). The person who registered the testimony wrote down, phonetically, "Cleuboudunguen."

Chapter 10. The Camp at Dora in 1944

1. Rassinier, *Passage de la ligne,* pp. 65–67.
2. Birin, *Seize Mois de bagne,* p. 68.
3. Sadron, *A l'usine de Dora,* p. 206.
4. Georges Soubirous, letter, AADE.
5. Spitz, *Cellule 114,* p. 180 sq.
6. Pierre Gabrion, letter, AADE.
7. Maurice de La Pintière published a collection of thirty-five wash drawings, entitled *Dora, la mangeuse d'hommes* (Presse d'aujourd'hui, 1993).
8. Spitz, *Cellule 114,* pp. 184–85.
9. Butet, *Cinquante Ans après!,* pp. 71–72.
10. Birin, *Seize Mois de bagne,* p. 94.
11. Albert Besançon, CV Fondation with appendix, AADE.
12. André Bérard (Guido Schreve), *Pierre Lalande,* pp. 174–76.
13. Michel, *Dora,* p. 197.
14. Rogerie, *Vivre, c'est vaincre,* p. 76.
15. J. B. de Korwin-Krokowski, letter, AADE.
16. Spitz, *Cellule 114,* p. 196.
17. Adrien Bramoullé, CV Fondation, AADE.
18. Birin, *Seize Mois de bagne,* p. 96.
19. Paul Butet, *Cinquante Ans après!,* p. 72.
20. Sadron, *A l'usine de Dora,* p. 210.
21. Georges Soubirous, letter, AADE.
22. Louis Garnier, narrative account, AADE.

23. Étienne Eckert, letter, AADE.
24. Jean Gouvenaux, letter, AADE.
25. Bailly, *Un lycéen à Buchenwald,* p. 120.
26. Mialet, *Le Déporté,* chapter 7.
27. Marcel Martin, letter, AADE.
28. Serge Sermot, letter, AADE.
29. Mialet, *Le Déporté,* pp. 125–32.
30. Joseph Jourdren, letter, AADE.
31. Marcel Martin, letter, AADE.
32. Delarbre, *Dora, croquis clandestins.*
33. Pierre Géhard, letter, AADE.
34. Jean Le Puillandre, CV Fondation, AADE.
35. Serge Sermot, letter, AADE.
36. André Bérard (Guido Schreve), *Pierre Lalande,* pp. 173–74.
37. Sadron, *A l'usine de Dora,* p. 210.
38. Maurice Gérard, letter, AADE.
39. Gérard Pichot, letter, AADE. Léonce Pichot joined his son in Block 8 in February 1945.
40. Roger Combarel, letter, AADE. Martial Bel, CV Fondation, AADE.
41. Leopold Claessens, letter, AADE.
42. Pierre Maho, narrative account, p. 53, AADE.
43. Neander, *Das Konzentrationslager Mittelbau,* chapter 4.4., with tables and graphics.
44. Rassinier, *Passage de la ligne,* pp. 74–75.
45. P. André Lobstein, "Le Block 39A du Revier de Dora," *Témoignages strasbourgeois,* 3rd ed., 1989, pp. 233–36.
46. André Lobstein went over the entire text concerning the *Revier.*
47. Rassinier, *Passage de la ligne,* p. 74.
48. Ibid., pp. 44–47.
49. Paul Le Goupil, *Un Normand dans . . .* (Paris: Tiresias, 1991), p. 173.
50. Olivier Richet, interview, 17 February 1994, AADE.
51. Testimony of Roger Latry. Michel, *Dora,* p. 237.
52. Jean-Paul Renard, *Chaînes et Lumières,* AADE.
53. Gustave Leroy, *A chacun son dû,* AADE.
54. Birin, *Seize Mois de bagne,* p. 87.
55. Louis Coutaud, letter, AADE.
56. François Heumann, letter, AADE.
57. Eudes de Galzain, *Dora, souvenirs d'avenir* (Villeurbanne: Golias, 1994), p. 63.
58. Pierre Durand, *La Résistance des Français à Buchenwald et à Dora* (Paris: Messidor, 1991), pp. 29–30.
59. Louis Garnier, narrative account, AADE.
60. Rassinier, *Passage de la ligne,* pp. 24–25.
61. Courtaud, *L'Expérience concentrationnaire,* p. 36.
62. Paul Le Goupil, "La vérité sur les départs en Kommandos," *Le Serment,* no. 252, March–April 1997.
63. Marcel Baillon, interview with the author.
64. Michel, *Dora,* pp. 226–28.
65. Jacques Chamboissier, CV Fondation, AADE.
66. Maurice Gérard, letter, AADE.
67. Wincenty Hein, *Conditions de vie et de travail des prisonniers dans le camp de concentration Dora-Mittelbau* (Warsaw, 1969; in French), pp. 76–78.
68. Michel, *Dora,* chapter 18, "L'évasion de Gaston Pernot."
69. Luc Clairin, *Requiem pour un pêcheur breton,* pp. 10–12, AADE.
70. Pierre Jacquin, *A propos d'une déportation,* pp. 16–21, AADE.
71. Auguste Henner, narrative account, AADE.
72. Roger Couëtdic, narrative account, AADE.
73. Birin, *Seize Mois de bagne,* pp. 97–98.
74. Marcel Petit, narrative account, pp. 42 sq.
75. Langbein, *La Résistance dans les camps de concentration,* p. 301.

76. Michel, *Dora,* p. 205.
77. d'Hainaut and Somerhausen, *Dora,* pp. 68–69.
78. Roger Predi, narrative account, AADE.
79. Jean Duale, narrative account, AADE.
80. Pierre Pinault, narrative account, AADE.
81. Pierre Pujol, letter, AADE.
82. Jean Fournier, *Vacances à Peenemünde,* AADE.

Chapter 11. Kammler's New Work Sites

1. Bornemann, *Geheimprojekt Mittelbau,* p. 86.
2. There is a town called Bischofferode between Duderstadt and Bleicherode. The Bischofferode of the Sonderstab Kammler is a place name around Woffleben. These sorts of confusions are frequent in the region—with regard to Osterode for instance.
3. Marcel Colignon, interview with the author.
4. Ibid., pp. 87–95.
5. Aimé Bonifas, *Détenu 20.801,* 2nd ed. (Pau: Marrimpouey, 1966), pp. 59–100.
6. Tauzin, *Quatre Ans dans les bagnes hitlériens,* pp. 51–58.
7. René André, article from 1945 in the internal bulletin of the GMF in Le Mans, AADE.
8. Courtaud, *L'Expérience concentrationnaire,* pp. 38–45, AADE.
9. Bonifas, *Détenu 20.801,* pp. 92–93.
10. Pierre Inchauspé, letter, AADE.
11. Bornemann, *Geheimprojekt Mittelbau,* p. 98.
12. Ibid., pp. 96–99.
13. Bailly, *Un lycéen à Buchenwald,* pp. 93–111.
14. Manfred Bornemann, *Chronik des Lagers Ellrich 1944/45* (Nordhausen, 1992), p. 73.
15. Jean de Sesmaisons, *Journal,* p. 71.
16. Bornemann, *Chronik des Lagers Ellrich,* p. 74.
17. Rassinier, *Passage de la ligne,* p. 82.
18. Bonifas, *Détenu 20.801,* pp. 101–20.
19. Ibid., pp. 116–18.
20. Ibid., pp. 121–41.
21. Ibid., pp. 137–38.
22. Bornemann, *Chronik des Lagers Ellrich 1944/45,* pp. 78 and 82.
23. Denis Guillon, narrative account, pp. 129–65, AADE.

Chapter 12. Harzungen, Ellrich, and Woffleben

1. Bornemann, *Geheimprojekt Mittelbau,* p. 72.
2. Joseph Jourdren, narrative account, AADE.
3. René Gilbert, letter, AADE.
4. Lucien Fayman, letter, AADE.
5. Bornemann, *Chronik des Lagers Ellrich 1944/45,* pp. 27–28.
6. Louis Garnier, narrative account, AADE.
7. Mialet, *Le Déporté,* p. 181.
8. Ibid., pp. 183–84.
9. Ibid., pp. 189–90.
10. Ibid., p. 206.
11. Maxime Cottet, *Journal,* p. 42, AADE.
12. François Poiré, narrative account, AADE.
13. Mialet, *Le Déporté,* p. 182.
14. Albert Bannes, narrative account, AADE.
15. Clément-Robert Nicola, letter, AADE.
16. Mialet, *Le Déporté,* p. 215.
17. Raymond Wautrecht, narrative account, AADE.
18. Maxime Cottet, letter, AADE.

19. Mialet, *Le Déporté,* pp. 190–92.
20. Lucien Fayman, narrative account, AADE.
21. Jean de Sesmaisons, *Journal,* pp. 75–76.
22. Raymond Wautrecht, narrative account, AADE.
23. Jean Marillier, CV Fondation, AADE.
24. Lucien Maronneau, letter, AADE.
25. Dienstplan du Revier de Harzungen, December 12, 1944, AADE.
26. Michel, *Dora,* p. 124.
27. Lucien Fayman, letter, AADE.
28. Bornemann, *Chronik des Lagers Ellrich 1944/45,* appendix, map 11.
29. *Mémorial des camps de Dora-Ellrich* (Paris, 1949), "Histoire d'un Block," p. 69, AADE.
30. Courtaud, *L'Expérience concentrationnaire,* pp. 49–50.
31. Bornemann, *Chronik des Lagers Ellrich 1944/45,* passim.
32. Miller, *Le Laminoir,* p. 114.
33. Jean-Pierre Couture, letter, AADE.
34. René Gilbert, letter, AADE.
35. Joseph Jourdren, letter, AADE.
36. Étienne Lafond, letter, AADE.
37. Pierre Goasguen, letter, AADE.
38. *Arbeitseinteilung* of the Ellrich camp, January 29, 1945, AADE.
39. Max Oesch, narrative account, AADE.
40. Jules Bouvet, CV Fondation, AADE.
41. Tauzin, *Quatre Ans dans les bagnes hitlériens,* pp. 67–68.
42. Miller, *Le Laminoir,* p. 149.
43. *Mémorial des camps de Dora-Ellrich,* "La journée d'un Kommando," pp. 62–63.
44. Jean Gineston, letter, AADE.
45. Miller, *Le Laminoir,* pp. 214 sq.
46. Courtaud, *L'Expérience concentrationnaire, Ellrich,* pp. 46–121.
47. Jacques Grandcoin, CV Fondation, AADE.
48. Ernest O. Abel, letter, AADE.
49. Jacques Vern, letter, AADE.
50. Claude Marchand, CV Fondation, AADE.
51. Tauzin, *Quatre Ans dans les bagnes hitlériens,* pp. 94–95.
52. Eugène Greff, "A Ellrich, près Dora," *Témoignages strasbourgeois,* 3rd ed., 1989, pp. 237–45.
53. Bronchart, *Ouvrier et Soldat,* pp. 158–61.
54. Pierre Walter, CV Fondation, AADE.
55. Bernard d'Astorg, letter, AADE.
56. *Mémorial des camps de Dora-Ellrich,* "Lager Woffleben," p. 94.
57. Ibid., p. 95.
58. Ernest O. Abel, letter, AADE.
59. *Mémorial des camps de Dora-Ellrich,* "Histoire d'un Block," p. 70.
60. Ernest O. Abel, letter, AADE.
61. *Mémorial des camps de Dora-Ellrich,* "Histoire d'un Block," pp. 70–71.
62. Roger Agnès, *De la ville rose aux bagnes nazis,* AADE.
63. Miller, *Le Laminoir,* p. 191.
64. René André, narrative account, AADE.
65. Étienne Lafond, *Survie* (Louviers: Drai, 1945), p. 35.
66. Miller, *Le Laminoir,* p. 231.
67. Lafond, *Survie,* p. 67.
68. Bornemann, *Chronik des Lagers Ellrich 1944/45,* pp. 53–54.
69. Courtaud, *L'Expérience concentrationnaire, Ellrich,* p. 67.
70. *Mémorial des camps de Dora-Ellrich,* "Le Revier," pp. 75–81.
71. Max Oesch, narrative account, AADE.
72. Greff, *A Ellrich, près Dora,* p. 244.
73. Miller, *Le Laminoir,* p. 233.
74. Jacques Brun, narrative account, AADE.
75. Jean-Pierre Couture, letter, AADE.

76. René Gilbert, letter, AADE.
77. Tauzin, *Quatre Ans dans les bagnes hitlériens,* p. 107.
78. Charles Mandelbaum, letter, AADE.
79. Max Oesch, narrative account, AADE.
80. Raymond Grand, letter, AADE.
81. Georges Virondeau, narrative account, AADE.
82. Albert Besançon, CV Fondation and appendix, AADE.
83. Paul von Gunten, letter, AADE.
84. Guy Marty, letter, AADE.
85. Pierre Auchabie, *Les Rayés,* AADE.
86. Lafond, *Survie,* p. 64.
87. Max Oesch, narrative account, AADE.
88. This evidence was gathered by Jacques-Guy Dussud, former prisoner in Peenemünde and in Dora, AADE.
89. Dossier of testimonies concerning the Puiseaux deportees, AADE.
90. Lafond, *Dora,* dedication.
91. Dossier de Puiseaux, AADE.
92. Pierre Maho, narrative account, p. 53, AADE.
93. Bornemann, *Geheimprojekt Mittelbau,* pp. 176–78.
94. Robert Lançon, CV Fondation, AADE.

Chapter 13. Rottleberode, Blankenburg, Langenstein, and Other Nearby Camps

1. Victor Letourneux, letter, AADE.
2. Jean Rougier, letter, AADE.
3. Bornemann, *Geheimprojekt Mittelbau,* p. 89.
4. Fernand Maistriaux, *Souvenirs tragiques d'avril 1945,* AADE.
5. Robert Gandar, letter, AADE.
6. Stéphane Hessel, *Danse avec le siècle* (Paris: Seuil, 1997), pp. 73–77.
7. Ibid., pp. 84–85.
8. Jean Michel, *De l'enfer aux étoiles* (Paris: Plon, 1986), chapters 8 and 12.
9. Hessel, *Danse avec le siècle,* pp. 86–88.
10. Ibid., pp. 89–92.
11. Rassinier, *Passage de la ligne,* p. 76.
12. Albert Van Hoey, narrative account, AADE.
13. French president of former deportee Jehovah's Witnesses.
14. Neander, *Das Konzentrationslager Mittelbau,* pp. 415–16.
15. Ibid., p. 234.
16. Jules Hofstein, "D'évacuation en évacuation," *Témoignages strasbourgeois,* 3rd ed., 1989, pp. 514–15.
17. Paul Le Goupil, "Mémorial des Français déportés au camp de Langenstein-Zwieberge," Buchenwald Kommando, 1996.
18. Hélie de Saint-Marc, "Le lieu de l'absolue vérité des êtres," in *Leçons de ténèbres* (Paris: Plon, 1995), pp. 226–27.
19. Georges Petit, "Témoignage d'un ancien déporté," *Vingtième Siècle,* no. 54, April–June 1997, pp. 89–101.
20. Association of former deportees to Neu Stassfurt, *Un pas, encore un pas pour survivre* (Amiens: Martelle Éditions, 1996).
21. André Cozette, interview with the author.
22. David Rousset, *Les Jours de notre mort* (Paris: Éd. du Pavois, 1947), pp. 78–79, 105–18.
23. Pierre Bleton, *Le Temps du purgatoire* (Paris: Téqui, 1953), pp. 49–93.
24. Wieslaw Kielar, *Anus mundi* (Paris: Laffont, 1980), pp. 282–92.
25. Rousset, *Les Jours de notre mort,* pp. 280 sq.
26. Albert Rohmer, "Helmstedt, mine de sel," *Témoignages strasbourgeois,* 3rd ed., 1989, pp. 297–322.
27. André Chicaud, narrative account from 1945, AADE.
28. Robert Antelme, *L'Espèce humaine* (Paris: Gallimard, 1957), pp. 15–211.

29. André Lacaze, *Le Tunnel* (Paris: Julliard, 1978).

30. Pierre Volmer, "Avec Desnos à Flöha," in *Le Déporté,* September 1990.

Chapter 14. The End of Auschwitz and Peenemünde

1. Alphonse Kientzler and Paul Weil, "A Stutthof," *Témoignages strasbourgeois,* 3rd ed., 1989, pp. 333–40.

2. Wieviorka, *Déportation et Génocide,* pp. 231–32.

3. Kielar, *Anus mundi,* pp. 23 sq.

4. Claudine Cardon-Hamet, *Mille Otages pour Auschwitz* (Paris: Graphein, 1997).

5. Rogerie, *Vivre, c'est vaincre,* pp. 72–73.

6. Hermann Langbein, *Hommes et Femmes à Auschwitz* (Paris: Fayard, 1975).

7. Kielar, *Anus mundi,* pp. 281–82.

8. Cardon-Hamet, *Mille Otages pour Auschwitz,* pp. 413–17.

9. Rogerie, *Vivre, c'est vaincre,* pp. 85–88.

10. Marc Klein, "D'Auschwitz à Gross Rosen et à Buchenwald," *Témoignages strasbourgeois,* 3rd ed., 1989, pp. 502–4.

11. Maurice Szafran, *Simone Veil, destin* (Paris: Flammarion, 1994), pp. 87–89.

12. Jules Hofstein, *D'évacuation en évacuation,* pp. 511–12.

13. Primo Levi, *La Trêve* (Paris: Grasset, 1963), pp. 9–10.

14. Roger Climaud, CV Fondation, AADE.

15. Rogerie, *Vivre, c'est vaincre,* pp. 88–90.

16. Klein, *D'Auschwitz à Gross Rosen et à Buchenwald,* pp. 504–5.

17. Cardon-Hamet, *Mille Otages pour Auschwitz,* pp. 419–20.

18. Léon-E. Halkin, *A l'ombre de la mort* (Brussels: Pauli), pp. 99–143.

19. Michel Poiteau, CV Fondation, AADE.

20. Charles Vedel, CV Fondation, AADE.

21. Bleton, *Le Temps du purgatoire,* chapter 5.

22. Klein, *D'Auschwitz à Gross Rosen et Buchenwald,* pp. 507–10.

23. Neufeld, *The Rocket and the Reich,* pp. 204–5.

24. Ibid., p. 256.

25. Ibid., p. 257.

26. Ibid., p. 257.

27. Ibid., p. 259.

28. Ibid., p. 257.

29. Ibid., p. 260.

30. Sadron, *A l'usine de Dora,* p. 225.

31. Guy Raoul-Duval, *Témoignage de déportation,* pp. 42–43.

32. Jean Fournier, *Vacances à Peenemünde,* AADE. Roger Predi, narrative account, AADE. Pierre Pinault, narrative account, AADE.

Chapter 15. The Final Months at Dora and the Boelcke Kaserne in Nordhausen

1. Bonifas, *Détenu 20.801,* p. 123.

2. Durand, *La Résistance des Français à Buchenwald et à Dora,* p. 186.

3. Amicale d'Oranienburg-Sachsenhausen, *Sachso* (Paris: Plon, 1982), pp. 446–47.

4. Michel, *Dora,* p. 256.

5. Ibid., pp. 239 sq.

6. Ibid., p. 317.

7. Pierre Maho, narrative account, p. 59, AADE.

8. Jean-Pierre Couture, narrative account, AADE.

9. Halkin, *A l'ombre de la mort,* pp. 168–69.

10. Clément-Robert Nicola, narrative account, AADE.

11. Pierre Maho, narrative account, p. 61, AADE.

12. Pierre Maho, narrative account, pp. 63–64, AADE.

13. Hofstein, *D'évacuation en évacuation,* pp. 513–14.

14. Halkin, *A l'ombre de la mort,* pp. 145–51.
15. Sadron, *A l'usine de Dora,* p. 220.
16. René Chapuy, CV Fondation et appendix, AADE.
17. Michel Thomas, narrative account, AADE.
18. Hessel, *Danse avec le siècle,* pp. 93–94.
19. Pierre Gabrion, letter, AADE.
20. Henri Barbier, letter, AADE.
21. Robert Roulard, narrative account, AADE.
22. Halkin, *A l'ombre de la mort,* pp. 155–56.
23. Szafran, *Simone Veil, destin,* p. 91.
24. *Le Figaro,* "Carnet du jour."
25. Jean-René Durand, narrative account, AADE.
26. Marcel Petit, narrative account, pp. 79 sq., AADE.
27. André Lobstein, dossier, AADE.
28. Boris Pahor, *Pèlerin parmi les ombres* (Paris: La Table ronde, 1990), passim.
29. René Bordet, narrative account, AADE.
30. Lobstein, *Le Block 39A du Revier de Dora,* pp. 233–36.
31. Mialet, *Le Déporté,* p. 241.
32. René Morel, *Perliris* (Oyonnax, 1993).
33. Hofstein, *D'évacuation en évacuation,* p. 514.
34. Charles Vedel, CV Fondation and appendix, AADE.
35. Sadron, *A l'usine de Dora,* p. 223.
36. Rogerie, *Vivre, c'est vaincre,* p. 91.
37. Pierre Auchabie, *Les Rayés,* p. 21, AADE.
38. Michel, *Dora,* pp. 330–32.
39. Halkin, *A l'ombre de la mort,* p. 146.
40. Christian Bernadac, *Les Médecins de l'impossible* (Paris: France-Empire), XXXII, Les garages de Nordhausen.
41. Pierre Maho, narrative account, pp. 71–72. AADE.
42. Hofstein, *D'évacuation en évacuation,* p. 516.
43. The term "block" refers in this case to a place for prisoners to sleep. It was often a shack. In Nordhausen it was a hangar. In the tunnel in the early months it was an underground gallery.
44. Pierre Maho, narrative account, p. 71, AADE.
45. Sadron, *A l'usine de Dora,* pp. 224–25.
46. Ibid., p. 226.
47. André Sellier, narrative account, AADE.
48. Spitz, *Cellule 114,* pp. 207–9.
49. Michel, *Dora,* p. 337.
50. Spitz, *Cellule 114,* pp. 204–5.
51. Sadron, *A l'usine de Dora,* pp. 216–17.
52. Wincenty Hein, *Conditions de vie et de travail à Dora-Mittelbau,* p. 179.

Chapter 16. A Chronicle of the Last Days

1. Bailly, *Un lycéen à Buchenwald,* pp. 188–89.
2. McGovern, *La Chasse aux armes secrètes allemandes,* pp. 99–102.
3. André Ribault, narrative account, AADE.
4. Sadron, *A l'usine de Dora,* p. 227.
5. McGovern, *La Chasse aux armes secrètes allemandes,* pp. 98–99.
6. André Ribault, narrative account, AADE.
7. Pierre Maho, narrative account, pp. 74–75, AADE.
8. Jean-Pierre Couture, narrative account, AADE.
9. Xavier Delogne, narrative account, p. 46, AADE.
10. Michel, *Dora,* pp. 351–52.
11. Xavier Delogne, narrative account, p. 46, AADE.
12. Halkin, *A l'ombre de la mort,* pp. 172–73.
13. Jean-Pierre Couture, narrative account, AADE.

14. Michel, *Dora,* pp. 353–55.
15. Pierre Maho, narrative account, pp. 75–76, AADE.
16. Cardon-Hamet, *Mille Otages pour Auschwitz,* p. 440. Interview with Abada by Henri Alleg in 1972.
17. Ernest Gaillard, *Les Nouvelles littéraires,* April 27, 1965.
18. Hofstein, *D'évacuation en évacuation,* p. 516.
19. Xavier Delogne, narrative account, pp. 47–48, AADE.
20. Clément-Robert Nicola, narrative account, AADE.
21. Jean-Pierre Couture, narrative account, AADE.
22. Xavier Delogne, narrative account, pp. 46–47, AADE.
23. Pierre Maho, narrative account, p. 78, AADE.
24. Béon, *La Planète Dora,* pp. 233–35.
25. André Ribault, narrative account, AADE.
26. Paul Hagenmuller, "L'évacuation de Dora," *Témoignages strasbourgeois,* 3rd ed., 1989, p. 248.
27. Sadron, *A l'usine de Dora,* p. 109.
28. Ibid.
29. André Ribault, narrative account, AADE.
30. Jean Fournier, *Vacances à Peenemünde,* AADE.
31. Joachim Neander, *Das Konzentrationslager Mittelbau,* tables on pp. 323 and 328.
32. Michel, *Dora,* pp. 345–46.
33. *The Buchenwald Report,* pp. 323–24.
34. André Ribault, narrative account, AADE.
35. Sadron, *A l'usine de Dora,* pp. 229–30.
36. André Ribault, narrative account, AADE.
37. Jacques Maillard, CV Fondation and appendix, AADE.
38. André Lobstein, dossier, AADE.
39. Pierre Maho, narrative account, *Bulletin Dora-Ellrich,* March–April 1947, AADE.
40. Hofstein, *D'évacuation en évacuation,* p. 516.
41. Ernest Gaillard, *Les Nouvelles littéraires,* April 27, 1965.
42. Cardon-Hamet, *Mille Otages pour Auschwitz,* p. 446.
43. Michel, *Dora,* pp. 357–72.
44. Clément-Robert Nicola, narrative account, AADE.
45. Halkin, *A l'ombre de la mort,* pp. 175–76.
46. Xavier Delogne, narrative account, pp. 49–50, AADE.
47. Pierre Auchabie, *Les Rayés,* pp. 23–24, AADE.
48. Jean-Pierre Couture, narrative account, AADE.
49. René Bordet, narrative account, AADE.
50. Maurice Lemière, *Retour de Buchenwald* (Condé-sur-Noireau: Corlet, 1980), pp. 78–82.
51. Pierre Maho, narrative account, p. 82, AADE.
52. Roger Couëtdic, narrative account, AADE.

Chapter 17. The Great Dispersion of April 1945 and the "Liberation" of Dora

1. For instance, Daniel Jonah Goldhagen, *Hitler's Willing Executioners* (New York: Alfred A. Knopf, 1996), part V: "Death Marches: To the Final Days."
2. Woolner, Frank, Murray H. Fowler, and United States Army Third Infantry Division, *Spearhead in the West: The Third Armored Division* (Frankfurt am Main-Schwanheim: F.J. Henrich, 1945), pp. 147–48.
3. Hoegh, Leo A. and Howard J. Doyle, *Timberwolf Tracks: The History of the 104th Infantry Division, 1942–1945* (Washington, D.C.: Infantry Journal Press, 1946), p. 329.
4. Pierre Maho, narrative account, p. 82, AADE.
5. René Bordet, narrative account, AADE.
6. Tauzin, *Quatre Ans dans les bagnes hitlériens,* pp. 117–18.
7. Xavier Delogne, narrative account, p. 52, AADE.
8. Clément-Robert Nicola, narrative account, AADE.
9. Pierre Maho, narrative account, p. 82, AADE.

10. Jean-Pierre Couture, narrative account, AADE.
11. Halkin, *A l'ombre de la mort,* p. 173.
12. Jean-Pierre Couture, narrative account, AADE.
13. Pierre Auchabie, *Les Rayés,* p. 24, AADE.
14. Jacques Can, CV Fondation, AADE.
15. Georges Virondeau, narrative account, AADE.

Chapter 18. From Dora, Ellrich, and Harzungen to Bergen-Belsen

1. *Mémorial des camps de Dora-Ellrich,* "Lager Woffleben," pp. 98–99.
2. Charles Vedel, CV Fondation and appendix, AADE.
3. Béon, *La Planète Dora,* pp. 246–47.
4. Jean Fournier, *Vacances à Peenemünde,* AADE.
5. Béon, *La planète Dora,* pp. 249–50.
6. Pierre Pinault, narrative account, AADE.
7. Spitz, *Cellule 114,* p. 216.
8. Mialet, *Le Déporté,* p. 289.
9. Lucien Fayman, narrative account, AADE.
10. Michel, *Dora,* pp. 385–86.
11. Jacques Courtaud, *L'Expérience concentrationnaire,* pp. 123–24, AADE.
12. Miller, *Le Laminoir,* pp. 267 sq.
13. Hessel, *Danse avec le siècle,* p. 95.
14. Jean Voisin, CV Fondation, AADE.
15. G. L. Fréjafon, *Bergen-Belsen, bagne-sanatorium* (Paris, 1947).
16. Szafran, *Simone Veil, destin,* pp. 91–93.
17. Jean-Pierre Renouard, *Un uniforme rayé d'enfer* (Monaco: Éd. du Rocher, 1993), pp. 93–94.
18. Eberhard Kolb, *Bergen-Belsen de 1943 à 1945* (Göttingen: Vandenhoeck, 1985).
19. Bronchart, *Ouvrier et Soldat,* p. 168.
20. Jacques Courtaud, *L'Expérience concentrationnaire,* p. 124, AADE.
21. Raoul-Duval, *Témoignage de déportation,* p. 70.
22. William E. Roach, *The First Four Days in Belsen,* AADE.
23. Fliecx, *Pour délit d'espérance,* pp. 92–93.
24. Delarbre, *Dora, croquis clandestins.*
25. Maurice Druon, letter-preface to the book by Jean-Pierre Renouard.
26. Louis Jadaud, letter, AADE.
27. Paul Butet, *Cinquante Ans après!* pp. 93–94, AADE.
28. *Le Déporté,* no. 500, July 1996.
29. Jacques Courtaud, *L'Expérience concentrationnaire,* p. 138, AADE.
30. Renouard, *Un uniforme rayé d'enfer,* pp. 111–24.
31. Wieviorka, *Déportation et Génocide,* pp. 93 sq.
32. Szafran, *Simone Veil, destin,* p. 104.
33. Jean Gineston, narrative account, AADE.
34. Recent correspondence between Theodor Braun and Yves Béon, AADE. Braun has lived in the United States since 1968.

Chapter 19. The Five Convoys in Altmark, and the Gardelegen Tragedy

1. d'Hainaut and Somerhausen, *Dora,* p. 128.
2. Albert Besançon, CV Fondation and appendix, AADE.
3. Lafond, *Survie,* pp. 77–83.
4. *Mémorial des camps de Dora-Ellrich,* "L'évacuation d'Ellrich," pp. 126–30.
5. Yves Aleste, report, AADE.
6. d'Hainaut and Somerhausen, *Dora,* pp. 80–83.
7. André Ribault, narrative account, AADE.
8. Georges Soubirous, narrative account, AADE.
9. Neander, *Das Konzentrationslager Mittelbau,* p. 371.
10. The city of Wittenberg should not be confused with the city of Wittenberge, both situated along

the Elbe. Wittenberg is the "city of Luther," upstream from Magdeburg on the right bank of the river. Wittenberge on the other hand is downstream between Magdeburg and Hamburg, but also on the right bank.

11. Pontoizeau, *Dora-la-Mort,* pp. 139–42.
12. Robert Roulard, narrative account, AADE.
13. Hessel Groeneveld, narrative account, AADE.
14. Rassinier, *Passage de la ligne,* chapter 6.
15. Robert Roulard, narrative account, AADE.
16. Jacques Brun, narrative account, AADE.
17. Robert Roulard, narrative account, AADE.
18. Guy Marquet, letter, AADE.
19. Gérard Pichot, letter, AADE.
20. Pontoizeau, *Dora-la-Mort,* pp. 143–44.
21. Kielar, *Anus mundi,* pp. 294–96.
22. Rousset, *Les Jours de notre mort,* pp. 727–31.
23. Fernand Maistriaux, *Souvenirs tragiques d'avril 1945,* AADE.
24. Robert Gandar, letter, AADE.
25. Fernand Maistriaux, *Souvenirs tragiques d'avril 1945,* AADE.
26. Morel, *Perliris,* p. 72.
27. Lucien Colonel, narrative account, AADE.
28. Bonifas, *Détenu 20.801,* pp. 148 sq.
29. Alain de Lapoyade, narrative account, AADE.
30. Lucien Colonel in *Le Serment,* no. 292, August–September 1993.
31. Bonifas, *Détenu 20.801,* pp. 158–59.
32. Fernand Maistriaux, *Souvenirs tragiques d'avril 1945,* AADE.
33. Bonifas, *Détenu 20.801,* pp. 161–63.
34. Guy Chamaillard, narrative account in *Bulletin de l'Amicale d'Ellrich,* March–April 1946, AADE.
35. Georges Cretin, narrative account, AADE.
36. Article dated October 17, 1997, in the Magdeburg newspaper *Volksstimme,* translated in the bulletin of the Belgian former prisoners' association *Dora,* 1997, 4th quarter, by Vladislas Mydlak.
37. Fernand Maistriaux, *Souvenirs tragiques d'avril 1945,* AADE.
38. Albert Van Dijk, CV Fondation and appendix, AADE.

Chapter 20. Death Marches Toward the East, and the Odyssey of the Blankenburg Kommando

1. d'Hainaut and Somerhausen, *Dora,* p. 125.
2. Ibid., p. 125.
3. Rogerie, *Vivre, c'est vaincre,* pp. 94–100.
4. Jean de Sesmaisons, *Journal,* pp. 80–81, AADE.
5. René Chapel, CV Fondation, AADE.
6. Jean Marillier, CV Fondation, AADE.
7. Rogerie, *Vivre c'est vaincre,* pp. 102–3.
8. Wolf Wexler, narrative account, AADE.
9. Primo Levi, *La Trêve.*
10. André Cozette, interview with the author.
11. André Chicaud, *Narrative account de 1945,* AADE.
12. Neander, *Das Konzentrationslager Mittelbau,* pp. 436–37.
13. Antelme, *L'Espèce humaine,* pp. 215–19.
14. Paul Le Goupil, *Mémorial des Français déportés au camp de Langenstein-Zwieberge,* Kommando de Buchenwald, 1996.
15. Jean de Sesmaisons, *Journal,* p. 81, AADE.
16. Denis Guillon, narrative account, pp. 171–83, AADE.
17. Dutillieux, *Le Camp des armes secrètes,* pp. 147–52.

18. Max Dutillieux, "Le curé Jean Uhl," *La Mémoire de Dora-Mittelbau*, no. 26, 2nd semester, 1997.
19. *Le Serment*, special issue, 1995, pp. 58–59.
20. Dossier by Narcisse Dufrane and Albert Van Hoey, AADE.
21. Neander, *Das Konzentrationslager Mittelbau*, pp. 421–23.
22. Albert Van Hoey, narrative account, AADE.
23. Paul Le Goupil, *Mémorial des Français de Langenstein*.
24. Le Goupil, *Un Normand dans . . . ,"* pp. 231–48.
25. Antelme, *L'Espèce humaine*, pp. 213–306.
26. Dossier communicated by Paul Le Goupil, AADE.
27. René Haentjens, *Au-delà de l'imaginable* (Vanier, Canada, no date).
28. Bulletin Sachso, March 1995.
29. Neander, *Das Konzentrationslager Mittelbau*, pp. 394–95.
30. Paul Le Goupil, "Les tombeaux flottants," *Le Serment*, special issue 1995, p. 57.
31. Bulletin Sachso, March 1995.
32. Neander, *Das Konzentrazionslager Mittelbau*, pp. 445–50.
33. Christine Schäfer, *Die Evakuierungstransporte des KZ Buchenwald und seiner Aussenkommandos* (Weimar-Buchenwald, 1983), pp. 33–34.
34. Ibid., p. 32.
35. Dossier communicated by Paul Le Goupil, AADE.
36. Neu Stassfurt Former Prisoners' Association, *Un pas, encore un pas, pour survivre*.
37. d'Hainaut and Somerhausen, *Dora*, p. 125.
38. Goldhagen, *Hitler's Willing Executioners*, pp. 339–54.
39. Brigitte Friang, *Regarde-toi qui meurs* (Paris: Éd. du Félin, 1997), pp. 174–217.
40. Hofstein, *D'évacuation en évacuation*, pp. 516–18.
41. Antelme, *L'Espèce humaine*, pp. 287–99.
42. François Bertrand, *Notre devoir de mémoire* (Pau: Héraclès, 1997).
43. Wieviorka, *Déportation et Géocide*, p. 100.
44. Dossier communicated by Paul Le Goupil, AADE.
45. Neander, *Das Konzentrationslager Mittelbau*, p. 451.
46. Ibid., pp. 349–53.

Chapter 21. From Sachsenhausen and Ravensbrück to the Schwerin Region

1. Sereny, *Albert Speer: son combat avec la vérité*, p. 515.
2. Ibid., pp. 521–36.
3. Ibid., pp. 538–39.
4. Bezaut, *Oranienburg, Sachsenhausen*, chapters 1 to 5.
5. Oranienburg-Sachsenhausen Former Prisoners' Association, *Sachso*, chapter 4.
6. Raymond Wautrecht, narrative account, AADE.
7. Jean Bezaut, *Oranienburg, Sachsenhausen*, p. 332.
8. Dutillieux, *Le Camp des armes secrètes*, p. 156.
9. Rémy Vincent, *KLB 52230* (Nantes, 1993).
10. Pierre Choquenet, interview with the author.
11. Harry Paylon, letter, AADE.
12. David Rousset, *L'Univers concentrationnaire* (Paris: Éd. du Pavois, 1946), pp. 171–74.
13. Kielar, *Anus mundi*, pp. 299–300.
14. Benès, *Détenu en Allemagne*, pp. 114–15.
15. Litomisky, *Les Mémoires du prisonnier 113.359*, p. 109.
16. Georges Schmidt, narrative account, AADE.
17. Numerous testimonies.
18. Very numerous testimonies.
19. André Ribault, narrative account, AADE.
20. Letter to the author.
21. Margarete Buber-Neumann, *Déportée à Ravensbrück* (Paris: Seuil, 1988), pp. 208–324.
22. Benès, *Détenu en Allemagne*, pp. 118–19.

23. Kielar, *Anus mundi,* p. 309.
24. Jean Mabire, *Mourir à Berlin* (Paris: Livre de poche, 1977), pp. 78–109, 487–88.
25. Georges Jouanin, letter, AADE.
26. Louis Garnier, narrative account, AADE.
27. André Bérard (Guido Schreve), *Pierre Lalande,* pp. 193–203.
28. André Fortané, narrative account, AADE.
29. Robert Thiercelin, narrative account, AADE.
30. Author's recollections.
31. Antoine Cirieco, CV Fondation, AADE.
32. Dutillieux, *Le Camp des armes secrètes,* p. 157.
33. Max Oesch, narrative account, AADE.
34. Raymond Wautrecht, narrative account, AADE.
35. Lafond, *Survie,* pp. 85–86.
36. Oranienburg-Sachsenhausen Former Prisoners' Association, *Sachso,* pp. 566–73.
37. Jean Cormont, narrative account, AADE.
38. Pouzet, *Dora,* pp. 210–12.
39. Jean Doucet, CV Fondation, AADE.

Chapter 22. The Dora-Mittelbau Toll

1. Wincenty Hein, *Conditions de vie et de travail à Dora-Mittelbau.*
2. Neander, *Das Konzentrationslager Mittelbau,* p. 335, chapter 6–1: "Transportbilanz der Evakuierung der Lager des Mittelbau," April 1945.
3. Juliane Wetzel, "Les camps pour personnes déplacées juives en Allemagne (1945–1957)," in *Vingtième Siècle. Dossier sur les camps de concentration du XXe siècle,* no. 54, April–June 1997.
4. Pineau, *La Simple vérité,* p. 356.
5. Jorge Semprun, *Quel beau dimanche!* (Paris: Grasset, 1980), p. 210.
6. Semprun, *L'Écriture ou la vie,* p. 308.
7. Le Goupil, *Un Normand dans . . . ,* p. 163.
8. Wieviorka, *Déportation et Génocide,* pp. 448–72.
9. *Témoignages strasbourgeois,* "Nos morts," pp. 541–46.
10. Bornemann, *Geheimprojekt Mittelbau,* p. 108. Bornemann quotes David Irving, *Die Geheimwaffen des Dritten Reiches* (Gütersloh, 1965).
11. Dossier communicated by Yves Le Maner.

Chapter 23. After the War: Between Missiles and Trials

1. Alfred Grosser, *L'Allemagne de notre temps, 1945–1978* (Paris: Livre de poche, 1978).
2. Joseph Rovan, *Histoire de l'Allemagne* (Paris: Seuil, 1994), chapter 21. Dennis L. Bark and David R. Gress, *Histoire de l'Allemagne depuis 1945* (Paris: Laffont, 1992).
3. Following reunification, this territory was returned to Lower Saxony.
4. McGovern, *La Chasse aux armes secrètes allemandes,* pp. 111–21.
5. Ibid., pp. 121–26.
6. Ibid., pp. 89–94.
7. Ibid., pp. 134–42.
8. Ibid., pp. 127–33.
9. Ibid., pp. 143–48.
10. Sereny, *Albert Speer: son combat avec la vérité,* p. 551.
11. Ibid., pp. 551–58.
12. Linda Hunt, *L'Affaire Paperclip* (Paris: Stock, 1995), p. 106.
13. McGovern, *La Chasse aux armes secrètes allemandes,* pp. 151–55.
14. Ibid., p. 151.
15. Ibid., pp. 156–57.
16. Ibid., pp. 159–63.

17. Kohler and Germain, *Von Braun contre Korolev,* pp. 113–18.
18. Ibid., pp. 127–29.
19. Ibid., p. 130.
20. Ibid., p. 135.
21. McGovern, *La Chasse aux armes secrètes allemandes,* p. 194.
22. Kohler and Germain, *Von Braun contre Korolev,* pp. 131–35.
23. Hunt, *L'Affaire Paperclip,* pp. 89–93.
24. Kohler and Germain, *Von Braun contre Korolev,* pp. 118–19.
25. Jean Sellier and André Sellier, *Atlas des peuples d'Orient* (Paris: La Découverte, 1993), p. 91.
26. Kohler and Germain, *Von Braun contre Korolev,* pp. 119–23.
27. Jacques Villain, *La France a-t-elle hérité de Peenemünde?* Lecture published in October 1992.
28. Kohler and Germain, *Von Braun contre Korolev,* pp. 143–45.
29. Michel, *De l'enfer aux étoiles,* pp. 255–56.
30. Émile Copfermann, *David Rousset. Une vie dans le siècle* (Paris: Plon, 1991), pp. 75–83.
31. Author's correspondence with K. S. Karol, February 1998.
32. Lutz Niethammer (ed.), *Der "gesäuberte" Antifaschismus* (Berlin: Akademie Verlag, 1994), pp. 495–519 (biographical notes).
33. On the special conditions regarding the functioning of Blocks 46 and 50 in the Buchenwald *Revier,* see the passages on Stéphane Hessel and Alfred Balachowsky in chapter 17.
34. Copfermann, *David Rousset. Une vie dans le siècle,* pp. 113–30.
35. Niethammer, *Der "gesäuberte" Antifaschismus,* pp. 77–91.
36. Ibid., pp. 131 and 414–31.
37. Ibid., p. 89.

Chapter 24. Solidarity and Memory

1. Wieviorka, *Déportation et Génocide,* pp. 121–40.
2. *Bulletin mensuel de l'Amicale,* nos. 6 and 7, June–July 1946, AADE.
3. *Le Lien, Bulletin de l'association "L'aide aux orphelins" du Réseau CND Castille et des déportés de la Résistance des camps Dora-Ellrich,* between no. 1, March 1950, and nos. 49–50, April–July 1962, AADE.
4. *Mémorial des camps de Dora-Ellrich,* "Tunnels de mort et tabernacles vivants," pp. 30–46.
5. Jean-Pierre Couture, letter, AADE.
6. Peter Reichel, *L'Allemagne et sa mémoire* (Paris: Odile Jacob, 1998), pp. 118–19.
7. Langbein, *La Résistance dans les camps de concentration,* pp. 381–82.
8. Jacques Delarue, lecture given at the historical symposium on Dora, Vincennes, April 25, 1990.
9. Maurice Rolland, letter dated March 28, 1967, AADE.
10. *Le Lien,* no. 65, June 1970, AADE.
11. McGovern, *La Chasse aux armes secrètes allemandes,* p. 71.
12. *Operation Crossbow,* a film by Michael Anderson made in 1965 with George Peppard, Trevor Howard, and Sophia Loren; produced by Carlo Ponti.
13. Hunt, *L'Affaire Paperclip,* pp. 312 sq.
14. Ibid., pp. 324 sq.
15. Ibid., p. 331.
16. Olga Wormser and Henri Michel, *Tragédie de la déportation, 1940–1945* (Paris: Hachette, 1955).
17. Michel de Bouard, "Mauthausen," *Revue d'histoire de la Seconde Guerre mondiale,* nos. 15–16, July–September 1954, on "Le système concentrationnaire allemand."
18. Germaine Tillion, *Ravensbrück* (Paris: Seuil, 1973).
19. Milan Filipcic, *Dora, KL Mittelbau, Zbornik* (Ljubljana: Borec, 1989).
20. *Dora—Ellrich—Harzungen—Ko, 1943–1945* (Paris: Presses d'aujourd'hui, 1989).
21. Florent Brayard, *Comment l'idée vint à M. Rassinier* (Paris: Fayard, 1996), chapters 1 and 2.
22. Anne Le Turdu, *Étude des témoignages oraux d'anciens déportés du camp de Dora,* master's thesis in history, University of Paris-IV-Sorbonne, 1990–91.
23. Bernard d'Astorg, letter, AADE.

Chapter 25. Dora Today

1. Reichel, *L'Allemagne et sa mémoire,* p. 119. See also Étienne François, "La postérité des camps en zone soviétique et en Allemagne de l'Est" in *La Déportation, le système concentrationnaire nazi* (Nanterre: BDIC, 1995), pp. 228–33.
2. Rovan, *Histoire de l'Allemagne,* p. 765.
3. *Bulletin Dora de l'amicale belge,* 1989, 2.
4. *Bulletin Dora de l'amicale belge,* 1990, 2, 3.
5. Dossier communicated by Jacques Brun, AADE.

Afterword

1. Götz Dieckmann and Peter Hochmut, "KZ Dora-Mittelbau. Produktionsstätte der V-Waffen: Kampffront gegen faschistischen Terror und Rüstungsproduktion" (Nordhausen, 1971).
2. An example is Manfred Bornemann, *Geheimprojekt Mittelbau: Vom zentralen Öllager des Deutschen Reiches zur größten Raketenfabrik im Zweiten Weltkrieg* (Bonn, 1994). Similar books are Kurt Pelny and Manfred Weisshaupt, *Geheimwaffen im Kohnstein* (Nordhausen, 1964); Fred Dittmann/Jürgen Michels, *Grösster Geheimwaffenproduzent des Dritten Reiches* (Kelbra, 1992); Frank Baranowski, *Geheime Rüstungsprojekte in Südniedersachsen und Thüringen während der NS-Zeit* (Duderstadt, 1995).
3. Eugen Kogon, *Der SS-Staat: Das System der deutschen Konzentrationslager* (Munich, 1946); Christopher Burney, *The Dungeon Democracy* (London, 1945); David Rousset, *L'univers concentrationnaire* (Paris, 1946).
4. Eberhard Kolb, *Bergen-Belsen. Geschichte des "Aufenthaltslagers" 1943–1945* (Hannover, 1962); Enno Georg, *Die wirtschaftlichen Unternehmungen der SS,* Schriftenreihe der Vierteljahreshefte für Zeitgeschichte, 7 (Stuttgart, 1963).
5. Martin Broszat, *Das System der nationalsozialistischen Konzentrationslager 1933–1945*, in Hans Buchheim, et al., *Anatomie des SS-Staates* (Olten/Freiburg, 1965), pp. 9–160; and Olga Wormser-Migot, *Le système concentrationnaire Nazi (1933–1945)* (Paris, 1968); a first study on the theme with Henri Michel, in 1955, was entitled *Tragédie de la Déportation 1940/1945* (Paris, 1955). A few years earlier an East German study that, as a comprehensive examination, hardly met scientific standards was Heinz Kühnrich's *Der KZ Staat: Rolle und Entwicklung der faschistischen Konzentrationslager* (Berlin, 1960).
6. Manfred Bornemann and Martin Broszat, "Das KL Dora-Mittelbau," in *Studien zur Geschichte der Konzentrationslager*, Schriftenreihe der Vierteljahreshefte für Zeitgeschichte, 21 (Stuttgart, 1970) pp. 154–198.
7. Joseph Billig, *Les camps de concentration dans l'économie du Reich Hitlerien* (Paris, 1973).
8. Falk Pingel, *Häftlinge unter SS-Herrschaft: Widerstand, Selbstbehauptung und Vernichtung im Konzentrationslager* (Hamburg, 1978). See also Herwarth Vorländer, ed., *Nationalsozialistische Konzentrationslager im Dienst der totalen Kriegsführung: Sieben württembergische Aussenkommandos des Konzentrationslager Natzweiler/Elsaß* (Stuttgart, 1978).
9. In addition to the above-mentioned Vorländer collective volume, note should also be taken of other examples, such as Rainer Fröbe, et al., *Konzentrationslager in Hannover: KZ-Arbeit und Rüstungsindustrie in der Spätphase des Zweiten Weltkrieges* (Hildesheim, 1985); Florian Freund, *"Arbeitslager Zement": Das Konzentrationslager Ebensee und die Raketenindustrie* (Wien, 1989); Bertrand Perz, *Projekt Quarz: Steyr-Daimler-Puch und das Konzentrationslager Melk* (Wien, 1991); Edith Raim, *Die Dachauer KZ-Aussenkommandos Kaufering und Mühldorf: Rüstungsbauten und Zwangsarbeit im letzten Kriegsjahr 1944/45* (Landsberg, 1992 [diss., München, 1991]).
10. The only studies thus far on this subject were presented by Christa Naumann on the satellite camps of Buchenwald and by Wolfgang Kirstein on the camp complex of Natzweiler. Cf. Christa Naumann, *Das arbeitsteilige Zusammenwirken von SS und deutschen Rüstungskonzernen 1942–1945: Dargestellt am Beispiel der Aussenkommandos des Konzentrationslagers Buchenwald* (diss. Humboldt-Univ. Ost-Berlin, 1973); Wolfgang Kirstein, *Das Konzentrationslager als Institution totalen Terrors: Das Beispiel des Kl. Natzweiler,* Freiburger Arbeiten zur Soziologie der Diktatur, 2 (Pfaffenweiler, 1992).

11. Cf. Gudrun Schwarz, *Die nationalsozialistischen Lager* (Frankfurt/New York, 1990), p. 4.
12. Exceptions, apart from the author's Mittelbau monograph (Jens-Christian Wagner, *Produktion des Todes: Das KZ Mittelbau-Dora* (Göttingen, Stiftung Gedenkstätten Buchenwald und Mittelbau-Dora, 2001), at least initially, are Isabell Sprenger, *Gross-Rosen: Ein Konzentrationslager in Schlesien*, Neue Forschungen zur Schlesischen Geschichte, 6 (Köln/Weimar/ Wien, 1996); Michel Fabreguet, *Mauthausen: Camp de concentration national-socialiste en Autriche rattachée (1938–1945)* (Paris, 1995).
13. Cf. Ulrich Herbert, Karin Orth and Christoph Dieckmann, eds., *Die nationalsozialistischen Konzentrationslager: Entwicklung und Struktur,* 2 vols. (Göttingen, 1998).
14. Cf. Sybille Steinbacher, *Dachau: Die Stadt und das Konzentrationslager in der NS-Zeit: Die Untersuchung einer Nachbarschaft* (München, 1994), and Jens Schley, *Nachbar: Die Stadt Weimar und ihr Konzentrationslager 1937–1945* (Köln/Weimar/Wien, 1999).
15. Joachim Neander, *Das Konzentrationslager Mittelbau: Zur Geschichte des letzten im "Dritten Reich" gegründeten selbständigen Konzentrationslagers unter besonderer Berücksichtigung seiner Auflösungsphase* (Clausthal-Zellerfeld, 1970 [diss., Univ. Bremen]).
16. For example, Broszat gives two brief citations of Mittelbau in his 1965 study.
17. Cf. Bornemann and Broszat, *KL Dora-Mittelbau.*
18. Wincenty Hein, "Zaglada wie, z'nów obozu Mittelbau (Dora)," *Biuletyn Glównej Komisji Badania Zbrdoni Hitlerowskich* 16 (1967), pp. 66–157. Hein's study is based on research that he assembled in 1945, at the request of the Americans, immediately after the liberation of Mittelbau-Dora and his discovery of SS documents.
19. Walter Bartel (1904–1992) while a prisoner chaired the illegal international camp committee in the Buchenwald concentration camp. In 1962 he was professor of modern and contemporary history at the Institute for German History, Humboldt University, East Berlin.
20. Cf. the literature survey in Bornemann and Broszat, p. 155, n1. Noteworthy are the dissertations of Götz Dieckmann and Laurenz Demps: G. Dieckmann, *Existenzbedingungen und Widerstand im Konzentrationslager-Dora-Mittelbau unter dem Aspekt der funkionellen Einbeziehung der SS in das System der faschistischen Kriegswirtschaft* (Berlin, 1968); L. Demps, *Zum weiteren Ausbau des staatsmonopolistischen Apparates der faschistischen Kriegswirtschaft in den Jahren 1943 bis 1945 und zur Rolle der SS und der Konzentrationslager im Rahmen der Rüstungsproduktion, dargestellt am Beispiel der unterirdischen Verlagerung von Teilen der Rüstungsindustrie* (Berlin, 1970). The intensive research on the history of Mittelbau-Dora in the GDR was certainly also impacted by the 1967–1970 West German Dora trial in Essen, in which the GDR lawyer Friedrich-Karl Kaul participated as a co-plaintiff. Götz Dieckmann and Laurenz Demps participated in the Essen trial as Kaul's colleagues and wrote the contemporary expertise statement that Walter Bartel provided for the trial: Walter Bartel, *Wehrwirtschaftsführer, Geheimwaffen, KZ. Gutachten über Rolle und Bedeutung des KZ Dora-Mittelbau und die Funktion der SS bei der A4-Produktion,* Schriftenreihe des Präsidiums der VVN, 13 (Frankfurt, 1970). Cf. Georg Wamhof, "Prozessgebundene Kampagnenpolitk. Die 'DDR-Nebenklage' im Essener KZ-Dora Prozeß (1967–1970)," in Sabine Moller, et al., eds., *Abgeschlossene Kapitel? Zur Geschichte der Konzentrationslager und der NS Prozesse* (Tübingen, 2002), pp. 173–186.
21. Naumann, *Das arbeitsteilige Zusammenwirken,* and Manfred Pautz, "Ein Arbeitslager der SS—der Ausbau und die Häftlings—und SS-Organisation des KZ 'Dora' und seine Aussenkommandos" (unpublished Dipl.-Arb., Humboldt Univ. East Berlin, 1966).
22. See, for example, Erhard Pachaly and Kurt Pelny, *Konzentrationslager Mittelbau-Dora: Zum antifaschistischen Widerstandskampf im KZ Dora, 1943–1945* (East Berlin, 1990).
23. Bornemann and Brozsat, *KL Dora-Mittelbau.*
24. Manfred Bornemann, *Geheimprojekt Mittelbau: Die Geschichte der deutschen V-Waffen Werke* (München, 1971). An expanded edition was published in 1994 under a new title: *Geheimprojekt Mittelbau: Vom zentralen Öllager des Deutschen Reiches zur grössten Raketenfabrik im Zweiten Weltkrieg* (Bonn, 1994).
25. Cf. Heinz-Dieter Hölsken, *Die V-Waffen: Entstehung—Propaganda—Kriegseinsatz* (Stuttgart, 1984); David Irving, *Die Geheimwaffen des Dritten Reiches* (Gütersloh, 1963); also Karl-Heinz Ludwig, *Technik und Ingenieure im Dritten Reich* (Königstein/Düsseldorf, 1979). A particularly discouraging example of pure technical historical presentation is Walter Dornberger's

autobiography entitled *V-2—Der Schuß ins Weltall* (Esslingen, 1952). This culprit's empirical report demonstrates the personal and social suppressive and exculpatory strategies in West Germany in the 1950s. Camp Dora, in contrast to the Mittelwerk, is nowhere mentioned.

26. Cf. Rainer Eisfeld, "Von Raumfahrtpionieren und Menschenschindern. Ein verdrängtes Kapitel der Technikentwicklung im Dritten Reich," in Rainer Eisfeld and Ingo Müller, eds. *Gegen Barbarei: Essays Robert M. Kempner zu Ehren* (Frankfurt, 1989); Eisfeld, *Die unmenschliche Fabrik: V-2 Produktion und KZ Mittelbau-Dora* (Erfurt, 1993); Eisfeld, *Mondsüchtig: Wernher von Braun und die Geburt der Raumfahrt aus dem Geist der Barbarei* (Reinbek bei Hamburg, 1966); and Michael J. Neufeld, *The Rocket and the Reich: Peenemünde and the Coming of the Ballistic Missile Era* (New York, 1995).

27. See Neander, *Konzentrationslager Mittelbau.*

28. Oliver Tauke, *"Genesung" und "Selektion": Zur Funktion der Häftlingskrankenbauten im KZ-Komplex Mittelbau-Dora* (unpublished ms., Univ. Göttingen, 1996); Olaf Mussmann, " 'Bunte Lagerprominenz'?: Die Funktionshäftlinge im Rüstungs-KZ Mittelbau-Dora," *Beiträge zur Geschichte der nationalsozialistischen Verfolgung in Norddeutschland,* 4 (1998), 82–96; see also Mussmann, "Italienische Häftlinge im KZ Mittelbau," *Verfolgung als Gruppenschicksal, Dachauer Hefte,* 14 (1998), 245–253.

29. Cf. Walter Naasner, *Neue Machtzentren in der deutschen Kriegswirtschaft 1942–1945: Die Wirtschaftsorganisation der SS, das Amt des Generalbevollmächtigten für den Arbeitseinsatz und das Reichsministerium für Bewaffnung und Munition/Reichsministerium für Rüstung und Kriegsproduktion im nationalsozialistischen Herrschaftssystem,* Schriften des Bundesarchivs, 45 (Boppard a. Rhein, 1994); Jan Erik Schulte, *Zwangsarbeit und Vernichtung: Das Wirtschaftsimperium der SS. Oswald Pohl und das SS-Wirtschafts-Verwaltungshauptamt 1933–1945* (Paderborn, 2001); Michael Thad Allen, *The Business of Genocide: The SS, Slave Labor, and the Concentration Camps* (Chapel Hill, 2002). Allen's study deserves special mention because he was the first to do research in the voluminous Mittelwerk GmbH administration files in the Bundesarchiv Berlin (Bestand R 121, Industriebeteiligungsgesellschaft).

30. Cf. Jutta Holzhaus, *Die Verbindung der Zivilbevölkerung der Stadt Nordhausen und des Kreises Hohnsteinsche Forst zu den Häftlingen des faschistischen KZ Mittelbau-Dora und seinen Außenlagern: Möglichkeiten und Formen der antifaschistischen Zusammenarbeit und Hilfe* (unpublished Dipl.-Arb., Päd. Hochschule Erfurt/Mühlhausen, 1979).

31. Ibid., p. 25.

32. Cf. Schley, *Nachbar Buchenwald*; Steinbacher, *Dachau;* Wagner, *Produktion des Todes.*

33. Communication of Dora Miethe (Abt. Hist. Gedenkstätten) to Committee of the Anti-Fascist Resistance Fighters in the GDR, January 25, 1973, at the documentation center of Gedenkstätte Mittelbau-Dora (DMD), without signature.

34. A counterpart, similar in its apologetic effect on the historical picture, is the West German "seduction" thesis; cf. Hans-Ulrich Thamer, *Verführung und Gewalt: Deutschland 1933–1945* (Berlin, 1986).

35. Yves Béon, *Planet Dora: A Memoir of the Holocaust and the Birth of the Space Age*, with an intro. by Michael J. Neufeld (Boulder, Colo., 1997).

36. For the "de-coupling" (*Entkopplung*) thesis, derived from the science of cybernetics and chaos theory, cf. Ludolf Herbst, *Das nationalsozialistische Deutschland 1933–1945* (Frankfurt, 1996), pp. 16ff.

37. Cf. in detail Wagner, *Produktion des Todes*, pp. 405ff. On the annihilation of the Hungarian Jews beginning in spring 1944, see Randolph L. Braham, compiler, *The Destruction of Hungarian Jewry: A Documentary Account* (New York, 1963). See also Christine Gerlach and Götz Aly, *Das letzte Kapitel: Realpolitik, Ideologie, und der Mord an den ungarischen Juden 1944/45* (Stuttgart, 2002).

38. The number of Jews in the "evacuation transports" from Auschwitz and Gross-Rosen is difficult to establish on the basis of the rudimentary prisoner lists. According to careful estimates it is likely that at least a fourth of sixteen thousand "evacuees" were Jewish.

39. Cf. weekly report of "Krankenrevier" Harzungen, March 25–31, 1945, NARA, Microfilm M-1079, Roll 1, Fr. 577.

40. Cf. below, Anlage (file percentages doc.).

41. Neander estimates the total number of dead in the Mittelbau-Dora camps (including the victims of the death marches) at 27,000; cf. Joachim Neander, *"Hat in Europa kein annäherndes*

Beispiel": Mittelbau-Dora—ein KZ für Hitlers Krieg (Berlin, 2000), p. 173. Because most of the inmates died at the construction sites, it is difficult to arrive at an accurate number of those who died in Dora and in the other camps as a *direct* consequence of forced labor in V-2 production. But it is certain that more people died in the production than in the use of the weapons.

42. Cf. Broszat, *System der nationalsozialistischen Konzentrationslager*, pp. 113–114.

43. Ibid; Kogon, *SS-Staat*, pp. 262ff. A comprehensive monograph on the *Nacht und-Nebel* prisoners has not yet appeared. Joseph de la Matinière, in his 1981 study, deals extensively with the prehistory and evolution of the Keitel edict as well as with the *Sondergericht* (special German courts) trials and conditions in German prisons, but not with the deportation to the camps; cf. his *Le décret et la procedure Nacht und Nebel (nuit et brouillard)* (Orléans, 1981); cf. also his *Nuit et Brouillard à Hinzert* (Tours, 1984).

44. Hermann Kaienburg, *"Vernichtung durch Arbeit": Der Fall Neuengamme. Die Wirtschafts-bestrebungen der SS und ihre Auswirkungen auf die Existenzbedingungen der KZ-Gefangenen* (Hamburg, 1991), p. 469. A similar argument is made by Miroslav Karny in "Vernichtung durch Arbeit: Sterblichkeit in den NS-Konzentrationslager," *Beiträge zur nationalsozialistischen Gesundheits- und Sozialpolitik* (Berlin, 1987), 5:133–158.

45. Ulbricht Herbert, "Arbeit und Vernichtung," in Dan Diner, ed., *Ist der Nationalsozialismus Geschichte?* (Frankfurt, 1987), p. 236.

46. Alf Lüdtke, "Die Praxis von Herrschaft: Zur Analyse von Hinnehmen und Mitmachen im deutschen Faschismus," in Brigitte Berlekamp and Werner Röhr, eds., *Terror Herrschaft und Alltag im Nationalsozialismus: Probleme einer Sozialgeschichte des deutschen Faschismus* (Münster, 1995), pp. 226–245, specifically p. 235.

47. Bernd-A. Rusinek, *Gesellschaft in der Katastrophe: Terror, Illegalität, Widerstand—Köln 1944/45* (Essen, 1989), pp. 198ff, especially pp. 216–217.

48. David Rousset, "Die Tage unseres Sterben," *Die internationale Umschau*, 1, no. 1 (September 1946), pp. 33–41; specifically p. 41.

Sources

I have used two types of sources, under very different conditions: I read and analyzed a great number of testimonies as well as several other documents in order to do entirely original historical work in piecing together the history of Dora. Drawing upon other works, I sought out elements enabling me to situate this history in the political, military, and economic context of the time.

The Testimonies

The testimonies used are almost exclusively those of former Dora prisoners. They come first of all from the archives assembled by the historical commission of the association of former prisoners from Dora-Ellrich, headed by Lucien Fayman and Georges Soubirous. The collection was enriched with subsequent inquiries and exchanges of correspondence that I had with various people. Certain documents were photocopied for me by Pierre Goasguen from his personal archives. All texts not in the public domain are indicated in the notes section by the acronym AADE, meaning "Archives de l'Amicale Dora-Ellrich" [the Dora-Ellrich Former Prisoners' Association Archive]. They may have been taken from other such organizations, such as the former prisoners' association of our Belgian friends. The testimonies are presented in three forms: published works; continuous accounts, whether published in bulletins or in typescript or manuscript form; and elements of information contained in letters, answers to questionnaires, or interviews. The distinction between these three forms is often rather unclear.

Some of the published works concern accounts written upon their author's return, printed under the conditions of the time, often at the author's expense. Others on the contrary are recent works, written by former prisoners now in retirement. The difference, however, is not clear-cut: the recent works are often based upon older texts, personal diaries, abandoned sketches, and so on, whereas the older works have been republished. I expected to discover significant differences between the accounts written upon their author's return and the recent works. But this turned out to be the case only in terms of the tone of the commentaries accompanying the account, more passionate in the 1940s, more sober today—but that is also true of newspaper articles and filmed news. In terms of lived experience the difference is no longer appreciable.

On this note I would like to emphasize the high quality of the texts I have quoted. However dramatic the account, there are rarely exaggerated formulations. Indeed, the witnesses generally remain somewhat short of actual reality. The fact that I was placed in similar conditions myself—at certain moments at any rate—gives me the authority to authenticate the testimonies to which I refer, which often tally in unforeseen ways.

I have used my fellow prisoners' texts to retrace the history of the camp and to illustrate its various episodes. But for this very reason I left out everything that reflects the personal experience of each person—his beliefs and doubts, hopes and fears, revolts and projects. I hope readers of this book will subsequently turn to these accounts to discover the unity of each of the individuals involved.

This also holds for those texts that have not been published and deserve to be. Distribution, generally speaking, has not extended beyond the circle of friends and family, and I am grateful to all those who enabled me to have access to these documents. A look at the notes accompanying the text reveals the importance of many of these testimonies.

I also found a great deal of substance in the answers to questionnaires and in personal letters. Many people lacking the practice or the temper to launch into carefully considered accounts responded relevantly to particular points. I have endeavored not to overlook more modest contributions. That enabled me to appreciate, for instance, the importance of certain events that remained, more than others, in collective memory. As will be noted in the index of names, in the course of my work I met other prisoners, witnesses, or companions of witnesses by the hundreds.

Virtually all the documents I have used are in French and come from France, Belgium, or the Netherlands (Van Dijk and Groeneveld). I have used them without distinction, for my purpose was not to speak particularly about the French at Dora. Through the European Committee I obtained access to two particularly interesting Czech testimonies. And my personal relations with Milan Filipcic enabled me to see that there was no discrepancy between our experience and that of the Slovenians.

For political reasons, no cross-checking was available as regards the Poles and above all the Russians. I have mentioned them in this book as well as I have been able, but I was unable to have them speak for themselves—a considerable lacuna.

One last remark regarding the testimonies. When writing about a concentration camp, one comes up against the objection that the author is in some respects speaking from the point of view of the survivors. This was already the case for the soldiers of the First World War. I am not sure in either case that the remark is well-founded, insofar as the extreme cases are recognized for their full importance—which is large indeed—and this I have endeavored to do. And it is true that all the situations were not permanently extreme. But no one was sheltered from a twist of fate.

Documentation on the Context

The great difficulty with regard to Dora and the other Mittelbau camps was to sort out the relationship between the various German authorities who held our fate in their hands. It was no easy task: there were the SS as well as Kammler himself; there were the Wehrmacht artillerymen, like Dornberger; there were von Braun and the team of scientists and engineers from Peenemünde; there were Speer and his technocrats, such as Sawatzki. It was Michael Neufeld, thanks to his fundamental work *The Rocket and the Reich,* who enabled me to get a firm grasp on these questions.

With regard to Dora and Mittelwerk, I am much indebted to three authors: the Polish prisoner Wincenty Hein, who prepared the case with the Americans for the 1947 trial; the German historian Manfred Bornemann, who situated our adventure in the history and geography of the region; and my friend Joachim Neander, who critically examined the available sources on how Mittelbau functioned and how the evacuation process was carried out. I refer to the classic works on the deportation, with which I was already familiar. I was careful not to go into overly great depth in the study of Buchenwald. But a total dissociation of the two camps was not conceivable.

Bibliography

PUBLISHED TESTIMONIES ON DORA-MITTELBAU

De l'Université aux camps de concentration. Témoignages strasbourgeois, 3rd ed. (Presses universitaires de Strasbourg, 1989), including the texts by: Charles Sadron, "A l'usine de Dora." P. André Lobstein, "Le Block 39 A du Revier de Dora." Eugène Greff, "A Ellrich, près Dora." P. Hagenmuller, "L'évacuation de Dora." J. Hofstein, "D'évacuation en évacuation."

Mémorial des camps de Dora-Ellrich (Paris, 1949). Significant collection of anonymous testimonies.

Dora, KL Mittelbau, Zbornik (Ljubljana: Zalozba Borec, 1989), in Slovenian. Collection of thirty-four testimonies of former Slovenian deportees, with a study by Milan Filipcic.

d'Hainaut (Brigitte) and Somerhausen (Christine), *Dora, 1943–1945* (Bruxelles: Didier-Hatier, 1991). Study based on testimony from former Belgian prisoners.

Bailly (Jacques-Christian), *Un lycéen à Buchenwald* (Paris: Ramsay, 1979).

Benès (Jiri), *Détenu en Allemagne* (translated from the Czech).

Béon (Yves), *Planet Dora* (Boulder, CO: Westview Press, 1997); *La Planète Dora* (Paris: Seuil, 1985).

Birin (frère), *Seize Mois de bagne, Buchenwald-Dora* (Épernay: Dautelle, 1947).

Bleton (P.), *Le Temps du purgatoire* (Paris: Téqui, 1953).

Bonifas (Aimé), *Détenu 20.801* (Pau: Marrimpouey, 1966).

Bronchart (Léon), *Ouvrier et Soldat* (Vaison-la-Romaine: Meffre, 1969).

Dutillieux (Max), *Le Camp des armes secrètes* (Rennes: Éd. Ouest-France, 1993).

Fliecx (Michel), *Pour délit d'espérance* (Nice: Récits de vie, 1989).

Fuchs (Gottlieb), *Le Renard* (Paris: Albin Michel, 1973).

Galzain (Eudes de) and Cardonnel (Jean), *Dora. Souvenirs d'avenir* (Lyon: Éd. Golias, 1994).

Gaussen (Dominique), *Kapo* (Paris: France-Empire, 1966; republished 1985).

Giquel (Raoul), *Le Prix de la liberté* (Nantes: Opéra Éditions, 1996).

Haentjens (René), *Au-delà de l'imaginable* (Vanier, Canada: Éd. L'Interligne, 1993).

Halkin (Léon-E.), *A l'ombre de la mort* (1945; updated edition, Bruxelles: Pauli, 1965).

Hessel (Stéphane), *Danse avec le siècle* (Paris: Seuil, 1997).

Julitte (Pierre), *L'Arbre de Goethe* (Paris: Presses de la Cité, 1965).

Lafond-Masurel (Étienne), *Survie* (Louviers: Jacques Drai, 1945; republished by Presse d'aujourd'hui [Paris], 1993).

Lemière (Dr. Maurice), *Retour de Buchenwald* (Condé-sur-Noireau: Éd. Charles Corlet, 1980).

Litomisky (Otakar), *Les Mémoires du prisonnier 113 359* (translated from the Czech).

Mialet (Jean), *La Haine et le Pardon. Le Déporté* (Paris: Fayard, 1981; republished by Laffont [Paris], 1997).

Michel (Jean), in collaboration with Louis Nucera, *Dora* (Paris: J.-C. Lattès, 1975).

Michel (Jean), *Dora* (New York: Holt, Rinehart and Winston, 1979); *De l'enfer aux étoiles* (Paris: Plon, 1986; republished by Presse d'aujourd'hui, 1993).

Miller (Serge), *Le Laminoir* (Paris: Calmann-Lévy, 1947).

Morel (René), *Perliris* (Oyonnax, 1993).

Morel (René), *Dix-sept plus six* (Oyonnax, 1995).

Morel (René), *Les derniers supplices* (Oyonnax, 1999).

Pahor (Boris), *Pèlerin parmi les ombres* (Paris: La Table ronde, 1990). Translated from the Slovenian by Andrée Lück-Gaye.
Pescadère (Georges), *77 023, Quarante-quatre ans après* (IMF Productions, 1991).
Pontoizeau (Andrès), *Dora-la-mort* (Tours: COSOR, 1947).
Pouzet (Richard), *Dora* (Paris: Castet, 1946).
Raoul-Duval (Guy), *Témoignage de déportation* (Paris: Éd. Christian, 1997).
Rassinier (Paul), *Passage de la ligne*, 6th ed. (Paris: La Vieille Taupe, 1979).
Rogerie (André), *Vivre, c'est vaincre* (Paris: Curial-Archereau, 1946; republished by Hérault-Éditions [Maulévrier], 1992).
Tauzin (Jean-Henry), *Quatre Ans dans les bagnes hitlériens* (Corbeil, 1945).
Spitz (Charles), *Cellule 114* (Cahors: Le Soutien par le livre, 1988).
Vincent (Rémy), *KLB 52 230* (Nantes, 1996).

Leroy (Gustave), *A chacun son dû.* Collection of poems from 1944–45, published in 1962.
Renard (Jean-Paul), *Chaînes et Lumières.* Collection of text, particularly poems, from 1942 to 1949.

Delarbre (Léon), *Croquis clandestins, Auschwitz, Buchenwald, Bergen, Dora* (Paris: Michel de Romilly, 1945).
La Pintière (Maurice de), *Dora, la mangeuse d'hommes* (Paris: Presse d'aujourd'hui, 1993). Collection of thirty-five wash drawings.

TESTIMONIES ON OTHER CAMPS OR KOMMANDOS DIRECTLY OR INDIRECTLY LINKED WITH DORA-MITTELBAU

Le Goupil (Paul), *Un Normand dans . . .* (Paris: Tiresias, 1991).
Pineau (Christian), *La Simple Vérité* (Paris: Julliard, 1960).
Semprun (Jorge), *Le Grand Voyage* (Paris: Gallimard, 1963).
Semprun (Jorge), *Quel beau dimanche!* (Paris: Grasset, 1980).
Semprun (Jorge), *Literature or Life,* translated by Linda Coverdale (New York: Penguin, 1998).

Antelme (Robert), *The Human Race,* translated by Jefferey Haight and Annie Mahler (Northwestern University Press, 1998).
Amicale des anciens déportés à Neu Stassfurt, *Un pas, encore un pas, pour survivre* (Amiens: Martelle Éditions, 1996).
Bertrand (François), *Notre devoir de mémoire* (Pau: Héraclès, 1997).

Rousset (David), *L'Univers concentrationnaire* (Paris: Éd. du Pavois, 1946).
Rousset (David), *Les Jours de notre mort* (Paris: Éd. du Pavois, 1947).
Kielar (Wieslaw), *Anus mundi* (Paris: Laffont, 1980), translated from the German by Frank Straschitz, with a preface by David Rousset.
Renouard (Jean-Pierre), *Un uniforme rayé d'enfer* (Monaco: Éd. du Rocher, 1993), with a letter-preface by Maurice Druon.
Amicale d'Oranienburg-Sachsenhausen, *Sachso* (Paris: Plon, coll. "Terre humaine," 1982).

Tillion (Germaine), *Ravensbrück* (Paris: Seuil, 1973; new edition, 1988).
Buber-Neumann (Margarete), *Déportée à Ravensbrück* (Paris: Seuil, 1988).

ANTHOLOGIES AND COMMEMORATIVE WORKS ON THE DEPORTATION IN GENERAL

Wormser (Olga) and Michel (Henri), *Tragédie de la déportation, 1940–1945* (Paris: Hachette, 1955).
FNDIRP (Fédération nationale des déportés et internés résistants et patriotes), *La Déportation* (Paris: Éd. Le Patriote résistant, 1968).
FNDIRP, *Le Grand Livre des témoins* (Paris: Ramsay, 1995).
FNDIR/UNADIF (Fédération nationale des déportés et internés de la Résistance/Union nationale

des associations de déportés, internés et familles de disparus), *Leçons de ténèbres. Résistants et déportés* (Paris: Plon, 1995, s.d. Jean Mansion).

FNDIR/UNADIF, Fillaire (Bernard), *Jusqu'au bout de la résistance* (Paris: Stock, 1997).

Ruby (Marcel), *Le Livre de la déportation. La vie et la mort dans les 18 camps de concentration et d'extermination* (Paris: Laffont, 1995).

Bédarida (François) and Gervereau (Laurent) (s.d.), *La Déportation. Le système concentrationnaire nazi* (Nanterre: Bibliothèque de documentation internationale contemporaine, 1995).

Bernadac (Christian), *La Libération des camps. Le dernier jour de notre mort* (Paris: Michel Lafon, 1995).

Vingtième Siècle. Les camps de concentration du XXe siècle, no. 54 (April–June 1997).

STUDIES ON NAZI CONCENTRATION CAMPS LINKED TO DORA-MITTELBAU

Sofsky (Wolfgang), *Die Ordnung des Terrors. Das Konzentrationslager* (Frankfurt-am-Main: S. Fischer Verlag, 1993). French translation: *L'Organisation de la terreur* (Paris: Calmann-Lévy, 1995). English translation: *The Order of Terror: The Concentration Camp* (Princeton: Princeton University Press, 1997).

Kogon (Eugen), *Der SS Staat. Das System der deutschen Konzentrationslager* (Frankfurt am Main: Europäische Verlagsanstalt, 1946). French edition in 1947, under the title *L'Enfer organisé* (Paris: Éd. de la Jeune Parque). A full French translation was published in 1993, under the title: *L'État SS. Le système des camps de concentration allemands* (Paris: Seuil, 1993).

Hackett (David A.), ed., *The Buchenwald Report,* translated, edited, and with an introduction by David A. Hackett (Boulder: Westview Press, 1995).

Langbein (Hermann), *Nicht wie die Schafe zur Schlachtbank* (Frankfurt am Main: Fischer Taschenbuch Verlag, 1980. French translation: *La Résistance dans les camps de concentration nationaux-socialistes, 1938/1945* [Paris: Fayard, 1980]).

Durand (Pierre), *La Résistance des Français à Buchenwald et à Dora* (Paris: Messidor, 1991).

Bezaut (Jean), *Oranienburg 1933–1935, Sachsenhausen 1936–1945* (Maulévrier: Hérault-Éditions, 1989).

Hilberg (Raul), *The Destruction of the European Jews* (New York: Holmes & Meier, 1985).

Langbein (Hermann), *Hommes et Femmes à Auschwitz* (Paris: Fayard, 1975).

Cardon-Hamet (Claudine), *Mille Otages pour Auschwitz* (Paris: Graphein, 1997).

Kolb (Eberhard), *Bergen-Belsen de 1943 à 1945* (Göttingen: Vandenhoeck, 1985).

NAZI GERMANY AND THE SECRET WEAPONS

Broszat (Martin), *Der Staat Hitlers* (Munich: D.T.V., 1970). French translation: *L'État hitlérien* (Paris: Fayard, 1985).

Mommsen (Hans), *Le National-Socialisme et la Société allemande* (Paris: Éditions de la Maison des sciences de l'homme, 1997).

Ayçoberry (Pierre), *La Société allemande sous le IIIe Reich, 1933–1945* (Paris: Le Seuil, "Points-Histoire," 1998).

L'Histoire. L'Allemagne de Hitler (Paris: Seuil, "Points-Histoire," 1991).

Delarue (Jacques), *Histoire de la Gestapo* (Paris: Fayard, 1962).

Delarue (Jacques), *Trafics et Crimes sous l'occupation* (Paris: Fayard, 1968).

Sereny (Gitta), *Albert Speer: His Battle with Truth* (New York: Alfred A. Knopf, 1995). French translation: *Albert Speer, son combat avec la vérité* (Paris: Seuil, 1997).

Zwangsarbeit und die unterirdische Verlagerung von Rüstungsindustrie (Berlin/Bonn: Westkreuz-Verlag, 1994).

Masson (Philippe), *Histoire de l'armée allemande, 1939–1945* (Paris: Perrin, 1994).

Neufeld (Michael J.), *The Rocket and the Reich: Peenemünde and the Coming of the Ballistic Missile Era* (New York: Free Press, 1995).

Bornemann (Manfred), *Geheimprojekt Mittelbau. Von zentralen Öllager des Deutschen Reiches zur grössten Raketenfabrik im Zweiten Weltkrieg* (Bonn: Bernard & Graefe Verlag, 1994).

Eisfeld (Rainer), *Mondsüchtig. Wernher von Braun und die Geburt der Raumfahrt aus dem Geist der Barbarei* (Reinbeck: Rowohlt, 1996).

Metzler (Georg), *"Geheime Kommandosache." Raketenrüstung in Oberschwaben. Das Aussen-lager Saulgau und die V2 (1943–1945)* (Bergatreute: Verlag Wilfried Eppe, 1996).

HISTORY OF DORA

Hein (Wincenty), *Conditions de vie et de travail des prisonniers dans le camp de concentration Dora-Mittelbau* (Warsaw, 1969, in French).

Bartel (Walter), *Wehrwirtschaftführer Geheimwaffen KZ Gutachten ber die Bedeutung des KZ Dora-Mittelbau und die Funktion der SS bei der A4-Produktion* (Frankfurt am Main, 1970).

Bornemann (Manfred), *Chronik des Lagers Ellrich 1944/45* (Hamburg, 1987; Nordhausen, 1992).

Bornemann (Manfred), *Aktiver und passiver Widerstand, im KZ Dora und im Mittelwerk* (Berlin/Bonn: Westkreuz-Verlag, 1994).

Neander (Joachim), *Das Konzentrationslager Mittelbau, in der Endphase der NS-Diktatur* (Clausthal-Zellerfeld: Papierflieger, 1997).

Le Maner (Yves) and Sellier (André), *Images de Dora* (La Coupole: Centre d'Histoire de la Guerre et des Fusées, 1999).

THE POST-DORA PERIOD, SINCE 1945

McGovern (James), *Crossbow and Overcast* (New York: William Morrow and Co., 1964). French translation: *La Chasse aux armes secrètes allemandes* (Paris: Stock, 1965).

Kohler (Pierre) and Germain (Jean-René), *Von Braun contre Korolev. Duel pour la conquête de l'espace* (Paris: Plon, 1994).

Hunt (Linda), *Secret Agenda: The United States Government, Nazi Scientists, and Project Paper-clip, 1945 to 1990* (New York: St. Martin's Press, 1991). French translation by Yves Béon: *L'Af-faire Paperclip. La récupération des scientifiques nazis par les Américains, 1945–1990* (Paris: Stock, 1995).

Rovan (Joseph), *Histoire de l'Allemagne, des origines à nos jours* (Paris: Seuil, 1994).

Grosser (Alfred), *L'Allemagne de notre temps, 1945–1978* (Paris: Fayard, 1970; updated edition, 1978, Livre de poche).

Bark (Dennis L.) and Gress (David R.), *History of Germany Since 1945* (Hoover Institution: Stanford University Press, 1989).

Niethammer (Lutz), *Der "gesäuberte" Antifaschismus. Der SED und die roten Kapos von Buchen-wald* (Berlin: Akademie Verlag, 1994).

Copfermann (Émile), *David Rousset. Une vie dans le siècle* (Paris: Plon, 1991).

Brayard (Florent), *Comment l'idée vint à M. Rassinier. Naissance du révisionnisme* (Paris: Fayard, 1996), with a preface by Pierre Vidal-Naquet.

Reichel (Peter), *Politik mit der Erinnerung* (Munich/Vienna: Carl Hanser Verlag, 1995). French translation: *L'Allemagne et sa mémoire* (Paris: Éd. Odile Jacob, 1998).

Wieviorka (Annette), *Déportation et Génocide. Entre la mémoire et l'oubli* (Paris: Plon, 1992).

Chaumont (Jean-Michel), *La Concurrence des victimes. Génocide, identité, reconnaissance* (Paris: La Découverte, 1997).

Maps

This section of maps is a key component of *A History of the Dora Camp*. It came together in parallel with the writing of the text and was worked out with the assistance of my son, Jean. It was then assembled by Anne Le Fur. The three of us had previously worked together on the *Atlas des peuples d'Europe centrale (Atlas of the Peoples of Central Europe)* along similar lines.

Because the maps and plans that comprise this section often correspond to a number of chapters, it seemed preferable to group them together at the end of the work following a logical order. The last maps thus correspond to the final phase of the evacuations. All these maps were designed to make up a homogeneous whole. The information was drawn to some extent from the important works already quoted in the text of the book, including Michael Neufeld's, Manfred Bornemann's, and Joachim Neander's. Paul Le Goupil was of great assistance in reconstituting the itineraries of the evacuations described in chapter 20.

The maps' origins vary. The Dora map is based upon a document from the time; every attempt has been made to render it as intelligible as possible. The Harzungen map was reconstituted by the Belgian prisoners' association on the basis of a recently discovered aerial photograph; the preceding map, based upon memories, was in fact not very different. That of Ellrich is far more uncertain. Clément-Robert Nicola drew up the plan of the Boelcke Kaserne, and André Lobstein drew up the plan of the two blocks of the Dora *Revier.* The plan showing the block of the Dora camp corresponds to the barracks at the camp entrance. The blocks at the back of the camp had a more rudimentary plan, but there were always two *Flügel*, or wings. The plan of the Peenemünde base is reliable; that of the Bergen-Belsen camp is far less reliable.

Among the underground work sites of the Sonderstab Kammler the layout of B 3 is best known, on the basis of Bornemann's reproductions. The plan shown corresponds to the projected layout and not to the situation at the time of the Allies' arrival. The same goes for the plan of the Wizernes bunker. The interest of these two plans is to show the extent of the work sites undertaken from 1943 on—which led to so many victims.

The Greater Reich and the Principal Deportation Camps

The limits of the Greater Reich were unilaterally established by the German government, in the west as well as in the east. They did not result from any treaty.

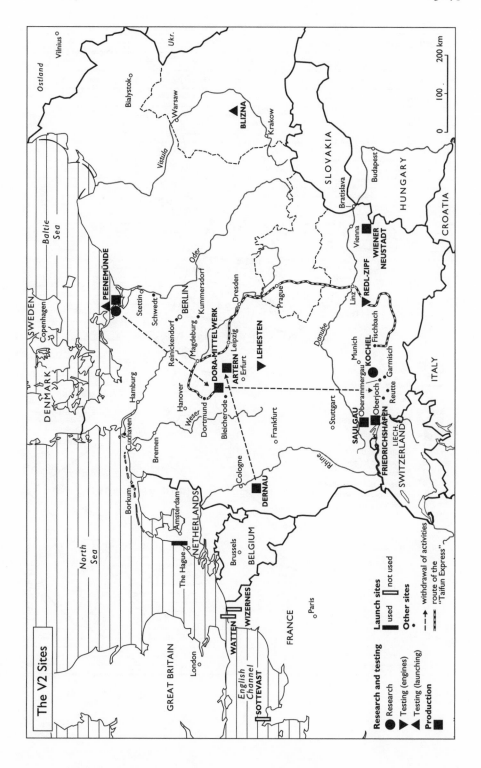

The V2 Sites

Research and testing
● Research
▼ Testing (engines)
▲ Testing (launching)
■ Production

Launch sites
■ used ▯ not used

Other sites
●
- - -→ withdrawal of activities
≈≈≈ route of the "Taifun Express"

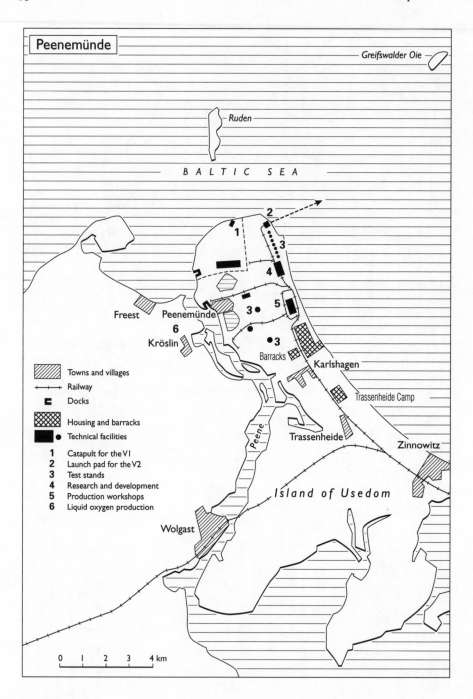

Peenemünde

Greifswalder Oie

Ruden

BALTIC SEA

Freest   Peenemünde
6
Kröslin

Barracks

Karlshagen

Trassenheide Camp

Trassenheide

Zinnowitz

Peene

Island of Usedom

Wolgast

Towns and villages
Railway
Docks
Housing and barracks
Technical facilities

1   Catapult for the VI
2   Launch pad for the V2
3   Test stands
4   Research and development
5   Production workshops
6   Liquid oxygen production

0   1   2   3   4 km

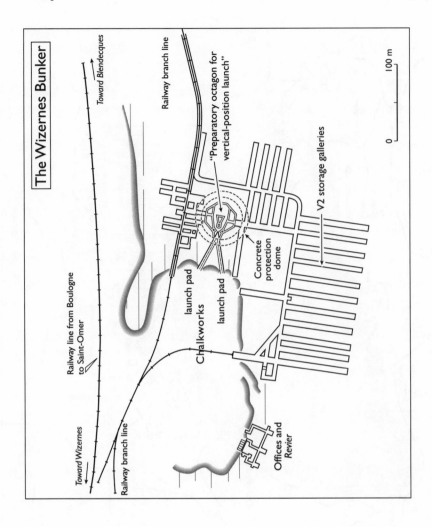

The Wizernes Bunker

Toward Blendecques

Railway branch line

"Preparatory octagon for vertical-position launch"

V2 storage galleries

Railway line from Boulogne to Saint-Omer

Concrete protection dome

launch pad

Chalkworks

launch pad

Toward Wizernes

Railway branch line

Offices and Revier

0   100 m

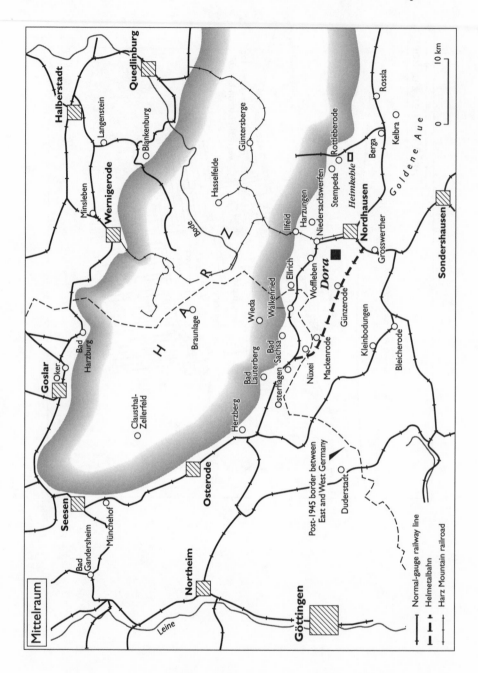

Mittelraum

Quedlinburg

Halberstadt

Langenstein

Blankenburg

Wernigerode

Minsleben

Güntersberge

Hasselfelde

Bode

H A R Z

Braunlage

Bad
Harzburg

Goslar

Oker

Clausthal-
Zellerfeld

Bad
Lauterberg

Wieda

Walkenried

Bad
Sachsa

Osterhagen

Nüxei

Herzberg

Osterode

Seesen

Münchehof

Bad
Gandersheim

Northeim

Leine

Göttingen

Rossla

Rottleberode

Berga

Kelbra

Niedersachswerfen

Stempeda

Heimkehle

Goldene Aue

Harzungen

Ilfeld

Nordhausen

Grosswerther

Ellrich

Woffleben

Dora

Günzerode

Kleinbodungen

Mackenrode

Bleicherode

Sondershausen

Post-1945 border between
East and West Germany

Duderstadt

10 km

0

Normal-gauge railway line

Helmetalbahn

Harz Mountain railroad

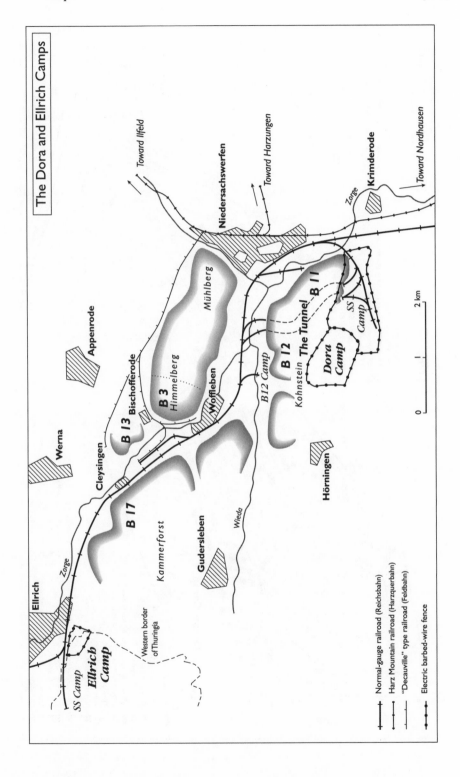

The Dora and Ellrich Camps

Toward Ilfeld

Toward Harzungen

Toward Nordhausen

Niedersachswerfen

Zorge

Krimderode

Mühlberg

Appenrode

B 13 Bischofferode

B 3
Himmelberg

Woffleben

B 12 Camp

Kohnstein **The Tunnel**

B 11

SS
Camp

**Dora
Camp**

Werna

Cleysingen

B 17

Kammerforst

Wieda

Gudersleben

Hörningen

0   1   2 km

Ellrich

Zorge

SS Camp

**Ellrich
Camp**

Western border
of Thuringia

┼┼┼┼ Normal-gauge railroad (Reichsbahn)

├──┤ Harz Mountain railroad (Harzquerbahn)

─── "Decauville" type railroad (Feldbahn)

●─●─● Electric barbed-wire fence

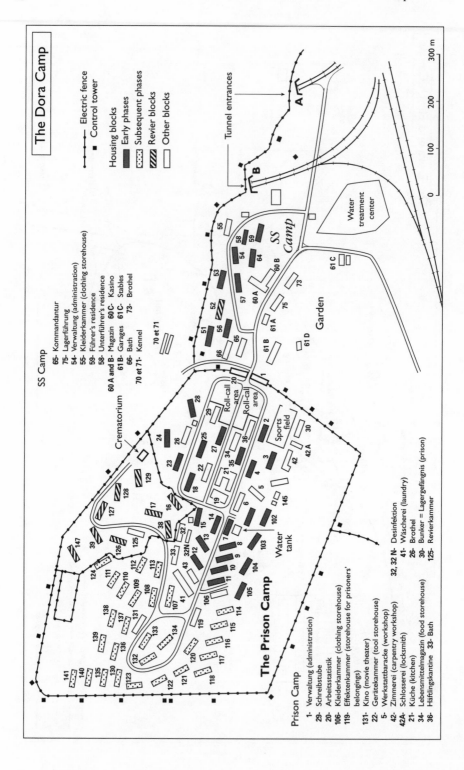

The Dora Camp

Legend:

—•—•— Electric fence
■ Control tower

Housing blocks
- Early phases
- Subsequent phases
- Revier blocks
- Other blocks

Tunnel entrances → A
B

Water treatment center

SS Camp

Garden

Crematorium

Roll-call area
Sports field
Water tank

The Prison Camp

SS Camp
- 65- Kommandantur
- 75- Lagerführung
- 54- Verwaltung (administration)
- 55- Kleiderkammer (clothing storehouse)
- 59- Führer's residence
- 58- Unterführer's residence
- 60 A and B- Magazin   60-C- Kasino
- 61-B- Garages   61-C- Stables
- 66- Bath   73- Brothel
- 70 et 71- Kennel

Prison Camp
- 1- Verwaltung (administration)
- 29- Schreibstube
- 20- Arbeitsstatistik
- 106- Kleiderkammer (clothing storehouse)
- 119- Effektenkammer (storehouse for prisoners' belongings)
- 131- Kino (movie theater)
- 22- Gerätekammer (tool storehouse)
- 5- Werkstattbaracke (carpentry workshop)
- 42- Zimmerei (carpentry workshop)
- 42A- Schlosserei (locksmith)
- 21- Küche (kitchen)
- 34- Lebensmittelmagazin (food storehouse)
- 36- Häftlingskantine   33- Bath
- 32, 32 N- Desinfektion
- 41- Wäscherei (laundry)
- 26- Brothel
- 30- Bunker = Lagergefängnis (prison)
- 125- Revierkammer

Block Layouts

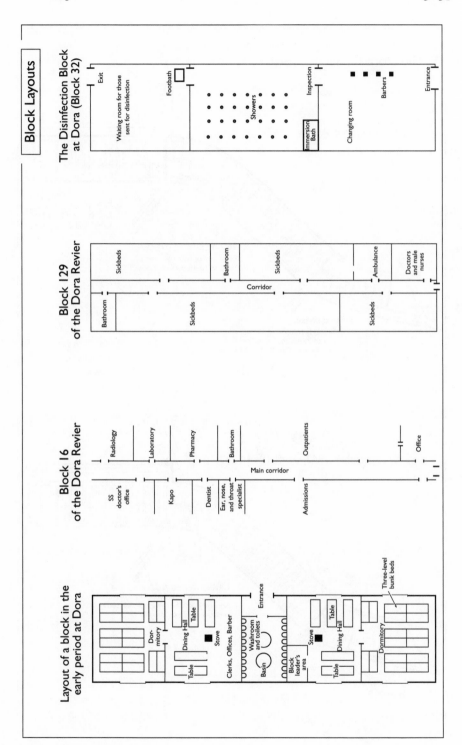

The Disinfection Block at Dora (Block 32)

Exit

Waiting room for those sent for disinfection

Footbath

Showers

Inspection

Immersion Bath

Changing room

Barbers

Entrance

Block 129 of the Dora Revier

Sickbeds

Bathroom

Sickbeds

Ambulance

Doctors and male nurses

Corridor

Bathroom

Sickbeds

Sickbeds

Block 16 of the Dora Revier

Radiology

Laboratory

Pharmacy

Bathroom

Outpatients

Office

Main corridor

SS doctor's office

Kapo

Dentist

Ear, nose, and throat specialist

Admissions

Layout of a block in the early period at Dora

Dormitory

Dining Hall

Table

Stove

Clerks, Offices, Barber

Entrance

Washroom and toilets

Basin

Block leader's area

Stove

Table

Dining Hall

Table

Dormitory

Three-level bunk beds

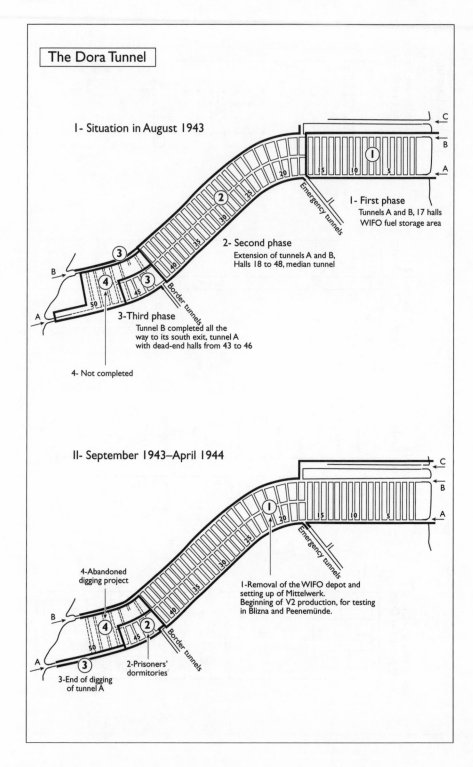

The Dora Tunnel

I- Situation in August 1943

1- First phase
Tunnels A and B, 17 halls
WIFO fuel storage area

2- Second phase
Extension of tunnels A and B,
Halls 18 to 48, median tunnel

3-Third phase
Tunnel B completed all the
way to its south exit, tunnel A
with dead-end halls from 43 to 46

4- Not completed

II- September 1943–April 1944

4-Abandoned
digging project

1-Removal of the WIFO depot and
setting up of Mittelwerk.
Beginning of V2 production, for testing
in Blizna and Peenemünde.

2-Prisoners'
dormitories

3-End of digging
of tunnel A

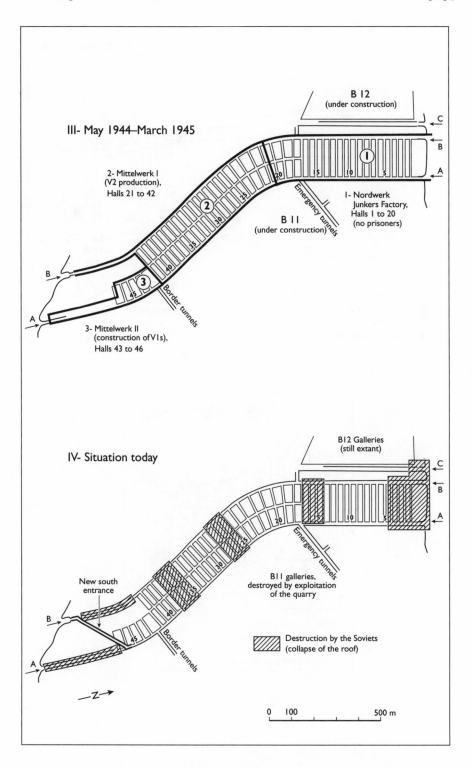

III- May 1944–March 1945

2- Mittelwerk I
(V2 production),
Halls 21 to 42

B 12
(under construction)

1- Nordwerk
Junkers Factory,
Halls 1 to 20
(no prisoners)

B 11
(under construction)

3- Mittelwerk II
(construction of V1s),
Halls 43 to 46

IV- Situation today

B12 Galleries
(still extant)

New south
entrance

B11 galleries,
destroyed by exploitation
of the quarry

Destruction by the Soviets
(collapse of the roof)

0   100   500 m

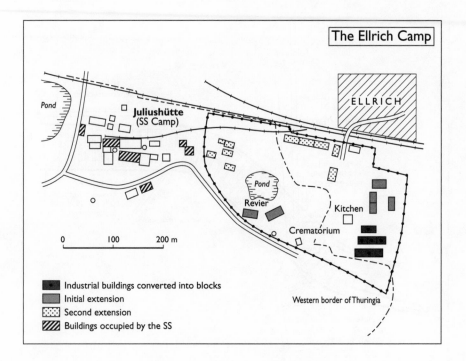

The Ellrich Camp

Pond

Juliushütte
(SS Camp)

ELLRICH

Pond

Revier

Kitchen

Crematorium

0   100   200 m

Western border of Thuringia

■ Industrial buildings converted into blocks
▨ Initial extension
▦ Second extension
▨ Buildings occupied by the SS

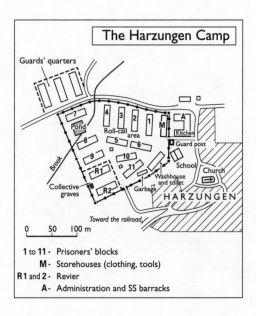

The Harzungen Camp

Guards' quarters

7   4 3 2   1 M A

Pond   Roll-call   Kitchen
        area

8   Guard post

9   5   6   School   Church

R1   10   11   Washhouse
                     and toilet

Collective   Garbage   HARZUNGEN
graves   R2

Toward the railroad

0   50   100 m

1 to 11 - Prisoners' blocks
M - Storehouses (clothing, tools)
R 1 and 2 - Revier
A - Administration and SS barracks

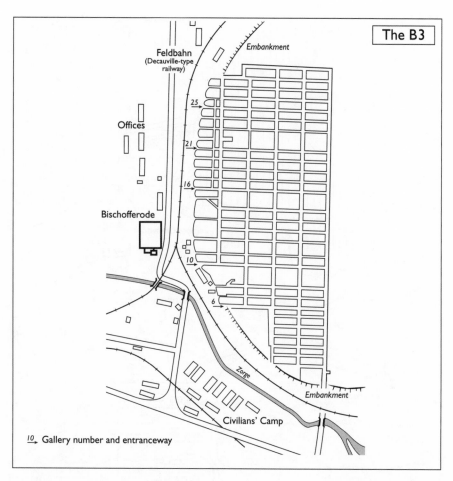

The B3

Feldbahn
(Decauville-type railway)

Embankment

Offices

25

21

16

Bischofferode

10

6

Zorge

Embankment

Civilians' Camp

<u>10</u> Gallery number and entranceway

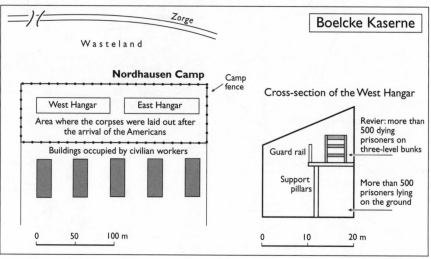

Zorge

Boelcke Kaserne

Wasteland

Nordhausen Camp

Camp fence

West Hangar

East Hangar

Area where the corpses were laid out after the arrival of the Americans

Buildings occupied by civilian workers

Cross-section of the West Hangar

Revier: more than 500 dying prisoners on three-level bunks

Guard rail

Support pillars

More than 500 prisoners lying on the ground

0   50   100 m

0   10   20 m

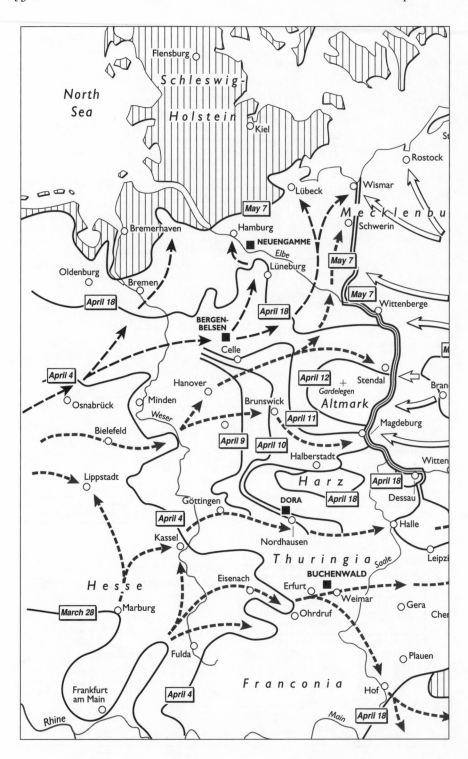

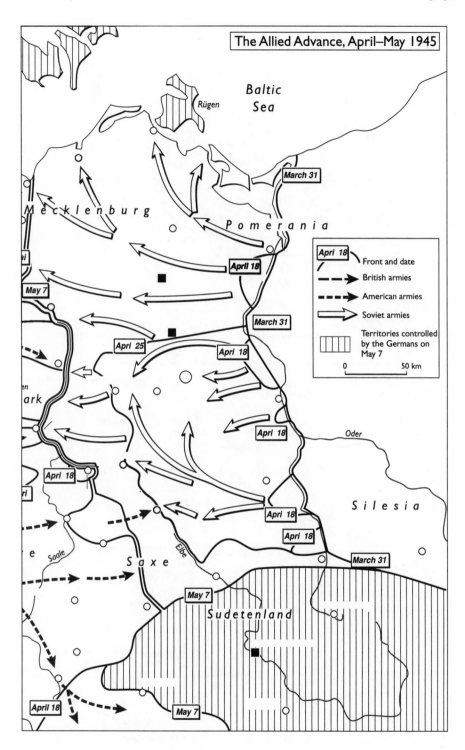

The Allied Advance, April–May 1945

Baltic
Sea

Rügen

Mecklenburg

Pomerania

March 31

April 18

May 7

March 31

Apri 25

Apri 18

April 18

April 18

Oder

April 18

Silesia

April 18

April 18

March 31

Saale

Saxe

Elbe

May 7

Sudetenland

April 18

May 7

ark

Legend:

April 18 — Front and date

▪▪▪▶ British armies

▪ ▪ ▪▶ American armies

⇨ Soviet armies

▦ Territories controlled by the Germans on May 7

0   50 km

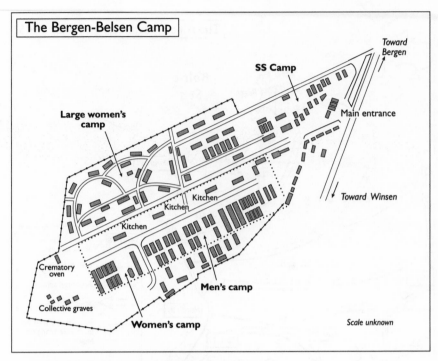

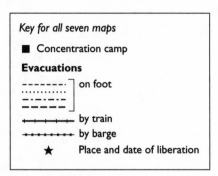

The Evacuations

Key for all seven maps

■ Concentration camp

Evacuations

-------- ⎤
.... ⎬ on foot
-.-.-.- ⎥
-----   ⎦

┣━┿━┿━┿━┫ by train

┣━•━•━•━┫ by barge

★ Place and date of liberation

From Karlshagen to Ellrich
From Dora-Mittelbau to Bergen-Belsen

From Blankenburg, Osterode, and Porta Westfalica toward the north

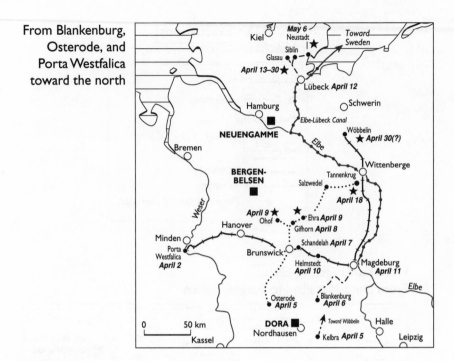

The last convoy from Dora to Ravensbrück and Parchim, arrival April 14

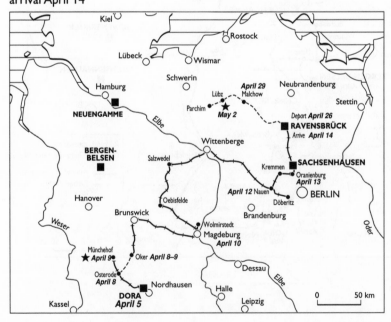

From Ellrich, Rottleberode, and Schönebeck to Sachsenhausen, and the evacuation of Sachsenhausen toward Schwerin

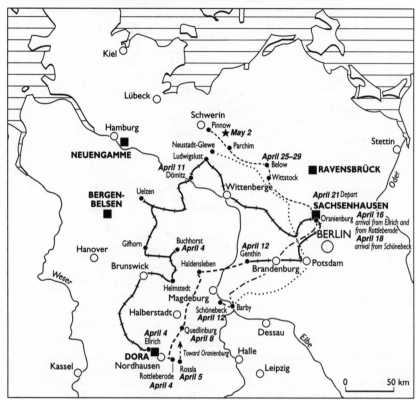

The Gardelegen tragedy

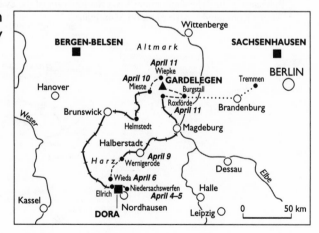

The itineraries from Arten, Langenstein, Neu Stassfurt, and neighboring Kommandos

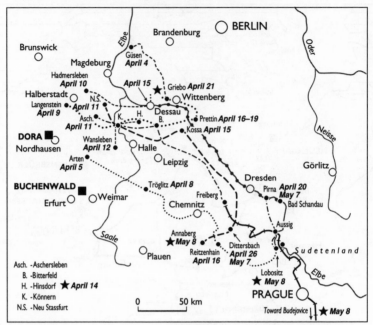

Certain evacuations have been studied in depth by the various associations established by prisoners from the Kommandos concerned. This is the case for the "death marches" of the Langenstein and Neu Strassfurt Kommandos, dependent on Buchenwald, whose itinerary is known on a day-to-day basis. Only the principal stages are indicated. The crucial importance of the crossing of the Saale over the Könnern Bridge is noteworthy. The evacuation columns from Aschersleben and Wansleben crossed the river at that same point. The same map shows the itinerary of the evacuation of the Artern Kommando, dependent on Mittelbau.

From the *Mittelraum* to the Sudetenland by various means

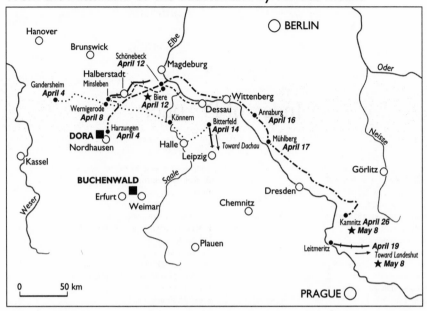

Among the most notable evacuations starting from *Mittelraum*, that of Gandersheim must be borne in mind: it began with a march all the way to Bitterfeld and was followed by an interminable trip by rail all the way to Dachau. The columns that left Harzungen on foot suffered various fates, as indicated on the map.

Between *Mittelraum* and the Sudetenland any number of other crisscrossing itineraries of evacuation could have been shown—ultimately rendering the map illegible.

Index of Prisoners

Abada, Roger, 30, 238, 293–294
Abel, Ernest, 7, 210, 216, 448
Ackermann, 279
Agnès, Roger, 211, 282, 302
Alcaras, François, 282, 302
Aleste, Yves, 339, 341
Alliens, Gabriel, 269
Amate, Albert, 68, 132, 137–139, 143
Amyot d'Inville, Gérald, 18
André, René, 184, 212
Anfriani, Mathieu, 143, 339
Anker, Daniel, 431
Anna (Wyglendatz), 153, 323
Antelme, Robert, 222, 231, 357, 369–371
Argoux, Georges, 55, 69
Astor, Fernand, 86
Aubin, Bernard, 388–389
Auchabie, Pierre, 81, 86, 194, 216, 217, 218, 292, 302, 315, 316

Bacanelli, Giuseppe, 118
Bachkir, 111, 144, 164
Baillon, Marcel, 56, 134, 137, 169, 389–391
Bailly, Jacques-Christian, 135, 137, 141, 157, 185–187, 288
Balachowsky, Alfred, 223
Balachowsky, Serge, 222, 223–224
Bannes, Albert, 195–196, 198
Baranton, Jacques, 219
Barbier, Henri, 333
Bartel, Walter, 3, 429, 430–431, 433, 438, 439, 458
Bazelaire de Lesseux, Florent de, 276
Bazelaire de Lesseux, Hubert de, 276
Bedel, Michel, 134, 143
Beham, Christian, 150, 161, 163, 170, 297
Bel, Martin, 159
Belin, Paul, 87
Benes, Jiri, 43, 58–59, 65, 68–69, 89, 135, 137, 141, 382, 385
Béninger, Joseph, 8, 111, 115, 142, 143, 144, 151
Béon, Yves, ix, 7, 124, 321, 322
Bérard-Shreve, André, 299
Berrod, Maurice, 355
Berthelot, Robert, 134
Berthéol, Jean, 190

Berthereau, Roger, 50–51, 70
Berthet, Marcel, 70, 138
Berthier, Georges, 219
Berthier, Germain, 219
Bertrand, François, 369–370
Besançon, Albert, 154–155, 216, 336–337, 379
Bezaut, Jean, 376
Bignon, 133, 138, 143
Birin, Alfred (Untereiner), 124, 134, 152, 154, 156, 166, 169, 171–173, 269, 328, 331, 333, 427
Bischoff, Franz, 391
Blanchet, Emmine, 118
Blanchou, Jean, 86
Bleton, Pierre, 229, 238, 279, 282, 301–302
Boisot, Guy, 143, 151, 387–388; drawings by, 245, 250
Bollaert, Emile, 156, 164–165, 331, 333
Bolteau, Paul, 126–127
Bonifas, Aimé, 183–184, 187–188, 267, 345, 346, 347, 350
Bordeaux Montrieux, Étienne, 78
Bordet, René, 8, 143, 279, 299, 302–303, 314, 316
Bordier-Brunschwig, Jacques, 164, 269, 285, 293, 294, 331
Bossue, Roland, 337
Bouchez, Maurice, 226
Boudon, Paul, 165
Boulard, Robert, 132
Bourdet, Claude, 426
Bourdois, Raymond, 219
Bourget, Didier, 78, 148
Bourgogne, Jean, 86
Bouvet, Jules, 205
Boyer, André, 165, 173, 268, 279, 285, 293, 294, 331
Bramoullé, 156
Braun, Theodor, 120, 334
Brembéche, Lucie, 393
Breton, Pierre, 124, 386–387
Brière, Marcel, 294, 315, 316
Bronchart, Léon, 55, 56, 57, 58–59, 65–66, 69–70, 78, 81, 208, 332, 377; biography, 70–71; on exhaustion, 328; relationship with *Kapos*, 88; repatriation, 333; writing of, 71
Brossolette, Pierre, 165
Brun, Jacques, 7, 214, 299, 343, 449
Buber-Neumann, Margarete, 385, 429
Buchet, Marius, 76, 79, 86

Buigne, Francis de, 219
Burney, Christopher, 426, 457
Busse, Ernst, 425, 428–429, 430, 433
Butet, Paul, 60, 66, 74, 79, 129, 130, 131, 143, 154, 156, 266, 331, 333

Calès, Henri, 134, 388–389
Can, Jacques, 316–317
Canivet, Frans, 161, 299
Cardon, André, 7, 132, 393
Carlebach, Emil, 428
Caruana, André, 269, 331
Caruana, Pierre, 269, 331
Castellevi, Amaro, 346, 347, 348, 350
Caton, Paul, 338
Cauchois, Maurice, 85
Caussin, Edmond, 147, 161
Cayrol, Jean, 430
Cespiva, Jan, 73, 161, 172–173, 268–269, 279, 439
Chabaud, André, 279, 299
Chaloupka, Jan, 172, 173
Chamaillard, Guy, 346, 347, 348–349
Chamboissier, Jacques, 124, 169–170
Chanteloup, Claude de, 132, 253
Chapel, René, 355
Chapuy, René, 274
Chevalier, André (Schock), 165, 197, 331
Chevalier, Rémy, 199
Chicaud, André, 230
Chlique, Daniel, 42
Choquenet, Pierre, 380
Choquet, Marcel, 70
Cimek, Otto, 73, 173
Cirieco, Antoine, 390
Claessens, Leopold, 7, 159
Clairin, Luc, 114, 333
Clavé, André, 197
Clergue, Maurice, 124, 386–387
Climaud, 280
Cluyou, Joseph, 218
Cogny, René, 134, 173–174, 185, 269, 331
Colignon, Marcel, 181
Colombel, Ivan de, 219
Colonel, Lucien, 187, 346, 347
Colonna, Martin, 115
Combarel, Roger, 159
Combes, Sylvain, 86
Commandeur, André, 85
Corbin de Mangou, Paul, 86
Cormont, Jean, 7, 132, 393
Cottet, Maxime, 7, 194–195, 196, 197–198, 334
Coty, Roland, 192, 199, 328
Coudert, Emile-Louis, 391
Couëtdic, Roger, 114, 170, 171, 185, 304
Coulardot, Marcel, 134
Coupa, François, 218
Coupa, Grégoire, 218
Courtaud, Jacques, 168, 183, 184, 193, 207, 213, 216, 219, 319, 323–324, 328, 333–334, 435–436
Coutaud, Louis, 124, 133, 166, 340

Couture, Jean-Pierre, 8, 203, 214, 216, 271, 282, 292, 294, 302, 315, 316
Cozette, André, 229, 357
Cratès, Eugène, 218
Crémieux, Benjamin, 168
Cretin, Georges, 348, 350
Croizat, Georges, 73, 299
Croze, René, 129, 137

Daguin, 354–355
Dahlem, Franz, 433
Daix, Pierre, 430
Dancourt, Christian de, 219
D'Astorg, Bernard, 8, 85–86, 114, 445
Daubèze, Georges, 199
Davesnes, René, 141
Dayan, Agop, 132
De la Pintière, Maurice, 114, 153; drawings by, 246, 259
De Poortère, 293
Debeaumarché, Edmond, 148, 165, 173, 268–270, 331, 333
Debeauvais, Michel, 219
Deconninck, 346
Defiliquier, 333
Deglane, Robert, 134
Dejussieu, Pierre, 114, 164, 173–174, 331, 333, 440
Dejussieu-Pontcarral, 134, 169
Deknibber, Jean-Baptiste, paintings by, 361
Delarbre, Léon, 139, 158; drawings by, 248–249, 255–258, 261, 330
Delarue, Jacques, 33, 440, 443–444
Delaunnois, 391
Delaval, Michel, 114, 124, 386
D'Elbée, Philippe, 219
Delogne, Xavier, 7, 292, 294, 301–302, 315, 316, 338
Delogne, Yves, 393
Demuyter, Jean, 65, 114, 134–135
Denais, 285, 293
Depierre, Michel, 137, 299, 316
Desnos, Robert, 222, 231, 369
Despierres, Louis, 426
Desprez, Dr. Jacques, 73, 77, 198, 323, 328
Desseaux, Christian, 130
Detoux, Georges, 219
Deviataev, 175
D'Honincthun, Cazin, 173–174
Diquelou, Pierre, 218
Dondon, Henri, 279
Donnier, 285, 293
Douay, Claude, 69, 134, 299, 343
Doucet, Jean, 161, 299, 394
Doumeau, Arsène, 156, 333
Drung, Roman, 424
Duale, Jean, 174, 242, 331
Dubois, Albert, 215–216
Ducoloné, Guy, 7, 426
Duflot, Henri, 215
Dufrane, Narcisse, 225
Dumont, Jean, 199
Dunouau, Francis, 65, 133, 136

Dupuy, Emile, 86, 334
Durand, Jean-René, 276–278, 299
Durand, Pierre, 167, 299, 426
Dutillieux, Max, 7, 114, 391; evacuation, 359, 377–378, 379; the Green prisoners, 115; and liberation, 391; living conditions, 62, 65, 75; *Revier*, 75, 76; Sachsenhausen, 379; *Schonung*, 76, 78; working conditions, 69, 87, 88, 146
Dutois, 293
Dutzmann, 137
Duvernois, 333

Ebel, Jean-Pierre, 115, 161, 299
Eckert, Étienne, 7, 115, 157
Ego, 187
Eiden, Hans, 428
Erler, Gerhart, 215
Ertlen, Henri, 379
Estadès, Gustave, 124, 127–128
Estiot, Maurice, 86
Eymard, André, 86

Falaise, Richard de la, 219
Fayman, Lucien, 7, 193, 197, 198, 199, 323, 328, 444
Feliziani, Aurelien, 151
Fernand, 124
Filiatre, Roland, 393
Filipcic, Milan, 7, 130, 144, 384, 443
Filipcic, Zmagoslava, 384
Finelli, Francis, 8, 115, 138, 143, 387–388
Finkenzeller, Georg, 138–139, *256*
Fisher, Claude, 134
Flamatti, Elisio, 118
Fliecx, Michel, 27–28, 40, 57, 62, 63, 73–75, 76–77, 78–79, 81–82, 329
Foiret, 333
Foiret, Serge, 141
Foiry, Maurice, 219
Forcinal, Albert, 426
Fortané, André, 8, 143, 151, 166, 387–388
Fournier, Jean, 174–175, 241, 242, 296–297, 322, 333
Fourquet, René, 143
Frager, Henri, 223
Frank, Anne, 326
Frank, Josef, 431, 432
Franssen, Job, 199
Friang, Brigitte, 368
Fuches, Gottlieb, 199

Gabrion, Pierre, 153, 275
Gaillandre, Paul, 426
Gaillard, Ernest, 30, 238, 276, 282, 293–294, 316
Gaillot, Jean-Louis, 161
Gaillot, Pierre, 161
Galzain, Eudes de, 167
Gamisch, Joseph, 150, 161, 163, 270, 297
Gandar, Robert, 115, 223, 345
Garault, Francoise, 132
Garnavault, Pierre, 346

Garnier, Louis, 7, 114, 124, 157, 168, 386
Gáti, Pierre, 8, 143, 341
Gaude, Mélanie, 393
Gaussen, Dominique, 139
Géhard, Pierre, 158
Gentil, Col. Louis, 141, 148, 164, 165, 173, 268–270, 298
Gérard, André, 115, 129–130, 143, 144
Gérard, Maurice, 158, 170
Gilbert, René, 192–193, 203, 214
Gineston, Jean, 7, 206, 334
Giquel, Raoul, 147, 185
Girard, Louis, 56, 73, 161–162, 299
Girardi, André, 346
Girardin, Bernard, 185
Goasdoué, Georges, 218
Goasdoué, Pierre, 218
Goasguen, Pierre, 204, 216, 331, 333
Golfier, Robert, 132
Gos, Georges, 199
Gouju, Marcel, 143, 147
Gouvenaux, Jean, 133, 157
Graf, Albert, 161
Grand, Raymond, 215–216, 336–337, 379
Grandcoin, Jacques, 207, 216
Greff, Eugène, 115, 208, 214, 216
Grignola, Jean, 211
Grimaux, Jacques, 168, 223, 400
Groeneveld, Dr. H. L., 73, 225, 299, 342
Gross, Bernard, 143
Grozdoff, André, 173, 269, 298, 425
Gruat, Justin, 225, 361
Guégen, Aimé, 218
Guichard, André, 56, 132, 143
Guillon, Denis, 189–190, 358–359
Guinvarch, Edgar-Félix, 218
Guinvarch, François, 218
Guinvarch, Jean, 218
Gunten, Paul von, 216
Gutzkow, Alfred, 215
Guyon des Diguères, Jean, 143

Haentjens, René, 114, 194, 197
Hagenmuller, Paul, 115, 295
Halkin, Léon-E., 238, 271, 273–274, 275–276, 279, 282, 292, 301, 316
Hassen, Ben Chérif, 124
Hein, Wincenty, 170, 283, 287, 395, 397, 423, 458
Hémery, Pierre, 143
Henner, Auguste, 170, 171, 304
Herrou, François, 143
Hessel, Stéphane, 171, 214, 222, 223–224, 275, 324
Heumann, François, 115, 120, 132, 166
Heuzé, Marcel, 341, 382
Hlavac, Vlada, 135
Hofstein, Jules, 226–227, 238, 272–273, 276, 279, 283, 284, 294, 300–301, 368–369

Inchauspé, Pierre, 184, 193

Jacob, Raymond, 59, 63, 70, 194, 197
Jacob, Simone, 238, 276, 326, 334
Jacquin, Pierre, 170
Janek, 110
Jansch, 134, 284
Jazbinsek, Joseph, 138
Jelinek, 141
John, Rudolf, 362–363
José, 387
Jouanin, Georges, 138, 386
Jougier, Georges, 184, 187
Jourdain, Roger, 185
Jourdren, Joseph, 158, 192, 203
Julien, Henri, 86
Julitte, Pierre, 134, 165, 331

Kaczmarek, Hans, 110
Katz, Raphael, 452
Kemeter, Kurt, 63
Kielar, Wieslaw, 229–230, 237, 343–344, 380, 381, 385
Kientzler, Alphonse, 236
Kilian, Joseph, 424
Klein, Marc, 238
Koch, Justus, 391
Koehren, Maurice, 69
Korenfeld, Élie, 132
Korwin-Krokowski, J.B. de, 110, 270
Kroneberg, August, 88
Kump, Aleksander, 144
Künder, Emil, 230, 429, 430
Kuntz, Albert, 1, 88, 125–126, 150, 156, 161, 174, 270, 297, 424, 432, 438–439

La Falaise, Richard de, 219
La Guéronnière, Jean de, 86
Lacoste, Gabriel, 134, 164, 388–389
Lacour, Alfred, 136
Lafond, Étienne, 7, 203–204, 212, 213, 216, 217–218, 219, 337–338, 378, 392–393
Lagey, Paul, 198, 199
Lalba, Abel, 86
Lambert, 215
Lamothe, Xavier, 114
Lançon, Robert, 221
Lanemajou, Jean, 86
Langbein, Hermann, 3, 43, 45, 89, 108, 110, 171, 172–173, 237, 433
Lange, Marcel, 218
Lapoyade, Alain de, 124, 187, 346, 350
Laroche, André, 185
Lassus, Jean, 115, 279, 299
Latappy, François, 124
Latry, Roger, 165, 269, 331, 332
Laurent, Eugène, 340
Lauth, Claude, 148, 169, 173, 268–270, 331
Laval, René, 73
Lavallard, Charles, 36
Le Bris, Gilbert, 218
Le Goupil, Paul, 8, 163, 164, 168–169, 227, 362–363, 401, 505

Le Lionnais, François, 143, 339
Le Puillandre, 158
Leboucher, Marcel, 391
Leciejewski, Boleslas, 225, 361
Legrand, André, 87
Leineweber, Ludwig, 88
Lemière, Dr. Maurice, 73, 299, 302, 303, 315
Lemoine, Robert, 171, 224
Lemoine, Valentin, 86
Lenoir, Georges, 299, 316
Lepinay, Robert de, 114
Lepretre, Marcel, 124
Leroy, Gustave, 134, 164, 166, 173–174, 299, 440
Leschi, Marien, 156, 164, 331
Leteuil, Marc, 185
Letourneux, Victor, 223
Levi, Primo, 238, 356
Lévy, Louis, 380
Lhoste, Robert, 346
Liedekerke, Baudouin de, 279
Liedekerke, Guillaume de, 279
Lisle, Xavier de, 114, 148
Litomisky, Otakar, 43, 63, 80, 89, 135, 382
Lizeaux, Albert, 86
Lizeaux, André, 86
Lizeaux, Pierre, 86
Lobstein, André, 7, 115, 160, 161, 279, 299–300, 302, 505
London, Artur, 431, 433
Lucas, Pierre, 132
Luzius, 297

Maho, Pierre, 29, 159, 270–272, 282–283, 293, 294, 300, 303, 314, 315, 316
Maillard, Jacques, 299
Maire, Marc, 185
Maisonnial, Antoine, 86
Maisonnial, Pierre, 86
Maistriaux, Férnand, 223, 344, 345, 347, 348–350
Maloubier, Alfred, 86
Mandelbaum, 215
Manhès, Frédéric-Henri, 168
Manhès, Frédéric, 426
Marchand, Claude, 207
Marie, André, 426
Marienne, Edmond, 219
Marillier, Jean, 198, 355
Maris, Louis, 219
Maronneau, Lucien, 90, 194, 198
Marquet, Guy, 343
Martin, Marcel, 65, 157–158, 195
Martin-Chauffier, Louis, 326, 427, 430
Marty, Guy, 193, 217
Massoni, Carlo, 118
Masure, Henri, 219
Mathieu, Marcel, 302
Mattéoli, Jean, 326
"Maufaix," 168
Maupoint, Jacques, 133, 166, *253*
Mazeau, Antonin, 86

Mazellier, Georges, 199
Méfret, Joannès, 70, 194
Merker, Paul, 431, 433
Meunier, Pierre, 124
Mével, Louis, 114
Mialet, Jean, 7, 114, 157, 158, 333, 449; at Bergen-Belsen, 328; deaths at camp, 79–80, 85; evacuation, 323; friendships, 194; Harzungen, 194, 195, 196, 197, 199; living conditions, 58–59, 328; repatriation, 333; *Revier,* 279, 323; working conditions, 87, 196, 197
Michel, Jean, 72, 279, 301, 331, 333, 441; at Bergen-Belsen, 328, 331; bureaucracy, 155; escapes, 301; evacuations, 323, 328; repatriation, 333; resistance within camp, 171, 172–173, 268, 269–270, 279, 285–286, 297, 298; *Revier,* 72, 73, 169, 198, 328; transports of prisoners, 77–78; working conditions, 68; writing of, ix, 441
Michelet, Edmond, 427
Miller, Serge, 128, 201–202, 205, 207, 211–213, 214, 216, 219, 266–267, 324
Minguet, Marcel, 388–389
Miribel, Raymond de, 70, 78, 143, 382
Montrieux, Étienne Bordeaux, 78
Morand, Guy, 138
Morel, René, 73, 161, 279, 299, 345
Moutel, André, 170
Moz, Ernesto, 118

Naegelé, Maurice, 165, 173, 268–270, 425
Navaro-Mora, Léon, 133
Navet, Yvon, 143
Nérot, Emile, 59, 65, 146
Neumann, Heinz, 385
Nicholaï, 172, 173
Nicola, Clément-Robert, 8, 196, 271, 282, 294, 315, 316, 505
Nicolas, Johnny, 225, 383
Nimwegen, Erich, 240
Noël, Jacques, 133
Normand, Jacques, 282, 283, 294, 302

Oesch, Max, 185, 205, 215, 216, 218, 219, 336–337

Pagnier, Paul, 136
Pahor, Boris, 279
Patte, Marcel, 187
Patzer, Tadek, 110
Paucard, André, 86
Paucard, François, 86
Paul, Marcel, 168, 426
Paylon, Harry, 380
Pernot, Gaston, 170, 299
Perrin, Marcel, 218
Perrot, Bernard, 187
Pescadère, Georges, 156, 216
Peskar, Anton, 144
Petit, Jean, 199, 299
Petit, Marcel, 73, 124, 161, 167, 168, 169, 171–173, 228, 299

Pétré, Yves, 283
Petrenko, Nicolas, 269–270
Peuleve, 224
Pichot, Gérard, 158, 343
Pichot, Léonce, 158, 343
Pierrel, Marcel, 62, 136
Piétrois, Lucien, 219
Piguet, Xavier, 359
Pinault, Pierre, 174, 241, 242, 323
Pineau, Christian, 168, 223, 400, 426
Pintière, Maurice de la, 114, 153; drawings by, 246, 259
Ploton, Robert, 427
Pointe, Pierre, 194
Poiré, François, 195
Poiteau, Michel, 238, 280
Pontoizeau, Andrès, 136–137, 339, 341–342, 343
Porocevalec, 238
Pouget, Antoine, 86
Poupault, Jacques, 161, 165, 173, 268, 279, 285, 292–293, 294, 301, 331
Pouzet, Richard, 143, 382, 393–394, 440
Predi, Roger, 174, 241, 242
Priser, Paul, 133
Pröll, Fritz, 73, 116, 150, 160–161, 174, 270, 279, 297, 439
Pujol, Pierre, 174
Puppo, Joseph, 268

Ramet, Gabriel, 280
Ramillon, Bernard, 132, 133, 142
Ranchain, Marcel, 148
Raoul-Duval, Guy, 43, 56, 114, 132, 133, 137, 138, 140, 143, 145, 241, 328
Rassinier, Paul, 124–125, 127, 152, 160, 161, 163, 168, 187, 343, 426–427, 444, 471
Ratineaud, Fernand, 86
Raymond, 196
Reimann, Claude, 79
Reimann, Marius, 79
Rémy, Jean, 199
Renard, Jean-Paul, 135, 137, 153, 166–167, 341, 382, 427, 437; religious activities, 166–167, 288
Renouard, Jean-Pierre, 326–327, 334
Renty, Robert de, 219
Reschke, Erich, 429, 430, 433
Retaureau, Henri, 219
Ribault, André, 135, 137, 140, 141, 289, 291, 295, 296, 298, 299, 339
Richet, Olivier, 148, 163–164, 169
Rieg, Jean, 59, 75, 78, 133
Riquet, Michel, 430
Roche, Germain, 134
Rogerie, André, 7, 40, 76, 78, 86, 114, 276, 280–281, 391; at Boelcke Kaserne, 280–281; bureaucracy, 155; deaths, 79, 218, 237–238, 276; identity number, 40, 114; liberation, 354–356, 391; *Schonung,* 76; transports of prisoners, 78; writing of, 354, 402
Rohmer, Alfred, 230
Ropers, Georges, 226

Roulard, Robert, 275, 299, 342, 343
Roure, Rémy, 426, 430
Rousseau, Fernand, 147
Rousset, David, 168, 222, 229, 230, 344, 380, 425–426,
    427, 429–430, 433, 457, 468
Roye, René de, 219
Rozan, Pierre, 7, 77–78, 155, 169, 299, 387
Runki, 297
Ruskon, 285

Sadron, Charles, 115, 130; camp living conditions,
    60–62, 127, 152, 156, 280, 283–284; convoys from
    Auschwitz and Gross Rosen, 274; crematorium
    description, 158; evacuations, 323; executions, 286;
    factory work, 134, 136, 138, 141, 284, 289–290;
    friendships, 143, 296; last day of camp, 298, 299; on
    news sources, 144; refuge by evacuated ministry, 241;
    Von Braun's meeting with, 105–106
Saint-Marc, Hélie de, 228
Sanchidrian, Georges, 435
Sänger, Jack, 199
Scharf, Hermann, 300
Schimmeck, Arthur, 202
Schmidt, Georges, 156, 383
Schmidt, Rudi, 88
Schmidt, Willy, 88, 146, 424
Schmitt, Albert, 115
Schneider, Ernst, 72–73, 160–161, 279, 297
Schock, André (Chevalier), 165, 197, 331
Schreck, Paul, 428
Schreve, Guido, 155, 387
Schweitzer, Karl, 73, 88
Schwertz, François, 115, 132
Scola, Giovanni, 118
Sczymczak, Ludwig, 88, 89, 149, 270, 297, 424
Ségelle, Pierre, 165, 215, 336–337, 435
Seifert, Willi, 432
Sellier, André, ix–x, 40, 130, 134, 141, 143, 144–145,
    151, 157, 323, 341, 382, 389–391, 444, 454, 457
Sellier, Louis, 6, 426
Semprun, Jorge, 36, 37, 119, 168, 223, 400–401, 431
Serge, 363
Sermot, Serge, 65
Sesmaisons, Jean de, 114, 185, 194, 197, 355, 358
Simonin, 79
Skodas, Otto, 283
Slansky, Rudolph, 431
Sommer, Peter, 138
Sommerhausen, Jean, 391
Soubirous, Georges, 7, 65, 70, 114, 153, 157, 339, 444
Souquet, René, 8, 143, 151, 389–391
Spitz, Charles, 120, 121, 127, 153–154, 285, 323, 328,
    331
Sprung, Gabriel, 337
Sudreau, Pierre, 426
Svetic, Franc, 144

Tartinville, Guy, 114, 133
Tauzin, Jean-Henry, 183, 184, 193, 205, 207–208,
    214–215, 216, 299, 314, 316

Terral, Louis-Clément, 216
Thälmann, Ernst, 438
Theo, 210, 211
Thibault, Roland. *See* Korenfeld, Elie
Thiercelin, Robert, 388–389
Thomas, Eugène, 426
Thomas, Georg, 88, 89, 149, 270, 297, 424
Thomas, Michel, 274–275, 282, 301
Thomas, Yeo, 224
Tinet, Emile, 218
Tinet, Étienne, 218
Traxler, Josef, 363
Tricoire, Roger, 78
Tumerelle, Hubert, 225, 361

Ulbricht, 224
Untereiner, Alfred (Birin), 124, 134, 152, 154, 156, 166,
    169, 171–173, 269, 328, 331, 333, 427
Uyttenhoef, Joseph, 337

Vagnon, Pierre, 70
Vaillant-Couturier, Marie-Claude, 381
Vallier, Louis, 185
Valois, Georges, 326
Van der Meer, Georges, 302
Van Dijk, Albert, 80–81, 187, 350–351, 449, 450
Van Hoey, Albert, 7, 225–226, 446, 448, 449, 450, 453
Vedel, Charles, 238, 276, 279–280, 320
Vern, Jacques, 71, 207
Vidal, Michel, 370
Vincent, Rémy, 219, 379–380
Virondeau, Georges, 56, 216, 317, 336
Voisin, Jean, 147, 185, 324–325
Voland, Maurice, 218
Vuillermoz, Albert, 136

Waitz, Dr., 334
Walenta, Richard, 202, 424
Walter, Pierre, 208, 224
Wautrecht, Raymond, 7, 8, 196, 197, 378, 391–392
Weil, 236
Weil, Simone, 238, 276, 326, 334
Wellner, 134, 284, 289
Wells, 134
Wexler, Wolf, 193, 355–356, 391
Wiesel, Elie, 36, 120
Wieviorka, Annette, 334, 402–403, 434
Wodruzeck, 215
Woussen, Joseph, 117, 174, 339, 341, 383
Wyglendatz, Eric (Anna), 153, 323

Yanouk, 323

Zadravec, Matija, 78
Ziller, Pierre, 154, 165
Zilliox, Raymond, 136
Zwiener, Willy, 149–150

Index of Persons Other Than Prisoners

Akselrad, Richard, 37
Allen, Michael Thad, 459
Andrae, Kurt, 423
August, Dorothea, 454
Axster, Herbert, 410

Baer, SS-Sturmbannführer Richard, 284, 423, 469
Ball, George, 414
Beauchamp, Georges, 370
Becher, Kurt, 329
Becker, Col. Karl Emil, 20–21, 23
Bernadotte, Count Folke, 361, 374, 375, 381
Biberfeld, Ernest S., 37
Billig, Joseph, 457
Bischoff, SS-Obersturmbannführer Helmut, 268, 425, 469
Blochwitz, Mrs. Bloch von, 347
Bonhoeffer, Dietrich, 298
Bormann, Martin, 97, 375, 422
Bornemann, Manfred, 30, 31–32, 65, 88, 193, 201, 213, 220, 439, 445, 448, 458–459, 505
Bradley, Gen. Omar Nelson, 401
Brähne, Werner, drawings of, 246
Braun, 346
Brauny, Hauptscharführer Erhard, 344–345, 346–347, 424, 469–470
Brayard, Florent, 444
Bringer, Heinz, 420
Brinkmann, Otto, 202, 424
Brodniewicz, Bruno, 210
Bromley, Maj., 411
Broszat, Martin, 439, 457, 458
Busta, SS-Hauptscharführer Erwin ("Horse Head"), 139, 255, 286, 371, 372, 425, 470

Canaris, Adm. Wilhelm, 298
Castille, William, 313–314
Chandon-Moët, Paul, 173, 185, 269
Chapman (Major), 33, 329, 332
Churchill, Winston, 29
Clay, Gen. Lucius, 413
Crossman, Richard, 426

De Bouard, Michel, 443
De Gaulle, Gen. Charles, 333, 420

Degenkolb, Gerhard, 24, 25, 29, 49, 91, 104, 470
Delestraint, Charles, 298
D'Hainaut, Brigitte, 443
Dieckmann, Götz, 439
Dietzsch, Arthur, 224
Ding-Schuler, Erwin, 224
Dönitz, Karl, 97, 375, 376, 413
Dornberger, Gerhard, 470
Dornberger, Walter, 21–27, 30, 50–51, 52, 470; Dora role, 30, 68, 91, 98, 100, 101, 104, 105; evacuations, 50–51, 91, 240, 410; and Hitler assassination attempt, 103; Hitler's relationship with, 52; Peenemünde, 21–27, 240; postwar activities, 372, 410, 415–416, 418, 420; V2 rocket firings, 104, 105, 133
Dorsch, Xaver, 14, 98
Drung, Roman, 284
Drunon, Maurice, 330
Du Bois de Vroylande, Marie-Claire, 7, 449

Eicke, Theodor, 15, 16, 38, 237, 278
Eisenhower, Gen. Dwight, 401, 414
Eisfeld, Rainer, 445, 459

Figge, Paul, 148
Finkenzeller, George, 28, 256
Fleck, Egon W., 426
Fleischer, Karl Otto, 411
"Folette," 153, 330
Förschner, SS-Sturmbannführer Otto, 50, 53, 100, 126, 140, 156, 268–269, 284, 422, 423, 438–439, 470
Francois-Poncet, Henri, 334
Fréjafon, Dr., 326, 334
Frentz, Walter, 243–244; photographs by, 251–254
Friedeburg, Hans von, 376
Fröbe, Rainer, 457
Fromm, Friedrich, 103
Funk, Walter, 97

Gaïdoukov, Gen., 418–419
Galbraith, John Kenneth, 414
Georg, Enno, 457
Germain, Jean-René, 439–440
Glücks, Richard, 16, 17–18

Goebbels, Joseph, 12, 97, 375
Goethe, Johann Wolfgang, 438
Goldhagen, Daniel J., 368, 468
Göring, Hermann, 15, 97, 99, 180, 240, 375, 414, 422
Greese, Irma, 329
Grihon, Renée, 454
Grotewohl, Otto, 438
Gröttrup, Helmut, 98, 416, 418–419, 420
Guderian, Gen. Heinz, 97

Haas, Adolf, 325, 327
Hackett, David A., 432
Hamill, Maj. James, 411, 417, 418, 420
H. D., 315, 316
Heinkel, Ernst, 414
Herbert, Ulrich, 457–458, 465
Hermann, Rudolf, 22, 52, 418
Hettlage, Karl, 49
Heydrich, Reinhard, 15
Himmler, Heinrich, 15, 16–17, 47, 103, 237, 267, 329,
    379; Buchenwald constructions by, 42; negotiations
    with Bernadotte, 375, 381; political machinations of,
    26, 98; Red Cross arrangements with, 361, 374; and
    the World Jewish Congress, 375
Hitler, Adolf: aircraft industry involvement, 180;
    assassination attempt on, 96, 103; final days, 311,
    375–376; rocket program involvement, 23, 52, 99,
    101, 240; scorched-earth policy, 287, 289, 298, 312;
    and Speer, 13–14, 97, 98, 376
Hochmuth, Peter, 439
Hodges, Courtney Hicks, 242, 310
Hoftoy, Holger, 415
Holtzman, Elizabeth, 441
Holz, 137
Holzmann, Philipp, 125–126
"Horse Head" (Busta), 139, 255, 286, 371, 372, 425, 470
Höss, 202
Hössler, Franz, 327–328, 329, 422, 470
Hunt, Linda, 442
Huzel, Dieter, 289, 410, 411, 420

Jäckel, Eberhard, 450
Jaeger, Joachim, 450
Jeschonneck, suicide of, 12
Jodl, Alfred, 375, 376, 413
Jones, Dr. R. V., 29
Jüttner, SS-Obergruppenführer Hans, 103, 104

Kahr, Dr. Karl, 72, 160, 328, 471
Kaienburg, Herman, 465
Kaltenbrunner, Ernst, 15, 375
Kammler, Brigadeführer Dr. Hans, 104–105, 240, 242,
    290, 410, 471; Auschwitz construction by, 16; Dora
    camp role, 30, 49, 53, 111, 116, 123, 140, 240, 442,
    465–466; Harzungen and Ellrich, 191, 192, 199; and
    postwar trials, 242, 423; responsibility for deaths,
    221; rocket program role, 49, 53, 90, 91, 99, 104–105,
    240, 290, 442; work sites, 179
Keating, F. A., 349–350

Keitel, Marshal Wilhelm, 97, 375, 376, 379, 413
Kessel, Joseph, 36
Kettler, Kurt, 50, 53, 100, 192
Kimenthal, Max M., 37
Kleeman, Hermann, 210, 284, 320, 327
Klose, Cornelia, 450
Koch, Friedrich, 97
Kogon, Eugen, ix–x, 3, 37–38, 44, 108, 111, 224, 298,
    421, 425–426, 427, 432–433, 457
Kohler, Pierre, 98, 439–440
Kolb, Eberhard, 457
Koniev, 373
Korolev, Serge, 416, 420, 440
Kramer, Joseph, 116, 327, 329–330, 422
Kravtchenko, Victor, 429
Krüger, 134, 137, 144, 284
Kuhn, Capt. Joseph, 346, 347
Kummer, 410
Kunze, Heinz, 49, 53, 100, 104
Kurzke (SS doctor), 279, 299, 328

Lammers, Hans, 97
Lamster, Otto, 301
Lang, Fritz, 19
Le Fur, Anne, 8, 505
Le Maner, Yves, 8
Le Turdu, Anne, 444
Leeb, Gen. Emil, 23, 240
Ley, Robert, 375
Lindenberg, 410

Manko, Alexander, 112
Mascolo, Dionys, 370
Masson, Philippe, 11
McGovern, James, 103, 289, 440–441
McNarney, Joseph, 413
Michel, Henri, 443
Miel, 346, 347
Milch, Field Marshal Erhard, 24, 25, 97, 99
Milz, Col. Walter, 346, 347
Mitterand, François, 370
Monicke, Ruth, 446, 448
Möser, Hans, 340, 424, 471
Moureu, 419–420
Mussolini, overthrow of, 12

Naasner, Walter, 459
Neander, Joachim, 8, 65, 395, 396, 397–398, 445, 454,
    505
Neu, Karl Wilhelm, 50, 64, 91, 125, 192
Neufeld, Michael J., 19, 65, 240, 444–445, 505;
    commentary by, ix–x
Niethammer, Lutz, 430–431, 432
Nitze, Paul, 414
Nucera, Louis, 441

Oberth, Hermann, 19, 420

Paraz, Albert, 427
Patton, George Smith, 310–311, 401
Pauler, Stefan, 201
Pelny, Kurt, 439
Petersen, Walter, 25
Piech, Anton, 148
Pieck, Wilhelm, 429
Pingel, Falk, 457
Piskunov, Mikhail, 112
Pister, SS-Oberführer Hermann, 126, 150, 268, 422
Plaza, Dr. Heinrich, 72, 116, 423
Pohl, Oswald, 16, 17, 325, 376
Porsche, Ferdinand, 414
Porter, Richard, 410, 412, 415, 417
Praeger, Frederick A., 432

Rees, Eberhard, 411
Reichel, Peter, 447
Resnais, Alain, 113
Ribbentrop, Joachim von, 375
Rickhey, Georg, 100, 123, 418, 421, 423, 424, 471
Riedel, Klaus, 998
Riedel, Walter, 21
Ritz, Hans Joachim, 202
Roach, William E., 328, 329, 331, 332
Röhm, Ernst, 15
Rokossovsky, Konstantin, 382
Rolland, Maurice, 440
Rommel, Erwin, 12
Rosenbaum, 441
Rosenberg, Lt. Albert G., 37, 426, 432
Rossmann, Gen. Josef, 100, 104
Rovan, Joseph, 448
Rudolph, Arthur, ix, 21, 26, 49, 68, 91, 100, 418, 423,
    424, 441–442, 445, 471–472
Ruland, Bernd, 440
Rusinek, Bernd, 467

Sampson, Alfred H., 37
Sanchidrian, Mrs., 435
Sander, Kriminal-Assistant and SS-Oberscharführer
    Ernst, 268–270, 284, 285, 286, 297, 425, 472
Sandys, Duncan, 28–29
Sauckel, Fritz, 14, 97, 111
Sauer, 99
Saur, Karl Otto, 14, 25, 30, 53, 99, 241, 376, 472
Sawatzki, Albin, 25–26, 49–50, 53, 54, 91, 100, 130, 132,
    138, 414–415, 424, 472
Schacht, Hjalmar, 414
Schellenberg, Walter, 374, 375
Scheufelen, Dr. Klaus, 371–372
Schneeman, Günther, 215, 216
Schneider, Erich, 103
Schulte, Jan-Erik, 459
Schumann, Dr. Erich, 20
Sellier, Caroline, 8
Sellier, Jean, 505
Sereny, Gitta, 98
Sher, Neal, 442
Simon, Dr., 128–129

Simon, Wilhelm, 424, 441–442, 472
Simon, William, 371
Simpson, 242, 336, 358
Sofsky, Wolfgang, 44–45
Somerhausen, Christine, 443
Speer, Albert, 13–14, 17, 29–30, 52–53, 96–98, 128, 375,
    376, 379; camp construction, 125–126; Hitler's
    relationship with, 13–14, 97, 98, 376; illness of,
    97–98; photographs commissioned by, 243–244; on
    prisoner living conditions, 69, 89–90, 125; rivalries
    with "inner circle," 5, 97, 103; rocket program role,
    23–26, 49–50, 53, 97–98, 100, 471; and scorched-
    earth policy, 287; trial of, 422
Staver, Maj. Robert, 411, 412, 415
Steinhoff, Erich, 22, 100
Steinhoff, Ernst, 418, 420
Storch, Paul, 100, 101, 104

Tenenbaum, Edward A., 426
Thiel, Walter, 22, 29
Thiele, Gerhard, 346–347
Tillion, Germaine, 443
Todt, Dr. Fritz, 13, 14, 23
Toftoy, Col. Holger, 411, 416, 418, 420
Trichel, Col. Gervais William, 411, 415

Udet, Ernst, 21

Von Blomberg, Werner, 20
Von Brauchitsch, Walter, 20
Von Braun, Eva, 376
Von Braun, Magnus, 98, 410
Von Braun, Sigismund, 440
Von Braun, Wernher, 20–22, 25, 29, 51, 53, 91, 100,
    101–102, 105–106, 372, 421, 469; archive protection
    by, 289; arrest and release of, 97–98, 416;
    evacuations, 239–241, 290, 410; honors accorded to,
    440; postwar activities, 410, 415–418, 420, 439–440;
    postwar controversies over, 439–440, 445; and
    prisoners, 105–106, 138, 445; responsibility for
    deaths, 421; SS registration, 22, 26
Von Friedeburg, Hans, 376
Von Richtofen, Wolfram, 21

Wagner, Jens-Christian, commentary by, 455–468
Walter, Wilhelm, 186
Wehling, Franz, 49
Weisshaupt, Manfred, 439
Wirths, Eduard, 284, 472
Woodruff, Louis, 411
Wormser-Migot, Olga, 443, 457

Ximenes, Dr., 394

Zanssen, Leo, 22, 26, 51, 103
Zhukov, Marshal Georgi Konstantinovich, 373
Zweiner, Willy, 424
Zwerger, Sepp, 210

Subject Index

"À l'usine de Dora" (Sadron), 134

A2 rockets, 21

A4 rockets, 21–26; test launchings, 25. *See also* V2 rockets.

Abteilung Kontrolle, 133–134

Achersleben, 364–365

Administration, Nazi Party, 13, 346, 374, 375–376, 460, 466, 467–468; rocket program, 53, 97–98, 104–106. *See also* Camp administration.

AEG Kommando, 208, 331

Air war. *See* Aircraft industry; Allied bombing of Germany; Rocket program.

Aircraft industry, 99, 179–184, 222–223, 230–231, 377, 466

Allied bombing of Germany, 12, 13, 28–30, 50, 52, 102–103, 283–284, 345, 362; British intelligence, 28–29; Dora, 295–296; Éperlecques, 52; evacuation transport trains, 290–294, 295, 321–322; Operation Crossbow, 102–103, 440–441; Peenemünde, 28–30, 50, 57, 102; prisoner deaths due to, 291–294, 362, 397–398

Allies, 37, 421, 425–426; administration of camps, 314–316, 331–332; intelligence, 28–29, 102–103, 440; liberation of camps, 35–38, 144–145, 242, *260,* 280, 327, 328–330, 421; offensives in France, 96, 103–104, 145; offensives in Germany, 235–236, 239, 240, 242, 283–284, 307–308, 310–318, 336, 342, 345–346, 349–351, 354–356, 357, 358, 359, 364, 367, 369, 373–374, 378, 379, 382, 383–385, 387, 389, 390, 402, *518–519. See also* Allied bombing of Germany; Liberation of camps; WWII aftermath.

Alsace-Lorraine, prisoners from, 115–116

Americans: control of Dora factory, 408, 410–412; liberation of camps, 242, *260,* 303, 312–318, 328–329, 380–381, 401–402, 426; occupation of Germany, 408–409, 413; offensives on German territory, 242, *263,* 310–318, 324, 328–329, 336, 342, 345–346, 349–350, 354–356, 357, 358, 359, 373–374, 379, 382, 383–384, 387, 390, *518–519;* Operation Overcast, 410–412, 414–415, 416–418, 420, 440–441; Soviet Union and, 409, 432, 439; war criminal trial role, 5–6, 421–422

Ancillary camp facilities, 156–158

Anhydrit work site, 182–183, 195–196, 197, 204, 206–207, 220, 221, *517*

Anhydrite, 31–32, 182, 447, 452

Antiaircraft missile development at Peenemünde, 105, 371

"Anus mundi" (Kielar), 380

Arbeitsstatistik, 39, 80, 154; burning of papers, 295; employment organization by, 154, 179; transport organization by, 87–89

Archives of rocket construction, 289, 410–412

Arms policies, 23

Army Ordnance Office (Heereswaffenamt), 20–21

Arrest of Nazi Party members, 97–98

Arrest of prisoners within camp, 165, 171, 173–174, 268–270

Art in camp, 152, 153, 158, 166, 243–244, *245–250. See also* Music; Writing in camps.

Artern, 365–366, *524*

Artillerymen and the rocket program, 20–23, 90, 100, 133–134

Assassination attempt on Hitler, 96, 103

Assembly-line production of rockets, 24–28, 131–133, 403

Association of Political and Resistance Deportees of Dora, Ellrich, Harzungen, and Annex Kommandos, 435–437

Associations of survivors, 6–7, 434–445, 449–450; camp commemoration initiatives, 448–449; Dora association, 449–450; Dora-Ellrich association, 435–437; Kommando associations, 6, 435; publications by, 4, 377, 436–437, 443–444; service activities, 435–436. *See also* Commemoration of camps.

Auschwitz, 236–238, 272–276, 284, 326, 378

Autonomy of Dora camp, 265–266

Autopsies, 277–278

B3 (project), 182–183, 195–196, 197, 204, 206–207, 220, 221, *517*

B11 (project), 159, 182–183, 195, 204, 206, 220–221

B12 (project), 182, 202, 204, 206, 208–209, 210–211, 220, 221

B13 (project), 183, 204, 221

B17 (project), 182, 204, 221

Backfire (Operation), 414–415

Barracks construction, 67–68, 123–128

Baubrigade Kommandos. *See* Work sites.

Beatings, 136, 137–139, 170–171, 200, 277; death from, 87, 219

Belgian prisoners, 116–117, 195
Belongings of prisoners, 155, 218. *See also* Mail; Thefts of food.
Berga, 365–366
Bergen-Belsen, 325–335, *520–523;* deaths, 398; evacuation of, 312; evacuations to, 319–328, 398; hygiene, 334, 391; liberation, 328–330; maps, *520–523;* mortality rate, 78, 334, 335; numbers of prisoners, 326; *Revier*, 332, 391; transports to, 78–79, 86, 184, 217, 297; trial of officials, 422
Berlin: occupation of, 408, 413; siege of, 373–374
Berlin Wall, fall of, 446–447
Black market, ROGES activities, 33–34
Blacks (prisoners), 40, 202
Blankenburg camps, 225–226, 266, 353, 360–362, *522*
Blasting rock, 65–66
Block organization, 150–151
Blockältester, 13, 150–151, 152
Blockführer, 38, 151, 152
Boelcke Kaserne camp, 270–272, 280–281, 291–294, 301, 312–313, 317, 326, 397, 401–402; commemoration, 452; maps, *517*; trial of officials, 422–423. *See also* Nordhausen.
Bohemia, convoys through, 369–371
Bombing. *See* Allied bombing of Germany; Rocket program.
Brauny convoy, 344–345, 346
Britain. *See* Allied bombing of Germany; British.
British: administration of camps, 331–332: intelligence, 28–29, 440–441; liberation of camps by, 329–330; occupation of Germany, 409; offensives in Germany, 390, *518–519;* rocket program interest, 415–416
British prisoners, 426
Buchenwald, 35–46, 220; administration, 38–39; associations of survivors, 434–435; commemoration, 447–448, 451, 453; convoys from, 45–46; cremations, 81–82; Dora compared to, 62–63, 162–167, 400–401, 438–439; Dora's links with, 35, 54–57, 88, 90, 149, 265–266; evacuation, 365–366, 369–371; industrial facilities, 42–46; liberation of, 35–38, 242, 438; living conditions, 35–38, 41–42, 43, 57, 123; political activity within, 167–169, 224, 426; postwar, 422, 423, 425–433, 437–439; prisoner categories, 40–41, 111; prisoner identification numbers, 39–40; prisoner mortality rates, 36; prisoner nationalities, 55–57, 426; prisoner transport, 42, 55–57, 377; quarantine, 41–42; statistics, 44–46; trial of officials, 422, 423; working conditions, 42
"Buchenwald Mahnung und Verpflichtung" (ed. Bartel), 433, 438
Buchenwald Report, The (Kogon), 425–426, 432–433
Bünemann Kommando, 133, 143
Bunkers: punishments bunker, 170–171; Watten Bunker, 24; Wizernes bunker, 52, *509*
Bureaucracy, 153–156, 218, 275–276, 278; burning of records, 295. *See also* Administration, Nazi Party; Arbeitsstatistik.
Burning of prisoners, *262*, 347–349. *See also* Cremations; Crematorium.
Burning of records, 295

Camouflage, 207, 237. *See also* Security measures.
Camp administration, 38–45, 95, 149–162, 180, 284–287, 294, 326–327, 465–468; Allied administration, 314–316, 331–332; Arbeitsstatistik, 39, 80, 154, 179; belongings of prisoners, 155, 218; block organization, 150–151; bureaucracy, 153–156, 218, 275–276, 278; corpse disposal, 79–80, 158, 171, 183, 218, 226, 228, *256–260*, 273, 274–276, 280, 313, 326–327, 341, 348, 380, 400; dismantling of Dora and, 294; Ellrich, 201–202, 210; evacuations, 240, 284; extraction of teeth from corpses, 218; factory, 68–69, 90, 133–148; by Luftwaffe, 194, 195, 201, 202, 215, 221, 300, 371–372; Politische Abteilung, 154–155; by prisoners, 149–156; by Wehrmacht, 375, 466–467; Woffleben, 210; work sites, 99, 180. *See also* Bureaucracy; Evacuation of camps; *Kapos*; Living conditions; *Meister*; Prisoner administrators; SS (Schutzstaffel); Transportation of prisoners; Working conditions.
Cannibalism, 212–213, 380
Canteen, 156
Care packages, 62–63, 76, 77
Casualties. *See* Deaths; Mortality rate.
Centre d'études des projectiles autopropulsés (CEPA), 420
CEPA (Centre d'études des projectiles autopropulsés), 420
"Chant de déportés" ("Prisoners' Song") (Chlique), 42
Child prisoners, 203–204, 463
"Chronik des Lagers Ellrich 1944/1945" (Bornemann), 445, 448
Cinema, 157
CIOS (Combined Intelligence Objectives Subcommittee), 412
Citadel (Operation), 11–12
Civilian clothing for escapes, 387, 389
Civilian workers, 183, 185–186, 219–220, 229, 267, 289, 290, 311–312, 313; *Meister*, 87, 136, 137–138, 140, 142; as news sources, 144; secretaries, 135; as witnesses, 423–424, 459–460
Civilians. *See* Civilian workers; German civilians.
Clothing, 30, 211–212, 216, 220, 275–276, 281, 295, 304, 338, 362; civilian clothing for escapes, 387, 389
Code names, 53–54, 180–181, 265–266, 417
Cold living conditions in camps, 60–62, 171, 183, 188, 197, 241, 272–274, 282
Colditz, 365–366
Combined Intelligence Objectives Subcommittee (CIOS), 412
Comit, européen de Dora, Ellrich, Harzungen et Ko "Pour la mémoire," 449
Commemoration of camps, 437–439, 446–454, 460; Buchenwald, 447–448, 451, 453; Dora tunnels, 451–454, 455–456; Ellrich, 448–449, 451, 454; Jugend für Dora, 454; pilgrimages, 438–439, 454. *See also* Associations of survivors.
Communism, in concentration camps, 43, 88–89, 110, 114, 126, 150, 153, 161, 164, 167–168, 174, 184, 268, 297–298, 402, 407, 426, 438–439; and postwar camp considerations, 428–433, 439, 447–448
Compiègne camp, 112–113

Complicity: among prisoners in camp deaths, 87–89, 288; of German civilians with SS, 459–460, 466–468; of SS with prisoners, 266–267, 298

Compulsory Work Service, 12

Concealment of Dora, 5–6, 439–441, 443–444, 458–459

Concentration camps, 15, 16–18, 43–46, 116, 235, 455–468; administration, 38–45, 95, 149–162; aircraft industry and, 99; communism in, 43, 88–89, 110, 114, 126, 150, 153, 161, 164, 167–168, 174, 184, 268, 297–298, 402, 407, 426, 428–433, 438, 439; evolution of, 43–45, 460–462; French inquiries into, 430; identification numbers, 39–40, 80–81, 378; identification triangles, 40–41; images of, x, 3–4, 6–7, 447–449, 457–460; mortality rates, 17–18, 28, 36; postwar, 425–433, 437–439, 446–454; prisoner categories, 40–41, 107–108; socialism in, 43; trusteeship of, 450–451; work allotments, 39, 128–129, 154, 179; WVHA, 16. *See also* Associations of survivors; Death camps; Gulags; Liberation of camps; Numbers of prisoners; Prisoner nationalities; Transportation of prisoners; Work sites; *individual camps by name.*

Concrete pouring, 66–67

"Conditions de vie et de travail des prisonniers dans le camp de concentration Dora-Mittelbau" (Hein), 423

Construction at new work sites, 179–221. *See also* Construction of camp; Construction of factory.

Construction of camp, 123–128, 150, 157; design, 124–125, 126, 127, 150–151, 156–158, 250, 461–462, 512–513; fencing, 124; Kuntz's role, 125–126; sanitation, 123, 127; Schlempp construction group, 125–126; Speer's role, 125–126; SS barracks, 67–68. *See also* Construction at new work sites; Construction of factory.

Construction of factory, 54–55, 64–67; design, 64, 68, 131–133, 505, 514–515

Convoys from camps. *See* Evacuation of camps; Transportation of prisoners.

Corpse disposal, 79–81, 158, 171, 183, 218, 226, 228, 256–260, 273, 274–276, 280, 313, 326–327, 341, 348, 350, 380, 400; after bombings, 29; cannibalism and, 212–213, 380; identifying corpses, 80–81; tooth extraction from corpses, 218

Crafts by prisoners, 143, 207

Cremations, 81–82

Crematorium, 158, 258

Criminal activity files, 154–155

Crossbow (Operation), 102–103, 440–441

Crossbow and Overcast (McGovern), 440–441

Czech prisoners, 63, 109, 120, 124, 135, 146, 155, 173

Dachau, 130, 421–422

"Danse avec le siècle" (Hessel), 224

"Das Konzentrationslager Mittelbau" (Neander), 445

DAW (Deutsche Ausrustungswerke), 42

Death camps: camouflage of, 207, 237; selection of workers from, 130; transports to, 77–79, 86, 88, 184, 217, 296, 297, 312, 319–328. *See also* Concentration camps.

Death marches, 352–372, 382, 461, 522–525; 365–366, 524; Aschersleben, 364–365, 370–371; Berga, 365–366; Blankenburg, 360–362, 522; Colditz, 365–366; Flöha, 365–366; Gandersheim, 364–365; Günzerode, 358–359; Hadmersleben, 365; Harzungen, 353–356, 365; Langenstein, 362–363, 366, 524; Leitmeritz, 367; maps, 522–525; Neu Stassfurt, 366–367, 524; Rossla, 359; Rottleberode, 360, 523; Sachsenhausen, 379, 523; Saxony, 363–364; Schönebeck, 360; Schwarzheide, 365, 368–369; Sudetenland, 363–364, 368, 525; Thekla, 365; Theresienstadt, 367, 368–369; Wansleben column, 356–357. *See also* Evacuation of camps.

Deaths, 395–404, 462, 463–465; Auschwitz, 237; autopsies, 277–278; beatings causing, 87, 219; Bergen-Belsen, 398; Boelcke Kaserne, 272, 280–281, 312, 401–402; bombings as cause of, 291–294, 362, 397–398; corpse disposal, 79–81, 158, 171, 183, 218, 226, 228, 256–260, 273, 274–276, 280, 291, 313, 326–327, 341, 348, 350, 380, 400; cremation, 81–82, 158, 258; evacuation of camps, 237–238, 272–276, 280, 300, 321–325, 379, 382, 397–398; exhaustion, 79–81, 86, 277–278, 398; food eaten after starvation, 391–392; from rocket firings, 404; identifying corpses, 80–81; Nordhausen, 282–283, 401–402; Peenemünde workers, 29; records of, 154, 155, 423; religious ceremonies, 36, 85, 226, 350; responsibility for, 86–91, 147, 221, 421, 456, 459; in *Schonung*, 76–77; in Strasbourg, 403; transportation of prisoners, 77–79, 86, 88, 217, 272–274, 280, 281, 309–310, 319–328, 337–351, 397; V2 rockets, 404; Wöbbelin, 380. *See also* Executions; Extermination of prisoners; Mortality rate; *Revier.*

Debate over concentration camps (postwar), 425–433

DEFA (Direction des études et fabrications d'armement), 419–420

DEMAG factories, 377

"Déportation et Génocide" (Wieviorka), 402–403, 434

"Der SS Staat" (Kogon), 37, 425–426

Design: Bergen-Belsen, 520; Dora camp, 124–125, 126, 127, 150–151, 156–158, 250, 460–462, 512–515; Ellrich camp, 199, 511, 516; factory, 64, 68, 131–133, 505, 514–515; Harzungen camp, 193–194, 516; *Revier*, 72, 160

Desprez, Georges, 198–199, 353, 360

Deutsche Ausrustungswerke (DAW), 42

Diaries in camp, 194–195

"Die nationalsozialistischen Konzentrationslager 1933–1945" (Broszat), 457

Digging of tunnels: Dora, 31–33, 57, 58, 59, 64, 65–67, 90, 162, 245, 452; work sites, 182–183, 191, 195–198, 206, 207, 220–221, 226, 228, 229

Dining room (Dora), 152

Direction des études et fabrications d'armement, 419–420

Disinfection of prisoners, 60–62, 90, 211–212, 282, 513

Dismantling of Dora, 294–300; burning of records, 295; destruction of equipment, 299; factory shutdown, 289–290. *See also* Evacuation of camps.

Doctors, 72–73, 198, 213–214, 215, 224, 226, 276–278, 279, 284–285, 299–300, 302, 439

Dora: commemoration, 452–454, 455–456, 460;
international committee, 449–450; maps, 505,
510–515; numbers of prisoners, 43–46, 55–57, 60,
113–114, 159, 266; prisoner nationalities, 40–41,
46–47, 55–57, 82–83, 107–121, 143–144; trial of
officials, 422–425

*Dora: In the Hell of the Concentration Camp Where the
Nazi Scientists Prepared for the Conquest of Space*
(Michel and Nucera), ix, 441

"Dora: le cimetière des Français" (Rogerie), 402

Dora, 1943–1945 (d'Hainaut and Somerhausen), 443

Dora KL Mittelbau (Slovenian association of deportees),
443

Dora Kommando (from Dachau), 130

Dora-Ellrich association, 435–437

Dormitories, 59–60, 126–128, 396, 513

Draftsmen, 134, 135

Drawings of camp, 243–244, 245–250

Dungeon Democracy, The (Burney), 426

Dust and noise, 59, 65, 196

Dutch prisoners, 118, 135

EAC (European Advisory Commission), 413

Earthworks projects, 67, 205–206, 226, 228, 246. See
also Digging of tunnels.

Eastern Front, 11–12

Eastern Galicia, 112

Economy, SS involvement in, 16–18, 42, 111, 159, 457,
461–462

Educated prisoners, 105–106, 109, 111–112, 115, 124,
129–130, 134, 135, 143, 164–165, 276–278, 279

Eicke-style camp administration, 38–39, 237, 278

Elecktromechanische Werke GmbH (EW), 104

Electric cable installation, 67, 253

Electrical work, 69–70, 130, 133, 197, 206–207, 208,
228–229, 331

Electricians, 69–70, 130, 197, 206–207, 228–229, 331

Ellrich camp, 191–193, 199–221, 257, 505, 511, 516;
child prisoners, 203–204, 463; commemoration,
448–449, 451; evacuation, 296–297, 319–320, 323,
337–338, 344–345, 357, 523; Harzungen camp
compared to, 195; liberation, 317; living conditions,
200–204, 208–213; maps, 505, 511, 516; mortality
rate, 216–221; numbers of prisoners, 193, 202–203,
204, 265–266; prisoner nationalities, 193, 202; *Revier*,
198–199; Woffleben camp, 208–210, 220, 297,
319–320, 511, 517; Woffleben farm, 192–193;
working conditions, 204–208, 220–221

Employment offices for prisoners, 128–129. See *also*
Arbeitsstatistik.

Engineers, 137–138

Éperlecques, bombing of, 52

Escapes, 170–171, 175, 224, 292–294, 300–302, 304,
324, 345, 346, 354–355, 358–359, 380, 383, 386–391

Essen, Dora trial, 424–425

European Advisory Commission (EAC), 413

European Dora, Ellrich, Harzungen Ko Committee "For
Memory," 449

"European Propulsion Company" (SEP), 420

Evacuation of camps, 235–242, 261–262, 272–276, 284,
294–300, 307–308, 336–372, 373, 463, 521–525;
Artern, 365–366, 524; Aschersleben, 364–365,
370–371; Auschwitz, 236–238, 272–276, 284, 326,
378; Berga, 365–366; Blankenburg camps, 353,
360–362, 522; Buchenwald, 45–46, 365–366,
369–371; Colditz, 365–366; convoys to Bergen-
Belsen, 319–328, 398; deaths, 237–238, 272–276,
280, 300, 321–325, 379, 382, 397–398; Dora, 45–46,
241, 261, 290, 294–300, 336–343, 357–358, 371–372,
381–382, 521–522; Ellrich, 296–297, 337–338,
344–345, 357, 523; Flöha, 365–366; Gandersheim,
364–365, 369–371; Gross Rosen, 238–239, 272–276,
368; Hadmersleben, 365; Harzungen, 297, 357, 365;
Karlshagen, 241–242, 521; Langenstein, 362–363,
366, 524; Leitmeritz, 367; maps, 505, 521–525;
medical care, 353, 358, 360, 391; mortality rate,
397–398; Neu Stassfurt, 366–367, 524; Peenemünde,
239–241, 410; Porta Westfalica, 343–344; prison
administrators, 299–300; prisoner nationalities as an
organizing factor, 379; procedures, 309; rations, 323,
361, 369, 382–383; Ravensbrück, 379, 381–386, 393,
522; *Revier*, 299–300, 323, 328; Rossla, 359;
Rottleberode, 360, 523; Sachsenhausen, 378–381,
391, 393, 523; Saxony, 363–364, 371; Schwarzheide,
365, 368–369; specialist workers, 290, 298–299, 410;
Stutthof, 236; Sudetenland, 363–364, 368, 525;
Thekla, 365; Theresienstadt, 367, 368–369;
Woffleben, 297, 319–320. See *also* Death marches;
Liberation of camps; Transportation of prisoners.

EW (Elecktromechanische Werke GmbH), 104, 239

Executions: of German civilians, 169–170; of prisoners,
118, 169–170, 174, 213, 224, 258, 285–287, 297, 300,
424, 438–439; of war criminals, 422, 423, 424, 425,
431. See *also* Extermination of prisoners.

Exhaustion, deaths from, 79–81, 86, 277–278, 398

Extermination of prisoners: by German civilians,
346–349, 360, 467; by SS, 171, 309–310, 312, 317,
323, 324, 328, 330, 339–340, 346–349, 357–358, 364,
366, 378–379, 407, 460–461, 462, 465, 467. See *also*
Executions; Punishments.

Factories, aircraft industry factories, 179–184, 222–223,
230–231, 377, 466. See *also* Factory (Dora).

Factory (Dora), 128–148, 243–244, 246, 251–255,
263–264, 283–284, 289–290, 402, 454–456;
administration, 68–69, 90, 138–140; Allied takeover
of, 314–318, 408, 410–412, 437, 452; construction,
54–55, 64–67; deaths due to, 90–91; design, 64, 68,
131–133, 505, 514–515; engineers, 137–138;
friendships among prisoners, 142–144, 296;
inspectors, 133–135, 142; *Kapos*, 138–139; labor
needs, 71, 100, 442, 455–456; *Meister*, 87, 136,
137–138, 140, 142; postwar film versions, 140–142,
173, 441; secretaries, 135; setup, 68–69, 131–133,
246; shutting down of, 289–290, 294, 313; specialist
workers, 128–131, 290, 298–299; SS supervision,
139–140; supply warehouses, 146–147; technical
work, 134–135; tours by officials, 100–102, 138;
WWII aftermath, 408, 416, 437–438. See *also*
Kommandos; Work; Workers; Working conditions.

Famine, 212–213. *See also* Food; Hunger; Rations.

Fencing of camp, 124

Fi 103. *See* VI rockets.

FIAT (Field Information Agency, Technical), 414

Field Information Agency, Technical (FIAT), 414

Firnrohr Kommando, 131–132, *253*

First Four Days in Belsen (Roach), 328

Flöha, 365–366

Food: after liberation, 314, 329–330, 331, 381, 382, 388, 390, 391–393; canteen, 156; care packages, 62–63, 76, 77; distribution of, 62–63, 379, 382; hunger, 62–63, 212–213, 273, 280–281, 314–315, 328, 341, 361, 380, 392; rations, 62–63, 81, 151, 200, 210–213, 280–281, 294, 303, 323, 328, 329–330, 341, 342, 361, 369, 379, 382–383; Red Cross distributions, 379, 382; scavenging of, 294, 295, 301, 328, 388, 390; thefts of, 62–63, 152, 163, 379, 380, 382–383

Forge Kommandos, 207

Fort Bliss, 417–418

France: Allied entry into, 96, 103–104, 145; concentration camp debate, 426–427; concentration camp inquiry, 430; occupation by Germany, 12, 33–34; occupation of Germany, 409, 413; Resistance movement, 12, 46, 70–71, 223–224, 436; rocket program interest, 419–420; Service du travail obligatoire (STO), 12; trial of war criminals, 425. *See also* French prisoners.

French prisoners, x, 55–57, 101, 108, 112–115, 285–286, 315, 325, 402–403; Alsace–Lorraine natives, 115–116; Buchenwald, 426; Ellrich, 204; Harzungen, 193; morale, 144–145; mortality rate, 84–86, 218–219, 367; political activities among, 168–169; Ravensbrück, 381; work assignments, 124, 130–133, 155, 156, 197

French SS, 385–386, 389

Friendships among prisoners, 7, 143–144, 194, 206–207, 296, 386–388; Buchenwald and Dora compared, 163–164; Ellrich, 206–207; Harzungen, 194

Friseur, 151

Fuel depot evacuation, 65

Fuel tanks, *251*

Galicia, Eastern, 112

Gandersheim Kommando, 230–231, 357, 364–365, 369–371

Gardelegen, *262*, 346–350, 398, 401, *523*

Geheime Staatspolizei (Gestapo), 15, 38–39, 278–279, 467

"Geheimprojekt Mittelbau" (Bornemann), 30, 31–32, 445

"Geheimwaffen im Kohnstein" (Pelny and Weisshaupt), 439

German civilians: aid to prisoners by, 356, 361, 387; citizenship categories, 107–108; 15, 38–39, 278–279, 467; complicity with SS, 459–460, 466–468; corpse burial by, 313; extermination of prisoners by, *262*, 346–350, 360, 398, 401, *523;* police control of, 169–170, 267–268; as witnesses, 423–424, 459–460. *See also* Civilian workers.

German prisoners, 107–108, 115–116, 121, 195, 295, 299, 368

German prisoners of war, health care by, 314

Germany, *506;* Allied bombing of, 12, 13, 28–30, 50, 52, 57, 102–103, 283–284; annexation of Poland, 110; arms policy, 23; commemoration of camps, 447–448, 450–451; concentration camp locations, *506, 510;* economy, 16–18, 42, 111, 159, 457, 461–462; Harz Mountain area, 30–32, 182, *510; Länder* divisions, 446–447; military situation, 11–13, 33–34, 96, 118–119, 145, 171, 175, 235–236, 239, 240, 242, 265, 283–304, 307–308, 310–318, 336, 341–342, 345–346, 349–351, 354–356, 357, 358, 359, 364, 367, 369, 373–376, 378, 379, 382, 383–385, 387, 389, 390, *518–519;* occupation of France by, 12, 33–34; occupation of Yugoslavia by, 118–119; occupied zones (postwar), 408–409, 413; partition of, 407–409, 412–413, 427–428; reunification of, 446–447; surrender to Allies, 375–376, 408, 413; Treaty of Versailles denounced by, 21; WWII aftermath, 407–433. *See also* Luftwaffe; Nazi Party; Wehrmacht.

Germany and Its Memory (Reichel), 447

Gestapo (Geheime Staatspolizei), 15, 38–39, 278–279, 467

Greens (prisoners), 40, 89, 108, 114–115, 135, 149–150, 163, 184, 195, 202, 231, 267, 277, 283

Greffier list, 84

Gross Rosen camp, 238–239, 272–276, 368, 464

Grosswerther Kommando, 371–372

Gulags, 425, 429–430, 433

Günzerode camp, 189–190, 358–359

Gustloff factories, 42

Gypsy prisoners, 121, 193, 195, 202, 237

Hadmersleben, 365

Halupka, Jan, 172, 173, 268–269, 279

Hamburg, destruction by bombing, 322

Hangings, *258*, 285–287. *See also* Executions.

Harz Mountains, 30–32, 182, *510*

Harzungen camp, 191–199, 505, *516;* evacuation, 323, 353–356, 357, 365, 368; liberation, 353–356; living conditions, 194–195; maps, 505, *516;* mortality rate, 216–221, *257;* numbers of prisoners, 193, 265–266; prisoner nationalities, 193, 195; *Revier*, 198–199, 332; Woffleben farm, 192–193; working conditions, 195–198

Haukohl Kommando, 132, 138–139, 143

Heckbau group, 143

Heckbau Kommando, 132

Heckmontage group, 143

Heereswaffenamt (Army Ordnance Office), 20–21

Heinkel factories, 377

Heinkel Kommando, 377

Helmetalbahn work sites, 184–189, 220–221

Helmstedt, 229–230, 242

Hémery, Pierre, 169, 341

Hermes group, 412

Himmelberg work sites, 182–183, 219–221

History: images of concentration camps in, x, 3–4, 6–7, 447–449, 457–460; rocket program, 19–20, 444–445

Hitler's Willing Executioners (Goldhagen), 368

Human Race, The (Antelme), 231
Hungarian prisoners, 119–121, 148, 193, 203–204, 223, 236, 325, 463
Hunger, 6, 62–63, 212–213, 273, 280–281, 314–315, 328, 341, 380, 392
Hygiene of prisoners, 59–63, 123, 127, 210, 212, 326, 334, 391

I Chose Freedom (Kravtchenko), 429
Identification numbers, 39–40, 80–81, 266, 378; for corpses, 80–81
Identification triangles, 40–41
Illness. *See* Deaths; Medical care of prisoners; Mortality rate; *Revier*; *Schonung.*
Illustrations, 243–244, *245–264;* drawings, *245–250;* maps, 505, *506–525;* photographs, *243–244, 251–255. See also* Art in camp.
Images of Dora, x, 3–4, 6–7, 400–404, 441, 442–443, 447–448, 453–454, 457–460
Indifference to prisoners by Nazis, 26–27, 91, 101, 442, 455, 462
Inspection of camp: Nazi officials, 150; Red Cross, 127–128
Inspection of factory, 133–135, 142
Intelligence: Allied bombing due to, 28–29, 102–103; CIOS (Combined Intelligence Objectives Subcommittee), 412; on German weaponry sites, 102–103, 314, 440–441; Psychological Warfare Division, 37, 421, 425–426
Interallied Information Commission, 330
International Red Cross, 369, 374, 375, 382. *See also* Red Cross.
Italian prisoners, 118–119
Italy, occupation of, 12

Jägerstab, 99
Jehovah's Witnesses as prisoners, 374
Jewish prisoners, 36, 68, 119–121, 148, 193, 203–204, 223, 226, 236, 239, 299–300, 325–326, 327, 365–366, 367, 368–369, 371, 374, 434, 463–464; commemoration, 452; mortality rate, 203–204, 237, 276; repatriation, 334–335, 399, 400; trials of, 431; World Jewish Congress negotiations, 375
Jugend für Dora, 454
Junkers factories, 42–43, 99, 227–228

Kabelsir Kommando, 67
Kaolin work site, 182
Kapos, 39, 88–89; at the *Revier*, 72–73, 215; factory *Kapos* 138–139; Finkenzeller, 138–139, *256*, 424; responsibility for deaths, 87–89, 347–348; trial of, 430, 432. *See also* Prisoner administrators.
Karlshagen camp, 241–242, *521*
Kleinbodungen Kommando, 147, 324–325
Klosterwerke camp, 225–226
Koenig Kommando, 70
Kohnstein hill, 30–34
Kohnstein work sites, 182, 219–221

Kommando 32, 270–272
Kommando associations, 6, 435
Kommandos, 39, 44–45, 87, 131–133, 146–148, 157–160, 179–190; AEG Kommando, 208, 331; B11 Kommando, 159; Baubrigade Kommandos, 179–190; Bünemann Kommando, 133, 143; camp construction by, 123–128, 157; Dora Kommando (from Dachau), 130; Firnrohr Kommando, 131–132, *253;* forge Kommandos, 207; Grosswerther Kommando, 371–372; Haukohl Kommando, 132, 138–139, 143; Heckbau Kommando, 132; Heinkel Kommando, 377; inspection kommandos, 133–134; Kabelsir Kommando, 67; Kelbra Kommando, 146–147; Kleinbodungen Kommando, 147, 324–325; Koenig Kommando, 70; Kommando 32, 270–272; Kommando associations, 6, 435; Kommandos, friendships within, 7, 143–144, 164, 206–207, 296, 387–388; Kontrolle Scherer Kommando, 130; Lagerkommando, 157–158; Mackenrode Kommandos, 187–189; Maurer Kommando, 87; Neu Stassfurt Kommando, 228–229; Niedersachswerfen Kommando, 146–147; Nüxel Kommandos, 187–189; Ohrdruf Kommando, 220, 357, 401; Osterhagen Kommando, 187–189; painter kommandos, 207; Rossla Kommando, 146–147, 359; Sawatzski Kommandos, 132, 138; Schachtkommando, 157, 171; Scherer Kommando, 7, 111–112, 134, 136, 138, 143, 144, 151, 279, 296; Schönebeck Kommando, 231, 355–356, 360; Schreiber Kommando, 135, 144; Sonderkommando, 158; specialist kommandos, 71, 206–207, 208, 298–299; Speer Kommando, 377; statistics, 44–45; technical work kommandos, 134; tractor factory kommando, 159; *Transportkolonnen* kommandos, 135–137, *255;* woodworking kommandos, 207; work site construction by, 179–190; Zaunbau Kommando, 124, 143. *See also* Electrical work; Work sites; Workers.
Kontrolle Scherer Kommando, 130
"Konzentrationslager Buchenwald," 425
Kummersdorf, rocket experiments, 20–21
"KZ Dora. Produktionsstätte des Todes" (Dieckmann and Hochmuth), 439

LÄ (Lagerältester), 38
"La Résistance dans les camps de concentration nationaux–socialistes" (Langbein), 43, 45
"La Simple Vérité" (Pineau), 400
"La Tregua" (Levi), 356
Labor, forced. *See* Workers.
Laboratoire de recherches balistiques et aérodynamiques (LRBA), 420
Lagerältester (LÄ), 38
Lagerkommando, 157–158
Lagerschutz, 39
Land clearing, 203
Länder divisions, 446–447
Langenstein camp, 227–228, 358, 362–363, 366, *524*
Latrines, 59, 206
Laura camp, 183–184
"Le Mensonge d'Ulysse" (Rassinier), 426–427

"Leçons de ténèbres" (de Saint–Marc), 228
"L'Écriture ou la vie" (Semprun), 400–401
Lehesten factory, 184
Lehesten rocket test center, 52
Leitmeritz, 367
"Les jours de notre mort" (Rousset), 229, 425, 429
"L'Espèce humaine" (Antelme), 231
"L'État SS" (Kogon), 37, 224, 425–426
"L'Expérience des autres" (Rassinier), 427
Liberation of camps, 5–6, *260*, 280, 307–318, 327,
   356–358, 383; by Americans, 5, 242, *260*, 303,
   312–318, 328–329, 380–381, 401–402, 426; Bergen-
   Belsen, 328–330; Boelcke Kaserne, 312–313,
   401–402; by British, 329–330; Buchenwald, 35–38,
   45–46, 242, 438; Dachau, 422; Dora, 144–145, 280;
   Ellrich, 317; food, 314, 329–330, 331, 381, 382, 388,
   390, 391–393; Gross Rosen camp, 368; Günzerode,
   358–359; Harzungen, 317, 353–356; Langenstein,
   358; Mauthausen, 422; medical care, 332, 343, 356,
   361–362, 391, 392–394; Nordhausen, 6, 312–313,
   401–402; Ravensbrück, 385, 428; Red Cross role,
   374, 375, 381, 399; repatriation, 316–317, 332–334,
   342–343, 355, 357, 359, 362, 383–384, 387, 389, 390,
   392, 394, 407; Sachsenhausen, 391–393, 428; by
   Soviets, 391, 393–394, 399–400, 427–428, 437–438;
   trial witnesses of, 421; truce, 356, 390–391;
   Wansleben, 356–357; Wöbbelin, 380–381. *See also*
   Evacuation of camps.
Libraries, 157
Lice, 60–62, 90
Living conditions, *245–250;* art, 152, 153, 158, 166,
   243–244, *245–250;* Bergen-Belsen, 326–328;
   Blankenburg camps, 226; Boelcke Kaserne, 270–271,
   280–281; bombing of camps by Allies, 290–294;
   Buchenwald, 35–38, 41–42, 43, 57, 123; Buchenwald
   and Dora compared, 162–167; clothing, 211–212,
   216, 220, 275–276, 281, 295, 301, 304, 337–338, 362;
   cold, 60–62, 171, 183, 188, 197, 241, 272–274, 282;
   construction of camp, 123–128, 150; crafts by
   prisoners, 143, 207; diaries, 194–195; dining room,
   152; disinfection of prisoners, 60–62, 90, 211–212,
   282, *513;* Dora, 54–55, 58–63, 90–91, 123–128,
   151–153, 156–158, 265; dormitories, 59–60,
   126–128, 396, *513;* dust and noise, 59, 65, 196;
   Ellrich camp, 200–204, 208–213; Günzerode camp,
   189–190; Harzungen camp, 194–195; hunger, 62–63,
   212–213, 273, 280–281, 314–315, 328, 341, 361, 380,
   392; hygiene, 59–63, 123, 127, 210, 212, 326, 334,
   391; Langenstein, 227; latrines, 59, 206; Laura camp,
   183–184; lice, 60–62, 90; Mackenrode, 187–188;
   mail, 62–63, 76, 77, 151–152; mortality rate and, 396;
   Neu Stassfurt, 228; Nordhausen, 282–283;
   Osterhagen, 188; political activity, 43, 88–89, 110,
   114, 126, 150, 153, 161, 164–165; prisoner
   administrators and, 149–150, 184, 209–211, 283;
   quarantine, 41–42; rations, 62–63, 81, 151, 200,
   210–213, 280–281, 294, 303, 323, 328, 329–330, 341,
   342, 361, 369, 379, 382–383; reading, 157; release
   from tunnels, 126–128, 396; roll call, 89–90, 154,
   211, *248–249*, 328; *Schonung*, 76–77, 271; Speer on,
   69, 89–90, 125; thefts, 62–63, 152; tunnels, 54–55,

58–63, 90–91; Wieda, 185–186, 188; Wöbbelin,
   380–381; Woffleben camp, 208–210; work sites,
   179–180, 183–184, 193–221; writing, 165–166,
   194–195, 289. *See also* Construction of camp; Deaths;
   Mortality rate; Punishments; *Revier;* Working
   conditions.
Locations: Bergen-Belsen, *520–523;* concentration
   camps within German territory, *506, 510;* Dora,
   30–33, 95, *506, 510;* Ellrich camp, 199–200; work
   sites, 181–182, *518. See also* Maps.
LRBA (Laboratoire de recherches balistiques et
   aérodynamiques), 420
Luftwaffe: disintegration of, 12; as prison wardens, 194,
   195, 201, 202, 215, 221, 300, 312, 371–372, 387;
   rocket program involvement, 21, 24, 104, 148
"L'Univers concentrationnaire" (Rousset), 380, 425

Mackenrode Kommandos, 187–189
Maïdanek camp, transports to, 77–78, 86
Mail, 151–152; care packages, 62–63, 76, 77
Maps, 8, 505, *506–525;* Allied offensives in Germany,
   518–519; B3, *517;* Bergen-Belsen, *520–523;* Boelcke
   Kaserne, *517;* concentration camp sites in German
   territory, *506;* Dora, 505, *510–515;* Ellrich, 505, *511,
   516;* evacuation of camps, 505, *521–525;* factory,
   514–515; Harzungen, 505, *516;* Nordhausen, *517;* V2
   sites, *507–515. See also* Design.
Maurer Kommando, 87
Mauthausen camp, 422, 443
Medical care of prisoners: after liberation, 332, 343, 356,
   391, 392–394; evacuation, 353, 358, 360, 361–362,
   383, 391; SS directives, 18. *See also* Disinfection of
   prisoners; Doctors; Quarantine; Red Cross; *Revier.*
Medical experiments, 224
Mediterranean Front, 11, 12
Meerschaum (Operation), 56
Meister, 87, 136, 137–138, 140, 142
"Mêmorial des camps de Dora-Ellrich" (Dora-Ellrich
   Association), 436–438
Memorials. *See* Associations of survivors;
   Commemoration of camps.
Mibau Werke factory, 42
Military situation of Germany, 11–13, 33–34, 96,
   118–119, 145, 171, 175, 235–236, 239, 240, 242, 265,
   283–284; last days, 284–304, 307–308, 310–318, 336,
   341–342, 345–346, 347, 349–351, 354–356, 358, 359,
   364, 369, 373–376, 378, 379, 382, 383–385, 387, 389,
   390. *See also* Allied bombing of Germany; Allies;
   Occupied zones; Partition of Germany.
"Miners," 196
Mittelbau complex, 54, 95
Mittelraum, 54, 95
Mittelwerk GmbH, 49–50, 53, 64, 100, 104–105, 122,
   125, 133, 146–147, 243; policy toward prisoners, 140;
   V1 construction, 147–148
*"Mondsüchtig. Wernher von Braun und die Geburt der
   Raumfahrt aus dem Geist der Barbarei"* (Eisfeld),
   445, 459
Mortality rate, 17–18, 82–86, 398; Bergen-Belsen, 78,
   334, 335; Blankenburg camps, 226; Buchenwald, 36;

Mortality rate (*cont.*)
  child prisoners, 203; Dora, 63, 116, 118, 395–396,
    398; Ellrich, 216–221, 257; evacuation of camps,
    397–398; Greffier list, 84; Jewish prisoners, 203–204,
    237, 276; Karlshagen, 241; Langenstein, 227–228,
    363; Laura camp, 183–184; living conditions and,
    396; Peenemünde, 28, 241; prisoner nationalities and,
    82–83, 116, 118; time of arrival and, 83–85, 219, 276;
    Transportkolonnen Kommandos, 137, *255;* working
    conditions and, 396. *See also* Deaths; Extermination
    of prisoners.
Music, 42, 121, 166, 186, 195, 284, 285, 314, 389

Nacht und Nebel (NN) prisoners, 113, 464
Natzweiler camp, 464
Nazi Party: administration, 13, 15, 346, 374, 375–376,
    460, 466, 467–468; arrest of members by Party
    authorities, 97–98; German citizenship categories, 15,
    38–39, 107–108, 278–279, 467; indifference to
    prisoners, 26–27, 91, 101, 442, 455, 462;
    responsibility for deaths, 90–91, 456, 459; rivalries
    within, 5, 26, 96–98, 104; summit meetings on V2
    program, 100–102, 123, 129; trials for war crimes, ix,
    5–6, 414, 418, 421–425, 441–442. *See also* SS
    (Schutzstaffel).
Neu Stassfurt, 228–229, 366–367, *524*
Neu Stassfurt Kommando, 228–229
Neuengamme, prisoner transports to, 113
News sources, 144–145, 161, 210, 216
Nicolas, Jean Marcel, 225, 301
Niedersachswerfen Kommando, 146–147
NN *(Nacht und Nebel)* prisoners, 113, 464
Nordhausen, *260,* 269, 271, 281–283, 300–302, 317,
    401–402; bombing of, 290–294, 295; liberation, 6,
    312–313, 401–402; living conditions, 282–283; maps,
    517; transports to, 217, 281–282, 285; trial of
    officials, 422–423; trusteeship, 450. *See also* Boelcke
    Kaserne camp.
Nordhausen prison, 292
"Notre devoir de mémoire" (Bertrand), 369–370
Numbers of prisoners, 43–46, 55–57, 60, 113–114, 159,
    239, *260;* Auschwitz, 239; Bergen-Belsen, 326; Dora,
    43–46, 55–57, 60, 113–114, 159, 266, 396; Ellrich,
    202–203, 204, 265–266; Harzungen, 193, 265–266;
    Langenstein, 227–228; Osterode camps, 226;
    Rottleberode, 223, 266; Sachsenhausen, 377, 378–379;
    Theresiendstadt, 327. *See also* Identification numbers.
Nüxel Kommandos, 187–189

Oberammergau, Peenemünde personnel refuge in, 410
Occupied zones, 408–409, 413
Office of the Military Government of the United States
    (OMGUS), 413
"Ohne Kleider," 211–212, 220
Ohrdruf Kommando, 220, 357, 401
OMGUS (Office of the Military Government of the
    United States), 413
Operation Backfire, 414–415
Operation Citadel, 11–12

Operation Crossbow, 102–103, 440–441
Operation Meerschaum, 56
Operation Overcast, 412, 414–415, 416–418, 440–441
Operation Paperclip, 417–418
Operations (surgical), 75–76, 147, 161, 162, 302
Oranienburg, 336–338, 376–378. *See also* Sachsenhausen
    camp.
Oranienburg 1933–1935, Sachsenhausen 1936–1945
    (Bezaut), 376
Orphans' aid by survivor associations, 435–436
Ostarbeiter, 111
Osterhagen Kommando, 187–189
Osterode camps, 226–227, 266, 341–342; evacuations,
    339, *522*
Outside work. *See* Construction at new work sites;
    Construction of camp; Construction of factory;
    Earthworks projects.
"Ouvrier et Soldat" (Bronchart), 71
Overcast (Operation), 412, 414–415, 416–418, 440–441

Packages, care packages, 62–63, 76, 77
Painter Kommandos, 207
Paperclip (Operation), 417–418
Parades of repatriated prisoners, 333
Partition of Germany, 407–409, 412–413, 427–428
"Passage de la ligne" (Rassinier), 343, 426–427
Peenemünde, 21–30, 50–53, 101–102, 104–106,
    174–175, 235, 239–241, *508;* antiaircraft missile
    development, 105, 371; bombing of, 28–30, 50, 57,
    102; Elecktromechanische Werke GmbH (EW), 104,
    239; evacuation of, 239–241, 410; facilities, 22,
    27–28; film versions, 441; map, *508;* mortality rate,
    28, 241; personnel, 22, 23–26; sabotage, 50–51;
    security measures, 29, 53; workers, 25, 26–28, 129;
    working conditions, 27–28, 57; WWII aftermath,
    410–412, 445. *See also* Rocket program.
"Perliris" (Morel), 279
Photographs of camp, 243–244, 251–255
Pilgrimages to former concentration camps, 438–439, 454
Pinks (prisoners), 40–41
Planet Dora (Béon), ix
Poetry, 165–166
Poland, annexation by Russia and Germany, 109–110
Police control of civilians, 169–170, 267–268
Polish prisoners, 109–110, 156, 193, 287, 295, 399–400
Political activity in camps, 164–165, 297–298, 434–435;
    Buchenwald, 167–169, 224, 426; communism, 43,
    88–89, 110, 114, 126, 150, 153, 161, 164, 167–168,
    174, 184, 268, 297–298, 402, 407, 426, 428–433, 438,
    439. *See also* Politics in Germany; Resistance within
    camps.
Political careers of former prisoners, 164–165, 426, 427,
    429, 431, 432
Politics in Germany: Dora and Germany's military
    situation, 95–106, 145, 171, 175, 265, 283–284,
    294–300, 307–308, 310–318; rocket program and, 5,
    22, 69, 96–98, 104. *See also* Nazi Party; Political
    activity in camps.
"Politik mit der Erinnerung" (Germany and Its Memory)
    (Reichel), 447

Politische Abteilung, 38–39, 154–155
Porta Westfalica, 229–230; evacuation of, 343–344
Prisoner administrators, 149–156, 162–163, 184, 202, 209–210, 266–267, 286, 299, 312, 426; *Blockältester,* 13, 150–151, 152; Buchenwald, 426; complicity with other prisoners, 87–89, 288, 431; evacuation, 299–300; executions of, 297–298; *Friseur,* 151; Lagerkommando, 157–158; living conditions and, 149–150, 184, 209–211, 283; political struggles, 237, 426; in the *Revier,* 160–161, 188, 198, 210, 215–216, 223–225, 277, 279; *Schreiber,* 38, 151, 153–156; *Stubendienst,* 150–151, 152; trial of, 424, 429, 430–432. *See also* Communism, in concentration camps; Doctors; *Kapos.*
Prisoner categories, 40–41, 463–465; Blacks, 40, 202; educated prisoners, 105–106, 109, 111–112, 115, 125, 129–130, 134, 135, 143, 164–165, 276–278, 279; Greens, 40, 89, 108, 114–115, 135, 149–150, 163, 184, 195, 202, 231, 267, 277, 283; Gypsies, 121, 193, 195, 202, 237; Jehovah's Witnesses, 374; Jewish prisoners, 119–121, 148, 193, 203–204, 223, 226, 236, 239, 299–300, 325–326, 327, 334–335, 361, 365–366, 367, 368–369, 371, 374–375, 399, 400, 452, 463–464; NN prisoners, 113; Pinks, 40–41; Purples, 41; Reds, 40, 43, 88, 108, 114, 149–150, 160–161, 162–163, 266, 270, 279; women prisoners, 326, 332, 381, 384, 385, 393.
See also Numbers of prisoners; Prisoner nationalities.
Prisoner identification numbers, 39–40, 80–81, 266, 378
Prisoner identification triangles, 40–41
Prisoner nationalities, 40–41, 44–47, 462–464; Alsace–Lorraine natives, 115–116; at Auschwitz, 236–237; at Bergen-Belsen, 331; at Buchenwald, 55–57, 426; at Dora camp, 40–41, 46–47, 55–57, 82–83, 107–121, 147; at Ellrich camp, 193, 202; at Gross Rosen camp, 238–239, 464; at Harzungen camp, 193, 195; at Langenstein camp, 227; at Laura camp, 183; at Stutthof, 236; at Wieda, 185; Belgian prisoners, 116–117, 195; bloc groupings by, 328; British prisoners, 426; camp commemoration committees and, 450, 451; Czech prisoners, 63, 109, 120, 124, 135, 146, 155, 173; Dutch prisoners, 118, 135; evacuation by, 379; French prisoners, x, 55–57, 84–86, 101, 108, 112–116, 130–131, 144–145, 155, 156, 168–169, 193, 197, 204, 218–219, 285–286, 315, 325, 367, 381, 390, 402–403, 426; German prisoners, 107–108, 115–116, 121, 195, 295, 299, 368; Hungarian prisoners, 119–121, 148, 193, 203–204, 223, 236, 325, 463; Italian prisoners, 118–119; mortality rates and, 82–83, 116, 118; Polish prisoners, 109–110, 156, 193, 287, 295, 399–400; repatriation and, 398–400; and resistance within camp, 171–172; Soviet Union natives, 111–112, 175, 193, 269–270, 285–287, 295, 325, 330, 385, 400; Spanish prisoners, 119; and work assignments, 131–137, 153–156; Yugoslavian prisoners, 118–119. *See also* Prisoner categories.
Prisoner transportation. *See* Evacuation of camps; Transportation of prisoners.
Prisoners of war at Dora, 111–112, 118
"Prisoners' Song" ("Chant de déportés") (Chlique), 42

Privileged workers, 69–70, 71, 126, 131, 133–135, 153–156, 159, 198, 204, 228–229, 427. *See also* Specialist workers.
Prominente, 39
Psychological Warfare Division intelligence teams, 37, 421, 425–426
Punishments, 87, 89–90, 137, 285, 328; beatings, 87, 136, 137–139, 170–171, 200, 219; bunker, 170–171; for escapes, 170–171, 175, 224, 300–301, 346, 383, 387; execution, 118, 169–170, 174, 213, 224, 258, 285–287, 297–298, 300; for resistance, 268–270. *See also* Extermination of prisoners.
Purples (prisoners), 41

Quarantine, 41–42; "Ohne Kleider", 211–212, 220; worker selection from, 130. *See also* Revier.
"*Quel beau dimanche!*" (Semprun), 400

Rabe Institut, 416
Radio transmitters in camp, 172–173
Rail installation, 68–69
Railway construction, 184–185, 197
Railway transport, 309–310, 320–322, 336–351, 369–372
Rain, 197, 208
Rapportführer, 38
Rations, 62–63, 151, 200, 210–213, 280–281, 294, 303, 328, 329–330; corpse rations, 81, 272, 283; evacuation rations, 323, 341, 342, 361, 369, 379, 382–383. *See also* Food.
Ravensbrück: evacuation, 379, 381–386, 393; liberation, 385, 428; studies of, 443; transports to, 296, 297, 340–341, 522
Records: burning of, 295; of deaths, 154, 155, 423. *See also* Administration, Nazi Party; Archives of rocket construction; Bureaucracy; Prisoner administrators.
Red Cross, 361–362, 369, 379; food distributions, 379, 382; inspection of camp, 127–128; International Red Cross, 369, 374, 375, 382; liberation of camps, 374, 375, 381, 399; Swedish Red Cross, 361–362, 374, 381; Swiss Red Cross, 38
Redl-Zipf, 52
Reds (prisoners), 40, 43, 88, 108, 114, 149–150, 160–161, 162–163, 266, 270, 279
"*Regarde-toi qui meurs*" (Friang), 368
Reichsdeutsche, 107–108, 115
Reichssicherheitshauptamt (RSHA), 15
Religious activities in camp, 36, 85, 166–167, 195, 226, 288
Repatriation of prisoners, 316–317, 332–334, 342–343, 355, 357, 359, 362, 383–384, 387, 389, 390, 392, 394, 407; prisoner nationalities and, 398–400
Resistance fighters in camps, 6, 46, 70–71, 73, 113, 114, 117, 134, 165, 166–167, 168, 173, 197, 223–224, 316, 331, 370
Resistance movement, 12, 46, 70, 223–224; postwar activities, 436
Resistance within camps: arrests of prisoners within camp, 165, 171, 173–174, 268–270; Buchenwald, 224, 268; Dora, 89, 161, 165, 167–175, 267;

Resistance within camps (*cont.*)
  Günzerode, 358–359. *See also* Political activity in
    camps; Sabotage.
Responsibility for deaths, 86–91, 147, 221, 346–351,
  421, 456, 459
Revier, 39, 72–76, 160–162, 214–215, 247, 276–281,
  285, 302–303, 427, *513;* autopsies, 277–278; Bergen-
  Belsen, 332, 391; Blankenburg camps, 226; Boelcke
  Kaserne, 271–272; doctors, 72–73, 160–161, 198,
  213–214, 223–225, 226, 276–278, 279, 284–285,
  299–300, 302, 439; Ellrich, 213–216; evacuation,
  299–300, 323, 328; Gestapo intervention, 278–279;
  Günzerode camp, 190; Harzungen, 198–199; as a
  hiding place, 299–300, 302; layout of, 72, 160, 505,
  513; liberation, 314–315; medical experiments, 224;
  as a news source, 161, 216; Nordhausen, 282–283,
  294; prisoner administrators (other than doctors),
  160–161, 188, 198, 210, 277, 279; Ravensbrück, 382;
  Rottleberode camp, 223, 225; Sachsenhausen, 391;
  Schonung, 76–77; surgeries, 75–76, 147, 161, 162,
  302; transport to death camps from, 77–79; treatment,
  75–76, 160, 214, 215–216, 224; Wieda, 188;
  Wöbbelin, 380; Woffleben, 210
Rock blasting, 65–66
Rocket and the Reich, The (Neufeld), 19, 444–445
Rocket program, 4–5, 19–34, 455–456, 461–462; A
  rocket series, 21–26; administration, 53, 97–98,
  104–106; Allied bombing's effect on, 28–30, 50, 52,
  57, 102, 404; Allied takeover, 408, 410–412,
  414–415, 416–418, 440–441; archive protection, 289,
  410–412; artillerymen and, 20–23, 90, 100, 133–134;
  assembly-line production, 24–28, 403; history, 19–20,
  444–445, Hitler's involvement in, 23, politics and, 5,
  22, 69, 96–98, 104; responsibility for deaths, 90–91,
  456, 459; rivalries among Nazi Party members, 5,
  96–98, 104; Soviet Union, 20, 416, 418–419, 420,
  437; test launchings, 25, 51, 52, 97, 99–100, 101–102,
  147, 184; V1 rockets, 5, 24, 25, 101, 102–103, 104,
  120, 122, 145, 147–148, 157, 165, 240, 403–404, 419,
  463; writing on, 444–445; WWII aftermath, 410–412,
  414–421. *See also* Peenemünde; V2 rockets.
Rocket scientists. *See* Rocket program; V2 rockets;
  scientists by name.
ROGES (Rohstoffhandelsgesellschaft), 33–34
Rohstoffhandelsgesellschaft (ROGES), 33–34
Roll call, 89–90, 154, 211, *248–249*, 328
Rossla Kommando, 146–147, 359
Rottleberode camp, 222–225, 266, 297, 357, 360,
  451–452, *523*
RSHA (Reichssicherheitshauptamt), 15

SA (Sturmabteilung), 15
Sabotage, 140–142, 173; Peenemünde, 50–51. *See also*
  Political activity in camps; Resistance within
  camps.
Sachsenhausen camp, 376–381, 391–393, 428, *523*
Sachso (association of French deportees of
  Sachsenhausen), 377, 443
Salvage of V2s, 147
Saxony, 363–364, 371

Schachtkommando, 157, 171
Scherer Kommando, 7, 111–112, 134, 136, 138, 143,
  144, 151, 279, 296
Schlempp construction group, 25–126
Schönebeck Kommando, 231, 355–356, 360
Schonung, 76–79, 271
Schreiber, 38, 151, 153–156
Schreiber Kommando, 135, 144
Schreibstube, 38, 153, 154
Schutzstaffel. *See* SS (Schutzstaffel).
Schwarzheide, 365, 368–369
Scorched-earth policy, 287, 289, 298, 312, 367, 460–461,
  467. *See also* Extermination of prisoners; Indifference
  to prisoners by Nazis.
SD (Sicherheitsdienst), 15
Secretaries, 135
Security measures, 53–54, 140–142, 267–268, 456;
  agencies, 267–268; camouflage, 207, 237; code names,
  53–54, 180–181, 265–266, 417; Peenemünde, 29, 53
SEP ("European Propulsion Company"), 420
Service du travail obligatoire (STO), 12
Setup of factory, 68–69, 131–133, *246*
Sicherheitsdienst (SD), 15
Sicily, invasion of, 12
SIPO (Security Police), 15
Slansky trial, 431
Social life. *See* Friendships among prisoners; Political
  activity in camps.
Socialism in concentration camps, 43
Sonderinspektionen, 180–184
Sonderkommando, 158
Sonderstab, 99
Sonderstab Kammler, 179, 180–184, 191, 204, 222–223,
  227, 229, 367, 505
Soviet Union: American relations with, 409, 432, 439;
  annexation of Poland, 109; education in, 111–112;
  gulags, 425, 429–430, 433; invasion by Germany,
  11–12; liberation of camps, 391, 393–394, 399–400,
  427–428, 437–438, 452; occupation of Germany, 408,
  409, 412, 413, 416, 428; offensives on German
  territory, 235–236, 239, 240, *264*, 311, 317, 350–351,
  364, 367, 369, 373–374, 378, 382, 383, 384–385, 387,
  389, 402, *518–519;* prisoners from, 111–112, 175,
  193, 269–270, 285–287, 295, 325, 330, 385, 400,
  462–463; return of Western prisoners from, 433;
  rocket development in, 20, 416, 418–419, 420, 437;
  space race, 439–440
Space race (Soviet/U.S.), 439–440
Spanish prisoners, 119
Specialist workers, 128–131, 197, 206–207, 208, 290,
  298–299, 410. *See also* Privileged workers; Technical
  work.
Speer Kommando, 377
SS (Schutzstaffel), 14–18; adherence to policy, 266–267,
  312, 367, 465, 467; aircraft industry role, 99; barracks
  construction, 67–68; camp administration roles, 151,
  152, 218, 221, 376; complicity with prisoners,
  266–267, 298; economic ambitions, 16–18, 42, 111,
  159, 457, 461–462; Ellrich, 201–202, 210, 212–213;
  empire, 14–15; executions, 118, 169–170, 174, 213,
  224, *258*, 300, 424, 438–439; extermination of

prisoners by, 171, 262, 309–310, 312, 317, 323, 324, 328, 330, 339–340, 346–349, 357–358, 364, 366, 378–379, 407, 460–461, 462, 465; factory supervision by, 139–140; French SS (Schutzstaffel), 386, 389; isolation from other prisoners by Allies, 331; Peenemünde guards, 28; prisoner shootings of, 303; and prisoner transports, 77–78, 272–273, 276–277, 281, 309–310, 321, 326–327, 337, 339–340, 342, 354, 358–359, 363, 364, 366–367, 369, 378–379, 382–383, 384; privileges and powers, 15, 16, 108; refuge in tunnels by, 241; responsibility for deaths, 89–90, 221; Speer on, 69; surrender, 385–386; Totenkopf Division, 16; Waffen-SS, 16; Wieda intervention, 186–187; Woffleben, 210; WVHA, 16. *See also* Administration, Nazi Party; Concentration camps; Evacuation of camps; Punishments.

Stiftung Gedenkstötte Buchenwald und Mittelbau-Dora, 451

STO (Service du travail obligatoire), 12

Stockpiling, 33, 64, 65, 183

Struthof camp, 115–116

Stubendienst, 150–151, 152

"Studien zur Geschichte der Konzentrationslager" (Wormser-Migot and Broszat), 457, 458

Sturmabteilung (SA), 15

Stutthof camp, 236

Successful firings of V2s, 403–404

Sudetenland, 363–364, 368, *525*

Suicides, 12, 270, 279, 311, 376, 385

Summit meetings on V2 program, 100–102, 123, 129

Supply warehouses for factory, 146–147

Surgical operations, 75–76, 147, 161, 162, 302

Surrender: of German soldiers, 385–386; of Germany, 375–376, 408, 413

Survivors of concentration camps. *See* Associations of survivors; *individuals by name.*

Swedish Red Cross, 361–362, 374, 381

Swiss Red Cross, 38

Taifun Express, 371–372

Tank transport in factory, 136

Technical work, 134–135. *See also* Specialist workers.

"Témoignages strabourgeois" (University of Strasbourg), 403

Tessman, Bernhard, 289, 410, 411

Test launchings of rockets, 25, 51, 52, 97, 99–100, 101–102, 147, 184

Thefts of food, 62–63, 152, 163, 379, 380, 382–383

Thekla, 365

Theresiendstadt, 327, 367, 368–369

Thuringia: commemoration of former camps in, 450–451; occupation of, 412, 416, 418–419, 437–438

Time of arrival: and friendships, 143; and mortality rates, 83–85, 219, 276

Todt Organization, 13–14, 24, 98, 125–126, 225, 226

Totenkopf Division (Waffen-SS), 16

Tractor factory kommando, 159, 271

"Trafics et Crimes sous l'Occupation" (Delarue), 33

"Tragédie de la déportation" (Wormser-Migot and Michel), 443

Trains. *See* Railway construction; Railway transport.

Transportation of prisoners, 43–46, 278, 308, 402–403, 463; Brauny convoy, 344–345, 346; Buchenwald, 42, 55–57, 113–114, 308; death marches, 352–372, 382, 461, *522–525;* deaths, 77–79, 86, 88, 217, 272–274, 280, 281, 309–310, 319–328, 337–351, 397; Gardelegen, 346–350, 398, 401, *523;* railway transport, 309–310, 320–322, 336–351, 369–372; repatriation, 316–317, 332–334, 342–343, 355, 357, 359, 362, 383–384, 387, 389, 390, 392, 394, 398–400, 407; to Dachau, 370–371; to death camps, 77–79, 86, 88, 184, 217, 296, 308, 312, 319–328; to Dora, 55–57, 112–114, 116–117, 193, 194, 214–215, 217, 218–219, 220, 272–277, 281, 377; to Ellrich, 184, 193, 194, 202–203, 218–219, 220, 290, 296; to Harzungen, 194, 294–295; to Langenstein, 227, *524;* to Lehesten, 184; to Nordhausen, 217, 281–282, 285; to Rottleberode, 223; trucks, 309. *See also* Evacuation of camps.

Transportkolonnen Kommandos, 135–137, *255*

Treatment of diseases, 75–77, 214, 215–216, 224

Treaty of Versailles, denunciation of, 21

Trials for war crimes, 5–6, 421–425; Jewish prisoners, 431; Nazi Party officials, 414, 418, 421–425, 441–442; Nuremberg trials, 422; prisoner administrators, 424, 429, 430–432; scientists, ix, 415, 418, 421, 423

Triangles, identification triangles, 40–41

Truce, 356, 390–391

Trucks for transporting prisoners, 309

Truman, Harry S., 417

Trusteeship of camps, 450–451

Tunnel A, 58–60, 65–67, 245, *514*

Tunnel B, 32, *514*

Tunnels, 31–33, 49–53, 57, 58–59, 63, 64, 65–67, 90, 162, 241, 313–314; coming outside of, 126–128, 396; commemoration, 451–454, 455–456; digging of, 31–33, 57, 58, 59, 64, 65–67, 90, 162, 182–183, 191, 195–198, 206–207, 220–221, 226, 228, 229, 245, 452; executions in, 286–287; factory setup, 68–69, 131–133, *246;* living conditions, 54–55, 58–63, 90–91, 126–128; maps, *514–515;* as a refuge, 241, 313; Soviet destruction of, 437, 452; stockpiling in, 33, 64, 65; tunnel A, 65–67, 245, *514;* tunnel B, 32, *514;* V2 rockets transfer to, 49–53; water in, 58–59, 63; work site tunnels, 182–183, 191, 206–207, 226, 228, 229. *See also* Factory (Dora); Living conditions; Working conditions.

Turmalin camp, 226

Ukrainian prisoners, 111–112

"Un Normand dans..." (Le Goupil), 401

"Un pas, encore un pas...pour survivre" (Amicale des anciens déportés Neu Strassfurt), 229

United States. *See* Americans.

United States Strategic Bombing Survey (USSBS), 414

USSBS (United States Strategic Bombing Survey), 414

V1 rockets, 5, 24, 25, 101, 102–103, 104, 120, 122, 145, 147–148, 157, 165, 240, 403–404, 419, 463

V2 rockets, 4–5, *243–244, 251–254*, 403–404, 455–456, 461–462; Allied concerns, 102–103, 402; Allied takeover, 408, 410–412; deaths from firings, 404; factory facilities, 50; Fort Bliss, 417–418; Lehesten factory, 184; maps of sites, *507–515;* Mittelwerk GmbH, 49–50, 53, 64, 100, 104–105, 122, 125, 133, 140, 146–147, 243; priority of, 101–102, 103–104, 125; problems with, 100; production of, 50, 122–123, 131–133, *243–244, 251–254*, 289–290, 403; salvage, 147; security program, 29, 53–54, 140–142, 180–181, 265–266, 267–268, 417, 456; shutting down of operations, 289–290, 294, 313; successful firings, 403–404; summit meetings on, 100–102, 123, 129; test launchings, 51, 52, 97, 99–100, 101–102, 147, 184; transfer to Dora Tunnel, 49–53; Wasserfall missile guidance, 101–102, 105; welding, 142; Wizernes bunker, 52, *509. See also* A4 rockets; Factory (Dora); Operation Overcast; Peenemünde.
Veterans' associations, 434
Victim swapping, 431
Volksdeutsche, 108, 115
"Von Braun contre Korolev" (Kohler and Germain), 439–440

Waffen-SS, 16
Wansleben camp, 356–357
War. *See* Allied bombing of Germany; Allies; Military situation of Germany; Scorched-earth policy.
War crime trials. *See* Trials for war crimes.
War Crimes Investigating Team, 421
Warehouses for factory, 146–147
Wasserfall missile guidance, 101–102, 105
Water in Dora tunnels, 58–59, 63
Watten Bunker, 24
Weapons, rockets as, 22–23, 404
Weather conditions at Dora, 31
Wehrmacht: administration, 375, 466–467; complicity with prisoners, 301, 302, 312; and prisoner transports, 321–322; westward migration at end of war, 385
"Wehrwirtschaftführer Geheimwaffen KZ. Gutachten über Rolle und Bedeutung des KZ Dora-Mittelbau und die Funktion der SS bei der A4 Produktion" (Bartel), 439
Welding of V2s, 142
Whorehouse, 156, 157, 171
Wieda work site, 185–187, 188, 345, 357
Wiener Neustadt site, 57
WIFO (Wirtschaftliche Forschungsgesellschaft), 30, 32–34, 50, 64–65, 125, 462; black market activities, 33–34, 64, 65
WIFO workers, 64–65, 87, 462
Wirtschaft- und Verwaltungshauptamt (WVHA), 16
Wirtschaftliche Forschungsgesellschaft (WIFO), 30, 32–34, 50, 64–65, 125, 462
Wizernes bunker, 52, *509*
Wöbbelin camp, 380–381
Woffleben camp, 208–210, 220, 297, 319–320, *511, 517*
Women prisoners, 26, 332, 381, 384, 385, 393
Woodworking Kommandos, 207
Work: allotments of work, 39, 128–129, 154, 179;

blasting rock, 65–66; clearing land, 203; concrete pouring, 66–67; digging tunnels, 31–33, 57, 58, 59, 64, 65–67, 90, 162, 182–183, 191, 195–198, 206–207, 220–221, 226, 228, 229, *245*, 452; earthworks, 67, 205–206, 226, 228, *246;* electric cable installation, 67, *253;* electrical work, 69–70, 130, 133, 197, 206–207, 208, 228–229, 331; forges, 207; nationalities and work assignments, 131–137; rail installation, 68–69; woodwork, 207. *See also* Construction of camp; Construction of factory; Kommandos; Workers; Working conditions.
Work sites, 179–231, 345, 461; administration, 99, 180; *Anhydrit,* 182–183, 195–196, 197, 204, 206–207, 220, 221, *517;* Blankenburg camps, 225–226, 266, 360–362; construction, 179–221; digging of tunnels, 182–183, 191, 195–198, 206–207, 220–221, 226, 228, 229; Ellrich, 91–193, 199–221; Gandersheim Kommando, 230–231, 357, 364–365, 369–371; Günzerode, 189–190; Harzungen, 191–199; Helmetalbahn, 184–189, 220–221; Helmstedt, 229–230, 242; *Kaolin,* 182; Langenstein camp, 227–228, 358, 362–363, 366, *524;* Laura camp, 183–184; living conditions, 179–180, 183–184, 193–221; locations, 181–182, *518;* Mackenrode, 187–188; maps, 505, *511, 516–518;* Neu Stassfurt, 228–229; Osterode camps, 226–227, 266, 339, 341–342, *522;* Porta Westfalica, 229–230; railway construction, 184–185, 197; Rottleberode, 222–225, 266, 357, 360, 451–452, *523;* Schönebeck Kommando, 231, 355–356, 360; Wieda, 185–187, 188, 345, 357; *Zinnstein,* 182. *See also* Kommandos.
Workers, 17–18, 26–28, 42; civilian workers, 87, 136, 137–138, 140, 142, 183, 185–186, 219–220, 229, 267, 287, 289, 290, 311–312, 313, 423–424; draftsmen, 134, 135; electricians, 69–70, 130, 197, 206–207, 228–229, 331; engineers, 137–138; indifference to by Nazis, 26–27, 91, 101, 442, 455, 462; labor needs, 71, 100, 220, 442, 455–456, 461; "miners," 196; Peenemünde, 25, 26–29; privileged workers, 69–70, 71, 126, 131, 133–135, 153–156, 159, 198, 204, 228–229; quarantine for selecting, 41–42, 130; recruiting of, 12, 14, 16, 111, 128–131; specialist workers, 128–131, 197, 206–207, 208, 290, 298–299, 410; WIFO workers, 64–65, 87, 462. *See also* Kommandos; Prisoner administrators; Working conditions.
Working conditions, 65–70, 122–123, 131–148, *245–246, 253, 255*, 400–401; Blankenburg camps, 226; Buchenwald, 42; civilian workers, 87, 136, 137–138, 140, 142, 183, 185–186, 219–220, 229, 267, 287, 289, 311–312, 313; digging tunnels, 31–33, 57, 58, 59, 64, 65–67, 90, 162, 182–183, 191, 195–198, 206–207, 220–221, 226, 228, *245;* dust, 59, 65, 196; earthworks, 67; earthworks projects, 67, 205–206, 226, 228, *246;* electrical work, 69–70, 130, 197, 206–207, 228–229, 331; Ellrich, 204–208, 220–221; Günzerode camp, 189–190; Harzungen, 195–198; Kabelsir Kommando, 67; Langenstein, 227–228; Mackenrode, 187–188; mason Kommandos, 87; mortality rate and, 396; Neu Stassfurt, 228–229; Osterhagen, 188–189; Osterode camps, 226;

Peenemünde, 27–28, 57; rain, 197, 208; Speer on, 69, 89–90; tractor factory, 159, 271; *Transportkolonnen*, 135–137, 255; Woffleben camp, 220. *See also* Deaths; Kommandos; Living conditions; Punishments; Workers.

World Jewish Congress, 375

World War I veterans as prisoners, 70

Writing in camps, 165–166, 194–195, 289

WVHA (Wirtschaft- und Verwaltungshauptamt), 16

WWII aftermath, 407–433; Buchenwald, 422, 423, 425–433; communism and postwar camp considerations, 428–433, 439, 447–448; concealment of Dora, 5–6, 439–441, 443–444, 458–459; concentration camp debate, 425–433; inquiry by Western powers, 414–415, 416–417; occupied zones, 408–409, 413; partition of Germany, 407–409, 412–413, 427–428; publications, 442–445; rocket programs, 410–412, 414–421, 440–444; trial of Nazi Party officials, 414, 418, 421–425; trial of scientists, 415, 418, 421, 423. *See also* Associations of survivors.

Young prisoners block, 157. *See also* Child prisoners.

Yugoslavia, partition of, 118–119

Yugoslavian prisoners, 118–119

Zaunbau Kommando, 124, 143

Zinnstein work site, 182

A NOTE ON THE AUTHOR

André Sellier, historian and former diplomat, is the co-author (with his son, Jean) of *The Atlas of the Peoples of Central Europe*, *The Atlas of the Peoples of Western Europe*, and *The Atlas of the Peoples of the Orient*, published in France. He lives in Picardy.